Handbook of Central Banking, Financial Regulation and Supervision

T0314182

Handbook of Central Banking, Financial Regulation and Supervision

After the Financial Crisis

Edited by

Sylvester Eijffinger
CentER, European Banking Center and TiasNimbas Business School, Tilburg University and CEPR

Donato Masciandaro
Department of Economics and Paolo Baffi Centre, Bocconi University and SUERF

Edward Elgar
Cheltenham, UK • Northampton, MA, USA

Published by
Edward Elgar Publishing Limited
The Lypiatts
15 Lansdown Road
Cheltenham
Glos GL50 2JA
UK

Edward Elgar Publishing, Inc.
William Pratt House
9 Dewey Court
Northampton
Massachusetts 01060
USA

A catalogue record for this book
is available from the British Library

Library of Congress Control Number: 2011925773

ISBN 978 1 84980 313 7 (cased)

Printed and bound by MPG Books Group, UK

Contents

Contributors

Fabian Amtenbrink, Erasmus University Rotterdam, The Netherlands

Jaromír Baxa, Institute of Economic Studies, Charles University, Prague and Institute of Information Theory and Automation, Academy of Sciences of the Czech Republic

Benjamin Born, University of Bonn

Pierre C. Boyer, Department of Economics, University of Mannheim

Gerard Caprio, Williams College and Trinity College, Dublin

Martin Čihák, International Monetary Fund

Alex Cukierman, Berglas School of Economics and CEPR

Lucia Dalla Pellegrina, University of Milan-Bicocca and Paolo Baffi Centre, Bocconi University

Jakob De Haan, De Nederlandsche Bank and University of Groningen, The Netherlands

Michael Ehrmann, European Central Bank

Barry Eichengreen, University of California, Berkeley

Sylvester Eijffinger, CentER, European Banking Center and TiasNimbas Business School, Tilburg University and CEPR

Yiwei Fang, Lally School of Management, Rensselaer Polytechnic Institute

Marcel Fratzscher, European Central Bank

Francesco Giavazzi, Bocconi University

Alberto Giovannini, Unifortune Asset Management

Charles A.E. Goodhart, London School of Economics

Iftekhar Hasan, Rensselaer Polytechnic Institute and Bank of Finland

Roman Horváth, Czech National Bank and Institute of Economic Studies, Charles University, Prague

Donato Masciandaro, Department of Economics and Paolo Baffi Centre, Bocconi University and SUERF

Loretta J. Mester, Federal Reserve Bank of Philadelphia and the Wharton School, University of Pennsylvania

Maria J. Nieto, Banco de Espana

Rob Nijskens, CentER and European Banking Center, Tilburg University

Athanasios Orphanides, Central Bank of Cyprus

Rosaria Vega Pansini, Paolo Baffi Centre, Bocconi University

Jorge Ponce, Banco Central del Uruguay

Marc Quintyn, International Monetary Fund

Marcelo Rezende, Board of Governors of the Federal Reserve System

Pierre L. Siklos, Wilfrid Laurier University

Alexander Tieman, International Monetary Fund

Bořek Vašíček, Universitat Autonoma de Barcelona

Introduction

Sylvester Eijffinger and Donato Masciandaro

The objective of this volume is to offer an updated and systematic discussion of the relationship between central banks, financial regulation and supervision after the financial crisis. The current crisis has raised important questions about:

1. the compatibility of monetary and financial stability and consequently

2. the changing face of central banking, as well as

3. the architecture of financial regulation and supervision.

Before the crisis, in the past two decades, changes in the financial landscape and architecture were characterized by two distinctive features: consolidation and specialization.

Supervisory regimes can be classified as follows: the vertical (silos) model, which follows the boundaries of the financial system in different business sectors, and where every sector is supervised by a different agency; the horizontal (peaks) model, which follows the difference among the public goals of regulation, and where every goal is supervised by a different authority; and the unified (integrated) model, where a single authority supervises the entire financial system in pursuing all public goals.

On one hand, reforms of institutional settings were driven by a general trend to reduce the number of supervisory and regulatory agencies, to reach the unified model – unknown before 1986 – or the vertical model. In both models financial supervisors have specialized themselves with a well-defined mission.

On the other hand, the trend towards specialization has become particularly evident, if we observe the route that the major central banks have followed. The central banks with full responsibility for monetary stability – the Federal Reserve System (Fed), the European

Central Bank (ECB), the Bank of England, the Bank of Japan – did not have full responsibility of financial stability. This does not mean that these central banks are not concerned with financial stability, but it is generally dealt with from a macro-economic perspective only in function of their primary mission, i.e., preserving monetary stability. Among the central banks which do not have full responsibility for monetary policy, such as those in the countries belonging to the euro zone, the most prudent banks have chosen or will choose the route of specialization in vigilance: the cases of Czech Republic, Finland, Ireland, the Netherlands and the Slovak Republic, for example, can be looked at. In general, it has been noted that the national central banks in the euro zone have become increasingly financially stable agencies.

After the crisis, the concern for the stability of the banking and financial industry has caused renewed attention to the architecture of the supervisory and regulatory regimes and the role of the central banks. Policymakers in all countries have wondered and are still wondering whether to reshape their supervisory and regulatory regimes. New proposals to reform these regimes have already been enacted both in the European Union and in the United States. In both cases the consolidation process seems to be stopped, with an increased involvement of the main central banks, i.e., the European Central Bank and the Federal Reserve System, at the same time, using the new territory of macro-prudential supervision. However, the responsibility for micro-prudential supervision is less clearly settled, including the issues of the lead supervisor and burden sharing.

Therefore the topic is in an interesting state of flux. The aim of the book will be to shed light on both the economics and political economy of central banking and financial supervision and regulation to understand where, why and how reforms of financial supervisory and regulatory structure and the role of the central banks can be designed and implemented.

Part I Central Banking, Regulation and Supervision

In Chapter 1, Francesco Giavazzi and Alberto Giovannini argue that financial systems are inherently fragile because of their very function, which makes them valuable: liquidity transformation. Regulatory reforms can strengthen the financial system and decrease the risk of liquidity crises, but they cannot eliminate it completely. This leaves monetary policy with a very important task. In a framework that recognizes the interactions between monetary policy and liquidity transformation, optimal monetary policy would consist of a modified Taylor rule, in which the real interest rate reacts to the possibility of liquidity crises and recognizes the possibility that liquidity transformation may get subsidized. Failure to recognize this point risks leading the economy into a low interest rate trap: low interest rates induce too much risk taking and increase the probability of crises. These crises, in turn, require low interest rates to keep the financial system alive. Raising interest rates becomes extremely difficult in a severely weakened financial system. Therefore, monetary authorities remain stuck in a low interest rate trap. They consider this a reasonable description of the situation we have experienced throughout the past decade.

Athanasios Orphanides provides a policymaker's perspective on some lessons from the recent financial crisis in Chapter 2. He focuses on questions in three areas. First, what lessons can be drawn regarding the institutional framework for monetary policy? Has the experience changed the pre-crisis consensus that monetary policy is best performed by an independent central bank focused on achieving and maintaining price stability? Second, what lessons can be drawn regarding the monetary policy strategy that should be followed by a central bank? How activist should a central bank be in dampening macro-economic fluctuations? Should the 'output gap' serve as an important policy guide? Are there lessons regarding the stability-oriented approach followed by the ECB? How activist should a central bank be in tackling perceived asset price misalignments? Third, is monetary policy pursuing price stability enough to ensure overall stability in the economy? Or is there room for improvement regarding how central banks can contribute to financial stability? Should the role of monetary policy be seen as completely separate from the broader institutional environment governing financial markets and institutions in our economy? Or would greater central bank involvement in regulation and supervision pertaining to credit and finance allow better management of overall economic stability?

In Chapter 3 Alex Cukierman discusses the problems exposed by the global financial crisis in the areas of financial regulation and supervision and possible solutions. He describes and evaluates current proposals regarding the role of the central bank as a systemic regulator, the pros and cons of locating financial supervision in the central bank, and the conflicts and synergies that such an arrangement entails. Once a crisis erupts, central bank liquidity injections constitute a first line of defense. But in the longer term these injections create a trade-off between price and financial stability, and may compromise central bank independence. Problems exposed by the crisis include the growth of a poorly regulated shadow financial system, a short horizon in executive compensation packages and consequent adverse incentive effects, the too-big-to-fail problem, procyclicality in the behavior of financial institutions, conflicts of interest in the rating agencies industry and the trade-off between the scope of intermediation through securitization and transparency in the valuation of assets. He also discusses international dimensions including international cooperation in regulatory reform and the scope for limiting exchange rate variability. The conclusion points out inherent difficulties in distinguishing ex ante between a fundamentals based expansion and a 'bubble'.

According to Rob Nijskens and Sylvester Eijffinger's Chapter 4, banking regulation has proven to be inadequate in guarding systemic stability in the recent financial crisis. Central banks have provided liquidity and ministries of finance have set up rescue programs to restore confidence and stability. Using a model of a systemic bank suffering from liquidity shocks, they find that the unregulated bank keeps too much liquidity and takes excessive risk compared to the social optimum. A Lender of Last Resort can alleviate the liquidity problem, but induces moral hazard. Therefore, they introduce a fiscal authority that is able to bail out the bank by injecting capital. The fiscal authority faces a trade-off. When it imposes strict bailout conditions, investment increases but moral hazard ensues. Milder bailout conditions reduce excessive risk taking at the expense of investment. This resembles the current situation on financial markets, in which banks take less risk but also provide less credit to the economy.

In Chapter 5, Pierre Siklos states that the events since the financial crisis of 2007–2009 are likely to increase the breadth and scope of central bank responsibilities. Since the individuals responsible for running both institutions are unelected, there should be, going forward, more effort devoted to measuring the overall quality of the monetary authorities. To this end, he proposes an index of central bank governance derived from an existing index of central bank transparency. The proposed indexes, however, represent only the first step. Many improvements that can be made to the measures are introduced in this chapter. In particular, any improved index of central bank governance will have to consider how institutional quality is influenced by how well monetary authorities coordinate their actions with other regulatory institutions, both domestic and international. One way to hold monetary authorities as reasonably accountable as possible is to ask how well central banks are governed. It is with this in mind that he argues that we need to go beyond indicators of central bank independence and transparency and think in terms of indicators of central bank governance. Such indicators are commonplace for other governmental institutions. It is high time the same indicators are applied to central banks.

Pierre Boyer and Jorge Ponce analyze in Chapter 6 whether or not central banks should be in charge of micro-prudential, as well as of macro-prudential supervision. They discuss this question, which is at the core of current reform efforts on the fields of banking supervision. Their analysis builds on a recent strand of the literature that considers the effects of different supervisory arrangements on the incentives of bank supervisors under the threat of being captured by bankers. They argue that, while there are good reasons for central banks to conduct macro-prudential supervision, it is socially optimal that another supervisor conducts micro-prudential supervision. Their results suggest that policy makers in many countries would like to reconsider the current trend toward the concentration of supervisory powers into central banks because the monopoly in information acquisition may be a curse when regulatory capture is a concern.

In Chapter 7, Yiwei Fang, Iftekhar Hasan and Loretta Mester conduct an empirical analysis of the institutional structure and effectiveness of central banks during the financial crisis. Their main focus is to investigate how central bank independency, transparency, and supervisory regimes affect their policy effectiveness, measured by inflation, exchange rate volatility, GDP growth, unemployment rates, and non-performing loans. They also examine governor characteristics such as term length and prior working experience and relate them to central bank performance. Preliminary findings from cross-country comparison show that central bank independency, transparency, and financial supervision are significantly correlated with the policy effectiveness during the financial crisis. Moreover, governor characteristics also play an important role. First of all, the financial crisis can be thought of as 'exogenous shocks', which to a great extent reduces the endogeneity concern of potential reserve causality from economic performance to central bank structure. Secondly, the financial crisis hit almost every country, thereby allowing us to conduct a cross-country comparison among central banks with varying institutional characteristics. Lastly and most importantly, in the financial crisis when the global economy was suffering from increased unemployment and low GDP growth, central banks were more vulnerable to the political pressure and became deeply involved in government-led efforts to rescue the economies.

Lucia Dalla Pellegrina, Donato Masciandaro and Rosaria Vega Pansini empirically investigate whether central bank independence and the monetary policy setting can influence the likelihood that policymakers assign banking supervision to central banks in Chapter 8. They find that, with the condition of the government being benevolent, higher central bank operational freedom (economic independence) is associated with a reduced degree of supervisory powers. They motivate this with the possibility that governments fear the risk of a discretionary misuse of monetary tools. However, it turns out that having tight monetary policy goals (a specific form of political independence) becomes a commitment device mitigating the risk of discretion and increases the odds of central bank involvement in supervision. Their study suggests that central bank independence can be relevant not only for the alleged beneficial effects on macroeconomic variables, but also in influencing policymakers' decisions in terms of banking supervision. From the policymakers' point of view, the involvement of the central bank in macro-prudential supervision means greater potential benefits in terms of information. They can also presume that the potential costs of central bank involvement are smaller compared to those related to micro-prudential supervision. In other words, the separation between micro- and macro-prudential supervision can be used to reduce the arguments against central bank involvement.

In Chapter 9, Benjamin Born, Michael Ehrmann and Marcel Fratzscher focus on the new challenges for central banks in terms of communicating about macro-prudential supervision. With regard to the role of communication in enhancing the effectiveness of macro-prudential policy, they differentiate between communication during 'normal' times and during times of crisis. In the former, it is important to be transparent about the aims of the central bank, the processes at work, and the instruments that the central bank will use. In this fashion, the central bank can affect the incentives of economic agents, and thus contribute to crisis prevention. Communication during 'normal' times should, in their view, be very much in line with the principles of monetary policy communication, which typically stress the importance of clarity, transparency and predictability. This will also help in making the central bank accountable. In contrast, during times of crisis, there might well be legitimate limits to transparency, as central bank communications which are too transparent could possibly destabilize the financial system, e.g. by triggering bank runs. They show that both communication instruments exert effects on a broad set of financial markets, and that these instruments do so in a very different way. For instance, Financial Stability Reports tend to reduce volatility in financial markets on release dates, whereas speeches and interviews tend to increase it. This underlines the importance of choosing a careful communication strategy on macro-prudential policy which should be adopted over time and across countries, as there is clearly no one size fits all solution.

Jaromír Baxa, Roman Horváth, and Bořek Vašíček investigate the empirical relationship between monetary policy rules and financial stress in Chapter 10. They examine whether and how main central banks responded to episodes of financial stress over the last three decades and employ a new methodology for monetary policy rules estimation, which allows for time-varying response coefficients and corrects for endogeneity. This flexible framework applied to the US, UK, Australia, Canada and Sweden together with a new financial stress dataset developed by the International Monetary Fund (IMF). This dataset does not only test whether the central banks responded to financial stress, but it also detects the periods and types of stress that were the most worrying for monetary authorities and quantifies the intensity of policy response. Their findings suggest that central banks often change policy rates: mainly decreasing rates in the face of high financial stress. However, the size of a policy response varies substantially over time as well as across countries, with the 2008–2009 financial crisis being the period of the most severe and generalized response. With regards to the specific components of financial stress, most central banks seemed to respond to stock market stress and bank stress, while exchange rate stress is found to drive the reaction of central banks only in more open economies.

Part II The Architecture of Regulation and Supervision

According to Charles Goodhart in Chapter 12, financial regulation has always been a-theoretical, a pragmatic response by practical officials and concerned politicians to immediate problems, following the dictum that 'We must not let that happen again'. When the Basel Committee on Banking Supervision was established in 1974–75 to handle some of the emerging problems of global finance and cross-border banking, the modus operandi then developed was to hold a round-table discussion of current practice in each member state with the objective of trying to reach an agreement on which practice was 'best', and then to harmonize on that. Little or no attempt was made to go back to first principles, and to start by asking why there should be a call for regulation on banking – whether purely domestic or cross-border – in the first place. The current financial crisis has forced a fundamental reconsideration of financial regulation; and rightly so since much of the focus, and the effects, of the existing system were badly designed, with its concentration on individual, rather than systemic, risk and its procyclicality. In response, we now have a ferment of new ideas, many touched upon here. A great deal of further work needs to be done to discern which of these ideas are good and which less so.

Barry Eichengreen discusses eight out-of-the-box ideas about the international financial architecture in Chapter 13. Some of these are even further out of the box than others. They fall under three headings: measures to buttress financial stability, steps to smooth the operation of the international monetary system, and reforms of the IMF. He admits that none of these ideas will be adopted in the short term, but they are the kind of things that policy makers should be pondering once they move beyond the current crisis. His out-of-the-box ideas are:

1. countercyclical IMF capital charges;
2. a price-based scarce currency clause;
3. convertible Special Drawing Rights (SDRs);
4. global Glass-Steagall-like restrictions;
5. a global systemic risk facility;

6. a multilateral insolvency trust for international banks;
7. a World Financial Organization (WFO) and
8. a thorough reform of IMF governance in order to enhance its legitimacy and accountability.

For out-of-the-box ideas to have legs, they must be accompanied by a roadmap for how to get from here to there in the space of, say, ten years. It is clear that reform of IMF governance is a prerequisite for many of the other ambitious ideas entailing a role for the Fund. Without meaningful governance reform, emerging market members would not agree to a significant expansion of the IMF's resources and implement these out-of-the-box ideas.

In Chapter 14, Gerard Caprio analyzes the role of countercyclical regulatory requirements in improving safe and sound banking. Most explanations of the financial crisis of 2007–2009 emphasize the role of the preceding boom in real estate and asset markets in a variety of advanced countries. As a result, an idea that is gaining support among various groups is how to make Basel III or any regulatory regime less procyclical. He addresses the rationale for and likely contribution of such policies. Making provisioning (or capital) requirements counter-cyclical is one potential way of addressing procyclicality, and accordingly it looks at the efforts of the authorities in Spain and Colombia, two countries in which countercyclical provisioning has been tried, to see what the track record has been. As explained there, these experiments have been at best too recent and limited to carry much weight, but they are much less favorable for supporting this practice than is commonly admitted. Finally, he discusses his concerns and implementation issues with countercyclical capital or provisioning requirements, including why their impact might be expected to be limited, and concludes with recommendations for developing country officials who want to learn how to make their financial systems less exposed to crises.

Martin Čihák and Alexander Tieman conduct an empirical analysis of the quality of financial sector regulation and supervision around the world in Chapter 15. Unlike studies that collect and analyze data on regulation and supervision 'on the books', their study also analyzes available information on supervisory implementation, making use of data from IMF-World Bank assessments of compliance with international standards and codes. Incorporating supervisory implementation into the study provides an improved means of assessing countries' regulatory systems. They find, among other things, that countries' regulatory frameworks score, on average, one notch below full compliance with the standards (on a four-notch scale). The analysis suggests that financial supervisory systems in high-income economies are generally of higher quality than those in medium- or low-income economies. However, supervision in high-income countries also faces bigger challenges, as they are characterized by more complex financial systems. On balance, therefore, their research cautions that despite the higher grades obtained by high-income countries, the supervisory knowledge about the financial strength of their institutions may not be higher than that of low- or middle-income countries. Indeed, the developments in the global financial system in late 2007 and early 2008 suggest that the higher quality of supervisory systems in high-income countries may not have been sufficient given the complexity of their financial systems.

Donato Masciandaro and Marc Quintyn give an overview of the worldwide trends, causes and effects during the 1998–2008 period in reforming the financial supervision architecture and the role of the central bank in Chapter 16. Today policymakers in all countries, shaken by the financial crisis of 2007–2008, are carefully reconsidering the features of their supervisory architecture. Over the last ten years the financial supervision architecture and the role of the central bank in supervision therein has undergone radical transformation. In the wake of the 2007–08 financial crisis, more countries are considering reforms, while others, who went through a round of reforms, are looking at the architecture once again. They review the insights gained by the literature on this topic and, based on updated information on 102 countries for the 1998–2008 period, they address three questions:

(a)   Which main features are reshaping the supervisory architecture?,

(b)   What explains the increasing diversity of the institutional settings? and

(c)   What are the effects so far of the changing face of banking and financial supervisory regimes on the quality of regulation and supervision?

In Chapter 11, Sylvester Eijffinger in his second contribution to this volume discusses defining and measuring systemic risk. With the planned implementation of the European Systemic Risk Board (ESRB) in 2011, European authorities are trying to identify and avoid future financial crises before they start. The ESRB chaired by the President of the ECB will have to deal with the macro-prudential supervision of the financial sector in the European Union and is mandated to detect 'systemic risks'. However, the ECB does not have a clear concept of systemic risk itself and even in academia no generally accepted definition exists. He stresses the conceptual issues of systemic risk, stressing that the ESRB's tasks will be risk detection, risk assessment and ultimately issuing risk warnings. First, the different definitions of systemic risk are discussed, to be able to pinpoint the common components of systemic risk. Then he moves to risk detection and assessment, for which accurate 'early-warning indicators' should be developed together with the gathering of appropriate data. Finally, he argues that this new way of defining and measuring systemic risk should be translated into new ESRB policy, taking into account that the indicators can and should be refined over time.

In their second contribution to this volume in Chapter 17 Donato Masciandaro and Marc Quintyn, this time with co-author Maria Nieto, discuss the measuring convergence in the new European System of Financial Supervisors (ESFS). In June 2009 a new financial supervisory framework for the European Union was endorsed, consisting of a macro-prudential pillar and a micro-prudential pillar. The latter is composed of a Steering Committee, three supranational supervisory authorities (ESAs) and a network of national supervisory authorities at the bottom, de facto establishing a complex, multiple principals, multiple agents network. The ESAs will have far-reaching powers vis-à-vis the national supervisory authorities. However, the latter will also retain their full powers with respect to the oversight of the domestic financial system. Intertwined in this network of European and national supervisors are also the existing home-host supervisor relations, as well as the supervisory colleges, in charge of the oversight of cross-border institutions. So the emerging structure is a complex, multiple principals, multiple agents web, which, in order to produce efficient and effective supervision, needs to be governed by incentive-compatible arrangements. This paper focuses on the network of national agencies. Starting from an analysis of supervisory architectures and governance arrangements, they assess to what extent lack of convergence could undermine efficient and effective supervision. Their main conclusion is that harmonization of governance arrangements towards best practice would better align supervisors' incentive structures and hence be beneficial to the quality of supervision.

Marcelo Rezende empirically investigates in Chapter 18 how joint supervisors examine financial institutions, in particular state banks. He studies what determines whether federal and state supervisors examine state banks independently or together. The results suggest that supervisors coordinate examinations in order to support states with lower budgets and capabilities and more banks to supervise. He finds that states with larger budgets examine more banks independently, that they accommodate changes in the number of banks mostly through the number of examinations with a federal supervisor and that, when examining banks together, state banking departments that have earned quality accreditation are more likely to write conclusion reports separately from federal supervisors. The results also indicate that regulation impacts supervision by changing the characteristics of banks. Independent examinations decrease with branch deregulation, which is consistent with the facts that this reform consolidated banks within fewer independent firms and that state and federal supervisors are more likely to examine large and complex institutions together.

In the last contribution to this volume Jakob de Haan and Fabian Amtenbrink discuss the role of credit rating agencies (CRAs) in general and particularly during the financial crisis. They argue that CRAs play a crucial role in the global financial system as it is currently organized. This role is not limited to the elimination of an information asymmetry in favor of investors that readily take over the advice provided by CRAs in the form of credit rating. It actually extends to the fulfillment of a quasi-regulatory and thus public function in determining capital requirements for financial institutions, a crucial aspect of the prudential supervision and thus ultimately of financial stability as such. What is more, CRAs do not only cast a judgment on the creditworthiness of companies, such as financial institutions and their financial products, but also on states. The current euro zone crisis highlights the vast implications which a sovereign downgrading can have not only in the financial markets but also for the respective state itself. The recent financial crisis highlights that assigning such a key role to CRAs bears considerable risks, when not accompanied by an adequate regulatory framework. Certainly in the past, the business model of CRAs left room for conflicts of interest, while their rating methodologies remained opaque and arguably ill-suited for the application to the complex structured financial products that currently make such a large portion of the rating business of CRAs. Moreover, a large concentration in the rating business has left little or no room for new CRAs with other business models and rating methods to enter the market.

Conclusion

The relationships between central banking on one hand and financial regulation and supervision on the other hand must heed the lessons of the financial crisis. Everybody agrees about this issue. But how?

As we already stressed above the most interesting innovation to have taken place over the last decade is the split between responsibility for monetary policy and responsibility for micro supervision, assigning each function to a different regulatory actor. In a country the central bank should be the only lender of last resort and the sole monetary policy authority. Consequently, at least in normal times, three key features of modern central banking can be identified: the central bank should focus mainly on maintaining price stability; the central bank should be politically independent from the government and at the same time accountable and transparent; the central bank should be operationally independent in influencing interest rates as well as bank reserves to safeguard monetary stability.

The extraordinary times of the crisis confirmed that monetary policy and micro supervision should be separated, given that expected disadvantages have outweighed expected advantages. Those who still favor the coupling of the two policy monopolies within the central bank object that there are significant benefits in terms of information. But there are other ways to improve information flows, beyond such coupling.

On the other hand, the coupling of the micro supervision function with the monetary function poses certain dangers. There is the risk of distorting the behavior of financial intermediaries, by augmenting their propensity to risk. When the controller is the same actor that can save you by printing money, the moral hazard is likely to increase. There is a further risk in terms of central bank behavior, which can turn into an all-powerful bureaucracy, with related consequences.

The coupling of micro supervision and monetary policy tends to not keep banks, the central bank and the political system at arm's length from each other, with all the consequent risks. These risks are more relevant today, if one thinks how much tighter the relations between these agents have become in the wake of the financial crisis. Both micro supervisory policy and monetary policy must be managed by independent authorities: independent from banks, government, and their own bureaucratic appetites. The trend away from having micro supervision done inside the central bank should be completed.

Still the architecture of central banks should follow to ensure that the government of money not be subjected to either the vagaries of the electoral cycle or political ideology. The expressions 'independence' and 'accountability' have entered everyday language, but they need to be given more significant meaning. It is crucial to guarantee the correct perimeter of the triangle of power linking the central bank to banks and the political system, particularly if two of the corners are already so close to each other, after the extensive bailouts.

At the same time the crisis reminded us that in extraordinary times the central banks are still expected to utilize their policy instruments to safeguard the systemic stability of the financial system. The implications of the role of the central banks in maintaining financial stability concern its abilities in facing the potential tradeoffs that can occur in terms of goals, institutional relationships and instruments.

Our general suggestion is that future effectiveness of the central banking architecture will depend on its ability to ensure the consistency between the central bank actions in normal times – when the main goal is monetary stability – and extraordinary times – when the need is to rebuild public trust in financial stability. The central bank should be free to set the right policy instruments from time to time, so they are accountable and transparent, but not dependent or captured in any case.

In order to face banking panics and maintain financial stability, the central bank can be in the position to implement both conventional and non conventional policies. These policies can have implications on both the dimension and the riskiness of the central bank balance sheet. In a financially unstable environment the central bank may need to lend to anyone and to be the sole judge of whether the credit conditions – including collateral – are acceptable. Consequently, central bank policies may have potentially fiscal consequences, given that any negative payoffs ultimately must be funded by the fiscal authority. During the crisis the monetary and fiscal decisions become temporarily more intertwined. It is crucial that the institutional design avoids the risks that such temporary interactions produce permanent effects on central bank independence, accountability and transparency. The solution of the trading off between fiscal and monetary considerations will crucially depend on the different institutional solutions which characterize the relationships between the central bank, the government and the legislative bodies country by country. It is clear, for example, that the different position of the Anglo-Saxon central banks – the Fed and the BoE – compared to the ECB will be likely to matter.

This conclusion raises important and novel questions about how to manage the crucial differences in monetary policy strategies during normal and extraordinary times – i.e., unusual and exigent circumstances – as well as their consequences in central bank institutional design. In this respect at least three intertwined questions are today on the table. First, should the potential tradeoff between monetary stability and financial stability be explicitly considered and eventually disciplined in the central bank goal setting? In other words, should the central bank be made the explicit macro prudential regulator? Second, should central banks be independent, accountable and transparent following different procedures? Third, in order to prevent credit-based bubbles, should the central bank operational setting be enriched, possibly though regulatory instruments?

This handbook cannot have definite answers, but we have tried to offer robust frameworks and results to orientate future research. Now we are where the Ancient Romans called *Terra Incognita* ('Unknown Land'), or *Hic Sunt Leones* ('Here Are Lions'). Let us share the hope of the Medieval cartographers by offering maps to be used for avoiding nasty meetings!

A warm word of thanks goes also to Rosaria Vega Pansini for her excellent editorial assistance.

PART I

Central Banking, Regulation and
Supervision

1. Central Banks and the Financial System

Francesco Giavazzi and Alberto Giovannini[1]

Introduction

This chapter reviews the factors that make a financial system fragile and discusses the interaction between financial fragility and monetary policy. We argue that financial fragility is a deeper phenomenon than that which manifests itself when the price of some financial assets appear to follow a bubble. The fundamental fragility of a financial market does not arise from irrational behavior (although such irrationality seems to be routinely observed in financial markets).

The fundamental fragility of a financial system arises from its role in liquidity transformation. We shall illustrate a few examples of liquidity transformation, and the nature of the market fragility associated with it. As it will be apparent from the different examples, liquidity transformation is a central and ever-present function of financial markets. And therefore the 'fragility' of financial markets is an unavoidable fact of life. The challenge for policymakers, including central banks, is how to minimize the occurrence of financial crises which arise from a breakdown of liquidity transformation, and how to design their policy taking into account the possibility that such crises might occur.

We argue that a crucial variable in the Taylor rule, the tool most central banks use, albeit in quite different forms, to set the level of interest rates, is the real rate of interest the rule targets. Central banks

---

[1] This paper was originally written for the Conference in Honour of Pentti Kouri: Helsinki, 10–11 June, 2010. We thank Ricardo Caballero, Stephen Cecchetti and Fausto Panunzi for very useful discussions and Bengt Hölmstrom and Philip Lane for their comments.

typically treat the real rate as a constant, failing to recognize that the ex-ante real rate should be set so as to correct the inefficiency which arises by the incentive of financial intermediaries to borrow too much and borrow too short. This risks leading the economy into a low interest rate trap. Low interest rates induce too much risk taking and increase the probability of crises. These crises, in turn, require low interest rates to maintain the financial system alive. Raising rates becomes extremely difficult in a severely weakened financial system, so monetary authorities remain stuck in a low interest rates equilibrium. Following this introduction the paper is organized in four sections. We start by taking some distance and asking why were central banks created and to what extent and for what reasons do modern central banks differ from their precursors at the turn of the 20th century. We then ask to what extent has the crisis influenced the thinking of central bankers. After these introductory comments, we come to the core of the chapter: Why are financial systems fragile? We conclude by discussing possible remedies.

The Functions of Central Banks

There have been a number of comments regarding the role of central banks in the 2007–2008 crisis. While we think we can characterize the economics profession as largely unanimous on the broad appropriateness of central banks' interventionism and interventions as the crisis unfolded, within the larger business and financial community there have been a number of critics. Much less uniform views, even among economists, can be found on the question of whether central banks could have prevented the crisis or, worse, whether central banks caused the crisis through policies that provided the support to a credit bubble, especially in the United States.

The business of central banking has evolved tremendously in recent decades. Among the most notable evolutions we list the diffusion of legally-sanctioned forms of central bank independence, the spreading of inflation targeting as a guide to monetary policy and the establishment of the European Central Bank managing a currency for a group of 16 countries. A common conceptual thread in these reforms has been the view that the effectiveness of central banks could only be enhanced by limiting their mandate and allowing them to pursue such a mandate free from external influences. Until the 2007–2008 crisis, such reforms have been regarded as highly successful, bringing about a period of low and stable inflation and sustained growth in the 1990s.[2]

The direction of central banking in recent decades, focusing on the management of inflationary expectations with the ultimate task of price stability, contrasts with the experience of the early years of central banking in the two countries where substantial financial activities had developed: England and the United States.

The Bank of England was created to arrange finances for the government: it was supposed to be the government debt manager. Yet, after a succession of financial crises in the 19th century, it transformed into the guardian of the financial stability of the City of London, adopting a modus operandi in line with Walter Bagehot's (1873) influential suggestions.

The case of the US Federal Reserve is paradigmatic.[3] The US National Monetary Commission, chaired by Senator Nelson Aldrich, was set up in 1910 to investigate the workings of foreign financial systems and central banks, to find out whether setting up a US central bank would help prevent the liquidity crises, followed by widespread financial crises, that characterized the US financial system during the National Banking Period (from 1863 to 1913). During this period, two notable attempts to set up entities performing the functions of a central bank were the evolution of the Independent Treasury, which during the tenure of Leslie Shaw (between 1902 and 1907, on the eve of the last and arguably most serious crisis of the National Banking Period) actively injected and withdrew funds into the money market with the explicit objective of stabilizing it, and the clearinghouse associations, such as the New York Clearinghouse Association (1854), which by netting payments reduced the circulation of specie thus attempting to reduce the risk of liquidity shortages due to failures in the payments system.

Sprague (1910) was the best known advocate of a creation of a US central bank. Writing on the 1907 crisis he concludes (p. 320):

---

[2] With the notable exception of the experience in Japan.
[3] See Miron (1989).

Somewhere in the banking system of a country there should be a reserve of lending power, and it should be found in its central money market. Ability in New York to increase loans and to meet the demands of depositors for money would have allayed every panic since the establishment of the national banking system. Provision for such reserve power may doubtless be made in a number of different ways. This investigation will have served its purpose if in showing the causes and consequences of its absence in the past it brings home to the reader the need not only of this reserve power, but also of the readiness to use it in future emergencies.

A stable financial system is a necessary condition for a central bank to carry out a macroeconomic mandate (this is the argument often cited by the European Central Bank) such as inflation targeting: a corollary of this statement is that the central bank should be the guardian of financial stability. Conversely it has also been argued that macroeconomic stability, to which the central bank can contribute with its actions, is a prerequisite for financial stability. Indeed, many have suggested that one of the prime causes of the 2007–2008 crisis was the buildup of global imbalances in savings and investment across different macro regions. The arguments cited above are consistent with the following proposition: *the central bank should pursue its macroeconomic mandate with all means at its own disposal, including interventions in the money markets; the concern for financial stability does not imply deviations of interest rates from the path dictated by the objectives of macroeconomic stability (i.e., price stability).* What this proposition more specifically implies, is that the path of interest rates which results from a maximization problem that does not take into account the potential and determinants of financial crises is equal to one that solves out financial markets and their instabilities into the maximization problem. Moreover, the pursuit of an inflation target does not preclude the ability of the central bank to take action in the event of a crisis and use a wide and changing array of tools to avoid a chain of liquidations among financial intermediaries, with severe impacts on economic activity.

In this chapter we want to challenge the proposition in the paragraph above, hoping to contribute to a discussion on the development of central banking in the years to come. As the evolution of the financial systems of New York and London shaped the way for the development of the US Federal Reserve and the Bank of England in the early 20th century, so the development of financial markets throughout the globe witnessed in the past two decades will have to induce an equally important evolution of the structure and operations of central banks.

Lessons From the Crisis

When discussing central banks' roles in financial markets it is essential to distinguish ex-ante and ex-post. Ex-post, once a financial crisis has materialized, few disagree with the need for the central bank to intervene employing all the tools at its disposal. The typical telltale of a financial crisis is a spike in the demand for liquidity (more on this in the following sections). Since Bagehot (1873), the recipes for responding to financial crises have been routinely applied by central banks: abundant liquidity supply through low interest rates and open market operations; access to the discount window; and, as we have seen in recent months, a much enlarged universe of collateral instruments to obtain credit from the central bank (that is to obtain loans in central bank money), as well as access to central bank credit by a wider variety of financial intermediaries. Because the central bank is the monopolist supplier of the safest means of payment, i.e. central bank money, it is only to be expected that it will play an active role during times of financial stress. The lessons of Bagehot and Sprague have been well absorbed.

Matters, however, are very different ex-ante. Thinking of what central banks should do ex-ante, that is when financial markets work smoothly, economists have mostly focused on the question whether central banks should worry about the buildup of 'bubbles' in financial asset prices, under the implicit assumption that a financial crisis is the bursting of a financial bubble. Below, we shall review arguments in favor of and against central banks' intervention in the buildup of financial markets bubbles. These arguments, however, can and should be extended to the more general case and the more general question of whether and how central banks should take into account, in their day-to-day operations in normal times, the possibility of financial instabilities.

The argument that monetary policy should not be influenced by the concern for the fragility of financial markets is a prominent and well argued one among academics and policy-makers. A common view (see for example, Bernanke and Gertler, 1999) is that financial stability and price stability are 'highly complementary and mutually consistent objectives' which can be jointly pursued through a flexible inflation targeting regime, whereby central banks adjust monetary policy actively and pre-emptively to offset incipient inflationary or deflationary pressures. This prescription derives from a model of monetary transmission (see, for example, Bernanke, Gertler and Gilchrist, 1999) which allows for financial intermediation by assuming that policy interest rates induce changes in the external finance premium, the difference in cost between external funds and retained earnings, which is a characteristic of credit markets with asymmetric information. The channel through which interest rates affect the external finance premium are balance sheets and bank lending. The basic conclusion is that the richer and more realistic description of the monetary transmission mechanism to include financial intermediaries and balance sheet effects makes monetary policy more potent than simpler models would lead us to believe. In these models the complementarity between macroeconomic stability and financial stability arises essentially because the procyclicality of policy interest rates, rising during inflationary periods and declining in deflationary periods, dampens asset price fluctuations, as asset price booms tend to go together with inflationary pressures and, vice versa, busts with deflationary conditions.[4] For these reasons, Bernanke and his co-authors argue that central banks should not worry about the possible buildup of 'bubbles' in financial markets, and even less about pricking them. They should simply be aware of the effects on aggregate spending of presumed bubbles or of other fluctuations in asset prices, and be prepared to respond in the case of sudden changes in the price of financial assets. Recently Fed chairman Ben Bernanke (2010) has reiterated the argument in a discussion of monetary policy in the United States around the boom and bust of the housing market. He illustrates the output of a vector autoregression (VAR) of seven

---

[4] The experience of the years leading up to the recent crisis, years characterized by low and stable inflation and asset price booms, naturally puts into question this view.

variables, including measures of economic growth, inflation, unemployment, residential investment, house prices, and the federal funds rate, estimated using data from 1977 to 2002. He then uses the estimated model to simulate the federal funds rate in the intervening years as well as the behavior of house prices. The exercise shows that the actual federal funds rate moved broadly in line with the predictions of the model, while housing prices were widely outside the model's predictions. His conclusion is that house prices movements from 2002 to 2009 are hardly connected to either monetary policy or the broader macroeconomic environment. This lack of a systematic relation between the dynamics of asset prices and monetary policy leads Bernanke to conclude that it would be inefficient for monetary policy to deal actively with asset prices, before potential disruptions manifest themselves. The absence of a systematic relation between the evolution of asset prices and monetary policy instruments (together with other relevant macroeconomic variables) is consistent with the hypothesis that monetary policy instruments may not have an effect on financial asset prices in a robust and reliable way.[5] In particular, Bernanke claims it is impossible to detect asset 'bubbles' before they burst and therefore central banks should not engage in the activity of detecting bubbles and pricking them. At the same time, however, he recognizes that the damage produced by the rapid deleveraging caused by precipitous asset deflations justifies that central banks 'must be especially vigilant in ensuring that the recent experiences are not repeated'. This remark is in line with Greenspan (2003) who describes a kind of risk management approach to monetary policy: 'Recognizing that monetary policy decisions have to be taken in conditions of uncertainty, and that certain low-probability events may have large negative consequences on the economy, monetary policymakers may take actions that are difficult to justify in terms of the observable state of the economy, but find an explanation as hedges against tail events'.

These statements represent a significant departure from the view that central banks should not worry about the possible buildup of 'bubbles' in financial markets, and much less about pricking them,

---

[5] The notable exception here is the linear-quadratic optimal control result that the instrument has no detectable correlation with the equilibrium realizations of the target variable when at an optimum: the only fluctuations of the target variable are due to uncontrollable idiosyncratic disturbances.

and that they should simply be aware of the effects of presumed bubbles or other fluctuations in asset prices on aggregate spending. Yet, both Bernanke and his predecessor at the Federal Reserve do not offer specific guidance as to the role of monetary authorities vis-à-vis financial markets in 'normal' times: this is what we are going to discuss in the next section.

The Fragility of Financial Markets

Many commentaries on financial markets identify their 'fragility' with the phenomenon of bubbles: sustained and often sudden increases in the prices of certain financial assets that make them attractive to investors, whose investments further drive up prices, well beyond what is justified by the expected returns from those assets. Bubbles 'burst' when investors realize their enthusiasm is unjustified. This is clearly an important phenomenon in financial markets, one that will always be present because information about the value of assets is always incomplete, and therefore investors think that other investors are, through their behavior, revealing incremental information about the value of assets.

However, the fundamental fragility of financial markets does not require investors to behave in a way that ultimately proves irrational (although such irrationality seems to be routinely observed in financial markets): it is associated with liquidity transformation. Through liquidity transformation different agents, with different transactional needs, can be pooled together to provide long-term funding for productive investments. The pooling of diverse transactional needs permits, in principle, the stability of long-term funding. Liquidity transformation is a socially productive activity because it is generally the case that production possibilities become more attractive whenever investment horizons can be lengthened.

Liquidity transformation is produced by different intermediation technologies. The two simplest technologies for producing liquidity transformation are a bank and a securities market. Consider a bank. First: it issues short-term debt, in the form of short-term deposits or checking accounts, and with them it finances long-term loans. As long as the liquidity needs of depositors and checking account holders are sufficiently diversified, the bank is viable and profitable. However, were the bank compelled to provide funds to a large fraction of its depositors or account holders simultaneously, the value of its investments would likely fall short of the value of its short-term debt. A securities market is very similar. Through it, an issuer can raise, in principle, long-term funding. Trading activity in the (secondary) market allows investors with diverse liquidity needs to enter and exit the market flexibly. If the securities market did not exist many fewer investors would be willing or able to commit funds for maturities matching those needed by the issuers. The secondary market would break down if the smooth mechanism that brings together buyers and sellers stopped working. What would make a bank or a securities market experience a crisis? What is sufficient is the fear of not recouping the value of one's investment. This can happen any time to the bank clients, if they fear that all may want to withdraw their cash at the same time (because all know that there is not enough value to satisfy every depositor). But this can also happen in securities markets: investors will be unwilling to buy securities if for any reason they suspect not being able to sell them when they need to. Such market breakdowns are market failures, i.e. spontaneous market equilibria that generate inferior welfare levels. When markets break down, funding for long-term projects dries up and society is forced to less efficient productions, implying lower income for everybody. In this section of the paper we shall illustrate a few examples of the market fragility associated with liquidity transformation. As it will be apparent from the different examples, liquidity transformation is a central and ever-present function of financial markets. And therefore the 'fragility' of financial markets is an unavoidable fact of life. The challenge for policymakers, including central banks, is how to minimize the occurrence of financial crises which arise from a breakdown of liquidity transformation, and how to design their policy taking into account the possibility that such crises might occur.

The first example (which elaborates on Hölmstrom and Tirole, 2011) illustrates one aspect of the fragility induced by liquidity transformation. It shows that an amount of 'inside' liquidity, i.e., liquidity created by financial intermediaries, that is sufficient in the aggregate may not be enough to make sure that every actor in the marketplace has access to a sufficient amount of liquidity when she needs it. In such a situation 'outside liquidity', i.e., liquidity created by the monetary authorities may be needed even in the absence of macroeconomic shocks.

The second example also borrows the analytical framework developed in Hölmstrom and Tirole (2011) to show how financial intermediaries may be subject to 'runs' and face spikes in liquidity demand in a way that is similar to the 'runs on banks' studied in the time-honored Diamond-Dybvig model. These examples illustrate two different aspects of the market fragility associated with liquidity transformation and show how central banks can intervene to accommodate spikes in the demand for liquidity. In the following paragraph we shall move one step further, showing that inappropriate monetary policy can induce excessive liquidity transformation and, through this channel, raise the probability of a crisis. In this context we shall show that the ex-ante 'optimal' monetary policy differs from the policy that is optimal ex-post, that is after a crisis has developed, as the two need to move in opposite directions: relatively higher interest rates ex-ante to reduce the incentive to engage in excessive liquidity transformation and, to the extent that sudden needs for liquidity still arise, relatively accommodative monetary policy ex-post to limit the damage to the real economy.

Liquidity transformation and financial fragility

The first two examples illustrate the fragility associated with liquidity transformation. We take the amount of liquidity transformation as given and discuss why it makes financial markets fragile. In the third example we shall discuss why monetary policy may induce 'excessive' liquidity transformation, thus contributing to making markets more fragile.

Dispatching inside liquidity

A well functioning financial market should be able to produce enough 'inside liquidity' to meet the liquidity shocks it needs to withstand. The ability to do this hinges on an efficient dispatching of available liquidity toward those intermediaries in need of cash. This can be accomplished by pooling the available liquidity at the level of financial intermediaries, who then re-dispatch it through a mechanism that Hölmstrom and Tirole (2011) describe as akin to drawing from credit lines. This is clearly a superior arrangement compared to a situation in which each intermediary hoards liquidity to withstand a possible shock: hoarding results in a waste and therefore a potential shortage of liquidity, as intermediaries that end up awash with cash do not lend it to those with a shortage of liquidity. What can cause this efficient distribution of inside liquidity to break down? The most relevant case are macroeconomic shocks, when inside liquidity is insufficient because all intermediaries face the same need for liquidity and all at the same time. In the presence of macroeconomic shocks (as illustrated in Hölmstrom and Tirole 1998) even if intermediaries were to diversify holding the stock market index (i.e. claims on the aggregate economy) they could not create a store of value that can be resold in case of liquidity needs that hit the entire economy. But the efficient distribution of inside liquidity can break down also in the absence of macro shocks: this can happen if, for some reason, financial intermediaries are unable or unwilling to redistribute efficiently an otherwise sufficient level of inside liquidity. We shall illustrate this point elaborating on an example described in Hölmstrom and Tirole (2011). There are three periods and the real interest rate between each period is zero. In $t = 0$, an entrepreneur finances a project whose initial cost is I; borrowing B from investors and contributing E in equity, so that $B + E = I$. The project does not generate any revenue at $t = 1$; actually with probability $1/2$ an overrun (a 'liquidity shock') of L arises, that must be covered if the project is to go on and produce income at $t = 2$, otherwise the project is liquidated and yields no income. With probability $1/2$, there is no overrun and therefore no extra expense at $t = 1$. At $t = 2$, revenue accrues (provided that the overrun, if it happened, has been covered). The total proceeds are then shared between investors and the entrepreneur. The share that goes to the entrepreneur (in case of a success) must be large enough to make sure that he puts enough 'effort' into running the project. To compute the pledgeable income, that is the maximum amount that the entrepreneur can credibly promise to investors, note that, as of $t = 0$, the expected contribution of investors to this project is $B+I=2L$: this is the minimum that must be promised to bring them in at date 0. In fact, under perfect competition it is all that is needed to bring them in. Thus the pledgeable income at $t = 0$ is:

$$P = B + 1/2\, L \qquad (1.1)$$

All that remains goes to the entrepreneur. (In computing P this way we are assuming that the return on the project, which we have not specified, is large enough for the entrepreneur to have an incentive to put in enough effort). Thus, if investors are promised P as of $t = 0$, the project will be financed even if investors know that it might need refinancing and, in case of success, a large enough share of the revenue will have to be turned over to the entrepreneur. However, what looks feasible as of $t = 0$ may no longer be feasible at $t = 1$. Assume an overrun occurs in $t = 1$. The entrepreneur could look for new investors who are willing to refinance his project, but it is not clear he would find them. The reason is that all he can promise is P in $t = 2$; but to keep the project going he needs L. If $L > P$ (that is if $L > 2B$) he will find no investors and the project will be abandoned. (Note that offering the new investors, those that come in $t = 1$, seniority with respect to the investors that came in the period before does not help. If $L > P$ the project is abandoned even if the entrepreneur were to give 0 to the original investors and P to the new ones). There are two ways an entrepreneur can insure against such liquidity shocks. The inefficient way is to hoard liquidity in case an overrun occurs. This is inefficient because capital would remain idle. Hölmstrom and Tirole (2011) suggest that the entrepreneur could instead negotiate a credit line with a bank. For a fee F paid in $t = 0$, the bank could commit to pay L in $t = 1$. If the overrun occurs and the credit line is drawn, the bank becomes the senior creditor (the original creditors get nothing) and therefore receives P in $t = 2$. The commitment fee is:

$$F = (1/2)\,(L - P) = (1/4)L - (1/2)B \qquad (1.2)$$

The value of F can be computed observing that the bank makes money if the credit line is not drawn, and loses money if the firm faces an overrun: for the value of F shown above the bank's expected profit is zero. Note that the credit line must be pre-arranged in $t = 0$. Come $t = 1$ financing the overrun is a money-losing operation: the bank would not be willing to do it unless it is bound by a contract: an example of a situation of time inconsistency. Outside investors will still finance the project in $t = 0$. They will also pay for the commitment fee: you can check this noting that they pay $B + F =$

1/2B + 1/4L in *t = 0* and their expected return is also *(1/2) P = 1/2B + 1/4L*; thus they come out even. The bank is also fine, provided that it diversifies the credit lines across all firms in the economy, and that the overruns net out in the aggregate, i.e., provided that the sum of all that is drawn from the credit lines in *t = 1* is zero. In other words, provided that there is no aggregate shock to the economy. In this case the bank makes a profit of *F* on one half of the firms to which it has extended credit lines (we are assuming that all firms are identical) and a loss of *–F +(L – P) = F* on one half of the firms who draw the lines. Thus it would seem that if liquidity shocks are uncorrelated there is always enough inside liquidity and no project will ever be abandoned.

What could go wrong? Inside liquidity need not only be sufficient in the aggregate: as we have seen it also needs to be dispatched to those who need it This condition breaks down if 'banks' are not perfectly diversified. In the previous example there is only one bank: thus, if shocks are idiosyncratic and cancel out in the aggregate, the bank is perfectly diversified by definition. But consider a situation where there is more than one bank and banks are not perfectly diversified. Consider an extreme case: assume there are only two firms and two banks. Each bank extends a credit line to one firm only. There is no aggregate liquidity shock: one firm faces an overrun and thus draws on its credit line; the other pays the commitment fee but does not draw on its credit line because it does not face an overrun. In this case one bank makes a profit of F, the other a loss of F. More importantly, the firm which faces an overrun cannot rely on its bank to finance it and must fold up its project. There is still enough liquidity in the aggregate, but it is not dispatched to the firm that needs it because the bank which makes a profit has no incentive to give it up and transfer it to the other bank so that this can deliver on its committed credit line.[6]

---

[6] The literature has investigated many reasons why the dispatching of inside liquidity may break down. Adverse selection: if you sell it, it must be a lemon, thus I don't buy it. Bad news (Dang, Gorton and Hölmstrom, 2009) which not only lowers the value of an asset but gives rise to adverse selection problems resulting in secondary markets drying up. Fire sales. Institutions which hoard liquidity to be ready to snap up the assets of distressed firms. Gambling for resurrection: distressed firms have the assets and could sell them to deep-pocket investors, but because the price of these assets is low, they rather wait.

The lesson from this example is that inside liquidity may be insufficient to prevent liquidation of otherwise productive projects, even absent macroeconomic shocks: financial fragility can result in productive capital being destroyed. The central bank has two ways to deal with this. It can use regulation to make sure that all banks are perfectly diversified, so that none is exposed to idiosyncratic shocks. This is the superior, though probably unrealistic solution. Alternatively, if regulation fails to achieve perfect diversification, it can step in to provide outside liquidity to those firms to which liquidity fails to be dispatched.

The fragility of securities markets

Our second example uses the same analytical framework used in the first: it is also inspired by Hölmstrom and Tirole (2011). But here we extend that framework to study the liquidity shocks that might affect, rather than an entrepreneur, a portfolio manager. Our purpose is to show how financial intermediaries may be subject to 'runs' in a manner that is similar to the 'runs on banks' studied in Diamond and Dybvig (1983). There are still three periods. At date 0, a fund manager creates a fund purchasing a set of securities to construct a portfolio. The total outlay for the purchase of the securities is I, which the fund manager finances borrowing B from investors and contributing E of his own, so that $B+E = I$. In $t = 2$ (and not before) the portfolio yields a return greater than I which is distributed between the fund manager and the investors (as above in such a way as to make sure that the manager puts in enough effort). In $t = 1$ the fund is subject to a random liquidity shock: with probability *1/2* investors withdraw B. Why would this happen? In $t = 0$ investors know that the securities yield a return only in $t = 2$, but they also know that there is the chance of an early withdrawal. (This is a short-cut that should be more carefully thought out. Investors could suddenly discover that instead of 'patient', they are 'impatient' and want to withdraw, maybe there is a shock to their preferences, maybe some macro news has scared them.) Whatever the reason, we assume it does not alter the expected return on the portfolio. In $t = 0$ the pledgeable income (following the same logic of the previous example) is

$$P = B + 1/2B = 1.5B \qquad (1.3)$$

To attract investors the fund must promise that they will at least break even: investors contribute B in $t=0$ and again B with probability $1/2$ in $t = 1$. Thus in $t = 0$ they must be promised at least *1.5 B*. How can the fund manager liquidate his investors if he needs to in $t = 1$? He could either sell the portfolio or raise fresh funds from new investors. Because $P = 1.5 \, B > B$, he will always be able to survive the liquidity shock by attracting new investors: he needs to raise B and can promise $P > B$. So, this case is not particularly interesting. But let's instead assume that the option of attracting new investors is ruled out, perhaps because when some investors withdraw nobody is willing to come in. Then the only way for the fund manager to survive the withdrawals is to sell the portfolio. Let p be the price at which the portfolio can be sold in $t = 1$. Assume that p is a firesale price, so that $p < P$: in other words, p is lower than the 'value' of the portfolio in $t = 1$. The minimum price that allows the fund manager to survive is $p \geq B$. For $p < B$, anytime investors want to get out in $t = 1$, the intermediary is broke. Thus there are multiple equilibria which depend on investors' preferences. The possibility that a fund subject to sudden withdrawals may fail can have real effects and result, as in the previous example, in a destruction of capital. Here again the central bank can address this fragility by stepping in to provide outside liquidity to the funds that experience sudden withdrawals.

Excessive liquidity transformation

In the previous section we took the amount of liquidity transformation as given and discussed why it makes financial markets fragile. We now move on and allow for monetary policy to determine the amount of liquidity transformation. Drawing on a contribution by Jeremy Stein (2011) we show that the central bank may induce 'excessive' liquidity transformation, thus contributing to making markets more fragile. The Stein model considers a bank which faces the following investment opportunity: by investing I in $t = 0$, if a 'good state' prevails (which happens with probability p) total output at time 2 is $f(I) > I$. If instead a 'bad state' prevails, total expected output in $t = 2$ is $\lambda I \leq I$, where λ could be as low as 0. The state of the world, good or bad, is revealed in $t = 1$. At that time it is possible for the bank to sell its investment at a (possibly firesale price) k, where $0 \leq k \leq 1$: The bank finances I borrowing from investors. It can do so by issuing either short-term (maturing in $t = 1$) or long-term (maturing in $t = 2$) debt claims. Long term debt is risky because there is a positive probability of the assets yielding zero output at time two. Short term deposits pay a return R^M and are by assumption riskless: they are de-facto 'private money'. Because the interest rate on risky assets is above the interest rate on riskless assets, the bank has an incentive to finance as much as possible of its project with short term debt: by doing this it appropriates the value that investors attribute to the services of 'money', i.e., to liquidity. The constraint is that 'money' must always be repaid, no matter what the state of the world is in period 1. Let m be the fraction of the project financed issuing short-term deposits. In $t = 1$ the bank owes its short-term creditors $mIR^M \equiv M$. For the bank to meet this promise in the bad state by selling assets (i.e., the project it has financed) it must be that:

$$M \le k\lambda I \qquad\qquad (1.4)$$

which implies an upper bound for m

$$m \le m^{\text{max}} = \frac{k\lambda}{R^M} \qquad\qquad (1.5)$$

so that

$$M^{\text{max}} = \frac{k\lambda I}{R^M} \qquad\qquad (1.6)$$

$m = m^{max}$ whenever the difference between the return on risky and riskless assets is sufficiently high, i.e., when the bank's incentive to issue short term liabilities is large. Note that for $m = m^{max}$ the bank faces a collateral constraint: the only way it can raise M (and thus appropriate the value investors attribute to the services of liquidity) is to raise I. To issue additional short term debt it must invest more which is the way it can raise its collateral. As Stein observes, the collateral constraint gives rise to an externality which can be understood as follows. When a given bank raises I, and thus M, it takes into account the fact that, in the bad state, this will force it to sell more assets at a discount in order to pay off its own short-term debt. What it fails to internalize, however, is that by raising M it reduces the equilibrium value of k, thus lowering the collateral value of all other bank's assets. The bottom line is that for a large-enough spread between the return on risky and riskless assets the bank engages in inefficient liquidity transformation.

What happens in a 'bad' state when the bank, to make good on M, needs to sell its project at a price k ? Who will buy it, and how is k determined? In $t = 1$ there will be new investors in the economy and new projects to be financed (new to distinguish them from the investors who have financed the 'old' project in $t = 0$). They are the buyers of the old project. Let W be the total resources of the new investors, and $g(W)$ the output of the new projects they could finance. In principle these investors could use all of W to finance new projects, obtaining a marginal return $g'(W)$. If instead they buy M from the bank they will only invest $(W–M)$ and their return will fall to $g'(W – M) < g'(W)$. In the bad state the need to reimburse M crowds out good projects. To convince the new investors to buy M, $g'(W–M)$ must equal the marginal return from buying the old project from the bank: this pins down the firesale discount k:[7]

$$g'(W - M) = \frac{1}{k} \qquad (1.7)$$

As in the examples of the previous section, when a bad state occurs, and the spread between risky and riskless assets induces excessive liquidity transformation, the central bank can limit the crowding out by injecting outside liquidity, that is by supplying M (or a fraction of M) to the bank, thus limiting how much of the project it will need to sell. But the model has an additional implication for monetary policy[8]: the smaller the difference between the return on

---

[7] We are left with the problem of determining the optimal levels of m and of I. We show this in Appendix 1.

[8] The model has another interesting, though somewhat paradoxical implication. A way to induce the bank to limit m is to allow it to increase the riskiness of its balance sheet, for example by holding 'derivatives', i.e., assets that resemble pure 'bets'. When a bank holds a 'bet', its balance sheet becomes more fragile, and this is normally bad. But there is also a silver lining. The 'bet' reduces the amount of safe deposits the bank can issue, and thus the distortion associated with this incentive. There are two reasons why a bank may decide to hold 'bets'. They may be part of its proprietary trading

risky assets and the risk-free rate, the smaller the bank's incentive to increase I in order to relax its collateral constraint; in other words, the smaller is the incentive to engage in excessive liquidity transformation. There is a level of this spread below which liquidity transformation is no longer 'excessive'.

We shall discuss what this implies for central banks in the next section.

Liquidity Transformation, Financial System Reforms and Monetary Policy

The examples in the previous sections have illustrated the basic fragility of financial intermediation which arises from the possibility that investors rush to liquidity. This risk is compounded by the possibility that monetary policy might induce excessive liquidity transformation. In this section we start by asking if financial system reforms can limit financial fragility; we shall then discuss how central banks can avoid subsidizing liquidity transformation.

Financial system reforms

The basic ingredients of financial fragility are liquidity transformation as well as asymmetric information. Liquidity transformation is itself a good thing, because it allows access to more productive technologies. Imperfect information is a characteristic of any financial system where the providers of funds are different from the users of funds. In addition, the imperfect information problem is multiplied the greater is the distance between users and providers of funds. With the multiple

---

activities: in this case the bank holds pure bets with the purpose of affecting the risk profile of its own equity. Alternatively it may hold them as part of the services it offers to its clients: one example is a bank that sells insurance (options) that allows a firm to protect itself against, for instance, fluctuations in commodity prices. By doing this the bank exposes itself to fluctuations in such prices. In this case 'bets' have a social value: for instance they can raise the productivity of the technology the bank's clients operate. We analyze this case in Appendix 2.

layers of intermediaries and the pervasiveness of securities markets, the potential guises liquidity or financial crises can take also multiply.

Another factor contributing to the spreading as well as the magnification of liquidity crises is, in the intermediaries' business, the process of risk management. Exposures to financial risks are hedged dynamically (or equivalently through contingent derivative contracts), thus giving rise to nonlinear reactions to price changes. Furthermore, risk management leads to contagion, as losses in some markets lead to a deficit of capital that can only be recouped through the liquidation of assets not necessarily related to the original losses.

These observations highlight, just as the analytical examples in the previous sections, that liquidity crises are as much outside the banking system as within the system itself. The evolution of the financial system outside of banks is well illustrated by Gorton (2007). Banks have exited the traditional borrowing/lending business (whereby loans are held in the balance sheet until maturity) because it is not any more profitable. They sell their loans through various structures, including special investment vehicles (SIVs), asset backed securities (ABSs), collateralized loan obligations or collateralized bond obligations (CLOs, CBOs). The different capital tranches of these structures are bought by different classes of investors, including long term investors like pension funds, money market mutual funds and hedge funds. As far as fund-raising is concerned, banks use the repo market, where cash is exchanged with securities in a buy/sell type contract: the securities provided as collateral are those created through the various structures mentioned above, which in part banks retain for themselves. According to Gorton, the size of the repo market in the United States has reached roughly US$ 12 trillion. A liquidity crisis in this market, a run on the banks, involves an increase in margin requirements in repo transactions, leading to liquidations of the underlying assets and therefore further increases in margin requirements (these illiquidity spirals have been described, among others, by Brunnermeier and Pedersen, 2008). The final observation needed to describe the nature of financial crises in the contemporary financial system is that, especially through risk management and the development of over-the-counter derivative contracts, the number and frequency of transactions in securities has increased tremendously (the total value of securities transactions in the United States is valued in the quadrillions): with it, counterparty risk has multiplied. As a result, the potential of chains of failures has gone up.

Recognizing the increased fragility of the financial system due to the spreading and multiplying of liquidity risk well outside the banking system, a number of authors, including one author of this chapter (Giovannini, 2010), have suggested structural reforms to make the financial system less prone to crises. These reform proposals include:

1. a decrease of counterparty risk in the financial system through a much wider use of central counterparties, which play the role of 'black holes' of counterparty risk in the system, as well as the adoption of orderly resolution rules for the large balance sheets of financial intermediaries.
2. a role for regulatory authorities to mitigate the information problem by accessing all data in securities and derivatives market transactions and positions, as well as risk positions of all financial intermediaries, by elaborating an aggregate picture of systemic risks, and by publishing their analysis and (aggregate) information for all market participants to see. This way, authorities would be in a position of carrying out their systemic risk manager duties much more effectively than in the recent past.
3. the re-establishment of an appropriate correspondence between the regulatory framework that defines different financial organizations in the marketplace and the functions they effectively perform (to avoid conflicts of interest, excessive risk taking, implicit puts to the government, etc.): a concept that inspires the so-called 'Volcker rule', as well as initiatives to make the regulatory framework for hedge funds converge onshore.

Low interest rate traps

Structural reforms can strengthen the financial system and decrease the risk of liquidity crises, but they cannot eliminate them completely. The reason is that liquidity breakdowns can only be eliminated by eliminating liquidity transformation. By now it should be apparent that liquidity transformation is a function that almost defines the financial system. Thus, even successful structural reforms do not take away from our conclusion in the previous section, that is, interest rates have to reflect the risk of financial crises. In other words, all actors in the marketplace have to know that liquidity could be less than what they observe in normal times, because there is always the possibility of breakdowns: interest rates have to properly reflect this. Discussions of monetary policy in the years preceding the crisis (including Bernanke 2010) mostly focus on the extent to which interest rates have been set according to the 'Taylor rule'. They concentrate on the variables in the Taylor rule – the deviation of inflation expectations from the central bank target – but tend to overlook the other variable in the rule: the real rate of interest. Empirical applications of the Taylor rule tend to use, for the real rate, a long average of past real rates – the argument being that since the real rate is a stationary variable the average of past real rates is a good proxy for the equilibrium real rate today. This argument, however, overlooks the point made in the previous section, namely that the ex-ante real rate affects the banks' incentive to engage in liquidity transformation. To the extent that this incentive has changed over time (or has been overlooked when setting interest rates in the past) so should the ex-ante real rate. If central banks set interest rates overlooking the risk of financial crises, rates in 'normal times' will be too low and liquidity transformation will be subsidized, as recent experience has shown. This could push the economy into a low-interest-rate trap. Low interest rates induce too much risk taking and increase the probability of crises. These crises, in turn, require low interest rates to maintain the financial system alive. Raising rates becomes extremely difficult in a severely weakened financial system, so monetary authorities remain stuck in a low interest rates equilibrium.

Summing Up and Looking Forward

Two main messages come out from our paper. Financial systems are inherently fragile because the reason for their fragility is the very function which makes a financial system so precious: liquidity transformation. Regulatory reforms can strengthen the financial system and decrease the risk of liquidity crises, but they cannot eliminate it completely. This leaves monetary policy with a very important task. In a framework that recognizes the interactions between monetary policy and liquidity transformation, 'optimal' monetary policy would consist of a modified Taylor rule in which the real rate reflects the possibility of liquidity crises and recognizes that liquidity transformation gets subsidized. Failure to recognize this point risks leading the economy into a low interest rate trap: low interest rates induce too much risk taking and increase the probability of crises. These crises, in turn, require low interest rates to maintain the financial system alive. Raising rates becomes extremely difficult in a severely weakened financial system, so monetary authorities remain stuck in a low interest rates trap. This seems a reasonable description of the situation we have experienced throughout the past decade. What is the empirical implication of the analysis in this paper? What does it mean that the short term real interest rate should not subsidize liquidity transformation? And importantly, if what matters for the possibility of such a subsidy is the spread between the policy rate and the return on risky assets, does the central bank have control over it? These are issues for further research. As concerns the first question one way to go about it could be investigating whether different monetary policy rules (across time or countries) are correlated with differences in the duration of investment: in particular the share of residential investment in total investment or in GDP (for an attempt see Dew-Becker 2009). The idea being that a monetary policy that subsidizes liquidity transformation might be associated with a longer duration of investment and a higher share of residential investment.

Appendix 1

Determining the optimal values of *m* and *M*

The bank's profits are:

$$\left[pf(I) + (1-p)\lambda I - IR^{B} \right] - mI\left(R^{B} - R^{M} \right) - (1-p)zmIR^{B}$$

The FOC with respect to *m*, the share of the project financed with short term debt, is:

$$I\left[\left(R^B - R^M\right) - \left(1-p\right)zR^B\right]$$

If the excess return on the risky asset, R^B, over the return on money R^M, is larger than the expected losses associated with a firesale, $(1-p)zR^M$, m has a corner solution

$$m^* = m^{\text{max}} = \frac{k\lambda}{R^M}$$

The optimal quantity of M (note that finding a *max* with respect to M or I is equivalent) is determined by the following FOC

$$\left[pf' + (1-p)\lambda - R^B\right]\frac{dI}{dM} + \frac{R^B - R^M}{R^M} - z(1-p)$$

If $m = m^{max}$ the sum of the last two terms is positive: the optimal level of M then requires the first term to be negative: this means that the optimal level of I, I^*; is larger than the level that would be chosen if the project was financed only with risky debt at the rate R^B, that is $I^* > I^B$. The intuition for this result is as follows. For $m = m^{max}$ the bank runs up against a collateral constraint: it can raise M (thus appropriating the social value of money) only by investing more, that is raising I, because m is fixed. It can do this choosing $I^* > I^B$, the amount the bank would invest if it financed the project only with risky bonds.

I^* is not only larger than I^B: it is also larger than the level a social planner would choose for a given spread $R^B - R^M$. To see this note that a social planner would maximize

$$U = \left[pf(I) + (1-p)\lambda I - IR^B\right] - M\frac{R^B - R^M}{R^M} + E\left[g(K) - K\right]$$

The social planner's FOC with respect to M is identical to the FOC faced by the individual bank with one difference

$$\frac{dM}{dI}\bigg|_{planner} = \frac{k\lambda}{1 - \lambda I \dfrac{dk}{dM}} < \frac{dM}{dI}\bigg|_{bank} = k\lambda$$

when a single bank raises its investment, and thus the amount of money it issues, it takes k as given. For this to happen, that is for k not to change, all other banks must compensate lowering the money they create. The externality works like in a Cournot equilibrium: one firm raises its output, the other firm cuts it, but by less, so that aggregate output increases and the price falls. This is the externality the social planner corrects, thus the result that the planner, for any increase in I, would raise M by less.

Appendix 2

Bets, capital and private money

Consider the effect of introducing a 'bets' in the balance sheet of the bank studied in Stein (2010). Let B be the amount of 'bets' the bank holds. 'bets' are securities which yield B with probability α and $-B$ with probability $(1-\alpha)$. Define $b \equiv B / I$. By raising the risk of the balance sheet, B reduces m^{max}. By how much depends on whether it is a pure 'bet', or a 'bet' held to provide a service to the bank's clients. We shall consider the two cases separately.

- A pure 'bet' with no direct value

  The 'bet' has no value, i.e., it does not affect the return on the project the bank finances. In this case

  $$m^{max} = \frac{k\lambda - B / I}{R^M} < \frac{k\lambda}{R^M}$$

  the higher B, the lower m^{max}: the 'bet' reduces the externality moving the share of short term financing closer to the level a social planner would choose.

- A 'bet' which increases the amount a firm can invest for any given amount of financing

The way we model this is as follows. Think of this 'bet' as insurance the bank sells to a firm. Insurance makes I less risky. Assume then that the project yields $f(I)$ by investing $I(1-b)<I$.

In this case

$$m^{\max} = \frac{k\lambda - b}{R^M (1-b)}$$

Now the bank has two ways to increase the value of the collateral and issue more short term debt: it can raise I, or it can raise B. For $B = 0$, the collateral is, as before, $k\lambda I$. For $B > 0$ it is $\frac{k\lambda - b}{(1-b)}$.

The total amount of safe demand deposits the bank can issue, M, is $M = m^{\max} I/1 - b$ and increases with b provided $k\lambda > b$

$$\frac{dM}{db} = I \frac{k\lambda - b}{(1-b)^2}$$

Note that this condition is reasonable because it compares the value of the collateral that is constraining the amount of short term debt the bank can issue, $k\lambda$, with b that measures the crowding out effect. As b raises, M rises provided $k\lambda > b$. The 'bet' has two effects, both of which are a reasonable description of the consequences of allowing the bank to take up risks that help the economy insure: it crowds out short term debt, thus working against the externality, and it expands lending allowing it to issue a larger amount of short term debt.

References

Bagehot, W. (1873), *Lombard Street*, New York: Scribner, reprinted by John Wiley and Sons.

Bernanke, B. (2010), 'Monetary Policy and the Housing Bubble,' Annual Meeting of the American Economic Association, Atlanta Georgia, 3 January.

Bernanke, B. and M. Gertler (1999), 'Monetary Policy and Asset Price Volatility' in *New Challenges for Monetary Policy*, Kansas City: Federal Reserve Bank of Kansas City.

Bernanke, B., M. Gertler and S. Gilchrist (1999), 'The Financial Accelerator in a Quantitative Business Cycle Model', in J.B. Taylor and M. Woodford (eds.), *Handbook of Macroeconomics*, Amsterdam: North Holland.

Brunnermeier, M.K. and L.H. Pedersen (2008), 'Market Liquidity and Funding Liquidity,' *Review of Financial Studies*, **22**(6), 2201–2238.

Dang, T.V., G. Gorton and B. Hölmstrom (2009), 'The Optimality of Debt in Liquidity Provision', notes.

Dew-Becker, I. (2009), 'Investment and the Cost of Capital in the Cross-Section: The Term Spread Predicts the Duration of Investment', mimeo, Harvard University.

Diamond, D. and P. Dybvig (1983), 'Bank Runs, Deposit Insurance, and Liquidity,' *Journal of Political Economy*, **91**, 401–419.

Giovannini, A. (2010), 'Financial System Reform Proposals from First Principles', Center for Economic Policy Research, Policy Insight No. 45, January.

Gorton, G. (2007), *Slapped by the Invisible Hand: The Panic of 2007*, Oxford: Oxford University Press.

Greenspan, A. (2003), 'Opening Remarks', in *Monetary Policy and Uncertainty: Adapting to a Changing Economy*, Kansas City: Federal Reserve Bank of Kansas City.

Hölmstrom, B. and J. Tirole (1998), 'Private and Public Supply of Liquidity,' *Journal of Political Economy*, **106,** 1–40.

Hölmstrom, B. and J. Tirole (2011), *Inside and Outside Liquidity*, Cambridge, MA, USA: MIT Press.

Miron, J.A. (1989), 'The Founding of the Fed and the Destabilization of the Post-1914 US Economy,' in M. De Cecco and A.

Giovannini (eds.), *A European Central Bank?*, Cambridge: Cambridge University Press.

Sprague, O.M.W. (1910), *History of Crises Under the National Banking System*, Washington, DC: Government Printing Office.

Stein, J.C. (2011), 'Monetary Policy as Financial Stability Regulation,' mimeo, Harvard University, January.

2. Monetary Policy Lessons from the Crisis

Athanasios Orphanides[1]

Introduction

The assignment I accepted for this chapter is not straightforward. The task is to provide a policymaker's perspective on some lessons from the great financial crisis for monetary policy. Having studied earlier challenging episodes in monetary history, I am well aware of the pitfalls of attempting to draw lessons from a crisis while the experience is still raw. Better to wait a decade or more, to have time to evaluate with greater clarity whether, how and under what conditions things could have evolved differently. On the other hand, there is no time to waste on suggested improvements in the policy framework if the objective is to improve the odds of better outcomes for the future. What better opportunity to offer some early thoughts on the lessons, then, than the occasion presented by this colloquium honouring Lucas Papademos, taking place right after the last meeting of the Governing Council of the European Central Bank (ECB), before the end of his tenure as Vice-President of this institution.

I focus on questions in three areas. First, what lessons can be drawn regarding the institutional framework for monetary policy? Has the experience changed the pre-crisis consensus that monetary policy is best performed by an independent central bank focused on achieving and maintaining price stability?

[1] Prepared for *The great financial crisis: lessons for financial stability and monetary policy: colloquium in honour of Lucas D. Papademos*, Frankfurt, 20–21 May 2010. I would like to thank Gregory Hess, Lucrezia Reichlin and George Tavlas, for helpful comments and suggestions. The opinions expressed are those of the author and do not necessarily reflect views of the Governing Council of the European Central Bank.

Should central banks be more or less independent? Should their aim be higher inflation instead of price stability, as some suggest?

Second, what lessons can be drawn regarding the monetary policy strategy that should be followed by a central bank? A perennial debate in monetary economics has raged over how ambitious monetary policy should be, how activist it should be in dampening fluctuations and tackling perceived disequilibria and imbalances. Where does the historical behaviour place the ECB in this debate? In the history of central banking, one can identify shifts in the consensus from waves of optimism that policies could be fined-tuned to achieve more to waves of caution when the limits of our knowledge are reconfirmed by reality. Has the recent experience shifted the centre of gravity in this continuing debate?

Third, is monetary policy pursuing price stability enough to ensure overall stability in the economy? Or is there room for improvement regarding how central banks can contribute to greater stability? Would greater central bank involvement in regulation and supervision pertaining to credit and finance allow better management of overall economic stability? Or should the role of monetary policy be seen as completely separate from the broader institutional environment governing financial markets and institutions in our economy?

It is not necessary to elaborate on the consequences of what became 'the great financial crisis'. Its severity is evident in the evolution of euro area real GDP (Figure 2.1). It suffices to note that the level of real GDP fell by nearly 5 percent from its peak in 2008Q1 to its trough in 2009Q2. Events during the crisis, the decisive policy responses, and implications for the future of macro-prudential supervision, were analysed by Lucas Papademos in a number of timely and insightful speeches (Papademos, 2007, 2008, 2009a,b,c,d, 2010). As the person responsible for both financial stability and economic research at the ECB during the crisis, Lucas has been in a unique position to provide insights into the events and guidance on the appropriate policy responses.

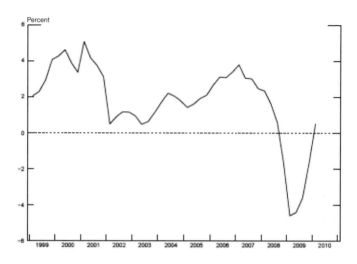

Note: Year-on-year growth of euro area seasonally adjusted quarterly real GDP.

Figure 2.1 Real GDP Growth

The Institutional Framework of Monetary Policy

The founders of the European Union ensured that the ECB, more than any other central bank that has ever existed, would be an independent institution fully committed to ensuring price stability. The independence of the ECB as well as its clear mandate are enshrined in the Treaty on the Functioning of the European Union. According to the Treaty, the primary objective of the ECB 'shall be to maintain price stability'. In light of this mandate, the Governing Council of the ECB aims to maintain inflation rates at levels below, but close to, two percent over the medium term. Inflation is measured by the year-on-year rate of increase in the Harmonised Index of Consumer Prices (HICP).

It should not be necessary to remind ourselves why price stability is so important. The economic costs of inflation are well known[2]. High

---

[2] See, e.g., Fischer and Modigliani (1978) and Fischer (1981, 1984). See also

and variable inflation is detrimental to productivity and growth; uncertainty and unpredictability about future prices leads to inefficient decisions. The social costs of failing to preserve price stability can be far reaching.

Inflation is one of the most virulent and corrosive forces in a democratic society, eroding the functioning of a market economy. The key to securing price stability is to ensure that businesses and households do not need to worry about protecting themselves from the inflationary disease. Temporary upward and downward fluctuations in inflation may occur but they must not be embedded permanently in high inflation or deflation. This result is assured only when inflation expectations over suitably long horizons are well anchored at levels of inflation sufficiently low to constitute effective price stability. The ECB's definition of price stability, that is a rate of increase of the HICP close to but below two percent a year, meets this criterion. Delivering on this goal of price stability is the best way monetary policy can contribute to economic welfare over time.

Since the birth of the euro, the ECB has been successful in delivering on this task. Figure 2.2 plots HICP inflation as well as the long-term expectations regarding inflation from the ECB's quarterly Survey of Professional Forecasters (SPF).[3] As can be seen, the average of the SPF responses (the dashed line) has consistently been in line with the ECB's price stability mandate despite fluctuations in actual inflation which, over the past three years, have been relatively large. There are differences of opinion among the survey respondents that are also informative. The thin lines in the figure show the 25th and 75th percentiles of the cross-sectional distribution of responses in each quarter. As can be seen by the fairly narrow width of the shaded area, disagreement, as measured by the interquartile range of responses, has been limited. This speaks volumes for the credibility of the ECB.

Papademos (2001) for a more recent ECB perspective.
[3] The survey has been conducted towards the end of the first month of every quarter since 1999. Its results are published in the ECB Monthly Bulletin of the second month of each quarter.

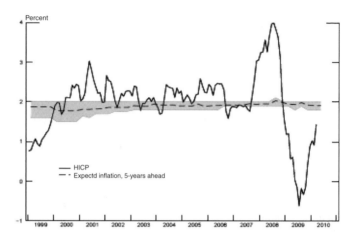

Note: HICP shows the rate of increase of the index over 12 months. Expected inflation is the average five-year ahead forecast reported in the ECB SPF. The thin lines denote the 25 percent and 75 percent percentiles and the shaded area reflects the interquartile range of the cross-sectional distribution of the individual responses.

Figure 2.2 Inflation and Long-Term Inflation Expectations

But price stability cannot be assured by a central bank unless it enjoys absolute political independence that can be used to shield it from short-sighted political inflationary pressures that harm the common good over the long haul. The temptations are asymmetric and well known. Inflationary policies can temporarily ease budgetary pressures, buying time for profligate governments. Necessary adjustments may be delayed. A democratically elected government facing an unfriendly electorate, could be tempted to pursue inflationary policies that might temporarily raise employment and income as well as its electoral prospects. The detrimental effects of inflation, which far exceed any temporary gains for society, would only appear later on. An unavoidable social cost of a democratic society is that the damage from irresponsible government policies can sometimes be hidden from the electorate until after the next election.

The problem, and its obvious solution, have been recognized for a very long time. Early in the 19th century, English economist and member of Parliament David Ricardo explained the main concern that led him to the conclusion that a central bank responsible for the issuance of paper money should be independent as follows:

> 'It is said that Government could not be safely entrusted with the power of issuing paper money; that it would most certainly abuse it; and that, on any occasion when it was pressed for money to carry on a war, it would cease to pay coin, on demand, for its notes; and from that moment the currency would become a forced Government paper. There would, I confess, be great dangers of this, if Government – that is to say, the Ministers – were themselves to be entrusted with the power of issuing paper money' (Ricardo, 1824).

Ricardo thought it critical for the bank to be governed by individuals who, in his words, would be 'entirely independent' of the government's ministers and stressed that the individuals governing the bank 'should never, on any pretence, lend money to Government, nor be in the slightest degree under its control or influence.' The object of Ricardo's inquiry was the Bank of England, but his analysis has had lasting appeal and was adopted when the ECB was created. By the end of the 20th century, the need for an independent central bank to ensure price stability became the consensus view. Increasingly, independence was granted to more and more central banks (including the Bank of England in 1997). Today virtually all of the world's major central banks enjoy a substantial degree of independence. The credibility that an independent central bank can establish with its actions over time does not only facilitate the success of monetary policy in normal times. It can be invaluable during critical times when unusual actions may be required that might otherwise risk raising questions regarding the central bank's continued commitment to price stability.

A complicating factor, especially since the last quarter of 2008, has been that numerous central banks around the world, including the ECB, the Federal Reserve and the Bank of England, have reduced interest rates to or near historical lows and, as a result, considerations regarding the zero bound on nominal interest rates have become pertinent. When policy operates very close to the zero bound, unconventional policy measures may be undertaken for engineering additional monetary policy easing.[4] These measures operate through

---

[4] See Bernanke (2002), Clouse et al (2000), and Yates (2002) for reviews of

expanding or changing the composition of the balance sheet of the central bank. At times, monetary policy and fiscal policy may blur as some monetary policy decisions may unavoidably have a temporary fiscal dimension.[5] Under such circumstances, an independent central bank that is credibly committed to ensuring that inflation remains low in line with price stability, can have much greater flexibility to take actions that would otherwise risk stoking inflationary fears.

Events during the past three years have provided practical demonstrations of these points. One example has been the massive provision of liquidity by the ECB and other central banks, first when money markets malfunctioned in August 2007 and then during subsequent periods of stress. Were it not for the independence of the central banks in question, and the credibility earned by their earlier success in maintaining price stability, the ensuing rapid increases in the monetary base could have raised the spectre of inflation in the public's conscience.

Some purchases of assets by central banks over the past two years may also be seen as examples of such unusual actions. These actions were taken either to repair market functioning or, in light of the zero bound, to engineer further monetary policy easing and defend against deflation, or both. In the United States, for example, the Federal Reserve bought large quantities of asset-backed securities to prop up an ailing financial sector and the housing market and to stimulate economic activity. In the United Kingdom, the Bank of England engaged in quantitative easing by purchasing UK government bonds. And very recently, the ECB decided to conduct targeted interventions in some euro area public and private debt securities markets to address their dysfunction. In each of these cases, the unusual central bank interventions could potentially have been questioned if the central banks undertaking these interventions were not seen as independent, credible and committed to safeguarding price stability.

One lesson I draw from this experience is that the greater the independence and credibility enjoyed by a central bank in ordinary times, the greater the flexibility to engage in unusual and forceful

---

unconventional tools available to a central bank at the zero bound and Curdia and Woodford (2010) and Gertler and Karadi (2010) for recent equilibrium models.

[5] See Goodfriend (2010).

corrective policy measures during times of crisis. Independence and credibility cannot be taken for granted, however, and must be continuously defended, especially in jurisdictions where the independence of the central bank is not enshrined in a constitutional treaty. The risk that the corrective actions taken by a central bank during a crisis become part of a short-sighted political agenda cannot be ruled out.

Another issue that has surfaced in academic debates concerns the appropriateness of price stability as the primary objective of a central bank. The zero bound on nominal interest rates suggests that if interest rates are already low under normal circumstances, the scope of engineering a conventional monetary policy easing by cutting rates is limited. In light of the recent experience, when several central banks cut short-term nominal interest rates close to zero, it has been suggested that the price stability objective should be replaced with the objective of aiming for a stable higher rate of inflation, say 4 percent. This, it is argued, would provide flexibility for greater policy easing, if needed in the future.

Such proposals to abandon price stability seem to be the unfortunate consequence of a fundamental misconception about monetary policy. They seem to draw on the false premise that the zero lower bound on nominal interest rates poses a limit on the effectiveness of monetary policy to protect against deflation. But when policy rates are close to the zero lower bound, they no longer suffice as indicators of the monetary policy stance and of how expansionary monetary policy may be. In these circumstances, unconventional policy measures acquire an elevated role. To evaluate policy, it is important to look at the complete policy package, accounting both for conventional and unconventional policy easing. In fact, monetary policy can continue to engage in unconventional policy easing even without changing very short-term interest rates near the zero bound. The room for conventional easing may be limited but the ammunition for unconventional policy easing is unlimited. A more legitimate concern is that we have much less experience with unconventional policy-easing measures and face greater uncertainty in calibrating their impact. But this uncertainty is only a matter of degree. Policymakers also face considerable dynamic multiplier uncertainty with respect to conventional policy changes.

One of the lessons that can be drawn from the experience with near-zero interest rates over the past year or so is that, when needed, unconventional monetary policy measures can be effectively deployed to engineer additional easing to prevent deflation. With this in mind, I see absolutely no reason to tolerate corrosive higher inflation in order to reduce the probability that policy rates may occasionally have to be very close to zero.

The Strategy of Monetary Policy

There are a number of areas of broad consensus regarding what constitutes good monetary policy practice. Two such elements are common to the monetary policy strategy of numerous central banks around the world today, including the ECB. The first is the usefulness of a clear definition of the central bank's price stability objective, as discussed in the previous section. The second is a forward-looking policy orientation and the associated monitoring of economic projections and, in particular, close attention to inflation forecasts and inflation expectations. Since long and variable lags are an inherent feature of monetary policy, a forward-looking approach is a necessary part of policy strategy.

Monitoring short-term inflation expectations is valuable because expectations are important determinants of actual price and wage setting behavior and thus actual inflation over time. Monitoring the stability of inflation expectations is also important to gauge the extent to which a central bank can respond to real economic disturbances without compromising its price stability mandate. When private inflation expectations become unmoored from the central bank's objectives, macroeconomic stabilization can be considerably harder to achieve. Well-anchored inflation expectations facilitate the monetary policy response to adverse supply shocks, thereby enabling central banks to better stabilize economic fluctuations. Indeed, one lesson from the crisis is the confirmation of this stabilizing role of well-anchored inflation expectations when the economy is under stress.

There is less agreement, however, about a third aspect of monetary policy strategy. This concerns the degree of policy activism that should be employed as a central bank seeks to dampen economic fluctuations and address perceived disequilibria. We may distinguish between two alternative views: the activist view and the stability-oriented view. The activist view suggests that, in addition to price stability, an equally important goal of monetary policy is to guide the economy towards attainment of its ideal 'potential' level of activity. That is, an important guide to policy is the 'output gap', which measures how far GDP deviates from its potential. In contrast to the activist view, the stability-oriented approach could be characterized as attempting to dampen economic fluctuations by promoting stable economic growth over time, subject to a primary focus on maintaining price stability. The stability-oriented view more closely describes the monetary policy strategy of the ECB than the activist view. A perennial debate in monetary economics has raged over how activist policy should be in terms of closing output gaps. In the next two sections, I review in greater detail some lessons that can be drawn from the experience of the ECB regarding these two approaches.

Monetary Policy Activism

The activist view is motivated by the fact that the academic literature sometimes poses the monetary policy problem as the solution to a maximization problem with not one but two main objectives: getting inflation close to its assumed target, consistent with price stability, and getting real economic activity close to its ideal 'potential' level, defined as the equilibrium or natural level of output that is consistent with price stability.[6] Let p and q denote (the logarithms of) the price level and real output, respectively, and define the rate of inflation $\pi \equiv \Delta p$. Then, using 'stars' to mark the ideal target values of respective variables, we can use π^* to denote the numerical definition of price stability and q^* to denote the level of potential GDP. The activist approach to monetary policy imparts greater symmetry on closing the inflation gap $(\pi - \pi^*)$ and the output gap $(q - q^*)$ than alternative approaches. Thus, to the extent that this is feasible, activist policies

---

[6] Equivalent definitions may also be expressed in terms of the natural rate of employment and unemployment and are robust to alternative models of the process of inflation determination, as explained by Modigliani and Papademos (1975) in the discussion that defined the NIRU (non-inflationary rate of unemployment) concept.

prescribe that monetary policy should not only focus on achieving its price stability objective (that is closing the inflation gap) but also on closing the output gap. A constraint in achieving both results is presented in the form of a Phillips curve. A policy tightening can, by opening a negative gap, lead to dampening inflation pressures and vice versa. There are two types of activist policies: those that rely on a simple activist policy rule and those that claim broader optimality properties. The latter can be seen as attempting to devise a policy plan that balances the inflation and output gaps in the outlook, accounting as precisely as possible for model dynamics.[7,8] The alternative approach, that relies on an activist monetary policy rule to achieve an approximate balance, is simpler. A common reference to the latter approach is the Taylor (1993) rule:

$$i = r^* + \pi + \theta_\pi(\pi - \pi^*) + \theta_q(q - q^*) \tag{2.1}$$

where i is the policy rate and r^* the natural or equilibrium rate of interest.[9] Either approach to activism potentially suffers from a crucial practical pitfall: the need for accurate measurements of the level of potential output to measure the output gap, $(q - q^*)$. Output gaps are notoriously difficult to construct in real time, and without reliable estimates these activist approaches can run into problems.[10]

---

[7] The so-called 'flexible' inflation targeting approach to monetary policy is sometimes presented in this manner by some authors. See, among others, Svensson (2002) and McCallum and Nelson (2005).

[8] The intellectual underpinnings of the approach relate to the optimal control approach to monetary policy that was developed in the 1970s. This was an active area of research to which Lucas Papademos, starting with his Ph.D. thesis, contributed considerably (Athans et al (1977), Papademos (1977, 1981), Modigliani and Papademos (1976, 1978)).

[9] Taylor (1999), Orphanides (2003b) and Taylor and Williams (2010) review the development and rationale for this and related simple monetary policy rules. The specification of such simple rules for a central bank's policy rate abstracts from the zero-lower-bound problem. As mentioned earlier, unconventional policy measures come into play when short-term rates approach zero.

[10] This is not the only difficulty. Another related problem is associated with the need for reliable estimates of the natural rate of interest. For expositional ease, I focus on the output gap issue here, which I consider to be more critical in practice. See, e.g., Clark and Kozicki (2005), Laubach and Williams

Next, I review some illustrative evidence regarding the potential usefulness of the activist approach drawing on the recent experience of the ECB. However, since the ECB's policy cannot be characterized by this approach and the ECB does not even publish estimates of the output gap for the euro area, this illustrative evidence must be based on other sources. In what follows, I rely on the pertinent analysis presented by the International Monetary Fund (IMF) in its World Economic Outlook (WEO) publications. The WEO is useful for two reasons: first, it presents the necessary data and analysis either in the publication or in the associated electronic databases and second, in the years examined, the policy recommendations appear to have been influenced by readings of the output gap and, in this sense, they have had an activist bent.

Two specific episodes, when the ECB was concerned about inflation and was in a policy tightening mode, present interesting case studies. They correspond to the Spring 2000 WEO and the Spring 2006 WEO. On both occasions, the economy was growing at a brisk pace, but, according to the IMF analysis at the time, had not reached its potential. These are occasions when the differences between the activist and stability-oriented approaches become easier to isolate.

In the Spring of 2000 WEO, the IMF analysis suggested that the euro area suffered from a significant output gap that was projected to persist into 2001. (The forecasts suggested an output gap equal to -1.2 percent for 2000 and -0.5 percent for 2001.) This was a factor in the assessment that inflation prospects appeared benign and a policy recommendation that the ECB should hold back on a rapid tightening. Specifically, the IMF noted:

'Higher energy prices will temporarily affect headline inflation in the short term, but inflationary pressures should remain subdued due to the large output gap (projected at about 1 1/4 percent in 2000) and increased competitive pressures caused by the deregulation and restructuring across the area. While the ECB needs to maintain a strong anti-inflationary stance, and a gradual shift to a less accommodative stance is to be expected as slack is absorbed, inflation prospects remain benign and it is

---

(2003), Orphanides and Williams (2002) and Orphanides and van Norden (2002) for additional discussions of these measurement issues.

important currently to avoid holding back the ongoing recovery through a rapid tightening of policy' (IMF, 2000, p. 18).

A similar analysis is present in the spring 2006 WEO, and brings us closer to the crisis. Again, the IMF projected a significant (negative) output gap for 2006 that was seen as persisting into 2007. Specifically, the forecasts suggested a euro area output gap equal to -1.4 percent for 2006 and -1.3 percent for 2007. Indeed, the significant negative output gap on this occasion was seen as a global phenomenon. Drawing on these estimates, the Spring WEO noted: 'Quiescent inflation, partly because of a significant global output gap, allowed monetary policy to be very accommodative. Now as the global output gap narrows, monetary accommodation is being withdrawn' (IMF, 2006, p. xii). The IMF went on to suggest that the ECB should hold back on its policy tightening: '[W]ith underlying inflationary pressures contained and domestic demand still fragile, there appears to be no need to rush to normalize rates' (IMF, 2006, pp. 25–26).

On both of these occasions, the ECB emphasized the risks to inflation and continued its tightening. In retrospect, this proved to have been the right call. Retrospective analysis using the IMF's subsequent estimates of the output gap can be read as confirmation of the ECB's policy. How is this so? Simply, the large real-time negative output gap readings for these two years were subsequently revised away, and eventually became positive estimates of the output gap. The annual evolution of the estimates for the output gap for 2000, from Spring 2000 to Spring 2004, and that for the output gap for 2006, from Spring 2006 to Spring 2010, are shown in Figure 2.3. As can be seen, on both occasions, the real-time estimate proved to be of the wrong sign and was revised by more than two percentage points over the subsequent four years. Such revisions are not specific to the IMF estimates of the output gap. The pattern of revisions is rather typical of other estimates as well. For comparison, the figure shows the evolution of corresponding estimates of the output gap prepared by the European Commission (EC) each Spring.[11] How much does this

---

[11] These are typically produced one month after the IMF estimates. The 2001 estimate of the 2000 gap in the figure is from the Autumn 2001 forecast, as it is missing in the Spring forecast of that year.

matter for policy? To get a sense, recall that Taylor (1999) suggested considering two values for the output-gap response coefficient in rule (1), $\theta_q = 1/2$ (the classic rule), and $\theta_q = 1$ (the more activist revised rule). Thus, a two percentage point revision in the output gap corresponds to a 100 basis points difference in the classic rule and 200 basis points in the revised rule. Considering the size of typical policy changes, these are remarkably large.

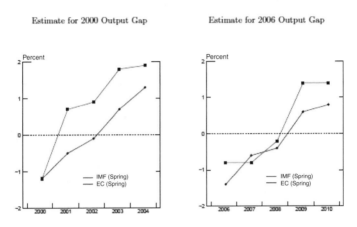

Note: Evolution of IMF and European Commission (EC) estimates of the output gap for year 2000 (left panel) and year 2006 (right panel). IMF estimates are from the spring WEO of each year. EC estimates are from the Spring forecast of each year, except for 2001 when only the Autumn estimate is available.

Figure 2.3 Evolution of Output Gap Estimates: Two Examples

Figure 2.4 plots the time series of real-time estimates of the output gap from each spring WEO against the latest vintage (spring 2010). Note also that the real-time estimates appear to be systematically biased downward. Since the birth of the euro, the real-time estimate of the euro area output gap in the Spring WEO has been negative every single year. Looking at the first ten years of this sample (1999–2008), on seven of ten occasions the sign of the 2010 estimate of potential output is the reverse of the sign of the real-time estimate.[12] The average bias for the first ten years is quite large, around 2.1 percentage points. The pattern of revisions is consistent with a gradual downward update of the rate of growth of potential GDP, which characterizes various estimates over the past decade.

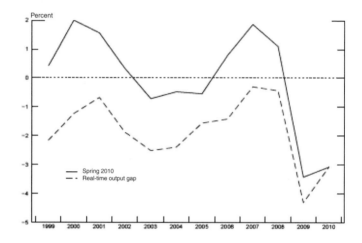

Note: The Spring 2010 series shows the historical output gap estimates from the latest IMF WEO (Spring 2010). The real-time series shows, in each year, the output gap estimate from the IMF Spring WEO of that year.

Figure 2.4 Real-time vs Retrospective Output Gap Estimates

One reason for the pronounced difference between the real-time and the recent estimates of the output gap is the dramatic revisions in prospects regarding potential GDP, partly as a result of the recent crisis. Figure 2.5 traces successive vintages of the output gap, starting with Spring 2000 to show how large the revisions were in the early years of the euro area. Figure 2.6 plots the successive vintages of the output gap from 2006 to the present. As can be seen, these estimates vary rather little for the early part of the sample shown but are

---

[12] Random selection would have suggested that the sign should be expected to be correct five out of ten times.

drastically different for the past few years. The crisis has forced a reevaluation of the euro area's productive capacity, as it has elsewhere in the world. According to the Spring 2010 IMF analysis, the output gap of all advanced economies for 2006 and 2007 is now estimated to have been large and positive (+0.9 and +1.5 percent, respectively) and not significantly negative as was projected in 2006 (−0.6 and −0.5 percent, respectively).

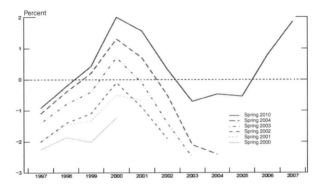

Note: Each line shows IMF output gap estimates from the corresponding Spring WEO.

Figure 2.5 Evolution of the Output Gap from 2000

Thus, the crisis has reconfirmed the lesson that activist monetary policy cannot work, simply because of our inability to possess reliable estimates of the output gap in real time. All in all, the size of revisions in estimates of the output gap for the euro area, as shown in the IMF analysis, suggests that the ECB is correct to eschew the activist approach to policy. This lesson against activism in monetary policy is not new. It is just a reconfirmation of earlier similar experiences, for example the disastrous experience of the Federal Reserve during the 1970s when warnings against the activist approach were not heeded.[13]

---

[13] See e.g. Orphanides (2003a) and Orphanides and Williams (2005, 2010).

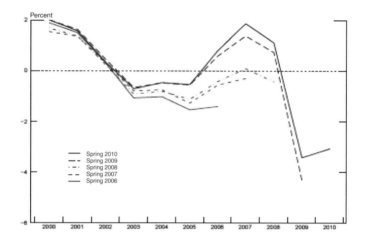

Note: Each line shows IMF output gap estimates from the corresponding Spring WEO.

Figure 2.6 Evolution of the Output Gap from 2006

The Stability-Oriented View and Robust Simple Rules

It is not necessary to rely on activist guidelines to formulate effective monetary policy. The alternative, stability-oriented approach appears less ambitious. Its relative strength is in consistently preserving price stability, stressing robustness over optimality. As an illustration, in this section I provide an example of a simple policy rule along these lines that I have found useful to monitor, among other things, over the past several years.[14] The policy rule is a simple difference rule that can be thought of as providing prescriptions for quarterly changes of the policy rate based on the evolution of inflation and real GDP growth:

$$\Delta i = \theta_\pi(\pi - \pi^*) + \theta_{\Delta q}(\Delta q - \Delta q^*) \qquad (2.2)$$

---

[14] This is based on a similar illustration I originally presented at The ECB and Its Watchers VIII conference in May 2006.

Rules of this type have been extensively investigated in quantitative evaluations and have been found to be robust to various sources of misspecification and to the possibility (in reality the certainty) of imperfect knowledge on the part of policymakers and of businesses and households in the model economies.[15]

The intellectual underpinnings of this rule connect with the writings of Knut Wicksell at the end of the 19th century and those of Milton Friedman in the middle of the 20th century, as well as numerous other authors. The common thread is the desire to find a simple monetary policy guide that can lead to reasonably robust policy without requiring precise information about theoretical concepts such as the various 'natural rates' (e.g. the definition of full employment or potential output, or the equilibrium real interest rate) that cannot be reliably observed or measured when policy is set. Estimates of output gaps are not needed for guiding policy in this approach, only a sense of the economy's trend growth, which is subject to considerably less uncertainty.

The link to Friedman comes from the idea that a robust rule for ensuring long-term monetary stability is for the central bank to maintain a constant rate of growth of the money supply – Friedman's k-percent rule. This is an example of a policy rule that does not require knowledge of either the natural rate of output or the natural rate of interest, but with a money instrument (Friedman, 1960). The Friedman rule draws on the equation of exchange that can be expressed in growth rates (approximated with log-differences) as follows:

$$\Delta m + \Delta v = \pi + \Delta q \qquad (2.3)$$

where m and v are (the logarithms of) the money stock and its velocity, respectively. Selecting the constant growth of money, k, to correspond to the sum of a desired inflation target, π^*, and the economy's potential growth rate, Δq^*, and adjusting for any secular trend in the velocity of money, Δv^*, suggests a simple rule that can achieve, on average, the desired inflation target, π^*:

---

[15] See, e.g., Orphanides and Williams (2002, 2008) and the references cited therein.

$$\Delta m = \pi * + \Delta q * - \Delta v. \qquad (2.4)$$

Further, if the velocity of money were fairly stable, this simple rule would also yield a high degree of economic stability. Unpredictable fluctuations in the equilibrium velocity of money that may take time to ascertain and operational difficulties in controlling the money supply in the short run for all but the most narrow monetary aggregates, however, do not speak well for relying on the money supply as the main instrument for monetary policy.

While monetary aggregates can serve to cross-check the stance of monetary policy, especially with regard to medium-to-long term risks to inflation, short-term nominal interest rates are usually more suitable to serve as day-to-day policy instruments.

The simple interest rate rule (2.2) may be seen as relating to Friedman's k-percent rule described above. To see the relationship between rule (2.2) and money growth targeting, substitute the money growth in rule (2.4) into the equation of exchange so that the rule can be stated in terms of the velocity of money:

$$\Delta v - \Delta v * = (\pi - \pi *) + (\Delta q - \Delta q *). \qquad (2.5)$$

Consider now the simplest formulation of money demand as a (log-) linear relationship between velocity deviations from its equilibrium and the rate of interest. In difference form this is:

$$\Delta v - \Delta v * = a \Delta i + e \qquad (2.6)$$

where $a > 0$ and e summarizes short-run money demand dynamics and temporary velocity disturbances. To reformulate the k-percent money growth rule in terms of an interest rate rule, while avoiding the short-run velocity fluctuations, e, one may substitute the remaining part of (2.6) into (2.5). This yields rule (2.2) for some $\theta = \theta_\pi = \theta_{\Delta q} > 0$.

The link to Wicksell derives from his work on interest and prices, where he argued that price stability could be maintained in an economy if the market interest rate were always equal to the economy's natural rate of interest, $r*$. Wicksell examined how the central bank might adjust the rate of interest to achieve price stability. Recognizing that the natural rate of interest is unavoidably an abstract concept, however, Wicksell did not advise that the central bank first take a stand on what the natural rate is in order to formulate policy: 'This does not mean that the bank ought actually to *ascertain* the natural rate before fixing their own rates of interest. That would, of course, be impracticable, and would also be quite unnecessary' (Wicksell, 1898[1936], p. 189, emphasis in the original). Rather, Wicksell pointed out that a simple method for a central bank to maintain approximate price stability would be to follow a simple prescription adjusting its interest rate in a systematic manner to developments in prices: 'If prices rise, the rate of interest is to be raised; and if prices fall, the rate of interest is to be lowered; and the rate of interest is henceforth to be maintained at its new level until a further movement in prices calls for a further change in one direction or the other' (p. 189). In algebraic terms, Wicksell's proposal can be interpreted as rule (2.2), but ignoring the response of interest rates to the difference between the economy's growth from its potential, that is $\theta_\pi > 0$ and $\theta_{\Delta q} = 0$.

Implementation of rule (2.2) at a quarterly frequency requires summary indicators of the quarterly evolution of inflation and output growth, an assessment of trend or potential output growth and, of course, a numerical definition of price stability, π^*. Implementation also requires the rule coefficients which are set to $\theta_\pi = \theta_{\Delta q} = 0.5$ for this illustration. Since monetary policy is forward looking, near-term forecasts are more useful summary indicators of inflation and output for guiding policy. I therefore rely on the ECB's SPF for the illustration presented here. Specifically, I employ the average of the survey responses regarding year-on-year forecasts for inflation and output growth with horizons ending about one year ahead from the data available when the survey is conducted. These 'year-ahead' forecasts have approximately the same horizon from quarter to quarter.

Figure 2.7 shows the one-year ahead inflation forecast from the SPF together with two numerical guides for the definition of price stability to be used in the rule: an upper guide of two percent and a lower guide of one and a half percent. Comparing the inflation forecast with the corresponding guide, therefore, indicates whether the rule prescribes that the policy rate should be raised or lowered on account of the near-term inflation outlook.

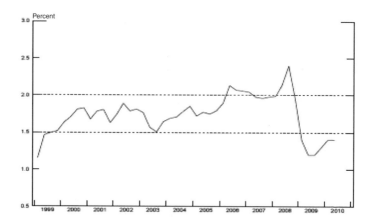

Note: Expected inflation, one-year ahead, is the average response in the ECB SPF.

Figure 2.7 Outlook for Inflation

Figure 2.8 shows the one-year ahead GDP growth forecasts from the SPF together with two alternative indicators of what trend or potential GDP growth is. One indicator is from the survey itself, the average response to a question asking what GDP growth is expected to be five years ahead. Because cyclical dynamics are expected to dissipate in a few years, this long-term forecast provides information about what the respondents view as the long-term growth potential of the economy. The second indicator is a rough real-time estimate of potential GDP growth based on the analysis presented in the IMF's WEO. In each year, the figure plots the potential GDP growth estimate for that year as reflected in the Spring WEO. The same estimate from the Spring WEO is plotted for all four quarters of the year.

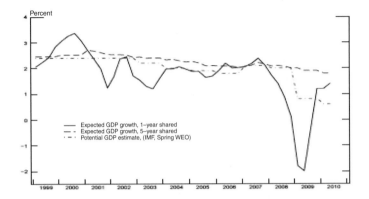

Note: Expected growth one-year ahead and five-years ahead are the average responses in the ECB SPF. Potential output growth in each year reflects the real-time estimate from that year's IMF Spring WEO.

Figure 2.8 Outlook for GDP Growth

As can be seen, the WEO estimates are generally close to the five-year ahead SPF forecast. A substantial difference appears for 2009 and 2010, however. The WEO estimates reflect an unusually large drop in potential GDP growth, not seen in the SPF forecast. According to the WEO analysis, however, this drop is expected to be temporary: thus, the implied five-year ahead forecast of potential output growth would be much closer to the corresponding SPF forecast shown in the Figure (IMF, 2009). The comparison of the GDP forecast with its underlying estimated trend, indicates whether the economy is expanding faster or slower than its normal limit in the near term, and therefore signals whether the rule prescribes that the policy rate should be raised or lowered on account of the near-term inflation outlook.

The combination of two alternative estimates for trend GDP and the upper and lower guide for the definition of price stability results in four different values for the quarterly change in the policy rate suggested by the rule. Figure 2.9 compares the resulting envelope of rule prescriptions (the shaded area in the figure) with the actual quarterly change in the ECB policy rate (more precisely, the rate on the main refinancing operations, MRO). For actual policy, in each quarter I use the MRO rate following the policy meeting of the second month of the quarter. This provides the closest match to the timetable of the SPF. As already noted, the survey is conducted towards the end of the first month in every quarter and the results are available to the Governing Council at the policy meeting of the second month. Figure 2.10 shows the prescriptions for the level of the policy rate that emerge from applying the prescribed quarterly changes to the level of the policy rate a quarter earlier.

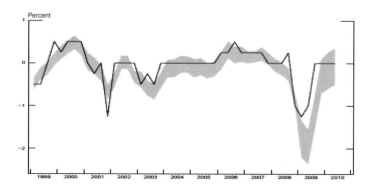

Note: The shaded area represents the envelope of prescriptions from the simple policy rule: $\Delta i = 1/2\ (\pi-\pi^*) + 1/2\ (\Delta q-\Delta q^*)$. $(\pi-\pi^*)$ reflects the deviations in the SPF one-year ahead inflation forecasts from either of two bounds as shown in Figure 2.7. $(\Delta q-\Delta q^*)$ reflects the deviations in the SPF one-year ahead GDP growth forecasts from either of two trend measures as shown in Figure 2.8. The solid line shows the quarterly change in the ECB policy rate (MRO) following the policy meeting of the second month in each quarter.

Figure 2.9 Policy Rate and Simple Rule Prescription: Quarterly Change

As can be seen in the figures, the contours of the policy prescriptions from this simple robust rule line up reasonably well with the actual policy decisions taken by the Governing Council of the ECB. In that sense, this rule is also descriptive of ECB policy. However, several complications should be kept in mind in treating the resulting illustration as an exercise in description. These complications would imply that if the rule described above were implemented it may result in distorted policy prescriptions. The complications arise from the fact that the inputs to the rule may not coincide with either the ECB/Eurosystem staff analysis or the Governing Council's views. Thus, the rule prescriptions would be tighter than indicated if, for example: (i) the inflation forecast were higher, (ii) the output growth forecast were stronger, or (iii) the potential output growth were more pessimistic than assumed in the exercise.

Even if a simple rule such as the one shown captured actual policy decisions reasonably well most of the time, deviations would be expected, reflecting factors that may importantly influence policy on some occasions but are not captured by the simple rule. Two such noteworthy deviations in the period since the financial turbulence began can be seen in Figures 2.9 and 2.10.

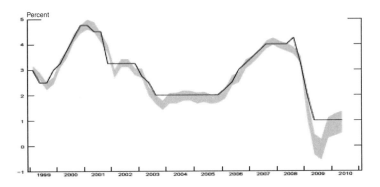

Note: The shaded area represents the envelope of prescriptions from the simple policy rule: $\Delta i = 1/2 \, (\pi - \pi^*) + 1/2 \, (\Delta q - \Delta q^*)$, that emerge from applying the prescribed change to the level of the policy rate a quarter earlier. $(\pi - \pi^*)$ reflects the deviations in the SPF one-year ahead inflation forecasts from either of two bounds as shown in Figure 2.7. $(\Delta q - \Delta q^*)$ reflects the deviations in the SPF one-year ahead GDP growth forecasts from either of two trend measures as shown in Figure 2.8. The solid line shows the quarterly change in the ECB policy rate (MRO) following the policy meeting of the 2nd month in each quarter.

Figure 2.10 Policy Rate and Simple Rule Prescription

The first deviation concerns the policy rate increase in 2008Q3, reflecting the tightening on 3 July 2008. According to the rule prescriptions, the evidence that the economy was weakening would have argued against the tightening during that summer. An important consideration at the time was a serious concern that inflation expectations risked becoming unmoored, a concern not adequately captured by the summary indicator reflecting the near-term deterioration in the inflation outlook. In the summer of 2008, the euro area, together with other parts of the world, experienced an inflation scare. This was toward the tail end of a long spell of increases in energy and commodity prices. For many months, despite some signs of weakness in the economy and despite continuing tensions in financial markets, there were successive deteriorations in the outlook for headline inflation. Signs of the emerging inflation scare appeared in financial market indicators and also in survey expectations.

For example, as seen in Figure 2.2, the ECB's SPF showed a shift in the distribution of forecasters' responses regarding their expectation of inflation five years ahead. As seen in the Figure, the survey that was published in August 2008 was the only one in the history of the survey where more than a quarter of the respondents thought inflation five-years ahead would exceed two percent. The mean of the forecasts, also shown, was the highest recorded in the history of the survey and slightly exceeded two percent (although the reading still rounded to two). This was also the only occasion in the history of the survey when the calendar-year after-next as well as the two-year-ahead forecast exceeded two percent. (They both registered 2.1 percent.)

In the Introductory Statement released after the meeting, the Governing Council stressed that: 'Against this background, it is imperative to ensure that medium to longer-term inflation expectations remain firmly anchored at levels in line with price stability' (ECB, 2008). On this occasion, ensuring that long-term inflation expectations remained well-anchored, proved to be a decisive factor.

Another deviation from the policy rule is evident during 2009. According to the policy rule prescriptions shown in Figure 2.10, additional policy easing (reflected in the reduction of the ECB policy rate on main refinancing operations) would have been suggested by the simple policy rule. The lower bound of the range even suggests that, according to the rule, the policy rate would have been set to a negative number for a couple of quarters, if that were possible. This episode, of course, involves near-zero short-term nominal interest rates. As already noted, under these circumstances, the stance of monetary policy cannot be adequately represented by the conventional policy changes embedded in short-term interest rates alone. On this occasion, faced with the zero nominal interest rate bound, the Governing Council supplemented its conventional policy easing that brought the main policy rate (MRO) to the historically low one percent level with unconventional policy measures, including liquidity provision at longer maturities and the purchases of assets for monetary policy purposes. Some of these measures were unprecedented in scale and scope. Indicatively, I mention the decision to offer unlimited liquidity for one year at the rate of one percent, upon presentation of adequate collateral, which resulted in the unprecedented liquidity injection of 442 billion euro in June 2009. The decisive unconventional policy measures adopted in the first half of 2009 drove overnight interest rates considerably below the policy rate and also influenced other interest rates and asset prices. A comparison of the behaviour of overnight interest rates (eonia) as well as the three-month interbank rate (euribor) compared to the policy rate (MRO) illustrates the point. As seen in Figure 2.11, for example, since the Spring of 2009, the three-month euribor has been trading consistently substantially below the policy rate, whereas under normal circumstances it should exceed it.

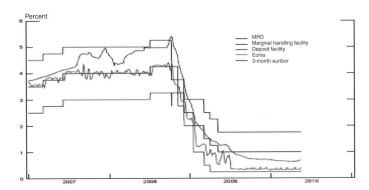

Note: Eonia is the 5-day trailing moving average.

Figure 2.11 Money Market and ECB Policy Interest Rates

This analysis suggests that the simple rule illustrated above can be viewed as an informative proxy of the ECB's economic analysis, aiming at assessing the role of short-run forecasts of inflation and economic activity on policy. In this sense, it may form a useful element in policy discussions. However, it should not be misinterpreted as coming close to providing the full range of considerations pertinent to any policy decisions. It should be recalled, for example, that the ECB's two-pillar approach to policy cross-checks economic analysis with the monetary analysis that focuses on a longer-term horizon. This two-pillar approach is designed to ensure that no relevant information is lost in the assessment of the risks to price stability and that appropriate attention is paid to different perspectives in order to come to an overall judgement on the risks to price stability.[16]

Activism and Asset Prices

Another area of continuing debate regarding the monetary policy strategy concerns the treatment of suspected asset price misalignments. In light of the large costs of the recent financial crisis, the origins of which could be related to such a misalignment, a re-assessment of the role of central banks in promoting financial stability is certainly in order. But how activist should monetary policy be in order to counter suspected asset price misalignments?

Broadly speaking, there are two main strategies for dealing with financial imbalances and suspected asset price bubbles. The conventional, non-activist strategy advocates that a central bank should focus its attention on the total risks to the outlook of inflation and real economic activity in evaluating policy alternatives.[17] Interest rate policy adjustments should only react to suspected asset price misalignments to the extent that changes in asset prices might affect prospective output and inflation prospects over the pertinent horizon. Thus, if a suspected bubble translates into ebullience in consumption and investment decisions, a policy tightening responding to the demand imbalance would be in order. And if a suspected bubble bursts, thus dampening aggregate demand, a monetary loosening

---

[16] See Beck and Wieland (2007, 2008) for a formalization of this cross-checking.

[17] Bernanke (2002), Greenspan (2010), Kohn (2006, 2009) and Posen (2009), among others, have argued in favor of this approach.

would reduce the possible damage – the so-called 'mop-up' approach to treating financial bubbles.

The alternative, more activist approach to responding to suspected asset price misalignments suggests that monetary policy should 'lean against the wind' of emerging financial imbalances over and above the implicit policy reaction suggested by the effect of the suspected asset price developments on the evaluation of the risks to the outlook for inflation and real economic activity.[18] This approach calls for 'extra action' to be taken on account of asset price movements (Kohn, 2006). The suggested rationale is that tempering emerging financial imbalances while they are developing can reduce the probability of costly financial instability in the future.

There are a number of practical concerns that bring into question the appropriateness of this activist approach. Even if the presence of a bubble is ascertained, one concern regards the difficulty in calibrating the size of an 'appropriate' interest rate response. Another concern regards the appropriate direction and timing of an activist monetary response to suspected asset price misalignments. Should policy tighten to arrest a brewing bubble or ease in anticipation of its crash? The most obvious concern, however, is that suspected asset price misalignments cannot be identified with enough accuracy in real time. Early identification is intrinsically difficult as it presupposes the ability to determine the fundamental value of assets when market forces fail to do so. This problem is fundamentally similar to the difficulty in assessing real-time estimates of the output gap for stabilisation policy. Only here the difficulty is far greater. Policymakers are asked to take a definitive position questioning the collective wisdom reflected in market valuations.

The non-activist approach need not mean that suspected asset price misalignments are ignored in setting interest rates, however, and if the risk evaluation framework is sufficiently encompassing, it may nest the concerns of the proponents of the activist view. In particular, to the extent that a misalignment is detected, and concerns regarding the possibility of a financial collapse emerge, these concerns can and should be mapped into the risk analysis concerning the outlook of the economy. An asset boom stokes inflationary dynamics. And an asset

---

[18] Borio and Lowe (2002), Borio and White (2003), Cecchetti et al. (2002) and White (2006), among others, have argued in favor of this approach.

price collapse can create the risk of a deflationary dynamic in the economy. These undesirable outcomes that are associated with asset price booms and busts can be accounted for as part of the overall risk analysis for monetary policy, provided the horizon for the analysis is sufficiently long. Indeed, as Papademos (2009c) points out, because asset price booms are often associated with robust money and credit expansion, accounting for the longer-term risks reflected in the ECB's monetary analysis provides an appropriate framework for incorporating the pertinent information in formulating policy. Closely monitoring money and credit can alert policymakers to the potential for financing unsustainable runs in asset prices in the medium to long-run. An advantage of the ECB monetary policy strategy in using information from the monetary analysis pillar in this manner, is that it can account for the risks from potential misalignments in an integrated risk management approach, without the need to take a definitive position on identifying asset price misalignments (Issing, 2009a,b).

The pertinent trade-off may be viewed as one regarding a comparison of the risks to price stability over shorter horizons against tail risks at longer horizons. If an adjustment in interest rates can reduce the tail risks to price stability associated with a suspected price misalignment at a more distant horizon, without significantly raising risks of deviating from price stability over nearer horizons, such an adjustment would seem warranted. That said, the interest rate does not seem to be the most appropriate instrument for minimizing the tail risks associated with a possible asset market collapse at distant horizons. Interest rates have always been and remain too blunt a tool for this purpose.

Enhancing financial stability is certainly a worthwhile goal. The great financial crisis has provided a reminder of the value of longer-term risk analysis, such as reflected in the ECB's monetary analysis pillar. But it has not provided concrete additional evidence that monetary policymakers should use their interest rate policy instrument to respond to emerging financial imbalances over and above what could be justified by a thorough analysis of the risks to price stability. Rather, regulatory tools should be brought to bear in order to minimize the risks associated with suspected asset price misalignment. Which brings us to the question regarding central bank involvement in regulation and supervision.

Is Price Stability Enough?

The crisis has confirmed that a central bank with a price stability objective and insufficient regulatory powers cannot ensure broader financial stability in the economy. The question is broader than that regarding the treatment of asset price misalignments and extends to other suspected imbalances in the economy such as overextended households and businesses, high levels of private and public debt, persistent current account deficits, highly leveraged positions in finance, etc.

The crisis has revealed a general underappreciation of systemic risks in micro-prudential supervision, and highlighted the need for a more system-wide macro-prudential approach towards supervisory oversight to ensure overall stability in the financial system. By definition, micro-prudential supervisors focus on individual institutions and cannot effectively assess the broader macroeconomic risks that pose a threat to the financial system as a whole. This is a task best suited to central banks.

However, for central banks to better enhance financial stability they must be provided with the right tools. In general, a central bank does not face a trade-off between price stability and financial stability. Rather, most of the time these two goals tend to reinforce each other. But there may be occasions when interest rate policy directed at preserving price stability is clearly insufficient to reduce risks to financial stability. Consider, for example, an episode of persistently high credit growth in an environment of price stability. Adjusting the interest rate tool is unlikely to be the most appropriate response. Ideally, under such circumstances, the central bank should have at its disposal macro-prudential levers with which to contain the risk of a potential financial disturbance. These could comprise the power to vary capital requirements, leverage ratios, loan-to-value ratios, margin requirements and so forth.

This highlights the importance of ongoing efforts to strengthen the macro-prudential supervision role of central banks (de Larosiére, 2009). Macro-prudential policies could aim to contain the build up of financial imbalances and ensure that the financial system is sufficiently resilient to withstand a disorderly unwinding (Papademos, 2009d).

The task of the central bank in its role as macro-prudential supervisor is to identify and assess risks and, if needed, to issue warnings and recommendations for remedial action. An issue that remains open, however, is the degree of effectiveness of such warnings and recommendations in the absence of an appropriate enforcement mechanism for heeding such warnings. Can macro-prudential supervision succeed in preventing the accumulation of large imbalances without the tools of enforcement? Can the macro-prudential recommendations issued by a central bank be enforced without the intimate involvement of the central bank in regulation and supervision pertaining to credit and finance?

Prior to the crisis, there was a tendency to separate monetary policy from supervision and regulation, though both could be viewed as central banking functions. Although, in numerous jurisdictions, the functions of bank supervision and regulation have traditionally been the responsibility of the central bank, in some cases these functions were separated from the core monetary policy function of the central bank. A lesson from the crisis is that this trend should be reversed. Indeed, some jurisdictions have already moved in that direction.

The crisis has revealed not only the need for more effective micro- and macro-prudential regulation and supervision but also the need for better coordination between the micro and macro parts. Considering the important informational synergies between micro-prudential supervision and systemic risk analysis, bringing micro-supervision under the same roof as other central bank functions seems an attractive proposition. Central banks can benefit from, and rely on, extended access to supervisory information and intelligence, especially on systemically relevant intermediaries, in order to better assess risks and vulnerabilities of the financial system as a whole. Overall, a lesson of the crisis is that greater central bank involvement in regulation and supervision pertaining to credit and finance should contribute to better management of overall economic stability. In turn, by reducing the prospects of tail events, this would contribute to the enhancement of price stability.

Concluding Remarks

Unlike the natural sciences, in central banking we do not have the luxury of running controlled experiments to improve our understanding of the world. Our only guide is history. As a result, crises are unique 'natural experiments' that we can mine for information to advance our learning. Reflecting on lessons from the current crisis, Lucas Papademos observed that not only has it been 'great' and 'beyond compare', but that it has also been 'a learning experience 'beyond compare' for market participants and policymakers, including central banks' (Papademos, 2009c). From the numerous ensuing lessons, I would like to end by returning to two fundamentals that the crisis has reminded us. First, *principles*: By staying true to its principles, by always being committed to preserving price stability, a central bank can have the credibility and flexibility required to take forceful corrective measures and serve as the cornerstone of stability during a crisis. Second, *humility*: We must always strive to avoid hubris. We must avoid the temptation to overpromise on what monetary policy can achieve and remain mindful of the limits of our knowledge.

References

Athans, M., E. Kuh, T. Ozkan, L.D. Papademos, R. Pindyck and K. Wall (1977), 'Sequential open-loop optimal control of a nonlinear macroeconomic model', in M.D. Intrilligator (ed) *Frontiers of Quantitative Economics, Vol. III*, Amsterdam: North-Holland.

Beck, G.W. and V. Wieland (2007), 'Money in monetary policy design: A formal characterization of ECB-style cross-checking', *Journal of the European Economic Association,* **5**(2–3), April–May, 524–533.

Beck, G.W. and V. Wieland (2008), 'Central bank misperceptions and the role of money in interest-rate rules', *Journal of Monetary Economics*, **55**:S1-S17.

Bernanke, B. (2002), 'Asset price bubbles and monetary policy', remarks before the New York National Association of Business Economics, October

Borio, C. and P. Lowe (2002), 'Asset prices, financial stability and monetary stability: exploring the nexus', BIS Working Paper 114.

Borio, C. and W.R. White (2003), 'Whither monetary and financial stability? The implications of evolving policy regimes', in

Monetary Policy and Uncertainty: Adapting to a Changing Economy, Kansas City, pp. 131–212.

Cecchetti, S.G., H. Genberg and S. Wadhwani (2002), 'Asset prices in a flexible inflation targeting framework', in W. Hunter, G. Kaufman and M. Pomerleano (eds.) *Asset Price Bubbles: The Implications for Monetary, Regulatory and International Policies* Cambridge, MA, USA: MIT Press, pp. 427–444.

Clark, T. and S. Kozicki (2005), 'Estimating equilibrium real interest rates in real time', *The North American Journal of Economics and Finance*, **16**(3):395–413, December.

Clouse, J., D. Henderson, A. Orphanides, D. Small and P. Tinsley (2000), 'Monetary policy when the nominal short-term interest rate is zero', Board of Governors of the Federal Reserve System, Finance and Economics Discussion Series 2000–51.

Curdia, V. and M. Woodford (2010), 'The central-bank balance sheet as an instrument of monetary policy', working paper, April.

de Larosiére, J. (2009), *Report of the High-Level Group on Financial Supervision in the EU*, 25 February.

European Central Bank (2008), 'Introductory Statement', Press Release, 3 July.

Fischer, S. (1981), 'Towards an understanding of the costs of inflation: II', *Carnegie-Rochester Conference Series on Public Policy*, **15**(1): 5–41.

Fischer, S. (1984), 'The benefits of price stability', paper presented at the Federal Reserve Bank of Kansas City Symposium on Price Stability and Public Policy, Jackson Hole, Wyoming, 2–3 August.

Fischer, S. and F. Modigliani (1978), 'Towards an understanding of the real effects and costs of inflation', *Review of World Economics*, **114**(4): 810–833.

Friedman, M. (1960), *A Program for Monetary Stability*, New York, NJ, USA: Fordham University Press.

Gertler, M. and P. Karadi (2010), 'A model of unconventional monetary policy', working paper, April.

Goodfriend, M. (2010), 'Central banking in the credit turmoil: an assessment of Federal Reserve practice,' working paper, April.

Greenspan, A. (2010), 'The Crisis', working paper, March.

International Monetary Fund (2000), *World Economic Outlook*, May.

International Monetary Fund (2006), *World Economic Outlook*, April.

International Monetary Fund (2009), *World Economic Outlook*, October.

Issing, O. (2009a), 'Some lessons from the financial crisis', *International Finance*, **12**(3): 431–444.

Issing, O. (2009b), 'Asset prices and monetary policy', *Cato Journal*, **29**(1):45–51.

Kohn, D.L. (2006), 'Monetary policy and asset prices', speech delivered at the European Central Bank Colloquium on *Monetary Policy: A Journey from Theory to Practice* held in honour of Otmar Issing, Frankfurt, 16 March.

Kohn, D.L. (2009), 'Monetary policy and asset prices revisited', *Cato Journal*, **29**(1):31–44.

Laubach, T. and J.C. Williams (2003), 'Measuring the natural rate of interest', *Review of Economics and Statistics*, **85**(4), November, 1063–1070.

McCallum, B., and E. Nelson (2005), 'Targeting vs. instrument rules for monetary policy', *Federal Reserve Bank of St. Louis Review* **87**, Sept./Oct., 597–611.

Modigliani, F. and L.D. Papademos (1975), 'Targets for monetary policy in the coming year', *Brookings Papers on Economic Activity*, **6**(1):141–165.

Modigliani, F. and L.D. Papademos (1976), 'Monetary policy for the coming quarters: the conflicting views', *New England Economic Review*, March/April: 2–35.

Modigliani, F. and L.D. Papademos (1978), 'Optimal demand policies against stagflation', *Weltwirtschaftliches Archiv*, **114**(4): 736–782.

Orphanides, A. (2003a), 'The quest for prosperity without inflation', *Journal of Monetary Economics*, **50**(3):605–631, April.

Orphanides, A. (2003b), 'Historical monetary policy analysis and the Taylor Rule', *Journal of Monetary Economics*, **50**(5): 983–1022.

Orphanides, A. and S. van Norden (2002), 'The unreliability of output gap estimates in real time', *Review of Economics and Statistics*, **84**(4):569–583, November.

Orphanides, A. and J.C. Williams (2002), 'Robust monetary policy rules with unknown natural rates', *Brookings Papers on Economic Activity*, **2**:63–118.

Orphanides, A. and J.C. Williams (2005), 'The decline of activist stabilization policy: natural rate misperceptions, learning, and expectations', *Journal of Economic Dynamics and Control*, **29**(11): 1927–1950, November.

Orphanides, A. and J.C. Williams (2008), 'Learning, expectations formation, and the pitfalls of optimal control monetary policy', *Journal of Monetary Economics*, **55**, Supplement 1, October, S80–S96.

Orphanides, A. and J.C. Williams (2010), 'Monetary policy mistakes and the evolution of inflation expectations', Central Bank of Cyprus Working Paper 2010–2.

Papademos, L.D. (1977), *Optimal Aggregate Employment Policy*, Doctoral Dissertation, Cambridge, MA, USA: Massachussets Institute of Technology.

Papademos, L.D. (1981), 'Maximum employment anti-inflation policy', *Greek Economic Review*, **3**(2): 93–127.

Papademos, L.D. (2001), 'Why price stability?', in A.G. Herrero, V. Gaspar, L. Hoogduin, J. Morgan and B. Winkler (eds.) *Why price stability?*, Proceedings of the First ECB Central Banking Conference, European Central Bank.

Papademos, L.D. (2007), 'The financial market turmoil, the European economy, and the role of the European Central Bank', paper presented at an event organised by the European Institute New York, 27 September.

Papademos, L.D. (2008), 'Financial market excesses and corrections: a central banker's perspective', speech at the International Research Forum on Monetary Policy, Frankfurt, 26 June.

Papademos, L.D. (2009a), 'Tackling the financial crisis: policies for stability and recovery', speech at the Annual Dinner of the Society of Business Economists, London, 11 February.

Papademos, L.D. (2009b), 'Strengthening macro-prudential supervision in Europe', speech at the conference on *After the Storm: the Future Face of Europe's Financial System*, Brussels, 24 March.

Papademos, L.D. (2009c), 'Monetary policy and the Great Crisis: lessons and challenges', speech at the 37th Economics Conference, *Beyond the Crisis: Economic Policy in a New Macroeconomic Environment*, Oesterreichische Nationalbank, Vienna, 14 May.

Papademos, L.D. (2009d), 'Financial stability and macro-prudential supervision: objectives, instruments and the role of the ECB', speech at the conference *The ECB and Its Watchers,* Frankfurt, 4 September.

Papademos, L.D. (2010), 'Financial integration, development and stability: lessons from the crisis', speech, Frankfurt, 12 April.

Posen, A.S. (2009), 'Finding the right tool for dealing with asset price booms', speech at the *MPR Monetary Policy and the Economy Conference*, London, 1 December.

Ricardo, D. (1824), 'Plan for the Establishment of a National Bank', reprinted in J.R. McCulloch (ed) *The Works of David Ricardo*, London: John Murray, 1888.

Svensson, L.E.O. (2002), 'Inflation targeting: should it be modeled as an instrument rule or a targeting rule?', *European Economic Review*, **46**(4–5): 771–780.

Taylor, J.B. (1993). 'Discretion versus policy rules in practice', *Carnegie-Rochester Conference Series on Public Policy*, **39**:195–214.

Taylor, J.B. (1999), 'A historical analysis of monetary policy rules', in Taylor, J.B. (ed), *Monetary Policy Rules*, Chicago, USA: University of Chicago.

Taylor, J.B. and J.C. Williams (2010), 'Simple and robust rules for monetary policy', Federal Reserve Bank of San Francisco, Working Paper Series 2010–10, April.

White, W. (2006), 'Is price stability enough?', BIS Working Paper 206.

Wicksell, K. (1898), *Interest and Prices*, London: Macmillan for the Royal Economic Society (translated by Richard Kahn), 1936.

Yates, T. (2002), 'Monetary policy and the zero bound to interest rates: a review', ECB Working Paper 190.

3. Reflections on the Crisis and on its Lessons for Regulatory Reforms and for Central Bank Policies

Alex Cukierman[1]

When the music stops, in terms of liquidity, things will be complicated. But as long as the music is playing, you've got to get up and dance. We're still dancing.[2]

Introduction

The global financial crisis (GFC) has exposed numerous problems of moral hazard and of asymmetric information in financial intermediation. In good times such problems are not as salient because various excesses – such as exaggerated commissions, large compensation packages, biased financial advice and outright fraud – are overshadowed by the generally good performance of the economy. When everybody is making money and credit is plentiful the general public, as well as politicians, are not inclined to be inquisitive and various excesses are more likely to be glossed over. Easy access to credit makes it possible to maintain such excesses and even outright fraud over long periods of time.[3]

---

[1] An earlier version of this work was published in the *Journal of Financial Stability* and was presented as a keynote lecture at the Finlawmetrics Conference on 'After the Big Bang: Reshaping Central Banking, Regulation and Supervision', June 2009, Bocconi University, Milan, Italy.
[2] Interview with Citigroup CEO in the *Financial Times*, 9 July 2007.
[3] A salient example is the Madoff case.

Many of those problems call for substantial reforms in the regulation and supervision of financial institutions and some reconsideration of the way central bank policies operate. Paradoxically, a benefit of the crisis is that it has exposed the fact that in a world with serious asymmetries of information, vigorous financial innovations and incomplete regulatory frameworks, 'self-regulation' does not work. This realization will, no doubt, induce institutional changes designed to reduce the likelihood of systemic crises through reforms of the current regulatory and supervisory systems. Some of this process is already taking place. The crisis also presents new challenges for recent conventional wisdom regarding monetary policy procedures.

Many reasons – such as inadequate regulation of financial institutions, overly expansionary monetary policy and a global savings glut – have been suggested as reasons for the crisis.[4] With an eye to potential reforms in the regulation of financial institutions, the chapter focuses mainly on inadequate regulation and supervision. It takes the view that suggestions for reforms must start with an identification of the factors that contributed to the eruption of the subprime crisis in the US and then to its transformation into a GFC.[5] The most glaring regulatory failures are the rise of an unregulated shadow banking system, the existence of compensation packages that encourage excessive risk taking behavior, the too-big-to-fail problem, procyclicality in the behavior of financial institutions, and moral hazard problems in the rating agencies sector. Section two describes the roles of those factors in the generation of the crisis and suggests detailed regulatory reforms to address the problems that surfaced in each of those areas.

Contrary to the great depression, both fiscal and monetary policies in the US, and to a lesser extent in Europe, have responded swiftly and vigorously to the crisis and are likely to be maintained for some time. It is highly likely that in the absence of those quick and large policy responses the crisis would have been deeper and more sustained. Particularly notable here is the response of the Fed which, unlike fiscal policy that requires a longer legislative process, was very quick

---

[4] See respectively Roubini (2008), Taylor (2009) and Bernanke (2005).
[5] A companion discussion that focuses on the reasons for the crisis and the regulatory reform in the UK appears in Goodhart (2008).

and determined. This swift response maintained financial markets afloat in face of the panic that took hold following the bankruptcy of Lehman Brothers. This experience revealed the crucial role of the central banker as a first line of defense in the face of a panic. Section three discusses this 'old–new' aspect of short run central bank policy and argues that it is likely to lead to a resuscitation of this function in parallel with the (recently) more traditional inflation targeting regime.

Although warranted by the seriousness of the crisis, the short-run response of monetary policy, and subsequently of fiscal policy, created a new state of affairs in which the central bank (CB) holds a large (and more risky) share of debt in the economy and in which the share of public debt in GDP is expected to increase substantially. This is particularly notable in the case of the Fed. When the US ultimately emerges from the crisis, this new state of affairs may create a painful trade-off between price stability and financial stability. However, price and financial stability may also reinforce each other, as was the case during the Savings and Loan Association crisis in the US. Section four discusses those issues along with other longer-term lessons for regulatory reform and for the role of the CB within the newly created regulatory environment. The section discusses the pros and cons of delegating responsibility for financial stability and regulation to the CB, and in particular, its potential role as a macro-prudential regulator. It also discusses the long-term risks posed by the crisis for CB independence as well as the independence and professionalism of other financial regulators.

The globalization of financial flows and of trade in conjunction with the central role of the US in both of these areas contributed to the quick transformation of the subprime crisis into a GFC. Thus, along with its substantial benefits, globalization also contributed to a quick transmission of the adverse effects of the subprime crisis to the rest of the world. This suggests that although the crisis originated in the US, other countries have to adapt their institutions as well. In the presence of globalization, regulatory reforms should not be confined to the US and should be sufficiently coordinated in order to prevent regulatory arbitrage.[6] The onset of the crisis dramatically increased volatility on

---

[6] The 2 April 2009 declaration on strengthening the financial system following the London summit of the G20 is well aware of this requirement. But its translation into specific recommendations is only partial at this stage.

forex markets. In times of global crisis, when much of the world is hit by a common shock, there may be room for beneficial coordination of monetary policies among major central banks in order to offset some of this volatility. Those international dimensions are discussed in section five. This is followed by concluding thoughts including, inter alia, some conjectures about the relation between the likelihood of bubbles and the effectiveness of regulation and of supervision.

Regulatory Problems Exposed by the Subprime Crisis in the US and Potential Remedies

This section reviews the contributions of supervisory forbearance and of regulatory incompleteness to the emergence of the crisis as a starting point for possible remedial measures in those areas.[7] It centers mainly on the US for two reasons. First, the crisis originated in that country. Second, the swift adoption and spreading of financial innovations in the US, many of which were driven by regulation avoidance, quickly led to an increasing gap between the sophistication of private financial operators and the abilities of financial supervisors to effectively regulate the financial system. This occurred through several channels, such as the emergence of lightly regulated shadow banking institutions, compensation packages that encouraged short-termism and excessive risk taking, various conflicts of interest related to the operation of rating agencies and of financial research departments within investment banks, and overly sophisticated financial assets whose fundamental values became more and more opaque as the state of the real economy gradually moved from boom to recession.

The Growth of Poorly Regulated Segments of the Financial System

Parts of the US financial system, such as commercial banks, are subject to reasonable levels of regulation and supervision, while other parts such as hedge funds are very lightly regulated, or not regulated at

---

[7] An early discussion of some of those issues appeared in Roubini (2008).

all[8]. The Glass Steagall Act of 1933 separated commercial banking from other financial activities like underwriting, brokerage and securitization that were performed by such institutions as investment banks. As long as the act was in force commercial banks were largely confined to narrow banking. Bowing to pressures from the financial community, the 1999 Gramm-Leach-Bliley Act effectively repealed this separation, widely opening the door for universal banking and the growth of a shadow banking system. This led to regulatory arbitrage that transferred a significant fraction of financial intermediation to non-bank financial institutions such as broker dealers and hedge funds. Commercial banks also participated in this expansion by setting up special investment vehicles (SIV), conduits and other legal entities that allowed them to shift a rising fraction of their business away from tightly regulated activities into unregulated or lightly regulated activities.

The growth of the shadow financial system had the following consequences. First, the fraction of intermediation not subject to capital requirements increased. Second, many institutions in this segment of the market did not have access to the lender of last resort facility, making them potentially subject to runs – not by bank depositors who are insured by the Federal Deposit Insurance Corporation (FDIC), but by the more sophisticated holders of their liabilities. Third, like banks, many institutions in the shadow system had liabilities whose average maturity was shorter than that of their assets. This created a liquidity risk akin to the classic liquidity run analyzed in Diamond and Dybvig (1983). Fourth, some of those institutions, such as hedge funds, engaged in highly leveraged operations. Finally, with light or nonexistent regulation, the shadow banking institutions could afford to be opaque and even secretive about their assets and liabilities.

Remedies

The main lesson for regulatory institutions is that the scope of regulation should be extended to *all* financial institutions. Extending regulation and supervision to *all* financial institutions is essential for restoring the shattered credibility and normal functioning of financial

---

[8] This statement refers to the period preceding the crisis outbreak.

institutions in the US and world financial markets as well as for the minimization of regulatory arbitrage. Although the details of the extended regulation may have to be tailored to the different types of financial intermediaries, the general principles – such as maintenance of risks, and particularly of systemic risks, below critical levels and assurance of adequate levels of disclosure and transparency – should be uniform. A practice that facilitated regulatory arbitrage in the US is the fact that, within some limits, financial institutions can choose their regulators. I believe any post-crisis reasonable regulatory system should largely eliminate this option.

Amidst the public policy discussions about the future of the US regulatory system, free-market advocates have been preaching in favor of self-regulation. My feeling is that the crisis has provided substantial evidence in favor of the view that self-regulation cannot be relied upon to prevent future crises in the US financial system. The 'taste' for taking risks and producing new financial instruments to generate profits is simply too strong in that country. Self-regulation may have a better chance in Canada whose banks are less innovative and more conservative in their lending policies. This view appears to be supported by the observation that although Canada has a large subprime mortgage market, this market has performed to date much better than its US counterpart.

Compensation Packages that Encourage Short-termism and Excessive Risk Taking

The crisis has drawn public attention and anger to the large compensation packages of senior- and mid-level financial executives. In addition to their size, which often appears exaggerated on distributional equity grounds, those packages raise two principal-agent issues and another one regarding their implications for systemic stability. The first principal-agent question is whether the compensation packages are justified in view of the contribution of those executives to the long-run performance of their respective institutions. The other concerns the effect of those packages on the incentives of top managers to make decisions leading to risks/return patterns that are in line with the long-term interests of their shareholders. Those microeconomic questions are discussed in this subsection; the macro type implication of existing compensation packages for systemic stability is discussed in the following subsection.

A typical remuneration package is composed of a fixed payment plus yearly bonuses paid for performance above a threshold level. Above the threshold, the bonus increases with the performance of the institution. As a consequence, financial executives are remunerated in good years but not fined for poor performance in other years. This creates a structure of incentives that encourages short-run profit maximization at the expense of longer-term average returns as well as excessive risk taking. Actions that increase the current year's performance, even if quite costly in terms of longer-run risks and returns, are individually rational since executives get extra pay now and are not fined for subsequent bad performance. Furthermore, this structure of incentives is likely to lead to decisions that increase the variability of profits and the overall risk of the financial institution over time.

This has important consequences for the chosen leverage ratio. The main instrument through which executives control the distribution of risks and returns is leverage. By raising leverage, they raise profits in case of success but also the magnitude of losses in case of failure. The typical compensation package lowers the individual executive's downside risk below that of the financial institutions leading to leverage ratios that are excessive for shareholders. Furthermore, bonuses often take the form of options on the stock of the institution. Since, by design, options are highly leveraged instruments relative to the institution's profits, the overall incentive of financial officers to aim at quick large profits is even higher.[9] Short-termism was further encouraged by the relatively high turnover of skilled financial individuals in the US and by the built-in short horizons of politicians in democratic countries.[10]

---

[9] A fuller analysis appears in Bebchuk and Spamann (forthcoming).

[10] In a recent book, Padoa-Schioppa and Romano (2009) describe the numerous channels through which short-termism contributed to the creation of the GFC.

Remedial devices

How should financial regulation be devised to reduce those distortions? The general principle is that executives' compensation should be aligned, as much as possible, with the long-term performance of the institution for which they work. In particular, bonuses should be based on average performance over several years. Should regulation of those matters be applied only to top executives or also to mid-level managers? One view is that it should suffice to align the incentive of top managers with those of shareholders, since it would then be in their interest to design packages with similar features for mid-level portfolio managers as well. Since short-termism at many levels was a basic factor in the creation of the crisis, my own view is that bonuses to all individuals who make risk/return decisions within a financial institution should be based on average performance over several years.

One problem with bonuses that are based on longer-term performance is that some shareholders of banks, such as hedge funds, have been focusing on short-term profits. This focus was most likely nurtured by the fact that managers and traders of such funds were being remunerated on the basis of short-term performance. Consequently, a possible way to deal with this problem is to extend the requirement that bonuses be based on longer-term performance to hedge funds and other institutions that hold large blocks of shares like mutual funds. The wider the circle of financial institutions to which this longer-term principle is applied, the better the chances that short-termism is moderated without major misalignment of incentives between managers of banks and their institutional shareholders.

Systemic or Macro Risks and the Too-Big-to-Fail Problem (TBTF)

Even when compensation packages are such that the incentives of shareholders and of managers are perfectly aligned, the latter take excessive risks from a social perspective because they do not internalize the impact of their actions on the likelihood of a systemic crisis. Although, for small financial institutions this negative externality is negligible, it is sizable for large institutions. Managers of large institutions expect therefore that, if they fail, the government will come to the rescue and bail out their institution. As a consequence they choose portfolios that carry risk levels higher than the socially optimal levels, not only because they do not internalize systemic risks, but also because they expect to be bailed out. This is the 'too-big-to-fail' problem. The large amounts of funds used by the Fed to keep AIG and Citibank afloat, as well as the financial markets disruptions induced by Lehman Brothers' bankruptcy, dramatically illustrate the dilemma of the Fed and of the US Treasury. Those authorities found themselves between a rock and a hard place. By bailing out large failing institutions they assumed high risks on behalf of taxpayers. But when they did not, they were faced with a severe crisis of confidence in financial markets.

Remedial devices

Once a crisis develops it is likely that bailouts of systemically important institutions are preferable to the financial disruptions that would otherwise occur. But the longer-run drawback of such policies is that they encourage systemically important institutions to assume excessive risks. The wide-scale bailouts implemented by both fiscal and monetary authorities during the GFC most likely reinforced such tendencies. It is therefore imperative to devise mechanisms that would offset those tendencies and possibly collect up-front payments from systemically important institutions for the risks they collectively impose on taxpayers.

   Those objectives can be achieved through a number of non-mutually-exclusive devices. Direct ways are the ex ante mandatory breakup of financial institutions that are TBTF and the imposition of absolute limits on the amounts of leverage and of risks that an institution can assume through derivatives (CDSs (credit default swaps) for example), as well as through the imposition of adequate capital requirements. The ex ante breakup of large institutions reduces the need to bail out the institution if it fails and, therefore, also its incentive to assume excessive risks. Ceilings on leverage and minimal capital requirements reduce risk taking by operating directly on the balance sheets of financial institutions. Some combinations of such devices are being considered in recently proposed legislation in both the US and the European Union. There are different views about whether authority over such instruments should be vested with the central bank or with a council of regulators. The pros and the cons of those alternative arrangements are discussed in section four.

A more market-oriented device to induce internalization of systemic risks by TBTF institutions is via a tax schedule whose structure is proportional to the systemic risks induced by the decisions of such institutions. Since larger institutions generate higher systemic risks, they should pay relatively higher taxes. In addition, the burden of the tax could be structured so that it is higher during expansions, when financial institutions tend to assume higher risks, and lower during recessions, when financial institutions are naturally more cautious. By collecting a larger share of the tax during expansions, such a schedule would offset at least part of the procyclical risk-taking tendencies of financial operators discussed in the following subsection. The average tax (or insurance premium) could be set at a level that covers, on average, the costs of prospective future bailouts. This method has two advantages. First, it operates through the price system rather than through quantitative restrictions. Second, in the presence of an appropriately chosen tax level, realized bailouts would be covered in the long run from fees on TBTF institutions without burdening taxpayers. On the other hand the appropriate insurance premium level may be hard to determine – at least initially.

Procyclicality in the Behavior of Financial Institutions and Investors

The decisions of financial institutions and of investors tend to be procyclical. During the upper phases of the cycle they accept higher risks in order to increase expected returns; during the down phases the reverse happens (in markets' language – a 'flight to safety'). As a consequence, credit and leverage expand during expansions and contract during recessions. This widely observed phenomenon is caused by economic and psychological factors as well as by some features of existing financial regulation. Among the economic factors are:

1. The countercyclical behavior of the external finance premium (EFP). The EFP is the difference between the cost of external

finance and the alternative cost of own funds.[11] It goes down during booms leading to the expansion of leverage and up during recessions leading to the contraction of credit and leverage. Related to that is the procyclical behavior of collateral also known as the 'balance sheet effect.' During expansions the value of collateral goes up, raising the willingness of lenders to extend credit, while during contractions the opposite occurs. This reinforces the procyclicality in leverage. An additional reinforcing factor is the Basel II requirement to mark collateral to market.[12]

2. Evaluation of risks by financial institutions tends to be based mainly on developments during the preceding several years. As a consequence, after several years of expansion, statistical measures of risk are likely to be biased downward. With the benefit of hindsight it appears that this was the case during the second half of the subprime crisis. On the other hand, following the downfall of Lehman Brothers the markets' risk evaluations jumped to levels which turned out to be exaggerated (at least with the benefit of hindsight). It appears that dramatic bad news, such as the downfall of Lehman Brothers, induces violent fluctuations in the risk assessments of financial institutions and other market participants. The impact of such news appears to be stronger when it comes following a substantial build-up of leverage. How much of the resulting waves of optimism and pessimism are due to changes in economic fundamentals and how much to human psychology is a widely open question. Some observers like Shiller (2000, 2008) attribute such fluctuations to 'irrational exuberance' or 'social contagion'. But more traditional economic thinking could argue that these wide gyrations are rational in a world of highly imperfect and asymmetric information. As a matter of fact, frameworks like those of Morris and Shin (2002) and Morris, Shin and Tong (2005), in which fully rational individuals overreact to public information because they know that everybody else has access to the same information, go a long way toward reconciliation of the two approaches. Nonetheless, it is likely that

---

[11] Due to asymmetric information and moral hazard problems between lenders and borrowers this premium is generally positive. For a quick survey see Bernanke (2007).

[12] A fuller discussion appears in chapter four of Brunnermeier et al. (2009).

the reactions of financial decision makers to unfolding events are affected by both economically rational calculations as well as by psychological considerations. An insightful discussion that combines both factors informally appears in White (2008, section three).

3. With the benefit of hindsight it became clear that an additional reason for the large risk evaluation mistakes made by financial officers prior to the eruption of the subprime crisis was due to their overreliance on evaluation of micro risks and relative disregard for macroeconomic risks created by systemic effects. As a consequence they underestimated the correlations between adverse states of nature across different segments of financial markets.[13] In particular, it is likely that they underestimated the correlations between credit default at the level of a single institution and at the level of the entire economy. This is probably due to their better understanding of micro than of macro risks. Besides contributing further to the procyclical behavior of leverage, this factor may also explain the speed with which the boom turned into bust following dramatically adverse news.

Remedial devices

Although regulation and supervision alone cannot fully offset the cumulative procyclical impact of those factors, they can be devised in ways that reduce them to tolerable levels. Through such devices, appropriately devised regulation of financial institutions can contribute to lowering the likelihood of bubbles and of the largely inevitable busts that follow their bursting. The general objective of regulation of financial institutions should be to create built-in mechanisms that attenuate the impact of procyclical behavior on the likelihood of a crisis.

Several, not mutually exclusive, regulatory devices can be used to achieve this objective. The most obvious is to raise capital requirements during booms and loosen them during recessions. Furthermore, capital requirements need not be the same for all institutions. They should rise with the riskiness of assets held by a financial institution, so that institutions with higher risk profiles are

---

[13] This issue is a main theme of Brunnermeier et al. (2009)

forced to maintain larger levels of capital as a cushion against the higher risks they impose on counterparties. One of the mechanisms proposed to handle the TBTF problem discussed above was to impose insurance levies on systemically important institutions. This mechanism can be refined to simultaneously offset procyclicality by spreading the systemic internalization levies discussed in the preceding subsection over the cycle, so that most of those levies are collected in good times when financial institutions enjoy large profits and robust balance sheets.

Other regulatory reforms could include the mandatory conversions of bonds into stocks in bad times in order to maintain the capital ratio in such times. Recent legislative proposals in the UK and the US would give regulators resolution authority under prespecified circumstances. Those devices are particularly important in the case of TBTF institutions. In addition, an appropriate systemic regulator should develop and maintain early warning signals for macroeconomic risks, particularly during booms, and publish them.[14] This may be supplemented by imposing upper limits on the levels of credit and of CDSs in large institutions, when those levels appear to move into a dangerous area. Authority for setting the specifics of those mechanisms would be vested with an appropriate macro-prudential regulator. The controversial issue concerning the powers of the CB in macro regulation is discussed in section four.

Regulation of Rating Agencies

The subprime crisis exposed an important conflict of interest between the public interest on one hand and securitizers (like investment and mortgage banks) and rating agencies on the other. Securitizers have an interest in embellishing the prospects of the financial assets that they repackage. Since rating agencies were paid by securitizers, they obviously had an interest in partially catering to those incentives of their clients within limits determined by the requirement that this did not visibly affect their ex ante credibility. The problem was

---

[14] Borio and Drehmann (2009) show that excessive increases in the credit-to-GDP ratio and in real estate prices perform reasonably well as advance indicators of a bubble that might burst.

compounded by the fact that regulators were using some of these ratings to determine the risk levels assumed by the regulated financial institutions. Interestingly, a similar conflict of interest – that involved manipulation of information through collusion between the research and marketing departments of investment banks at the expense of the general public – emerged already in the mid-eighties and was finally settled in 2003. Following lengthy investigations and litigation by the SEC and the NY Attorney-General, ten of the US top investment firms have settled enforcement actions involving conflict of interest between research and investment banking.[15] The fact that such conflicts of interest continued in another guise for several years after the settlement demonstrates that those measures did not suffice and further supports the view that self-regulation is unlikely to be effective in the US.

Remedial actions

It is clear that rating agencies should not be allowed to be remunerated by any institution that has a stake in the assets that are being rated. It is less obvious how the problem should be handled; different economists may have different views about this question, depending on their a priori views regarding the ability of rating agencies to self-regulate. My own view is that some public involvement in this matter is inescapable. Rating agencies should be monitored by appropriate public bodies and tightly regulated to detect conflicts of interests early on. They should be licensed by the regulatory authority and the latter should have the authority to revoke their license in case of unethical behavior. In addition, serious consideration should be given to the creation of independent public rating agencies parallel to the private ones. These rating agencies should have some authority to demand information from financial institutions and corporations. Their compensation should be totally divorced from the conclusions of their research, but may be tied to the ex post accuracy of their predictions.

---

[15] The settlement required payment of $487.5 million by the investment banks to fund independent research and investor education. Some of the investment banks involved were Bear Sterns, Goldman Sachs, Lehman Brothers, J.P. Morgan Securities, Merrill Lynch, Morgan Stanley and Citigroup. Further details appear in EC NewsDesk (2003).

If appropriately devised, such agencies may set a standard for the private rating agencies.

Securitization and the Trade-Off Between Transparency and Efficient Intermediation

Securitization of mortgages was initially introduced in the US by the National Mortgage Association (Fannie Mae) already in 1981 by issuing Mortgage Backed Securities (MBS) backed by the 'full credit' of the US government. Soon after, securitized products for prime loans without the backing of government emerged in the private US sector.[16] The main advantage of securitization is that it widens the scope for financial intermediation between final borrowers and final lenders. By repackaging mortgages (or other types of loans) it produces financial assets designed to better fit the risk/return preferences of different classes of lenders, thereby increasing the volume of intermediation and, presumably, its allocative efficiency.

However, by disconnecting the direct link between the mortgage originator and the final holder of the MBS, it makes the monitoring of the borrower and the evaluation of the fundamental value of the securitized asset difficult and opaque. This problem becomes more acute when market circumstances change. It is further compounded when there are several layers of securitization. The recent inability of highly sophisticated financial institutions to price the MBSs they owned clearly demonstrates that excessive, and poorly regulated, securitization also carries a cost. This cost, which is related to opaqueness about the value of securitized assets, was largely responsible for the drying out of the interbank market following the demise of Lehman Brothers. The upshot is that securitization creates a trade-off between larger volumes of intermediation on the one hand, and monitoring plus transparency with respect to the fundamental value of securitized assets, on the other.

---

[16] The European asset securitization market developed later during the nineties. Further details appear in Mizen (2008).

Remedial measures

An extreme solution to the consequent problems of monitoring and opaqueness is to forbid securitization altogether. This amounts to 'throwing out the baby together with the bathwater.' I believe an 'optimal' solution should maintain the option to securitize and to assure adequate levels of monitoring and of transparency through appropriate regulation. How this general principle is to be translated into specific details is a difficult open question that requires further research and thinking. One possibility is to require that the originators of MBSs and other securitized instruments retain a substantial fraction of the equity tranche of those assets. This would leave the incentive to monitor final borrowers with the institution that has a comparative advantage in achieving this task. In addition, excessive levels of securitization should be limited by regulators. It is likely that beyond a certain level, the monitoring and transparency losses outweigh the benefits in terms of the volume of intermediation.

Another dimension through which regulation may improve the trade-off between transparency and the scope of intermediation is by enhancing transparency regarding the valuation of securitized assets. This may be achieved by measures such as requiring securitizers to better inform the public about how to value securitized assets and possibly maintain an active secondary market for securitized assets.

The Central Bank as a First Line of Defense Against an Impending Financial Crisis

Although the subprime crisis was largely triggered by the 2006 reversal in the trend of prices in the US housing sector, it is essentially a crisis of the financial system. Due to factors discussed in the previous section, the flow of credit within the arteries of the financial system dried up. This was particularly dramatic after the downfall of Lehman Brothers in September 2008. Opaqueness about the value of assets in counterparty institutions made valuation of their assets highly uncertain. Banks and other financial institutions became reluctant to lend to each other, even for short periods of time. Well oiled and liquid financial markets like the interbank market and the subprime mortgage market dried up, and banks became reluctant to lend to the real economy. Highly leveraged institutions such as hedge funds were forced to engage in 'fire sales', further decreasing the value of assets, increasing uncertainty about their valuation and reducing their liquidity. These adverse effects quickly spread to derivatives like the huge CDS market further reinforcing the impact of the crisis on the financial system and on the supply of credit to the real sector of the economy.

The central bank (CB) constitutes the first (ex post) line of defense against such swift adverse developments and is naturally – and rightly so – expected to step in and react quickly. As a matter of fact, the Fed was originally created in order to offset the adverse effects of periodic financial panics and to reduce their impact on the variability of interest rates and on liquidity.[17] However, those necessary immediate reactions also create new challenges for the central bank, when the economy returns to normal. This section focuses on lessons from the crisis and from the Fed's response to date for CB policy during the crisis for the short and intermediate runs, while the impacts of the crisis are still substantial. Lessons for longer term reforms designed to reduce the ex ante likelihood of a crisis are discussed in the subsequent section.

The Central Bank as a 'Fire Fighter'

The GFC demonstrated that the presence of persistent regulatory problems induces serious credibility problems about the solvency and liquidity of financial institutions, and may eventually lead to the drying up of financial intermediation, to a severe contraction of credit to the private sector and, eventually, to a recession. Such structural problems can be handled only in the longer run, leaving an important open question about the role of the CB in the short run. In this run the CB is akin to a fire fighter. It first has to put out the fire and let society worry about future prevention after the fire has been put out. In the context of the financial system the 'fire' is the drying up of financial intermediation. In its role as lender of last resort the CB should, under such circumstances, step in and use its policy instruments to maintain adequate liquidity by assuming a greater share of financial intermediation in the economy. A by-product of such policy is that it

---

[17] See Meltzer (2003).

may restore some of the shattered credibility of the private financial system.

This lesson was learnt the hard way after the great depression (Friedman and Schwartz (1963)). Since September 2008 the Fed has supplied huge amounts of short-term liquidity and some longer-term funds to the economy, demonstrating that it has internalized this distant lesson.[18] This policy prevented the level of financial intermediation from dropping at very fast rates in spite of deleveraging by the private financial sector. A substantial part of intermediation by the private sector was replaced by intermediation through the central bank, and the interbank market (which dried up due to opaqueness about the credit worthiness of private financial institutions) was replaced by intermediation through the Fed. The fact that banks with excess funds abstained from lending to other financial institutions but were willing to do so through the intermediation of the Fed made it possible to maintain reasonable levels of credit flows. The ECB responded in qualitatively similar ways. It is now apparent (December 2009) that those policies averted a substantially worse financial crisis and restored a measure of confidence to global financial markets.

Longer Term Reform: The Role of Central Banks in Regulation and Supervision of Financial Institutions

Following the crisis there is broad consensus that financial regulation should be reinforced and supervision tightened. An important element of this consensus is that, in addition to existing micro regulatory authorities, a macro regulatory authority that would monitor systemic risks and possess policy instruments able to deal with such risks should be set up. However, views differ on the scope of reform and on

---

[18] By contrast, during the first three years of the great depression, monetary policy was passive and became expansionary only after Roosevelt was elected in 1933 (further details appear in Cukierman (2009)). No doubt, one factor that contributed to the swift and vigorous reaction of monetary policy during the current crisis is the fact that the Fed's chairman devoted much of his early academic career to studying the consequences of monetary passivity during the great depression (Bernanke (1983)).

the allocation of regulatory authority across different regulatory institutions. In particular there are disagreements about the allocation of responsibility for financial stability and of the closely related systemic regulation function to the CB or to one or several other regulatory institutions. Existing practices vary widely across countries. In the US the Fed regulates most of the banking system including banking holding companies while the Federal Deposit Insurance Corporation (FDIC) implements deposit insurance and handles the resolution of insolvent banks.[19] The Securities and Exchange Commission (SEC) regulates securities markets and the Commodity Futures Trading Commission (CFTC) handles futures markets. But many other derivative markets like the Credit Default Swap (CDS) market, that expanded by leaps and bounds prior to the crisis, are not regulated at all. Clearly, the structure of US financial regulation is fragmented and incomplete. Regulatory coverage and supervision in Europe are generally tighter. But the structure of regulation varies substantially across countries within Europe. Thus, since 1997, authority for regulation and supervision of banks in the UK is vested with the Financial Services Authority (FSA) and the Bank of England has no regulatory or supervisory authority. By contrast, in Germany regulation and supervision are shared between the Bundesbank and the German Federal Banking Supervisory Office (GFBSO).[20]

Regulatory Reform Proposals and the Role of the Central Bank

In view of its broad macroeconomic focus and expertise, the CB is a natural candidate for monitoring systemic risks and for evaluating the economy-wide risks induced by the behavior of large financial institutions. However, this does not necessarily mean that the CB should be the *only* institution in charge of those functions. This is where the consensus ends.

---

[19] The Fed regulates banks that are members of the Federal Reserve System. The remaining banks are regulated by state regulators and by the Office of the Comptroller of the Currency (OCC).

[20] Further details about German regulation appear in Fischer and Pfeil (2003). Masciandaro, Quintyn and Taylor (2008) provide a wider cross-country comparison of regulatory institutions.

The US

In June of 2009 the US Treasury produced a comprehensive plan for regulatory reform that includes the Fed as systemic risk regulator and supervisor of TBTF institutions, the creation of a 'Council of Regulators', the regulation of all financial derivatives for the first time in US history, a new resolution mechanism for failing institutions and the creation of a consumer protection agency. The central role of the Fed in regulating and potentially breaking up systemically important institutions and in setting leverage limits and liquidity rules was further upheld in October 2009 in a House Draft Law provision. But in November 2009 Senator Chris Dodd, Chair of the Senate Banking Committee, proposed alternative legislation that would create a Financial Institutions Regulatory Administration (FIRA) as the single national regulator. This council of regulators would include the Treasury, the Fed, the FDIC, a consumer agency (to be created), the SEC and the CFTC. The main difference between these two draft law provisions is that the house draft basically delegates the authority for systemic regulation and supervision to the Fed, whereas the Senate proposal assigns it to a council of regulators in which the Fed is only one of several institutions. The Senate proposal's revealed reluctance to vest systemic regulatory authority mainly with the Fed derives from its perception that this institution was partly responsible for the outbreak of the financial crisis.[21]

The European Union

Although the existing European regulatory structure provides better coverage of European financial institutions, it is more fragmented than that of the US. Consequently a first order of business of the Larosiere Committee appointed to recommend regulatory and supervisory reforms in Europe was to find ways to harmonize those functions across the EU while maintaining the involvement of national regulators. In February 2009 the committee came up with recommendations summarized in the Larosiere Report (2009). In

---

[21] Senator Dodd expressed this view at the Banking Committee hearings for the nomination of Ben Bernanke as the Fed's chairman for a second four-year term.

September 2009 the European Commission (EC) in Brussels endorsed those recommendations with the intention of having them eventually ratified by the 27 EU member countries.

The report recommends the establishment of a new body called the European Systemic Risk Council (ESRC) that would be responsible for systemic macro-prudential issues. The ESRC will be chaired by the European Central Bank (ECB) president and logistically supported by the ECB. In parallel, three pan-European supervisory agencies will be created to enforce a common rule-book for banks, insurance companies and security markets across the EU. These agencies' formal titles are the European Banking Authority (EBA), the European Insurance Authority (EIA) and the European Securities Authority (ESA). The ESRC will be composed of all the members of the general council of the ECB, the chairs of the EBA, the EIA and the ESA, as well as one representative of the EC. These bodies will have more powers and resources than the existing EU committees that they are supposed to replace. They will draw common rules in a wide range of financial services areas that would then have to be enforced by national regulators.[22] The three authorities would also be able to rule in the event of a dispute with or between member states – although there would be an appeal process, ultimately to European Council level, where the final decision would be by qualified majority voting. Finally, the principle of 'fiscal responsibility' would be formally recognized in the legislation, meaning that the new supervisory structure should not intrude on states' finances.

Comparison of US and EU reform proposals

The proposed US and EU regulatory legislations are similar in that they both create a top council of regulators (the FIRA in the US and the ESRC in the EC). But the European model clearly assigns a major role in macro-prudential regulation to the ECB, while this role is envisaged for the Fed only in the House Draft Law Provision. Another difference is that the EU formula creates three new pan-European regulatory agencies for banking, insurance and securities activities.

---

[22] Under the proposed legislation, their rules would still have to be endorsed by the European Commission before coming into effect, but this could become a largely 'rubber-stamping' exercise.

Since US wide regulatory institutions in those areas already exist, no additional regulatory organs are planned.[23] Hitherto unregulated segments of the US financial system would come under the responsibility umbrella of existing US regulatory agencies. Last but not least, European regulatory reform proposals recognize that, to the extent that maintenance of financial stability requires fiscal decisions, those are left to the discretion of the 27 national governments.

Should the Central Bank be Responsible for Financial Stability and Should it Regulate Financial Institutions? Pros and Cons

Central banks were originally created mainly in order to maintain financial stability and to prevent liquidity crises by acting as lenders of last resort (LLR), and later through regulation and supervision. Following the experience of the great depression and the inflationary experiences of the twentieth century, they were also assigned the additional dual objective of adequate employment and price stability. During the last two decades these two objectives were embedded into explicit or implicit inflation targeting (IT) frameworks in which the maintenance of financial stability, although implicitly present, took a back seat. The GFC propelled the financial stability objective and the LLR function back into the front seat, raising a fundamental question about whether regulatory and supervisory responsibilities should be located within the CB or in separate institutions.

This subsection considers the trade-offs and synergies between price and financial stability when the responsibility for achieving the second objective is placed with the CB. In this case the objective function of the standard IT framework should be expanded to include three objectives and (excluding initially possible additional instruments) only one instrument, to which I refer as the stance of monetary policy.[24] The presence of only one instrument and several objectives may create trade-offs between the various objectives. Following the extraordinary expansionary policies that major central

---

[23] An exception is the planned consumer regulatory agency that would protect the interest of consumers in matters such as credit card and ATM fees.

[24] The stance may be more or less expansionary. Although a given stance can be achieved by various combinations of interest rates and of quantitative easing policies, what matters is the degree of monetary stimulus to the economy and to the financial system which I consider as only one instrument.

banks have deployed in response to the GFC, a current concern is that excessive focus on financial stability may interfere with the objective of long-run price stability. This concern is particularly strong in the case of the Fed, whose monetary policy stance has been particularly expansionary and is expected to remain in such a state for some time.

Price and financial stability: complements or substitutes?

At a more general level, price and financial stability are not always competing objectives. Whether they compete or complement each other depends on the origin of shocks that affect the economy. This point is illustrated by means of two episodes from the recent history of the financial sector in the US. The first draws on the experience of the current crisis and the second on the Savings and Loans Associations (S&L) crisis during the seventies and the eighties of the previous century. The current crisis originated in the bursting of a real estate financial bubble against a backdrop of price stability. In conjunction with opaque financial instruments, this led to panic within the financial sector and to a stoppage of credit flows. To restore confidence and the flow of credit, monetary policy responded by flooding the financial system with liquidity. If not removed when the economy rebounds, this liquidity will be inflationary in the longer run, thus creating a trade-off between financial and price stability.

The S&L crisis was due to disintermediation in the S&L segment of the financial system. At a deeper level this was caused by the fact that the assets of a typical firm in this sector had longer maturities than its liabilities in conjunction with the acceleration of inflation. Together with the then-prevailing structure of deposit and loan contracts, inflation led to a faster rise in interest rates on deposits than on loans and to bankruptcies in the S&L sector. Thus, in contrast to the current crisis, inflation was an important contributing factor to the S&L crisis. When finally restored under Volcker, price stability also removed this kind of financial instability. Clearly, during the S&L crisis there were strong synergies between price and financial stability.

The broader conclusion from those two episodes is that, depending on the existing structure of financial contracts and on aggregate developments, price and financial stability may either compete or complement each other. Obviously, when they reinforce each other there is no harm in putting the financial stability objective under the

CB responsibility. The harder problem arises when those two objectives compete with each other. In such cases CB concern about financial stability may interfere to some extent with price stability and even create an inflation bias during times of financial stress.[25] On the other hand, periods of financial stress which necessitate large liquidity injections are not frequent events. Furthermore, during the last twenty years most CBs demonstrated their ability to overcome the well known, employment motivated, Kydland and Prescott (1977), Barro and Gordon (1983) inflation bias. There is therefore reason to believe that they are also capable of overcoming the financial stability motivated inflation bias.

The Central Bank as a macro-prudential regulator and supervisor

The CB appears to be the natural institution for monitoring systemic risks and for determining which institutions in the economy induce such risks for the entire economy. Modern central banks possess a broad macroeconomic outlook supported by professional research departments characterized by a broad aggregate outlook on the economy. Due to the complexity of financial markets, it is probably unrealistic to concentrate the regulation and supervision of the entire financial sector under the umbrella of a single institution, and a single regulatory formula may not fit all countries. I believe nonetheless that any future regulatory reform should at least fulfill the following criteria: First, the entire financial system should be regulated and supervised and the limits of responsibility across regulators delineated in ways that eliminate regulatory 'holes.' Second, a constant flow of two-way information between regulators should be assured. Third, in any sensible regulatory structure the CB is likely to occupy a central position as a macro-prudential regulator, particularly of TBTF institutions.

Devices for reining in the systemic risks induced by the behavior of TBTF institutions have been discussed in section two. They include, inter alia, the breakup of such institutions and appropriate up-front taxation of their activities commensurate with the systemic risks that they impose on the economy. Here again the CB appears to be the

---

[25]A formal analysis and demonstration of this point appears in chapter seven of Cukierman (1992).

most suitable institution to evaluate those externalities. It therefore appears efficient that the CB, perhaps with the cooperation of other suitable regulators and a representative of the Treasury, be in charge of setting those additional instruments. It is important to observe that since the regulation of TBTF institutions comes with additional new instruments, its location within the CB does not conflict with the price stability objective.[26] Last but not least, the macro-prudential regulator should closely monitor the evolution of financial innovations and evaluate their potential implications for systemic stability in real time. With the benefit of hindsight it is clear that, had there been an institution with a clear mandate to perform such a function, the buildup of the subprime crisis would have been detected earlier. Thus, Barth et al. (2009) note that over the period between 2003 and 2006 there was a rapid increase in the proportion of increasingly complex nontraditional mortgages which allowed and encouraged borrowers to postpone the amortization of mortgage debt. They claim that clear-sighted monitoring of information such as this by regulators should have set off the credit extension alarm bell sooner. In the future this kind of information should be reported to the systemic regulator sooner rather than later. Since many financial innovations are likely to be of microeconomic nature, this episode suggests that even when it is the main macro-prudential regulator, the CB should cooperate and exchange information with other more specialized regulators.

Other Long-Term Implications for Central Bank Policy and Independence

Once a crisis sets in, the immediate policy responses described in section three appear to be inevitable or at least a lesser evil. But they create longer-term challenges for monetary policy and the standing of the CB within the public sector. These challenges arise because, when the crisis starts to subside, there is a huge amount of liquidity in the economy and the CB finds itself holding a substantial fraction of

---

[26] At the positive level, Klomp and de Haan (2009) present empirical evidence which supports the view that the instrument independence of the central bank is associated with lower levels of financial instability. Masciandaro (2009) proposes a theory that separates circumstances under which politicians tend to vest regulatory authority with the central bank from circumstances under which they prefer to delegate it to one or several other institutions.

private and public debt. This creates two potential problems. One is to identify the shifts in the relative risks of inflation and of financial instability in real time, in order to decide when to start to remove liquidity from the economy and by how much. The objective here should be to maintain monetary policy as near as possible to an optimal trade-off between those two risks.[27] Success in achieving this goal depends mainly on the forecasting ability of the monetary authority. Qualitatively, this problem is no different from a similar problem during normal times. However, in the aftermath of a crisis, the public's mood is more volatile and uncertainty about the optimal response, therefore, substantial. This implies that the CB should devote more resources to monitoring the economy and possibly rely on additional indicators for evaluation of the state of the economy and for its mood, particularly within the financial community. This problem may be exacerbated if inflationary pressures develop before a sufficient level of stability has been restored to the financial system.

The second problem concerns the ability of the CB to maintain its independence. As the crisis subsides, it is likely that the substantial increase in public debt required to finance the ongoing US fiscal packages will raise the temptation for government to partly alleviate the debt burden by means of inflation. This will raise, at least implicitly, pressures on the CB to be more lenient on inflation. In addition, the balance sheet of the CB will, very likely, show substantial accumulated losses due to various ongoing rescue packages. If substantial, such accumulated losses are likely to make it more politically difficult for the CB to implement anti-inflationary policies. The experience of CBs that have accumulated large capital losses which led to negative CB capital shows that in such cases, CB independence is often compromised, making it more difficult to take a determined stance against inflation when the state of the economy requires it. Such institutional problems should be addressed sooner rather than later. In particular the political establishment (for example Congress in the US) should be made aware of the importance of recapitalization of the CB, if needed, when the economy returns to normal. With a view to the long run, it would be desirable to implement such recapitalization by means of legislation. But if that turns out not to be politically feasible, a long-term recapitalization

---

[27] This has been recently dubbed as the 'exit strategy.'

agreement between the CB and the Treasury would be a second best. Further discussions of these and related issues appear in Stella (2005) and Cukierman (2011)).

Independence, Professionalism and Remuneration of Regulatory Authorities

Since their decisions have non-negligible distributional consequences, regulators are natural candidates for pressures from the financial sector (regulatory capture) as well as from politicians. It is therefore important that, like central banks, all regulators be given an adequate level of legal independence. In view of the potency of pressures and of potential temptations from the private sector, additional safeguards are desirable. Individuals with authority within the regulatory establishment should be paid well, prohibited from moving to the financial community for some time after serving as regulators and have long enough terms of office. Finally they should be highly qualified professionals in their respective areas with substantial prior experience in the regulated sector. All things being equal, the appointment of individuals who are approaching final retirement age could provide greater assurance that they will not be lured by the temptations offered by the private financial sector.

Effective regulation depends to a great extent on the quality of regulators and on their motivation to do a good job. It bears repeating in this context that attracting suitable individuals requires a level of remuneration that does not deviate too much from income levels in the private financial sector. When the income discrepancy is overly large, able individuals are lured away from the regulatory sector into the sector that is being regulated. Maintaining the income differential between these two sectors below an appropriate threshold can be achieved in two ways. The obvious direct way is to raise the remuneration of regulators. A more roundabout way is to impose limits on remunerations within private financial institutions. Since such limits are currently being considered for institutions that benefited from Federal bailouts, it is worth remembering that such limits also provide the added benefit of attracting able personnel into regulation at more reasonable costs.

International Dimensions

This section briefly discusses additional international issues regarding regulatory reform and the future conduct of monetary policy. It is based on the presumption that globalization of financial markets is here to stay.

International Aspects of Regulatory Reform

Due to globalization, the reach of markets transcends that of nation states. Consequently, regulatory reform in one country leads to the creation of tax havens, regulatory arbitrage across borders and a race to the bottom in regulation. A world-wide unified regulatory system would, therefore, be a first best. The main practical impediment to such a solution is that nation states are unlikely to abrogate the privilege to regulate financial activity in their respective jurisdictions. Also, experience shows that a national budget is the most likely source to finance a bailout when the need arises. This yields support to the view that national governments should also retain the ultimate responsibility for setting up their regulatory systems. In addition, due to idiosyncrasies in national financial systems, the optimal modalities of regulation are likely to differ across countries. For all those reasons, cross-border minimization of regulatory arbitrage will have to be achieved by international cooperation rather than by full unification of regulation.

One option is to coordinate the national systems by setting good practice guidelines for regulation and supervision, preventing regulatory competition and – in extreme cases such as tax havens and non-cooperative jurisdictions – having the authority to enforce sanctions. Here central banks and international bodies like the Financial Stability Forum (FSF) and the recently established Financial Stability Board (FSB) can play a useful role. The G20 meeting in April 2009 has engaged on this route (G20 (2009)). Although the G20 declaration on strengthening the global financial system opens the way for many useful cooperative initiatives, their ultimate test will be in their worldwide implementation. In addition, the declaration ignores some areas in which future international cooperation may be needed under extreme circumstances. For example, the declaration is silent about the thorny issue of how the costs of rescuing a worldwide systemically important financial institution of a small country will be allocated across countries, if and when such a course of action is required. It is interesting to note in this context that, as of November 2008, the assets of the two largest Swiss banks (UBS and Credit Suisse) amounted to roughly four and two-and-a-half times Swiss GDP.

Obviously to the extent that they are partly responsible for regulation and supervision, those considerations apply inter alia to central banks.

Implications for the European Community and the Euro Area

An important particular case of the previous issue concerns the future of financial regulation in the European Union (EU) and/or the Euro area. Unlike the US that comprises one monetary authority and one fiscal authority, the Euro area (and a fortiori the EU) is composed of many national fiscal authorities. If and when a systemically important European financial institution needs to be bailed out, this fragmentation of bailout authority is likely to set in motion dangerous processes for the stability of the European financial system. The absence of one fiscal body may lead to protracted negotiations between the different fiscal authorities about sharing the bailout costs. In the absence of prior agreement about a sharing rule, such negotiations are likely to take time raising concerns about the liquidity and solvency of the entire system within the financial community.[28] This may clog financial markets and trigger a financial panic.

Within the Euro area, the ECB can act as a first line of defense (as it did during the current crisis). However, for systemically important financial institutions whose activities are well diversified over the Euro area this may not suffice. In case longer-term bailouts are considered, national governments may object to bailouts conducted by the ECB on the grounds that this involves fiscal decisions and that such decisions should be made by the democratically elected national governments. Buiter (2009) points out that the 'single passport' policy of the EU allows financial services operators legally established in one

---

[28] The recent adoption of the recommendations of the Larosiere Report (2009) by the EU implies that in case of bailouts, fiscal responsibilities remain decentralized.

member state to provide their services in other member states without further authorization requirements. Since this facilitates cross-border financial operations, the need to bail out a large European financial institution with operations all over the community is likely to arise sooner than later.

Clearly, resolution of such potential problems should be coordinated in advance among member countries rather than ex post under the menace of a financial panic. Clear and well publicized principles for sharing the burden of bailouts – if and when they become necessary – are essential. One important by-product of such agreements is that they reduce the likelihood of a financial crisis and the associated drying-up of credit. On the regulatory front a first best would be a unified European system, preferably well coordinated with regulators outside Europe. In the absence of such a system, national regulatory systems should operate under a similar set of conventions and have relatively tighter regulatory and supervisory systems in order to partially compensate for the fragmentation in the fiscal area. A not-mutually-exclusive measure would be the establishment of a European bailout tax that would be collected from systemically important European financial institutions by a European-wide organization whose proceeds would be used in case of a bailout. Open questions remain, such as by whom and how should a bailout decision be made?

Should Central Banks Dampen Exchange Rate Volatility Under Extreme Circumstances?

As the crisis developed and gathered momentum, volatility on exchange-rate markets increased dramatically, as can be seen from Figure 3.1 Thus, between February and April 2008 the Euro/US Dollar rate climbed from a range of 1.45 to around 1.60. It stayed in this range till the beginning of July when it started a deep descent, culminating at a bottom of around 1.25 at the beginning of November 2008.

Figure 3.1

In December of that year it managed to hit the 1.45 mark again and subsequently briefly revisited the 1.25 range at the end of February 2009. During the last week of May 2009 it was back in the 1.40 range. Some of those fluctuations were caused by unsynchronized changes in the monetary policies of the Fed and of the ECB, and others by frequent shifts between flight to safety and risk appetite. While it may be argued that the first class of factors represent 'fundamental' adjustments, it is more difficult to defend this position with respect to the frequent shifts between risk appetite and flight to safety. It is noteworthy that some of those large fluctuations occurred in the vicinity of major financial news, like the rescue of Bear-Stern in March 2008, the downfall of Lehmann Brothers in September of that year, the announcement of the Public-Private Partnership Investment Program (PPIP) for buying toxic assets from banks' balance sheets in March 2009, and the increase in yields on ten-year US Treasury bills in May 2009.

Direct intervention

It appears that as the crisis intensified so did volatility on foreign-exchange markets. This raises a difficult old question about whether central banks should try to dampen some of this volatility by direct intervention in the market. Although the answer may be positive for small open economies like Chile, Switzerland and Israel, it is less clear for key currencies like the US Dollar and the Euro.[29] Due to the large volume of trade in such currencies, direct intervention is likely to be ineffective unless the respective central banks agree to cooperate via swap arrangements. As a matter of fact, such arrangements were implemented during the last quarter of 2008 between the Fed and the ECB when the Fed provided dollars to the ECB in order to satisfy a large temporary demand for US Dollars in the Euro area.

Should such swap arrangements be utilized during periods of large exchange rate fluctuations due to excessive uncertainty in international capital markets? The answer probably depends on whether the two central banks involved are reasonably confident that sizable exchange rate fluctuations are temporary. If so, intervention is indicated. Otherwise the question remains open.

Synchronization of monetary policy decisions between key currencies

For key currencies like the Euro/US Dollar rate, a good part of the volatility during the last three years was due to asynchronization in interest rate (and quantitative easing) decisions between the Fed and the ECB. With the benefit of hindsight it appears that the policies of those two institutions turned out to be strongly correlated, on average, during the last year. But since those decisions were not synchronized on a weekly or even monthly basis, asynchronization of policy actions contributed to high volatility. Some of this volatility might have been

---

[29] Israel recently implemented a preannounced program of direct intervention designed to moderate the impact of capital inflows on the exchange rate of the shekel. Between early July 2008 and fall 2009 the Bank of Israel has been buying $100 million per business day on average. Investigation of the economic consequences of sterilized intervention in a small open economy within a DSGE framework appears in Benes et al. (2009).

avoided if the two central banks had put some effort into tighter synchronization of their policy decisions.

Most likely, such an objective is not practical for the agenda of national monetary authorities if economic developments in their respective economic areas are expected to be persistently different. But in years like 2008 and 2009, during which the US and the Euro area were hit by large common shocks to the financial and the real sectors of the economy, it was individually rational for the monetary policies of the two blocks to generally move in the same direction. Under such circumstances an attempt to increase synchronization of policy actions is likely to be beneficial for the following reason: When monetary policy decisions are asynchronized, the forex market overreacts to new information about policy decisions and this raises short-run volatility in the forex market. Morris and Shin (2002) have shown that traders tend to rationally overweight public information relative to the social optimum, implying that this volatility reduces welfare. The public information in this case concerns the highly advertised monetary policy decisions of the two central banks.[30]

Concluding Thoughts and Open Questions

In view of the large costs imposed by various aspects of incomplete regulation that led to the financial crisis, the task of appropriately reforming this system is of paramount importance. The discussion in this paper is based on the premise that globalization is desirable and that it is here to stay. Financial globalization broadens the scope of intermediation, thereby increasing the efficiency of flows between savers and investors. But the same efficient channels quickly transmit the adverse impacts of a crisis across countries. It is therefore important that regulatory and supervisory reform be sufficiently coordinated across countries. The remainder of this closing section is devoted to some conjectures triggered by the evolution of the crisis and open questions.

---

[30] Hence, when the policies of the two CBs move on average in the same direction, synchronization of policy decisions reduces suboptimal short-run volatility.

Can appropriately devised regulation and supervision reduce the probability of a crisis, and if so through which channels? This paper suggests that the answer is yes, and points to several channels. First, by assuring adequate transparency about the valuation of assets, regulation can alleviate mutual suspicions among financial institutions, contribute to the uninhibited flow of funds between them and reduce uncertainty and volatility. In particular, it is quite likely that in the presence of adequate transparency about financial assets, the interbank market would not have dried up as it did during the last quarter of 2008. Second, direct and efficient regulation of all financial institutions and rating agencies would have reduced the leverage buildup and the subsequent bust induced by the unwinding of this leverage. Third, built-in countercyclical measures of the type discussed in section two also operate in the same direction through their moderating effect on booms and busts.

The crisis vividly demonstrated the need for a systemic regulator that would produce and disseminate information about macroeconomic risks and regulate TBTF financial institutions. An important issue, currently debated by legislators in the US, concerns the role of the CB as a potential systemic regulator. Although there is room for different institutional regulatory arrangements, I believe it is clear that in any of those the role of the CB as a systemic regulator is central. Section four discusses and evaluates current proposals for regulatory reform and the role of the CB and discusses the relation between price and financial stability when the CB plays an important role in assuring the stability of the financial system. It is argued that, depending on the nature of shocks to the financial system, those two objectives may be either complements or substitutes. In the first case there is no harm in charging the CB with financial stability; in the second there is a tradeoff between price and financial stability. In such cases additional regulatory instruments should be developed to maintain financial stability in order to leave interest-rate policy free to focus on the price stability objective.

Financial crises usually occur following expansionary periods nurtured by overly optimistic expectations that induce financial institutions and the general public to assume higher risks. When this overoptimism is sufficiently controverted by reality, expectations become overly pessimistic and the boom turns into bust. In the jargon of economists, the first phase is identified as a 'bubble' and the second as the 'bursting of the bubble.' A widely accepted tenet of economic theory is that a bubble may develop through the interaction between self-fulfilling expectations and economic developments, when the possible range of paths for those expectations is larger than one. In the presence of opaqueness and a shadow banking system, there are potentially many such self-fulfilling paths, since there are less constraints regarding expectations about feasible outcomes. By imposing tighter constraints on behavior and assuring adequate transparency, regulation is likely to reduce the scope for 'wild' self-fulfilling expectations and with it the likelihood of booms and busts associated with bubbles. As a by-product it also reduces the probability of errors on the part of financial institutions, policymakers and the general public. By reducing the magnitude of the positive interaction between expectations and cyclically oriented behavior, built-in countercyclical regulation of financial institutions can also contribute to the reduction of 'wild' self-fulfilling expectations.

It would be highly desirable to have a procedure for identifying bubbles ex ante. Unfortunately, economists do not possess a clear-cut recipe for distinguishing between a bubble and a healthy expansion based on fundamentals for both conceptual and practical reasons. The conceptual difficulty originates in the observation that (as far as theory is concerned) all expansions are driven by self-fulfilling expectations blurring the distinction between what is a bubble and what is not. One possibility would be to rank self-fulfilling paths as being 'more bubbly' if the amplitudes of cycles created through their booms and busts is larger. Even if we accept such a notion, theoretically based indicators for more bubbly paths do not currently exist.[31] However, as we have seen above, it is still possible to make statements about the relation between the institutional framework, such as regulation, and the likelihood of a bubble. It is also possible, based on the experience of past crises, to draw inferences about circumstances that increase the likelihood of bubbles.

---

[31] But there are some empirically based early warning indicators (Borio and Drehmann (2009)).

References

Barro, R. J. and R. Gordon (1983), 'A positive theory of monetary policy in a natural rate model', *Journal of Political Economy*, **91**, 589–610.

Barth, J., T. Li, W. Lu, T. Phumiwasana and G. Yago (2009), *The rise and fall of the US mortgage markets*, Hoboken, NJ: John Wiley and Sons.

Bebchuk, L. and H. Spamann (Forthcoming), Regulating bankers' pay, *Georgetown Law Journal*.

Benes, J., A. Berg, R. Portillo and D. Vavra (2009), Modeling sterilized interventions and balance sheet effects of monetary policy, August, Manuscript, Czech National Bank and IMF.

Bernanke, B. (1983), 'Non-monetary effects of the financial crises in the propagation of the great depression', *American Economic Review*, **71**(3), June, 393–410.

Bernanke, B. (2005), The global saving glut and the US current account deficit, Board of Governors of the Federal Reserve System. Available at: http://www.federalreserve.gov/boarddocs/speeches/2005/200503102/

Bernanke, B. (2007), The financial accelerator and the credit channel, Board of Governors of Federal Reserve System. Available at: http://www.federalreserve.gov/newsevents/speech/Bernanke20070615a.htm

Borio, C. and M. Drehmann (2009), 'Assessing the risk of banking crises – revisited', *BIS Quarterly Review*, March, 29–46.

Brunnermeier, M., A. Crockett, C. Goodhart, A. Persaud and H. Shin (2009), The fundamental principles of financial regulation, Geneva Reports on the World Economy 11, ICBM and CEPR, Preliminary.

Buiter, W. (2009), 'Why Weber is half right but completely wrong', *Financial Times*, April 23.

Cukierman, A. (1992), *Central bank strategy, credibility and independence – theory and evidence*, Cambridge, MA: The MIT Press.

Cukierman, A. (2009), 'The great depression, the current crisis and old versus new Keynesian thinking – What have we learned and what remains to be learned?', in A. Arnon, J. Weinblatt and W.

Young (eds.), *Perspectives on Keynesian Economics*, Berlin and Heidelberg: Springer-Verlag.

Cukierman, A. (2011), 'Central bank finances and independence – How much capital should a central bank have?', in S. M. and P. Sinclair (eds.), *The capital needs of central banks*, London, UK: Routledge.

Diamond, D. and P. Dybvig (1983), 'Bank runs, deposit insurance and liquidity', *Journal of Political Economy*, **91**, 401–419.

EC NewsDesk (2003), US authorities settle with US investment banks, Ethical Corporation, April 29, Available at: http://www.ethicalcorp.com/content.asp?ContentID=548

Fischer, K.-H. and C. Pfeil (2003), Regulation and competition in German banking: An assessment, *CFS Working Paper* No. 2003/19, June.

Friedman, M. and A. Schwartz (1963), *A monetary history of the US, 1867–1960*, Princeton, NJ, USA: Princeton University Press.

G20 (2009), *The Global Plan for Recovery and Reform*, April 2, London.

Goodhart, C. A. E. (2008), 'The regulatory response to the financial crisis', *Journal of Financial Stability*, **4**(4), 351–358.

Klomp, J. and de Haan J.(2009), 'Central bank independence and financial instability', *Journal of Financial Stability*, **5**(4), 321–338.

Kydland, F. E. and E. C. Prescott (1977), 'Rules rather than discretion: The inconsistency of optimal plans', *Journal of Political Economy*, **85**, 473–92.

Larosiere Report (2009), The high-level group on financial supervision in the EU report, February 25, Brussels.

Masciandaro, D. (2009), 'Politicians and financial supervision unification outside the central bank: Why do they do it?', *Journal of Financial Stability*, **5**(2), 124–146.

Masciandaro, D., M. Quintyn and M. Taylor (2008), 'Inside and outside the central bank: independence and accountability in financial supervision trends and determinants', *European Journal of Political Economy*, **24**, 833–848.

Meltzer, A. (2003), *A history of the federal reserve, Vol. 1: 1913–1951*, Chicago, USA: University of Chicago Press.

Mizen, P. (2008), 'The credit crunch of 2007–2008: A discussion of the background, market reactions and policy responses', *Federal Reserve Bank of St Louis Review*, **90**(5), September/October.

Morris, S. and H. Shin (2002), 'Social value of private information', *American Economic Review*, **92**(5), 1521–1534.

Morris, S., H. Shin and H. Tong (2005), 'Reply to 'social value of private information: Morris and Shin (2002)' is actually pro transparency not con', *American Economic Review*, **96**(1), 435–455.

Padoa-Schioppa, T. and B. Romano, (2009), *Contre la courte vue – entretiens sur le grand krach*, Paris, France: Odile Jacob.

Roubini, N. (2008), 'Ten fundamental issues in reforming financial regulation and supervision in a world of financial innovation and globalization', *RGE Monitor*, March.

Shiller, R. (2000), *Irrational exuberance*, Princeton, NJ, USA: Princeton University Press,

Shiller, R. (2008), *The subprime solution*, Princeton, NJ, USA: Princeton University Press,

Stella, P. (2005), 'Central bank financial strength, transparency and policy credibility', *IMF Staff Papers*, **52**(2), 355–365.

Taylor, J. (2009), *Getting off track: How government actions and interventions caused, prolonged, and worsened the financial crisis*, Stanford, CA, USA: Hoover Institution Press.

White, W. R. (2008), 'Past financial crises, the current financial turmoil, and the need for a new macrofinancial stability framework', *Journal of Financial Stability*, **4**(4), 307–312.

4. The Lender of Last Resort: Liquidity Provision versus the Possibility of Bailout

Rob Nijskens and Sylvester Eijffinger

Introduction

The financial crisis of the last two years has shown that banking regulation is not adequate to safeguard the stability of the financial system. While prudential regulation (such as the Basel II capital requirements) has allowed for regulatory arbitrage, the existence of a lender of last resort has been insufficient to deter banks from taking risks that are harmful to the financial system. Furthermore, (ex post) policies for crisis management have not been able to resolve the crisis in a clean way.

In 2008 and 2009, central banks around the world have had to provide substantial amounts of liquidity to alleviate liquidity shortages and to prevent the interbank market from breaking down completely. They have provided this liquidity on very generous terms, letting virtually every bank access their facilities. Among the many banks that received liquidity assistance, several were in fact insolvent. This goes against the principle advocated by Bagehot (1873): insolvent banks should not be provided with liquidity. However, as these banks constitute a risk for the financial system as a whole, regulators have had no choice but to save them. This suggests that the Too-Big-to-Fail problem still exists, although many now call it a Too-Connected-to-Fail problem. This means that the interlinkages between banks are so dense that contagion of bank failures has become inevitable (Nijskens and Wagner, 2011).

In addition to the liquidity provision by central banks, governments around the world have constructed very large rescue packages to restore confidence in the financial system.

These packages consist of capital injections into banks, all-out nationalizations, explicit guarantees on bank lending and purchases of troubled assets. Halfway through 2009, total resources committed in these packages amounted to €5 trillion or 18.8 per cent of GDP for 11 large western countries[1], whereas actual outlays were €2 trillion (Panetta et al., 2009) at that time. This large-scale intervention has turned out to be absolutely necessary to restore confidence and stability.

To provide a correct assessment of crisis management after large systemic shocks, we should consider the recent crisis and its main aspects. In managing this crisis, central banks (as providers of liquidity) and fiscal authorities (by providing capital or guarantees) have both acted vigorously and at the same time. It is thus imperative to perform a simultaneous analysis of liquidity provision and solvency regulation. Moreover, we need to consider large, systemically relevant banks and examine their interaction with both the central bank and the fiscal authorities. The analytical model in this paper will provide a framework for doing this. Furthermore, our analysis incorporates two principles regarding lender of last resort practices. One is the abovementioned principle of Bagehot, stating that central banks should only provide liquidity to solvent banks. The other is the idea that bailout assistance (e.g., capital injections or loan guarantees) should be made costly for banks (Eijffinger, 2008), as a punishment for threatening financial stability.

The results of our analysis indicate that without any safety net, banks take excessive risk and hoard too much liquidity. The introduction of a safety net, in the form of a central bank providing liquidity, can decrease excessive liquidity hoarding but also leads to engagement in moral hazard by banks. To alleviate the moral hazard problem we extend the safety net to comprise also capital provision, which can be made costly for banks. Ultimately we find that the regulators face a trade-off. On the one hand, making capital assistance very costly for the bank increases productive investment, but also increases excessive risk taking. On the other, relatively less costly capital assistance decreases moral hazard at the expense of investment. This reflects the current situation in the financial world:

---

[1]Australia, Canada, France, Germany, Italy, Japan, the Netherlands, Spain, Switzerland, the United Kingdom and the United States.

due to conditions on bailout assistance by governments, banks are facing harsher funding requirements and can thus extend less credit for risky investment. On the other hand, the risks they are taking are less excessive than before the crisis.

In what follows, we will first provide a short overview of existing literature on LLR and solvency regulation in section two. Our model will be described in section three, while section four presents the analytical results derived from this model. Section five concludes.

Related Literature on LLR Policy and Solvency

The academic literature on the Lender of Last Resort (LLR) is not very extensive. It is even more limited when we restrict our attention to that part also considering solvency decisions. Since the United States' Savings and Loans (S&L) crisis in the 1980's, the literature has focused on the role of the Central Bank (CB) as an LLR to prevent and manage crises, and on the role of the CB and other institutions in resolving bank failures. Analogously, the current financial crisis has stimulated research in this area and we are bound to see many more research efforts in the near future.

A good overview of two decades of research on LLR and closure policy has been provided by Freixas and Parigi (2008). The authors begin their survey paper by mentioning the classic Bagehot principle, which has been a starting point of analysis for many authors. It states that the LLR should always provide liquidity to illiquid but solvent banks at a penalty rate and against good collateral. Freixas and Parigi then note that banking has become much more complex since 1873, which has led to problems such as the inability to distinguish liquidity from solvency issues (Goodhart, 1987), interbank market imperfections, moral hazard caused by penalty rates, the increasing difficulty in determining the quality of collateral, and the change of the banking system in general. The authors end with the recommendation that we should not only look at the role of the LLR, but also study '*what architecture of prudential regulation, risk supervision, monetary policy, deposit insurance and ELA is best to guarantee financial stability*'. We will review the recent literature relevant to this recommendation. As this literature has evolved after Bagehot (1873), we order our review according to improvements on his principle.

One issue with Bagehot's LLR view is the idea that the CB should always provide liquidity to banks. Many authors argue instead that a bank should face some uncertainty about whether it will receive liquidity. This so-called 'creative ambiguity' doctrine is analyzed by, among others, Freixas (1999), Goodhart and Huang (1999), Repullo (2005) and Cordella and Levy-Yeyati (2003), with contrasting results. While Freixas (1999) finds that ambiguity may have its merits in some cases (by reducing moral hazard), he also provides a rationale for a Too-Big-to-Fail (TBTF) policy: the CB will always assist large banks with liquidity, which can be detrimental to welfare if the bank is insolvent. Essentially the same result is found by Goodhart and Huang (1999): the optimal degree of ambiguity decreases strongly in bank size, leading ultimately to a TBTF policy motivated by contagion concerns. Repullo (2005) finds that certainty about liquidity provision does not increase moral hazard, although banks hold too little liquidity. The introduction of penalty rates, however, does cause moral hazard since penalty rates decrease the expected return in the illiquid state. The bank tries to offset this by taking a higher risk, thereby increasing its return in the good state. Cordella and Levy-Yeyati (2003) also conclude that moral hazard alone is not sufficient to justify criticism on standard LLR policies, as the possible moral hazard effect of having an LLR can be compensated by an increase in bank charter value. This increase is generated by the CB's commitment to an unambiguous LLR policy, conditional on an aggregate macroeconomic shock and certain 'good practice' conditions on funding.

Furthermore, Bagehot did not yet consider systemic risk and contagion; two principles that have turned out to be important during the recent crisis. Although we do not explicitly model these two phenomena, systemic risk is implied in our analysis and we thus review briefly the literature on this topic. We consider two different perspectives on the risk that banks pose to the financial system: 'Too-Connected-to-Fail' (TCTF) and 'Too-Many-to-Fail' (TMTF).

Freixas, Parigi and Rochet (2000) have been among the first to model systemic risk in the interbank market, leading to a TCTF problem. Coordination failures in this market can lead to a gridlock, which may lead to inefficient closure of solvent banks facing a lack of liquidity. Moreover, in this model money center banks are not allowed to fail as their failure might lead to contagion. More recently, Acharya and Yorulmazer (2007, 2008) have considered systemic risk in a different way. They have modeled interlinkages between banks that invest in similar projects, leading to a TMTF situation. Problems arise in their model if the correlation between these projects is high and many banks fail simultaneously. The central bank (CB) has to choose whether to bail them out or liquidate them, the latter of which can be very costly because of asset specificity. This leads to a time inconsistency problem, as the CB cannot credibly commit to not bail out these banks.

Although the models discussed above can explain several phenomena present in the financial system, they also suffer from one deficiency: they focus mainly on the CB as a lender of last resort (LLR), without considering other authorities. According to Bagehot's rule, the CB should provide liquidity assistance only when the bank is deemed solvent. However, because of a lack of information at the CB, banks may be inefficiently closed. Furthermore, as described above and noted by e.g., Boot and Thakor (1993) and Rochet (2004), the inability to discriminate between liquidity and solvency problems can lead to regulatory forbearance. Freixas, Parigi and Rochet (2004) thoroughly examine the issue of indistinguishable liquidity and solvency problems. They explicitly model liquidity and solvency shocks separately, under the assumption that the CB cannot determine ex ante whether the bank is only illiquid or also insolvent. Their model finds that a CB providing LLR support is optimal under three conditions: insolvent banks are not detected by the market, it is costly for banks to screen borrowers, and interbank market spreads are high. This resembles crisis episodes with inefficient supervision, such as the recent financial crisis. In Rochet and Vives (2004), the indistinguishability problem does not stem from failing supervision, but is caused by coordination failures between market participants. In their model participants in the interbank market cannot distinguish between illiquid and insolvent banks. Below a certain threshold for bank fundamentals, participants in the interbank market are not willing to lend to the bank anymore. Although the bank may still be solvent in this case, the interbank market will see it as insolvent. This suggests a role for the CB as an LLR, complemented with prompt corrective action or closure policy to implement the incentive-efficient solution.

To incorporate the idea of prompt corrective action, some authors have considered the co-existence of multiple regulators in the banking system. Repullo (2000), for instance, suggests a model of a bank suffering liquidity shocks and thus requiring LLR emergency liquidity. His model contains two regulatory agencies with different preferences: the central bank and the deposit insurance fund (DIF). These agencies can provide liquidity using nonverifiable information on the bank's asset quality. Additionally, he assumes that the allocation of liquidity can be made contingent on the size of the shock. The main result of this model is that the CB should be the LLR in case of small shocks, and that the DIF should fulfil this role in case of large shocks. Kahn and Santos (2005) extend this model significantly by considering closure authority, in addition to liquidity decisions. This allows for a clearer distinction between illiquidity and insolvency and, additionally, for examining how the institutional allocation influences the regulator's information gathering incentives. The authors find that having only one regulator deciding on both LLR and closure leads to regulatory forbearance and suboptimal bank investment. Like Repullo (2000), they also find that multiple regulators may improve this situation, especially when supervision is allocated to the DIF. However, when the liquidity shortage is small the forbearance problem may be exacerbated.

Additional to having two regulatory bodies, it is argued that capital provision may complement liquidity provision and help to solve the problem of inefficient closure. Diamond and Rajan (2005), for instance, have set up a general equilibrium model in which an endogenous liquidity problem occurs as entrepreneurs need to refinance their projects (Holmstrom and Tirole, 1998). This leads to an aggregate liquidity shortage, which the CB can partly alleviate. Furthermore, they find that a capital injection may improve banks' ability to raise liquidity. They note that this intervention does not work when the bank is fundamentally insolvent, in line with Bagehot's principle: genuinely insolvent banks should not receive liquidity.

Building on this body of literature, we acknowledge that there are indeed often two different authorities responsible for financial crisis management. These authorities have a division of tasks, where the central bank is generally responsible for liquidity provision and a fiscal authority (Treasury or Ministry of Finance) has to decide whether the bank receives a capital injection or not. We will argue that the existence of a fiscal authority beside a central bank can reduce excessive risk taking. The model with which we show this builds on that of Repullo (2005). We take a similar game theoretic approach, but we introduce an additional regulatory authority into the model. Our model will be explained in the next section.

The Model

Let us consider an economy with risk-neutral agents and three dates: $t = 0,1,2$. In this economy, there is one systemically important bank that collects deposits and has equity capital. These quantities are exogenously given, and the bank operates under limited liability. The economy also contains two regulatory agencies: a central bank (CB) fulfilling the role of Lender of Last Resort (LLR) and a fiscal authority that, in case of a bank failure, has to decide on the failure resolution procedure.

The bank's size is equal to one[2], and its balance sheet is described by the following equation:

$$I + M = E + D \qquad (4.1)$$

Investments I provide a random gross return[3] R per unit of investment in period two, with:

$$\tilde{R} = \begin{cases} R_H = R(p) > 1 & \text{with probability } p \\ \\ R_L = 0 & \text{with probability } 1 - p \end{cases} \qquad (4.2)$$

Where $p \in [0,1]$ is the success probability of investment, increasing in the efforts of the bank to monitor this investment. The assumptions on $R(p)$ are:

---

[2]Since we have assumed that there is only one bank and thus bank failure is costly for society, we may abstract from letting bank size determine bank closure policy.

[3]Note that all returns in our model are gross returns.

$$R'(p) < 0, \ R''(p) \le 0 \tag{4.3}$$

$$R(1) \ge 1, \ R(1) + R'(1) < 0 \tag{4.4}$$

This return function implies that expected return $E(\tilde{R}) = pR(p)$ will be maximized at $\hat{p} \in (0,1)$ where $\hat{p}$ is defined by $R(\hat{p}) + \hat{p}R'(\hat{p}) = 0.$[4] Furthermore, $E(\tilde{R})$ is greater than one, and investments are illiquid since they cannot be sold before $t = 2$. The other item on the asset side is M, holdings of liquid assets. These are called 'liquid' since they represent investment in a storage technology, which provides a riskless return of $R_M = 1$ per unit of M. This implies that the riskless interest rate in our model is equal to zero.

On the liability side we find equity and deposits. Equity capital E comes from the bank owner, who operates under limited liability. Deposits D are fully insured, which means they are riskless, and thus yield a return $R_D = 1$ at $t = 2$. To abstract completely from deposit insurance issues, we assume that the bank pays no deposit insurance premium.

We will further assume that $I > E$, to give the bank owner the opportunity to work with leverage. This assumption reflects that holding liquidity may be costly as the bank foregoes potential returns on I. Since $E(R) \ge 1$, it is profitable for the bank owner to invest the bank's funds in the risky asset. Finally, given the above assumptions, we can write bank value at $t = 2$ as follows:

$$V_2 = p\left[\left(R(p) - 1\right)I + E\right] \tag{4.5}$$

---

[4]Note that, for $p = 0, dpR(p)/dp = R(0) > 0$ and, for $p = 1$, $R(1) + R'(1) < 0$. The second order condition for a maximum is $d^2 pR(p)/dp^2 = 2R'(p) + pR''(p) < 0$ for all $p > 0$. This suffices for an interior maximum at $\hat{p} > 0$.

A Liquidity Shock

In its operation, the bank is subject to stochastic liquidity shocks. A liquidity shock, consisting of depositors withdrawing a fraction x of their deposits, occurs at date $t = 1$.[5] The shock is uniformly distributed on the interval $(0,1)$ with cumulative density $F(x) = x$ and probability density $f(x) = 1$. The size of the shock is public information when it occurs. Taking into account that we have two regulatory agencies, we can distinguish three cases:

1. $x \leq M/D = \underline{x}$, in which the liquidity shock can be resolved using liquid reserves;

2. $\underline{x} < x \leq \overline{x}$, in which the bank is illiquid and will apply for emergency lending at the LLR. $\overline{x}$ is a threshold that is determined by the Central Bank, as described below; and

3. $\overline{x} < x$, in which the solvency of the bank is insufficient to warrant LLR borrowing and the fiscal authority will have to take a closure/continuation decision.

In case one, the shock is small and the bank can repay the withdrawn deposits using its liquid reserves M. Note that we assume there is no interbank market; the bank's only liquidity comes from the amount of liquid reserves it has kept at $t = 0$.[6]

In case two, when $\underline{x} < x < \overline{x}$, the bank cannot finance the liquidity shortage by itself, so it has to apply for emergency liquidity from the LLR at an amount of $xD - M$. The LLR will ask a repayment rate

---

[5]Taking the credit crisis as a reference point, this kind of liquidity shock is very similar to investors in asset-backed securities selling their claims back to the bank. Banks were obliged to return the money, which led to severe liquidity problems. We can see this as analogous to deposit withdrawals.

[6]This assumption can be justified since we are focusing on crisis management. In the financial crisis the interbank market nearly broke down (Allen, Carletti and Gale, 2009; Diamond and Rajan, 2009). Massive intervention by central banks seemed to be the only way to get it going again.

equal to one (we assume no penalty rate) at $t = 2$ and will only lend to solvent banks.

In fulfilling its role of LLR, the central bank (CB) will want to minimize the social cost of a bank's risk taking. This is reflected in the bankruptcy cost C, which will be realized if the bank fails. The CB will therefore provide liquidity up until a certain threshold[7]. This follows from the generally accepted principle stated by Bagehot: central banks should not lend to banks that are both illiquid and insolvent. In determining this so-called solvency threshold, the CB takes into account an expected cost of $(1 - p)[\alpha C + (xD - M)]$ when it supports the bank with emergency liquidity. When it does not support the bank, the CB incurs the certain loss αC. In these expressions, α is the weight the regulator attaches to the bankruptcy cost. This can be interpreted as the political or reputational cost to the central bank and is assumed to be greater than zero[8].

Comparing the two above expressions, $(1 - p)[\alpha C + (xD - M)] \leq \alpha C$ we can deduce the solvency threshold for the CB at $t = 1$, denoted by $\bar{x}$:

$$x \leq \bar{x} \equiv \frac{p}{1 - p} \frac{\alpha C}{D} + \frac{M}{D} \tag{4.6}$$

Otherwise stated: the bank will apply for an amount of $xD - M$ and the CB will only provide liquidity when (4.6) holds. This means that the certain cost of a bank failure at $t = 1$ is greater than the expected cost of failure at $t = 2$. In this case the bank is considered to be solvent ($x \leq \bar{x}$), but illiquid.

Therefore, when $x > \bar{x}$, the bank cannot borrow from the LLR (case three). The bank will enter into a prompt corrective action programme by the fiscal authority (FA). A bailout from the FA is needed to continue the bank's business, and the FA will require a certain repayment that is potentially costly for the bank owner.

---

[7] Depositors get D back in case of insolvency, but this is dealt with by the DIF (a separate authority). We assume that the deposit insurance is not part of the loss functions.

[8] $\alpha > 1$ in Kahn and Santos (2005), but Repullo (2000) assumes $\alpha < 1$ and Repullo (2005) assumes $\alpha = 1$. We will not yet make any assumptions other than $\alpha > 0$. The same holds for β in the case of the fiscal authority.

In a bailout, the FA has to provide an amount of funds equal to $xD - M$ to make the bank solvent; we will call these funds 'capital'. The FA then decides upon the conditions on which this capital will be provided. These are meant to discipline the bank owner for taking too much risk and letting the bank become insolvent, and will consist of the regulator determining the amount of gains it appropriates from the bank. The FA will require a share γ of bank value at $t = 2$ in case of success, and will incur the bankruptcy cost βC in case of failure. However, when it does not provide assistance, it will incur the cost βC with certainty.

The FA will then choose the repayment γ such that it at least breaks even in expectation:

$$\gamma \geq \frac{xD - M - p\beta C}{p[(R(p)-1)I + E]} \qquad (4.7)$$

where β is the weight the FA attaches to the cost of bankruptcy in the same vein as the CB's α. Note, however, that these weights may differ for the CB and the FA. This reflects the political relation between the CB and the FA; they may have different responsibilities regarding financial stability.

This possibility of bailout, with a required period two return of γ, is a stylized representation of the situation in which a bank is nationalized, recapitalized or provided with guarantees on its borrowing. These measures have been used extensively in crisis management during the last two years. Of course, these measures have not been free for banks: regulators have set a premium on the rates to be paid for access to these facilities, as the government has taken over part of the risk from the bank. This is epitomized by the γ in our model, which may contain the abovementioned risk premium. Bailout assistance thus comes at a cost for the bank owner.

The Bank's Objective

Taking the liquidity shock and the regulatory system into account, the bank owner will maximize total bank value at $t = 2$. The bank operates with an exogenously given capital structure (following Wagner, 2007), consisting of positive amounts of both equity and deposits. The choice variables for the bank owner are the effort put into monitoring, embodied by the probability of success p, and the amount of investment I. The probability of success, which increases with monitoring effort at $t = 0$, is the inverse of the amount of risk taken.

Using the properties of the liquidity shock and the aforementioned conditions $\bar{x}$ and γ set by the regulatory authorities, we can refine the bank's objective function. We assume that there is no time discounting. Let us first write down the bank owner's $t = 2$ payoff, denoted by $\tilde{V}_2$, in the different scenarios:

$$\tilde{V}_2 = \begin{cases} V_2^L(p) = p[R(p)I + M - D] & \text{w.p.} \quad \underline{x}, \\ V_2^M(p) = p[R(p)I - (1-x)D - (xD - M)] & \text{w.p.} \quad \bar{x} - \underline{x}, \\ V_2^H(p) = (1-\gamma)p[R(p)I + M - D] & \text{w.p.} \quad 1 - \bar{x}, \end{cases}$$

where 'w.p.' means 'with probability' and the superscripts denote the magnitude of the shock: low, medium or high. We can thus write the bank's objective function at $t = 0$ as follows:

$$\max_{p,I}\left\{E(\tilde{V}(p,I)_2) = p[R(p)I + M - D][1 - \gamma(1 - \bar{x})]\right\} \qquad (4.8)$$

The fact that expected bank value is not only varying with p, but also with $\bar{x}$ and γ, indicates that it depends on the choices made by the bank owner as well as those made by the regulators. In the next section we will characterize this interdependence.

Liquidity or Liquidation

To summarize the previous sections, we can systematically go through the sequence of events. Following Repullo (2005), we let the bank simultaneously choose its risk p (determined by its monitoring effort) and its portfolio of risky investments I at $t = 0$, taking into account the possibility of liquidity shocks at $t = 1$ and responses by the CB and the FA. At $t = 1$, the liquidity shock realizes and it is observable.

If $x \leq \underline{x}$, the bank pays depositors out of its liquidity reserves. If $\underline{x} < x \leq \overline{x}$, the bank applies for liquidity and the CB will provide it. Finally, if $x > \overline{x}$, the CB is not willing to provide liquidity and the FA will take action. This will lead to a required repayment γ, which depends in turn on the amounts of investment and monitoring chosen by the bank at $t = 0$. Finally, at $t = 2$ returns on I realize and assistance has to be repaid.

First Best

As a benchmark, we first analyze the socially efficient solution to the problem of choosing optimal investment and risk taking. In the first best case, there is a central planner who chooses risk, investment and the regulatory instruments such that the social value of bank investments is maximized. The gains to society are the total value of bank investments at $t = 2$ minus the value of investments. The central planner's problem thus is

$$\max{}_{p,I} \; p[(R(p)-1)I + M] + (1-p)[M-I]. \qquad (4.9)$$

As we have assumed $E(\tilde{R}) = pR(p) > 1$, this function is strictly increasing in I and it is optimal to set I equal to one. Furthermore, the derivative of (4.9) with respect to p is $[R(p) - pR'(p)]I$. The optimal quantities of p and I are thus given by

$$R(p^{fb}) + p^{fb}R'(p^{fb}) = 0 \qquad (4.10)$$

$$I^{fb} = 1 \qquad (4.11)$$

which means that p^{fb} is such that equation (4.10) is satisfied. It is optimal to set $M = 0$ and invest all funds into the risky asset I; with this knowledge, monitoring effort (and thus p) is chosen to maximize the expected return on these investments.

Of course the central planner/regulator takes into account the full social value when setting a solvency threshold for liquidity provision. The threshold rule will thus be determined by comparing the expected

cost of providing liquidity $(1-p)(C+(xD-M))-p(R(p)I-(xD-M))$
with the cost of failure C (from society's point of view). This leads to
the following solvency threshold:

$$\bar{x}^{fb} = p^{fb}[R(p^{fb})+C] \quad (4.12)$$

Which says that the bank only fails when its expected return on
investment at $t=2$ plus the possible bankruptcy costs is less than the
liquidity shock. As $x \in (0,1)$ and $p^{fb}R(p^{fb}) \geq 1$, we see that this
threshold is larger than 1 and thus not binding. The bank will always
get a liquidity injection from the government in the first best scenario:
socially optimal risk taking and investment justify unconditional
liquidity assistance.

Bank Optimization Without Regulation

Let us now consider the case of a private bank choosing an optimal
portfolio, and analyze whether it reaches the first best allocation. We
assume that there are no regulatory authorities, such as a Lender of
Last Resort or a fiscal authority, which may provide assistance. There
is also no interbank market, as mentioned above. The bank thus has to
cope with liquidity shocks on its own, which means that the bank fails
if $x > \underline{x} \equiv M/D$, i.e. when the sudden demand for liquidity is larger
than the bank's liquid assets. In case of failure, the returns at $t=2$ are
zero, since effectively $\gamma=1$ when there is no FA. The bank's expected
value is thus equal to

$$E(V(p,I)_2) = p[(R(p)-1)I + E][\underline{x}]. \quad (4.13)$$

The bank simultaneously chooses optimal values $p=p^n$ and $I=I^n$
to maximize $E(V(p,I)_2)$. We can analyze the decision process by first
letting the bank choose p^n, assuming I is already at its optimum I^n;
subsequently, the bank chooses I^n taking p^n as given. The choice of p^n
is given by the following first order condition (FOC), replacing M by
$1-I$:

$$R(p^n) + p^n R'(p^n) = 1 - \frac{E}{I^n} \qquad (4.14)$$

which holds since $I < 1$: if $I = 1$, $\underline{x} = 0$ and the bank would always fail. The bank would thus choose $I^n < 1$ to receive a positive payoff at $t = 2$. Next, taking p^n as given, we can analyze the bank's choice of I^n. The following FOC holds:

$$I^n = \frac{1}{2}\left[1 - \frac{E}{R(p^n) - 1}\right] \qquad (4.15)$$

where we have used $\partial \underline{x}/\partial I = -1/D$. Under the assumptions on $R(p)$ these FOCs also fulfill the second order conditions for a maximum.

We can deduce from equations (4.14) and (4.15) that the bank takes more risk than is desirable from a social perspective. This follows from our assumption that the bank invests with leverage (i.e. $D > M > 0$), which means $I^n > E$ and thus $R(p^n) + p^n R'(p^n) > 0$. As $R(p^n) + p^n R'(p^n)$ is decreasing in p, we see that $p^n < p^{fb}$. Furthermore, we can state that $I^n < I^{fb}$, which follows from assuming that $E > 0$ and $R(p^n) > 1$ (otherwise it would not be profitable to invest in the risky asset):

$$I^n - I^{fb} = \frac{1}{2}\left[1 - \frac{E}{p[R(p^n) - 1]}\right] - 1 < 0 \qquad (4.16)$$

The bank owner thus generates too little productive (but risky) investment compared to the first best case, and takes too much risk while doing so. The investment decision follows from the assumption that there is no safety net in the form of a central bank able to provide emergency liquidity; the bank has to reserve part of its funds to cope with liquidity shocks. As it has to keep more liquidity on its balance sheet, the bank tries to make up for the foregone investment returns by taking more risk. This means the bank owner 'gambles' for a higher return in the case of success, which is harmful to social welfare.

Introducing a Lender of Last Resort

It may be possible to improve this situation by setting up a central bank (CB) that can provide temporary liquidity to an illiquid bank. The bank owner then chooses risk-taking and the amount of investment in this new situation by setting p and I, with equilibrium values p^l and I^l (where l denotes that we are dealing with the possibility of liquidity provision). As in Repullo (2005) and Kahn and Santos (2005), bank and CB play a simultaneous Bayesian Nash game in the determination of p and $\bar{x}$. In this game, the CB can only observe the choice of I (from the bank's balance sheet) when it has to make a liquidity provision decision at $t = 1$; this observation of I is not verifiable. The CB does not know the choice of p at this moment. However, the CB can form a belief about p^l through its knowledge of I and x. Expressing M as $1 - I$, the threshold can be written as:

$$\bar{x} = \frac{p^l}{1 - p^l} \frac{\alpha C}{D} + \frac{1 - I}{D} \tag{4.17}$$

with equilibrium value $\bar{x}^l = \bar{x}(p^l, I^l)$. This threshold shows that the CB only faces downside risk; the bank gets the upside. We can also see that the threshold depends only on the bank's actual choice of I; it doesn't change directly with the actual choice of p. Instead, it is determined by p^l, the equilibrium value of p. Furthermore, if $x > \bar{x}$ the bank finds itself in a crisis situation and it will be taken over completely by the fiscal authority; this means that $\gamma = 1$. The depositors will be compensated by the DIF, and the remaining parts of the bank will be sold by the FA at $t = 2$. The bank owner will thus get a zero return in this case; we will relax this assumption in the next section.

At $t = 0$, the bank will take all this into account while choosing p and I. It maximizes the new objective function:

$$E(V(p, I)_2) = p[(R(p) - 1)I + E][\bar{x}^l] \tag{4.18}$$

taking into account the equilibrium decision by the CB. The corresponding FOC with respect to p and I are:

$$R(p^l) + p^l R'(p^l) = 1 - \frac{E}{I^l} \qquad (4.19)$$

$$I^l = \frac{1}{2}\left[\frac{p^l}{1-p^l}\alpha C + 1 - \frac{E}{R(p^l)-1}\right] \qquad (4.20)$$

where we can see that p^l and I^l are determined in a similar way as p^n and I^n. However, we also see that $I^n \neq I^l$ when $\alpha > 0$, which means that $\bar{x}^l > \underline{x}$. To determine the relative size of I^n and I^l, we note that a decrease in α means that the Central Bank cares very little about bank failure. This leads to very little liquidity injections: the equilibrium threshold $\bar{x}^l$ will fall towards $\underline{x}$. Analogously, when $\alpha = 0$ the CB will never intervene as it will not incur any political cost from failure. This is equivalent to the earlier situation without a Lender of Last Resort. It is thus straightforward to perform comparative statics regarding α by taking the derivative of I^l with respect to α:

$$\frac{dI^l}{d\alpha} = \frac{C}{2}\frac{p^l}{1-p^l} > 0 \qquad (4.21)$$

This expression indicates that I^l decreases when α decreases: $I^l \to I^n$ when $\alpha \to 0$. This means that $I^l > I^n$, or that an introduction of a Lender of Last Resort leads to an increase in productive investment.

However, regulation is also established to mitigate risk taking. Let us therefore analyze whether the riskiness of the bank has improved, by comparing p^l with p^n. To this end, we can totally differentiate equation (4.19) and perform comparative statics:

$$\frac{dp^l}{dI^l} = \frac{\dfrac{E}{I^l}\,\overline{x}^l\left(\dfrac{\overline{x}^l}{I^l} + \dfrac{1}{D}\right)}{[2R'(p^l) + p^L R''(p^l)]I^l} < 0 \tag{4.22}$$

where the inequality holds because of the assumptions on $R(p)$. As we have found that $I^l > I^n$, we must also conclude that $p^l < p^n$ because of equation (4.22).

The bank thus invests more in productive assets than in the situation without a liquidity provider: a positive development. However, it also takes more risks when doing so, which is worse from a social point of view. This may reflect a moral hazard effect caused by the introduction of a safety net: since there is a Lender of Last Resort, the bank takes more risk.

To illustrate this phenomenon, we have calibrated our model using reasonable parameter values. We have specified the returns as a concave decreasing function of p, namely $R(p) = 3 - 2p^2$ (satisfying the assumptions from the previous section), and the cost of bankruptcy is set to 0.10 or 10 per cent of the bank's balance sheet (Repullo, 2005). α is set to one (Cordella and Levy-Yeyati, 2003) and the capital ratio E is assumed to be at the minimum Basel II requirement, which is eight per cent of risk weighted assets. We assume that the risky asset I gets a 100 per cent weight.

Figure 4.1 shows that investment and the solvency threshold are indeed negatively related, as an increase in investment means a decrease in liquidity buffers. We also see that the probability of success and the solvency threshold are positively related. This means that an increase in investment should be met with an increase in its success probability to keep the threshold at the same level. The bank will thus face a trade-off between investment and risk-taking if it wants to induce the CB to set the optimal solvency threshold. In the end, this leads to a higher I but a lower p: there is more productive investment, but this goes with increased risk taking.

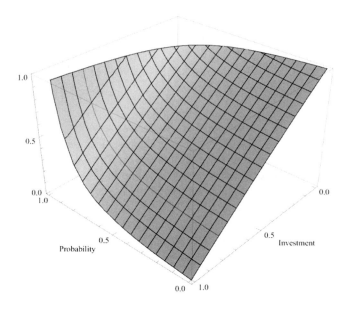

Figure 4.1 The Optimal Solvency Threshold $\bar{x}^l$

In this section, we have abstracted from penalty rates for emergency liquidity. Although this is one of Bagehot's key arguments, there are some issues with this view. One problem is that it may be rather difficult for a CB to commit to these penalty rates, especially in times of crisis. This is exemplified by the recent financial crisis, in which the ECB, Fed and other central banks have provided liquidity at far below market rates. Another problem is that banks may internalize this penalty rate by taking higher risk ex ante; the higher expected return in the good state will then compensate for higher expected LLR payments in the bad state (Repullo, 2005).

Furthermore, the concept of 'creative ambiguity' has been introduced (by e.g., Freixas (1999)) as a possible solution to mitigate moral hazard. However, this concept also suffers from commitment problems, as Freixas (1999) already noted himself: it may cause a Too-Big-to-Fail problem. Cordella and Levy-Yeyati (2003) have also shown that committing explicitly has a possible '[charter] value' effect that may outweigh the moral hazard effect. Acharya and Yorulmazer (2007, 2008) find similar results for systemically important banks.

We thus abstract from penalty rates and the 'creative ambiguity' principle, and instead focus on a situation in which the regulator will bail out the bank by injecting capital (as the bank is a systemic one). At the same time, the regulator can determine what cost will be attached to this assistance. We will analyze this situation in the next section.

The Possibility of Bailout

After analyzing the case where a bank goes simply bankrupt when a crisis occurs ($x > \bar{x}$), we will now introduce the possibility of the FA injecting capital into the bank. When doing so, the FA will stipulate its required share in the bank's value at $t = 2$; this is denoted by γ. The FA can thus discipline the bank for taking too much risk by setting a high γ.

It is assumed that the fiscal authority gets supervisory information from the central bank. Therefore, the bank and the FA, just as the bank and the CB, play a simultaneous Bayesian Nash game. We will assume additionally that the CB and the FA observe each other's actions, but take them for granted; there is no interaction between the CB and the FA.

The bank again chooses risk-taking and the amount of investment in this new situation by setting p and I , with equilibrium values p^c and I^c. The c indicates that we have added the possibility of capital provision. Furthermore, the fiscal authority chooses the repayment fraction such that it breaks even in expectation. This means that it chooses $\gamma = \underline{\gamma}$, with equilibrium value $\underline{\gamma}^c$. The $\underline{\gamma}$ is determined by the following equation, where we can see it depends on the bank's actual choice of I , but only on its *equilibrium* choice of p , which is p^c :

$$\underline{\gamma} \equiv \frac{xD - 1 + I - p^c \beta C}{p^c[(R(p^c) - 1)I + E]} \tag{4.23}$$

For the bank, this γ will be a function of the expectation of x, conditional on $x > \bar{x}$: $E(x/x) = (1/2)(\bar{x}^c + 1)$, where $\bar{x}$ is determined as in a previous section and $\bar{x}^c$ is its equilibrium value. We thus find an expected minimum repayment fraction of:

$$E(\underline{\gamma}) = \frac{\frac{1}{2}(\bar{x}+1)D - 1 + I - p^c\beta C}{p^c[(R(p^c)-1)I + E]} \qquad (4.24)$$

The bank's objective function in the case of bailout possibility is thus as follows:

$$\max_{p,I} E(V(p,I)_2) = p[(R(p)-1)I + E][1 - E(\underline{\gamma})[1-\bar{x}]] \qquad (4.25)$$

which is optimized according to the following FOCs:

$$R(p^c) + p^c R'(p^c) = 1 - \frac{E}{I^C} \qquad (4.26)$$

$$p^c \left\{ (R(p^c)-1)[1 - \underline{\gamma}^c(1-\bar{x}^c)] - [(R(p^c)-1)I^c + E] \left[\frac{\partial\underline{\gamma}^c}{\partial I^c}(1-\bar{x}^c) + \underline{\gamma}^c \left(\frac{1}{D} \right) \right] \right\} = 0 \qquad (4.27)$$

where $\bar{x}^c = \bar{x}(p^c, I^c)$ and $\underline{\gamma}^c = \underline{\gamma}(p^c, I^c)$. It is not straightforward to write an explicit solution for both p^c and I^c from these conditions. However, we can see that the FOC for p^c is similar to that of p^l; the only difference is that I^c may differ from I^l.

To gauge the effect of having the possibility of bailout on I and p, let us again perform comparative statics. Since the introduction of a bailout possibility means that $\gamma < 1$ (as opposed to $\gamma = 1$, when the bank is seized completely), our analysis should focus on the effect of this change. As in section 4.3, we perform comparative statics by totally differentiating equations (4.27) and (4.26), respectively:

$$\frac{dI^c}{d\gamma} = \frac{p^c[(R(p_1^c)-1)I^c + E]}{1/2 - \underline{\gamma}^c(R(p^c)-1)} \tag{4.28}$$

$$\frac{dp^c}{dI^c} = \frac{-[R(p^c)+ p^c R'(p^c)-1]}{I^c[2R'(p^c)+ p^c R''(p^c)]} \tag{4.29}$$

The sign of equation (4.29) is negative because of equation (4.26), $I \geq 0$ and the assumptions on $R(p)$. However, the sign of equation (4.28) is not unambiguous; it depends on the sign of the denominator (since the numerator, representing a part of expected bank value, is positive). We see that this sign depends on the relative size of $(R(p^c)-1)$ and the equilibrium $\underline{\gamma}^c$. To assess the effect of a possible bailout, we thus need to consider two situations.

First, when $\underline{\gamma}^c$ is relatively large, $(R(p^c)-1)\underline{\gamma}^c > 1/2$ and we find a negative effect of an increase in γ on investment. The $\underline{\gamma}^c$ is large when β is small, meaning that the regulator cares little about bankruptcy. This leads to a strict FA, which will discipline banks fiercely when in a crisis by making capital assistance costly.

The bank owner takes into account that he will thus lose a large share in period two profits. An increase in this expected repayment will induce him to invest less in risky assets and keep more reserves to fend off liquidity shocks. As $\underline{\gamma} \to 1$ and we move towards the case without an FA, we thus see that investment decreases. This means that the introduction of an FA with bailout capabilities (and $\underline{\gamma} < 1$) can stimulate productive investment: $I^c > I^I$.

There is also a downside to having a regulator that can provide bailout assistance. Because of equation (4.29) we also see that the banker takes more risk when investment increases: the p^c decreases with I. This is the negative effect of the introduction of a strict FA. It is similar to the moral hazard effect that may ensue when penalty rates on liquidity are introduced: the banker will compensate the higher expected repayment with higher risk taking, to increase the return when investment is successful.

However, the effect is reversed when $\underline{\gamma}^c$ is relatively small

$((R(p^c)-1)\underline{\gamma}^c < 1/2)$. In this case, $dI^c/d\gamma > 0$ which means that investment decreases when an FA is introduced (decreasing γ to $\underline{\gamma}^c = 1$). A reason for this small $\underline{\gamma}^c$ may be a large β, which means that the FA's political cost of a bank failure is large. This will thus lead to a small required repayment, which ex ante provides the banker with a relatively high expected return.

Counterintuitively, a small γ^c leads to a lower level of investment: the bank's optimal payoff is reached at $I^c < I^n$. Investing more than I^c in the risky asset is considered as 'gambling' by the bank. Similarly, we can see that the decrease in investment leads to a positive effect on risk taking (since $dp^c/dI^c < 0$). As γ^c is quite small, investments have a higher expected return. Less risk taking is thus necessary to achieve the optimal bank value at $t = 2$.

Table 4.1 summarizes the different situations described above. An FA that cares little about bankruptcy (low β) demands a large repayment for banks in a crisis, leading to an increase in investment, but also an increase in risk taking. On the other hand, an FA that cares a lot about bankruptcy (high β) demands a small repayment from crisis banks, thereby decreasing productive investment but also mitigating risk taking.

Table 4. 1 The Effect of Having an FA on I and p

	Low β	High β
Investment	+	-
Success Probability	-	+

Figure 4.2 shows the case of an FA that is much concerned about bankruptcy. This is probably the most realistic case, especially since we consider the bank to be systemic. In this situation β is relatively high; in our set of parameter assumptions we have set $\beta = 2$. This means that the weight the FA attaches to bankruptcy is twice as large

as that of the CB[9]. It also means that $\underline{\gamma}^c$ is relatively low[10]. We can clearly see that keeping $\underline{\gamma}^c$ low can lead to a low I, but a higher p and thus less risk taking. It is especially interesting to see that an increase (as well as a decrease) in risk taking is met with a punishment for the banker by increasing $\underline{\gamma}^c$.

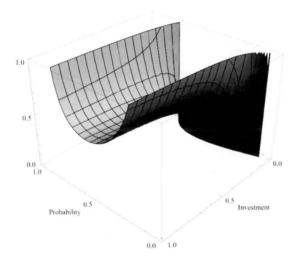

Figure 4.2 The Optimal Required Return $\underline{\gamma}^c$

We can conclude that a high β can mitigate risk taking, but also causes a decrease in investment; a low β induces more risk taking, but has a positive effect on investment. Regulatory authorities thus

---

[9]The exact size of this number is not very important; with $\beta = 1$ we get a similar result, but it is much more pronounced for $\beta = 2$.

[10]Only at the top left we see the situation where $dI / d\underline{\gamma} < 0$, caused by a very high $\underline{\gamma}^c$. Since we only consider cases with too *low* p and $p^{fb} = 0.71$ with our parameter values, this extreme range is not relevant.

face a trade-off when establishing regulation in the form of a safety net. They have to decide whether they attach more value to an increase in investment, or to a decrease in risk taking. This seems to be realistic: the nationalization, bailout and guarantee efforts by governments have led banks to mitigate their risk taking, while at the same time they have cut back on (risky) lending to entrepreneurs.

Conclusions

The recent financial crisis has provoked governments and central banks to supply unusually large amounts of capital and liquidity to banks. Regard for systemic stability is the main motivation with which this support to the financial system has been provided. However, the risk for financial stability (ultimately leading to the financial crisis) has arisen because of excessive risk taking by individual institutions that were central to the system. Since they thus posed a risk for the financial system as a whole, regulators had no choice but to prevent them from failing.

Because of the enormous costs that are associated with financial system failure, but also with its prevention, it is necessary to thoroughly assess the management of crises by regulatory authorities. In our analytical model, we have thus simultaneously allowed for liquidity provision (by a central bank) and capital assistance (by a fiscal authority) to examine how they interact with a bank facing a crisis.

We have assessed this interaction for a systemic bank suffering from liquidity shocks, with which it can only cope by keeping liquid reserves. There is no interbank market in our model, reflecting a crisis situation in which the interbank market does not function well. We find that being in this situation without any regulation leads a bank to hoard too much liquid assets and take too much risk, compared to the first best situation.

The introduction of a liquidity provider in the form of a central bank (CB) should alleviate this problem. This CB has no information other than the bank's investment level. It cannot observe the bank's choice of risk ex ante and can thus not condition its Lender of Last Resort (LLR) policy upon this information. We find that this measure indeed induces a higher investment level. However, the introduction of a safety net also increases moral hazard as found by Freixas (1999).

To improve the situation, we set up a second regulator in the form of a fiscal authority (FA) that is responsible for the bank closure decision. However, it can also decide to give the bank a capital injection if it deems the bank solvent. This FA has the same information as the CB. We find that this set-up leads to a trade-off between mitigating risk and promoting investment. When the FA is mild in its bailout conditions (demanding a low repayment) it can, counterintuitively, reduce moral hazard at the expense of investment. A strict FA achieves the opposite result: the investment level is higher, but there is an increase in moral hazard.

We must conclude that an additional regulatory authority with responsibility for solvency is not a completely satisfactory solution for curbing excessive risk taking. This result is in line with the current situation: although banks take less risk, they provide less credit to the economy partly due to the terms of their rescue packages. Furthermore, relative effects of CB and government policies are also likely to play a role: central banks continue to provide liquidity to stimulate lending, while banks are hoarding liquid reserves as the government induces them to reduce risk.

References

Acharya, V. V. and T. Yorulmazer (2007), 'Too many to fail - An analysis of time-inconsistency in bank closure policies.' *Journal of Financial Intermediation* **16**(1), 1–31.

Acharya, V. V. and T. Yorulmazer (2008), 'Cash-in-the-market pricing and optimal resolution of bank failures.' *Review of Financial Studies* **21**(6), 2705–2742.

Allen, F., E. Carletti, and D. Gale (2009), 'Interbank market liquidity and central bank intervention.' *Journal of Monetary Economics* **56**(5), 639–652.

Bagehot, W. (1873), *Lombard Street: A Description of the Money Market*, Henry S. King & Co: London.

Boot, A. and A. Thakor (1993), 'Self-interested Bank Regulation.' *American Economic Review* **83**(2), 206–212.

Cordella, T. and E. Levy-Yeyati (2003), 'Bank Bailouts: Moral hazard vs. Value Effect.' *Journal of Financial Intermediation* **12**(4), 300–330.

Diamond, D. W. and R. G. Rajan (2005), 'Liquidity Shortages and Banking Crises.' *Journal of Finance* **60**(2), 615–647.

Diamond, D. W. and R. G. Rajan (2009), Illiquidity and interest rate policy. *Working Paper 15197*, National Bureau of Economic Research.

Eijffinger, S. (2008), Crisis management in the European union. *CEPR Policy Insight* No.27.

Freixas, X. (1999), Optimal bail-out policy, conditionality and creative ambiguity. *CEPR Discussion Paper* No. 2238.

Freixas, X. and B. M. Parigi (2008), Lender of last resort and bank closure policy. *CESifo Working Paper Series* No. 2286.

Freixas, X., B. M. Parigi, and J. C. Rochet (2000), 'Systemic risk, interbank relations, and liquidity provision by the central bank.' *Journal of Money, Credit and Banking* **32**(3), 611–638.

Freixas, X., J. Rochet, and B. Parigi (2004), 'The Lender of Last Resort: A Twenty-First Century Approach.' *Journal of the European Economic Association* **2**(6), 1085–1115.

Goodhart, C. A. E. (1987), 'Why do banks need a central bank?' *Oxford Economic Papers*, **39**(1), 75–89.

Goodhart, C. A. E. and H. Huang (1999). A model of the lender of last resort. *Proceedings*, Federal Reserve Bank of San Francisco.

Holmstrom, B. and J. Tirole (1998), 'Private and public supply of liquidity.' *Journal of Political Economy* **106**(1), 1–40.

Kahn, C. and J. Santos (2005), 'Allocating bank regulatory powers: lender of last resort, deposit insurance and supervision.' *European Economic Review* **49**(8), 2107–2136.

Nijskens, R. and W. Wagner (2011), 'Credit risk transfer activities and systemic risk: How banks became less risky individually but posed greater risks to the financial system at the same time.' *Journal of Banking and Finance* **35**(6), 1391–1398.

Panetta, F., T. Faeh, G. Grande, C. Ho, M. King, A. Levy, F. M. Signoretti, M. Taboga and A. Zaghini (2009), An assessment of financial sector rescue programmes. *Questioni di Economia e Finanza (Occasional Papers)* 47, Economic Research Department Bank of Italy.

Repullo, R. (2000), Who should act as lender of last resort? An incomplete contracts model. *Journal of Money, Credit and Banking*, **32**(3), 580–605.

Repullo, R. (2005), 'Liquidity, Risk Taking, and the Lender of Last Resort.' *International Journal of Central Banking* **1**(2), 47–80.

Rochet, J. (2004), 'Macroeconomic shocks and banking supervision.' *Journal of Financial Stability* **1**(1), 93–110.

Rochet, J. and X. Vives (2004), 'Coordination failures and the lender of last resort: was Bagehot right after all?' *Journal of the European Economic Association* **2**(6), 1116–1147.

Wagner, W. (2007), 'The liquidity of bank assets and banking stability.' *Journal of Banking & Finance* **31**(1), 121–139.

5. Transparency is Not Enough: Central Bank Governance as the Next Frontier

Pierre L. Siklos[1]

Back to the Future?

Once the afterglow of the latest G20 summit dissipates policy makers will have returned home to begin the difficult task of delivering on the various undertakings agreed to since the Pittsburgh meeting in 2009. In the crisis atmosphere that has reigned since the sub-prime crisis hit the US beginning in the late summer of 2007, central banks and governments have acted decisively though, in retrospect, it seems increasingly evident that both actors were complicit in creating the conditions that continue to this day to pre-occupy policy makers and the public. Previously held beliefs about the limits of central banking and the role of fiscal policy were discarded in the belief, espoused most forcibly by the Chair of the FOMC, Ben Bernanke, to do 'whatever it takes' to avoid facing a Great Depression 2.0.[2]

While the circumstances facing the global economy are different than they were 20 years ago, the world does face a problem similar to the one that befell policy makers then, once the economic implications, let alone the social consequences, of the fall of the Berlin Wall in 1989 became abundantly clear. The problem then was to decide the sequencing of reforms necessary to convert previously centrally planned economies into market driven economies while, simultaneously, creating the institutions that would ensure adequate

---

[1] An early draft of this paper was written while the author was on leave at Princeton University. He is grateful for their hospitality.
[2] Apparently, as the financial crisis worsened, this expression defined Bernanke's mantra about what monetary (and fiscal) policy had to do to avert a repeat of the Great Slump of 1929. See Wessel (2009).

oversight and implement the appropriate policies.[3] In the event, different economies chose different paths, in part because circumstances drove them to a particular sequence of reforms. In other instances, however, when the 'luxury' of choosing the correct path to follow was available, deliberate choices were made with varying consequences. The situation at present is reminiscent of those times if only because economies, institutions, and policy makers, have finally come to the realization that the globalization of goods and financial markets has heightened the need for international surveillance of policies of a different kind than heretofore practiced.

At first glance it appears surprising that governments have reached this epiphany. After all, in the aftermath of the wreckage of World War II, governments also came to the same conclusion and this found expression in the creation of the UN, the World Bank and, most tellingly when it came to economic surveillance, the International Monetary Fund (IMF). However, all of these institutions eventually lost their way and a variety of explanations have been put forward for this state of affairs[4]. Nevertheless, focusing on the IMF by way of illustration, it became evident that the so-called article IV consultations, the device intended to let the world community know whether the right balance of economic policies was being implemented in individual countries, were either being ignored or, if problems requiring attention were highlighted, were felt to infringe on the sovereign right of nations to, first and foremost, be accountable to their own populations and, second, conduct their affairs as they saw fit. Moreover, and in spite of the IMF's attempt to become more 'relevant' by refreshing its surveillance strategy in 2007, it is becoming apparent that one failure of the new policy was to adequately consider how the broader implications of the adoption of economic strategies in one country affect economic outcomes elsewhere. This reflects the collective absence of the will to act globally, even if policy failures can be local. Perhaps inevitably, it

---

[3] Political reforms were also, of course, a preoccupation as all the economies involved were attempting to introduce democratically functioning governments.
[4] See the collection of studies published by what came to be known as the Meltzer Commission of the late 1990s. These can be found at http://www.house.gov/jec/imf/ifiac.htm. An alternative account of the IMF's role since Bretton Woods can be found in James (1996).

took the failure of policies in a very large economy to shake the complacency around the world about the necessity to adopt a different form of international surveillance.[5]

Back in the 1990s it was obvious to policy makers that enshrining adequate property rights was the logical first step to creating the right conditions for a well-functioning market economy. The next steps on the road to a market economy were much more difficult to get agreement on. Should the privatization of assets, not to mention the manner in which this would be implemented, precede economic stabilization? After all, the productive capacity of centrally planned economies was shattered and inefficiencies abounded, while the unleashing of previously unknown market forces threatened social and economic stability through inflation. As is often true in economics, one size did not fit all as subsequent retrospectives made clear.

The lessons for the current crisis are, therefore, also clear. Getting it right implies that while some common responses to the economic turmoil that has afflicted the global economy, such as fiscal expansion combined with monetary easing, were entirely appropriate, it is also the case that pre-existing conditions in individual countries imply that calibrating the response was also critical in preventing another Great Slump. Similarly, an idiosyncratic response to the fledgling economic recovery is also the correct way to proceed. This need not imply, however, that any exit toward economic 'normalcy' should be undertaken oblivious to its global repercussions. Indeed, this is where the commitment of governments, particularly in the advanced industrial economies, to consider the consequences of their actions for others, needs a voice and a roadmap. Therefore, cooperation, rather than coordination, is likely to produce more fruitful results and fulfill the Leaders' express wish to restore balanced economic growth.

---

[5] This is not the place to debate necessary reforms in policies and governance at the IMF. It is worth noting, however that the Bank of Canada, to name but one institution, has been very active in this debate. For example, see Maier and Santor (2008).

The Current Situation

Policy makers have now decided that the correct sequencing of policies as the world emerges from the crisis involves a re-balancing of sorts of economic policies followed by the introduction of improved regulatory oversight of the financial system. If successful this promises desirable outcomes. However, there are a number of caveats that must be considered before victory can be declared. First, and foremost, policy makers must recognize that, in a dynamic world, some imbalances will always persist. The key is to avoid the temptation of the Bretton Woods era to narrowly define them, for example, in terms of balance of payments considerations only. In this regard the proposal made by the US to impose a numerical limit on current account imbalances – though unlikely to be approved by the international community – may have the virtue of being transparent but is unlikely on its own to prevent future crises. Instead, varieties of imbalances must be considered, and these should include fiscal and monetary policy, as well as regulatory frameworks. Second, if individual countries adopt different models for assigning responsibility for the measurement and accountability for systemic risks, there needs to be a forum where decisive actions can be taken in the event that the balance of these risks once again threatens the global economy. Some broad principles are outlined later in this chapter.

Some will bemoan the fact that existing proposals do not provide for sanctions or penalties in case where reckless economic policies are pursued. Yet, powerful weapons are available to policy makers, namely accountability and transparency, and, properly structured, these can accomplish far more than sanctions for bad behavior.[6] Here

---

[6] The Stability and Growth Pact negotiated by members of the European Union is a recent illustration of the failure of sanctions to be taken seriously, in part because its most powerful members were unwilling to strictly follow the 'rules of the game' when financial penalties threatened them as opposed to other members thought more likely to display profligate fiscal policies. The recently created European Financial Stability Facility is too young an institution to provide an assessment of its impact. In any event, as It is currently constituted, it can only react to political decisions. It is not set up to provide oversight or provide an early warning indicator of a looming crisis. It is simply too small an institution to provide all of these functions. See http://www.efsf.europa.eu/about/index.htm.

again policy makers can learn a lesson or two from the recent history of central banking which is the focus of this Chapter.

The battle for central bank independence that was largely won by the early 1990s also ushered in an era of greater transparency. Monetary policy transparency differs across countries but one trend since the late 1990s is unmistakable: we have witnessed a substantial rise in the transparency of monetary policy worldwide. This is shown in Figure 5.1 adapted from Siklos (2010a). In contrast, attempts to raise the transparency with which fiscal policies are evaluated and implemented have, so far, failed to gain any traction in spite of laudable attempts to do so in a handful of countries (e.g., New Zealand).

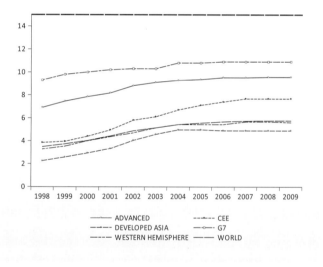

Note: The definitions are the ones used by the International Monetary Fund's International Financial Statistics. See Siklos (2010a) for the details.

Figure 5.1 Aggregate Index of Central Bank Transparency, 1998–2009

One lesson from the crisis then, in terms of the future of international governance, is clear. In order for the era of the G20 to be a success all countries will have to relinquish some sovereignty. Is this feasible? The simple answer is yes. Is this outcome likely? Here, a positive response needs to be couched in far more uncertain terms.

Making Sure Central Banks Don't Become the Fourth Branch of Government

A retrospective of the last two decades of macroeconomic history will conclude that while many countries around the world drove inflation rates to levels that were both low and stable the monetary policies that were eventually adopted in the early years of this century will have be shown to have created another, more pernicious, form of inflation, namely inflation in asset prices, notably in housing and equities. The fact that so many central banks acted in this manner suggests that the policy framework, under the guise that consumer price inflation was all that was needed to ensure permanently stable macroeconomic outcomes, produced conditions that allowed the 'black swan' of the global economic crisis to emerge. Consider the example of Figure 5.2 which plots the policy rate for the US (i.e. the Fed funds rate) against an index of (nominal) asset prices for the period 1998–2009.[7] It is important to note that while the two series appear to be cyclical, they do not coincide. More generally, this suggests that the coincidence between financial cycles and the business cycle is far from clear. Indeed, as found by Aikman, Haldane, and Nelson (2010), for several countries, the frequency and amplitude of business cycles differs from that of credit cycles. Hence, notions that '...curbing credit cycle frictions ...through monetary policy – either by ensuring that it moderates appropriately the business cycle (Taylor 2010) or, more ambitiously, by having it play a wider role in curtailing financial imbalances (Borio and White 2004)...is not very encouraging...' (op. cit., pp. 28–29).

---

[7] A plot using real asset prices would reveal a similar result. However, the data for this series were only made available to me by the BIS for a sample that ends in 2008.

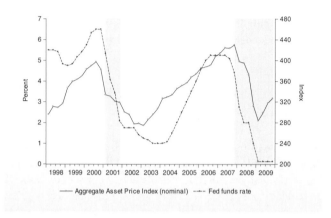

Note: Aggregate asset prices (right hand scale) are courtesy of the Bank for International Settlements. See Borio and Lowe (2002) for details of the construction of this series. The Fed funds rate (left hand scale) is the policy rate of the US Federal Reserve. The shaded areas are the NBER recession dates. See http://www.nber.org/cycles/cyclesmain.html.

Figure 5.2 Policy Rates and Assets Prices, 1998–2008: United States

When the G20 leaders, at the end of the Pittsburgh summit, announced the need to initiate '...a cooperative process of mutual assessment of our policy frameworks and the implications of those frameworks for the pattern and sustainability of global growth'[8] the natural reaction is to point out that the devil is, of course, in the details.[9] Presumably, given the remainder of the Leaders' Statement, the Leaders' remit implies a review of existing monetary and fiscal frameworks. In the case of monetary policy, Canada, as have many other countries since (Siklos, 2009), adopted inflation targeting. The Bank of Canada is already committed to a review of the inflation targeting framework and a joint decision with the Government on how

---

[8] 'Leaders' Statement: The Pittsburgh Summit', http://www.pittsburghsummit. gov/mediacenter/129639.htm.
[9] A little remarked flaw of the Bretton Woods system is that, as Bordo (1993, p. 28) points out '[T]he architects never spelled out how the system was supposed to work.'

to proceed after 2011 looms large. What if the sovereign decision of the Canadian government and its central bank proves incompatible with the wishes of the G20, or its most powerful partners? Rather than a threat, the lofty goals of the G20 should be seen by Canada as a challenge to reaffirm the success of the inflation targeting framework and underscore its central role in the country's policy framework. Steps to increase the transparency and accountability of fiscal policy is the other side of the two-sided coin that makes up a nation's macro-policy framework and it represents the missing element that will require some attention. More importantly, since Canada has not fully escaped the consequences of the financial crisis, the current environment offers an opportunity to experiment with different monetary policy frameworks, including a form of price level targeting.[10] Clearly, inflation targeting, even if it possesses a great many virtues, neither prevented an orderly exit from the asset price bust nor slowed the asset price boom that preceded it. The fact that, for example, Canada did not appear to be as adversely affected as others by the events of 2008–2009 provides little comfort. After all, the economies of other inflation targeting economies, such as the UK or Iceland, became seriously impaired. Of course, this is where the question of macro-prudential monitoring and regulation has been raised as solutions to the crisis. To be sure, such a response is appropriate but care must be taken to allow different economies to handle the work in a manner that is, to some extent, idiosyncratic. For example, while the US may hand over the responsibility for systemic concerns to one agency, namely the Federal Reserve, other countries, including Canada, may prefer a more collegial approach to monitoring systemic risks. Moreover, as this is written, we are aware that few tools for macro-prudential objectives have been developed and ones that have been proposed may or may not be sufficiently orthogonal to existing monetary tools (e.g., a policy rate or the direct purchase of financial assets by central banks) to be sure that they are completely effective. What we do know is that resorting to a single instrument is inappropriate in a world with multiple objectives as Tinbergen's

---

[10] Considerable research has been underway for some years on the desirability of inflation targeting. See, for example, Gaspar, Smets, and Vestin (2010).

principle reminds us or, at the very least, may be a heavy handed instrument to use in a crisis.[11]

Where Do We Go From Here?

As in many other endeavors, 'one size does not fit all', and the G20 Leaders should avoid the temptation to act collectively by imposing a particular menu of policies. It is worth reminding readers that the IMF, apparently re-energized as the global institution to watch over economies' performance and how they interact with each other, is also the agency that for years has been accused of supporting one size fits all policies that contributed to the Asian crisis. In any event, even if there is enough blame to spread around elsewhere, the danger going forward is that institutions such as the IMF are given responsibilities they are unable to carry out in a credible manner or are ill-defined, such as surveillance in the area of financial system stability. Therefore, while the IMF has a role as an agency that can channel funds from advanced economies to others in need of restructuring, or temporary financial support, its original mandate does not square very well with a role as the global monitor of systemic risks. The G20, together with the FSB, the BIS, or other agencies (e.g., the OECD), should retain this responsibility. The IMF should stick to its knitting and not be assigned responsibilities it is ill prepared to take on. No doubt one concern is that the more agencies are responsible for managing these systemic risks the greater are the risks of failure as competing agendas and the potential for non-cooperative behavior might well lead to a repeat of the failure of the FSA in the UK and the Bank of England to prevent the financial crisis from taking hold there. Yet, if the alternative is an institution that does practically everything the danger is equally great that its internal oversight mechanisms will not be up to the task, as the US experience apparently demonstrates. Perhaps, as Goodhart (2010) points out, though one wonders whether it is with a touch of wishful thinking, '[S]urely professional bodies can work in conjunction on one issue, e.g., financial stability, and with (delegated) independence on another, e.g., setting interest rates.'

---

[11] For more details about the role of Tinbergen's principle in a post-crisis world see Siklos (2010b).

Regardless of how systemic risks are managed, there are critical implications for central bank governance. It will be essential for all central banks to reconsider how the rules for intervention in financial markets, in particular, should be defined. Once again, while the rules ought to be tailored to the needs of individual central banks, there are certain common features in reforming central bank governance that could be agreed on across a wide spectrum of countries. First, where it is absent, the location of accountability in crisis situations needs to be clarified. Central banks cannot be open to the threat of retaliation or loss of independence because, in the absence of 'rules of engagement', legislatures perceive the central bank as overstepping the normal bounds of monetary policy.[12] Second, the limits of monetary policy interventions in private markets need to be more clearly defined. The experience of quantitative or credit easing in many parts of the world have left many observers uneasy, with considerable justification, because the lines of responsibility between fiscal and monetary policy became blurred, no more so than in the United States. In contrast, monetary policy authorities in other countries (e.g., the UK) were keenly aware that the division of responsibility for the consequences of fiscal and monetary policies do matter. This requires coordination, to be sure, but not the comingling of the two. History has amply demonstrated that when the two are inappropriately mixed the results can be catastrophic. Hence, the rules of indemnification in case of policies that are introduced due to '...unusual and exigent...' circumstances[13] need to be clarified and codified in central bank legislation.

---

[12] Legislation in the US Congress to audit the US Federal Reserve, and question its very existence, is gaining some traction. Unlike the economics profession which has tended, with some notable exceptions (e.g., Taylor 2009), to support the actions of the Fed, there is little affection displayed toward the Fed in Congress these days.

[13] Section 13(3) of the Federal Reserve Act. It was this section of the Act which permitted the Fed to initiate the series of lending programs to banks and private markets more generally that has raised concerns about whether the central bank effectively emerged as a fourth branch of government. Under the new legislation passed in 2010 the Fed's ability is circumscribed and requires the Treasury to sign off on unorthodox policy measures in some circumstances while the US Congress has also placed limits on how far the Fed can go as well as reserving the right to terminate the Fed's ability to do 'whatever it takes'.

Whether the G20 framework proves to be a watershed in promoting cooperative or coordinated policies remains to be seen. The Leaders have now issued their marching orders. The actual difficult work of carrying out the twin dreams of good governance and the development of policy frameworks that can guarantee balanced growth can now begin. If carried out the resulting reforms will have lasting positive consequences. One institution that is certain to be affected is the central bank. Since central banks can, with some justification, claim to have had a critical role in stabilizing financial markets and economies more generally, how their role evolves in the near future bears watching very closely. The ability of policy makers to weather the next crisis rests on what monetary policy frameworks will look like in the next decade.

Central Bank Transparency and Governance: A Preliminary Attempt at Measurement

Dincer and Eichengreen (2007), relying on the earlier work by Eijffinger and Geraats (2004), and Siklos (2002), created an index for central bank transparency for over 100 countries. Importantly, the Dincer and Eichengreen index contained a time series element since the data were constructed for the sample 1999–2006. Siklos (2010a) extends their data set, as well as updates and corrects a few elements in the original Dincer and Eichengreen data until the end of 2009.

The index is an aggregation of 15 attributes that describe the type and content of information released by central banks. However, the index also includes characteristics that can equally be considered as elements of an index of governance, that is, a measure of the overall quality of the institution. It is somewhat surprising that economists, fond of creating indicators of all kinds, starting with indexes of central bank independence through to indicators of transparency and accountability of the monetary authority, have not yet created an institutional quality indicator for central banks.[14] What follows is a

---

[14] For example, the World Bank has long published a governance indicator that, among other variables, includes a measure of government effectiveness, but not one of the effectiveness of monetary policy. See http://info. worldbank.org/governance/wgi/index.asp.

very preliminary attempt to do so. No doubt the addition of data from a variety of other sources, as well as other considerations that may influence measures of institutional quality, will, in future, improve the index developed below. Some are mentioned below.

The attributes in the Dincer and Eichengreen index are grouped into five broad categories. They are: political transparency, which measures how open the central bank is about its policy objectives; economic transparency, an indicator of the type of information used in the conduct of monetary policy; procedural transparency, which provides an indication of how monetary policy decisions are made; policy transparency, a measure of the content and how promptly decisions are made public by the central bank; and, finally, operational transparency, which summarizes how the central bank evaluates its own performance. Details about the construction of the index can be found in Dincer and Eichengreen (2007) and in the Appendix of this chapter. Even if everyone can agree that the individual components of the index are useful metrics for our understanding about how open central banks are, it is striking that certain elements of the index reflect longer term concerns of the central bank while others are more suited to an evaluation of how well the central bank is likely to communicate monetary policy in the short-term. Thus, for example, since political transparency is geared toward the provision of information stemming from the precision of policy objectives and the government's role in setting these objectives, these are likely to change slowly and infrequently. The slow moving nature of changes in the values in this category is likely also enhanced by the principle 'if it ain't broke, don't fix it'. In contrast, attributes included under the headings of policy and operational transparency, are focused on the day to day policy challenges a central bank is likely to face. As a result, an aggregate indicator of central bank transparency is less likely to indicate how well central banks have used their drive to become more transparent to calm markets' fears or in dealing with crisis type situations that directly impinge on the conduct of monetary policy. An additional consideration is likely to stem from the fact that central banks are apt to copy from each other what 'works', prompted also by advice from institutions such as the IMF and the BIS. Presumably, they are likely to promote what they consider as 'best standards of practice' when it comes to monetary policy.

It is also clear from the contents of the index that some relate more to governance matters, such as who sets the objectives of policy or the extent to which these are numerically specified, to elements that directly pertain to transparency as it is commonly understood, such as how promptly policy rate decisions are made or whether the central bank publishes an inflation forecast. Because the original Dincer and Eichengreen index equally weights the 15 attributes of their index – theory offers no real guidance as to what weight one might attach to individual components of the index – it cannot serve as a proxy for and index of central bank governance. Alternatively, it is conceivable that a suitably weighted, and possibly augmented, index might be interpreted as a first attempt to measure central bank governance, that is, the institutional quality of monetary authorities. After all, there is little doubt that good governance will partly be dictated by how much light central banks shed on their operations, successes and failures. Nevertheless, it is equally plausible that, by ignoring the political environment the central bank operates under, a factor that is not explicitly incorporated in the transparency index[15], a true measure of governance can be said to have been constructed. Therefore, the 15 attributes in the Dincer and Eichengreen index are augmented by other indicators that are likely to influence the overall institutional quality of the central bank. More precisely, two other factors are added. The polity indicator, an index that ranges from +10, indicating a strongly democratic state, to -10, the index value for a strongly autocratic state. Second, while political regimes come and go it is more likely that governance quality is inversely related to the length of time a particular regime is in place. Both these indicators are available in the time series – cross section dimensions from the Polity IV project (http://www.systemicpeace.org/polity/polity4.htm).[16]   While   other measures could well have been incorporated into a governance index for central banks, I chose not to simply because the aim of the Chapter is to raise the possibility that, in future, economists and others interested in central banks as an institution, should consider the overall governance of the monetary authority and not only its autonomy,

---

[15] Nor, interestingly, is this the case in existing measures of central bank independence, at least not directly.

[16] Indeed, the Polity IV data base refers to itself as a governance indicator. The data are available on an annual basis whereas the World Bank's governance indicator is available only every second year.

transparency, or accountability. Research is ongoing to improve the first measures of central bank governance.

Next, one has to decide how to weigh the attributes, whether relying on the original 15 or the augmented 17 attributes, into a new index. To do so I follow the approach recently used by Hatsius et al. (2010), who construct new measures of financial conditions relying on factor models. As noted by Dincer and Eichengreen (2007), there is likely an endogenous relationship between central bank objectives such as inflation and any indicator of institutional quality, whether it is an indicator of transparency or governance. Therefore, by regressing the various institutional attributes, for example, on past inflation the resulting principal components extracted from the residuals are likely to better reflect the exogenous contribution of the various attributes of governance and not the reaction to macroeconomic conditions.

Consequently, define G_{it} as attribute i at time t. Due to data limitations – there are, at most, only 12 years of time series data for over 100 countries – I estimate the principal components across countries.[17] Next, define Π_t as the inflation rate at time t. Once again, to economize on notation, it is to be understood that there is, in practice, another subscript, j, representing a particular country in question. If the following is estimated, namely:

$$G_{it} = A_i(L)\Pi_{it} + \xi_{it} \qquad (5.1)$$

Where all the variables were previously defined, $A(L)$ is a distributed lag function, and ξ is an error term that is the governance indicator purged from the effects of past inflation.[18] Now suppose that the

---

[17] There are obviously other improvements one can make to this approach which is done mainly to preserve the simplicity of the approach. For example, one might want to separately estimate the principal components in the manner described in the text for advanced, emerging market, or developing economies. This is left for future research.

[18] Conceivably, one can also consider real GDP growth or some output gap indicator. Since much of the literature on central bank independence and transparency focuses on its effects on inflation we retain this focus here. Future research might also consider the sensitivity of the results to relying on other macroeconomic indicators.

'exogenous' portion of the governance attributes can be decomposed as follows:

$$\xi_{it} = \lambda'_i F_t + \eta_{it} \tag{5.2}$$

Equation (5.2) describes the factors (F) that are unobserved but which are captured by their impact on ξ via λ'_i. A positive value for λ implies that the principal components of the governance attributes improve governance whereas the opposite is true, of course, for negative values of λ. The goal of the empirical analysis to follow is to estimate F. All the attributes, with the exception of the regime duration indicator, are defined in such a way that the larger their value, the better the governance. Hence, one would want to estimate the number of principal components with these signs in mind.[19] The estimated value for F, that is, $\hat{F}_t$ is the estimated governance indicator.

The empirical results below are based on a sample of 101 countries for the sample 1998–2009. Data limitations, as well as the necessary data transformations, imply that the resulting governance indicators are effectively generated for a slightly smaller set of countries and only for the period 2000 to 2009. A spreadsheet with the (standardized) values for the indices will be posted on the central bank communication network's website (http://www.central-bank-communication.net/about/index.htm).

Table 5.1 gives estimates of two versions of equation (5.1). Two lags for inflation were found to be sufficient for the two cases examined.

---

[19] Hatsius et al. (2010) provides references to the relevant literature on factor models and principal components analysis. While estimation via least squares is considered acceptable, the estimates shown below were obtained via maximum likelihood.

Table 5.1 Estimates of Equation (5.1)

Coefficients	Attributes 1	Attributes 2
Constant	0.37 (.003)*	2.40 (.08)*
Inflation (t-1)	-0.001 (.0003)*	-0.02 (.01)*
Inflation (t-2)	-0.001 (.0003)*	-0.0 (.01)*
R^2 (adjusted)	0.29	0.37
F (sign. Level)	358.7 (.00)	528.00 (.00)
Obs.	14325	16036

Note: Ordinary Least Squares estimate of equation (5.1). Fixed effects not shown to conserve space.

Source: authors' calculations.

The first set of estimates consists of the original 15 attributes used in the Dincer and Eichengreen transparency index; the second set of estimates adds the duration of political regimes and the polity index which measures how democratic or autocratic political regimes are. As expected, higher inflation reduces the index of transparency in both specifications but the effect is stronger when the political governance variables are added. This suggests that central bank governance need not be treated separately from economic governance. Next, as previously outlined, the residuals from equation (5.1) are used to estimate the factor model (5.2). Keeping in mind the theoretical expectation that all of the factors, save the duration variable, are expected to be positively related to an indicator of good governance this suggests that it is likely that a one-factor model will suffice.[20] Figure 5.3 then provides a bar chart with the estimates of λ. When the political governance variables are excluded the factor approach highlights the role of economic transparency, how promptly a central bank releases and explains its decision, and the extent to which it evaluates its performance and provides information about economic shocks. Other attributes receive smaller weights.

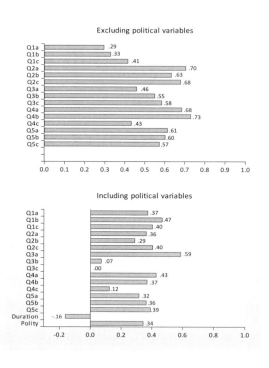

Note: See text for estimation details of lambda (λ_i')

Figure 5.3 Lambdas in Single Factor Model

Next, turning to the case where the political governance proxies are included we now find that political transparency matters relatively

---

[20] For similar reasons, Hatsius et al. (2010) also rely on a one-factor model to construct their financial conditions index.

more followed by the release of forecasts and an explanation of the central bank's strategy. The second version bears a closer resemblance to what most observers would consider to be essential ingredients of governance, that is, elements of accountability, transparency, and clarity in the relationship between the polity and the central bank. Nevertheless, a priori, it is not immediately clear that one version is to be preferred over the other. It is instructive to consider how well the various indexes are correlated through time and across countries. For the full data set the two governance indicators constructed here are positively and significantly correlated with a simple coefficient of 0.30. Interestingly, the correlations between the two governance indicators and the original Dincer and Eichengreen index are 0.32 when the political governance indicators are excluded and -0.25 when the polity related series are included. The latter correlation suggests that more transparency, in the sense of the Dincer-Eichengreen index, need not be equivalent to better governance.

If the same correlations are evaluated for the countries with the most experience with a numerical inflation target, namely Australia, Canada, New Zealand, Sweden and the UK, the correlation between the transparency index and, for example, the governance index including the polity-related variables is 0.60 which is highly statistically significant. Indeed, if we repeat the same calculation for a set of emerging market economies that also adopted a numerical inflation objective, namely Brazil, Chile, Mexico, Czech Republic, Hungary, Poland, South Africa, Korea, and Thailand, the same correlation falls to 0.41 and is also statistically significant. Hence, there is a little bit of evidence that inflation targeting can improve governance and more so the longer the regime has been in place, although the latter hypothesis has not been formally tested here. Of course, other factors, such as the rule of law to name one, may also play a role. These, and other extensions, are left for future research.

Finally, by way of illustration, Figure 5.4 displays the relationship between inflation and the (standardized) measure of governance that incorporates the polity variables for three countries. They are Canada and Korea, both of which target inflation, and the USA which does not target inflation and is sometimes used as a benchmark in similar

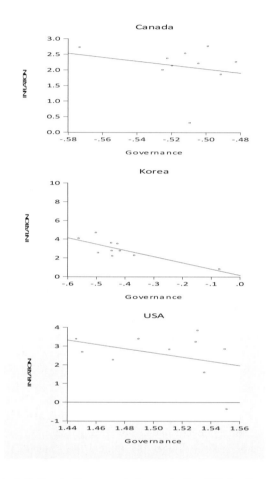

Note: Inflation is the percent change in the CPI for the years 2000–2009; Governance is the (standardized) value of the indicator derived in this study that includes political governance proxies.

Figure 5.4 Inflation and Governance: Canada, Korea, and the USA

studies. In all three cases there is an inverse relationship between contemporaneous inflation and the governance index. Hence, while inflation targeting may be associated with improvements in governance, it need not be the only factor. Moreover, the negative relationship reported in the Figure need not hold for every country in the sample.

Conclusions

Over three decades ago the economics profession began to build an empirical case in favor of central bank independence. This line of research proved successful. Next, economic analysis suggested that a concern for inflation, not to the exclusion of a concern over real economic performance, also represents an improvement in monetary policy. The theoretical rationale for this result also implied that central banks needed to become more transparent, as well as accountable, for their actions. Paralleling the creations of indexes of central bank independence a literature developed to measure how transparent central banks have been over the past decade. The events since the Global Financial Crisis of 2007–2009 are likely to increase the breadth and scope of central bank responsibilities. Already, the Bank of England and US Federal Reserve have taken on more important and powerful roles in the affairs of both nations. Since the individuals responsible for running both institutions are unelected there should be, going forward, more effort devoted to measuring the overall quality of the monetary authorities. To this end, this Chapter proposes an index of central bank governance derived from an existing index of central bank transparency. The proposed indexes represent, however, only a first step. There are many improvements that can be made to the measures introduced in this chapter, several of which were discussed above. In particular, any improved index of central bank governance will have to consider how institutional quality is influenced by how well the monetary authorities coordinate their actions with other regulatory institutions, of both the domestic and international varieties.

It is clear that central banking after the crisis will change in ways that remain to be determined. It is imperative, however, that these institutions which have built up an impressive capital of reputation and demonstrated considerable credibility through the crisis not lose sight of the fact that there were also failures which contributed to the substantial economic costs incurred as a result of the build-up of financial imbalances throughout the 2000s. One way to hold the monetary authorities as reasonably accountable as possible is to ask how well central banks are governed. It is with this in mind that this chapter argues that we need to go beyond indicators of independence and transparency and think in terms of indicators of governance. Such indicators are commonplace for other governmental institutions. It is high time the same applied to central banks.

Appendix

Index of Central Bank Transparency (Dincer and Eichengreen 2007)

This appendix describes the construction of the transparency index. The index is the sum of the scores for answers to the fifteen questions below (min = 0, max = 15).

Political Transparency

Political transparency refers to openness about policy objectives. This comprises a formal statement of objectives, including an explicit prioritization in case of multiple goals, a quantification of the primary objective(s), and explicit institutional arrangements.

a. Is there a formal statement of the objective(s) of monetary policy, with an explicit prioritization in case of multiple objectives?

No formal objective(s) = 0.
Multiple objectives without prioritization = 1/2.
One primary objective, or multiple objectives with explicit priority = 1.

b. Is there a quantification of the primary objective(s)?

No = 0.
Yes = 1.

c. Are there explicit contracts or other similar institutional arrangements between the monetary authorities and the government?

No central bank contracts or other institutional arrangements = 0.
Central bank without explicit instrument independence or contract
= 1/2.
Central bank with explicit instrument independence or central
bank contract although possibly subject to an explicit override
procedure = 1.

Economic Transparency

Economic transparency focuses on the economic information that is
used for monetary policy. This includes economic data, the model of
the economy that the central bank employs to construct forecasts or
evaluate the impact of its decisions, and the internal forecasts (model
based or judgmental) that the central bank relies on.

a. Is the basic economic data relevant for the conduct of monetary
    policy publicly available? (The focus is on the following five
    variables: money supply, inflation, GDP, unemployment rate and
    capacity utilization.)

    Quarterly time series for at most two out of the five variables = 0
    Quarterly time series for three or four out of the five variables =
    1/2
    Quarterly time series for all five variables = 1

b. Does the central bank disclose the macroeconomic model(s) it
    uses for policy analysis?

    No = 0
    Yes = 1

c. Does the central bank regularly publish its own macroeconomic
    forecasts?

    No numerical central bank forecasts for inflation and output = 0
    Numerical central bank forecasts for inflation and/or output
    published at less than quarterly frequency = 1/2
    Quarterly numerical central bank forecasts for inflation and output
    for the medium term (one to two years ahead), specifying the

assumptions about the policy instrument (conditional or unconditional forecasts) = 1

Procedural Transparency

Procedural transparency is about the way monetary policy decision are taken.

a.   Does the central bank provide an explicit policy rule or strategy that describes its monetary policy framework?

No = 0
Yes = 1

b.   Does the central bank give a comprehensive account of policy deliberations (or explanations in case of a single central banker) within a reasonable amount of time?

No or only after a substantial lag (more than eight weeks) = 0
Yes, comprehensive minutes (although not necessarily verbatim or attributed) or explanations (in case of a single central banker), including a discussion of backward and forward-looking arguments = 1

c.   Does the central bank disclose how each decision on the level of its main operating instrument or target was reached?

No voting records, or only after substantial lag (more than eight weeks) = 0
Non-attributed voting records = 1/2
Individual voting records, or decision by single central banker = 1

Policy Transparency

Policy transparency means prompt disclosure of policy decisions, together with an explanation of the decision, and an explicit policy inclination or indication of likely future policy actions.

a. Are decisions about adjustments to the main operating instrument or target announced promptly?
No or only after the day of implementation = 0
Yes, on the day of implementation = 1

b. Does the central bank provide an explanation when it announces policy decisions?

No = 0
Yes, when policy decisions change, or only superficially = 1/2
Yes, always and including forwarding-looking assessments = 1

c. Does the central bank disclose an explicit policy inclination after every policy meeting or an explicit indication of likely future policy actions (at least quarterly)?

No = 0
Yes = 1

Operational Transparency

Operational transparency concerns the implementation of the central bank's policy actions. It involves a discussion of control errors in achieving operating targets and (unanticipated) macroeconomic disturbances that affect the transmission of monetary policy. Furthermore, the evaluation of the macroeconomic outcomes of monetary policy in light of its objectives is included here as well.

a. Does the central bank regularly evaluate to what extent its main policy operating targets (if any) have been achieved?

No or not very often (at less than annual frequency) = 0
Yes but without providing explanations for significant deviations = 1/2
Yes, accounting for significant deviations from target (if any); or, (nearly) perfect control over main operating instrument/target = 1

b. Does the central bank regularly provide information on (unanticipated) macroeconomic disturbances that affect the policy transmission process?

No or not very often = 0
Yes but only through short-term forecasts or analysis of current macroeconomic developments (at least quarterly) = 1/2
Yes including a discussion of past forecast errors (at least annually) = 1

c. Does the central bank regularly provide an evaluation of the policy outcome in light of its macroeconomic objectives?

No or not very often (at less than annual frequency) = 0
Yes but superficially = 1/2
Yes, with an explicit account of the contribution of monetary policy in meeting the objectives = 1

Source: Dincer and Eichengreen (2007), Appendix.

References

Aikman, D., A. Haldane and B. Nelson (2010), 'Curbing the Credit Cycle', Paper Prepared for the Columbia University Centre on Capital and Society Annual Conference, New York, November 2010.

Bordo, M. (1993), 'The Gold Standard, Bretton Woods, and Other Monetary Regimes: An Historical Appraisal', *NBER working paper* No. 4310, April.

Borio, C. and P. Lowe (2002), 'Asset Prices, Financial and Monetary Stability: Exploring the Nexus', *BIS working paper* No. 114, July.

Borio, C. and W. White (2004), 'Whither Monetary and Financial Stability? The Implications for Evolving Policy Regimes', *BIS working papers* No. 147.

Dincer, N. and B. Eichengreen (2007), 'Central Bank Transparency: Where, Why, and with What Effects?', *NBER working paper* No. 13003, March.

Eijffinger, S.C.W. and P.M. Geraats (2004), 'How Transparent Are Central Banks?,' Cambridge Working Papers in Economics 0411, Faculty of Economics, University of Cambridge.

Gaspar, V., F. Smets and D. Vestin (2010), 'Is Time Ripe for Price Level Path Stability?', in P.L. Siklos, M.T. Bohl and M.E. Wohar (eds.), *Challenges in Central Banking* Cambridge, UK: Cambridge University Press.

Goodhart, C. (2010), 'The Role of Macro-Prudential Supervision', Paper Presented at the 2010 Atlanta Federal Reserve Financial Markets Conference 'Up from the Ashes: The Financial System After the Crisis', May.

Hatsius, J., P. Hooper, F. Mishkin, K. Schoenholtz and M. Watson (2010), 'Financial Conditions Indexes: A Fresh Look After the Crisis', *Princeton University working paper*, April.

James, H. (1996), *International Monetary Cooperation Since Bretton Woods*, Oxford, UK: Oxford University Press.

Maier, P. and E. Santor (2008), 'Reforming the IMF: Lessons from Modern Central Banking', *working paper* 2008–6, May.

Siklos, P.L. (2010a), 'Central Bank Transparency: An Updated Look', *Applied Economics Letters* (forthcoming).

Siklos, P.L. (2010b), 'Communication for Multi-Taskers: Perspectives on Dealing with both Monetary Policy and Financial Stability', *Wilfrid Laurier University working paper*.

Siklos, P.L. (2009), 'As Good as It Gets? The International Dimension to Canada's Monetary Policy Strategy Choices', *C.D. Howe Commentary* No. 292, July.

Siklos, P.L. (2002), *The Changing Face of Central Banking,* Cambridge, MA, USA: Cambridge University Press.

Taylor, J. (2010), 'Commentary: Monetary Policy After the Fall', Paper presented at the 2010 Jackson Hole Conference.

Taylor, J.B. (2009), *Getting Off Track: How Government Actions and Interventions Caused, Prolonged, and Worsened the Financial Crisis,* Stanford, CA, USA: Hoover Institution Press.

Wessel, D. (2009), *In Fed We Trust: Ben Bernanke's War on the Great Panic,* New York, NJ, USA: Crown Business.

6. Central Banks and Banking Supervision Reform

Pierre C. Boyer and Jorge Ponce[1]

Introduction

A series of reform proposals that have been envisaged since the subprime crisis started aim to concentrate regulatory and supervisory powers in the hands of central banks. For example, the Bank of England has received new responsibilities for guarding the overall system's stability, i.e., 'macro-prudential supervision'. Yet, the Conservative Party, now in office, has adopted as policy the investiture of full responsibilities to the Bank of England for the prudential oversight of all individual financial institutions, i.e., 'micro-prudential supervision' (see The Conservative Party, 2009). The US Federal Reserve System is accumulating huge control over the economy and banks. The Restoring American Financial Stability Act of 2010 gives the Federal Reserve primary responsibilities for supervising all firms that could pose a threat to financial stability in addition to its responsibilities for monitoring the operations of holding companies – including traditional banks – and for protecting consumers.

[1] The views expressed herein are those of the authors and do not necessarily represent the views of the institutions to which they are affiliated. The authors would like to thank the Editors Donato Masciandaro and Sylvester Eijffinger, as well as Germán Cubas, Umberto Della Mea, Alvaro Forteza, Diego Gianelli, Hans Peter Grüner, Friedrich Heinemann, Gerardo Licandro, José Antonio Licandro, David Martimort, Marc Rennert, and Leandro Zipitría for their valuable comments on earlier versions of this chapter. Boyer gratefully acknowledges the Collaborative Research Center 884 for financial support. Boyer is also grateful for the hospitality of the IGIER at Bocconi University and the Toulouse School of Economics where part of this research was conducted.

It is not hard to see why central banks are being given more responsibilities for macro-prudential supervision. Central banks are the natural source of liquidity. As lender of last resort, they play a crucial role preventing and managing banking crises. So having access to timely supervisory information would help them to better perform these activities. Financial instability affects the macroeconomic environment – with substantial consequences for price stability and the monetary policy transmission process – to the point that even central bankers now recognize that they have ignored macro financial stability to their peril. Moreover, the conduct of monetary policy provides central banks with an ideal position to monitor macroeconomic developments and better anticipate threats to the stability of the whole financial system (see, for instance, Blinder, 2010; Di Giorgio and Di Noia, 1999; Goodhart and Schoenmaker, 1995; and Masciandaro, 1995 and 2004).

Should central bankers also be in charge of micro-prudential supervision? On the one hand, Goodhart and Schoenmaker (1995) argue that the main opposition to giving supervisory responsibilities to central banks is that these responsibilities could conflict with monetary policy and reduce its efficiency. Claeys and Schoors (2007) present empirical evidence of conflicts between micro- and macro-prudential objectives in the Central Bank of Russia. On the other hand, Peek et al. (1999) show that having access to supervisory information may improve the efficiency of monetary policy because it helps central banks to better forecast economic variables. Therefore, from an efficiency point of view, it is not clear whether or not central banks are better positioned to monitor idiosyncratic developments in financial institutions.

In this chapter, we analyze the previous question from a different perspective. We argue that most of the current reform efforts in the field of banking supervision ignore the possibility that concentrating supervisory powers in the hands of central bankers could make them more prone to be captured by bankers. Following Barth et al. (2004), Djankov et al. (2002) and Quintyn and Taylor (2002), we consider the case where powerful supervisors may use their powers to benefit favored constituents instead of improving the well-being of the society. Certain features of banking supervision – e.g., the very specialized skills and the vast amount of data that are necessary to conduct banking supervision and the maintenance of confidentiality – may facilitate the capture of supervisors by bankers. Additionally, the regulated industry may be more willing to capture supervisors that are powerful.[2] Indeed, capture has already been a concern during the Savings & Loans debacle (see Kane, 1990a,b and 2001), and in past regulatory debates in the US and in Europe (see, for instance, Abrams and Settle, 1993; Gabillon and Martimort, 2004; and Heinemann and Schüler, 2004).

Hardy (2006) argues that the possibility of regulatory capture needs to be taken into account in designing governance arrangements for bank supervisors. In Boyer and Ponce (2010), we focus on the incentives that self-interested bank supervisors may have to use supervisory information for their own benefit. We examine the implications of these incentives for the design of banking supervision institutions when capture is a concern. We show that concentrating supervisory authority in the hands of a single supervisor, e.g., a central bank, may have a potential drawback: it may make the capture of the supervisor by banks more likely. Considering the allocation of bank supervisory powers as a contracting variable, we find that it is socially optimal that the micro- and the macro-prudential dimensions of banking supervision be conducted by different bank supervisors. Hence, policy makers in many countries would like to reconsider the current trend toward the concentration of supervisory powers in the hands of central banks.

In our analysis, each banker has private information about her bank's riskiness. The total riskiness of a bank is the sum of an idiosyncratic component (a micro risk) and of a systemic (macro) risk. A benevolent financial stability committee does not observe that information but uses one or two supervisors to attempt to bridge its informational gap. One can think of the financial stability committee as a legislature designing banking regulation and supervisory arrangements, and of the supervisors as two governmental agencies, e.g. the Bank of England and the Financial Services Authority. The

---

[2] In an article in *Bloomberg* we read 'With power from Congress to oversee the previously unregulated $615 trillion market for over-the-counter derivatives, it [the Commodity Futures Trading Commission] has become one of the hottest lobbying spots in town.' ('Wall Street Lobbyists Besiege CFTC to Shape Derivatives Rules', October 14, 2010.)

supervisors are endowed with imperfect informational technologies that allow them to get verifiable information on each dimension of the riskiness of a bank with some positive probabilities.[3]

If supervisors were benevolent, then the allocation of supervisory power is of no consequence. Bank supervisors always reveal truthfully their supervisory information about the riskiness of the bank to the financial stability committee. In turn, the latter can implement a socially optimal regulatory contract.

However, bank supervisors may pursue self interests rather than social welfare. As a matter of fact, supervision creates particular links between supervisors and the banking sector which increase the likelihood that supervisors deviate from socially optimal objectives. We model the pursuit of self interest by allowing the supervisors to hide supervisory information, so that the financial stability committee remains uninformed. Supervisory information gathered through audits and in situ inspections cannot be easily manipulated but can be easily concealed. Supervisors may have many reasons not to inform the financial stability committee about the riskiness of the bank.[4] We use the following modeling short-cut: a supervisor may be willing to hide supervisory information in exchange for some monetary bribes from the bank.

If supervisors are self-interested agents, then the allocation of supervisory powers may be a useful mechanism to improve social welfare. We discuss three possible supervisory arrangements. First, we consider the case where there is only one supervisor gathering information about the two dimensions of a bank's riskiness. Second, we study the arrangement where there are two supervisors endowed with a supervisory technology each; i.e., each supervisor only gathers information about one dimension of a bank's riskiness. Finally, we consider a hierarchical structure where one supervisor is under the authority of a second one; i.e., the superior supervisor observes the information gathered by its subordinate, but the latter does not observe the information gathered by its superior.

---

[3] Verifiability has a weak meaning as we do not require that the information can be verified by a jury but only that the financial stability committee can be convinced about it.

[4] For example, bank supervisors may prefer to conceal information in order to protect their reputation like in Boot and Thakor (1993), or in exchange of favors and post-career concerns like in Laffont and Tirole (1993).

We find that the separation of supervisory powers into different agencies is the superior arrangement. Intuitively, splitting supervisory powers into two different supervisors reduces their discretion by limiting the information at their disposal. Under separation, each supervisor does not observe the information gathered nor the bribe requested by the other supervisor, and then requests bribes based only on the piece of information it has gathered. Hence, each supervisor is constrained to request bribes that are always accepted by the bank whatever its riskiness and whatever the bribe requested by the other supervisor. As a result, the sum of the bribes requested by both supervisors is at most as large as the bribe requested by a single supervisor which is endowed with the two supervisory technologies. Since the financial stability committee has to offer greater than possible bribes, splitting supervisory powers reduces the costs for the financial stability committee to provide incentives to bank supervisors and so to get information. Thus, the separation of supervisory powers improves social welfare.

The introduction of capture concerns into bank supervision models has straightforward policy implications. Splitting supervisory powers among different bank supervisors is a superior arrangement in terms of social welfare to concentrating supervisory powers in a single supervisor. Since central banks seem to be natural candidates to perform macro-prudential supervision, micro-prudential supervision should be allocated to a different supervisor from the central bank supervisor. From an ex ante perspective, the design of two separated supervisory entities with precise objectives and specific supervisory technologies leads to more rules and less discretion in banking supervision. The move from discretion to rules is indeed a constitutional response to the threat of capture. Each supervisor then receives a single mission, i.e. to monitor a single dimension of risk, and follows stringent rules.

If it is not possible to split supervisory powers into two separated bank supervisors because, for example, it would be too costly to duplicate supervisory structures, then the policymaker should implement a hierarchical structure of banking supervision. The informational advantage of the superior supervisor implies that the hierarchical structure does strictly worse than having two independent supervisors. However, the lack of an informational advantage by the subordinated supervisor implies that social welfare improves with respect to the case in which only one supervisor is used. Summarizing, a hierarchical structure of banking supervision improves the social welfare with respect to using only one bank supervisor but does strictly worse than using two independent bank supervisors.

Recent literature on the institutional allocation of bank regulatory powers, e.g., Kahn and Santos (2005 and 2006), Ponce (2010) and Repullo (2000), studies the optimal allocation of lender of last resort responsibilities, deposit insurance and supervision among several bank regulators. Their guiding question is who should perform each of these activities. In this chapter, we focus on banking supervision and analyze whether or not more than one supervisor should be responsible for conducting such an activity. So, we contribute new results to that strand of the literature. In particular, we find new results about the optimal allocation of micro- and macro-prudential supervisory responsibilities. These results also inform the current debate about banking supervision reforms (see, for example, Brunnermeier et al. (2009) and Acharya and Richardson (2009)).

This chapter borrows extensively from the insights of the regulatory literature on collusion. Laffont and Tirole (1993) formally study issues such as the capture of regulators, favoritism in auctions and collusion in cost auditing. The general problem is that bureaucrats may fall under the influence of the industry and then fail to reduce the informational gap between uninformed policy makers and the privately informed industry. Revolving doors or post-career concerns[5] can lead the bureaucrats to manipulate their information in favor of the industry's interest. Those models have shown that the policy maker avoids collusion by reducing the discretion of the regulatory agency. The closest model to the one introduced in this chapter is by Laffont and Martimort (1999). They are also interested by the possibility that the separation of powers in regulation acts as a commitment device against the threat of regulatory capture. We adapt their framework to analyze the implications of capture on the optimal allocation of the micro- and the macro-prudential dimensions of banking supervision.

The rest of the chapter is organized as follows. First, we present a simple model to structure our arguments. Next, we analyze and discuss different supervisory arrangements in terms of social welfare. Finally, we offer some concluding remarks.

---

[5] On career-concerns and behavior of government agencies see Dewatripont et al. (1999a and b).

Sketch of the Model

In this section, we present a sketch of the model developed by Boyer and Ponce (2010) and consider the following three-tier hierarchy: benevolent financial stability committee; bank supervisors; bank.

Agents, preferences and information. A banker has private information about her bank's riskiness, r. The riskiness of the bank can be decomposed into two components. A first component of risk is idiosyncratic to the bank; it is a risk affecting the bank individually. Since it is bank-specific and not related to the rest of the banking system, we call this component a 'micro' risk. A second component of risk is systemic. It measures the contribution of the bank to the aggregate risk of the whole banking system. We call this component a 'macro' risk. We assume that these two components of risk are additive. Hence, r has the following structure:

$$r = \underline{r} + r_m + r_M \tag{6.1}$$

where $\underline{r}$ is the minimal level of risk, and r_m and r_M are two binary random variables with support in $\{0, \Delta r\}$ representing the micro and the macro components of risk respectively. Hence, the bank can have three levels of risk $\underline{r}$, $\hat{r} \equiv \underline{r} + \Delta r$ and $\overline{r} \equiv \underline{r} + 2\Delta r$.

The size of the bank's balance sheet is equal to the level of capital, k, put at risk by the banker. If the (net) profit of the bank is denoted by π, then the utility function of the banker is given by

$$B = \pi - rk \tag{6.2}$$

the reservation utility of the banker is such that $B \geq 0$.

A benevolent financial stability committee is responsible for the design of banking regulation and supervisory arrangements. The financial stability committee does not observe the riskiness of the bank. It can use, however, one or two supervisors in order to bridge its lack of information on r. If two supervisors are used, they can be independent or one of them can be the hierarchically superior of the other. Let w_i, for $i \in \{1, 2\}$, be the wage of each supervisor. If the financial stability committee uses only one supervisor, then that supervisor's utility level is:

$$S = w \qquad (6.3)$$

with the individual rationality constraint $w \geq 0$. If the financial stability committee uses two supervisors, then we have similarly

$$S_i = w_i \geq 0 \text{ for } i \in \{1,2\} \qquad (6.4)$$

Figure 6.1 summarizes the structure of the three-tier hierarchy in this simple model.

Bank regulation. The benevolent financial stability committee regulates banks using a set of regulatory instruments. First, the financial stability committee regulates the size of the bank's balance sheet, k, using capital regulations, mergers and acquisition regulations, and downsizing policies among other tools. For example, the Restoring American Financial Stability Act of 2010 introduces tough new capital and leverage requirements with the aim of making it undesirable for banks to get too big. Second, the financial stability committee may use instruments like fees, taxes, provisioning for expected and unexpected losses, and monetary penalties that directly or indirectly affect the profit of the bank, π.[6]

Bank regulation, as well as bank supervision, entails some costs due to, for example, the bureaucratic structures that are needed to enact regulations and to collect public funds in order to pay wages, w, to bank supervisors. For simplicity, we assume that these costs are equal to $\lambda(\pi + w)$ with $\lambda > 0$. The term $\lambda\pi$ measures the bureaucratic costs of enacting regulations affecting the profit of banks, while the term λw measures the costs of collecting public funds to pay bank supervisors.

---

[6] See Perotti and Suarez (2009) and Shin (2010) for proposals of bank regulation that use taxes and charges as prudential tools.

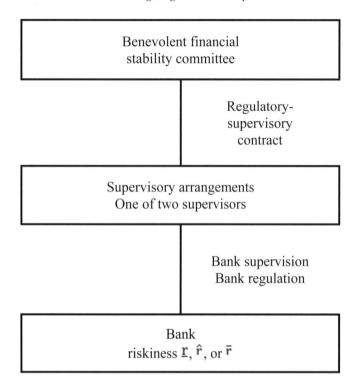

Figure 6.1 The Three-tier Hierarchy

Supervisory technologies. There are two risk-specific supervisory technologies. Each supervisory technology is imperfect in the sense that it provides hard information on one dimension of the bank's riskiness with a positive probability that is different from one. The information gathered by supervisors is hard in the sense that it can be justified by evidences.

Social welfare. The benevolent financial stability committee maximizes the following welfare function

$$W = \Psi(k) + B + S - (1+\lambda)(\pi + w) \qquad (6.5)$$

where $\Psi(k)$, with $\Psi'(k) > 0$ and $\Psi''(k) < 0$, is the utility that the customers of the bank derive from using its services. The surplus of customers, $\Psi(k)$, is assumed to be increasing in the size of the bank (which is measured by its capital, k) but with decreasing returns to scale. Indeed, larger banks generally offer more complete sets of products, which may better satisfy the preferences of customers. However, the marginal utility derived by customers from the introduction of a new product tends to zero when the current offer of products by the bank is large enough. Moreover, better capitalized banks offer better protection to their depositors. Whereas, the marginal utility of extra protection tends to zero when the bank is well capitalized. Recall that B and S are the utility functions of the banker and of bank supervisors respectively. Finally, the term $(1+\lambda)(\pi+w)$ represents the total costs of regulating and supervising banks. The welfare function can be restated as follows

$$W = \Psi(k) - (1+\lambda)rk - \lambda B - \lambda S \qquad (6.6)$$

Benchmark: benevolent supervision. We present the optimal regulatory scheme for the benchmark case in which bank supervisors are benevolent. Benevolent supervisors truthfully report their supervisory information to the financial stability committee for a zero reward (i.e., $w_i = 0$). Hence, to have one or two supervisors is indifferent from the perspective of the financial stability committee.[7]

The optimal regulation under benevolent supervision entails more severe regulations for the most risky banks such that (i) the most risky banks face more stringent capital (size) regulations than the less risky banks, and (ii) the less risky banks make more profits.

Under the optimal regulatory scheme, the less risky banks face the less severe capital or size regulations. Moreover, the size that is allowed by regulation for the less risky banks does not depend on the information gathered by supervisors. However, the profit of the less risky banks depends on the number of informative signals gathered by

---

[7] As we discuss in the case with hierarchical supervision, this conclusion would differ when appointing a second supervisor entails the duplication of some costs.

supervisors. In particular, the less risky banks gain more under asymmetric information, i.e., when no or only one informative signal is gathered by the supervisor, than under perfect information, i.e., when two informative signals are gathered. Intuitively, when benevolent supervisors observe the riskiness of a bank, the financial stability committee can leave less profit to that bank and still implement the level of capital that is socially optimal. Otherwise stated, as soon as at least one supervisory signal is not informative, the financial stability committee has to leave some informational rent to the banker in order that the latter chooses the regulatory scheme that is socially optimal for its bank level of risk.

Intermediate and high-risk banks face more stringent regulations than low-risk banks. Under asymmetric information, and due to incentive reasons, the financial stability committee restricts further the size of the most risky banks and their profits accordingly. By so doing, the financial stability committee has to leave less informational rents to bankers to encourage self-selection into the regulatory scheme that is designed for their category of risk. As a result, optimal regulation entails an inverse relationship between riskiness and size of banks.

Supervisory Arrangements

One Non-Benevolent Supervisor

We first consider the case in which the financial stability committee uses only one bank supervisor in order to bridge its informational gap on the riskiness of the bank. The single bank supervisor is endowed with the two supervisory technologies. Figure 6.2 represents this situation. The bank supervisor is non-benevolent and has some discretion in performing his tasks. In particular, he may hide supervisory information in exchange for some monetary bribes from the bank. Hence, the financial stability committee has to reward the supervisor to incentivize him to reveal his information about the riskiness of the bank.

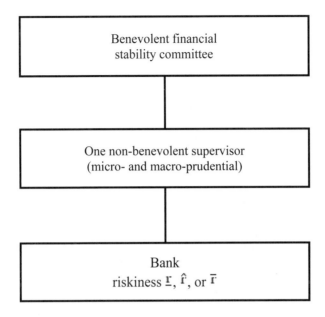

Figure 6.2 The Hierarchy with One Non-Benevolent Supervisor

If the supervisor obtains hard information about the riskiness of the bank, it could be the case that the banker is better off when such information is not revealed to the financial stability committee. In such a case, there is scope for a collusive agreement between the banker and the supervisor. Hence, the supervisor requests a monetary bribe from the bank that is consistent with the information at its disposal and with the extra benefit accruing to the banker when the information is not revealed to the financial stability committee. This kind of bribe request is 'safe' in the sense that it is always accepted by the banker. However, due to the illegal nature of bribes and the difficulties that arise when organizing such a collusive agreement, side-contracts between the banker and the supervisor are subject to transaction costs. These transaction costs imply that each unit of bribes paid by the banker increases the utility of the supervisor by only τ, with $\tau \in \{0,1\}$.[8]

---

[8] We assume that τ is exogenous and common knowledge. See Kofman and Lawarre (1993) for supervision models where the financial stability

In this setting, the financial stability committee has to offer a reward to the bank supervisor which is at least equal to the stake of bribes. There is not loss of generality in restricting the analysis to collusion-proof schemes, namely schemes that do not induce the bank and the supervisor to collude and motivate the latter to report truthfully to the financial stability committee.[9]

The threat of collusion between the supervisor and the bank leads to additional distortions on the optimal regulatory scheme. In particular, optimal regulation with one non-benevolent bank supervisor entails more capital restrictions for the most risky banks and lower profits for the less risky banks with respect to the case of benevolent supervision.

The intuition for this result is as follows. Non-informative signals are more likely to be observed by the financial stability committee when collusion between the bank and the supervisor is a concern. Hence, the financial stability committee has to reward the supervisor for truthfully reporting in order to revert his incentive to engage in collusive agreements with the banker. Since such a reward depends on the capacity of the banker to provide bribes to the bank supervisor, the financial stability committee reduces the social cost of being informed by decreasing the stake for collusion. This is achieved by reducing the profit of the bank in states where collusion is an issue and by introducing additional capital regulations such that the size of the most risky banks is lower than in the case in which supervisors are benevolent.

It is worth noting that the regulatory distortions that are necessary to provide incentives to the bank supervisor depend on the transaction costs of side-contracting between the banker and the supervisor. In particular, when these costs are extremely large, i.e. $\tau \to 0$, optimal regulation with a single non-benevolent supervisor tends to the optimal regulation under benevolent supervision. Increasing the transaction costs of side-contracting, e.g., via large scale policies

---

committee does not know τ. In Laffont and Martimort (1997 and 2000) transaction costs are endogenously generated by asymmetric information among agents who want to enter collusive agreements.

[9] The collusion-proofness principle holds in our context. See Laffont and Tirole (1993) for a formal exposition of this principle.

against corruption, is an effective policy to reduce the possibility of capture.

Two Non-Benevolent Supervisors

We now consider the case in which the financial stability committee uses two bank supervisors in order to bridge its informational gap on the riskiness of the bank. Each supervisor is endowed with only one supervisory technology as depicted in Figure 6.3. For example, the central bank, e.g. the Bank of England, monitors the contribution of the bank to the systemic risk and another bank supervisor, e.g. the Financial Services Authority, monitors the risks that are idiosyncratic to the bank. Hence, each supervisor observes only the signal coming from its supervisory technology and remains ignorant about the other supervisor's signal. In order to simplify the analysis, we assume that supervisors do not exchange information about their signals.[10]

As in the previous case, the threat of collusion between each of the bank supervisors and the banker leads to distortions on the optimal regulatory scheme with benevolent supervision such that we have: (i) more capital restrictions for the most risky banks, and (ii) lower profits for the less risky banks. However, the fact that now each bank supervisor is only partially informed about the riskiness of the bank implies that, for banks of riskiness $\hat{r}$ (respectively $\bar{r}$), optimal regulation is less (respectively more) distorted when two non-benevolent bank supervisors are used instead of using only one non-benevolent bank supervisor.

---

[10] In the absence of monetary bribes, central banks and bank supervisors do not have an incentive to voluntarily share supervisory information with each other (see, for example, Kahn and Santos, (2005) and (2006); and Ponce, (2010)). If monetary bribes were allowed, then it may be the case that one supervisor 'sells' its information to the other. However, the financial stability committee is likely to be able to better control and therefore prevent monetary bribes between supervisors than bribes between supervisors and banks.

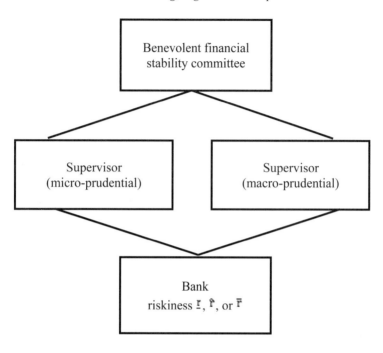

Figure 6.3 The Hierarchy with Two Non-Benevolent Supervisors

The use of two bank supervisors implies more severe regulation, i.e., more capital restrictions and less profits, for the most risky banks than the use of only one bank supervisor. Intuitively, if two supervisors are used, then a collusive agreement between one of the supervisors and the bank can only involve the non-report of one signal. Hence, the capacity of each supervisor to request bribes from the bank is reduced. As a consequence, the financial stability committee reduces the stake for collusion, and thus the social cost of being informed, by introducing additional capital regulations to only the most risky banks. However, there are now two bank supervisors rather than one. Hence, the distortion introduced to the optimal regulation for the most risky banks with respect to the case under benevolent supervision is larger when two supervisors are used than when one supervisor is used. In contrast to the case in which only one bank supervisor is used, the financial stability committee does not need to distort the optimal regulation for other categories of risk. Indeed, it is enough to apply more stringent regulations to the most risky banks in order to ensure that bank supervisors truthfully report their information at the lowest social cost.

Hierarchical Supervision

It is possible that some economic or political reasons prevent the implementation of two separated bank supervisors. For example, bank supervision may entail some fixed costs, e.g. buildings and bureaucracy, that need to be duplicated when supervisory powers are split. Formally, this can be modeled as a minimal fixed budget that has to be paid to each supervisor such that $w_i \geq \underline{w}$. If two supervisors are used, the financial stability committee faces twice this constraint. Hence, the result that separating supervisory powers implies welfare gains with respect to concentrating these powers holds as long as the cost of settling a bank supervisor, i.e. $\underline{w}$, is not too large.

It is indeed possible that in countries with relatively small banking systems the costs of duplicating supervisory structures exceed the benefits of separating supervisory powers. In this case, policy makers should empower the central bank with the authority to conduct micro- as well as macro-prudential supervision. Moreover, policy makers using the insights of this chapter would like to allocate supervisory technologies to two independent units within the central bank.

However, the allocation of all supervisory powers into central banks could lead to a hierarchical structure where the unit that is responsible for micro-prudential supervision is subordinated to the authority from the unit that is responsible for macro-prudential supervision, as depicted in Figure 6.4, or vice versa. In this case, the structure of information is slightly different with respect to the two cases that we have already analyzed in this chapter. More precisely, the micro-prudential supervisor cannot observe the signal that has been gathered by the macro-prudential supervisor, as it was the case when using two independent supervisors. However, the macro-prudential supervisor, which is superior in the hierarchy, can observe the signal that has been gathered by its subordinate, as it was the case when using only one supervisor.

The differences in the structure of information lead to differences in the distortions to the optimal regulatory policy. In particular, the distortions introduced by using hierarchical supervision are between the distortions introduced by using only one bank supervisor and the distortions introduced by using two bank supervisors. The distortions are larger than in the case in which two bank supervisors are used because the informational advantage of the macro-prudential supervisor allows him to request larger bribes from the banker. However, the distortions are smaller than in the case in which only one bank supervisor is used because the micro-prudential supervisor is only partially informed.

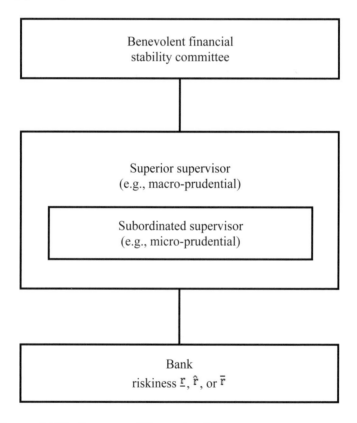

Figure 6.4 The Structure of Hierarchical Supervision

Comparison of Supervisory Arrangements

The three supervisory arrangements lead to different distortions to the optimal regulatory policy. In particular, the single-supervisor arrangement implies more capital restrictions for banks of riskiness $\bar{r}$ and $\hat{r}$ with respect to the case of benevolent supervision. Meanwhile, the two-supervisors arrangement implies no distortion for banks of riskiness $\hat{r}$ and further distortions for the most risky banks (i.e., for banks of riskiness $\bar{r}$). Finally, a hierarchy of bank supervisors introduces intermediate distortions between those under the single bank supervisor and those with separation of supervisory powers. Since the distortions generated go in opposite directions, the ranking of supervisory arrangements in terms of social welfare is then ambiguous. However, in Boyer and Ponce (2010) we prove that, from an ex ante point of view, the increase of social welfare from using two non-benevolent bank supervisors instead of only one non-benevolent bank supervisor is at least equal to zero. Moreover, a hierarchical structure of banking supervision improves social welfare with respect to using only one bank supervisor but does strictly worse than using two independent bank supervisors.

Splitting supervisory powers into two different bank supervisors reduces the social cost of obtaining two informative signals about the riskiness of the bank. Otherwise stated, it is less expensive for the financial stability committee to be informed by two bank supervisors endowed with separate risk-specific supervisory technologies, than by only one bank supervisor endowed with the two supervisory technologies. Under the two-supervisor arrangement, each bank supervisor is partially informed about the riskiness of the bank. Whereas a single supervisor may be perfectly informed about the riskiness of the bank and may use such a piece of information to ask for bribes that could never be requested under separation of supervisors. Hence, an optimal response to the threat of capture is the design of two separate supervisory entities with precise objectives and specific supervisory technologies. The separation of supervisory tasks introduces more rules to banking supervision and improves social welfare by reducing the discretion of bank supervisors. Each supervisor receives a single mission, i.e. to monitor a single dimension of risk, and follows stringent rules.

In the case of hierarchical supervision, the informational advantage of the macro-prudential supervisor implies that the hierarchical structure does strictly worse than having two independent supervisors. However, the lack of an informational advantage by the micro-prudential supervisor implies that the social welfare improves with respect to the case in which only one supervisor is used.

Concluding Remarks

In this chapter, we analyze whether or not the same bank supervisor should conduct both micro- and macro-prudential supervision when supervisors' capture is a concern. We find that supervisory tasks should be split into more than one bank supervisor. The concentration of supervisory powers in the hands of a single supervisor makes the capture of the supervisor by the banking industry more likely. Hence, it is more costly for a benevolent financial stability committee to provide incentives. The separation of supervisory responsibilities appears as an optimal organizational response to the threat of capture. Separation leads to more rules and reduces supervisors' discretion to pursue their private agendas by limiting the information at their disposal.

The results of our formal analysis have straightforward policy implications that inform current efforts to reform the architecture of banking supervision: the powers to conduct micro- and macro-prudential supervision should be allocated to different supervisors. A series of reform proposals that have been envisaged in the aftermath of the subprime crisis aim however to concentrate supervisory powers (both micro- and macro-prudential supervision) into central banks. Hence, our results suggest that policy makers would like to reconsider the current trend toward the concentration of supervisory powers because the monopoly in information acquisition may be a curse when capture is a concern.

Reconsidering the concentration trend of supervisory powers into central banks does not imply that central banks should have no role in banking supervision. There are good reasons for central banks to oversight the stability of the whole financial system. Nowadays it seems to be a consensus among academics and policy makers on the need that central banks conduct macro-prudential supervision. Hence, policy makers using the insights of this chapter would like to allocate micro-prudential supervision to a different supervisor from the central bank.

References

Abrams, B. and R. Settle (1993), 'Pressure-group influence and institutional change: Branch-banking legislation during the great depression', *Public Choice*, **77**, 687–705.

Acharya, V. and M. Richardson (eds) (2009), *Restoring financial stability*, New York, NJ, USA: John Wiley and Sons.

Barth, J.R., G. Caprio, and R. Levine (2004), 'Bank regulation and supervision: What works best?', *Journal of Financial Intermediation,* **117**(13), 205–248.

Blinder, A. (2010), 'How central should the central bank be', *Journal of Economic Literature*, **48**(1), 123–133.

Boot, A.W. and A.V. Thakor (1993), 'Self-interested bank regulation.' *American Economic Review*, **83**(2), 206–212.

Boyer, P.C. and J. Ponce (2010), 'Central banks, regulatory capture and banking supervision reform.' *Paolo Baffi Centre on Central Banking and Financial Regulation Research Paper Series, No. 2010–83,* Paolo Baffi Centre on Central Banking and Financial Regulation, Bocconi University.

Brunnermeier, M., A. Crocket, C. Goodhart, A. Persaud, and H. Shin (2009), 'The fundamental principles of financial regulation' *VoXEU.org.*

Claeys, S., and K. Schoors (2007), 'Bank supervision Russian style: Evidence of conflicts between micro- and macro-prudential concerns' *Journal of Comparative Economics*, **35**, 630–657.

Dewatripont, M., I. Jewitt and J. Tirole (1999a), 'The economics of career concerns, part I: Comparing information structures' *Review of Economic Studies*, **66**(1), 183–198.

Dewatripont, M., I. Jewitt and J. Tirole (1999b), 'The economics of career concerns, part II: Application to missions and accountability of government agencies' *Review of Economic Studies*, **66**(1), 199–217.

Di Giorgio, G. and C. Di Noia (1999), 'Should banking supervision and monetary policy tasks be given to different agencies?' *International Finance*, **3**.

Djankov, S., R. La Porta, F. Lopez-de Silanes and A. Shleifer (2002), 'The regulation of entry' *Quarterly Journal of Economics*, **117**(1), 1–37.

Gabillon, E. and D. Martimort (2004), 'The benefit of central bank's political independence' *European Economic Review*, **48**, 353–378.

Goodhart, C. and D. Schoenmaker (1995), 'Should the functions of monetary policy and banking supervision be separated?' *Oxford Economic Papers*, **47**, 539–560.

Hardy, D. (2006), Regulatory capture in banking. *IMF Working Paper* 06/34.

Heinemann, F. and M. Schüler (2004), 'A stiglerian view on banking supervision', *Public Choice*, **121**(1), 99–130.

Kahn, C.M. and J.A. Santos (2005), 'Allocating bank regulatory powers: Lender of last resort, deposit insurance and supervision', *European Economic Review*, **49**, 2107–2136.

Kahn, C.M. and J.A. Santos (2006), 'Who should act as lender of last resort? An incomplete contracts model: A comment', *Journal of Money, Credit and Banking*, **38**(4), 1111–1118.

Kane, E.J. (1990a), 'Principal-agent problems in S&L salvage', *Journal of Finance*, **45**(3), 755–764.

Kane, E.J. (1990b), *The S&L insurance mess: How did it happen?* Urban Institute Press.

Kane, E.J. (2001), 'Dynamic inconsistency of capital forbearance: Long-run vs. short run effects of too-big-to-fail policymaking', *Pacific Basin Financial Journal*, **9**(4), 281–299.

Kofman, F. and J. Lawarre (1993), 'Collusion in hierarchical agency', *Econometrica*, **61**(3), 629–656.

Laffont, J.-J. and D. Martimort (1997), 'Collusion under asymmetric information', *Econometrica*, **65**, 875–911.

Laffont, J.-J. and D. Martimort (1999), 'Separation of regulators against collusive behavior', *RAND Journal of Economics*, **30**(2), 232–262.

Laffont, J.-J. and D. Martimort (2000), 'Mechanism design with collusion and correlation', *Econometrica*, **68**(2), 309–342.

Laffont, J.-J. and J. Tirole (1993), *A theory of incentives in procurement and regulation*. Cambridge, MA, USA: The MIT Press.

Masciandaro, D. (1995), 'Designing a central bank: Social player, monetary agent or banking agent?', *Open Economies Review*, **6**, 399–410.

Masciandaro, D. (2004), 'Unification in financial sector supervision: The trade off between central bank and single authority', *Journal of Financial Regulation and Compliance*, **12**(2).

Peek, J. E. Rosengren and G. Tootell (1999), 'Is bank supervision central to central banking?', *Quarterly Journal of Economics*, **114**, 629–653.

Perotti, E. and J. Suarez (2009), 'Liquidity risk charges as a macroprudential tool' *Centre for Economic Policy Research, Policy Insight* **40**.

Ponce, J. (2010), 'Lender of last resort policy: What reforms are necessary?', *Journal of Financial Intermediation*, **19**(2), 188–206.

Quintyn, M. and M. Taylor (2002), 'Regulatory and supervisory independence and financial stability', *IMF Working Paper* 02/46.

Repullo, R. (2000), 'Who should act as lender of last resort? An incomplete contracts model', *Journal of Money, Credit and Banking*, **32**(3), 580–605.

Shin, H. (2010), Non-core liabilities tax as a tool for prudential regulation. Policy Memo.

The Conservative Party (2009), From crisis to confidence: Plan for sound banking. *Policy White Paper.*

7. Institutional Structure and Effectiveness of Central Banks during the Financial Crisis: An Empirical Analysis

Yiwei Fang, Iftekhar Hasan and Loretta J. Mester[1]

Introduction

A central bank is crucial for the functioning of any economy, since it is responsible for setting the country's monetary policy in order to achieve long-run price stability, sustainable economic growth, and a stable financial system. Given a central bank's importance, there is a large literature in economics examining how various central bank characteristics could influence the effectiveness of monetary policy. For example, the literature discusses the legal and institutional frameworks governing central banks throughout the world. Nowadays, it is widely accepted that central bank independence, accountability, and transparency are associated with more effective monetary policy and better economic outcomes (e.g., Grilli, et al., 1991; Cukierman, et al., 1992; Berger, et al., 2001; Eijffinger and Geraats, 2006; Hayo and Voigt, 2008). More recently, some attention has turned to the internal governance mechanisms of central banks (Lybek and Morris, 2004; Frisell, et al. 2007; Hasan and Mester, 2008). In light of some of the corporate governance literature, these studies argue that features of the governing body of the central bank, such as delegated boards of directors and the design of the optimal

---

[1]The views expressed in this paper are those of the authors and do not necessarily represent those of the Federal Reserve Bank of Philadelphia, the Board of Governors of the Federal Reserve System, or the Bank of Finland.

contract for bank supervisory tasks, are essential to achieving its objectives effectively and efficiently.

While much has been written about various central bank characteristics and the performance of the real economy, there is little work relating central bank governance structure to the performance of the banking sector. Given the vital role of bank intermediation in the economic growth of nations (Beck, et al., 2000; Levine, 2005), and given the regulatory reforms that are occurring in the aftermath of the recent financial crisis, it is important to have a good understanding of the role central bank governance plays in promoting banking performance from a policy perspective. Indeed, problems with banking sectors may not be as salient during good economic times when everyone is making money and bank credit is plentiful. However, in times of financial crisis, banking institutions face massive losses and liquidity stress. Numerous moral hazard problems and information asymmetry in financial intermediation might also arise. As a financial regulatory institution and as a lender-of-last-resort, a central bank typically plays a crucial role not only in setting monetary policy, but also in stabilizing and promoting the development of the financial system.

As suggested by the recent research findings in the corporate governance literature, we evaluate central bank governance structure by central banks' board size (number of directors), board independence (percentage of the board that are outside directors), governor turnover, and whether a governor has commercial banking experience. In addition to these internal governance mechanisms, we also look at central banks' financial supervisory role. To measure banking performance at a country level, we obtain bank-level financial data from 28 countries over the period of 2001–2008 and then calculate the mean value for profitability, loan losses, credit growth, and the cost-to-income ratio as proxies for banking sector performance. We first test whether there is a significant relationship between governance characteristics and banking performance during good economic times (2001–2006), controlling for various other country-level factors. To shed light on the recent financial crisis, we then examine whether, during the financial crisis period (2007–2008), the relationship between central bank governance features and banking sector performance differed from that found during normal times.

Our findings reveal some significant relationships between central bank governance characteristics and banking performance. When the economy is good, smaller board size, lower governor turnover, having commercial banking experience, and having financial supervisory responsibility are associated with higher profitability and lower operating costs of the banking sector. The relationships between board independence, governor turnover, and commercial banking experience on banking performance are statistically significantly different in the recent crisis period than they were before the crisis. We find that during the crisis period, greater board independence is associated with higher banking profits but lower credit growth, while higher governor turnover is related to higher profitability and credit growth. Governors' commercial banking experience is associated with lower loan losses and greater credit growth during the crisis period.

Some results are quite interesting. For example, the corporate finance literature generally suggests that outside board members are good monitors since they are independent and reputable (e.g., Perry and Peyer, 2005), while there is also evidence that outside directors are usually too busy to provide effective monitoring (Fich and Shivdasani, 2006). Our finding provides some new insights to the debate. During good economic times, outside board directors might not be as effective, since they are busy and they put in less effort. However, when the firm (in our case, the central bank) is operating in a difficult time, outside board members provide valuable inputs. Their expertise and reputation outweigh concerns of busy directorship during the crisis. As for the governor turnover, some research suggests that high turnover may indicate instability and less independence from the government, which might have a negative impact on central bank effectiveness (Berger, et al., 2001; Cukierman, et al., 1992). Our findings on this variable in the analysis of the pre-crisis period support this argument. However, we also find that governor turnover has a positive influence on banking performance during the crisis period and the coefficient estimates are significantly different from those of pre-crisis regression. We thus argue that greater governor turnover may indicate higher market discipline and monitoring from the government. During the crisis period, high governor turnover could be seen as a good governance mechanism. Arguably, it is possible that our central bank governance variables might capture some omitted factors that could affect banking performance. To deal with this concern, we control for various country-level factors, including share of the banking sector that is foreign owned, banking market concentration, country governance, macroeconomic conditions (GDP per capita and inflation), and financial structure of a nation. We therefore interpret our results as indicating that besides the main country-level factors, central bank governance structures also play a significant role in banking system performance.

This chapter contributes to the literature in several ways. First, as far as we know, it is the first effort to analyze the link between central bank governance structure and banking sector performance. Far from having a neutral effect, we show that various internal governance features as well as the supervisory regime of the central bank are all related to banking sector profitability, loan losses, and credit growth. In this regard, our study complements a number of recent papers, including Hasan and Mester (2008), who find that the board structure of central banks significantly affects the effectiveness of monetary policy on the real economy. Second, our research contributes to another stream of the literature that looks at country-level determinants of banking development. This literature has identified various factors related to financial development such as macroeconomic conditions, foreign bank presence, market competition structure, institutional environment, and bank regulation (e.g., Demirgüç-Kunt and Huizinga, 2000; Barth, et al., 2001; Laeven and Levine, 2009). However, the governance role of central banks and the possible trade-offs among achieving monetary policy, financial stability, and banking sector efficiency have received relatively little attention. This Chapter helps fill this void. Last, by focusing our study on the recent financial crisis we also bring additional insights to the growing literature on organizational form and central bank performance. Specifically, if we view the financial crisis as a set of 'exogenous shocks,' this reduces the endogeneity concern (Cukierman, Webb, and Neyapti, 1992) and we can ask, for example, whether organizational form causes good performance, or whether good performance leads to particular central bank organizational characteristics. Because the recent financial crisis affected many countries, including advanced and developing economies, we are able to conduct a cross-country comparison among central banks with varying institutional characteristics. In this regard, our paper complements prior studies that focused only on a single country's experience of a financial crisis.

The rest of the chapter is organized as follows. Section two discusses the literature on central bank governance structures and banking performance. Section three describes our data and methodology and provides some descriptive statistics. In Section four we present our empirical results. The final section concludes.

Literature Review

Central bank governance

The corporate finance literature has long recognized the importance of corporate governance. It suggests that delegated boards of directors, monitoring by large-block shareholders, and optimal management contracts are essential in ensuring that an organization achieves its objectives effectively and efficiently (Shleifer and Vishny, 1997; Hermalin and Weisbach, 1991; Murphy, 1999). Applying governance concepts to central banks, Shleifer and Vishny (1998) indicate that since there are multiple layers of delegation and political intervention, central banks are likely to suffer from diluted monitoring incentives. Moreover, as bankers' banks and lenders of last resort, they are also susceptible to the intrinsic opaqueness of the banking business as well as to the risk of the banks they regulate (Adams and Mehran, 2003; Caprio et al., 2004). Frisell, et al. (2007) discuss additional features of internal governance mechanisms that may apply to central banks. They argue that the only internal mechanisms that are likely to be effective are board supervision and incentive contracts. External governance mechanisms are almost absent for central banks because they are insulated from competition and the market for corporate control.

Some related literature also looks at the role of central bank governor in the process of making monetary policy. Kuttner and Posen (2010) find that markets react significantly to the appointment of a central bank governor, which also suggests that who the central bank governor is matters for the effectiveness of monetary policy. Berger et al. (2001) and Cukierman, et al. (1992) examine the turnover rate of the central bank governor (or chairman of the board). They suggest that a higher turnover rate indicates less independence from the government, which might have a negative impact on central bank effectiveness, but it could also signal the exit of less effective management. Göhlmann and Vaubel (2007) show that the education and profession of central bankers affect their effectiveness in controlling inflation.

Reform of the financial supervisory role of central banks also involves central bank governance issues. Nowadays, the supervisory framework of central banks is much more diversified than before. In some countries, such as the Netherlands, Austria, Belgium, and Germany, national central banks are no longer directly responsible for prudential supervision. In other countries, like Finland and transition countries involved in the EU enlargement process, supervisory powers are concentrated in the central bank. In the UK, micro-prudential bank regulation which had been moved from the Bank of England into the newly formed Financial Services Authority before the recent financial crisis is now being moved back (HM Treasury, July 2010). And in the US, bank supervision is shared among several agencies including the Federal Reserve, the Office of the Comptroller of the Currency, and the Federal Deposit Insurance Corporation. In the literature, the main argument in favor of the central bank's involvement in supervision is that a single supervisor could deal with supervisory problems more flexibly than multiple agencies (Abrams and Taylor, 2002, Čihák and Podpiera, 2007). Especially during the crisis, having a powerful supervisor might make policy more effective (Goodhart and Schoenmaker, 1995, Bernanke, 2007, Herring and Carmassi, 2008). An additional argument is linked to the efficiency gains from central bank capacity in skilled staff and physical infrastructure (Abrams and Taylor, 2002, Quintyn and Taylor, 2007). However, there are also arguments against unification of financial supervision. Schoenmaker (1992) demonstrates that a central bank with a concentration of power in financial supervision may face conflicts of interest among multiple objectives. On the one hand, as banking supervisors, central banks are obligated to ensure a sound banking system, and therefore, they might choose to hold down interest rates when price stability considerations might require higher rates. Hence, simultaneously striving for price stability and financial stability involves a time-dependent trade-off. Boot and Thakor (1993) argue that supervisory tasks within central banks could create some moral hazard problems in the banking system. In particular, banks might take on excessive risk if they thought that a central bank charged with supervisory responsibilities would be more likely to rescue them and provide emergency liquidity assistance. To protect their reputations, central banks might be induced to do this to cover up failures in supervisions.

Country-level determinants of banking development

Research in the banking literature has examined various country-level factors that may have a significant impact on banking performance. In a comprehensive study and using bank data for 80 countries, Demirgüç-Kunt and Huizinga (2000) show that differences in interest margins and bank profitability reflect a variety of determinants, such as bank characteristics, macroeconomic conditions, explicit and implicit bank taxation, deposit insurance regulation, overall financial structure, and several underlying legal and institutional indicators. They also find that foreign banks, as opposed to domestic banks, tend to have higher profits in developing countries, while the opposite holds in developed countries. Regarding the role of foreign ownership, various authors have reached similar conclusions, finding that foreign ownership is positively related to higher profit margins because foreign banks are better capitalized, have better governance structure and management expertise, and have parent banks as a safeguard (Hellman and Murdock, 1998; Moreno and Villar, 2005; Detragiache, et al., 2008; Hasan and Marton, 2003; Bonin et al., 2005).

Banking competition and financial structure may also significantly influence banking performance, although the direction of the effect is ambiguous. Some theoretical arguments suggest that a concentrated banking market may lead to enhanced market power, higher bank profits, and less chance of crisis (Allen and Gale, 2000, 2004; Beck, et al., 2006). An opposing view is that in a more concentrated banking market bank managers could enjoy a quiet life and therefore underperform (Berger and Hannan, 1998). Financial stability may also be reduced when banks have a lot of market power (Caminal and Matutes, 2002; Boyd and De Nicolo, 2005). Thus, theory provides conflicting predictions on whether market competition curtails or promotes bank performance. Several studies have examined the impact of international differences in bank regulation using cross-country data. In an earlier study, Barth, et al. (2001) find that greater regulatory restrictions are associated with a higher probability of a major banking crisis and lower banking-sector efficiency. They do not find countervailing positive effects from restricting banking-sector activities. Some studies examine the impact of institutional development on bank performance. Earlier empirical evidence shows that a weak institutional environment makes banking crises more likely (Demirgüç-Kunt and Detragiache, 1997). Demirgüç-Kunt and Huizinga (2000) show that several institutional factors, such as indices of credit rights and law and order and corruption, have more pronounced effects on interest margins and bank profitability in developing countries than in developed countries.

Data and Methodology

Measuring characteristics of central bank governance

To capture central bank governance structure, we focus on variables that are related to board composition, governor characteristics, and bank supervisory regimes that could potentially be correlated with the performance of the banking system. Our measures, which do not vary over our sample period for the countries included in this study, are as follows:

Directors = logarithm of the number of directors on the central bank's governing board;

Outside directors = percentage of the central bank's governing board that are outside directors;

Commercial banking experience = 1 if the central bank governor had worked in commercial banking before being appointed as governor;

Governor turnover = average rate of turnover of central bank governors since 1993, measured as the total number of years left in a term since 1993 as a percentage of the length of a governor's term specified by law divided by the number of governors since 1993;

Supervision = 1 if the central bank has bank supervisory responsibilities as well as monetary policy responsibilities and 0 otherwise.

Measuring banking sectors' performance

BankScope provides various bank-level financial variables. To measure country-level banking sector performance, we calculate the mean values of the following variables for each country each year by averaging over all banks with available information.

ROAA and ROAE: We measure profitability of the banking sector by these two ratios. ROAA is defined as return on average assets at a country level. ROAE is return on average equity at a country level. They are calculated by averaging bank-level ratios for each country each year. We expect that better quality central bank governance should be positively associated with ROAA and ROAE.

NPL and Relative Equity Ratio: These two measures are used to proxy for the financial stability of the banking sector. Specifically, NPL is the average of nonperforming loans divided by total loans. Everything else equal, we would expect the quality of central bank governance to be negatively related to NPL. Relative Equity Ratio is measured as the average of (total equity divided by total assets) minus the regulatory minimum capital ratio, which is 8 percent. We would expect that central bank governance should be positively related to the relative equity ratio to the extent that better governance would imply that the supervisor is less likely to be practicing forbearance and leaving undercapitalized banks open.

Asset Growth and Loan Growth: These two measures are used to capture industry growth and credit availability of the banking sector. Various empirical studies have uncovered evidence that bank credit sharply dropped in many countries during the financial crisis, especially after the Lehman collapse (e.g. Ivashina and Scharfstein, 2010; Aisen and Franken, 2010). The shortage of capital flows and the contraction of credit growth forced financially constrained firms to reduce investments (Duchin, et al.,

2010), which could ultimately affect long-term growth and development. As lender-of-last-resort, effective central banks try to ensure the continuation of bank funding and restore the confidence of market participants in the financial system. However, ensuring that banks are not lowering credit standards to engage in excessively leveraged asset growth might also be an appropriate strategy for central banks charged with financial supervisory responsibilities.

Cost Ratio: This measures the country average bank operating cost to income ratio in a sample year. A higher cost ratio suggests more expense and less cost efficiency (Berger and Hannan, 1998). We therefore would expect it to be negatively related to the effectiveness of central bank supervision.

Country governance, competition and macroeconomic controls

To control for country-level factors that are likely to affect banking sector performance, we include GDP per capita and inflation as proxies for economic development and stability. In addition, we consider several variables that are related to country-level governance, banking market competition, and foreign ownership.

KKZ index: This is an index of country-level governance constructed by Kaufmann, Kraay, and Mastruzzi (2008). The underlying indicators capture different dimensions of governance, which include political stability, government effectiveness, regulatory quality, rule of law, and government accountability and transparency. We sum individual indicators and use the aggregated value as a proxy for the overall level of country governance. We would expect a positive relationship between country governance and banking sector performance.

Foreign ownership: This is the percentage of foreign bank ownership in a given country. This information is obtained from Barth, et al. (2004). Recent cross-country studies on banking performance emphasize the importance of ownership structure (e.g., Demirgüç-Kunt and Huizinga, 2000; Laeven and Levine, 2009). Based on the literature, one would expect foreign ownership to be positively related to higher profit margins because foreign banks have been found to be better capitalized, to have better governance structure and management expertise, and to have parent banks that act as a safeguard (Hellman and Murdock, 1998; Moreno and Villar, 2005; Detragiache, et al., 2008). However, during the recent financial crisis, which originated in developed countries, a greater presence of foreign ownership could be seen as a channel of risk contagion. The experience during the financial crisis provides evidence that more integrated financial markets can be more exposed to financial turmoil due to contagion. Therefore, countries with less exposure to foreign banks might exhibit less volatility because they have lower access to capital flows from developed countries.

Bank concentration: This is a proxy for banking market structure, which is measured by the fraction of assets held by the three largest banks in the country in a given year. Regarding its impact on bank performance, some theoretical arguments suggest that a concentrated banking market may lead to enhanced market power, higher bank profits, and less probability of crisis (Demirgüç-Kunt and Huizinga, 2000; Allen and Gale, 2000 and 2004; Beck, et al., 2006). An opposing view is that in a more concentrated banking market bank managers could enjoy a quiet life and therefore underperform (Berger and Hannan, 1998). Financial stability may also be reduced when banks have high market power (Caminal and Matutes, 2002; Boyd and De Nicolo, 2005).

Mkt_vs_bk: This is an indicator equal to 1 if the financial system of a country is market-based and 0 if it is bank-based. We use it as a proxy for financial structure. According to Demirgüç-Kunt and Huizinga (2000), a larger stock market capitalization to GDP reflects possible complementarities between debt and equity financing and therefore could be negatively related to bank profitability but positively related to bank asset growth.

CB Independence: This is a dummy variable equal to 1 if the central bank is not part of the Ministry of Finance and can implement monetary policy without the direct approval of the government, and 0 otherwise.

Descriptive statistics

After cleaning the raw data, our final sample comprises 28 major economies from 2001 to 2008. Table 7.1 reports the countries and statistics on their average banking performance during our full sample period, 2001–2008. Table 7.2 reports the average banking performance of these countries in each year.

Table 7.1 Summary of banking performance measures of individual countries

Country	ROAA	ROAE	NPL	Asset growth	Loan growth	Cost ratio	Relative equity ratio
ARGENTINA	0.011	0.054	0.135	0.098	0.122	0.764	0.145
AUSTRALIA	0.010	0.109	0.008	0.020	0.041	0.610	0.051
BRAZIL	0.024	0.142	0.100	0.160	0.154	0.612	0.126
CANADA	0.012	0.084	0.013	-0.040	-0.029	0.669	0.060
CHINA	0.007	0.131	0.081	0.118	0.118	0.490	0.008
CZECH REPUBLIC	0.009	0.127	0.088	0.106	0.190	0.638	0.020
ESTONIA	0.018	0.155	0.027	-0.090	-0.054	0.626	0.095
GERMANY	0.006	0.049	0.042	0.066	0.072	0.710	0.070
HUNGARY	0.014	0.133	0.049	0.164	0.200	0.720	0.048
INDIA	0.010	0.155	0.071	0.212	0.260	0.509	0.000
ITALY	0.007	0.073	0.042	0.029	0.049	0.700	0.050
JAPAN	0.002	0.002	0.081	0.024	0.023	0.687	0.013
LATVIA	0.014	0.157	0.022	0.301	0.404	0.639	0.042
LITHUANIA	0.009	0.100	0.031	0.291	0.414	0.731	0.017
MEXICO	0.016	0.096	0.035	0.166	0.095	0.725	0.105
NETHERLANDS	0.014	0.091	0.018	0.059	0.064	0.577	0.104
NORWAY	0.010	0.078	0.015	0.165	0.127	0.663	0.079
POLAND	0.012	0.107	0.151	0.158	0.197	0.684	0.049
PORTUGAL	0.013	0.084	0.024	0.095	0.130	0.630	0.099

Table 7.1 Continued

Country	ROAA	ROAE	NPL	Asset growth	Loan growth	Cost ratio	Relative equity ratio
RUSSIA	0.018	0.117	0.025	0.072	0.147	0.651	0.123
SAUDI ARABIA	0.028	0.236	0.038	0.121	0.196	0.358	0.039
SLOVENIA	0.010	0.088	0.090	0.224	0.271	0.597	0.016
SOUTH AFRICA	0.025	0.159	0.095	0.228	0.224	0.624	0.197
SPAIN	0.007	0.083	0.017	0.232	0.286	0.613	0.051
SWITZERLAND	0.017	0.091	0.025	0.032	-0.017	0.661	0.126
TURKEY	0.025	0.141	0.079	0.071	0.187	0.607	0.137
UNITED KINGDOM	0.012	0.083	0.039	-0.027	-0.008	0.646	0.137
UNITED STATES	0.010	0.104	0.011	0.057	0.051	0.636	0.029

Notes: Our sample covers 8 years from 2001 to 2008. Table 7.2 reports the mean of various banking performance measures for each year. *ROAA* is country average return on assets. *ROAE* is country average return on equity. *NPL* is nonperforming loans to total loans ratio. *Relative equity ratio* refers to the equity divided by total assets minus regulatory minimum (8%). *Asset growth* is the growth rate of total assets from last year. *Loan growth* is the growth rate of total loans from last year. *Cost ratio* is total operating expense divided by total revenue.

Table 7.2 Summary of banking performance over years

Year	ROAA	ROAE	NPL	Asset growth	Loan growth	Cost ratio	Relative equity ratio
2001	0.011	0.092	0.070	0.051	0.068	0.654	0.073
2002	0.011	0.082	0.082	0.128	0.129	0.678	0.085
2003	0.013	0.107	0.063	0.109	0.139	0.655	0.071
2004	0.013	0.105	0.047	0.057	0.112	0.650	0.074
2005	0.015	0.130	0.038	0.111	0.168	0.617	0.068
2006	0.017	0.134	0.037	0.116	0.157	0.598	0.072
2007	0.016	0.135	0.034	0.134	0.145	0.597	0.073
2008	0.010	0.080	0.043	0.186	0.193	0.623	0.061

Table 7.3 reports the summary statistics of the analysis variables. Measures of banking sector performance are comparable with recent studies. Turning to central bank organizational structure, the average board size is 9.241, and on average, outside directors make up about 19.3 percent of the board. The mean (median) governor turnover rate

is 19.8 percent (15 percent), meaning that on average, each governor serves 80.2 percent of his/her full term (and that half of the governors serve less than 85 percent and half the governors serve more than 85 percent of their full terms).

We find that 64.5 percent of the governors have worked in commercial banking and that among the 28 central banks in our sample, 46.4 percent have a responsibility to oversee commercial banks of the country, and 32.3 percent are independent of government intervention in implementing monetary policy. Our other controls indicate that foreign bank ownership averages 31 percent; banking concentration (as measured by the asset share of the three largest banks) is 47.7 percent; country-level corporate governance (as measured by the KKG index) is 4.569. In our sample, 43.2 percent of our countries have market-based financial systems. The GDP per capita on average is $20,025.8 in US dollars, and inflation averages 4.4 percent.

Table 7.3 Descriptive statistics of key variables

Variable	N	mean	p50	sd	min	max
Banking performance						
ROAA	220	0.013	0.012	0.008	-0.003	0.049
ROAE	220	0.108	0.110	0.060	-0.133	0.346
NPL	220	0.052	0.033	0.051	0.003	0.345
Asset_growth	220	0.112	0.109	0.204	-0.664	0.838
Loan_growth	220	0.139	0.146	0.216	-0.661	0.749
Cost_income_ratio	220	0.634	0.645	0.098	0.267	0.934
Relative_Equity_ratio	220	0.072	0.061	0.054	-0.015	0.292
Central bank characteristics						
Directors	220	9.241	8.000	4.817	3.000	24.000
Outsidedirs_pct	220	0.193	0.092	0.249	0.000	0.842
Gov_turnover	220	0.198	0.150	0.182	0.000	0.930
Commercial_banking_exp	220	0.645	1.000	0.479	0.000	1.000
Supervisory	220	0.464	0.000	0.500	0.000	1.000
Other controls						
CB independence	220	0.323	0.000	0.469	0.000	1.000
Foreign ownership	220	0.310	0.184	0.315	0.019	0.989
Bank concentration	220	0.477	0.461	0.203	0.059	0.984
KKZ	220	4.569	5.302	4.460	-4.604	11.127
GDP_percap	220	20025.8	13960.8	17197.0	462.8	94567.9
Inflation	220	0.044	0.031	0.048	0.000	0.450
Mkt_vs_bank	220	0.432	0.000	0.496	0.000	1.000

Regression Analysis

Regressions on banking performance during pre-crisis period

First, we examine the impact that central bank governance structure has on banking sector performance during the pre-crisis period from 2001 to 2006. The estimation equation is as follows:

$$P_{i,t} = \alpha_0 + \alpha_t + \sum \beta_t \cdot \text{(central bank characteristics)}_i +$$
$$+ \sum \gamma_t \cdot \text{(country governance and bank competition)}_l + \quad (7.1)$$
$$+ \sum \delta_t \cdot \text{(macroeconomic controls)}_{i,t} + \varepsilon_{i,t}$$

where i indexes individual countries, and t indexes year. Our dependent variables ($P_{i,t}$) are banking performance measures of country i in year t, and the key independent variables are various central bank characteristics, including board size, percentage of the board that are outside directors, governor turnover rate, an indicator of a governor's commercial banking experience, and an indicator of a central bank's responsibility for banking supervision. The model also has year fixed effects (denoted by α_t), and controls for country governance, banking competition, and the macroeconomy. We estimate the model using ordinary least squares. In addition, the heteroskedasticity-robust standard errors clustered at the country level are used in computing the parameters' t-values. This treatment has been shown to be important in deriving robust and reliable results in cross-country studies (Beck, Demirgüç-Kunt, and Peria, 2007). The estimation results are reported in Table 7.4.

In column one and column two, we examine the relationship between central bank governance and the profitability of banking sectors. We find that the coefficients on *directors* in the ROAA and ROAE regressions are negative and significant, which suggests that smaller board size is correlated with higher banking profitability. This finding supports the argument that a larger board might hinder efficient decision making because it makes it more difficult to reach a consensus or to achieve individual accountability. Another interesting finding is that *governor turnover* also has a strong and negative correlation with banking sector profitability. The effect is both statistically and economically significant. Some of the literature, for example, Berger, et al. (2001) and Cukierman, et al. (1992), has examined the turnover rate of the central bank governor (or chairman of the board). They argue that high turnover may suggest less independence from the government, which might have a negative impact on central bank effectiveness, but it could also signal the exit of less effective management. We find that during the pre-crisis period, governor turnover is negatively correlated with banking sector profitability.

Table 7.4 Regression results on banking performance during pre-crisis period (2001–2006)

VARIABLES	(1) ROAA	(2) ROAE	(3) NPL	(4) Relative equity ratio	(5) Asset growth	(6) Loan growth	(7) Cost ratio
Central bank characteristics							
Directors	-0.0057***	-0.0270**	-0.0046	-0.0350**	0.0356	0.0524	0.0664***
	(-3.8741)	(-2.6804)	(-0.3001)	(-2.2441)	(0.8526)	(1.2712)	(5.5502)
Outsidedirs_pct	0.0032	0.0241	0.0672	0.0491	-0.0162	-0.0615	-0.0542
	(1.4352)	(0.8204)	(1.5464)	(1.4518)	(-0.1875)	(-0.6222)	(-1.6496)
Gov_turnover	-0.0140***	-0.1459***	0.0907*	0.0590	-0.0843	-0.0559	0.2189***
	(-4.3266)	(-5.8184)	(2.0423)	(1.4067)	(-0.9644)	(-0.4913)	(7.0066)
Commercial banking_exp	0.0032**	0.0223	-0.0254	-0.0036	-0.0267	-0.0149	-0.0605***
	(2.1622)	(1.4748)	(-1.1201)	(-0.1991)	(-0.5617)	(-0.2793)	(-3.4949)
Supervisory	0.0018	0.0294**	-0.0224	-0.0088	0.0461	0.0944*	-0.0691***
	(1.0825)	(2.1034)	(-1.0277)	(-0.6586)	(1.0238)	(1.7967)	(-3.9039)
Country controls							
Developed	-0.0078	-0.0728	-0.0435	0.0464	-0.1283	-0.1974*	0.1452***
	(-1.4228)	(-1.5311)	(-1.1827)	(1.4686)	(-1.3387)	(-2.0396)	(3.5561)
Foreign ownership	-0.0094*	-0.0426	0.0091	-0.0118	-0.0727	-0.1283*	0.2073***
	(-2.0233)	(-1.1114)	(0.2756)	(-0.3748)	(-0.9817)	(-1.7189)	(6.1843)
Bank concentration	0.0054	0.0399	-0.0528	0.0290	0.1036	0.1714	-0.0021
	(1.4013)	(1.0596)	(-1.1968)	(0.7141)	(0.8377)	(1.4414)	(-0.0435)
KKZ	-0.0006	0.0019	0.0024	-0.0082**	0.0090	0.0077	-0.0109**
	(-1.2208)	(0.4765)	(0.7774)	(-2.5605)	(0.8830)	(0.6925)	(-2.4905)
GDP_percap	0.0024**	-0.0069	0.0034	0.0204*	-0.0461**	-0.0580**	0.0067
	(2.1560)	(-0.6756)	(0.2893)	(1.9436)	(-2.0641)	(-2.3964)	(0.7726)
Inflation	0.0340***	0.1328	0.0979	0.1319	-0.4132	-0.8698***	-0.3259*
	(3.3705)	(0.8806)	(0.7771)	(0.8414)	(-1.1972)	(-2.8821)	(-2.0118)
Mkt_vs_bank	0.0029	0.0175*	-0.0283*	0.0164	-0.0086	0.0279	0.0014
	(1.2101)	(1.7188)	(-2.0464)	(0.7805)	(-0.2594)	(0.7983)	(0.0879)
CB independence	-0.0068***	-0.0390***	0.0231	-0.0372**	0.0163	0.0227	0.0944***
	(-5.8391)	(-2.8388)	(1.3704)	(-2.2269)	(0.4786)	(0.6032)	(6.2818)
Constant	0.0098	0.2058**	0.1311	0.1011	0.4674*	0.4476	0.4930***
	(0.8282)	(2.4150)	(1.1167)	(0.9516)	(1.7606)	(1.6429)	(5.2820)
Year and region dummies	Yes	Yes	Yes	Yes	Yes	Yes	Yes
Observations	165	165	165	165	164	164	165
R-square	0.671	0.604	0.506	0.666	0.157	0.262	0.777
Adjusted R-square	0.6196	0.5421	0.4298	0.6138	0.0255	0.1464	0.7429

Note: OLS regression results relating central bank governance characteristics and various banking performance measures during the pre-crisis period (2001–2006). Numbers in the parentheses are robust t-statistics clustered by country. *, **, and *** denote significance at 10%, 5%, and 1%, respectively.

In column three and column four we look at whether central bank organizational variables could also influence the banking sector's riskiness, as measured by NPL (the ratio of nonperforming loans to total loans) and relative equity ratio (ratio of equity to assets minus regulatory minimum). Consistent with the negative impact of *governor turnover* on profitability, we also find that *governor turnover* is positively correlated with nonperforming loans. Also, *directors* is significantly and negatively associated with relative equity ratio ($p < 5\%$). The coefficient is -0.035, meaning that one percentage increase in the number of directors is associated with a 0.035 decrease of the equity ratio relative to the regulatory minimum. Thus, larger board size is associated with higher equity risk in the banking sector. Columns five and six show results for asset growth and loan growth. Sufficient bank credit is crucial for economic development, as discussed in Barth, et al., (2004). Therefore, we expect that central banks with good governance might allow for greater levels of lending, all else equal (i.e., holding risk constant). However, we do not find any significant associations except that *supervisory* has a positive effect on loan growth rate at 10 percent significance level. The overall results imply that during good economic times, internal governance mechanisms including board size, independence, as well as governor characteristics are not correlated with credit availability and industry growth of the banking sectors. However, the central bank having bank supervisory responsibilities is associated with greater lending activity. Column seven reports the correlates of central bank governance characteristics with the cost ratio, which is often used as a proxy for operating efficiency. We see strong relationships between all central bank governance variables and the cost ratio. In line with our previous findings on profitability, larger board size and greater governor turnover are associated with higher costs. But the central bank governor's having commercial banking experience and the central bank having bank supervisory responsibilities are negatively related to operating costs.

Regressions on banking performance during crisis

In this subsection, we examine whether, during the financial crisis period (2007–2008), the relationships among the various characteristics of central bank governance and banking performance behaved differently than in good economic times. To do so, we re-estimate equation (7.1) for 2007 and 2008. The results are reported in Table 7.5.

Table 7.5 Regression results on banking performance during crisis period (2007–2008)

VARIABLES	(8) ROAA	(9) ROAE	(10) NPL	(11) Relative equity ratio	(12) Asset growth	(13) Loan growth	(14) Cost ratio
Central bank characteristics							
Directors	-0.0077***	-0.0266	0.0143**	-0.0446**	0.1472***	0.1745**	0.0246
	(-4.6225)	(-1.6494)	(2.1404)	(-2.6115)	(2.7943)	(2.3646)	(0.8321)
Outsidedirs_pct	0.0105**	0.0679*	-0.0076	0.0825*	-0.6748***	-0.5951***	-0.1988***
	(2.2069)	(1.8989)	(-0.3780)	(1.9949)	(-4.1066)	(-3.3677)	(-3.4623)
Gov_turnover	0.0019	0.0057	0.0011	0.0403	0.2367	0.4375**	0.1367**
	(0.3814)	(0.1782)	(0.0480)	(0.7740)	(1.2432)	(2.1359)	(2.5003)
Commercial banking_exp	-0.0009	0.0032	-0.0196*	0.0093	0.2065**	0.2119**	0.0077
	(-0.3321)	(0.1514)	(-1.9350)	(0.3836)	(2.2162)	(2.1371)	(0.1918)
Supervisory	-0.0010	0.0160	0.0020	-0.0115	0.1533	0.2213**	0.0097
	(-0.3692)	(0.7121)	(0.2170)	(-0.4780)	(1.5223)	(2.2941)	(0.2377)
Country controls							
Developed	-0.0051	-0.0645	0.0009	0.0275	-0.5266**	-0.7460***	0.0427
	(-0.7084)	(-1.2218)	(0.0382)	(0.4728)	(-2.4522)	(-3.6071)	(0.6433)
Foreign ownership	-0.0066	-0.0253	0.0258	-0.0405	-0.2437	-0.3453*	0.0359
	(-1.1467)	(-0.6331)	(1.3857)	(-0.8601)	(-1.3207)	(-1.9573)	(0.6690)
Bank concentration	0.0088	0.0764*	-0.0089	-0.0201	-0.2690	-0.3366	-0.1846**
	(1.4545)	(1.7427)	(-0.5098)	(-0.3567)	(-1.1674)	(-1.3796)	(-2.2774)
KKZ	-0.0006	-0.0003	-0.0015	-0.0027	-0.0064	0.0144	0.0023
	(-1.1813)	(-0.0769)	(-0.8217)	(-0.5734)	(-0.3553)	(1.0470)	(0.4239)
GDP_percap	0.0021	-0.0063	-0.0074	0.0098	0.1079**	0.1291**	-0.0127
	(1.4318)	(-0.3899)	(-1.1810)	(0.6153)	(2.1268)	(2.1765)	(-0.4008)
Inflation	-0.0069	-0.2415	-0.1710	0.2598	-3.0895*	-2.9557*	-0.5257
	(-0.1504)	(-0.7792)	(-1.0517)	(0.6617)	(-2.0313)	(-1.9115)	(-0.9841)
Mkt_vs_bank	0.0028	0.0118	-0.0016	0.0065	0.2201**	0.1926*	-0.0059
	(0.9870)	(0.8486)	(-0.2309)	(0.2128)	(2.3113)	(1.7678)	(-0.1284)
CB independence	-0.0041*	-0.0196	0.0203**	-0.0380	-0.1896**	-0.1723**	-0.0054
	(-1.9111)	(-1.0959)	(2.4716)	(-1.5995)	(-2.6583)	(-2.2387)	(-0.1787)
Constant	-4.6007**	-0.3847	-1.6536	-1.7713	-7.0195	2.3443	-1.0175***
	(-2.2367)	(-0.1620)	(-0.6024)	(-1.0886)	(-1.4345)	(0.8198)	(-3.0312)
Year and region dummies	Yes	Yes	Yes	Yes	Yes	Yes	Yes
Observations	55	55	55	55	55	55	55
R-square	0.702	0.695	0.620	0.622	0.466	0.451	0.764
Adjusted R-square	0.5526	0.5430	0.4295	0.4332	0.1997	0.1764	0.6459

Note: OLS regression results relating central bank governance characteristics and various banking performance measures during the crisis period (2007–2008). Numbers in the parentheses are robust t-statistics clustered by country. *, **, and *** denote significance at 10%, 5%, and 1%, respectively.

We also find that different from during the pre-crisis period, during the crisis period, a higher proportion of *outside directors* is associated with a higher equity ratio, lower credit growth, and lower operating costs. The coefficients are economically as well as statistically significant. This set of findings implies that outside directors are more likely to require the banking system to enhance capital reserves, reduce cost, and enhance bank profitability. However, they also tend to restrict banks' lending activities and asset growth. Examining governor characteristics, our results reveal that during the crisis, in countries in which governors have commercial banking experience, the level of nonperforming loans and the cost ratio are lower and loan growth and asset growth are higher. This set of results highlights the benefit of a governor's commercial banking experience during the recent banking crisis.

Table 7.6 compares the estimated coefficients in the pre-crisis regression (Table 7.4) with those in the crisis regression (Table 7.5). As can be seen clearly, in the crisis period, the effects of *outside director percentage*, *governor turnover*, and *commercial banking experience* are significantly different from those before the crisis.

The board independence is more strongly associated with higher banking profits and equity reserve and lower loan losses and operating costs. It is also associated with lower asset growth and loan growth during the financial crisis. As opposed to pre-crisis periods, in crisis period higher *governor turnover* is not associated with lower banking performance. The differences in the coefficients of the two regressions are statistically significant, implying that governor turnover may have a positive influence on banking performance during the crisis period. Lastly, the positive effects of *commercial banking experience* are significantly greater on asset and loan growth, but weaker on ROAA and cost ratio during crisis period than pre-crisis period.

Table 7.6 Comparison of the coefficients across pre-crisis regression and crisis regression

VARIABLES	Diff in ROAA	Diff in ROAE	Diff in NPL	Diff in Equity ratio	Diff in Asset growth	Diff in Loan growth	Diff in Cost ratio
	(8)-(1)	(9)-(2)	(10)-(3)	(11)-(4)	(12)-(5)	(13)-(6)	(14)-(7)
Directors	-0.0020	0.0004	0.0189	-0.0096	0.1116**	0.1221	-0.0418
	(-1.2504)	(0.0325)	(1.1339)	(-1.3815)	(2.1287)	(1.6939)	(-1.4426)
Outsidedirs_pct	0.0073*	0.0438	-0.0748*	0.0335*	-0.6586***	-0.5336***	-0.1446***
	(1.7630)	(1.1818)	(-1.7299)	(1.9729)	(-4.9621)	(-3.4489)	(-3.8117)
Gov_turnover	0.0159***	0.1516***	-0.0896*	-0.0187	0.3210*	0.4933***	-0.0822*
	(5.3615)	(4.9245)	(-2.0364)	(-0.9198)	(1.8740)	(2.8384)	(-1.9140)
Commercial banking_exp	-0.0041**	-0.0191	0.0058	0.0129	0.2332***	0.2267***	0.0682**
	(-2.3767)	(-1.0873)	(0.2435)	(1.2555)	(3.0819)	(2.8065)	(2.3166)
Supervisory	-0.0028	-0.0134	0.0243	-0.0026	0.1072	0.1269	0.0788**
	(-1.4932)	(-0.7244)	(1.0783)	(-0.1947)	(1.3917)	(1.4698)	(2.4030)
Country controls	Yes	Yes	Yes	Yes	Yes	Yes	Yes
Year and region dummies	Yes	Yes	Yes	Yes	Yes	Yes	Yes

Note: This table reports the differences in coefficient estimates across pre-crisis regression and crisis regression. Numbers in the parentheses are robust t-statistics clustered by country. They are computed by nesting the two regressions. *, **, and *** denote significance at 10%, 5%, and 1%, respectively.

Regressions on performance changes

At this point, we have shown evidence that central bank board characteristics and organizational features do have significant correlations with banking industry performance, during both good economic times and crisis periods. In the following tests, we use performance changes as dependent variables to control for persistence of the banking performance from the past. Specifically, we estimate the following equations:

$$P_{i,t} - P_{i,t-1} = \phi_0 + \phi_t + \sum \rho_t \bullet \text{(central bank characteristics)}_i +$$
$$+ \sum \lambda_t \bullet \text{(country governance and bank competition)}_i + \quad (7.2)$$
$$+ \sum \eta_t \bullet \text{(macroeconomic controls)}_{i,t} + \zeta_{i,t}.$$

where i indexes individual countries, and t indexes year. $P_{i,t} - P_{i,t-1}$ represents the change in performance measures from the previous year. The key variables are the same as equation (7.1). The model also has year fixed effects (denoted by ϕ_t), country governance and banking competition controls, and macroeconomic controls. We estimate the model using ordinary least squares with the heteroskedasticity-robust standard errors clustered at the country level. As shown in Table 7.7, Panel A looks at the yearly change of banking performance of all the non-crisis years (2001–2006). Panel B looks at 2007–2008 to test performance change during the crisis period, and Panel C looks at 2006–2008 to test performance change from the pre-crisis period. 2006 is the benchmark for the non-crisis years and 2007 is the benchmark for the start of the crisis.

Panel A shows that *directors* has a negative coefficient in the pre-crisis regression, which suggests that a smaller board is associated with an increase in profitability during the pre-crisis period. This result reverses the during the crisis period. As shown in Panel B, *directors* is positively associated with a change in profitability. It is possible that at the start of the crisis, a larger board helped to bring a diversity of views and skills to the decision-making process, which arguably led to less of a reduction in profitability. As shown in Panel B, we also find negative relationships between *outside directors* and loan losses and credit growth. In line with previous findings, this result suggests that boards with more independent directors tend to be associated with lower loan losses and lower levels of banking system lending during the crisis period. Examining governor turnover, our results reveal that during the crisis period, higher turnover of the governor is positively related to the change in profitability and equity ratio, but negatively related to credit growth. Lastly, columns five and six of Panel B indicate that the governance variables are all significantly correlated with the credit growth of the banking industry. In particular, larger boards, greater governor turnover, the governor's commercial banking experience, and central bank supervisory responsibility are all related to lower asset growth and loan growth. The share of outside directors, however, is associated with higher asset growth during 2007–2008.

Table 7.7 Regressions on performance changes

Panel A: Regression on yearly change of banking performance during non-crisis period (2001–2006)

VARIABLES	(1) chg ROAA	(2) chg ROAE	(3) chg NPL	(4) chg relative equity ratio	(5) chg asset growth	(6) chg loan growth	(7) chg cost ratio
Directors	-0.0012***	-0.0016	-0.0043	-0.0038	0.0207	0.0170	0.0027
	(-2.9385)	(-0.4306)	(-1.1557)	(-1.2629)	(0.8311)	(0.6812)	(0.2710)
Outsidedirs_pct	0.0021**	0.0070	0.0033	0.0029	0.0069	0.0105	-0.0225
	(2.6049)	(1.1170)	(0.4418)	(0.4838)	(0.1660)	(0.2579)	(-1.5492)
Gov_turnover	0.0030	0.0375**	-0.0217	-0.0176*	0.0650	-0.0613	-0.0648*
	(1.3673)	(2.2129)	(-0.9275)	(-1.8911)	(0.8480)	(-0.7699)	(-1.9370)
Commercial banking_exp	0.0002	-0.0061	-0.0047	-0.0051	-0.0301	-0.0209	0.0002
	(0.4493)	(-1.6813)	(-1.0119)	(-1.4063)	(-1.0653)	(-0.7748)	(0.0254)
Supervisory	0.0002	0.0053	-0.0072	-0.0102***	0.0109	-0.0185	-0.0029
	(0.6182)	(1.1066)	(-1.1283)	(-2.7888)	(0.4287)	(-0.7503)	(-0.3919)
Constant	-0.0073*	-0.0170	0.0272	-0.0112	-0.2524	0.0139	0.0798
	(-1.7287)	(-0.6075)	(0.9846)	(-0.4335)	(-1.2007)	(0.0633)	(1.0360)
Country controls	Yes	Yes	Yes	Yes	Yes	Yes	Yes
Year and region dummies	Yes	Yes	Yes	Yes	Yes	Yes	Yes
Observations	136	136	136	136	136	136	136
R-squared	0.153	0.192	0.275	0.185	0.0581	0.0399	0.179
Adjusted R2	-0.0033	0.0435	0.1417	0.0348	-0.1170	-0.1385	0.0282

Panel B: Regression on yearly change of banking performance during crisis period (2007–2008)

VARIABLES	chg ROAA	chg ROAE	chg NPL	chg relative equity ratio	chg asset growth	chg loan growth	chg_Cost ratio
Directors	0.0065**	0.0271	0.0019	0.0245***	-0.2684**	-0.2249*	-0.0406**
	(2.7213)	(1.0303)	(0.4760)	(2.9734)	(-2.3977)	(-1.7575)	(-2.2872)
Outsidedirs_pct	-0.0034	-0.0587	-0.0228**	-0.0226	0.9895***	1.1752***	-0.0931**
	(-0.5848)	(-0.8701)	(-2.2212)	(-1.1793)	(5.1780)	(5.7350)	(-2.6911)
Gov_turnover	0.0150**	0.0786	-0.0039	0.0497**	-0.4118*	-0.2340	0.0145
	(2.2245)	(0.9548)	(-0.4874)	(2.7158)	(-1.7860)	(-0.8261)	(0.3323)
Commercial banking_exp	-0.0007	0.0229	0.0026	0.0017	-0.2539**	-0.1794	0.0381
	(-0.1940)	(0.7006)	(0.5642)	(0.1613)	(-2.1651)	(-1.4445)	(1.5710)
Supervisory	-0.0007	0.0109	0.0114***	0.0108	-0.5432***	-0.3116**	0.0322
	(-0.1588)	(0.3228)	(2.8537)	(1.2915)	(-4.6809)	(-2.5404)	(1.0465)
Constant	-0.0277***	-0.1631***	0.0302***	-0.0294	0.2669	-0.1215	0.0909**
	(-4.9338)	(-3.7674)	(3.4828)	(-1.6546)	(1.4173)	(-0.4744)	(2.5014)
Country controls	Yes	Yes	Yes	Yes	Yes	Yes	Yes
Region dummies	Yes	Yes	Yes	Yes	Yes	Yes	Yes
Observations	27	27	27	27	27	27	27
R-squared	0.815	0.732	0.922	0.700	0.891	0.798	0.805
Adjusted R2	0.4663	0.2247	0.7752	0.1346	0.6839	0.4166	0.4356

Table 7.7 Continued

	(1)	(2)	(3)	(4)	(5)	(6)	(7)
Panel C: Regression on two-year change of banking performance during crisis period (2006–2008)							
VARIABLES	chg ROAA	chg ROAE	chg NPL	chg relative e quity ratio	chg asset growth	chg loan growth	chg_Cost ratio
Directors	0.0046	0.0367	0.0100	-0.0041	-0.1052	-0.0635	-0.0645**
	(1.3349)	(1.3232)	(1.1478)	(-0.3963)	(-0.5717)	(-0.2617)	(-2.6360)
Outsidedirs_pct	-0.0057	-0.0537	-0.0568*	0.0434	-0.0059	0.1640	-0.1084**
	(-0.6545)	(-0.7240)	(-1.9474)	(1.5760)	(-0.0227)	(0.5850)	(-2.0893)
Gov_turnover	0.0143**	0.0972	0.0044	0.0305	-0.0471	0.5158	0.0310
	(2.4464)	(1.5754)	(0.1339)	(0.8498)	(-0.1185)	(1.3387)	(0.3908)
Commercial banking_exp	-0.0035	0.0021	0.0191	0.0253*	0.0590	0.1460	0.0597
	(-1.0867)	(0.0665)	(1.3201)	(1.7770)	(0.4105)	(0.9110)	(1.5766)
Supervisory	-0.0006	0.0193	0.0179	0.0085	-0.2971	-0.0516	0.0719
	(-0.1716)	(0.5401)	(1.6210)	(0.7109)	(-1.5247)	(-0.2780)	(1.4863)
Constant	-0.0170**	-0.1270**	0.0354	-0.0270	-0.1788	-0.4833	0.0722
	(-2.3983)	(-2.6500)	(1.0283)	(-1.1099)	(-0.7349)	(-1.4964)	(1.1829)
Country controls	Yes	Yes	Yes	Yes	Yes	Yes	Yes
Region dummies	Yes	Yes	Yes	Yes	Yes	Yes	Yes
Observations	27	27	27	27	27	27	27
R-squared	0.844	0.792	0.646	0.839	0.799	0.696	0.748
Adjusted R2	0.5491	0.3987	-0.0226	0.5351	0.3720	0.0492	0.2711

Note: OLS regression results relating central bank governance characteristics and changes in bank performance. Numbers in the parentheses are robust t-statistics clustered by country. *, **, and *** denote significance at 10%, 5%, and 1%, respectively.

Conclusion

There is a large literature in economics examining central bank characteristics and linking them with various performance measures of the real economy. There is also a significant literature in banking that investigates different determinants of bank performance at the international level. Noticeably absent is an examination of the links between central bank characteristics and a country's banking performance. The limited research in this area is somewhat surprising given the important role bank intermediation plays in promoting economic growth (Beck, et al., 2000; Levine, 2005). The recent financial crisis, which affected both advanced and developing countries, has further intensified our interest. Policymakers in all countries, shaken by the sharp global contraction, are carefully reconsidering the regulatory regimes and governance structure of central banks.

This chapter provides preliminary evidence on this issue. Specifically, our findings reveal that central bank governance characteristics are correlated with banking performance. When the economy is good, smaller board size, lower governor turnover, governors with commercial banking experience, and the central bank having a bank supervisory role are associated with higher profitability, lower costs, and lower loan losses. During the crisis period, the effects of some governance variables are significantly different from those before the crisis. Our results indicate that during the crisis period, a higher percentage of outside directors was associated with higher banking profits and lower loan losses but lower credit growth, while higher governor turnover was related to higher profitability and credit growth. Governors' commercial banking experience is associated with lower loan losses and greater credit growth during the crisis period.

This chapter has several broad policy implications. First, we shed light on the central bank governance issue. Our findings suggest that corporate governance principles are applicable to central banking. Although not definitive, our results are sufficiently interesting to warrant further investigation of the important question of whether there is a discernable relationship between central bank governance structure and banking sector performance. Second, our research complements some of the banking literature that looks at country-level determinants of banking development. In particular, recent studies have identified various factors such as macroeconomic conditions, foreign bank presence, market competition structure, institutional environment, and bank regulation (e.g., Demirgüç-Kunt and Huizinga, 2000 Barth, et al., 2001 Laeven and Levine, 2009). However, the quality of central bank governance and the possible trade-offs between achieving monetary policy, financial stability, and banking sector efficiency have received relatively little attention. Last, our study provides more insights into the role of central banks during the recent financial crisis. Between 2001 and the end of 2006, financial markets were characterized by abundant liquidity and little perception of risk. Large parts of the world experienced a prolonged period of high economic growth. In good times like these, the issue of central bank governance may not be as salient. However, things have changed dramatically. Policymakers in all countries, shaken by the financial crisis of 2007–2008, are rethinking what the optimal institutional framework and governance structure of their central banks should be. This chapter provides a timely discussion of this issue by empirically examining the relationship between central bank governance structures and banking performance during the recent financial crisis.

To the best of our knowledge, we are the first to analyze this policy-related issue. However, given there is only one crisis in our data, we cannot conclude our results are representative of crisis periods more generally. Extending our analysis to include other banking crisis events is left for future work.

References

Abrams, R.K. and M. Taylor (2002), 'Assessing the Case for Unified Financial Sector Supervision,' *LSE Financial Markets Group Special Paper*, No. 134.

Adams, R. and H. Mehran (2003), 'Is corporate governance different for bank holding companies?' Federal Reserve Bank of New York *Economic Policy Review,* April, 123–142.

Aisen, A. and M. Franken (2010), 'Bank credit during the 2008 financial crisis: A cross-country comparison,' IMF Working Paper No. 10/47, International Monetary Fund, Washington, D.C.

Allen, F. and D. Gale (2000), *Comparing Financial Systems.* Cambridge, MA, USA: MIT Press.

Allen, F. and D. Gale (2004) 'Competition and financial stability,' *Journal of Money, Credit and Banking*, **36**, 433–480.

Barth, J.R., G. Caprio and R. Levine (2001), 'The Regulation and Supervision of Banks around the World: A New Database,' in Litan, R. and R. Herring (eds) *Brookings–Wharton Papers on Financial Services,* Washington DC: Brooking Institution Press, pp. 183–250

Barth, J.R., G. Caprio and R. Levine (2004), 'Bank regulation and supervision: What works best?' *Journal of Financial Intermediation,* **13**, 205–248.

Barth, J.R., G. Caprio and R. Levine (2006), *Rethinking bank regulation: Till angels govern.* Cambridge, MA, USA: Cambridge University Press.

Beck, T., R. Levine and N. Loayza (2000), 'Finance and the sources of growth,' *Journal of Financial Economics*, **58**, 261–300.

Beck, T., A. Demirgüç-Kunt, and R. Levine (2006), 'Bank concentration, competition, and crises: First results,' *Journal of Banking and Finance*, **30**, 1581–1603.

Beck, T., A. Demirgüç-Kunt and M. Peria (2007), 'Reaching out: access to and use of banking services across countries,' *Journal of Financial Economics*, **85**, 234–266.

Berger, A.N. and T.H. Hannan (1998), 'The efficiency cost of market power in the banking industry: A test of the 'quiet life' and related hypotheses,' *The Review of Economics and Statistics*, **80**(3), 454–465.

Berger, H., J. De Haan and S.C.W. Eijffinger (2001), 'Central bank independence: An update of theory and evidence,' *Journal of Economic Surveys*, 3–40.

Bernanke, B. (2007), Central banking and banking supervision in the United States, Allied Social Sciences Association, Annual Meeting, Chicago, mimeo.

Bonin, J., I. Hasan, and P. Wachtel (2005). 'Bank Performance, Efficiency and Ownership in Transition Countries,' *Journal of Banking and Finance*, **29**, 31–53.

Boot, A.W. and A.V. Thakor (1993), 'Self-interested bank regulation' *American Economic Review*, **83**(2), 206–212

Boyd, J.H. and G. De Nicolo (2005), 'The theory of bank risk-taking and competition revisited,' *Journal of Finance*, **60**(3), 1329–1343.

Caminal, R. and C. Matutes (2002), 'Market power and banking failures,' *International Journal of Industrial Organization*, **20**, 1341–1361.

Caprio, G., L. Laeven and R. Levine (2004), 'Governance and bank valuation,' National Bureau of Economic Research Working Paper No. 10158.

Čihák, M. and R. Podpiera (2007), 'Experience with integrated supervisors: Governance and quality of supervision,' in D. Masciandaro and M. Quintyn (eds.), *Designing Financial Supervision Institutions: Independence, Accountability and Governance*, Cheltenham, UK and Northampton, USA: Edward Elgar, pp. 309–341.

Cukierman, A., S. Webb, and B. Neyapti (1992), 'Measuring the independence of central banks and its effect on policy outcomes', *World Bank Economic Review*, **6**, 353–98.

Demirgüç-Kunt, A. and E. Detragiache (1997), 'The determinants of banking crises: Evidence from developed and developing countries.' Washington, D.C.:The World Bank, mimeo.

Demirgüç-Kunt, A. and H. Huizinga (2000), 'Determinants of commercial bank interest margins and profitability: Some international evidence,' *World Bank Economic Review*, **13**, 379–408.

Detragiache, E., T. Tressel, and P. Gupta (2008), 'Foreign banks in poor countries: Theory and evidence,' *Journal of Finance*, **63**(5), 2123–2160.

Duchin, R., O. Ozbas, and B.A. Sensoy (2010), 'Costly external finance, corporate investment, and the subprime mortgage credit crisis,' *Journal of Financial Economics*, **97**, 418–435.

Eijffinger, S.C. and P.M. Geraats (2006), 'How transparent are central banks?' *European Journal of Political Economy*, **22**(1), 1–21.

Fich, E., and A. Shivdasani, (2006), 'Are busy boards effective monitors?,' *Journal of Finance*, **61**, 689–724.

Frisell, L, K. Roszbach, and G. Spagnolo (2007), 'Governing the governors: A clinical study of central banks,' Working paper, Riksbank.

Göhlmann, S. and R. Vaubel (2007), 'The educational and professional background of central bankers and its effect on inflation: An empirical analysis,' *European Economic Review*, **51**, 925–941.

Goodhart, C. and D. Schoenmaker (1995), 'Should the Functions of Monetary Policy and Banking Supervision be Separated?' *Oxford Economic Papers,* No. 47, pp. 539–560.

Grilli, V., D. Masciandaro and G. Tabellini (1991), 'Political and monetary institutions and public financial policies in the industrial countries,' *Economic Policy,* **13**, 341–92.

Hasan, I. and K. Marton (2003), 'Development and Efficiency of a Banking Sector in a Transitional Economy: Hungarian experience', *Journal of Banking and Finance*, **27**, 2249–2271.

Hasan, I. and L.J. Mester (2008), 'Central bank institutional structure and effective central banking: Cross-country empirical evidence,' *Comparative Economic Studies*, **50**(4), 620–645.

Hayo, B. and S. Voigt (2008), 'Inflation, Central Bank Independence, and the Legal System,' *Journal of Institutional and Theoretical Economics*, **164**(4), 751–777.

Hellman, T. and K. Murdock (1998), 'Financial sector development policy: The importance of reputational capital and governance,' in

R. Sabot and I. Skékely (eds.) *Development Strategy and Management of the Market Economy*, 2, Oxford, UK: Oxford University Press.

Hermalin, B. and M. Weisbach (1991), 'The effects of board composition and direct incentives on firm performance', *Financial Management*, **20**, 101–112.

Herring, R.J. and J. Carmassi (2008), 'The structure of cross-sector financial supervision,' *Financial Markets, Institutions and Instruments*, **17**(1), 51–76.

HM Treasury (2010), *A new approach to financial regulation: judgement, focus, and stability*. July, United Kingdom.

Houston, J., C. Lin, P. Lin, and Y. Ma (2010), 'Creditor rights, information sharing, and bank risk taking,' *Journal of Financial Economics*, **96**, 485–512.

Ivashina, V. and D. Scharfstein (2010), 'Loan syndication and credit cycles,' *American Economic Review: Papers and Proceedings*, **100**(2), 1–8.

Kaufmann, D., A. Kraay, and M. Mastruzzi (2008), 'Governance matters VIII: Aggregate and individual governance indicators, 1996–2008' World Bank Policy Research Working Paper No. 4978

Kuttner, K.N. and A.S. Posen (2010), 'Do markets care who chairs the central bank?,' *Journal of Money, Credit and Banking*, **42**(2–3), 347–371

Laeven, L. and R. Levine (2009), 'Bank governance, regulation and risk taking', *Journal of Financial Economics*, **93**, 259–275.

Levine, R. (2005), 'Finance and growth: Theory and evidence,' in Aghion, P. and S. Durlauf (eds.), *Handbook of Economic Growth*, Amsterdam: North-Holland.

Lybek, T. and J. Morris (2004), 'Central Bank Governance: A Survey of Boards and Management,' IMF Working Paper No. 04/226.

Moreno, R. and A. Villar (2005), 'The increased role of foreign bank entry in emerging markets,' BIS Papers, chapter in *Bank for International Settlements, Globalisation and Monetary Policy in Emerging Markets*, **23**, 9–16.

Murphy, K.J. (1999), 'Executive compensation,' in O. Ashenfelter and D. Card (eds.), *Handbook of Labor Economics*, vol. 3, Amsterdam: North Holland.

Perry, T. and U. Peyer (2005), 'Board seat accumulation by executives: A shareholder's perspective,' *Journal of Finance*, **60**, 2083–2123.

Quintyn, M. and M.W. Taylor (2007), 'Building supervisory structures in sub-Saharan Africa – An analytical framework,' IMF Working Papers WP 07/18.

Schoenmaker, D. (1992), 'Institutional separation between supervisory and monetary agencies'. Financial Markets Group, London School of Economics, FMG Special Papers No. 52.

Shleifer, A. and W.R. Vishny (1997) 'A survey of corporate governance,' *Journal of Finance*, **52**(2), 737–83.

Shleifer, A. and W.R. Vishny (1998), *The Grabbing Hand: Government Pathologies and their Cures*. Cambridge, MA, USA: Harvard University Press.

8.   New Advantages of Tying One's Hands: Banking Supervision, Monetary Policy and Central Bank Independence

Lucia Dalla Pellegrina, Donato Masciandaro and Rosaria Vega Pansini

Introduction

In response to the 2007–2008 financial crisis, different countries and regions – the European Union, Germany, Ireland, United Kingdom and the United States, among others – are either implementing or evaluating the possibility of introducing reforms aimed at reshaping the role of their central banks in banking supervision.

On July 2010, for example, US President Barack Obama signed into law the Dodd-Frank Act, which is considered the most important US financial regulation overhaul since the Great Depression. A rethink of the Fed has been part of the broad financial legislation restyling. Despite the fact that during the discussion of the bill US lawmakers debated on the possibility of restricting some of the Fed's regulatory responsibilities (supervision of small banks, emergency lending powers), as well as to increase the political control on the central bank with changes in its governance (congressional audits of monetary policy decisions, presidential nomination of the New York Fed Presidents), the Dodd-Frank law ended up increasing the powers of the Fed as a banking supervisor. In Europe, policymakers are moving to finalize reforms concerning the extent of the central bank involvement in supervision, both at international and at national levels.

In 2009, the European Commission enacted a proposal inviting the establishment of a European Systemic Risk Council (ESRC) for macro prudential supervision which should be dominated by the ECB. Among the individual EU members, in 2008 the German grand-coalition government expressed its willingness to dismantle the unique financial supervisor (BAFIN) in favor of the Bundesbank. In June 2010, the UK government unveiled a reform of the bank supervisory system aimed at consolidating powers within the Bank of England. The key functions of the Financial Services Authority should then be moved inside the Bank of England, which will become the Prudential Regulatory Authority. Finally, in summer 2010 the Irish Financial Services Regulatory Authority was legally merged with the central bank.

These episodes provide signals of a sort of Great Reversal, given that it has been shown that before the crisis the direction of the changes in the supervisory structure was characterized by the specialization of central banks in pursuing the monetary policy as a unique mandate (Masciandaro and Quintyn, 2009; Orphanides, 2010). Given this general change, we question whether there is any particular institutional setting influencing the relationship between governments and their central banks in the allocation of banking supervisory powers.

Our empirical results provide evidence that, conditional on institutional features: a) banking supervision is in principle assigned to central banks by benevolent policymakers; b) higher central banks' operational independence[1] is associated to a lower involvement of central banks in bank supervision; c) central banks engaged with some specific monetary policy objectives, which can be interpreted as a specific feature of political independence[2], are more likely to be endowed with supervisory tasks.

This chapter is organized as follows. In the next section we overview the literature on the topic and highlight the motivation of the chapter. We then describe the dataset. In the successive section, we

---

[1] Operational independence entails operational freedom in defining the instruments of monetary policy (also defined 'economic independence' in Grilli, Masciandaro and Tabellini, 1991).

[2] Political independence indicates the lack of institutional political constraints in defining a final monetary policy objective different from price stability (Grilli, Masciandaro and Tabellini, 1991).

illustrate the estimation techniques adopted in the empirical analysis. We then present the results. The final section concludes with the discussion of policy implications.

Allocating Banking Supervision within Central Banks

In light of the recent financial turmoil, it is unquestionable that decisions concerning how to assign supervisory tasks should pay strong attention to interactions between the responsibility of monitoring the banking activity and the role of the central bank, which is normally in charge of monetary policy. Unfortunately, the economic literature has not so far provided any clear-cut indication in terms of the optimal way of assigning supervisory tasks, especially when the policymaker is a benevolent one (Masciandaro, 2008).

There are somehow contrasting arguments on this topic (for a survey, see Garcia and Del Rio, 2003 and Klomp and De Haan, 2010). The main argument in favor of the involvement of the central bank in supervision is its informational advantage, which unquestionably stems from managing liquidity tools. In fact, lending of last resort and open market operations may endow the central bank with a privileged view on the health of the banking system. Externalities could also go in the opposite direction, since having supervisory powers may both provide assistance in the monetary policy conduct and allow a more effective management of crises (Goodhart and Schoenmaker, 1995; Bernanke, 2007; Herring and Carmassi, 2008; Blanchard, Dell'Ariccia and Mauro, 2010). An additional argument is related to the central banks ability to attract more skilled staff thanks to the availability of financial resources and reputational concerns (Abrams and Taylor 2002, Quintyn and Taylor 2007).

However, these considerations go against the argument, often recurring in the literature, that the intertwined implementation of monetary policy and banking supervision can be costly for several reasons. First, any extension of the central bank's powers in the field of supervision can endogenously stimulate bank moral hazard behavior and, consequently, increase the risk of lenient monetary actions (Goodhart and Schoenmaker, 1995; Llewellyn, 2005; Herring and Carmassi, 2008). Moreover, if a central bank is empowered with an excessive discretion on the possibility of monetizing financial distress, systemic risk will be even more likely, since pouring central bank money into the financial system can both derail monetary policy and aggravate financial instability (Jacome, 2008). Second, the risk of reputational losses may increase if the central bank is deeply involved in supervision. In fact, given that the nature of supervision entails a higher visibility of failures compared to flagships, reputational benefits are less likely to emerge (Goodhart, 2000). Then, again, it may occur that in order to avoid reputational losses the central bank is more likely to accommodate bailout pressures using liquidity tools. Finally, although this argument is likely to be confined to grabbing-hand policymakers, governments should account for the threat represented by an extremely powerful central bank holding both monetary and supervisory functions (Padoa Schioppa, 2003; Masciandaro, 2006), since the latter is a bureaucratic organization (Oritani, 2010).

Summarizing these different views, we can conclude that policymakers are likely to face a trade-off between expected benefits and expected costs of central bank involvement in supervision. In particular, expected costs are crucially based on the possibility that the latter may relax monetary policy standards in order to mitigate problems in the financial sector. This could in turn exacerbate both financial and monetary instability. Although it is unquestionable that the central bank has to provide loans to banks, it is also advisable that it does so avoiding liquidity mismanagement. In other words, the risk of failures is likely to increase the greater the central bank discretion in the conduct of monetary policy.

The purpose of this chapter is to investigate under which institutional conditions it is more likely that policymakers choose to assign banking supervision to central banks. Besides not excluding other hypotheses, we offer an explanation based on the role of central bank independence (CBI, hereafter) in shaping the policymaker's choices. We consider the CBI as being both a threat for financial stability and a tying one's hands mechanism operating the other way around. On the one hand, it may allow an instrumental use of monetary policy. On the other hand, it may imply that the central bank cannot accommodate outside political and financial pressures. This, in particular, becomes a commitment device in face of the time inconsistency problems in financial stability policy making (Čihák, 2007; Klomp and De Haan, 2009)[3].

Our analysis is concentrated on the different role that central banks' political and operational (economic or functional) independence have on supervisory tasks assignment. In particular, central banks' binding monetary policy objectives (which are considered as a form of political independence) are here considered in the policymakers' view as a way to reduce the fear that the latter may make an instrumental use of monetary policy.

The chapter improves upon the existing literature from three different perspectives.

First, several studies have examined the effects of the financial crisis on central banks' strategies and policies under two distinct aspects. On the one hand, it has been observed that the greater CBI the greater the flexibility and the credibility to engage in unconventional monetary policy in normal times (Orphanides, 2010). A financial crisis can also threaten CBI. In fact, considerations in terms of financial stability can require that the central bank bears either effective or potential losses in order to reduce the risk of a systemic crisis. These losses can impact on CBI through the central bank's balance sheet position. The outcome of policies aimed at preventing financial stability shocks may result in a substantial amount of deteriorated assets in the central bank balance sheet. Besides this, CBI can be also severely limited by the need to cover government losses. Hence, the central bank cannot credibly operate in an independent way without proper financial means (Buiter, 2007; Bini Smaghi, 2008; Berriel and Bhattarai, 2009). On the other hand, the recent financial crisis poses new challenges to the classic Dynamic Stochastic General Equilibrium (DSGE) models, where monetary policy is conducted by an independent central bank which follows an interest rate rule-based approach to stabilize inflation (Goodhart, Osorio and Tsomocos, 2009; Curdia and Woodford, 2010; Gertler and Karadi, 2010; Giavazzi and Giovannini, 2010; Cohen-Cole and Morse, 2010). Hence, we also consider this additional feature, wondering if there is any potential

---

[3] Furthermore, this commitment device can be particularly useful if the banking supervision can be considered an instrument of electoral cycle policies (Keefer, 1999).

CBI effect on facilitating the policymaker's decisions in terms of central bank involvement in banking supervision, with particular attention to what occurred after the financial crisis.

Second, the economics of financial supervisory architecture has been so far empirically investigating both causes (Masciandaro, 2006 and 2007; Dalla Pellegrina and Masciandaro, 2008; Masciandaro and Quintyn, 2008) and effects (Barth et al., 2002; Arnone and Gambini, 2007; Čihák and Podpiera, 2007) of assigning the overall financial powers to one single authority rather than multiple ones. This chapter, instead, focuses on the drivers of the specific allocation of banking supervisory powers.

Finally, the chapter offers a contribution also in the research area of the effects of central bank independence. From its origins (Grilli, Masciandaro and Tabellini, 1991; Cukierman, Webb and Neyapti, 1992), legal central bank independence has been considered a significant determinant of several macroeconomic performances (Cukierman, 2008; De Haan et al., 2008; Carlstorm and Fuerst, 2009; Alpanda and Honig, 2010; Alesina and Stella, 2010; Klompt and De Haan, 2010). A recent literature has also been exploring the relationships between CBI and the conduct of monetary policy (Down, 2008; Maslowska, 2009; Alpanda and Honig, 2009), the effect of CBI on financial stability (Čihák 2007; Klomp and De Haan, 2009) as well as political and institutional factors influencing the effectiveness of CBI (Keefer and Stasavage, 2002 and 2003; Eijffinger and Stadhouder, 2003; Acemoglu et al., 2008; Gollwitzer and Quintyn, 2010). In particular, we explore the relationship between CBI and an institutional feature – banking supervision – rather than specific macroeconomic performances. Our view suggests that CBI can be relevant not only for the alleged beneficial effects on macroeconomic variables, but also in influencing the policymaker decisions, given that its importance seems to have been internalized by both the politicians and the public opinion (Alesina and Stella, 2010).

Dataset and Descriptive Statistics

The dataset contains information about 88 countries worldwide, at different stages of economic development. Data are collected using both countries' official documents and available surveys. Details are reported in Table 8.A1 in the Appendix.

First, in order to measure central bank involvement in banking supervision we built a dichotomous variable (*CBBA*) indicating whether the central bank is the main responsible authority for banking supervision[4]. The variable has been constructed using information available on both central banks' websites and other official documents (see Table 8.A2 in the Appendix for description and sources). Table 8.A3 in the Appendix provides information about the values assigned to the *CBBA* variable for each country in the sample.

Second, one of the novelties of our analysis is represented by the way we deal with the measurement of the degree of central banks' independence. In designing modern central bank governance economic theory attributes primary importance to the degree of independence, which should be then accompanied by accountability and transparency (Cukierman, 2008; Crowe and Meade, 2008). We focus our analysis on the legal aspects of independence, although we acknowledge that the level of actual independence, particularly in developing countries, can be lower than the one indicated by the law (Cukierman, 2008). We also recognize both that in more practical matters the legal rules can be necessary, although not sufficient, to ensure central bank independence (Bini Smaghi, 2008) and that every institutional measurement methodology inevitably suffers shortcomings, as at least subjectivity (Maslowska, 2007).

There are plenty of indexes proposed in the literature measuring both political and operational independence (for a survey, see Ahsan et al., 2006; Maslowska, 2007). We refer to the definition proposed by Grilli, Masciandaro and Tabellini (1991), in the updated version computed in Arnone and Gambini (2007), which is both widely used and recently evaluated as the more robust one for empirical analyses (Maslowska, 2008). Such index (hereafter *GMT*) evaluates central bank independence by aggregating scores over 15 different criteria,

---

[4] Masciandaro (2006, 2007) and Masciandaro and Quintyn (2009) use the degree of central bank's involvement in financial supervision (CBFA index). The CBBA variable is parallel to the CBFA index but it refers exclusively to central bank's involvement in the banking sector.

eight for political independence and seven for operational (economic) independence respectively.[5]

In the empirical analysis, we decompose the *GMT* index in order to better explore how the combination of different characteristics of both political and operational independence (hereafter respectively *GMTp* and *GMTo* indexes) affects the choice to assign central bank supervisory tasks for the banking sector.[6]

In fact, the *GMT* index provides a rather comprehensive assessment of the requirements that each central bank must fulfill in order to be autonomous. However, it suffers from major limitations

---

[5] The criteria used to construct the GMT index are the following:

Political independence:

1. governor is appointed without government involvement;
2. governor is appointed for more than five years;
3. board of directors is appointed without government involvement;
4. board is appointed for more than five years;
5. there is no mandatory participation of government representative(s) in the board;
6. no government approval is required for formulation of monetary policy;
7. central bank is legally obliged to pursue monetary stability as one of its primary objectives;
8. there are legal provisions that strengthen the central bank's position in the event of a conflict with the government.

Operational independence:

1. there is no automatic procedure for the government to obtain direct credit from the central bank;
2. when available, direct credit facilities are extended to the government at market interest rates;
3. this credit is temporary;
4. and for a limited amount;
5. the central bank does not participate in the primary market for public debt;
6. the central bank is responsible for setting the policy rate;
7. the central bank has no responsibility for overseeing the banking sector (two points) or shares responsibility (one point).

[6] We not only divide the (aggregate) *GMT* index into its two main components (respectively *GMTp* and *GMTo* indexes), but we provide also alternative construction of indexes of political and operational independence considering only a limited set of criteria. See the next section for further details.

since its aggregate components may have different implications on supervisory task assignment. In general it is possible that operational independence, intended as freedom of choosing monetary policy instruments, including the possibility of supporting the banking system with liquidity injections, has a substantial different impact on supervisory task assignment compared to the freedom of choosing monetary policy objectives.

More in detail, the *GMT* index implicitly states that, in order to achieve political independence, the central bank should be obliged to pursue monetary stability as its primary objective. The relevance to test separately the role of the price stability goal has been implemented in Klomp and De Haan (2010). However, this definition is rather general given the fact central banks are indeed the authorities in charge of monetary policy conduct. In our view, when looking at supervisory issues, one should be concerned about the tightness of the objective pursued by central banks.

Therefore, we combine the information contained in the *GMT* index and its individual components with specific information describing central bank's monetary policy goals. The latter have been carefully investigated analyzing central banks' official documents. More specifically, we built a set of dummy variables (*GOAL* (1) – *GOAL* (4)) indicating if the central bank's goal in pursuing monetary policy focuses, respectively, on:

1. price and inflation control;
2. liquidity (most frequently M2) control;
3. output control;
4. other goals characterized by a combination of objectives, including, among others, the maintenance of the external value of the national currency.

The choice to construct such new variables is justified by the need to disentangle the different styles with which central banks may have 'tied hands' in reaching a specific policy goal. For instance, Goals (1)–(3) are devoted to maintain either price or economic stability. This, in turn, could provide the central banker with a relatively low margin of discretion since any deviation from the declared objective would be blamed. Goal (4) is instead rather loose since it involves mixed tasks, so that several forms of trade-off between them could easily be invoked in case the central bank does not fulfill its goal(s). Table 8.A3 in the Appendix provides details about values assumed by this variable for each country in the sample.

The dataset contains also a set of variables describing other institutional and economic features of countries in the sample. The first is a proxy for the presence of grabbing-hand policymakers. It measures the perceived level of corruption in the public sector $(CORR)$[7]. Based on data constructed by Transparency International, it ranges from one to 10 with a higher score indicating a lower level of corruption. The idea to use a measure of the quality of governance in similar contexts has already been exploited in several previous studies[8]. In this particular case, controlling for the level of corruption is an attempt at minimizing the distortions originating from the presence of grabbing-hand policymakers. The empirical concern behind the choice of isolating this component aims at obtaining parameters for CBI which are indicative of the choice of benevolent governments in terms of supervisory task assignment.

Second, the choice to assign supervision to central banks may be influenced by both the level of wealth and economic development. In particular, richer countries may have a wider range of options in setting the level of central bank's involvement in banking supervision. However, using GDP as a control variable raises serious endogeneity issues. In this context, unemployment (UN) is instead better suited to describe the 'quality' of the economic development.

Then, we chose three specific proxies describing the level of development of the financial market (Beck et al. 1999). The first is the market versus bank based index (MvB), which takes value one if the dimension of the market is relatively larger than the banking sector. The second is the level of bank assets with respect to GDP $(BankAss\_GDP)$ calculated from World Bank data released in the 'Banking Regulation Survey'. The third is the country latitude (LAT)

---

[7] The best recognized measure of 'grabbing hand' politicians is the Kaufmann (2004) corruption index. In the empirical analysis that follows we control for this index in all the specifications of the equations we estimate. Therefore, conditioning on it, we minimize the effect of the presence of corrupt policymakers on the estimated parameters, as if the degree of grabbing-hands was the same in each country.

[8] See among others, Dalla Pellegrina and Masciandaro (2008); Masciandaro (2006 and 2007).

as a measure of the degree of competitiveness of financial markets[9] as provided by CIA.

Using World Bank's World Development Indicators, we also include population (*POP*) as a variable describing the relative size of the country. It is inserted as the number of inhabitants averaged over the period from 1996 to 2004[10]. Religion (*REL*) is included as a variable broadly describing the social and institutional landscape of each country. It can be used as a proxy of country's preference toward concentration versus division of powers through different authorities. Applied to the analysis of the probability that central bank is engaged also with supervisory tasks, it can help explain if countries prefer to concentrate powers into a single authority or to spread it into different ones. Finally, a set of continental fixed-effects (*CONT*) are also considered in order to control for 'mimic effects' among neighboring countries (Masciandaro 2008; and Dalla Pellegrina and Masciandaro, 2008). A dummy indicating if the country belongs to the OECD group has been also added.

Banking Supervision, Central Bank Independence and Monetary Policy Goals

Before analyzing results of the econometric analysis, it is worth looking at some features of the data. Table 8.1 shows the distribution of countries by geographical location, income group, level of corruption and inflation rate depending on values assumed by our focus variables, i.e., the dummy for central bank being the banking supervision authority (*CBBA*), the degree of central bank independence (*GMT* index) and the type of monetary policy goal (*GOAL*).

Out of 88 countries in our sample, 52 have central bank as the authority both in charge of monetary policy and bearing the main responsibility for banking supervision. As one can observe in column one, most of these countries are located in Europe (20 European

---

[9] The reason behind using latitude is to check if there is an 'endowment effect' (Beck, Demirgüç-Kunt and Levine 1999), i.e., if it is true that countries closer to the equator tend to be more inhospitable because of climate conditions, and therefore less favorable to the development of competitive financial markets.

[10] Data on population are collected for five points in time, respectively, 1996, 1998, 2000, 2002 and 2004 and then averaged.

countries out of 35 in our sample) and Asia (12 countries out of 17)[11.] Countries with a higher level of income[12] and a lower level of corruption are also those where central banks are more frequently assigned both supervisory powers and monetary policy tasks. It is also interesting to note that central banks are more frequently (in almost 50 per cent of cases) assigned supervisory powers where the level of inflation[13] is quite low, i.e., less than five per cent.

Table 8.1 also displays how countries are distributed depending on the level of central bank independence and its monetary policy goal. In order to do this, we calculate the mean value of the *GMT* index and its components (*GMTp* and *GMTo*) over the whole sample and count the number of countries where the central bank has a level of independence above or below the mean, depending on the level of economic development (income group), the average value of inflation rate, location, and average level of corruption.

Comparing columns two to four of Table 8.1, we derive interesting insights on the difference in frequency between the *GMT* scores and the single aspects of independence. Considering the degree of (total) independence (column two), Asian countries exhibit the highest frequency of central banks with a value below the sample mean (low independence). Conversely, Europeans set above the sample mean. American countries, instead, are equally distributed in these terms. Considering the two components of the *GMT* index (*GMTp* in column three; and *GMTo* in columns four), we find that political independence is below the mean in Asian and American countries almost in the same percentage. Operational independence is less frequent in American countries. European central banks, instead, experience the highest performance in terms of both political and operational independence. As a first conclusion, we can then say that the

---

[11] Note that this evidence may result from the fact that distributions are affected by a problem of selection bias.

[12] Countries are classified in four groups depending on the level of their gross national income per capita following the World Bank's criterion. For further details, see:http://web.worldbank.org/WBSITE/EXTERNAL/DATASTATISTICS/0,,contentMDK:20420458~menuPK:64133156~pagePK:64133150~piPK:64133175~theSitePK:239419,00.html

[13] Inflation is calculated as the average rate in the last five years, from 2004 to 2008. Data are taken from the IMF's International Financial Statistics.

operational side of central bank independence drives the distribution, by location, of the overall index of independence.

We also observe that countries reporting a lower level of inflation are those with both independent central banks[14] and high income levels (51 per cent of cases). The same is true considering the degree of corruption: when the latter is low, central banks have higher independence, in both the two dimensions.

Finally, 58 countries out of 88 have central banks with 'tied hands' in keeping a low inflation rate and pursuing price stability as an objective expressed in their official documents, only six care about liquidity control, while the remaining 22 countries distribute equally among targeting economic growth and other loose objectives. The majority of central banks having an eye on inflation control are located in Europe (48.28 per cent), an effect of the presence of the European Systems of Central Banks. Not surprisingly, among those having a commitment toward low inflation, most exhibit also a low inflation rate, while they distribute equally depending on their level of corruption[15]. Moreover, with respect to income level, it is more frequent that central banks with the objective of inflation control are located in the richest countries of our sample (50 per cent of cases compared to 1.72 per cent from low income countries).

---

[14] It should be underlined that results contained in Table 8.1 are simply frequency rates. Therefore, we cannot derive any conclusion about the causal relationship between variables considered. We can only say, for example, that where inflation is low, it is more frequent to have a central bank with a higher level of independence, both operational and political. Nevertheless, the analysis of distribution of countries in subcategories helps to identify which are the most interesting features of the sample that will be more deeply explored in the econometric analysis.

[15] Even though we cannot derive any causal relationship, differently from the other three monetary policy goals considered, having an objective on price and inflation control doesn't seem to depend on the level of corruption.

Table 8.1 Banking Supervision, Central Bank Independence and Monetary Policy Goals

	CBBA (1)	GMT (2)	GMTp (3)	GMTo (4)	GOAL (5)			
	= 1 in 52 countries	Average=0.67	Average=0.57	Average=0.76	1	2	3	4
		(above average)	(above average)	(above average)				
Continents								
America	17.31	24.49	19.51	7.14	20.69	83.33	27.27	9.09
Europe	38.46	65.31	65.85	85.71	48.28	0	18.18	45.45
Africa	19.23	6.12	7.32	7.14	10.34	16.67	27.27	9.09
Asia	23.08	4.08	7.32	0	17.24	0	27.27	36.36
Oceania	1.92	0	0	0	3.45	0	0	0
Inflation rate								
Below 5%	48.08	67.35	65.85	78.57	67.24	50	27.27	27.27
Betw. 5% and 10%	21.15	18.37	21.95	14.29	15.52	50	45.45	18.18
Above 10%	30.77	14.29	12.2	7.14	17.24	0	27.27	54.55
Income group								
Low income	5.77	0	0	0	1.72	0	0	9.09
Lower middle	26.92	18.37	21.95	14.29	20.69	33.33	54.55	9.09
Upper-middle	32.69	30.61	29.27	21.43	27.59	33.33	27.27	54.55
High income	34.62	51.02	48.78	64.29	50	33.33	18.18	27.27
Corruption (average=4.73)								
High corruption (below average)	30.77	51.02	46.34	53.57	50	33.33	18.18	27.27
Low corruption (above average)	69.23	48.98	53.66	46.43	50	66.67	81.82	72.73

Note:
Monetary policy goals considered in the last four columns are respectively: 1= price and inflation control; 2= liquidity control; 3= economic growth; 4= maintenance of the external value of the currency.

Source: authors' calculation.

Looking at characteristics of countries whose central banks have a monetary policy goal on liquidity control, they are American in most of the cases and they do not differ depending on their level of income. Inflation rate, even when it is below the 10 per cent level[16], doesn't help to distinguish them. Having a lower level of corruption, instead,

---

[16] No countries in our sample have central banks assigned with this objective and a high inflation rate.

seems to determine the preference to assign such a goal to the central bank.

Not surprisingly, mid-low income countries tend to delegate to the central bank the objective of enhancing economy expansion rather than inflation and liquidity control. As in the case of the second category of monetary policy goals, a country's 'integrity' level seems to drive the decision over this assignment (in almost 82 per cent of cases). Also not surprisingly, most of the central banks targeting growth are located in countries characterized by having an inflation rate between five and 10 per cent.

Finally, central banks with looser monetary policy objectives are more frequently located in countries with a low level of corruption (almost 73 per cent of cases). Also in this case, adopting this kind of goal does not seem to have a positive impact on both growth and inflation. More than half of the countries in our sample, in fact, have an inflation rate higher than 10 per cent and with the same proportion (54.55 per cent) we can find countries out of the richest group.

Table 8.A2 in the appendix provides summary statistics on the variables used for this analysis.

Estimation Techniques

We estimate the following equation:

$$CBBA_i = \alpha + \beta \, GMTp_i + \gamma \, GMTo_i + \sum_{n=1}^{N} \delta_n \, GOAL_{ni} + \sum_{m=1}^{M} \phi_m x_{mi} + \mu + \varepsilon_i \qquad (8.1)$$

where i identifies the country. The dependent variable $CBBA$ is a dummy taking the value of one if the central bank is the main supervisor of the banking sector, and zero otherwise.

Among the independent variables, $GMTp$ is the political independence component of the GMT index, while $GMTo$ is the operational independence component. $GOAL_n$ is the set of N binary variables describing monetary policy objectives pursued by the central bank in country i as mentioned in its official documents.[17]

---

[17] $N=3$ in our case. In the specific, we label $n=1$ price with inflation goal, $n=2$ liquidity control, $n=3$ real economy growth, while $n=4$ other. We treat the

The variable x_m represents the set of M standard controls described in the previous section, such as economic development indicators (OECD membership and unemployment rate), financial development indicators (bank assets to GDP, the market-versus bank-based index, latitude), country corruption scores, and religion. μ are continental fixed-effects. Finally, ε_i is an idiosyncratic normally distributed error term with zero mean and constant variance.

We estimate equation (8.1) by means of a Probit model. Therefore, the expected value of the dependent variable is the probability that bank supervisory activity is assigned to the central bank rather than other authorities.

The above specification poses issues concerning causality between the dependent and the independent variables. In particular, our analysis stands on the argument that the extent of central bank's political and operational independence in carrying out monetary policy is likely to represent a largely consolidated feature for most economies. Several central banks became rather independent far in the past, while many others did so more recently. It has been calculated that at least 84 countries increased the legal independence of their central banks from 1989 to 2008 (Rapaport et al. 2009). In the same period, several countries have reformed the structure of their overall financial supervision. From 1998 to 2008 at least 69 countries chose to reform their financial supervisory structure, by establishing a new supervisory authority and/or changing the powers of – at least – one of the already existing agencies (Masciandaro and Quintyn, 2009). Our view is based on the assumption that the current supervisory setting has been arranged assuming a given set-up of the overall institutional position of central banks in terms of independence. This should avoid the possibility of reverse/contemporaneous determination of central bank independence and supervisory powers.

So far the assumption seems confirmed. In Figure 8.1, we compare the year in which the present degree of central bank involvement in supervision was established (continuous line, data from Masciandaro, 2008) with the year of the most recent reform of the central bank

---

latter as the base-category and omit it in order to avoid the dummy variable trap. We do the same with other sets of covariates expressed in the form of dummy variables.

independence (dashed line, data from Acemoglou et al., 2008). Given the available data of 43 countries, we find that in most of the cases the last reform of the supervisory setting follows the last reform of the CBI (72 per cent of the countries).

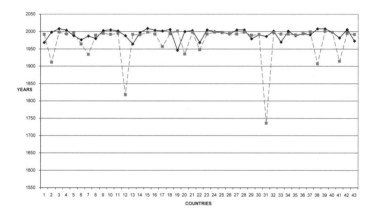

Source: authors' elaborations.

Figure 8.1 Supervisory Regime Reforms and CBI Reforms

Alternative Central Bank Independence Scores

As described in the previous section, in the original *GMT* index, political independence (*GMTp*) includes five principles related to government interference in the appointment of the central bank governor and composition of the board of directors (see previous section). Three additional questions, more related to monetary policy complete the original score: the first (*GMTp_6*) consists of the possibility that no government approval is required for the formulation of monetary policy, the second (*GMTp_7*) reports whether central bank is legally obliged to pursue monetary stability as one of its primary objectives, while the last one (*GMTp_8*) refers to legal provisions that strengthen the central bank's position in the event of a conflict with the government. It has to be noted, in particular, that principle *GMTp_7* is close to our concept of pursuing monetary policy goals, as captured by the variable *GOAL*.

Similarly, operational independence (*GMTo*) includes five principles related to the outstanding limits on public debt financing (see again previous section), while two additional questions refer to whether the central bank is responsible for setting the policy rate (*GMTo_6*), and whether it has no responsibilities for overseeing the banking sector (*GMTo_7*). Again, it is worth observing that *GMTo_7* is the reciprocal to our dependent variable *CBBA*.

Our hypothesis is that tighter monetary policy goals may mitigate the potential cons of the central bank involvement in supervision and then the benevolent policymakers' aversion to assign supervisory tasks to central banks. In general, different monetary policy goals should have different impact on delegation. This principle holds conditional on the fact that central banks are free to lend to the banking system. In fact, being able to set tough monetary policy standards would not be credible if the central bank was imposed to inject liquidity for government purposes.

Given these arguments, two requirements have to be fulfilled by a correct estimation of the effects we have in mind. The first is that the influence of monetary policy goals is evaluated conditional on the central bank position in terms of freedom from the duty of financing government deficits. In other words, both the first five principles of the *GMTo* index and the set of dummies related to monetary policy goals (*GOAL$_n$*) must always simultaneously enter equation (8.1). The second requirement is that, given its peculiar connotation to our purposes, principle *GMTp_7* is considered separately from the rest of the index.

Therefore, we estimate alternative specifications of equation (8.1) where the *GMTp* index is replaced by a 'narrow' definition (*GMTp_bis*) which excludes principle *GMTp_7*. The legal provision to pursue monetary stability is instead treated separately through the monetary policy goal dummies. In particular, the *GOAL$_n$* set goes beyond the binary statement defining whether monetary stability is delegated to the central bank, since it includes several alternatives.

Another restricted index, the *GMTp_ter*, excludes also principles *GMTp_6* and *GMTp_8* in order to better isolate the block of (first five) questions referring to the government interference with the composition of the central bank's board of directors.

As for the operational independence, serious problems stem from principle *GMTo_7*, since the latter tends to perfectly predict the dependent variable[18]. *GMTo_6* has instead the drawback of being correlated with the final objective of monetary policy included in the political independence score, since fixing the policy rate is often functional to pursuing a specific policy mandate freely defined by the central bank.

Therefore, parallel to what has been done with the *GMTp* index, we build 'narrow' *GMTo* scores. The first is the *GMTo_bis*, consisting in defining operational independence with the exclusion of principle *GMTo_7*, while the second, labeled *GMTo_ter* also excludes principle *GMTo_6*.

Finally, we estimate alternative specifications of equation (8.1) whereby the effects of *all* the *individual* components of both the *GMTo* and *GMTp* indexes on central bank supervisory task assignment are tested. We briefly discuss these alternative settings while commenting on results in the next section.

Results

Results of the estimation of both the basic version and alternative definitions of equation (8.1) are reported in Table 8.2. Estimates refer to the effect of aggregate central bank independence indexes (*GMT*, *GMTp*, and *GMTo*) and monetary policy goals (*GOAL_1*-*GOAL_4*) on supervisory power assignment. The dependent variable is the *CBBA* dummy.

In particular, in column (1) we use the 'full' definitions of the *GMTp* and *GMTo* indexes, while in column (2) these are replaced with the alternative *GMTp_bis* and *GMTo_bis*. Columns (3) and (4) differ from (2) in that they alternatively substitute *GMTp_bis* and *GMTo_bis* with *GMTp_ter* and *GMTo_ter*, which both preserve only pure government interference in the composition of central bank governance and in monetary policy management.

All alternative specifications in columns (1)–(4) include the set of monetary policy goals with the exception of $GOAL_4$ representing the

---

[18] More precisely, the probability of failure is perfectly matched.

residual category of all less defined monetary policy goals. We also account for all controls mentioned in the data Section[19].

The first crucial evidence that emerges from the estimates in Table 8.2 is that higher operational independence (*GMTo* and its alternative definitions *GMTo_bis* and *GMTo_ter*) is significant and reports a negative sign of the parameter. As has been previously discussed, freedom of lending to other financial institutions than the government is likely to represent the crucial device that allows central banks to instrumentally manage and channel liquidity towards individual, perhaps badly supervised intermediaries. In principle, policymakers' observed attitudes suggest a preference for equipping central banks with a low degree of supervisory powers when the latter have high operational independence. On the other hand, the absence of government interference in the central bank's governance (*GMTp, GMTp_bis*, and *GMTp_ter*), seems not to have the same role on task assignment. This may suggest that governments do not fear too politically powerful institutions.

The second important outcome that emerges from Table 8.2 is that parameters associated to tight monetary policy goals ($GOAL_1$, $GOAL_2$, $GOAL_3$) are positive and significant compared to the base-category, with the control of liquidity aggregates performing best. We interpret this result as a way of tying central banks' hands which leads benevolent policymakers to remove the fear of a possible sub-optimal behavior. This, in turn, ends up increasing the odds of a central bank involvement in supervision.

As for the controls, an interesting result is the negative – although weakly significant – sign of the corruption index. It means that the more virtuous the country (higher score) the lower the probability of assigning supervision to central banks. We interpret the negative sign as the possibility that in countries where corruption is low policymakers have a higher aversion towards a high involvement of the central bank in supervision.

---

[19] In the same vein as excluding one dummy variable for the monetary policy goal, we also exclude REL4 (Orthodox) and CONT5 (Oceania).

Table 8.2 Effects of Central Bank Independence and Monetary Policy Goals on Banking Supervision

Dependent variable: CBBA index (=1 if central bank is the main supervisor for the banking sector)	(1)	(2)	(3)	(4)
GMTp	1.179			
	(1.027)			
GMTo	-11.38***			
	(2.278)			
GMTp_bis		-0.0200	0.304	
		(0.736)	(0.715)	
GMTo_bis		-4.416**		-4.513**
		(1.925)		(1.969)
GMTo_ter			-3.956**	
			(1.818)	
GMTp_ter				-0.256
				(0.675)
GOAL1	3.897***	1.916**	1.727**	1.914**
	(1.095)	(0.774)	(0.758)	(0.768)
GOAL2	6.798***	3.843***	3.582***	3.880***
	(1.627)	(1.266)	(1.240)	(1.275)
GOAL3	4.149***	1.909**	1.728**	1.934**
	(1.030)	(0.868)	(0.815)	(0.863)
CORR	-0.230*	-0.131*	-0.0948	-0.132*
	(0.135)	(0.077)	(0.124)	(0.075)
Constant	8.437***	4.999**	4.264**	5.076**
	(2.117)	(2.377)	(2.117)	(2.410)
Country fixed-effects	yes	yes	Yes	yes
Religion dummies	yes	yes	Yes	yes
Population	yes	yes	Yes	yes
Financial development indexes[a]	yes	yes	Yes	yes
General development indexes[b]	yes	yes	Yes	yes
Observations	78	78	78	78

Notes:
Probit estimates. The dependent latent variable is the probability that the central bank is the (sole) authority responsible for banking supervision. Robust standard errors in parentheses. ***, **, * Significance at the 10, 5 and 1 per cent level.
[a] MvB, BankAss_GDP, Latitude.
[b] OECD, UN.

Source: authors' calculation.

The positive sign and significance of unemployment (*UN*) rate may instead capture the fact that several less-developed countries are more likely to assign supervisory powers to central banks (Goodhart, 2000).

Finally, Tables 8.3 and 8.4 split the aggregate GMT index in order to perform regressions including only its individual components. We find that results do not substantially change as compared to those reported in Table 8.2. In particular, the individual components of the *GMTo* index are still significant (Table 8.4), while those of the *GMTp* index are not (Table 8.3). As for the sign and significance of the monetary policy goals the results of Table 8.2 are also confirmed. In particular, one should note that goals become not significant when isolating the component relative to monetary stability. This supports the approach of interpreting that component as the practice of pursuing a clearly specified policy goal.

Table 8.3 Effects of Central Bank Political Independence and Monetary Policy Goals on Banking Supervision

Dependent variable: *CBBA* index (=1 if central bank is the main supervisor for the banking sector)	(1)	(2)	(3)	(4)	(5)	(6)	(7)	(8)
GMTp_1	0.330 (0.406)							
GMTp_2		-0.0140 (0.385)						
GMTp_3			-0.0210 (0.524)					
GMTp_4				0.537 (0.413)				
GMTp_5					-0.157 (0.371)			
GMTp_6						0.0653 (0.382)		
GMTp_7							0.0179 (0.482)	
GMTp_8								0.0706 (0.435)
GOAL1	0.368 (0.584)	0.382 (0.589)	0.389 (0.569)	0.486 (0.579)	0.393 (0.564)	0.388 (0.565)	0.385 (0.565)	0.377 (0.566)
GOAL2	1.884* (1.131)	1.878* (1.141)	1.874 (1.144)	2.003* (1.075)	1.986* (1.135)	1.856* (1.124)	1.875 (1.142)	1.882* (1.134)

Table 8.3 Continued

Dependent variable: CBBA index (=1 if central bank is the main supervisor for the banking sector)	(1)	(2)	(3)	(4)	(5)	(6)	(7)	(8)
GOAL3	0.452	0.499	0.506	0.516	0.544	0.499	0.500	0.501
	(0.699)	(0.686)	(0.673)	(0.715)	(0.679)	(0.674)	(0.672)	(0.679)
CORR	-0.0400	-0.0556	-0.0562	-0.0657	-0.0473	-0.0562	-0.0554	-0.0535
	(0.119)	(0.117)	(0.117)	(0.116)	(0.121)	(0.116)	(0.117)	(0.120)
Constant	1.647*	1.636*	1.625	1.830*	1.642	1.624	1.608	1.652*
	(0.938)	(0.926)	(1.225)	(1.091)	(1.245)	(1.222)	(1.382)	(0.997)
Country fixed-effects	yes	yes	yes	yes	yes	yes	yes	yes
Religion dummies	yes	yes	yes	yes	yes	yes	yes	yes
Population	yes	yes	yes	yes	yes	yes	yes	yes
Financial devel. indexes[a]	yes	yes	yes	yes	yes	yes	yes	yes
General devel. indexes[b]	yes	yes	yes	yes	yes	yes	yes	yes
Observations	78	78	78	78	78	78	78	78

Notes:

Probit estimates. The dependent latent variable is the probability that the central bank is the (sole) authority responsible for banking supervision. Robust standard errors in parentheses. ***, **, * Significance at the 10, 5 and 1 per cent level.

[a] MvB, BankAss_GDP, Latitude.

[b] OECD, UN.

Source: authors' calculation.

Table 8.4 Effects of Central Bank Operational Independence and Monetary Policy Goals on Banking Supervision

Dependent variable: CBBA index (=1 if central bank is the main supervisor for the banking sector)	(1)	(2)	(3)	(4)	(5)	(6)	(7)
GMTo_1	-1.389						
	(0.862)						
GMTo_2		-1.639***					
		(0.502)					

Table 8.4 Continued

Dependent variable: CBBA index (=1 if central bank is the main supervisor for the banking sector)	(1)	(2)	(3)	(4)	(5)	(6)	(7)
GMTo_3			0.166				
			(0.943)				
GMTo_4				-0.550			
				(0.875)			
GMTo_5					-1.465**		
					(0.582)		
GMTo_6						-1.196**	
						(0.583)	
GMTo_7							-3.399***
							(0.613)
GOAL1	0.862	0.951	0.359	0.573	0.530	0.783	-1.816***
	(0.718)	(0.581)	(0.611)	(0.712)	(0.658)	(0.663)	(0.682)
GOAL2	2.306*	2.415**	1.839	2.068*	2.787**	2.427*	2.266***
	(1.188)	(1.075)	(1.195)	(1.220)	(1.342)	(1.250)	(0.841)
GOAL3	0.950	0.707	0.469	0.696	0.805	0.889	0.242
	(0.797)	(0.664)	(0.726)	(0.808)	(0.725)	(0.796)	(0.497)
CORR	-0.0712	-0.103	-0.0553	-0.0572	-0.0429	-0.102	0.0579
	(0.119)	(0.127)	(0.117)	(0.117)	(0.118)	(0.121)	(0.190)
Constant	1.903	2.536	1.463	2.040	3.387*	3.155*	5.937***
	(1.498)	(1.706)	(1.919)	(1.697)	(1.822)	(1.834)	(1.437)
Country fixed-effects	yes	yes	yes	yes	yes	yes	yes
Religion dummies	yes	yes	yes	yes	yes	yes	yes
Population	yes	yes	yes	yes	yes	yes	yes
Financial devel. indexes [a]	yes	yes	yes	yes	yes	yes	yes
General devel. indexes [b]	yes	yes	yes	yes	yes	yes	yes
Observations	78	78	78	78	78	78	78

Notes:
Probit estimates. The dependent latent variable is the probability that the central bank is the (sole) authority responsible for banking supervision. Robust standard errors in parentheses. ***, **, * Significance at the 10, 5 and 1 per cent level.
[a] MvB, BankAss_GDP, Latitude.
[b] OECD, UN.

Source: authors' calculation.

Conclusions and Policy Implications

In this chapter, we investigate whether the institutional monetary setting can play a role in the policymakers' decision of assigning banking supervisory powers to central banks.

First, the econometric analysis shows that stronger central bank's operational independence implies less supervisory powers, while political independence – intended as the pure absence of government members in the central bank's board of directors – has no effect on task assignment. Since in our estimates we control for the presence of corruption practices in each country – a proxy for the presence of grabbing-hand politicians – the thesis of the fear of a too powerful institution seems insufficient to explain our outcome. Instead, we explain our result through the willingness of benevolent governments of not assigning supervision to central banks because these could make an instrumental use of monetary policy as a means to hide supervisory mismanagement.

Second, we provide evidence that a peculiar feature of political independence, namely the presence of clearly measurable monetary policy goals, can affect the way central banks tie their own hands in terms of the use of monetary policy. This should represent a commitment device mitigating the risk of discretion which increases the odds of a central bank involvement in supervision.

In this view, the analysis reveals that assigning supervision to highly operationally autonomous agencies might be a risk for policymakers. Having a monetary policy goal which ties central bank's hands thus minimizing operational liquidity mismanagement could help mitigate this problem.

In a policy perspective, the experience of the very last months seems characterized by an increasing involvement of central banks in supervision, in general using the 'new' formula of the macro-supervision, given the existing characteristics in terms of CBI. The explanation can be found in the effects of the financial crisis on the policymaker's perception of the pros and cons of the central bank involvement. In particular, the level of CBI can represent, case by case, a factor which either eases or complicates the final political decision. Let us qualify our statement with concrete examples.

The financial crisis has stressed the importance of overseeing systemic risks. In other words, it becomes crucial to monitor and assess the threats to financial stability that can arise from macro developments taking place both in the economic and the financial system as a whole (macro supervision). The increasing emphasis on macro supervision motivates policymakers to identify specific bodies, which should be responsible for this function. In order to carry out macro prudential supervisory tasks, information on the economic and financial system as a whole is required. The view is gaining momentum that central banks are in the best position to collect and analyze this kind of information (Orphanides, 2010), given their role in managing monetary policy both in regular and in exceptional times (through lending of last resort).

From the policymakers' point of view, the involvement of the central bank in macro supervision means greater potential benefits in terms of information. They can also presume that the potential costs of central bank involvement are smaller compared to those related to micro supervision. In other words, the separation between micro and macro supervision can be used to reduce the arguments against central bank involvement.

What are the possible effects of the existing degree of CBI? Both in the case of the European Union project and in the UK situation, we have two independent central banks committed to pursue the monetary stability goal; therefore political CBI is likely to represent a facilitating factor in increasing the central bank involvement in supervision. The same reasoning can be applied considering both the case of Germany and Ireland, which are countries belonging to the European Monetary Union. On the one hand, their central banks do not have full responsibilities for monetary policy any more; on the other hand these countries are members of a monetary agreement with an independent central bank committed to monetary stability. Both elements go in the same direction, i.e. to facilitate the political solution toward a greater central bank involvement in the banking supervision. In general, the recent episodes of greater central bank involvement in supervision through the macro responsibility assignment seem to be more an evolution of the central bank specialization as monetary agent rather than a new trend towards de-specialization.

Appendix

Table 8.A1 Variables Description and Data Sources

VARIABLE	DESCRIPTION	SOURCE
Central Bank as Banking Supervisory Authority (CBBA)	The variable takes value 1 if the central bank is the (sole) banking supervisory authority and zero otherwise.	Courtis (2009) and Central Banks' websites
Grilli Masciandaro Tabellini (GMT) Index of Central Bank Independence	The index is calculated as the sum of central bank's fulfillment of 15 criteria, 8 for political independence and 7 for operational independence. Political independence is defined as the ability of central bank to select the final objectives of monetary policy, based on the following eight criteria: (1) governor is appointed without government involvement; (2) governor is appointed for more than five years; (3) board of directors is appointed without government involvement; (4) board is appointed for more than five years; (5) there is no mandatory participation of government representative(s) in the board; (6) no government approval is required for formulation of monetary policy; (7) central bank is legally obliged to pursue monetary stability as one of its primary objectives; and (8) there are legal provisions that strengthen the central bank's position in the event of a conflict with the government. Economic independence is the central bank's operational independence based on seven criteria: (1) there is no automatic procedure for the government to obtain direct credit from the central bank; (2) when available, direct credit facilities are extended to the government at market interest rates; (3) this credit is temporary; (4) and for a limited amount; (5) the central bank does not participate in the primary market for public debt; (6) the central bank is responsible for setting the policy rate; and (7) the central bank has no responsibility for overseeing the banking sector (two points) or shares responsibility (one point).	Grilli, Masciandaro and Tabellini (1991) and Arnone et al. (2007)
GMTp	GMT index considering only the (8) criteria for political independence.	Grilli, Masciandaro and Tabellini (1991) and Arnone et al. (2007)
GMTp_bis	GMTp excluding criterion (7) in the political independence.	Grilli, Masciandaro and Tabellini (1991) and Arnone et al. (2007)
GMTp_ter	GMTp considering only the first 5 criteria for the political independence.	Grilli, Masciandaro and Tabellini (1991) and Arnone et al. (2007)
GMTo	GMT index considering only the criterion (7) for operational independence	Grilli, Masciandaro and Tabellini (1991) and Arnone et al. (2007)
GMTo_bis	GMTo excluding criterion (7) in the operational independence.	Grilli, Masciandaro and Tabellini (1991) and Arnone et al. (2007)

Table 8.A1 Continued

VARIABLE	DESCRIPTION	SOURCE
GMTo_ter	GMTo considering only the first 5 criteria for the operational independence.	Grilli, Masciandaro and Tabellini (1991) and Arnone et al. (2007)
Monetary Policy Goal (GOAL)	The variable takes different values depending on the type of objectives specified with respect to monetary policy: 1=price stability with inflation control; 2=liquidity control; 3=growth of means of payment in line with real economy growth; 4=other, mix of objectives.	Authors using central banks' websites and official documents.
Corruption index (CORR)	The index ranges from 1 to 10. A higher value indicates a higher score (lower corruption).	Transparency International (website), latest year available and Kaufman et al. (2003) and Kaufman (2004).
Bank Assets/GDP (BankAss_GDP)	Claims on domestic real nonfinancial sector by the Central Bank as a share of GDP.	Beck, Demirgüç-Kunt and Levine, (1999)
Market versus bank based country(MvB)	Market versus bank based country. The variable is constructed using different measures of financial and banking efficiency measures: see Demirgüç-Kunt and Levine (1999) for further details. Average values: 1996, 1998, 2000, 2002, 2004.	Beck-Demirgüç -Kunt and Levine (1999)
Latitude (LAT)	The value is calculated as in Beck, Demirgüç-Kunt and Levine (1999) as absolute value of country's latitude standardized on values between 0 and 1.	*FactBook*, CIA and Beck, Demirgüç-Kunt and Levine (1999)
Unemployment rate (UN)	Unemployment rate for 2007	*FactBook*, CIA
OECD membership (OECD)	The variable takes values: 1= OECD member; 2 = non-OECD member	Authors
Population (POP)	Million inhabitants. Average values 1996,1998,2000,2002, 2004	World Development Indicators (World Bank. 2007).
Religion (REL)	The variable takes values: 1= Buddhist; 2= catholic; 3= Muslim; 4= orthodox; 5= protestant	Djankov, McLiesh and Shleifer (2007)
Continent (CONT)	The variable takes values: 1= America; 2=Europe; 2=Africa; 4=Asia; 5= Oceania	Authors

Table 8.A2 Summary Statistics

	Mean	Standard Deviation	Min	Max
CBBA	0.590909	0.494484	0	1
GMT	0.667159	0.190118	0.25	1
GMTp	0.568966	0.306636	0	1
GMTp_bis	0.515599	0.344015	0	1
GMTp_ter	0.489655	0.352742	0	1
GMTp1	0.436782	0.498863	0	1
GMTp2	0.528736	0.502067	0	1
GMTp3	0.425287	0.497253	0	1
GMTp4	0.528736	0.502067	0	1

Table 8.A2 Continued

	Mean	Standard Deviation	Min	Max
GMTp5	0.528736	0.502067	0	1
GMTp6	0.574713	0.497253	0	1
GMTp7	0.942529	0.23409	0	1
GMTp8	0.586207	0.495368	0	1
GMTo	0.755747	0.178727	0.25	1
GMTo_bis	0.860153	0.172146	0	1
GMTo_ter	0.871264	0.199947	0	1
GMTo1	0.931035	0.254865	0	1
GMTo2	0.735632	0.443553	0	1
GMTo3	0.977012	0.150736	0	1
GMTo4	0.942529	0.23409	0	1
GMTo5	0.770115	0.423198	0	1
GMTo6	0.804598	0.398809	0	1
GMTo7	0.885058	0.841169	0	2
Monetary Policy Goal	1.709302	1.115308	1	4
Market vs Bank	0.250000	0.435494	0	1
Corruption Index	4.731818	2.473796	0	9.7
Bank_assets/GDP	2.596852	4.237759	0.087	35.267
Population	53.3858	171.1093	0.277	1250.632
Latitude	0.383082	0.190235	0.0111	0.7222
OECD	0.340909	0.476731	0	1
Buddhist	0.056818	0.232822	0	1
Catholic	0.363636	0.483802	0	1
Muslim	0.147727	0.356863	0	1
Orthodox	0.102273	0.304743	0	1
Protestant	0.159091	0.367857	0	1
Unemployment 2007	10.36932	10.9299	1.3	80
Continent	2.340909	1.123279	1	5

Source: authors' calculation.

Table 8.A3 Central Bank as Banking Supervisor, Independence and Monetary Policy Goals

COUNTRY	CBBA	GOAL	GMT	COUNTRY	CBBA	GOAL	GMT
Albania	1	1	0.75	Korea, Rep. Of	0	1	0.56
Argentina	1	2	0.75	Latvia	0	3	1
Australia	0	1	0.63	Lebanon	1	4	0.5
Austria	0	1	0.94	Libya	1	1	0.44
Bahamas, The	1	4	0.31	Lithuania	1	1	0.81
Belarus	1	4	0.44	Luxembourg	0	1	0.94
Belgium	0	1	0.94	Macedonia, FYR	1	4	0.88
Bolivia	0	2	0.75	Malaysia	1	1	0.5
Bosnia and Herzegovina	1	4	0.88	Malta	0	1	0.69
Botswana	0	1	0.44	Mauritius	1	3	0.5
Brazil	1	2	0.63	Mexico	0	1	0.69
Bulgaria	1	1	0.88	Moldova	1	1	0.75
Cameroon	0	2	0.69	Morocco	1	1	0.5
Canada	0	2	0.63	Netherlands	1	1	0.88
Chile	0	1	0.69	New Zealand	1	1	0.44
China	0	1	0.56	Nicaragua	0	1	0.56
Colombia	0	1	0.5	Norway	0	1	0.75
Costa Rica	0	1	0.69	Pakistan	1	1	0.5
Croatia	1	1	0.88	Panama	0		0.38
Cyprus	1	1	0.56	Peru	0	1	0.69
Czech Republic	1	1	0.88	Philippines	1	1	0.63
Denmark	0	4	0.75	Poland	0	1	0.88
Ecuador	0	3	0.94	Portugal	1	1	0.81
Egypt, Arab Rep.	1	3	0.38	Romania	1	1	0.69
El Salvador	0	3	0.81	Russian Federation	1	4	0.44
Estonia	0	4	0.81	Slovak Republic	1	1	0.63
Finland	0	1	0.94	Slovenia	1	1	0.81
France	1	1	0.94	South Africa	1	1	0.25
Georgia	1	3	0.75	Spain	1	1	0.88
Germany	0	1	0.88	Sri Lanka	1	1	0.56
Greece	1	1	0.81	Sweden	0	1	0.94
Guatemala	0	1	0.63	Switzerland	0	1	0.94
Hungary	0	1	0.94	Thailand	1	1	0.44
Iceland	0	3	0.75	Trinidad and Tobago	1	1	0.44
India	1	3	0.5	Tunisia	1	1	0.69
Iran, Islamic Rep.	1	3	0.38	Turkey	0	1	0.81
Ireland	1	1	0.81	Ukraine	1	1	0.81
Israel	1	3	0.38	United Arab Emirates	1	1	0.44
Italy	1	1	0.81	United Kingdom	0	1	0.69
Jamaica	1	3	0.38	United States	1	2	0.75
Japan	0	1	0.44	Uruguay	1	1	0.63
Jordan	1	4	0.38	Venezuela, RB	1	1	0.69

Table 8.A3 Continued

COUNTRY	CBBA	GOAL	GMT	COUNTRY	CBBA	GOAL	GMT
Kazakhstan	0	4	0.75	Vietnam	1	4	0.44
Kenya	1	1	0.44	Zimbabwe	1		0.44

Source: authors' calculation.

References

Abrams, R.K. and M.W. Taylor (2002), 'Assessing the Case for Unified Sector Supervision' *Financial Markets Group Special Papers* No.134, FMG, LSE, London.

Acemoglu D., S. Johnson, P. Querubin and J.A. Robinson (2008), 'When Does Policy Reform Work? The Case of Central Bank Independence', *NBER Working Paper Series* No.14033, National Bureau of Economic Research.

Ahsan A., M. Skully and J. Wickramanayake (2006), 'Central Bank Independence and Governance. Definitions and Modeling', *Journal of Administration and Governance*, **1**, 46–67.

Alesina A. and A. Stella (2010), 'The Politics of Monetary Policy', *Discussion Paper Series* No.2183, Harvard Institute of Economic Research.

Alpanda S. and A. Honig (2009), 'The Impact of Central Bank Independence on Political Monetary Cycles in Advanced and Developing Countries', *Journal of Money, Credit and Banking*, **41**(7), 1365–1389.

Alpanda S. and A. Honig (2010), 'Political Monetary Cycles and a de facto ranking of central bank independence', *Journal of International Money and Finance*, 1–21 (in press).

Arnone, M. and A. Gambini (2007), 'Architecture of Supervisory Authorities and Banking Supervision' in Masciandaro D. and M. Quintyn (eds), *Designing Financial Supervision Institutions: Independence, Accountability and Governance*, Cheltenham, UK and Northampton, MA, USA: Edward Elgar, pp. 262–308.

Barth, J.R., Nolle, D.E., Phumiwasana, T. and Yago, G. (2002), 'A Cross Country Analysis of the Bank Supervisory Framework and

Bank Performance', *Financial Markets, Institutions & Instruments*, **12**(2), 67–120.

Beck, T., A. Demirgüç-Kunt and R. Levine (1999), 'A New Database on Financial Development and Structure', *World Bank Economic Review,* **14**, 597–605.

Bernanke B. (2007), 'Central Banking and Banking Supervision in the United States', Allied Social Sciences Association, Annual Meeting, Chicago, mimeo.

Berriel T.C. and S. Bhattarai (2009), 'Monetary Policy and Central Bank Balance Sheet Concerns', *B.E. Journal of Macroeconomics*, **9**(1), 1–31.

Bini Smaghi L. (2008), 'Central Bank Independence in the EU: From Theory to Practice', *European Law Journal*, **14**(4), 446–460.

Blanchard O., G. Dell'Ariccia and P. Mauro (2010), 'Rethinking Macroeconomic Policy', *IMF Staff Position Note*, 10/03.

Buiter W.H. (2007), 'Seignorage', *NBER Working Paper Series,* No.11919, National Bureau of Economic Research.

Carlstrom C.T. and T.S. Fuerst (2009), 'Central Bank Independence and Inflation: a Note', *Economic Inquiry*, **47**(1), 182–186.

Čihák, M. (2007), *Central Bank Independence and Financial Stability*, IMF, mimeo.

Čihák, M. and R. Podpiera (2007), 'Experience with Integrated Supervisors: Governance and Quality of Supervision' in Masciandaro D. and M. Quintyn (eds) *Designing Financial Supervision Institutions: Independence, Accountability and Governance*, Cheltenham, UK and Northampton, MA, USA: Edward Elgar, pp. 309–341.

Cohen-Cole E. and J. Morse (2010), 'Monetary Policy and Capital Regulation in the US and Europe', *Working Paper Series* No.1222, European Central Bank.

Courtis, N. (2009), *How Countries Supervise their Banks, Insurers and Securities Markets*, London: Central Banking Publications.

Crowe C. and E.E. Meade (2008), 'Central Bank Independence and Transparency', *European Journal of Political Economy*, **24**, 763–777.

Cukierman A. (2008), 'Central Bank Independence and Monetary Policymaking Institutions: Past, Present and Future', *European Journal of Political Economy*, **24**, 722–736.

Cukierman A., G. Miller and B. Neyapti (2002), 'Central Bank Reform, Liberalization, and Inflation in Transition Economies. An International Perspective', *Journal of Monetary Economics*, **49**, 237–264.

Cukierman A., S. Webb and B. Nayapti (1992), 'Measuring the Independence of Central Banks and its Effect on Policy Outcomes', *World Bank Economic Review*, **6**(3), September, 353–98.

Curdia V. and M. Woodford (2010), 'The Central Bank Balance Sheet as an Instrument of Monetary Policy', *NBER Working Paper Series* No.16208, National Bureau of Economic Research.

Dalla Pellegrina, L. and D. Masciandaro (2008), 'Politicians, Central Banks and the Shape of Financial Supervision Architectures', *Journal of Financial Regulation and Compliance*, **16**, 290–317.

De Haan J., D. Masciandaro and M. Quintyn (2008), 'Does Central Bank Independence still Matter?' *European Journal of Political Economy*, **24**, 717–721.

Djankov, S., C. McLiesh and A. Shleifer (2007), 'Private Credit in 129 Countries', *Journal of Financial Economics*, **84**, May, 299–329.

Down I. (2008), 'Central Bank Independence, Disinflation and Monetary Policy', *Business and Politics*, **10**, 1–29.

Eijffinger, S. and P. Stadhouder (2003), 'Monetary Policy and the Rule of Law', CEPR *Discussion Paper Series* No. 3698, Center for Economic and Policy Research.

Garcia Herrero A. and P. Del Rio (2003), 'Financial Stability and the Design of Monetary Policy', *Working Paper Series* No.15, Banco de Espana.

Gertler M. and P. Karadi (2010), 'A Model of Unconventional Monetary Policy', *Journal of Monetary Economics*, forthcoming.

Giavazzi F. and A. Giovannini (2010), 'Central Banks and the Financial System', CEPR *Discussion Paper Series* No.7944, Center for Economic and Policy Research.

Gollwitzer S. and M. Quintyn (2010), 'The Effectiveness of Macroeconomic Commitment in Weak(er) Institutional Environment', *IMF Working Paper Series*, WP 10/193.

Goodhart, C.A.E. (2000), 'The Organisational Structure of Banking Supervision', *Financial Services Authority Occasional Paper*, Series 1.

Goodhart, C. and D. Schoenmaker (1995), 'Should the functions of monetary policy and banking supervision be separated?' *Oxford Economic Papers*, **47**, 539–560.

Goodhart C.A.E., C. Osorio and D.P. Tsomocos (2009), 'Analysis of Monetary Policy and Financial Stability: A New Paradigm', *CESifo Working Paper Series*, No. 2885.

Grilli V., D. Masciandaro and G. Tabellini (1991), 'Political and Monetary Institutions and Public Financial Policies in the Industrial Countries', *Economic Policy,* **13**, 341–92.

Herring R.J. and J. Carmassi (2008), 'The Structure of Cross-Sector Financial Supervision', *Financial Markets, Institutions and Instruments*, **17**, (1), 51–76.

Jacome L.I. (2008), 'Central Bank Involvement in Banking Crises in Latin America', *IMF Working Paper Series*, WP 08/135.

Kaufmann, D. (2004), *Corruption, Governance and Security: Challenges for the Rich Countries and the World,* Washington DC, USA: World Bank Institute.

Kaufmann, D., Kraay, A. and Mastruzzi, M. (2003), 'Governance matters III: governance indicators 1996–2002', *Policy Research Working Paper Series*, No. 3106, Washington DC, USA: The World Bank.

Keefer P. (1999), 'When Do Special Interests Run Rampant? Disentangling the Role of Elections, Incomplete Information and Checks and Balances in Banking Crises', *Policy Research Working Paper Series* No. 2543, The World Bank.

Keefer P. and D. Stasavage (2002), 'Checks and Balances, Private Information and the Credibility of Monetary Commitments', *International Organization*, **56**, 751–774.

Keefer P. and D. Stasavage (2003), 'The Limits of Delegation: Veto Players, Central Bank Independence, and the Credibility of Monetary Policy', *American Political Science Review*, **97**, 407–423.

Klomp J. and J. De Haan (2009), 'Central Bank Independence and Financial Stability', *Journal of Financial Stability*, **5**, 321–338.

Klomp J. and J. De Haan (2010), 'Central Bank Independence and Inflation Revisited', *Public Choice*, **144**, 445–357.

Llewellyn, D.T. (2005), 'Institutional Structure of Financial Regulation and Supervision: the Basic Issues' in A. Fleming, D.T. Llewellyn and J. Carmichael (eds), *Aligning Financial Supervision*

Structures with Country Needs, World Bank Publications, Washington D.C, USA: The World Bank, pp. 19–85.

Masciandaro, D. (2006), 'E Pluribus Unum? Authorities Design in Financial Supervision: Trends and Determinants', *Open Economies Review*, **17**(1), 73–102.

Masciandaro, D. (2007), 'Divide et Impera: Financial Supervision Unification and the Central Bank Fragmentation Effect', *European Journal of Political Economy*, 285–315.

Masciandaro, D. (2008), 'Politicians and Financial Supervision Unification outside the Central Bank: Why Do They Do It?', *Journal of Financial Stability*, **5**(2), 124–146.

Masciandaro D. and M. Quintyn (2008), 'Helping Hand or Grabbing Hand? Politicians, Supervisory Regime, Financial Structure and Market View', *North American Journal of Economics and Finance,* 153–174.

Masciandaro D. and M. Quintyn (2009), 'Reforming Financial Supervision and the Role of the Central Banks: a Review of Global Trends, Causes and Effects (1998–2008)', *CEPR Policy Insight*, **30**, 1–11.

Maslowska A. (2007), 'Discussion on the Inconsistency of Central Bank Independence Measures', *Discussion Paper Series* No.21, Aboa Centre for Economics.

Maslowska A. (2008), 'Quest for the Best: How to Measure Central Bank Independence and Show its Relation with Inflation?', *Discussion Paper Series* No.37, Aboa Centre for Economics.

Maslowska A. (2009), 'Using Taylor Rule to Explain Effects of Institutional Changes in Central Bank', *Discussion Paper Series* no.46, Aboa Centre for Economics.

Oritani Y. (2010), 'Public Governance of Central Banks: An Approach from New Institutional Economics', *BIS Working Papers* No. 299, Bank for International Settlements.

Orphanides A. (2010), 'Monetary Policy Lessons from the Crisis', *Discussion Paper Series* No.7891, CEPR.

Padoa Schioppa, T. (2003) 'Financial Supervision: Inside or Outside the Central Banks?' in J. Kremers, D. Schoenmaker, P. Wierts, *Financial Supervision in Europe*, Cheltenham, UK and Northampton, MA, USA: Edward Elgar, 160–175.

Quintyn, M. and Taylor, M.W. (2007), 'Building Supervisory Structures in sub-Saharan Africa – An analytical framework' *IMF Working Paper Series*, WP 07/18.

Rapaport O., D. Levi-Faur and D. Miodownik (2009), 'The Puzzle of the Diffusion of the Central Bank Independence Reforms: Insights from an Agent-Based Simulation', *Policy Studies Journal*, **37**(4), 695–716.

World Bank (2007), *World Development Indicators 2006*, Washington DC, USA: The World Bank.

9. How Should Central Banks Deal with a Financial Stability Objective? The Evolving Role of Communication as a Policy Instrument

Benjamin Born, Michael Ehrmann and Marcel Fratzscher[1]

Introduction

The financial crisis of 2007–2010 has brought the topic of financial supervision and regulation to the forefront of the policy debate. While micro-prudential supervision had already undergone a reform process prior to the crisis, with a trend towards unified national supervisory bodies *outside* the central banks,[2] a major overhaul of micro-prudential and macro-prudential regulation and supervision is on its way around the globe. Especially with regard to macro-prudential supervision, this reform process often assigns central banks a prominent role. There are a number of reasons for such an assignment.

Combining financial supervision with monetary policy tasks can

---

[1] We are grateful to a large number of colleagues in various central banks for useful discussions on the issues addressed in this chapter and for their help in retrieving some of the data employed in the empirical analysis. This chapter presents the authors' personal opinions and does not necessarily reflect the views of the European Central Bank.

[2] Recent reform efforts of micro-prudential regulation and supervision are discussed, e.g., in Herring and Carmassi (2008) and Masciandaro and Quintyn (2009).

lead to synergies, e.g., through information gains, thereby possibly leading to a more effective conduct of monetary policy and/or to more effective crisis prevention and management (Borio, 2009). Furthermore, the lender of last resort function gives central banks a natural role in this process (Blinder, 2010). Also, it has been argued that central banks should systematically incorporate systemic risk considerations in their monetary policy process (e.g., Feldstein, 2010), a point that has been strengthened by recent advances in our understanding of the transmission mechanism of monetary policy: the risk-taking channel, for instance, stipulates that if monetary policy keeps interest rates relatively low over an extended period this might cause an increase in the amount of risk that banks take on (e.g., Borio and Zhu, 2008; Jiménez et al., 2010).

Despite these considerations, macro-prudential tasks will bring a number of challenges for central banks. First, appropriate analytical tools need to be developed that allow assessing systemic risks (e.g., through early warning indicators and contagion models) with sufficient timeliness and precision. Once risks have been identified, it is necessary to gauge whether and how macro-prudential policy should react. For that purpose, realistic macro-finance models need to be developed that allow studying the propagation of financial stability risks to the broader economy, and that can be used to simulate the transmission channels of macro-prudential policy. The development of these tools constitutes a major task, especially given that the state of research in this area is far less advanced than, for instance, our understanding of monetary policy.

Second, to make these tools functional, the relevant data need to be made available. Also in this field, substantial progress is required, given that data availability is at times constrained by confidentiality restrictions, and because in many instances the relevant data are not yet collected. Third, in order to make macro-prudential policy effective, the policymaker needs to be equipped with a set of effective policy instruments. There is general agreement that the main instrument for monetary policy, an aggregate interest rate, is too blunt for macro-prudential purposes. Other tools are being devised, yet it also remains to be seen to what extent these will turn out to be sufficiently independent from policy rates in order to fulfill the

Tinbergen rule, which states that there must be one policy instrument for each objective.[3]

While central banks and the academic research community have started to devote a large amount of resources to address all these challenges, an issue that has attracted relatively little attention so far is the role of communication in the conduct of macro-prudential policy. This is rather surprising, given that communication is bound to be at centre stage of macro-prudential policy. As we will argue below, it will play a crucial role to address possible reputational risks for the central bank, to make macro-prudential policy more efficient, and to make the policymaker accountable.

Against this background, the aim of this chapter is to discuss the role of macro-prudential communication as well as a number of related challenges that central banks with macro-prudential policy tasks are likely to encounter (section two). Whenever possible, we will draw parallels to the role of communication in monetary policy-making, drawing on the emerging literature in this area. Furthermore, this chapter provides an empirical assessment of the effects of communication about financial stability and macro-prudential risks on financial markets in section three, building on the work by Born et al., (2010). In the final section, we will draw the main policy conclusions emerging from these considerations.

Some Conceptual Issues

The role of macro-prudential communication

Communication is bound to be at the centre stage of macro-prudential policy, for a number of reasons. First, central banks are often explicitly assigned to provide information, analysis and recommendations about systemic risks, thus making communication part of their macro-prudential mandate. Second, financial markets are inherently characterized by asymmetric information and co-ordination problems, characteristics which lie at the heart of the potential risks to financial stability. Co-ordinating the expectations of economic agents

---

[3] For a discussion on the possibility of conflicts among different goals, see, e.g., Goodhart and Shoenmaker (2005) or De Grauwe and Gros (2009).

can therefore be a powerful tool to address such problems, which in turn calls for clarity about the objectives of macro-prudential policy as well as about the way policy instruments are going to be used to that end (Aikman et al., 2010). Third, any body that is entrusted with macro-prudential supervision will need to be accountable, which calls for a clear mandate, and a transparent conduct of the assigned task. Although Oosterloo and de Haan (2004) found that there is often a lack of accountability requirements for central banks' financial stability objectives, this is very likely to change in the future, once financial stability has become a more important and explicit objective of central banks.

Fourth, the involvement in macro-prudential tasks might entail a risk for the reputation of a central bank, a point that has been raised in connection to micro-prudential supervision by Goodhart (2002), but equally applies in the macro-prudential arena. *Failures* in financial supervision do typically attract a lot of media attention, with possibly adverse effects on the confidence that the central bank enjoys with the public. In contrast, *successful* supervisory roles normally go unnoticed, implying that the reputational risks for the central bank are asymmetric. One might argue that this is the nature of the supervisory task, and that one institution will have to bear that risk, so it might just of well be the central bank. However, there is a possibility that a loss in confidence in the central bank, in turn, might adversely affect the effectiveness of the conduct of monetary policy, a trade-off that would not be relevant in the case of a separate macro-prudential body. In order to minimize the risk of a reputational loss, central banks that are entrusted with supervisory tasks will therefore need to carefully design their respective communication policies.

All these aspects of communication for financial stability closely resemble the role of monetary policy-related communication, as established in the recent literature on central bank communication (see, e.g., Blinder et al., 2008; Gosselin, Lotz and Wyplosz, 2007; Ehrmann and Fratzscher, 2007). Also in the monetary policy sphere, communication serves: i) to make central banks credible (mirroring the importance of financial stability communication for reputational purposes); ii) to enhance the effectiveness of monetary policy (just like good financial stability communication can contribute to financial stability); and iii) to make central banks accountable.

Communication channels and target groups

Having established the different objectives of macro-prudential communication, it is useful to think what these imply for the use of different communication channels, and which audiences should be addressed for the respective purposes. Over the recent past, the two channels most frequently used by central banks to convey messages about financial stability issues were Financial Stability Reports (FSRs) as well as speeches and interviews by members of the central banks' decision-making bodies. In some instances (e.g., Sweden's Riksbank), central banks have appointed spokespersons for financial stability matters, whereas in others, this task is performed jointly by the various members of the decision-making bodies.

Čihák (2006, 2007) provides a systematic overview of FSRs. He documents, on the one hand, that the reports have become considerably more sophisticated over time, with substantial improvements in the underlying analytical tools, and, on the other hand, that there has been a large increase in the number of central banks that publish FSRs. The frontrunners are the Bank of England, the Swedish Riksbank, and Norges Bank (Norway's central bank), all of which started publication in 1996/1997. It is probably no coincidence that these three central banks are typically also listed in the group of the most transparent central banks with regard to monetary policy issues (Eijffinger and Geraats, 2006; Dincer and Eichengreen, 2009). In the meantime, around 50 central banks have started to release FSRs.

A first empirical analysis of FSRs has been conducted by Oosterloo et al. (2007), with the aim to understand who publishes FSRs, for what motives, and with what content. Their results indicate that there are mainly three motives for publication, namely to increase transparency, to contribute to financial stability, and to strengthen co-operation between different authorities with financial stability tasks. They also find that the occurrence of a systemic banking crisis in the past is positively related to the likelihood that an FSR is published. Wilkinson et al. (2010) investigate the content of FSRs by four European countries, and find that these were generally successful in identifying the relevant risks prevailing during the global financial crisis, yet underestimated its severity.

Whereas FSRs typically have a pre-defined release schedule, speeches and interviews are a much more flexible tool. The intensity with which the central bank communicates with the public has been found to depend on market conditions, with more active communication occurring particularly during times of high volatilities in financial markets, as well as during bearish stock markets (Born et al., 2010). In the absence of a predefined release schedule, the mere occurrence of a speech, the fact that a policymaker feels compelled to make a statement about financial stability in a speech or interview, can already constitute news to financial markets (whereas for FSRs, the public knows the release dates ex ante, and therefore expects such statements). Other distinctive features of speeches and interviews are, on the one hand, that these are by nature much less comprehensive than FSRs (which aim to provide a broad coverage of all relevant aspects), and, on the other hand, that they often represent a personal view, whereas FSRs are typically approved by the entire decision-making body of the central bank.

Communication channels that have been used less regularly in the past, but that we would expect to grow in importance, are relevant data releases as well as regular press releases, and maybe even press conferences (as, for instance, practiced by the Financial Stability Board, which regularly issues press releases after its plenary meetings, and the chair of which often holds a press conference after the plenary meetings). Parliamentary hearings and testimonies are also likely to become much more frequent with explicit macro-prudential tasks assigned to central banks. Interestingly, all these changes would move the communication channels much closer to those currently employed for monetary policy purposes.

Similarities between monetary policy and financial stability communication also relate to the various target audiences. Governments and parliaments are important addressees of central bank communications in both policy domains with a view to establish accountability. Financial markets likewise are a major target given their importance for the conduct of monetary policy as well as for financial stability. Finally, also the general public will be an important audience for macro-prudential policymakers, as (just like in the case of monetary policy) the expectations of the general public and its trust in the policymaking institution are crucial for effective conduct of both policies. Van der Cruijsen et al. (2010b) have surveyed the knowledge and opinions about banking supervision among Dutch households. They find that the public's knowledge in this field is far from perfect.[4] In particular, respondents seem to have unrealistic expectations about what supervisors can deliver. Such misperceptions are bound to lead to disillusionment during crises, and thus possibly to a loss in confidence at times when this is most needed. Importantly, the survey also finds that respondents with better knowledge about banking supervision have more realistic expectations, which suggests that there are important benefits to educating the public about the aims of macro-prudential policies, but also about its limitations.

An aspect where macro-prudential communication might well differ from the monetary policy arena is owed to the fact that in several countries, a multitude of institutions is responsible for financial supervision, whereas there is typically only one monetary authority. The co-ordination of the content of communications is therefore essential (see also Siklos, 2010). Just as the discussion about whether central banks should speak with one voice about monetary policy, or convey the diversity of views on their decision-making bodies (see, e.g., Bernanke (2004) for a voice in favor of expressing diverse views, and Issing (2005) for a counterposition), the design of communication strategies for macro-prudential policy needs to consider to what extent the messages expressed by the various institutions should be consistent or express the whole range of views on the committee.

Communication during 'normal' and during crisis times

A crucial aspect that characterizes financial stability-related communications is the environment in which they are made. Principles of communication during 'normal' times of financial stability are necessarily very different from their counterparts during crisis times, or when there are substantial risks to financial stability. A first difference, of course, relates to the respective aims of communications – crisis prevention during 'normal' times, and crisis management and resolution otherwise.

---

[4] Which constitutes yet another analogy to monetary policy, see van der Cruijsen et al. (2010a).

This distinction is important with regard to how transparent the macro-prudential policymaker can be. In the monetary policy domain, we have seen central banks becoming much more transparent about their conduct of monetary policy over the last decades, along with an increasing importance given to communication. While here too there is a debate on possible limits to central bank transparency (e.g., Mishkin, 2004; Morris and Shin, 2002; Svensson, 2006), much more compelling arguments have been made in the case of financial stability-related communication. As demonstrated by Cukierman (2009), a clear case for limiting transparency can be made when the central bank has private information about problems within segments of the financial system. Release of such information may potentially be harmful, e.g., by triggering a run on the financial system. In this situation, limits to transparency are therefore easily justified.

At the same time, this line of reasoning is much less convincing when applied to normal times. Here, transparency should be the default option, as this can contribute to an effective crisis prevention. The model in Aikman et al. (2010), for instance, clearly shows that credit cycles result from a failure to co-ordinate the actions of economic agents, and that co-ordination of actions can be achieved once the agents' expectations are aligned. As the authors write (p. 31): 'Without absolute clarity about the objectives of any macro-prudential policy framework and the policy rule necessary to deliver these objectives, expectations will not adjust and policy will be impotent. Any lack of transparency or failure of communications is likely to inhibit seriously the effectiveness of macro-prudential policy.'

In a similar vein, Svensson (2003) discusses the role of Financial Stability Reports in the conduct of macro-prudential policy during normal times, stating that 'these reports serve to assure the general public and economic agents that everything is well in the financial sector when this is the case. They also serve as early warnings for the agents concerned and for the financial-regulation authorities when problems show up at the horizon. Early action can then prevent any financial instability to materialize, keeping the probability of future financial stability very low' (p. 26–27).

Another example relates to bank stress tests, which have become a common tool to assess systemic risks in the banking sector. If the central bank *ex ante* announces a rule that such tests will be conducted regularly, and that its results will be in the public domain, this clearly provides an incentive for banks to ensure that they will pass the stress tests. Transparency ex ante about the aims, tools, and procedures of macro-prudential policy is therefore a powerful instrument to steer the incentives of economic agents, and thereby to aid crisis prevention.

The very same (communication) instrument is much more controversial during crisis times. In the midst of the global financial crisis, bank stress tests have been conducted both in the European Union and in the United States. The results of the 2009 US Supervisory Capital Assessment Program, which assessed the financial conditions of the 19 largest US bank holding companies, and the subsequent actions by banks to raise new funds clearly had a calming impact on financial markets. In contrast, the 2010 European Union banking stress test exercise has been under heavy criticism, e.g. because the underlying assumptions were regarded as being too lax by some (e.g., Blundell-Wignall and Slovik, 2010).

These examples clearly illustrate that there is a very strong case for transparency in communication during normal times, or at early stages of a build-up in risk, when such communications can serve to align agents' incentives, to co-ordinate their expectations, and to steer their behavior in a way that helps to prevent crises. Only when it comes to crisis times, or in the presence of substantial risks to financial stability, do the arguments for limiting transparency gain their relevance. This distinction has rarely been made in the discussion about macro-prudential policies, but it is important to make. The evolution of monetary policy has clearly shown that a transparent, rule-based policy can very effectively steer agents' expectations and behavior, a lesson that should be taken into account when designing macro-prudential policies now.

Separating monetary policy and macro-prudential communications

Another aspect that needs considering is whether and how to separate communications about monetary policy from their macro-prudential counterparts if their sender is identical. According to what has been dubbed the 'Jackson Hole consensus' prior to the global financial crisis (Bean et al., 2010), many central banks worked under the assumption that price stability is a sufficient condition for financial stability. This consensus has clearly been challenged by the global financial crisis, leading to a common understanding that the two goals should be conceptually separated (which is the entire raison d'être for macro-prudential supervisors). As discussed above, according to the Tinbergen principle, in the presence of two goals, a policymaker requires two independent policy instruments. The same logic also applies to communications – in view of the possibility that the two goals might not always be fully aligned, and that there could even be conflicts between the goals, it is important to have two separate communication instruments at hand.

This has of course been well understood by central banks. The ECB's 'separation principle' is a case in point: from the onset of the global financial crisis, the ECB offered additional liquidity to banks with a view to ensuring the orderly functioning of the euro area interbank money market. These policy measures were taken from a financial stability perspective, given that the ECB had to ensure a proper transmission mechanism of its monetary policy actions, and wanted to avoid tensions in the money market spilling over to other markets and adversely affecting the real economy. Separate from this, the ECB's Governing Council had set the level of the key interest rates with a view to delivering price stability in the medium term. The ECB therefore carefully communicated two separate yet complementary messages, namely that it had implemented its exceptional interventions with a view to alleviating the tensions in the money market, but that this would not compromise the ECB's determination to deliver price stability (Trichet, 2008).

While there seems to be a strong case for separate communications, a complication arises for the following reason. The crisis has strengthened the case for 'leaning against the wind', whereby central banks react to asset prices beyond their effect on inflation and output objectives, with a view to prevent asset price bubbles. While there is still considerable controversy as to whether this is advisable (e.g., Bean et al., 2010), we should expect to see more leaning against the wind monetary policies in practice. In these cases, monetary policy and financial stability considerations are intertwined, such that a separation of the respective communications is not straightforward.

Distributional effects of macro-prudential policy – a communication challenge

A final aspect that we want to discuss in this section relates to the fact that macro-prudential policy is, in contrast to monetary policy, targeted at specific segments of the financial system. Accordingly, it is much more evident that macro-prudential policy actions affect particular parts of the financial system and/or the population. While monetary policy also has differential effects, e.g. across regions or sectors (Beckworth, 2010; Dedola and Lippi, 2005; Peersman and Smets, 2005), these are a by-product of a universal policy tool, not the intention of the policy. In both policy areas the famous quote by William McChesney Martin, the FOMC Chairman in the 1950s and 1960s applies, namely that the tasks imply 'to take away the punch bowl just as the party gets going'. The difference is that monetary policy takes away everyone's punch bowl (and this will lead to more or less disappointment of party guests depending on their preferences for punch), whereas macro-prudential policy has the task of barring only some guests from the punch bowl, whereas the other guests might continue (possibly receiving smaller helpings).

One can therefore expect much more controversy about macro-prudential policy actions than what we know from monetary policy, up to a point where a central bank might face a reputation risk (beyond those mentioned above, where reputation is lost in case of financial instability, whereas little reputation is gained in times of financial stability). An example relates to the decision of the Bank of Israel in May 2010 to restrict the loan to value ratio on mortgages, in order to cool the booming housing market. This measure has led to a controversial discussion in the media, where opponents argued that this policy harms young couples and other economically weak groups in a disproportionate manner (Katz and Katz, 2010; Landau, 2010). Being faced with such a challenge, central banks need to very carefully justify their policy measures, which in turn implies a central role for communication policies.

The Effects of Communication About Financial Stability and Macro-prudential Risks on Financial Markets

Having discussed various conceptual issues regarding financial stability-related communications by central banks, we will now move on to provide an empirical assessment on how such communications affect financial markets. A necessary (albeit not sufficient) condition for communications to affect the behavior of economic agents is that they get heard – which we hope to show by providing evidence that financial markets react to their release. A more stringent test is whether the central bank furthermore achieves that its views get reflected in the markets. For instance, if the central bank expresses a rather pessimistic view about the prospects for financial stability, and this view gets heard in financial markets, we would expect financial sector stock prices to decline. In that sense, these communications 'create news'. Another possible effect could be that they 'reduce noise', in the sense that a communication by the central bank contributes to reducing uncertainty in financial markets, thereby reducing volatility.[5]

To assess these questions, we estimate an exponential GARCH-model, which allows us to study the effects of financial stability-related communication both on the conditional mean and the conditional variance of important financial markets.

Data

The empirical analysis focuses on emerging economies[6], given that these have experienced relatively more periods of financial instability over the recent years, and therefore constitute an interesting sample. However, as is often the case when dealing with emerging economies, there are data availability restrictions when choosing the countries and markets to analyze. We settle for those emerging economies where the central banks publish FSRs, and for which daily data on financial stock market indices, overall stock market indices, short-term (three-

---

[5] These ideas are borrowed from the monetary policy communication literature, see Blinder et al. (2008).

[6] Emerging economies are defined following the IMF's country classification (see World Economic Outlook, IMF, 2010).

month) interest rates and (US-dollar) spot market exchange rates are available from Datastream.[7]

Identifying the exact publication dates and having a quantified measure of the contents of central bank communication about financial stability is of utmost importance for our econometric analysis. We use a new database, described in Born et al. (2010), providing this information about FSRs and speeches/interviews by the respective central bank governors. The release dates of FSRs are identified based on information provided on central banks' websites and by central bank press offices, and complemented with information from news reports about the release of FSRs as recorded in Factiva. Speeches and interviews are identified by extracting Factiva entries containing statements by the governors with a reference to financial stability issues.

Table 9.1 shows the distribution of the 87 FSRs and 89 speeches/interviews contained in our sample, by country and by year. Our sample starts in 2001, the year after the first FSR was published by a central bank in an emerging economy (Hungary) and ends on 30 September 2009.[8] The number of FSRs stays about constant from 2001 until 2003 and then makes a considerable jump and remains at this new level (because more and more central banks in the sample released such FSRs). On the contrary, the number of speeches/interviews is higher in the beginning of the sample and then drops for a couple of years only to jump up again in 2008. This is a good example of the difference in flexibility between FSRs and speeches/interviews. While FSRs are scheduled well in advance and only published few times a year, speeches and interviews can be used flexibly in times of crisis. In the early 2000s, the Argentinean crisis and the 9/11-attacks are reasons for the higher frequency of speeches/interviews. The increase in the number of speeches/interviews in 2008 can be clearly attributed to the global financial crisis.

---

[7] Although the FSR release dates for the Philippines could not be identified, we include the Philippines in the sample as a number of release dates for speeches/interviews are available.

[8] Convergence problems of our optimization algorithms forced us to drop the first year. As there was only one FSR published in 2000, starting in 2001 has a negligible effect on the overall results.

Table 9.1 Summary statistics for FSRs and speeches/interviews

		FSRs	Speeches & Interviews
By country	Argentina	12	8
	Brazil	14	0
	Chile	11	11
	China	5	16
	Hungary	16	14
	Philippines		9
	Poland	10	2
	South Africa	11	14
	Turkey	8	15
By year	2001	3	11
	2002	3	10
	2003	4	11
	2004	11	6
	2005	14	2
	2006	13	2
	2007	14	6
	2008	14	26
	2009	11	15
Overall		87	89

Note: The table shows the number of FSRs and speeches/interviews that are contained in the database, by country and by year.

To quantify the contents of communication, Born et al. (2010) employ the computerized textual-analysis software DICTION 5.0, which searches text for different semantic features. Based on this software, an optimism score is computed for each individual speech or interview, and for the overview part of each FSR. The resulting continuous scores are subsequently transformed into a discrete variable, which takes on the value -1 for the lowest tercile of the distribution, the value 0 for the middle tercile of the distribution, and the value +1 for the upper tercile of the distribution. That is, a value of +1 denotes a relatively optimistic text while a value of -1 indicates a relatively pessimistic text. We denote the resulting pooled indicators by $OPT_{i,t}^{FSR}$ and $OPT_{i,t}^{speech}$, where i denotes countries, and t time. While the database contains scores for two dimensions of communication, we will focus on the optimism dimension in our illustration. Optimism may be important as it provides agents with information about the central bank's views about the current state and the prospects of the financial system and underlying risks.

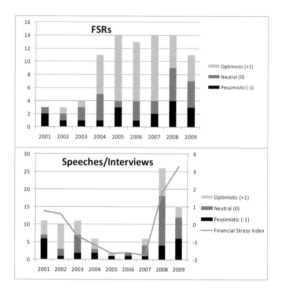

Notes: The figure shows the total number of FSRs (upper panel) and speeches/interviews (lower panel) in a given year together with the distribution of discrete codings on the left-hand axis. The lower panel also plots annual averages of the IMF's *'Emerging Markets Financial Stress Index'* (EM-FSI), an aggregate index designed to capture the most important episodes of financial stress in emerging economies (see Balakrishnan et al. 2009), on the right-hand axis.

Figure 9.1 Coding of FSRs and speeches/interviews

Figure 9.1 graphically emphasizes one of the main points of Table 9.1: speeches/interviews (depicted by the bars) occur more frequently in times of crisis, evidenced by the U-shaped pattern of the graph, which very closely follows the IMF's 'Emerging Markets Financial Stress Index' (shown by the solid line), an aggregate index designed to capture the most important episodes of financial stress in emerging economies (see Balakrishnan et al., 2009). What is also evident is that FSRs grew more and more optimistic until 2006, after which the number of optimistic FSRs started to fall again. It is also interesting to note that when the number of speeches concerned with financial stability rose to a record level in 2008, the large majority was optimistic or neutral rather than pessimistic, indicating that in many instances, central banks tried to lean against the wind. The reduction in the number of communications in 2009 is due to the sample ending in September, such that an entire quarter of data is missing compared to the earlier years.

Econometric Analysis

Our econometric approach closely follows Ehrmann and Fratzscher (2009) in employing Nelson's (1991) exponential GARCH (EGARCH) model to estimate the effects of central bank communication on markets. Specifically, let $x_{i,t}$ be the change in the variable of interest, and $x_{i,t-1}$ its lag. The conditional mean equation follows as

$$x_{i,t} = \alpha + \beta OPT_{i,t}^{C} + \gamma x_{i,t-1} + \delta z_t + \varepsilon_{i,t} \qquad (9.1)$$

where $OPT_{i,t}^{C}$ takes on the value +1 for optimistic communication, -1 for pessimistic communication, and 0 otherwise, and $C = \{FSR, speech\}$, z_t is a vector of day-of-the-week dummies, and $\varepsilon_{i,t} \sim (0, h_{i,t})$. The conditional variance for an EGARCH(1,1) can then be expressed as

$$\log\left(h_{i,t}\right) = \tau + \omega \left(\left| \frac{\varepsilon_{i,t-1}}{\sqrt{h_{i,t-1}}} \right| - \sqrt{2/\pi} \right) +$$
$$+ \varphi \log\left(h_{i,t-1}\right) + \kappa \left(\frac{\varepsilon_{i,t-1}}{\sqrt{h_{i,t-1}}} \right) + \lambda D_{i,t}^{C} + \xi z_t \qquad (9.2)$$

where $h_{i,t}$ is the conditional variance of $x_{i,t}$, $\varepsilon_{i,t-1}$ are past innovations, $D_{i,t}^{c}$ is a communication dummy that takes the value of 1 on days when a communication event is observed and 0 otherwise, and z_t is a vector of day-of-the-week dummies.

As explained in the previous section, the cross-section of markets considered in this study consists of financial sector stock market indices, overall stock market indices, short-term interest rates, and exchange rates. The model is estimated separately for each market via maximum likelihood. The effects of FSRs and speeches/interviews are estimated separately due to occasional convergence problems of the optimization algorithms (BHHH and BFGS).[9]

Table 9.2 presents the estimation results, focusing on the parameters of interest (β in the first column, and λ in the second column). There is clear evidence that the views expressed in FSRs get reflected in stock market returns, both for financial sector stock indices and overall stock indices: returns increase after optimistic FSRs, and decrease after pessimistic FSRs, with highly significant β's, and sizeable magnitudes: following an optimistic (pessimistic) communication, financial stock indices show higher (lower) returns in the order of 0.44 percent, and overall stock markets react slightly less, with 0.36 percent. This difference is intuitive, as we would expect financial stocks to be more receptive to financial stability-related news than other stocks. In addition, we find that the release of FSRs tends to calm stock markets, as our parameter estimates for λ are both negative and statistically significant. A similar volatility reduction is observed for exchange rates and interest rates, suggesting that FSRs tend to be rather effective in 'reducing noise'.

An interesting finding is that the FSR coefficient in the mean equation for interest rate changes is positive and significant. This can be interpreted as evidence for the existence of a signaling channel, whereby central bank assessments about financial stability risks are interpreted as signaling a monetary policy response.

In contrast, speeches and interviews have no significant effect in the mean equation, suggesting that the views expressed in these communications do not get reflected in corresponding changes in asset prices. At the same time, they tend to increase rather than decrease the volatility of interest rates and exchange rates, which is in stark contrast to the findings for FSRs.

---

[9] If there is not too much correlation between FSRs and speeches and interviews, separate estimation should yield similar results to estimating the joint model. We have run some joint models as a robustness check and the converging ones yielded very similar point estimates.

Table 9.2 Effect of communication on financial markets

	Mean		Volatility		No. obs.	Log. lik.
	Coef.	Std. err.	Coef.	Std. err.		
FSRs						
Financial stocks	0.442 ***	0.147	-0.127 **	0.060	20538	-4.281E+04
Overall stocks	0.359 **	0.175	-0.105 *	0.061	20538	-3.943E+04
Interest rates	0.014 ***	0.001	-0.409 ***	0.044	19856	1.006E+04
Exchange rates	0.024	0.039	-0.546 ***	0.057	20538	-2.117E+04
Speeches						
Financial stocks	0.021	0.276	0.055	0.050	20538	-4.281E+04
Overall stocks	0.334	0.240	0.053	0.052	20538	-3.944E+04
Interest rates	0.009	0.011	0.469 ***	0.029	19856	1.015E+04
Exchange rates	0.040	-	1.166 ***	0.009	20538	-2.045E+04

Notes: The table reports results of EGARCH models. The dependent variable in the mean equation is measured in log-differences multiplied by 100 for financial stock market indices, overall stock market indices, and exchange rates, and measured in differences for interest rates. Hence, a value of 0.01 for the coefficient on optimism implies, in the event of an optimistic FSR, a 1 basis point increase in the interest rate, and a 0.01 per cent higher return for financial stock market indices. ***, **, and * indicate statistical significance at the 1%, 5%, and 10% levels, respectively.

To summarize the main points of this empirical application, we find that speeches and interviews are used flexibly, in the sense that their frequency increases during periods of financial stress. While this might be a supply or a demand effect (central bankers wanting to raise the corresponding issues more frequently, or the media and the public asking more questions about financial stability), we find that the effects on markets are strikingly different from those of the pre-scheduled FSRs. Whereas the latter reduce noise consistently, i.e. lower market volatility, the former actually increase it. It also appears as if markets tend to dance to their own tune in response to speeches and interviews, whereas they are much more responsive to the views expressed in FSRs.

In any case, the empirical illustration demonstrates that macro-prudential communications get heard in financial markets, a necessary condition to steer the behavior of market participants. As such, communication could be an important policy tool for the macro-prudential supervisor. Yet the findings also show that such communication entails risks as it may unsettle markets. Hence central bank communication on macro-prudential issues needs to be employed with utmost care, stressing the difficulty of designing a successful communication strategy on financial stability.

Conclusion

Central banks will play a major role in macro-prudential supervision in the coming years. This new task brings a number of challenges, such as the development of appropriate analytical tools, the availability of relevant data, and the design of effective policy instruments, and it will impact on the way central banks communicate.

This chapter has looked at the latter aspect. It has discussed the various roles which communication will have to fulfill in macro-prudential policy, namely to enhance its effectiveness, to make the policymaker accountable, and to address possible reputation risks.

With regard to the role of communication in enhancing the effectiveness of macro-prudential policy, the paper has differentiated between communication during 'normal' times and during crisis times. In the former, it is important to be transparent about the aims of the central bank, about the processes at work, and about the instruments that the central bank will use. In this fashion, the central bank can affect the incentives of economic agents, and thus contribute to crisis prevention. One example for such an effect relates to bank stress tests, which, if pre-announced, create incentives for banks to pass the tests, and to behave accordingly. Communication during 'normal' times should, in our view, be very much in line with the principles of monetary policy communication, which typically stress the importance of clarity, transparency and predictability. This will also help to make the central bank accountable. In contrast, during crisis times, there might well be legitimate limits to transparency, as too transparent central bank communications could possibly destabilize the financial system, e.g., by triggering bank runs.

To counteract reputational risks, it is important that central banks manage expectations by clearly communicating what macro-prudential policy can and what it cannot do. This is even more important because macro-prudential tasks are targeted at specific segments of the financial system, such that one should expect much more controversy about individual actions than what central banks know from monetary policy. Finally, in that regard, it is also important to consider to what extent monetary policy communications should be separated from macro-prudential communications. To pursue two goals, a policymaker must be given at least two independent instruments, a principle that should also be considered in the arena of communications. A proper separation of the communications could also mitigate the risk that macro-prudential problems generate a loss of credibility of the monetary policy wing of the central bank. Of course, a monetary policy strategy that leans against the wind is bound to complicate the separation of the two.

Central banks will have several communication channels at hand, and they should be employed in a clearly differentiated manner. The two most frequent channels to date have been speeches and interviews on the one hand, and FSRs on the other hand. These serve very different purposes. Speeches and interviews can be used very flexibly to react to new developments in the financial system, whereas FSRs typically follow a fixed release schedule. Also, FSRs are much more comprehensive than speeches and interviews, and express the views of the entire decision-making body of the central bank as opposed to (possibly) the view of the individual speaker.

This chapter has shown that both communication instruments exert effects on a broad set of financial markets, and that they do so in a very different way. For instance, FSRs tend to reduce volatility in financial markets on release dates, whereas speeches and interviews tend to increase it. This underlines the importance of choosing a careful communication strategy on macro-prudential policy – which should be adopted over time and across countries, as there is clearly no one size fits all solution.

References

Aikman, D., A. Haldane and B. Nelson (2010), 'Curbing the Credit Cycle', speech at the Columbia University Center on Capitalism and Society Annual Conference, New York.

Balakrishnan R., S. Danninger, S. Elekdag and I. Tytell (2009), 'How Linkages Fuel the Fire: The Transmission of Financial Stress from Advanced to Emerging Economies', *IMF World Economic Outlook*, Chapter 4.

Bean, C., M. Paustian, A. Penalver and T. Taylor (2010), 'Monetary Policy after the Fall. Paper presented at the Federal Reserve Bank of Kansas City Annual Conference Jackson Hole.

Beckworth, D. (2010), 'One Nation Under the Fed? The Asymmetric Effects of US Monetary policy and Its Implications for the United States as an Optimal Currency Area', *Journal of Macroeconomics* **32**, 732–746.

Bernanke, B. (2004), 'Fedspeak', Remarks at the Meetings of the American Economic Association, San Diego, California, 3 January 2004.

Blinder, A. (2010), 'How Central Should the Central Bank Be?' *Journal of Economic Literature,* **48**(1), 123–133.

Blinder, A., Ehrmann, M., Fratzscher, M., de Haan, J. and D.J. Jansen (2008), 'Central Bank Communication and Monetary Policy: A Survey of Theory and Evidence', *Journal of Economic Literature,* **46**(4), 910–945.

Blundell-Wignall, A. and P. Slovik (2010), 'The EU Stress Test and Sovereign Debt Exposures'. OECD Working Papers on Finance, Insurance and Private Pensions No. 4.

Borio, C. (2009), 'Implementing the Macroprudential Approach to Financial Regulation and Supervision', *Banque de France Financial Stability Review,* **13**, 31–41.

Borio, C. and H. Zhu (2008), 'Capital Regulation, Risk-Taking and Monetary Policy: A Missing Link in the Transmission Mechanism' BIS Working Paper No. 268.

Born, B., M. Ehrmann and M. Fratzscher (2010), 'Macroprudential policy and central bank communication'. CEPR Discussion Paper No. 8094.

Čihák, M. (2006), 'How Do Central Banks Write On Financial Stability?' IMF Working Paper No. 06/163.

Čihák, M. (2007), 'Central Banks and Financial Stability: A Survey. Mimeo.

Cukierman, A. (2009), 'The Limits of Transparency', *Economic Notes* **38**(1–2), 1–37.

Dedola, L. and F. Lippi (2005), 'The Monetary Transmission Mechanism: Evidence from the industries of Five OECD Countries', *European Economic Review,* **49**, 1543–1569.

De Grauwe, P. and D. Gros (2009), 'A New Two-Pillar Strategy for the ECB', CESifo Working Paper No. 2818.

Dincer, N. and B. Eichengreen (2009), 'Central Bank Transparency: Causes, Consequences and Updates', NBER Working Paper No. 14791.

Ehrmann, M. and M. Fratzscher (2007), 'Communication and Decision-Making by Central Bank Committees: Different Strategies, Same Effectiveness?', *Journal of Money, Credit and Banking,* **39**(2–3), 509–41, March–April 2007.

Ehrmann, M. and M. Fratzscher (2009), 'Purdah – On the Rationale for Central Bank Silence Around Policy Meetings, *Journal of Money, Credit and Banking*, **41**(2–3), 517–27.

Eijffinger, S. and P. Geraats (2006), 'How Transparent Are Central Banks?' *European Journal of Political Economy,* **22**, 1–21.

Feldstein, M. (2010), 'What Powers for the Federal Reserve?' *Journal of Economic Literature,* **48**(1), 134–145.

Goodhart, C. (2002), 'The Organizational Structure of Banking Supervision', *Economic Notes,* **31**(1), 1–32.

Goodhart, C. and D. Schoenmaker (2005), 'Should the Functions of Monetary Policy and Banking Supervision Be Separated?', *Oxford Economic Papers,* **47**, 539–560.

Gosselin, P., A. Lotz and C. Wyplosz (2007), 'Interest Rate Signals and Central Bank Transparency', CEPR Discussion Papers No 6454.

Herring R.J. and J. Carmassi (2008), 'The Structure of Cross-Sector Financial Supervision', *Financial Markets, Institutions and Instruments,* **17**(1), 51–76.

IMF (2010), Emerging and Developing Economies List. World Economic Outlook Database, April 2010.

Issing, O. (2005), 'Communication, Transparency, Accountability – Monetary Policy in the Twenty-First Century', *Federal Reserve Bank of St. Louis Review,* **87**(2): 65–83.

Jiménez, G., S. Ongena, J.-L. Peydró and J. Saurina (2010), 'Hazardous Times for Monetary Policy: What do 23 Million Bank Loans Tell Us About the Impact of Monetary Policy on Credit Risk-Taking?', CentER Discussion Paper Series No. 2007-75.

Katz, H.V. and S. Katz (2010), 'Legal Ground: The End of Easy Mortgages?' *The Jerusalem Post*, May 28, 2010.

Landau, P. (2010), 'Global Agenda: The Me-Too Bubble', *The Jerusalem Post*, July 30, 2010.

Masciandaro, D. and M. Quintyn (2009), 'After the Big Bang and Before the Next One? Reforming the Financial Supervision Architecture and the Role of the Central Bank. A Review of Worldwide Trends, Causes and Effects (1998–2008)', Paolo Baffi Centre Research Paper No. 2009–37.

Mishkin, F.S. (2004), 'Can Central Bank Transparency Go Too Far?' in C. Kent and S. Guttmann (eds.). *The Future of Inflation Targeting*, Sydney: Reserve Bank of Australia, pp. 48–65.

Morris, S. and H.S. Shin (2002), 'Social Value of Public Information', *American Economic Review,* **92**(5), 1521–1534.

Nelson, D.B. (1991), 'Conditional Heteroskedasticity in Asset Returns: A New Approach', *Econometrica,* **59**, 347–370.

Oosterloo, S. and J. de Haan (2004), 'Central Banks and Financial Stability: a Survey', *Journal of Financial Stability,* **1**, 257–273.

Oosterloo, S., J. de Haan and R. Jong-A-Pin (2007), 'Financial Stability Reviews: A First Empirical Analysis', *Journal of Financial Stability,* **2**, 337–355.

Peersman, G. and F. Smets (2005), 'The Industry Effects of Monetary policy in the Euro Area', *The Economic Journal,* **115**, 319–342.

Siklos, P. (2010), 'Communication for Multi-Taskers: Perspectives on Dealing with Both Monetary Policy and Financial Stability', mimeo.

Svensson, L.E.O. (2003), 'Monetary Policy and Real Stabilization' NBER Working Paper No. 9486.

Svensson, L.E.O. (2006), 'Social Value of Public Information: Morris and Shin (2002) Is Actually Pro Transparency, Not Con', *American Economic Review,* **96**(1), 448–451.

Trichet, J.C. (2008), 'The Changing Role of Communication', Speech delivered at 'Internationaler Club Frankfurter Wirtschaftsjournalisten'.

van der Cruijsen, C., J. de Haan and D.J. Jansen (2010a), 'How Much Does the Public Know About the ECB's Monetary Policy? Evidence From a Survey of Dutch Households', ECB Working Paper No. 1265.

van der Cruijsen, C., J. de Haan, D.-J. Jansen and R. Mosch (2010b), Knowledge and Opinions about Banking Supervision – Evidence from a Survey of Dutch Households. Mimeo.

Wilkinson, J., K. Spong and J. Christensson (2010), 'Financial Stability Reports: How Useful During a Financial Crisis?', *Federal Reserve Bank of Kansas City Economic Review*, 41–70.

10. Time Varying Monetary Policy Rules and Financial Stress

Jaromír Baxa, Roman Horváth and Bořek Vašíček[1]

Introduction

The recent financial crisis has intensified the interest in exploring the interactions between monetary policy and financial stability. Official interest rates were driven sharply to historic lows and many unconventional measures were used to pump liquidity into the international financial system. Central banks pursued monetary policy under high economic uncertainty coupled with large financial shocks in many countries. The financial crisis also raised new challenges for central bank policies, in particular how to operationalize the issues related to financial stability for monetary policy decision-making (Goodhart, 2006; Borio and Drehmann, 2009).

This chapter seeks to analyze whether and how central banks reacted to the periods of financial instability, and in particular whether and how the interest-setting process evolved in response to financial instability over the last three decades. The monetary policy of central banks is likely to react to financial instability in a non-linear way (Goodhart et al., 2009). When a financial system is stable, the interest

[1] We gratefully acknowledge the support from Czech Science Foundation research grant no. P402/11/1487. We thank Øyvind Eitrheim, Ekkehart Schlicht, Miloslav Vošvrda and the seminar participants at the 7th Norges Annual Monetary Policy Conference, the Institute of Information Theory and Automation (Academy of Sciences of the Czech Republic), Universitat de Barcelona, Universitat de Girona, Universitat de les Illes Balears and Universidad Complutense de Madrid for helpful discussions. The views expressed in this paper are not necessarily those of the Czech National Bank.

rate setting process largely reflects macroeconomic conditions and financial stability considerations enter the monetary policy discussions only to a limited degree. On the other hand, central banks may alter monetary policy to reduce financial imbalances if these become severe. In this respect, Mishkin (2010) questions the traditional linear-quadratic framework[2] when financial markets are disrupted and puts forward the arguments for replacing it by nonlinear dynamics, describing the economy and the non-quadratic objective function resulting in the non-linear optimal policy.

To deal with the complexity of monetary policy and financial stability nexus as well as to evaluate monetary policy in a systematic manner, this study employs the recently developed time-varying parameter estimation of monetary policy rules appropriately accounting for endogeneity in policy rules. This flexible framework, together with a new comprehensive financial stress dataset developed by the International Monetary Fund (IMF), will allow not only testing whether the central banks responded to financial stress but also the quantification of the magnitude of this response and the detection of the periods and types of stress that were the most worrying for monetary authorities.

Although theoretical studies disagree about the role of financial instability for central bank interest rate setting policy, our empirical estimates of time-varying monetary policy rules of the US Fed, the Bank of England (BoE), Reserve Bank of Australia (RBA), Bank of Canada (BoC) and Sveriges Riksbank (SR) shows that central banks often alter the course of their monetary policy in the face of high financial stress, mainly by decreasing their policy rates. However, the size of this response varies substantially over time as well as across countries. There is a certain heterogeneity across countries and time as well when we look at central banks' consideration of specific types of financial stress: most of them seemed to respond to stock market stress and bank stress, and exchange rate stress drove central bank reactions only in more open economies.

The chapter is organized as follows: Section two discusses related literature. Section three describes our data and empirical methodology.

---

[2] Linear behavior of the economy and the quadratic objective function of monetary authority.

Section four presents our results. Section five concludes. An appendix with additional results follows.

Related Literature

First, this section gives a brief overview of the theory as well as empirical evidence on the relationship between monetary policy (rules) and financial instability. Second, it provides a short summary of various measures of financial stress.

Monetary policy (rules) and financial instability – some theories

Financial frictions, such as an unequal access to credits or debt collateralization, were recognized to have important consequences for monetary policy transmission and Fisher (1933) has already presented the idea that adverse credit-market conditions can cause significant macroeconomic disequilibria.

During the last two decades, the effects of monetary policy have been studied mainly within New Keynesian (NK) dynamic stochastic general equilibrium (DSGE) models, which assume the existence of nominal rigidities. The common approach to incorporate financial market friction within the DSGE framework is to introduce the financial accelerator mechanism (Bernanke et al., 1996, 1999), implying that endogenous developments in credit markets work to amplify and propagate shocks to the macroeconomy. Tovar (2009) emphasizes that the major weakness of the financial accelerator mechanism is that it only deals with one of many possible financial frictions. Goodhart et al. (2009) notes that many NK DSGE models lack the financial sector completely or model it in a rather embryonic way. Consequently, more recent contributions within this stream of literature examine other aspects of financial frictions such as the balance sheets in the banking sector (Choi and Cook, 2004), portfolio choice issue with complete (Engel or Matsumoto, 2009) or incomplete markets (Devereux and Sutherland, 2007) or collateral constraints (Iacovello and Neri, 2010).[3]

---

[3] The survey of this literature is provided by Tovar (2009).

A few studies focus more specifically on the relationship between the monetary policy stance (or the monetary policy rule) and financial stability. However, they do not arrive at a unanimous view on whether a monetary policy rule should include some measure of financial stability. Brousseau and Detken (2001) present an NK model where a conflict arises between short-term price stability and financial stability due to a self-fulfilling belief linking the stability of inflation to the smoothness of the interest rate path and suggests that monetary policy should react to financial instability. Akram et al. (2007) investigate the macroeconomic implications of pursuing financial stability within a flexible inflation-targeting framework. Their model using policy rule, augmented with financial stability indicators, shows that the gains of such an augmented rule vis-à-vis the rule without financial stability indicators highly depends on the nature of the shocks. Akram and Eitrheim (2008) build on the previous framework, finding some evidence that the policy response to housing prices, equity prices or credit growth can cause high interest rate volatility and actually lower financial stability in terms of indicators that are sensitive to interest rates. Ceccheti and Li (2008) show in a static and dynamic setting that a potential conflict between monetary policy and financial supervision can be avoided if the interest rate rule takes (procyclical) capital adequacy requirements into account, in particular that the policy interest rates are lowered when financial stress is high. Bauducco et al. (2008) extends the current benchmark NK model to include financial systems and firms that require external financing. Their simulations show that if a central bank responds to financial instability by policy easing it achieves better inflation and output stabilization in the short term at the cost of greater inflation and output volatility in the long term and vice versa. For the US Fed Taylor (2008) proposes a modification of a standard Taylor rule to incorporate adjustments to credit spreads. Teranishi (2009) derives a Taylor rule augmented by the response to credit spreads as an optimal policy under heterogeneous loan interest rate contracts. He finds that the policy response to a credit spread can be both positive and negative depending on the financial structure. However, he also puts forward that when nominal policy rates are close to zero a commitment rather than discretional policy response is the key for reducing the credit spreads. Christiano et al. (2008) suggest augmenting the Taylor rule with aggregate private credit and find that such a policy would raise welfare by reducing the magnitude of the output fluctuations. Cúrdia and Woodford (2010) develop an NK DSGE model with credit frictions to evaluate the performance of alternative policy rules that are augmented by a response to credit spreads and to aggregate the volume of private credit in the face of different shocks. They argue that the response to credit spreads can be welfare improving, but the optimal size of such a response is likely rather small. Like Teranishi (2009), they find little support for augmenting a Taylor rule by the credit volume given – that the size and even the sign of the desired response is sensitive to the sources of shocks and their persistence –which is information that is not always available during operational policy making.

The related stream of literature focuses on a somewhat narrower issue of whether or not monetary policy should respond to asset prices. Bernanke and Gertler (1999, 2001) argue that the stabilization of inflation and output provides a substantial contribution to financial stability and there are little if any gains to responding to asset prices. Faia and Monacelli (2007) extend the model developed by Bernanke and Gertler (2001) by a robust welfare metric confirming that strict inflation stabilization offers the best solution. Cecchetti et al. (2000) takes the opposite stand arguing that developments in asset markets can have a significant impact on both inflation and real economic activity, and central banks might achieve better outcomes considering the asset prices provided they are able to detect their misalignments. Borio and Lowe (2002) support this view claiming that financial imbalances can build up even in a low inflation environment, which is normally favorable to financial stability. The side effect of low inflation is that excess demand pressures may first appear in credit aggregates and asset prices rather than consumer prices, which are normally considered by the policy makers. Gruen et al. (2005) argues that responding to an asset bubble is feasible only when the monetary authority is able to make a correct judgment about the process driving the bubble. Roubini (2006) and Posen (2006) provide the summary of this debate from a policy perspective.

Monetary policy (rules) and financial instability – empirical evidence

The empirical evidence on central banks' reaction to financial instability is rather scant. Following the ongoing debate about whether central banks should respond to asset price volatility (e.g., Bernanke and Gertler, 1999, 2001; Cecchetti et al., 2000; Bordo and Jeanne, 2002), some studies tested the response of monetary policy to different asset prices, most commonly to stock prices (Rigobon and Sack, 2003; Siklos and Bohl, 2008; Fuhrer and Tootel, 2008). They find some evidence that asset prices either entered the policy information set (because they contain information about future inflation) or that some central banks were directly trying to offset its disequilibria.[4] All these papers estimate time-invariant policy rules, which means that they test a permanent response to these variables. However, it seems more plausible that if central banks respond to asset prices, they do it only when their misalignments are substantial, in other words their response is asymmetric. There are two additional controversies related to the effects of asset prices on monetary policy decisions: (i) The first concerns the measure, in particular whether the stock market index that is typically employed is sufficiently representative or whether some other assets, in particular the housing prices, should be considered as well, and (ii) the second issue is related to the (even ex-post) identification of the asset price misalignment. Finally, it is likely that the perception of misalignments is influenced by general economic conditions and that a possible response could evolve over time. Detken and Smets (2004) summarize some stylized facts on macroeconomic and monetary policy developments during asset price booms. Overall they find that monetary policy was significantly looser during the high-cost booms that were marked by the investment and real estate prices crash in the post-boom periods.

A few empirical studies measure monetary policy response using broader measures of financial imbalances. Borio and Lowe (2004) estimate the response of four central banks (Reserve Bank of Australia, Bundesbank, Bank of Japan and the US Fed) to imbalances

---

[4] A similar but somewhat less polemic debate applies to the role of the exchange rate, especially for small open economies (Taylor, 2001).

proxied by the ratio of private sector credit to GDP, inflation-adjusted equity prices and their composite. They find either negative or ambiguous evidence for all countries except for the USA confirming that the Fed responded to financial imbalances in an asymmetric and reactive way, i.e. that the federal fund rate was disproportionally lowered in the face of imbalance unwinding but it was not tightened beyond normal as imbalances built up. Cecchetti and Li (2008) estimate a Taylor rule augmented by a measure of banking stress, in particular a deviation of leverage ratios (total loans to the sum of equity and subordinated debt; total assets to the sum of bank capital and reserves) from its Hodrick-Prescott trend. They find some evidence that the Fed adjusted the interest rate in order to counteract the procyclical impact of a bank's capital requirements, while the Bundesbank and the Bank of Japan did not. Bulíř and Čihák (2008) estimate the monetary policy response to seven alternative measures of financial sector vulnerability (crisis probability, time to crisis, distance to default or credit default swap spreads) in a panel of 28 countries. Their empirical framework is different in the sense that the monetary policy stance is proxied along the short-term interest rate by measures of domestic liquidity and external shocks are controlled for. In the panel setting, they find a statistically significant negative response to many variables representing vulnerability (policy easing) but surprisingly not in country-level regressions. Belke and Klose (2010) investigate the factors behind the interest rate decision of the ECB and the Fed during the current crisis. They conclude that the estimated policy rule was significantly altered only for the Fed and they put forward that the ECB gave greater weight to inflation stabilization at the cost of some output loss.

Measures of financial stress

The incidence and determinants of different types of crises have been typically traced in the literature by means of narrative evidence (expert judgment). This was sometimes complemented with selected indicators (the exchange rate devaluation, the state of foreign reserves) that point to historical regularities (e.g., Eichengreen and Bordo, 2002; Kaminsky and Reinhart, 1999; Reinhart and Rogoff, 2009; Laeven and Valencia, 2008). The empirical studies (e.g. Goldstein et al., 2000) used binary variables that were constructed based on these narratives.

Consequently, some contributions strived to provide more data-driven measures of financial stress. Most of the existing stress indices are based on high-frequency data but they differ in the selected variables (bank capitalization, credit ratings, credit growth, interest rate spreads or volatility of different asset classes), country coverage and the aggregation method. An important advantage of continuous stress indicators is that they may reveal periods of small-scale stress that did not result in full-blown crisis and were neglected in studies based on binary crisis variables.

The Bank Credit Analyst (BCA) reports a monthly financial stress index (FSI) for the USA that is based on the performance of banking shares as compared to whole stock market, credit spreads and the slope of the yield curve, and the new issues of stocks, bonds and consumer confidence. JP Morgan calculates a Liquidity, Credit and Volatility Index (LCVI) based on seven variables: the US Treasury curve error (standard deviation of the spread between on-the-run and off-the-run US Treasury bills and bonds along the entire maturity curve), the 10-year US swap spread, US high-yield spreads, JP Morgan's Emerging Markets Bond Index, foreign exchange volatility (weighted average of 12-month implied volatilities of several currencies), the Chicago Board of Exchange equity volatility index VIX, and the JP Morgan Global Risk Appetite Index.

Illing and Liu (2006) develop a comprehensive FSI for Canada. Their underlying data covers equity, bond and foreign exchange markets as well as the banking sector. They use a standard measure and refined measure of each stress component, where the former refers to the variables and their transformations that are commonly found in the literature, while the latter incorporates the adjustments that allow for better extraction of the information about stressful periods. They explore different weighting schemes to aggregate the individual series (factor analysis, size of a corresponding market on total credit in economy, variance-equal weighting). Finally, they perform an expert survey to identify periods that were perceived as especially stressful, confirming that the FSI matches these episodes very well.

Carlson et al. (2009) propose for the Fed Board of Governors a framework similar to the option pricing model (Merton, 1974) that aims to provide a distance-to-default of the financial system, the so-called Index of Financial Health. The method uses the difference between the market value of a firm's assets and liabilities and the volatility of the asset's value in order to measure the proximity of a firm's assets being exceeded by its liabilities. They apply this measure to 25 of the largest US financial institutions, confirming its impact on capital investments in the US economy. The Fed of Kansas City developed the Kansas City Financial Stress Index (Hakkio and Keeton, 2009) that is published monthly and is based on eleven variables (seven spreads between different bond classes by issuers, risk profiles and maturities, correlations between returns on stocks and Treasury bonds, expected volatility of overall stock prices, volatility of bank stock prices and a cross-section dispersion of bank stock returns) that are aggregated by principal component analysis.

Finally, the IMF recently published financial stress indices for various countries. Cardarelli et al. (2009) propose a comprehensive index based on high-frequency data where the price changes are measured with respect to previous levels or trend value. The underlying variables are standardized and aggregated into a single index (FSI) using variance-equal weighting for each country and period. The FSI has three subcomponents: the banking sector (the slope of the yield curve, TED spread, the beta of banking sector stock), securities markets (corporate bonds spread, stock market returns and time-varying volatility of stock returns) and exchange rate (time-varying volatility of NEER changes). Balakrishnan et al. (2009) modify the previous index to account for specific conditions of emerging economies; on one hand including the measure of exchange rate pressures (currency depreciation and decline in foreign reserves) and sovereign debt spread, on the other hand downplaying the banking sector measures (slope of the yield curve and TED spread).[5] We will use the former index given its comprehensiveness as well as its availability for different countries (see more details below).

---

[5] The IMF Financial Stress Index has been recently applied by Melvin and Taylor (2009) to analyze the exchange rate crises.

Data and Empirical Methodology

The Dataset

We use monthly data (quarterly for Sweden and Canada, more details below). The sample period slightly varies due to data availability (the US 1981:1 M – 2009:6M; the UK 1981:1M – 2009:3M; Australia 1983:3M – 2009:5M; Canada 1981:1Q – 2008:4Q; Sweden 1984:2Q – 2009:1Q).

The dependent variable is typically the interest rate closely related to the official (censored) policy rate, in particular the federal fund rate (3M) for the USA, the discount rate (3-month treasury bills) for the UK, Canada and Sweden, and the 3-month RBA accepted bills rate for Australia. It is evident that policy rate is not necessarily the only instrument that the central bank uses, especially during the 2008–2009 global financial crisis when many unconventional measures were implemented (see Borio and Disyatat, 2009; Reis, 2010). So as to address this issue in terms of estimated policy rules, for robustness check we use the interbank interest rate (at a maturity of 3 months). While both rates are used in empirical papers on the monetary policy rules estimation without great controversy, the selection of the interest rate turns more delicate during financial stress periods (Taylor, 2008). While the former is more directly affected by genuine monetary policy decisions (carried by open market operations), the latter additionally includes liquidity conditions on the interbank markets and as such can be affected by some unconventional policies, though these are usually insulated (often intentionally) from policy interest rates.[6] This

---

[6] Borio and Disyatat (2009) characterize the unconventional policies as policies that affect the central bank's balance sheet size and composition and that can be insulated from the interest rate policy (so-called 'decoupling principle'). One common example of such a policy (not necessarily used during the time of crisis) is a sterilized exchange rate intervention. Given that we aim not at a single episode of stress but rather want to identify whether monetary authorities deviated from its systematic pattern (the policy rule) during these periods (by responding to indicators of financial stress), we need to use a consistent measure of policy actions that are adjusted during the periods of financial stress, though other measures can be in place as well. Therefore, we assume that the monetary policy stance is fully reflected in the interest rate, and we are aware that it might be subject to a downward bias on

represents a drawback but also a potential advantage of this alternative dependent variable. On the one hand, the changes in official policy rate may not fully pass through into interbank interest rates, in particular when the perceived counterparty risk is too high and the credit spreads widen (see Taylor and Williams, 2009). On the other hand the interbank rate may also incorporate the impact of policy actions such as quantitative easing aimed to supply additional liquidity into the system.[7]

The inflation is measured as a year-on-year change of CPI, apart from the United States where we use the personal consumption expenditures price index (PCE) and Sweden where the underlying inflation CPIX (excludes households' mortgage interest expenditure and the direct effects of changes in indirect taxes and subsidies from the CPI) is used.[8] The output gap is proxied by the gap of the seasonally adjusted industrial production index derived by the Hodrick-Prescott filter with smoothing parameter set to 14400. For Sweden and Canada, where we use quarterly data, the output gap was taken as reported in the OECD Economic Outlook (production function method based on NAWRU – non-accelerating wages rate of unemployment).

We proxy the financial stress by means of the FSI provided recently by the IMF (Cardarelli et al., 2009), which is a consistent measure for a wide range of countries but at the same time is comprehensive enough to track stress of a different nature. It includes the main components of financial stress in an economy and is available for a reasonably long period to be used for our empirical analysis (see Figure 10.1). We use both the overall index, which is a

---

the financial stress coefficient. The reader may want to interpret our results on the importance of financial stress on interest rate setting as a conservative estimate.

[7] There are other policy measures that can be used as a reactive or pre-emptive response to financial stress such as regulatory or administrative measures, although their effects are likely to appear only in the longer term and cannot be reasonably included in our empirical analysis.

[8] For Australia, the monthly CPI is not available because both the Reserve Bank of Australia and the Australian Bureau of Statistics only publish quarterly data. The monthly series was obtained using a linear interpolation of the CPI index.

sum of seven components, as well as each sub-index and component separately:

1. Banking-related sub-index components: the inverted term spread (the difference between short-term and long-term government bonds), TED spread (the difference between interbank rates and the yield on treasury bills), banking beta (12-month rolling beta, which is a measure of the correlation of banking stock returns to total returns in line with the CAPM);
2. Securities-markets related sub-index components: corporate bond spread (the difference between corporate bonds and long-term government bond yields), stock markets returns (monthly returns multiplied by -1), time-varying stock return volatility from the GARCH(1,1) model, and
3. Foreign exchange related sub-index: the time-varying volatility of monthly changes in NEER, from the GARCH (1,1) model.

We have examined the various alternative methods of aggregating the components: simple sum, variance-equal weighting, and PCA weighting, but failed to uncover any systematic differences among these in terms of the values of the overall index and consecutively in the empirical results.

The use of a composite index has a number of benefits. First, it approximates the evolution of financial stress caused by different factors and thus it is not limited to one specific type of instability. Second, the inclusion of additional variables into the stress index does not affect the evolution of the indicator markedly (Cardarelli et al., 2009). Third, the composition of the indicator allows breaking down the reactions of the central bank with respect to different stress sub-components. Nevertheless, one has to be cautious about the interpretation. The composite indicator might suggest a misleading interpretation as long as the stress is caused by variables not included within the FSI but highly correlated with some sub-component. An example is the case of Sweden during the ERM crisis. At the time of the crisis, Sweden maintained a fixed exchange rate and Riksbank sharply increased interest rates in order to sustain the parity. However, this is not captured by the exchange rate sub-component of the FSI, which measures the exchange rate volatility, because the volatility was actually close to zero. A closer look at the data shows that this period of stress is captured by the inverted term structure; hence it is incorrectly attributed to bank stress. A similar pattern can be observed for the UK, where the FSI increases after the announcement of the withdrawal from the ERM.

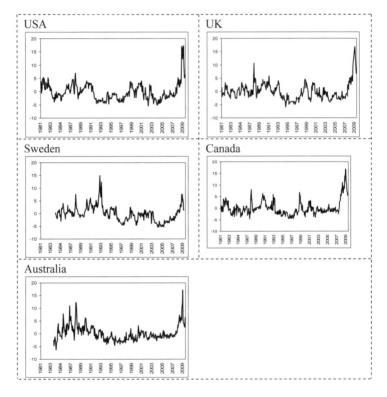

Note: The figure presents the evolution of the IMF stress index over time. Higher numbers indicate more stress (see Cardarelli et al., 2009).

Figure 10.1 IMF Financial Stress Indicator

The Empirical Model

Following Clarida et al. (1998, 2000), most empirical studies assume that the central bank sets the nominal interest rate in line with the state of the economy typically in a forward-looking manner:

$$r_t^* = \bar{r} + \beta \left(E\left[\pi_{t+i} \big| \Omega_t\right] - \pi_{t+i}^* \right) + \gamma E\left[y_{t+j} \big| \Omega_t \right] \tag{10.1}$$

where:

> r_t^* denotes the targeted interest rate;
> $\bar{r}$ is the policy neutral rate[9];
> π_{t+i} stands for the central bank forecast of the yearly inflation rate;
> i indicates periods ahead based on an information set Ω_t used for interest rate decision available at time t, and
> π_{t+i}^* is the central bank's inflation target.[10]
> y_{t+j} represents a measure of the output gap.

Nevertheless, equation (10.1) was found to be too restrictive to provide a reasonable description of actual interest rate setting. Notably it does not account for the interest rate smoothing of central banks, in particular the practice when the central bank adjusts the interest rate sluggishly to the targeted value. This is in empirical studies tracked by the simple partial-adjustment mechanism:

$$r_t = \rho r_{t-1} + (1-\rho) r_t^* \tag{10.2}$$

where $\rho \in [0,1]$ is the smoothing parameter. There is an ongoing controversy as to whether this parameter represents genuine policy inertia or reflects empirical problems related to omitted variables, dynamics or shocks (see e.g., Rudebusch, 2006). The linear policy rule in equation (10.1) can be obtained as the optimal monetary policy rule in the LQ framework where the central bank aims only at price stability and economic activity. Bauducco et al. (2008) propose an NK model with a financial system where the monetary policy has

---

[9] A policy-neutral rate is typically defined as the sum of the real equilibrium rate and the inflation target.

[10] An explicit definition of an inflation target exists only for countries with an inflation targeting (IT) regime. Most empirical studies assume, in line with Taylor (1993), that this target does not vary in time and can be omitted in the empirical model.

privileged information (given its supervisory function) on the health of the financial sector. In such a setting, the common policy rule represented by equation (10.1) shall be augmented by variables representing the health of the financial sector. Following this contribution we consider the forward-looking rule where central banks may respond to a comprehensive measure of financial stress rather than stress in a particular segment (Bulíř and Čihák, 2008). Therefore, we substitute equation (10.2) into equation (10.1), eliminate unobserved forecast variables, pass the inflation target to the generic intercept α and include measures of the financial stress described above, which results in equation (10.3):

$$r_t = (1-\rho)\big[\alpha + \beta\pi_{t+i} + \gamma y_{t+j}\big] + \rho r_{t-1} + \delta x_{t+k} + \varepsilon_t \qquad (10.3)$$

While in equation (10.1) the term α coincides with the policy neutral rate $\bar{r}$, its interpretation is not straightforward in our case. First, it is time varying as it encompass both changes in equilibrium real interest rate and inflation target. Second, the empirical model is augmented by an additional variable, the measure of financial stress. Note that the financial stress index x_{t+k} does not appear within the square brackets because it is not a variable that determines the target interest rate r_t^* but it is rather a factor such as the lagged interest rate, i.e., it may explain why the actual interest rate r_t deviates from the target. Moreover, placing it in the regression on the same level as a lagged interest rate, we can directly test whether this variable representing ad-hoc policy decisions decreases the interest rate inertia ρ as suggested by Mishkin (2009). The common logic also suggests that the coefficients ρ and δ shall move in the opposite direction because the central bank either smooths the interest rate changes or adjusts the rates in the face of financial stress. In the latter case, the response is likely to be quick and substantial. We set i equal to 2, j equal to 0 and k equal to -1.[11] Consequently, the disturbance term ε_t is

---

[11] Although the targeting horizon of central banks is usually longer (4–8 quarters), we prefer to proxy inflation expectations by inflation in $t+2$ for the following reasons: first, the endogeneity correction requires a strong correlation between the endogenous regressor and its instruments; second, the prediction error logically increases in longer horizons. In case of the output

a combination of forecast errors and is thus orthogonal to all information available at time t (Ω_t).

The empirical studies on monetary policy rules have moved from using time-invariant estimates (Clarida et al., 1998) through subsample analysis (Taylor, 1999, Clarida et al., 2000) towards more complex methods that allow an assessment of the evolution in the conduct of monetary policy. There are two alternative methods to model structural changes in monetary policy rules that occur on an unknown date: (i) regime switching models, in particular the state-dependent Markov switching models (Valente, 2003; Assenmacher-Wesche, 2006; Sims and Zha 2006) and (ii) state-space models, where the changes are characterized by smooth transitions rather than abrupt switches (Boivin, 2006; Kim and Nelson, 2006; Trecrocci and Vasalli, 2010). As argued in Baxa et al. (2010), we consider the second approach as preferable for the estimation of policy rules given that it is more flexible and allows the incorporation of a simple correction of endogeneity (Kim, 2006; Kim and Nelson, 2006), which is a major issue in forward-looking policy rules estimated from ex-post data.[12] The state-space approach or time-varying coefficient model seems also suitable when one wants to evaluate the effect of factors such as financial stress that can, for a limited length of time, alter (rather than permanently change) the monetary policy conduct.

---

gap, we instead assume a backward-looking reaction. The reason is that in the absence of real time data we have to rely on the output gap construction of statistical methods. It is arguable that besides the prediction error there is also a construction error that both might be magnified if an unobserved forecast is substituted by the output gap estimate for future periods. Finally, we assume that central bankers' response (if any) to financial stress is rather immediate (see Mishkin, 2009). Therefore, we use one lag of the FSI and its subcomponents in the benchmark case. However, as a robustness check we allow for different lags and leads, allowing the central bankers' response to be preemptive rather than reactive.

[12] The time-varying parameter model with the specific treatment of endogeneity is still relevant when real-time data are used (Orphanides, 2001). When the real-time forecast is not derived under the assumption that nominal interest rates will remain constant within the forecasting horizon (Boivin, 2006) or in the case of measurement error and heteroscedasticity (Kim et al., 2006).

The state-space models are commonly estimated by means of a maximum likelihood estimator via the Kalman filter or smoother. Unfortunately, this approach has several limitations that can turn problematic in applied work. First, the results are somewhat sensitive to the initial values of the parameters, which are usually unknown, especially in the case of variables whose impact on the dependent variable is not permanent and whose size is unknown, which is the case of financial stress and its effect on interest rates. Second, the log likelihood function is highly nonlinear and in some cases, optimization algorithms fail to minimize the negative of the log likelihood. In particular, it can either fail to calculate the Hessian matrix throughout the iterations process or, when the likelihood function is approximated to facilitate computations, covariance matrix of observation vector can get singular for provided starting values. The alternative is a moment-based estimator proposed by Schlicht (1981, 2005) and Schlicht and Ludsteck (2006), which is employed in our study and briefly described below. This framework is flexible enough so as to incorporate the endogeneity correction proposed by Kim (2006).

Kim (2006) shows that the conventional time-varying parameter model delivers inconsistent estimates when explanatory variables are correlated with the disturbance term and proposes an estimator of the time-varying coefficient model with endogenous regressors. The endogeneity may arise not only in forward-looking policy rules based on ex-post data (Kim and Nelson, 2006; Baxa et al., 2010), but also in the case of variables that have a two-sided relation with monetary policy. Financial stress unquestionably enters this category. Following Kim (2006) we rewrite equation (10.3) as follows:

$$r_t = \left(1 - \rho_t\right)\left[\alpha_t + \beta_t \pi_{t+i} + \gamma_t y_{t+j}\right] + \rho_t r_{t-1} + \delta_t x_{t+k} + \varepsilon_t \quad (10.4)$$

$$\alpha_t = \alpha_{t-1} + \vartheta_{1,t} \text{ with } \vartheta_{1,t} \sim i.i.d.N\left(0, \sigma_{\vartheta_1}^2\right) \quad (10.5)$$

$$\beta_t = \beta_{t-1} + \vartheta_{2,t} \text{ with } \vartheta_{2,t} \sim i.i.d.N\left(0, \sigma_{\vartheta_2}^2\right) \quad (10.6)$$

$$\gamma_t = \gamma_{t-1} + \vartheta_{3,t} \text{ with } \vartheta_{3,t} \sim i.i.d.N\left(0, \sigma_{\vartheta_3}^2\right) \quad (10.7)$$

$$\delta_t = \delta_{t-1} + \vartheta_{4,t} \text{ with } \vartheta_{4,t} \sim i.i.d.N\left(0, \sigma_{\vartheta_4}^2\right) \tag{10.8}$$

$$\rho_t = \rho_{t-1} + \vartheta_{5,t} \text{ with } \vartheta_{5,t} \sim i.i.d.N\left(0, \sigma_{\vartheta_5}^2\right) \tag{10.9}$$

$$\pi_{t+i} = Z_{t-m}'\xi + \sigma_\varphi \varphi_t \text{ with } \varphi_t \sim i.i.d.N\left(0, 1\right) \tag{10.10}$$

$$y_{t+j} = Z_{t-m}'\psi + \sigma_v v_t \text{ with } v_t \sim i.i.d.N\left(0, 1\right) \tag{10.11}$$

$$x_{t+k} = Z_{t-m}'o + \sigma_\iota \iota_t \text{ with } \iota_t \sim i.i.d.N\left(0, 1\right) \tag{10.12}$$

The measurement equation (10.4) of the state-space representation is the monetary policy rule. The transitions in equations (10.5) to (10.9) describe the time-varying coefficients as a random walk process without drift[13]. Equations (10.10) to (10.12) track the relationship between the potentially endogenous regressors (π_{t+i}, y_{t+j} and x_{t+k}) and their instruments, Z_t. We use the following instruments: π_{t-1}, π_{t-12} (π_{t-4} for CAN and SWE), y_{t-1}, y_{t-2}, r_{t-1}, and when $k \geq 0$ also x_{t-1} and x_{t-2}). Following Kim (2006), we assume that the parameters in equations (10.10) to (10.12) are time-invariant. The correlation between the standardized residuals ϕ_t, v_t and ζ_t and the error term ε_t is $k_{\phi,\varepsilon}$, $k_{v,\varepsilon}$ and $k_{\zeta,\varepsilon}$ respectively (note that σ_ϕ, σ_v, and σ_ζ are the standard errors of ϕ_t, v_t and ζ_t, respectively). The consistent estimates of the coefficients in equation (10.4) are obtained in two steps. In the first step, we estimate equations (10.10) to (10.12) and save the standardized residuals ϕ_t, v_t and ζ_t. In the second step, we estimate equation (10.13) below along with equation (10.5) to (10.9). Note that equation (10.13) now includes bias correction terms, i.e., (standardized) residuals from equation (10.10) to (10.12), to address the aforementioned endogeneity of the regressors. Consequently, the estimated parameters in equation (10.13) are consistent, as Z_t is uncorrelated with the regressors.

---

[13] Note that while a typical time-invariant regression assumes that $a_t = a_{t-1}$, in this case it is assumed that $E\left[a_t\right] = a_{t-1}$.

$$r_t = (1 - \rho_t)[\alpha_t + \beta_t \pi_{t+2} + \gamma_t y_{t-1}] + \rho_t r_{t-1} + \\ + \delta_t x_{t-1} + \kappa_{\zeta,\varepsilon} \sigma_{\varepsilon,t} \zeta_t + \kappa_{v,\varepsilon} \sigma_\varepsilon v_t + \kappa_{\varphi,\varepsilon} \sigma_\varepsilon \varphi_t + \zeta_t \qquad (10.13)$$

with $\zeta_t \sim N\left(0, (1 - \kappa_{v,\varepsilon}^2 - \kappa_{\varphi,\varepsilon}^2 - \kappa_{t,\varepsilon}^2) \sigma_{\varepsilon,t}^2\right)$

As we noted before, instead of the standard framework for second-step estimation, the maximum likelihood estimator via the Kalman filter (Kim, 2006), we use an alternative estimation framework, the 'varying coefficients' (VC) method (Schlicht, 1981; Schlicht, 2005; Schlicht and Ludsteck, 2006). This method is a generalization of the ordinary least squares approach that, instead of minimizing the sum of the squares of residuals $\sum_{t=1}^{T} \varepsilon^2$, uses the minimization of the weighted sum of squares:

$$\sum_{t=1}^{T} \zeta^2 + \theta_1 \sum_{t=1}^{T} \vartheta_1^2 + \theta_2 \sum_{t=1}^{T} \vartheta_2^2 + \ldots + \theta_n \sum_{t=1}^{T} \vartheta_n^2 \qquad (10.14)$$

where the weights θ_i are the inverse variance ratios of the regression residuals ζ_t and the shocks in time-varying coefficients ϑ_t, that is $\theta_i = \sigma^2 / \sigma_i^2$. This approach balances the fit of the model and the parameter stability. Additionally, the time averages of the regression coefficients, estimated by a weighted least squares estimator, are identical to their GLS estimates of the corresponding regression with fixed coefficients, that is $\frac{1}{T} \sum_{t=1}^{T} \hat{a}_t = \hat{a}_{GLS}$.[14] The method is useful in our case because:

1. it does not require knowledge of initial values even for non-stationary variables prior to the estimation procedure. Instead, both the variance ratios and the coefficients are estimated simultaneously,
2. the property of the estimator, that the time averages of estimated time-varying coefficients are equal to its time-invariant

---

[14] See Schlicht and Ludsteck (2006) and Baxa et al. (2010) for more details.

counterparts, permits an easy interpretation of the results in relation to time-invariant results,
3. it coincides with the MLE estimator via the Kalman filter if the time series are sufficiently long and if the variance ratios are properly estimated.[15]

However, this method suffers certain limitations of its own. In particular: (a) it requires that the time-varying coefficients are described as random walks and (b) the shocks in time-varying coefficients ϑ_t are minimized (see equation (10.14)). While this does not represent a major problem for the estimation of the coefficients of common variables such as inflation, where the monetary policy response is permanent, it can lead to a loss of some information about ad-hoc response factors in monetary policy-making that are considered by central bankers only infrequently but once they are in place the policy response can be substantial. A financial stress indicator x_{t+k} seems to be this kind of factor. The way to deal with this problem is the estimation-independent calibration of the variance ratios in equation (10.14) such that the estimated coefficient is consistent with economic logic, i.e. it is mostly insignificant and it can turn significant (with no prior restriction on its sign) during the periods of financial stress, i.e. when the financial stress indicator is different from zero. Therefore, we first estimate equation (10.13) using the VC method and study whether the resulting coefficients at the FSI correspond to economic intuition, and especially whether the coefficient is not constant or slowly moving (a so-called pile-up

---

[15] The Kalman filter as implemented in common econometric packages typically uses the diffusion of priors for its initiation but it still produces a lot of corner solutions and often it does not achieve convergence. Schlicht and Ludsteck (2006) compare the performance of the VC moment estimator and the Kalman smoother in terms of the mean squared error on simulated data and they conclude that the moment estimator outperforms the Kalman filter on small samples with a size of up to 100 observations. For comparison, we estimated Eq. (10.13) using the conventional Kalman smoother in the GROCER software using the function tvp (Dubois and Michaux, 2009). We parameterized the model by initial conditions taken from the OLS estimates of the parameters on the full sample and the initial forecast error covariance matrix set to 0. The matrix of the residuals of time-varying coefficients was assumed to be diagonal like in the VC method. The results were very similar to those obtained from the VC method when the estimated variances were the same in both methods.

problem, see Stock and Watson, 1998). When this problem occurs, we compare the results with models where k belongs to (-2, -1, 0, 1, 2) and calibrate the variance ratios in equation (10.13) by the variance ratios estimated for the model with the largest variances in the FSI. This step was necessary for Australia and Sweden. The Taylor rule coefficients were compared with the initial estimates and they were consistent in both cases.[16]

The results of our empirical analysis should reveal whether central banks adjusted the interest rate policy in the face of financial stress. However, the time-varying framework also allows inferring whether any response to financial stress led to the temporal dismissal of other targets, in particular the inflation rate. Therefore, we are mainly interested in the evolution of the financial stress coefficient δ_t. We expect it to be mostly insignificant or zero given that episodes of financial stress are rather infrequent and even if they occur the monetary authorities may not always respond to them. Moreover, the size of the estimated coefficient does not have any obvious interpretation since the FSI is a composite indicator normalized to have a zero mean. Consequently, we define the stress effect as a product of the estimated coefficient δ_t and the value of IMF financial stress index x_{t+k}. The interpretation of the stress effect is straightforward: it shows the magnitude of interest rate reactions to financial stress in percentage points or, in other words, the deviation from the target interest rate as implied by the macroeconomic variables due to the response to financial stress.

Results

This section summarizes our results on the effect of financial stress on interest rate setting. First, the results on the effect of the overall measure of financial stress on interest rate setting are presented. Second, the effect of specific components of financial stress on

---

[16] Stock and Watson (1998) propose a medium unbiased estimator for variance in the time-varying parameter model but its application is straightforward only in the case of one time-varying coefficient and, more importantly, it requires the variables being stationary.

monetary policy is examined. Third, we briefly comment on the monetary policy rule estimates that served as the input for the assessment of financial stress effects. Finally, we perform a series of robustness checks.

Figure 10.2 presents our results on the effect of financial stress on interest rate setting in all five countries (labelled as *financial stress effect* hereinafter). Although there is some heterogeneity across countries, some global trends on the effect of financial stress are apparent. While in good times, such as in the second half of the 1990s, financial stress has virtually no effect on interest rate setting or it is slightly positive,[17] the reaction of monetary authorities to financial stress was highly negative during the 2008–2009 global financial crisis. While the previous evidence on the effect of financial stress on monetary policy is somewhat limited, our results broadly confirm the time-invariant findings of Cecchetti and Li (2008), which show that the US Fed adjusted the interest rates to the procyclical impact of bank capital requirements in 1989–2000. Similarly, Belke and Klose (2010) estimate the Taylor rule on two sub-samples (before and during the 2008–2009 global financial crisis) and find that the Fed reacted systematically not only to inflation and output gap, but to asset prices, credit and money as well.

The size of financial stress effects on interest rate setting during the recent financial crisis is somewhat heterogeneous with the strongest reaction found for the UK. The results suggest that all central banks, except the Bank of England, kept their policy rates by about 50–100 basis points lower, as compared to the counterfactual of no reaction to financial stress. The size of this effect for the UK is assessed to be about three times stronger (i.e. 250 basis points). This implies that about 50 percent of the overall policy rate decrease during the recent financial crisis was motivated by the financial stability concerns in the UK (10–30 percent in the remaining sample countries), while the remaining half falls on unfavorable developments in domestic economic activity. This finding is interesting when confronted with the BoE's very low consideration of

---

[17] Note that the positive effect of financial stress on interest rate setting is to some extent a consequence of scaling the financial stress indicator; its zero value corresponds to a long run average stress. Hence, we do not give much attention to the positive values of stress unless caused by the temporarily positive and significant regression coefficient associated with the FSI.

expected inflation over the last decade (found Baxa et al., 2010, using the time-varying model and in Taylor and Davradakis, 2006, in the context of the threshold model) that further decreased during the current crisis similarly as for the USA but less so for the other central banks. It is also evident that the magnitude of the response is unusual for all five central banks. Yet, the results for Australia, Canada and Sweden show that a similar magnitude of the response to financial stress recorded during the recent financial crisis was already seen in previous periods of high financial stress.

Given that the 2008–2009 global crisis occurred right at the end of our sample (there is a peak in the stress indicator of five standard deviations that has not returned to normal values yet), we have performed an additional check to avoid possible end-point bias. In particular, we have run our estimation excluding the observation from the period of the 2008–2009 crisis: These results confirmed the robustness of the reported findings. With regards to the effect of the current crisis, the largest uncertainty is associated with the results for Canada, for which the shortest data sample was available, and it ends in the fourth quarter of 2008. When the possibility of a preemptive reaction of the central bank to financial stress is considered, the effect of financial stress in the current crisis is somewhere at 1–2 percent (see Appendix 10.3). These additional results suggest the response of the Bank of Canada is rather underestimated.

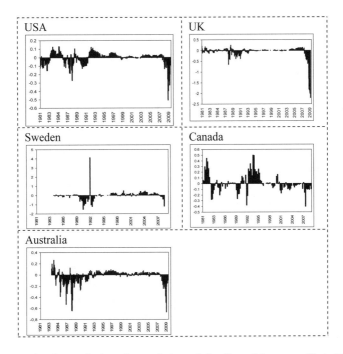

Notes: The figure depicts the evolution of the financial stress effect. The stress effect (y-axis) is defined as the product of the estimated coefficient on the financial stress indicator in monetary policy rule and the value of the IMF financial stress indicator. The stress effect shows the magnitude of the interest rate reaction to financial stress in percentage points.

Figure 10.2 The Effect of Financial Stress on Interest Rate Setting

The question of which components of financial stress influence interest rate setting is addressed in Figure 10.3. Some heterogeneity across countries is again apparent; although it seems that bank stress and stock market stress dominated the central bankers in less open economies. On the other hand, exchange rate stress matters in more open economies such as Canada and Sweden.

More specifically, the US Fed seemed to be worried about financial instability, especially during the 1980s. We can see that the main concern in the early 1980s was banking stress, which is arguably related to the Savings and Loans crisis. Another concern was that of stock market stress in particular during the stock market crash of 1987 when interest rates were lower by 30 basis points with respect to the benchmark case.

The Bank of England was, in general, much more perceptive to financial stress. We find its response mainly to stock market stress again notably in 1987. Interestingly, we find little response to exchange rate stress, not even during the 1992 ERM crisis. Nevertheless, it has to be emphasized that the interest rate reaction to speculative attack was subdued in comparison to, for example, the Riksbank (Buiter et al., 1998). The coefficient at the FSI remains constant until the devaluation of the pound sterling in September 1992. Since then the effect of financial stress on interest rate setting approaches zero from originally negative values. Besides this, the response of the Bank of England to inflation has decreased. From this perspective, it seems the pound sterling's withdrawal from the ERM allowed for both a more rule-based and less restrictive monetary policy.

The reaction of the Riksbank to the ERM crisis was different. First, after a series of speculative attacks on the Swedish krona in mid-September 1992, the Riksbank still tried to keep the current fixed exchange rate in place and the marginal interest rate jumped up 500 percent in order to offset the outflow of liquidity and other speculative attacks (see the large positive stress effect on the interest rate in 1992 in Figure 10.2). However, not even such an increase was sufficient and the fixed exchange rate had to be abandoned later in November. [18]

The Reserve Bank of Australia significantly loosened its policy during the 1980s, which can be attributed to the stress in the banking sector with an exception of the reaction to the stock market crash in 1987 (see Figure 10.3).

The exchange rate as well as bank stress seems to matter for interest rate considerations at the Bank of Canada. Interestingly, the results suggest that the Bank of Canada often responded to higher

---

[18] For Sweden, we add a dummy variable for the third quarter of 1992 (ERM crisis) to equation (10.13). At this time the Swedish central bank forced upward short-term interest rates in an effort to keep the krona within the ERM. From the perspective of our model, it was a case of a strong positive reaction to the actual stress that lasted only one period. When this dummy variable was not included, the model with a lagged value of the FSI was unable to show any link between stress and the interest and estimates of other coefficients were inconsistent with economic intuition.

exchange rate stress by monetary tightening. A possible explanation for this finding could be that the Canadian central bank tightened the policy when the currency stabilized at the level that the monetary authority considered to be undervalued.

We would like to highlight a comparison of Figures 10.2 and 10.3. First, it should be noted that the positive response to one stress subcomponent may cancel out against a negative response to another one, making the response to the overall stress negligible (as in the case of Canada). Second, the stress effects related to individual subcomponents need not necessarily sum up to the stress effect related to the entire FSI.

All in all, the results suggest that the central bank tends to react to financial stress and different components of financial stress matter in different time periods. The effect of financial stress on interest rate setting is found to be virtually zero in good times and economically sizable during the period of high financial stress.

Next, we briefly comment on our monetary policy rule estimates. The plot of the evolution of estimated parameters over time for all countries is available in Appendix 10.1. First, these results indicate that the interest rate smoothing is much lower than what time-invariant estimates of monetary policy rules typically suggest (see for example, Clarida et al., 1998, 2000). Our estimates of interest rate smoothing seem to be reasonable given the recent critique of Rudebusch (2006), who argues that the degree of interest rate smoothing is rather low. Moreover, for some central banks such as the RBA and the BoE in 2010 or the Sveriges Riksbank in late 1980 we find support for Mishkin's (2009, 2010) argument that central banks are less inertial during the crisis.[19] Second, the response of interest rates on inflation is particularly strong during the periods when central bankers want to break the record of high inflation such as in the UK or in Australia at the beginning of 1980s and it becomes less aggressive in the low inflation environment with subdued shocks. Third, some central banks are also found to react to output gap developments with the estimated parameter to be slightly positive on average (see more detailed results in Baxa et al., 2010).

---

[19] The correlation coefficient of the estimated time-varying coefficient of a lagged interest rate ρ and the financial stress index δ is -0.79 for Australia, 0.21 for Canada, -0.20 for Sweden, -0.68 for the UK and 0.60 for the US

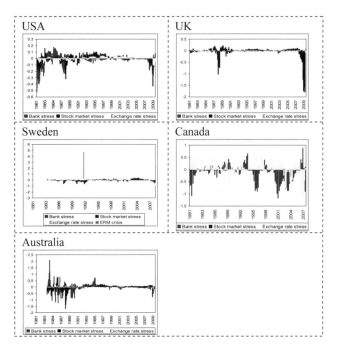

Note: The figure depicts the evolution of the components of the financial stress effect, namely bank stress effect, exchange rate stress effect and stock market stress effect. The stress effect (y-axis) is defined as the product of the estimated coefficient on the given component of the financial stress indicator in monetary policy rule and the value of the corresponding component of the IMF financial stress indicator. The stress effect shows the magnitude of the interest rate reaction to financial stress in percentage points.

Figure 10.3 The Effect of Financial Stress Components on Interest Rate Setting: Bank Stress, Exchange Rate Stress and Stock Market Stress

Finally, we perform a battery of robustness checks. First, following the argument put forward above, we use interbank interest rates as a dependent variable. These results are reported in Figures A.10.2.1–A.10.2.2. We can see that the overall stress effect on the interbank rate is larger for the US during the current crisis, where it explains two percent of the decrease of the interbank interest rate. For Sweden, we have found a strong positive effect of exchange rate volatility in the late 1980s; this might be linked to the aim of the central bank to keep the exchange rate fixed. In other cases, there is no substantial difference between the benchmark results and results obtained using this alternative dependent variable.

Second, in the benchmark model and all the results reported so far we use the first lag of the FSI in policy rule estimation. We stimulate this choice by the use of monthly data, the frequency of monetary policy meetings of most central bank boards and the assumption that the policy actions are likely to be implemented in a timely fashion. In addition, we employ different lags and leads, in the latter case allowing the policy to be preemptive rather than reactive. In this case, we use the future realized value of the FSI as a proxy of a central bank's expectation (in a similar manner as to how it is routinely executed for inflation expectations) and consequently treat the FSI as an endogenous variable (see Figure A.10.3.1 for the results). In order to get comparable results, we calibrate the variance ratios by the same values as in the baseline specification. Although we find rather mixed evidence on preemptive policy actions, which can be also related to the inadequacy of proxying the expected values of financial stress by actual values of the financial stress indicator as well as the fact that a central bank might not react to the stress preemptively, the reaction to financial stress in the current crisis is strongly negative for both expected and observed stress.

Third, we further break down the FSI sub-indices to each underlying variable to evaluate their individual contribution.[20] The corresponding stress effects appear in Figures A.10.4.1–A.10.4.2. Breaking down stock-market related stress, we find that the US Fed and the BoC react to the corporate bond spread, whereas the BoE and Sveriges Riksbank are more concerned by stock returns and volatility. While the RBA seem to be concerned with both corporate bond spreads and stock market volatility in the 1980s, the role of stock-related stress had substantially decreased by then. As far as bank-related stress is concerned, the TED spread plays a major role in all countries apart from the UK where the largest proportion of the effect on the interest rate can be attributed to an inverted term structure.

---

[20] This applies only to the banking and the stock market sub-components because the foreign exchange sub-component is represented by a single variable.

Fourth, since the verifications related to our econometric framework to obvious alternatives such as, first, the use of a maximum likelihood estimator via the Kalman filter instead of the moment-based time-varying coefficient framework of Schlicht and, second, the use of a Markov-switching model instead of a state-space model were provided in Baxa et al. (2010), we estimate simple time-invariant monetary policy rules for each country by the generalized method of moments, including various subsamples. This simple evidence reaffirms that the analyzed central banks seem to pay attention to overall financial stress in the economy. The FSI is statistically significant, with a negative sign of a magnitude between 0.05–0.20 for all countries. On the other hand, the coefficient of its sub-components often are not, and the exchange rate subcomponent in some cases has a positive sign. These results confirm that to understand the interest rate adjustment to financial stress, one should rely on a model allowing a differential response across time.

Concluding Remarks

The 2008–2009 global financial crisis awoke a significant interest in exploring the interactions between monetary policy and financial stability. This paper aimed to examine in a systematic manner whether and how the monetary policy of selected main central banks (US Fed, the Bank of England, Reserve Bank of Australia, Bank of Canada and Sveriges Riksbank) responded to episodes of financial stress over the last three decades. Instead of using individual alternative measures of financial stress in different markets, we employed the comprehensive indicator of financial stress recently developed by the IMF, which tracks overall financial stress as well as its main subcomponents, in particular banking stress, stock market stress and exchange rate stress.

Unlike a few existing empirical contributions that aim to evaluate the impact of financial stability concerns on monetary policymaking, we adopt a more flexible methodology that allows for the response to financial stress (and other macroeconomic variables) to change over time as well as deals with potential endogeneity (Kim and Nelson, 2006). The main advantage of this framework is that it does not only enable testing whether the central banks responded to financial stress at all, but it also detects the periods and types of stress that were the most worrying for monetary authorities. Our results indicate that central banks truly change their policy stance in the face of financial stress, but that the magnitude of such responses varies substantially over time. As expected, the impact of financial stress on interest rate setting is essentially zero most of the time when the levels of stress are very moderate. However, most central banks loosen monetary policy when the economy faces high financial stress. There is a certain cross-country and time heterogeneity when we look at central banks' considerations of specific types of financial stress. While most central banks seem to respond to stock market stress and bank stress, exchange rate stress is found to drive the reaction of central banks only in more open economies

Consistently with our expectations, the results indicate that a sizeable fraction of monetary policy easing during the 2008–2009 financial crisis can be explained by a direct response to the financial stress above what could be attributed to a decline in inflation expectation and output below its potential. However, the size of the financial stress effect differs by country. The result suggests that all central banks, except the Bank of England, kept their policy rates at 50 basis points lower on average solely due to financial stress present in the economy. Interestingly, the size of this effect for the UK is assessed at about five times stronger (i.e., 250 basis points). This implies that about 50 percent of the overall policy rate decrease during the recent financial crisis was motivated by financial stability concerns in the UK (10–30 percent in the remaining sample countries), while the remaining half falls on unfavorable developments in domestic economic activity. For the US Fed, the macroeconomic developments themselves (a low-inflation environment and an output substantially below its potential) explain the major fraction of the policy interest rate decreases during the crisis, leaving the further response to financial stress to be constrained by zero interest rate bound.

All in all, our results point to the usefulness of augmenting the standard version of monetary policy rule by some measure of financial conditions to get a better understanding of the interest rate setting process, especially when financial markets are not stable. The empirical results suggest that the main central banks considered in this study altered the course of their monetary policy in the face of financial stress. The recent crisis seems truly to be an exceptional period in the sense that the response to financial instability was substantial and coincided in all analyzed countries, which is evidently related to intentional policy coordination absent in previous decades. However, we have also seen that previous idiosyncratic episodes of financial distress were, at least in some countries, followed by monetary policy responses of similar if not higher magnitude.

Appendix 10.1
Time-varying Monetary Policy Rules Estimates

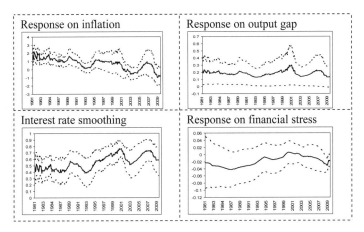

Note: The estimated coefficients of time-varying monetary policy rule are depicted with a 95% confidence interval.

Figure A.10.1.1 United States

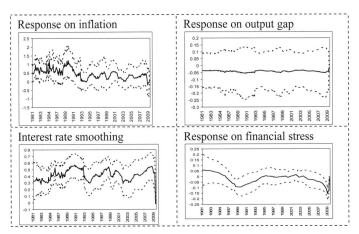

Note: The estimated coefficients of time-varying monetary policy rule are depicted with a 95% confidence interval.

Figure A.10.1.2 United Kingdom

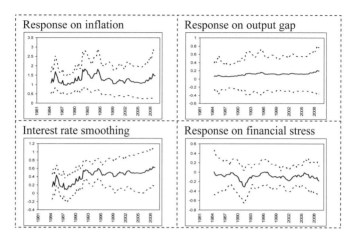

Note: The estimated coefficients of time-varying monetary policy rule are depicted with a 95% confidence interval.

Figure A.10.1.3 Sweden

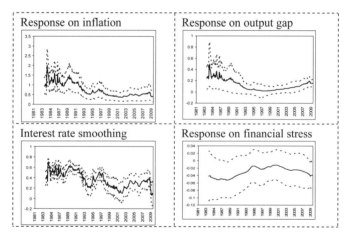

Note: The estimated coefficients of time-varying monetary policy rule are depicted with a 95% confidence interval.

Figure A.10.1.4 Australia

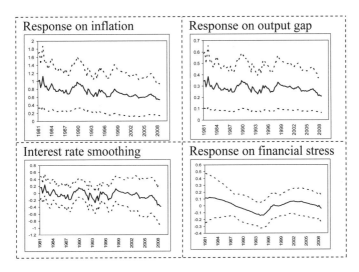

Note: The estimated coefficients of time-varying monetary policy rule are depicted with a 95% confidence interval.

Figure A.10.1.5 Canada

Appendix 10.2 The Results with the Interbank Rate as the Dependent Variable in the Policy Rule

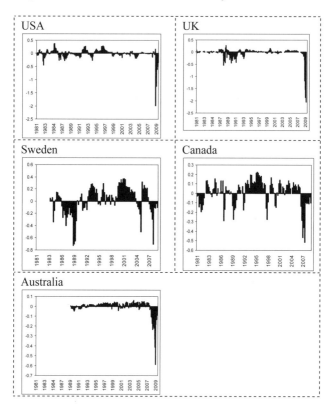

Notes: The figure depicts the evolution of the financial stress effect. The stress effect (y-axis) is defined as the product of the estimated coefficient on the financial stress indicator in monetary policy rule and the value of the IMF financial stress indicator. The stress effect shows the magnitude of the interest rate reaction to financial stress in percentage points.

Figure A.10.2.1   The Effect of Financial Stress on Interest Rate Setting

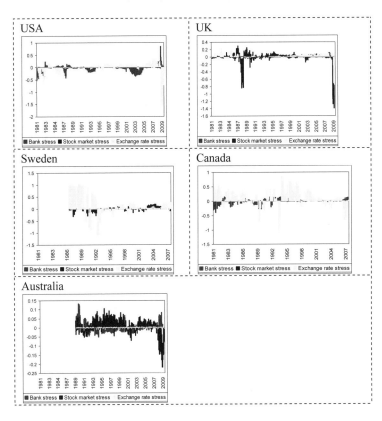

Notes: The figure depicts the evolution of the components of the financial stress effect, namely bank stress effect, exchange rate stress effect and stock market stress effect. The stress effect (y-axis) is defined as the product of the estimated coefficient on the given component of the financial stress indicator in monetary policy rule and the value of the corresponding component of the IMF financial stress indicator. The stress effect shows the magnitude of the interest rate reaction to financial stress in percentage points.

Figure A.10.2.2 The Effect of Financial Stress Components on Interest Rate Setting: Bank Stress, Exchange Rate Stress and Stock Market Stress

Appendix 10.3 The Results with Different Leads and Lag of the FSI

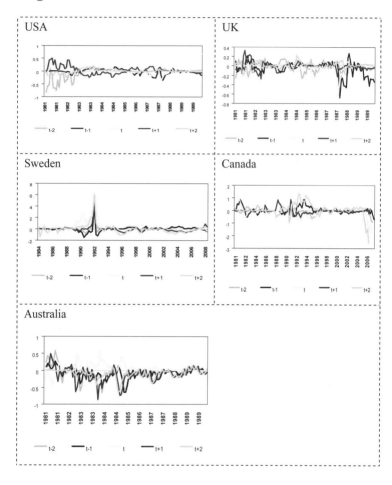

Figure A.10.3.1 The Effect of Financial Stress (t-1 vs. t-2, t, t+1, t+2) on Interest Rate Setting

Appendix 10.4 The Results with Individual Variables of Bank Stress and Stock Market Stress

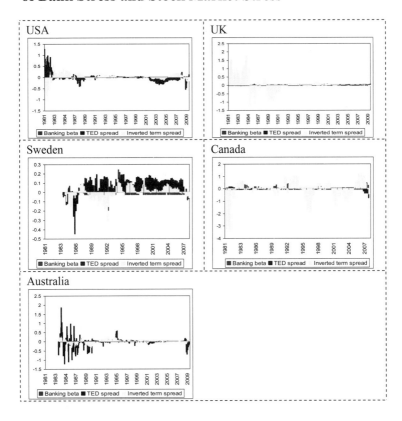

Figure A.10.4.1 The Effect of Bank Stress on Interest Rate Setting

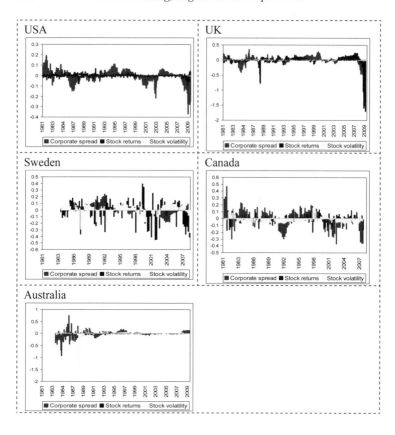

Figure A.10.4.2 The Effect of Stock Market Stress on Interest Rate Setting

References

Akram, Q.F. and Ø. Eitrheim (2008), 'Flexible Inflation Targeting and Financial Stability: Is It Enough to Stabilize Inflation and Output?', *Journal of Banking and Finance,* **32**, 1242–1254.

Akram, Q. F., G. Bårdsen and K.-G. Lindquist (2007), 'Pursuing Financial Stability under an Inflation-targeting Regime', *Annals of Finance,* **3**, 131–153.

Assenmacher-Wesche, K. (2006), 'Estimating Central Banks' Preferences from a Time-varying Empirical Reaction Function'. *European Economic Review*, **50**, 1951–1974.

Balakrishnan, R., Danninger, S., Elekdag, S. and I. Tytell (2009), 'The Transmission of Financial Stress from Advanced to Emerging Economies', *IMF Working Paper*, No. 09/133.

Bauducco, S., Bulíř, A. and M. Čihák (2008), 'Taylor Rule Under Financial Instability', *IMF Working Paper*, No. 08/18.

Baxa, J., Horváth, R. and B. Vašíček (2010), 'How Does Monetary Policy Change? Evidence on Inflation Targeting Countries', Working Paper No 2/2010, Czech National Bank.

Belke, A. and J. Klose (2010), '(How) Do the ECB and the Fed React to Financial Market Uncertainty? – The Taylor Rule in Times of Crisis', DIW Berlin, Discussion Paper No. 972.

Bernanke, B. and A. Blinder (1992), 'The Federal Funds Rate and the Channels of Monetary Transmission', *American Economic Review*, **82**(4), 901–921.

Bernanke, B. and M. Gertler (1999), 'Monetary Policy and Asset Price Volatility.' *Economic Review*, Federal Reserve Bank of Kansas City, 17–51.

Bernanke, B. and M. Gertler (2001), 'Should Central Banks Respond to Movements in Asset Prices?', *American Economic Review*, **91**(2), 253–257.

Bernanke, B., Gertler, M., and S. Gilchrist (1996), 'The Financial Accelerator and the Flight to Quality', *The Review of Economics and Statistics*, **78**(1), 1–15.

Bernanke, B., Gertler, M., and S. Gilchrist (1999), 'The Financial Accelerator in a Quantitative Business Cycle Framework', in J.B. Taylor and M. Woodford (eds.) *Handbook of Macroeconomics*. Amsterdam: North-Holland.

Boivin, J. (2006), 'Has US Monetary Policy Changed? Evidence from Drifting Coefficients and Real-Time Data', *Journal of Money, Credit and Banking*, **38**(5), 1149–1173.

Bordo, M.D. and O. Jeanne (2002), 'Boom-Busts in Asset Prices, Economic Instability, and Monetary Policy,' NBER Working Papers 8966, National Bureau of Economic Research.

Borio, C. and P. Disyatat (2009), 'Unconventional Monetary Policies: An Appraisal', BIS Working Papers, No. 292.

Borio, C. and M. Drehmann (2009), 'Towards an Operational Framework for Financial Stability: 'Fuzzy' Measurement and Its Consequences', BIS Working Papers, No. 284.

Borio, C. and P. Lowe (2002), 'Asset Prices, Financial and Monetary Stability: Exploring the Nexus.' BIS Working Paper, No. 114.

Borio, C. and P. Lowe (2004), 'Securing Sustainable Price Stability: Should Credit Come Back from the Wilderness?', BIS Working Papers, No. 157.

Borio, C. and I. Shim (2007), 'What Can (Macro-)Prudential Policy Do to Support Monetary Policy?', BIS Working Papers, No. 242.

Brousseau, V. and C. Detken (2001), 'Monetary Policy and Fears of Financial Instability.' ECB Working Paper, No. 89.

Buiter, W.H., Corsetti, G.M. and P.A. Pesenti (1998), 'Interpreting the ERM Crisis: Country-Specific and Systemic Issues', Princeton Studies in International Economics, 84, Princeton University.

Bulíř, A. and M. Čihák (2008), 'Central Bankers' Dilemma When Banks Are Vulnerable: To Tighten or Not To Tighten?' IMF mimeo.

Cardarelli, R., Elekdag, S. and S. Lall (2009), 'Financial Stress, Downturns, and Recoveries', IMF Working Paper, No. 09/100.

Carlson, M.A., King, T.B. and K.F. Lewis (2009), 'Distress in the financial sector and economic activity', Finance and Economics Discussion Series 2009–01, Board of Governors of the Federal Reserve System.

Cecchetti, S., Genberg, H., Lipsky, J. and S. Wadhwani (2000), 'Asset prices and central bank policy', *Geneva Reports on the World Economy*, No.2.

Cecchetti, S. and L. Li (2008), 'Do Capital Adequacy Requirements Matter for Monetary Policy?', *Economic Inquiry*, **46**(4), 643–659.

Choi, W. and D. Cook (2004), 'Liability Dollarization and the Bank Balance Sheet Channel', *Journal of International Economics*, **64** (2), 247–275.

Christiano, L., C. Ilut, R. Motto, and M. Rostagno (2008), 'Monetary Policy and Stock Market Boom-Bust Cycles', ECB Working Paper No. 955.

Clarida, R., Galí, J., and M. Gertler (1998), 'Monetary Policy Rules and Macroeconomic Stability: Evidence and Some Theory', *The Quarterly Journal of Economics*, **115**, 147–180.

Clarida, R., Galí, J., and M. Gertler (2000), 'Monetary Policy Rules in Practice: Some International Evidence', *European Economic Review*, **42**, 1033–1067.

Cúrdia, V. and M. Woodford (2010), 'Credit Spreads and Monetary Policy', *Journal of Money, Credit and Banking*, **42**, 3–35.

Detken, C. and F. Smets (2004), 'Asset Price Booms and Monetary Policy', ECB Working Paper, No. 364.

Devereux, M. and A. Sutherland (2007), 'Country Portfolios in Open Economy Macro Models', *Journal of the European Economic Association*, **5**(2–3), 491–499.

Dubois, É. and E. Michaux (2009), 'Grocer 1.4: an econometric toolbox for Scilab', available athttp://dubois.ensae.net/grocer.html.

Eichengreen, B. and M.D. Bordo (2002), 'Crises Now and Then: What Lessons from the Last Era of Financial Globalization', NBER Working Paper, No. 8716.

Engel, C. and A. Matsumoto (2009), 'The International Diversification Puzzle When Prices are Sticky: It's Really about Exchange-Rate Hedging not Equity Portfolios', *American Economic Journal: Macroeconomics*, **1**(2), 155–188.

Faia, E. and T. Monacelli (2007), 'Optimal Monetary Policy Rules, Asset Prices and Credit Frictions', *Journal of Economic Dynamics and Control*, **31**(10), 3228–3254.

Fisher, I. (1933), 'Debt-deflation Theory of Great Depressions', *Econometrica*, **1**(4), 337–357.

Fuhrer, J. and G. Tootell (2008), 'Eyes on the prize: How did the Fed respond to the stock market?', *Journal of Monetary Economics*, **55**(4), 796–805.

Goldstein, M., Kaminsky, G. and C. Reinhart (2000), *Assessing Financial Vulnerability: An Early Warning System for Emerging Markets*, Washington, DC: Institute for International Economics.

Goodhart, C. (2006), 'A framework for assessing financial stability?', *Journal of Banking and Finance*, **30**(12), 3415–3422.

Goodhart, C., Osorio, C., and D. Tsomocos (2009), 'An Analysis of Monetary Policy and Financial Stability: A New Paradigm', CESifo working paper, No. 2885.

Gruen, D., Plumb, M. and A. Stone (2005), 'How Should Monetary Policy Respond to Asset-Price Bubbles?', *International Journal of Central Banking, December*, 1–31.

Hakkio, C.S. and W.R. Keeton (2009): 'Financial Stress: What Is It, How is It to be Measured, and Why Does It Matter?', *Economic Review*, 2.Q 2009, Federal Reserve Bank of Kansas City, 1–50.

Iacovello, M. and S. Neri (2010), 'Housing Market Spillovers: Evidence from an Estimated DSGE Model', *American Economic Journal: Macroeconomics*, **2**(2), 125–164.

Illing, M. and Y. Liu, (2006), 'Measuring financial stress in a developed country: An application to Canada', *Journal of Financial Stability*, **2**(3), 243–265.

Kaminsky, G. and C. Reinhart (1999), 'The Twin Crises: The Causes of Banking and Balance-of-Payments Problems', *American Economic Review*, **89**(3), 473–500.

Kim, Ch.-J. (2006), 'Time-Varying Parameter Models with Endogenous Regressors', *Economics Letters*, **91**, 21–26.

Kim, Ch.-J. and Ch.R. Nelson (2006), 'Estimation of a Forward-Looking Monetary Policy Rule: A Time-Varying Parameter Model Using Ex-post Data', *Journal of Monetary Economics*, **53**, 1949–1966.

Kim, Ch.-J., Kishor, K. and Ch.R. Nelson (2006), 'A Time-Varying Parameter Model for a Forward-Looking Monetary Policy Rule based on Real-Time Data', mimeo.

Kiyotaki, N. and J. Moore (1997), 'Credit Cycles,' *The Journal of Political Economy*, **105**, 211–248.

Laeven, L. and F. Valencia (2008), 'Systemic Banking Crises: A New Database', IMF Working Paper, No. 08/224.

Melvin, M. and M.P. Taylor (2009), 'The crisis in the foreign exchange market', *Journal of International Money and Finance*, **28**(8), 1317–1330.

Merton, R. (1974), 'On the Pricing of Corporate Debt: The Risk Structure of Interest Rates', *Journal of Finance*, **29**(2), 449–470.

Mishkin, F. (2009), 'Is Monetary Policy Effective during Financial Crises?', *American Economic Review Papers & Proceedings*, **99**(2), 573–577.

Mishkin, F. (2010), 'Monetary Policy Flexibility, Risk Management and Financial Disruptions', *Journal of Asian Economics*, forthcoming.

Orphanides, A. (2001),'Monetary Policy Rules Based on Real-Time Data', *American Economic Review*, **91**, 964–985.

Posen, A. (2006), 'Why Central Banks Should Not Burst Bubbles', *International Finance*, **9**(1), 109–124.

Reinhart, C. and K. Rogoff (2009), *This Time is Different: A Panoramic View of Eight Centuries of Financial Crises*, Princeton, USA: Princeton University Press.

Reis, R. (2010), 'Interpreting the Unconventional US Monetary Policy of 2007–09', NBER Working Paper, No. 15662.

Rigobon, R. and B. Sack (2003), 'Measuring the Reaction of Monetary Policy to the Stock Market', *The Quarterly Journal of Economics*, **118**(2), 639–669.

Roubini, N. (2006), 'Why Central Banks Should Burst Bubbles', *International Finance*, **9**(1), 87–107.

Rudebusch, G. (2006), 'Monetary Policy Inertia: Fact or Fiction?', *International Journal of Central Banking*, **2**(4), 85–136.

Schlicht, E. (1981), 'A Seasonal Adjustment Principle and a Seasonal Adjustment Method Derived From this Principle', *Journal of the American Statistical Association*, **76**(374), 374–378.

Schlicht, E. (2005), 'Estimating the Smoothing Parameter in the So-called Hodrick-Prescott Filter', *Journal of the Japan Statistical Society*, **35**(1), 99–119.

Schlicht, E. and J. Ludsteck (2006), 'Variance Estimation in a Random Coefficients Model, Department of Economics', IZA Discussion Paper, No. 2031.

Siklos, P. and M. Bohl (2008), 'Asset Prices as Indicators of Euro Area Monetary Policy: An Empirical Assessment of Their Role in a Taylor Rule', *Open Economies Review*, **20**(1), 39–59.

Sims, Ch. and T. Zha (2006), 'Were there Regime Switches in US Monetary Policy', *American Economic Review*, **96**(1), 54–81.

Stock, J.H. and M.W. Watson (1998), 'Median Unbiased Estimation of Coefficient Variance in a Time-Varying Parameter Model'. *Journal of the American Statistical Association*, **93**(441), 349–358.

Taylor, J.B. (1993), 'Discretion versus Policy Rules in Practice', *Carnegie-Rochester Conference Series on Public Policy*, **39**, 195–214.

Taylor, J.B. (ed.) (1999), *Monetary Policy Rules*, Chicago: The University of Chicago Press.

Taylor, J.B. (2001), 'The Role of Exchange Rate in Monetary-Policy Rules', *American Economic Review*, **91**(2), 263–267.

Taylor, J.B. (2008), 'Monetary Policy and the State of the Economy', testimony before the Committee on Financial Services, US House of Representatives, February 26, 2008.

Taylor, M.P. and E. Davradakis (2006), 'Interest Rate Setting and Inflation Targeting: Evidence of a Nonlinear Taylor Rule for the United Kingdom', *Studies in Nonlinear Dynamics & Econometrics*, **10**(4), Article 1.

Taylor, J.B. and J. Williams (2009), 'A Black Swan in the Money Market', *American Economic Journal: Macroeconomics*, **1**(1), 58–83.

Teranishi, Y. (2009), 'Credit Spread and Monetary Policy', IMES Discussion Paper Series 2009-E-14, Bank of Japan.

Terrones, M. and Ch. Otrok (2004), 'The Global House Price Boom', in *IMF: World Economic Outlook*, Chapter 3, April. Washington: International Monetary Fund.

Tovar, C.E. (2009), 'DSGE Models and Central Banks'. *Economics: The Open-Access, Open-Assessment E-Journal*, **3**, 200916.

Valente, G. (2003), 'Monetary Policy Rules and Regime Shift', *Applied Financial Economics*, **13**, 525–535.

Zhang, Ch., Osborn, D.R. and H. Dong (2008), 'The New Keynesian Phillips Curve: From Sticky Inflation to Sticky Prices', *Journal of Money, Credit and Banking*, **40**, 667–699.

PART II

The Architecture of Regulation and
Supervision

11. Defining and Measuring Systemic Risk

Sylvester Eijffinger[1]

Introduction

With the planned implementation of the European Systemic Risk Board (ESRB) in 2010, European authorities are trying to identify and avoid future financial crises before they start. This board, under the lead of the European Central Bank (ECB) will have to deal with the macro-prudential supervision of the financial sector in Europe and is mandated to detect 'systemic risks'. However, the ECB does not have a clear concept of systemic risk itself and even in academia there exists no generally accepted definition.

Moreover, in his speech at the CEPR/ESI 13th Annual Conference on 'Financial Supervision in an Uncertain World' on 25–26 September 2009 in Venice, ECB Executive Board Member Mr. Lorenzo Bini Smaghi pointed out that 'firm-level data [...] have been recognized as essential for more accurate assessments of the potential impact of risks materializing. [...]. It should include better data coverage of non-regulated financial sectors, as well as more granular information on key node-institutions in the financial system and on potential inter-linkages between them.'

Bini Smaghi (2009) first stressed the conceptual issues of systemic risk, after which he stressed the tasks of the ESRB being risk detection, risk assessment and ultimately issuing risk warnings. This briefing chapter will be structured in the same way. First, the different definitions of systemic risk will be discussed, to be able to pinpoint

---

[1] The author gratefully acknowledges the very helpful comments of Mr. Edin Mujagic, MSc and the excellent research assistance of Mr. Rob Nijskens, MSc.

the common components of systemic risk. Then, we will move to risk detection and assessment, for which accurate indicators should be developed together with the gathering of appropriate data. Finally, this new way of defining and measuring systemic risk should be translated into new ESRB policy, taking into account that the indicators can and should be refined over time.

Defining Systemic Risk

The ESRB needs a clear concept of systemic risk to be able to measure it properly. There exist various definitions of systemic risk, which all share some common features. As Mr. Bini Smaghi also stressed, the definition introduced by the G10 provides a good starting point:

> '[Systemic risk is] the risk that an event will trigger a loss of economic value or confidence in, and attendant increases in uncertainty about, a substantial portion of the financial system that is serious enough to quite probably have significant adverse effects on the real economy'.

Important parts of this definition are the loss of confidence, increases in uncertainty, the fact that a substantial portion of the financial system is concerned and ultimately the significant adverse effects on the real economy. The last part warrants intervention by the ESRB at an early stage. This definition is also quite similar to that of the ECB, which is phrased in terms of financial stability (i.e., the absence of systemic risk):

> '[Financial stability is a] condition in which the financial system – comprising of financial intermediaries, markets and market infrastructures – is capable of withstanding shocks and the unraveling of imbalances, thereby mitigating the likelihood of disruptions in the financial intermediation process which are severe enough to significantly impair the allocation of savings to profitable investment opportunities'

In this definition it is clear that the financial system is stable when it can withstand the shocks that are mentioned in the G10 definition of systemic risk, i.e., those shocks that cause impairment to economic activity through affecting the ability of the financial system to allocate funds. The definition coined by Adrian and Brunnermeier (2009) is quite concise:

> *'The risk that institutional distress spreads widely and distorts the supply of credit and capital to the real economy'*

It is similar to that used by Acharya et al. (2009):

> *'[The risk] of widespread failures of financial institutions or freezing up of capital markets that can substantially reduce the supply of such intermediated capital to the real economy.'*

Hart and Zingales (2009) use an analogous definition, which also refers to the risk that the failure of one institution leads to a failure of other institutions in the system, having ultimate spillover effects on the real economy.

Borio and Drehmann (2008) have analyzed many definitions and concluded that they all have several elements in common, which are important to create a unifying understanding of systemic risk. All of them consider the whole financial system instead of individual institutions. Furthermore, they stress the risk of spillovers from the financial sector to the real economy and the costs in terms of welfare that are associated with these spillovers. Finally, most of them refer to the risk of financial instability, which is often more concrete and better measurable than financial stability.

Detecting and Assessing Systemic Risk

After having defined what is meant by systemic risk, it is imperative to design good measurement of this risk. This depends among others on sophisticated techniques that help in designing indicators that warn against a systemic crisis, and on the availability of detailed information as input for these indicators. Furthermore, the ESRB should take into account interlinkages between financial institutions; a factor that has been widely overlooked during the last years. However, let us first focus on how to measure systemic risk. We can divide the measurement of systemic risk into two components, which should complement each other. The first consists of detecting early warning indicators for asset bubbles and the second component refers to assessing the individual institutions' contribution to systemic risk. We will pick out the recent contributions to this literature.

Early Warning Indicators for Asset Bubbles

Borio and Drehmann (2009) improve upon earlier research by Borio and Lowe (2004) by constructing leading indicators for banking crises using both credit variables and asset prices. They argue that financial imbalances, which may lead to banking crises, manifest themselves when there is a coexistence of 'unusually rapid cumulative growth in private sector credit and asset prices'. This means asset price misalignments (usually a boom) exist in a financial system that has limited capacity to withstand the impending asset price reversal (bust). The indicators are measured as deviations of variables from their trends, issuing a signal when this gap exceeds a certain threshold. The authors construct indicators based on credit variables, equity prices and property prices (which is quite novel). They find that these joint indicators work quite well, also out of sample (i.e., in predicting the current crisis) according to standard measures such as the *noise-to-signal ratio*. Especially the indicators including all three categories (credit, equity and property) perform well. However, the authors stress that there are certain caveats. First, they confirm that the role of expert judgment is still quite large, as a complement to the signals the indicators provide. For policy purposes, they thus recommend a threshold range instead of specific points. Furthermore, the indicators could be improved in a few dimensions. One point is that cross-border exposures to asset price movements should be incorporated more systematically, preferably using data on individual institutions at the national level. Here lies an important improvement in terms of information provision, especially for national supervisors. Additionally, global measures of credit growth and asset price movements could be used (see below). Next, making the asset price series (especially property prices) more homogeneous across countries could greatly improve performance of the indicators in comparing countries. Furthermore, the authors stress that further asset price series, such as exchange rates and credit risk spreads, could be useful. Finally, the measures of leverage should be enhanced, especially concerning the leverage within the financial system that may indicate limited shock absorption capacity. This is also addressed in the second part of this section.

Very recently, Alessi and Detken (2009) have performed a thorough exercise to improve the early warning indicators for harmful (costly) asset booms leading to systemic crises. They consider a host of financial and real variables (a total of 89), for 18 OECD countries as well as for a subgroup of eight Euro Area countries. A main improvement of their method is that they determine the thresholds for indicators in real time, i.e., they dynamically update the optimal thresholds over time (as more crises have occurred). Another improvement is that they assess the usefulness of the many indicators using different criteria, which are determined by the weights that policy makers attach to *type I (missing crises)* and *type II (false alarm)* errors. In doing so, they confirm the usefulness results of Borio and Lowe and Borio and Drehmann and go even further in their assessment. Arguing that the usefulness of indicators for policy makers is determined by the relative preferences with respect to missing crises and providing false alarms, they set up a usefulness measure that depends on these relative preferences. They contend that central bankers on average have a stronger aversion to false alarms than to missing crises, especially because of credibility concerns. However, these preferences may also become more balanced when considering the severity of the recent financial crisis, which may explain the growing interest in early warning systems. The authors consider one indicator, the *global private credit gap*, that predicts 82 percent of the crises correctly and has a 32 percent share of false alarms as the best performing indicator when preferences are relatively balanced, for both the 18 country sample and the smaller Euro Area sample. It also has an average lead time for its first signal of 5.5 quarters before a crisis actually begins. Following Borio and Drehmann, the authors also construct joint indicators, which is a good way of reducing the noisiness of signals. However, they do not improve much upon the usefulness of individual indicators when using the preference weights. Furthermore, there is a large within-sample cross-country variation in these indicators, which raises issues when using aggregated data coming from individual countries.

Finally, Alessi and Detken conclude that global financial variables perform best in predicting costly booms, where global credit slightly outperforms global money. However, the authors also stress that signals should be interpreted very carefully and should definitely not be considered as the only input to the policy maker's information set. Furthermore, the co-dependence among variables should be further explored, as well as other balance sheet items of financial intermediaries (especially concerning leverage).

When potentially harmful asset booms that can lead to systemic crises are identified, we also need to single out the financial institutions (FIs) that constitute the highest risk for the system so regulatory action can be taken. Several financial experts have provided contributions to this literature on systemically relevant financial institutions.

Individual Institutions' Contribution to Systemic Risk

Acharya et al. (2009) adopt standard techniques that are used to manage risk within banks to consider the risk of the financial system as a whole. They begin by stressing that current regulation and measurement is aimed at limiting each institution's risk in isolation without paying enough attention to systemic risk. The authors specify a measure of *marginal expected shortfall* (MES) as used in Value at Risk (VaR) approaches applied by banks, which measures the loss in case returns go below a certain percentile of the distribution (i.e., one percent or five percent on the left side). This measure can be calculated for each individual group or trading desk within an institution, called MES^i; it measures how each group's risk taking adds to the financial institution's overall risk. However, the authors argue that this measure can also be calculated for a financial institution as a whole, where the MES^i measures the contribution of each FI to the risk of the complete financial system. Then, they define a measure of *systemic expected shortfall* (SES), which is related to the MES taking leverage and risk taking into account. It measures the effect of externalities from the banking sector to the real economy. These externalities take place when aggregate banking capital drops below a certain threshold (which can be optimally estimated) and thus certain institutions may fail; the externalities are also increasing in the size of the capital drop. The individual measure SES^i increases when a particular bank has high leverage (also subject to a bank-specific threshold) and takes high risks, in which case this bank has a high contribution to systemic risk (and thus a high SES^i). Finally, the authors estimate the SES^i for several large institutions, and the results confirm that the institutions that contributed most to the crisis indeed had a large SES^i. They conclude that the measurement SES^i can be improved when regulators gather more specific data on FIs, which constitutes a task for national regulators.

One possible drawback of the above method is that it is difficult to determine when the systemically relevant institutions are likely to fail and cause spillovers to the real economy. Hart and Zingales (2009) use credit default swap (CDS)[2] prices (which are market based) as an indicator of default for systemic institutions and as a trigger for regulatory action. This mechanism bypasses credit rating agencies, whose incentives and efforts have become regarded as flawed recently. The authors argue that if we want to maintain a system of large financial institutions (LFIs) that are too big to fail we need a mechanism that provides warnings when these institutions may experience distress. They set up a system similar to that of margin calls, with CDS prices on the LFI's debt as a trigger mechanism. Credit default swaps are instruments that are standardized and frequently traded, so their prices are a good indicator for the likelihood that a large FI will default. Hart and Zingales then set up a system in which a sufficiently high CDS price will trigger regulatory investigation of the LFI. The regulator will in the end decide whether the institution is adequately capitalized (i.e., debt is not at risk) or not and, in the latter case, will take over the company. It will then recapitalize and sell it, wiping out existing creditors and imposing a haircut on creditors. This threat, as argued by the authors, can be used to make LFIs issue sufficient capital ex ante so they will never be faced with the abovementioned regulatory procedure. The (anticipated) behavior of the CDS price will thus be an indicator for the solvency of systemically important institutions. The advantages of this method to measure systemic risk are that it uses data for individual institutions and is forward looking. However, the method is still relying mainly on market data and does not indicate which FIs are systemic.

---

[2] Ironically, CDS are seen as one of the causes of the current crisis. Hart and Zingales therefore state that "It would be only fitting if they were part of the solution".

Adrian and Brunnermeier (2009), besides considering the contribution of one institution to the stability of the system, additionally take into account the abovementioned point about the systemic interconnectedness of institutions and the effects they have on each other. This issue of financial network effects has already been stressed in the early 2000's, among others by Allen and Gale (2000) and Kiyotaki and Moore (2002). It has indeed become clear that financial institutions, regulated and non-regulated, were much more interconnected than regulators have been able to assess during the last decade.

Therefore, Adrian and Brunnermeier propose a measure called CoVaR^i, which is defined as the VaR of the whole financial system conditional on institution i being in distress. The difference between the CoVaR^i and the unconditional VaR of the financial system, denoted as ΔCoVaR, denotes (as in Acharya et al., 2009) the marginal contribution of a particular institution to the overall systemic risk. The authors argue that their measure has several advantages. First, it captures systemic risk per institution alongside the individual risk of this institution, opposite to current risk measures. The main conclusion here is that institutions may have a low VaR but a high CoVaR; something that is not captured in current regulation. Second, the CoVaR can also be used to gauge spillover effects from one institution to another: ΔCoVaR$^{i|j}$ denotes the increase in risk of institution i conditional on institution j already being in distress, or the effect that distress of institution j has on the risk of institution i. Finally, this measure can also be extended to expected shortfall (see above) so as to construct a Co-ES measure, which indicates the expected losses of the whole financial system when a systemic crisis occurs. The authors then delineate several methods to estimate CoVaR, including quintile regressions and panel data methods, which are dynamic enough to capture the changing nature of CoVaR. They then argue that their measure can be used as a basis for macro-prudential regulation by e.g., imposing systemic risk weighted capital charges.

The abovementioned measures of systemic risk contribution can complement each other: the methods of Acharya et al. and Adrian and Brunnermeier can be used to determine which institutions are possibly a threat to systemic stability (including their network effects), while the measure of Hart and Zingales can be employed to determine when this threat may materialize so regulators can take timely prudential action.

Policy Actions

The above mentioned measures of systemic risk can provide early warnings for a systemic crisis. The first part of them focuses on aggregate systemic risk, indicated by asset booms, while the second part focuses on the contribution of individual financial institutions to the risk of the financial system as a whole. It must be stressed that both types of measures should be used in tandem, and that the previous section of this chapter is not exhaustive but only a characterization of the measures necessary to gauge systemic risk properly. For the newly to be established ESRB this means that it should take into account all these indicators (and more) in the establishment of its regulatory policy. These indicators can be used by the ESRB to set up macro-prudential regulation for the European financial system and, together with national supervisors, for establishing the prudential regulation of individual institutions that contribute to a great extent to systemic instability. It is important to base new regulatory policy on a broad set of systemic risk measures, and evaluate their performance over time. It should be noted that it is an extremely difficult task. Too large a set of systemic risk measures will not solve anything but rather keep the confusion in place. For example, some of the indicators could send warning signals while others may not. It then comes to the question of interpretation and thus subjectivity, the very thing that must be avoided as much as possible. Too narrow a set of systemic risk indicators entails the danger that warning signals could not be picked up early enough. Therefore, the ESRB should approach this as a signal extraction problem, which can be solved by Bayesian updating until a compact set of useful indicators remains. This set, with appropriate weights on each indicator, can serve as a basis for European macro-prudential regulation.

The complicating factor according to Eijffinger and Mujagic (2009) is that the policy instruments of the ECB and ESRB must be independent of each other. The (interbank) money markets interest rates cannot be used for both price stability and financial stability, as the outlook for price stability could warrant higher interest rates, while ensuring financial stability might require a lower interest rate. Finding new instruments that are effective, easy to use, and independent of the interest-rate instrument seems to be an impossible task. And yet there is a solution. Central banks should give the *growth of (broad) money supply* more prominence in their monetary policy strategies. The ECB with its often criticized monetary pillar may have a head start. Important central banks, such as the Bank of England and the United States Federal Reserve, kept their key interest rates too low for too long leading to a long period of double-digit growth in money supply. The ECB was more cautious. To be sure, the fall of the risk premium on financial markets, the development of all kinds of exotic derivatives, and these derivatives' subsequent misuse sowed the seeds for this crisis, but those factors could not have caused the crisis without the plentiful rainfall that allowed those seeds to grow.

References

Acharya, V., L. Pedersen, T. Philippon, and M. Richardson (2009), 'Regulating Systemic Risk', in *Restoring Financial Stability: How to Repair a Failed System*. Wiley.

Adrian, T. and M.K. Brunnermeier (2009), 'CoVaR'. *Staff Report 348*, Federal Reserve Bank of New York.

Alessi, L. and C. Detken (2009), 'Real Time Early Warning Indicators for Costly Asset Price Boom/Bust cycles – A Role for Global Liquidity.' *ECB Working Paper Series 1039*, European Central Bank, Frankfurt-am-Main.

Allen, F. and D. Gale (2000), 'Financial Contagion'. *Journal of Political Economy*, **108**(1), 1–33.

Bini Smaghi, L. (2009), 'Macro-prudential Supervision'. Speech delivered at the CEPR/ESI 13th Annual Conference on 'Financial Supervision in an Uncertain World' on 25–26 September 2009 in Venice.

Borio, C. and M. Drehmann (2008), 'Towards an Operational framework for Financial Stability: 'Fuzzy' Measurement and its Consequences.' Paper presented at 12th Annual Conference of the Central Bank of Chile, Financial stability, monetary policy and central banking, Santiago, Chile.

Borio, C. and M. Drehmann (2009), 'Assessing the Risk of Banking Crises–Revisited.' *BIS Quarterly Review*, 29–46.

Borio, C.E.V. and P. Lowe (2004), 'Securing Sustainable Price Stability: Should Credit Come Back from the Wilderness?' *BIS Working Papers 157*, July, Bank for International Settlements.

Eijffinger, S.C.W. and E. Mujagic (2009), 'The Return of Monetarism, Project Syndicate, The Frontiers of Growth Series', New York, Columbia University, December.

Hart, O. and L. Zingales (2009), 'A New Capital Regulation for Large Financial Institutions'. *CEPR Discussion Papers 7298*, June, Centre for Economic Policy Research, London.

Kiyotaki, N. and J. Moore (2002), 'Balance-Sheet Contagion' *American Economic Review,* **92**(2), 46–50.

12.   Financial Regulation

Charles A.E. Goodhart[1]

Introduction

Financial regulation has always been a theoretical, a pragmatic response by practical officials, and concerned politicians, to immediate problems, following the dictum that 'We must not let that happen again'. When the Basel Committee on Banking Supervision (BCBS) was established in 1974/75, to handle some of the emerging problems of global finance and cross-border banking, the modus operandi then developed was to hold a roundtable discussion of current practice in each member state with the objective of trying to reach an agreement on which practice was 'best', and then to harmonize on that. Little, or no, attempt was made to go back to first principles, and to start by asking why there should be a call for regulation on banking, whether purely domestic or crossborder, in the first place.

Thus Basel I, the Accord on Capital Regulation in 1988, was propelled by concern that many of the major international banks, especially in the USA, would have been made insolvent, under a mark-to-market accounting procedure, by the MAB (Mexico, Argentina, Brazil) default crisis of 1982. Congress wanted to impose higher capital regulations on US banks, but was deterred by the 'Level Playing Field' argument that any unilateral move would just shift business to foreign, especially to Japanese, banks. Hence the appeal to the BCBS. Again little, or no, attempt was made to explore what was the fundamental need for holding capital, or what might be its optimal level (see Hellwig, 1996 and 2008). The target of eight percent was the outcome of a balance between a desire to prevent, and if possible to reverse, the prior long decline in that ratio counteracted by a

---

[1] An earlier version of this work was published in *The Future of Finance: The LSE Report*. See www.futureoffinance.org.uk. Reproduced with permission.

concern that any sharp rise in the required ratio above pre-existing levels could force banks into deleveraging and a slowdown on bank lending, which would be bad for the economy. It was a thoroughly practical compromise.

Basel I was hammered out by Central Bank officials behind closed doors, with little input from the commercial banks, the regulated. When, however, those same Central Bank practitioners sought to move on from attention to credit risk, the sole focus of Basel I, to a wider range of risks, notably market risk, in the mid-1990s their initial, *de haut en bas*, 'building block' approach to such risks was rejected by the commercial banks on the grounds that it was technically antediluvian, and that the banks had a much more up-to-date methodology of risk assessment, notably Value at Risk (VaR), (n.b., VaR was itself derived from earlier developments in finance theory by economists such as Markowitz and Sharpe). The officials seized on this eagerly. It enabled regulation to be based on the precept that each individual bank's own risk management should be brought up to the level of, and harmonized with, those of the 'best' banks, and had the added bonus that the methodology of regulation could be rooted in the (best) practices of the most technically advanced individual banks. The implicit idea was that if you made all banks copy the principles of the best, then the system as a whole would be safe. Hardly anyone critically examined this proposition, and it turned out to be wrong.

It was wrong for two main associated reasons. First, the risk management concerns of individual banks are, and indeed should be, quite different from those of regulators. A banker wants to know what his/her individual risk is under normal circumstances, 99 percent of the time. If an extreme shock occurs, it will anyhow be for the authorities to respond. For such normal conditions, the VaR measure is well designed. But it does not handle tail-risk adequately (see Danielsson, 2002). It is the tail risk of such extreme shocks that should worry the regulator.

Next, the whole process focused on the individual bank, but what should matter to the regulator is systemic risk, not individual risk. Under most measures of individual risks, each individual bank had never seemed stronger, as measured by Basel II and mark-to-market accounting, than in July 2007, on the eve of the crisis; Adair Turner emphasizes that CDS spreads on banks generally reached their all-time minimum then.

The Rationale for Regulation

Bankers are professionals. It should not be for the government, or for delegated regulators, to try to determine how much risk they take on board, nor to set out the particular way that they assess such risks, so long as any adverse fallout from adverse outcomes is internalized amongst themselves and their professional investors, debt or equity holders. Under these circumstances the authorities have no locus for any intervention, however risky the bank's business plan may seem.

This immediately indicates two of the three theoretical reasons for regulation/supervision, which are externalities and the protection of non-professional consumers of banking services (asymmetric information). There is a third reason for regulation, i.e., the control of monopoly power, but, with a few minor exceptions, e.g., access to Clearing Houses, this is not a relevant concern in the financial system. All this is set out at greater length in the Geneva Report (2009) on 'The Fundamental Principles of Financial Regulation'. Although externalities are the more important concern, in terms of the potential loss to society from lack of, or inappropriate, regulation/supervision, it is, perhaps, easiest to begin with customer protection (asymmetric information).

Asymmetric Information

The expertise of professionals, whether doctors, lawyers, independent financial advisors or bankers lies in their presumed greater knowledge. Since obtaining such knowledge is time-consuming and costly, the client is by definition at a disadvantage. In many cases we only need professional help rarely, but when we do it is vital, so repetition is not a safeguard. Shleifer (2010), 'Efficient Regulation' asks why a Coaseian appeal to the courts could not replace regulation in such circumstances and answers that the legal process is too time-consuming, costly and uncertain. Again while disclosure, and enforced dual capacity (i.e., the separation of advice from execution) can be partial safeguards, the former depends on the customer having the time/intelligence to interpret what is disclosed, and the latter adds greatly to the expense.

Moreover, when some shock makes depositors realize (eventually) that their bank may be in trouble, a run ensues, and once a run is perceived it is always rational to join it. With a fractional reserve banking system, any such run is likely to cause the bank involved to fail, unless supported by the Central Bank. If the loss from such a failure was entirely internalized that would only matter to that one bank's clients, and, apart from customer protection, would not matter (much) to the wider economy; but in many (but not all) cases there are serious externalities arising from such a bank failure.

So, there are two reasons to adopt deposit insurance, at least for non-professional retail depositors, both to protect customers and to prevent bank runs. Insurance is costly and provokes moral hazard. So the regulators/supervisors, who should themselves also be professionals, should, in principle, like any other professional investor, be in a position to assess the relative risk of the provision of such insurance and charge an appropriate levy or premium for so doing. In practice this has not happened in the past. No one can measure risk accurately in an uncertain (non-ergodic) world, so any attempt to do so has been put in the 'too difficult' category. Instead, insurance premia have usually been related, on a flat rate basis, to total insured deposits at a low, historically related, level. Following the recent crisis and the Obama (January 2010) initiative in proposing a tax on banks, that may now change with a possibly widespread introduction of bank taxes in many countries, one would hope ex ante rather than ex post, and risk-related rather than flat rate, or related to transactions (Tobin tax). We will see.

Some commentators have argued that the introduction of a risk-related bank levy is all that is needed to provide incentives for bankers to be appropriately prudent, and to provide a fund to support financial intermediaries that are too big to fail (TBTF), so that otherwise, and apart from other consumer protection measures, all other regulation/supervision could be removed. This is not so, since it ignores the role and importance of externalities, to which we now turn.

Externalities

Any market action taken by one player in a market is always likely to affect the economic position of all the other players in that market. If I buy (sell) an asset, its price will tend to rise (fall) and the current wealth of all players, as measured by current market prices tends to increase (fall). If I am more defensive (aggressive) in my lending practices by seeking more (less) collateral from my prospective borrowers, they in turn can purchase and hold fewer (more) assets, thereby lowering (raising) asset prices more generally. If I want to hold safer (riskier) assets, the risk spreads, and often the volatility, of riskier assets rises (falls), making such assets appear even riskier (less risky) in the market. Such pecuniary effects of market adjustments do not in themselves represent social externalities, nor are causes of systemic contagion, but can become so, in particular when extreme losses result in bankruptcies and liquidation, as described subsequently.

There are many such self-amplifying spirals in our financial system (see, for example, Adrian and Shin, 2008, Brunnermeier and Pedersen, 2005, and Geneva Report, 2009). Such inherent procyclicality becomes more immediately apparent when accounting is done on a fair value, mark-to-market basis. This is not, however, a knock-down argument against the adoption of such a measuring rod, since many partially informed (wholesale) counterparties, who are the most likely to run, can imagine the effect of current market price changes on underlying wealth, and, given the uncertainty, their imagination may lead to a picture worse than the reality. Anyhow if accounting is not to be at a 'fair' value, what 'unfair' value would be preferable? The conclusion from such considerations must surely be that a better way to handle procyclicality is to introduce contra-cyclicality into our macro-prudential regulations, a theme taken further in the *LSE Report* by Large (2010) and Smithers (2010).

Such self-amplifying market spirals would not matter in themselves, except to those directly involved, if all such losses/gains were internalized. There would then be no social externalities. This would be the case if all such losses/gains fell on shareholders, which would be so if all assets were backed by equity capital, or if the equity holders had unlimited liability (and the wealth to meet all debts). Indeed, in the early days of banking, until about 1850 in many countries, this was the intention of policy towards banks. As the scale of industry increased, however, relative to the size and the willingness and ability of the small, unlimited liability, private partnership banks to extend sufficient medium-term credit to such enterprises, a conscious choice was made to move towards limited liability joint stock banks, whose resulting greater riskiness was to be held in check by more transparency in their accounts and by external regulation.

The insiders, the executives, of any business know far more about it than everyone else, and are liable to use that information to extract rents from outsiders. That fact of life is the ultimate reason both for banks, who (should) have a comparative advantage in obtaining information about borrowers, and for the existence of certain contracts, e.g. fixed interest debt (and fixed nominal wage), whose purpose is to economize on information by imposing legal penalties on the borrower (employer) when she fails to meet the terms of the contract, in the guise of bankruptcy (and/or renegotiation under duress).[2] Unfortunately the societal costs of such bankruptcies are generally enormous in the case of large, inter-connected financial intermediaries, so much so that, following the bankruptcy of Lehman Bros in September 2008, it has been accepted by most governments that such intermediaries are indeed too big to close in bankruptcy (Too Big to Fail; TBTF). What are these costs? There are, perhaps, five such sets of costs:

1. the direct costs of using legal/accounting resources to wind down the enterprise. These can be sizeable;
2. the potential dislocation to financial markets and settlement/payment systems;
3. the loss of the specialized skills/information of those working in the bankrupt institution. Many will be deployed in similar jobs elsewhere after a time, but even so the loss could be considerable;
4. the immediate uncertainty, and ultimate potential loss, for all counterparty creditors of the financial intermediary. This will not only include bank depositors and those with insurance claims, but also those with uncompleted transactions, pledged or custodian

---

[2] This essentially is the reason why the proposals by L. Kotlikoff with various colleagues, Chamley, Ferguson, Goodman and Leamer, (2009) to transform all banking into mutual-fund, equity-based banking is a non-starter.

assets, other forms of secured or unsecured debt, etc., etc. Even when the ultimate loss may be quite small (as for example in the case of Continental Illinois), the interim inability to use the frozen assets and the uncertainty about both the ultimate timing of, and the valuation at, their release can be severe.

5. Besides creditors of the failing financial intermediary, potential debtors generally have an explicit or implicit agreement with the intermediary to borrow more, i.e., unused credit facilities. These disappear instantaneously on bankruptcy. While these may, or may not, be capable of replication elsewhere, this would take time, effort and perhaps extra cost. In the meantime potential access to money is lost.

Some of our colleagues, notably John Kay in his accompanying Chapter, (also see Kay, 2010, and the Treasury Select Committee, 2010), focus on the bankruptcy costs falling on bank depositors and payments systems, and argue that, once these are protected, no other financial intermediary need be regulated, or protected from bankruptcy. In my view that is to take far too narrow a view of the costs of bankruptcy. Lehman Bros was a 'casino' bank with few, if any, retail deposits and few links with the payment system. In the crisis of 2007–9, hardly any bank depositor lost a cent, and, following government guarantees, none need now expect to do so. In contrast, the crisis both generated, and was in turn deepened by, a sharp reduction in access to credit and a tightening in the terms on which credit might be obtained. A capitalist economy is a credit-based economy, and anything which severely restricts the continuing flow of such credit damages that economy. A sole focus on (retail) depositor protection is not enough.

One of the purposes of this section of this chapter is to demonstrate that the social externalities that provide a rationale, (beyond consumer protection), for financial regulation are intimately related to the governance structure of financial intermediaries, to which we now turn, and to the form, structure and costs of bankruptcy, to which we shall turn later.

The Governance Structure of Banks

There is no call for a generalized reversion to unlimited liability for the shareholders of banks, though there is a degree of regret about the earlier switch of the large investment houses (broker/dealers) in the USA from a partnership status to incorporation as a public company. Especially in view of the recent crisis, it would be impossible to raise sufficient equity funding to finance our financial intermediaries on an unlimited liability basis. In view, moreover, of the nature of a limited liability shareholding, equivalent to a call option on the assets of the bank, shareholders will tend to encourage bank executives to take on riskier activities, particularly in boom times. Northern Rock was a favorite of the London Stock Exchange until just a few months before it collapsed. It is, therefore, a mistake to try to align the interests of bank executives, who take the decisions, with those of shareholders, (Bebchuk and Fried, 2009, and Bebchuk and Spamann, 2010). Indeed as Beltratti and Stulz (2009) have shown, it was banks with the most shareholder friendly governance structures who tended to do worst in the recent crisis.

The payment structures for those in Wall Street and the City have been, arguably, more appropriate for a partnership structure than for limited liability. The wrath of the public was related more to the continuation of high remuneration following widespread disaster, than to the massive bonus rewards in good times. This raises the question whether more could be done to make (at least part of) the remuneration of bank executives once again more akin to unlimited liability, for example by some extended claw-back system (Squam Lake, 2010), by making bonus payments subject to unlimited liability (Record, 2010), or by requiring such executives' pensions to be invested wholly in the equity of their own bank (a suggestion once made by G. Wood). The case for doing so, however, rests, as yet, in some large part on public perception of what would be ethically appropriate, rather than on much empirical evidence that existing payment structures for bank executives led them consciously to take risks in the expectation that their bank would be bailed out by the taxpayer (Fahlenbrach and Stulz, 2009). The evidence is, instead, that top management were generally simply unaware of the risks that they were taking (but maybe in some cases they just did not want to know; in booms the warnings of risk managers can get brushed aside).

If there are limits to the extent that it is possible to lessen the social cost of bankruptcy by a reversion to unlimited liability, for shareholders or bank executives, then it may be possible to do so by increasing the ratio of equity to debt, i.e., reducing leverage, thereby allowing a larger proportion of any loss to be internalized. Moreover, the properly famous Modigliani/Miller theorem states (Modigliani and Miller, 1958) that, under some carefully structured assumptions, the value of a firm should be independent of its capital (liability) structure. The basic intuition is that, as equity capital increases proportionally, the risk premium on debt should fall away *pari passu.*

One reason why this does not happen is that debt is deductible for tax, so a shift from debt to equity gives up a tax wedge. While the tax advantages of debt are occasionally reconsidered – it was once mooted that the UK shadow-Chancellor was thinking along these lines – the international disadvantages of doing so unilaterally would be overwhelming, and there is no likelihood of this being enacted at an international level. The other main reason for debt to be seen as more advantageous is that the benefits of avoiding bankruptcy costs are social (external) rather than internalized, and that the implicit, or explicit, provision of safety nets for TBTF intermediaries, e.g. in the guise of liquidity and solvency support, guarantees and outright insurance, are not priced, yet.

This leads on to three (at least), not mutually exclusive, considerations. First, that, since the benefits of more equity, in avoiding bankruptcies in TBTF intermediaries are mostly social while the costs are private, society has the right to impose regulations, e.g., on capital, liquidity and margins, that should make the possibility of bankruptcy more remote. Such regulation is reviewed in the next section. Second, that since part of the problem is that the generalized insurance provided to TBTF intermediaries is not priced, a (partial) solution would be to price the risk of such insurance having to be provided, by having a specific risk premium levied. Such a response took a giant step forward when President Obama proposed a specific tax on banks in January 2010. To be sure this was only in small part risk-related, and to be levied on an ex post, not an ex ante, basis and so incapable of affecting behavioral incentives. Even so, it opened the door to consider how a more careful assessment of how a risk-related, ex ante tax/levy might be designed.

A major objection to this line of attack is that bureaucrats and regulators will never be able to price risk appropriately, and so TBTF intermediaries will engage in regulatory arbitrage. A suggestion put forward by Acharya, et al. (2009 and 2010a) is to require the private sector to price the insurance, but who would then insure the insurers? Acharya, et al., respond by suggesting that the private sector only provide a small percentage of such insurance, say five percent, large enough to get them to do the exercise carefully, but small enough for them to absorb any resulting loss without domino contagion. Meanwhile the public sector would provide the bulk of the insurance, but at a price determined by the private sector.

The third approach is to require, or to encourage, more equity to be obtained by TBTF intermediaries, not all the time but only at times of impending distress. The main version of this is the proposal to require banks to issue debt convertible into equity at times of distress, i.e. conditional convertible debt, or CoCos, (Squam Lake, 2009). While there has been some enthusiasm for this in principle, the details of its operation (e.g., triggers, pricing and market dynamics) still need to be worked out, and the relative advantages of CoCos compared with countercyclical macro-prudential capital requirements need to be considered in more detail.

Another version of this general approach has been put forward by Hart and Zingales (2009), who suggest that, whenever a TBTF intermediary's CDS spread rises above a certain level, it then be required to raise more equity in the market, or be closed. This can be viewed both as another version of prompt corrective action (trying to deal with a failing TBTF intermediary before it runs into insolvency), which general idea is dealt with further in the final section of this chapter, and also as a way to require banks to obtain more capital at times of distress. The problem with this particular proposal is that, in my view, the resulting market dynamics would be disastrous. A bank breaking the trigger would be required to issue new equity at a moment when the new issue market would be likely to be unreceptive, driving down equity values. That example would lower equity values, and raise CDS spreads, on all associated banks. It would, in my view, lead almost immediately to the Temporary Public Ownership (nationalization) of almost all banks in a country.

What is surprising, to me, is the enthusiasm of so many economists to conjure up quite complex financial engineering schemes to deal with such problems, when simpler and/or older remedies exist. Why not just require that no TBTF intermediary can pay a dividend, or raise executive compensation (on a per capita basis) when disastrous conditions prevail (Goodhart, et al., 2010). One problem with this is that if distress conditions are defined on an individual bank basis, it would provide even more incentive for manipulating accounting data; while, if done on an overall national basis, it would both have a differential impact on foreign vis à vis domestic banks and unfairly penalize the relatively prudent and successful banks. Perhaps an answer would be to make the requirement only effective when both of these conditions are triggered at the same time.

Another older proposal was to make the equity holder liable for a call for additional capital up to some amount, usually the par value of the share. While commonly adopted in the USA in earlier years, this fell into disuse after the 1930s, having failed to avert bank failures then. Moreover, it can lead to the net present value of a share becoming negative, leading not only to a collapse in equity values, but also to such equities being unloaded onto the ignorant.

What I observe (Goodhart, 2010) is that Europeans tend to focus more on the first of these mechanisms for reducing the frequency and costs of TBTF and bankruptcy in the guise of financial regulations. In contrast, Americans tend to put more emphasis on the second and third mechanism, i.e., introducing and pricing insurance via some kind of market mechanism. This reflects the greater skepticism of Americans about the efficacy of bureaucratic regulation, and the greater skepticism about the Europeans of the efficiency of market mechanisms.

However skeptical one may be about the efficacy of financial regulation, it is certain that one response to the recent crisis will be to tighten and to extend such regulation, and it is to this that we now turn.

Tighter Regulation

Any fool can make banks safer. All that has to be done is to raise capital requirements (on risk-weighted assets) and introduce (or constrict) leverage ratios, reestablish appropriate liquidity ratios and apply higher margins to leveraged transactions, such as mortgage borrowing (i.e., loan to value, LTV, and/or loan to income, LTI, ratios). Why then have our banks, and other systemic financial intermediaries, not been made safer already; just foolish oversight? The problem is that there is a cost to regulation; it puts banks into a less profitable, less preferred position, in their activities as intermediaries. Their previous preferred position may well have been partially due to receiving rents from the underpricing of social insurance to TBTF intermediaries. But even so, if such rents are removed, either by regulation or by pricing such risks, bank intermediation will become less profitable. If so, such intermediation will become considerably more expensive, i.e. higher bid/ask spreads, and less of it will be done, bank lending will continue to contract; a credit-less recovery then becomes more likely, as the IMF has warned (Cardarelli et al., 2009).

Many of the problems in our financial system have arisen because the trend growth of lending (credit expansion) has decisively exceeded the trend growth in retail bank deposits in recent decades, see Schularick and Taylor (2009), Table 1, p. 6, part of which is reproduced here as Table 12.1:

Table 12.1 Annual Summary Statistics by Period

	Pre-World War 2			Post-World War 2		
	N	Mean	s.d.	N	mean	s.d.
Δ log Money	729	0.0357	0.0566	825	0.0861	0.0552
Δ log Loans	638	0.0396	0.0880	825	0.1092	0.0738
Δ log Assets	594	0.0411	0.0648	825	0.1048	0.0678
Δ log Loans/Money	614	0.0011	0.0724	819	0.0219	0.0641
Δ log Assets/Money	562	0.0040	0.0449	817	0.0182	0.0595

Note: Money denotes broad money. Loans denote total bank loans. Assets denote total bank assets. The sample runs from 1870 to 2008. War and aftermath periods are excluded (1914–19 and 1939–47), as is the post WWI German crisis (1920–25). The 14 countries in the sample are the United States, Canada, Australia, Denmark, France, Germany, Italy, Japan, the Netherlands, Norway, Spain, Sweden and the United Kingdom.

This has induced banks to respond in three main ways:

1. to replace safe public sector debt by riskier private sector assets;

2.   to augment retail deposits by wholesale funding, with the latter often at a very short maturity because it is both cheaper, and easier to get whenever markets get nervous;
3.   to originate to distribute by securitizing an increasing proportion of new lending.

The danger to leveraged intermediaries from illiquidity is now being increasingly realized. Failure then arises from a combination of concern about ultimate solvency, which prevents other ways of raising new funds in the market, and illiquidity, the inability to pay bills coming due, which finally pushes institutions at risk over the edge. In a comparison of failing and more successful banks over the course of the recent crisis (IMF Global Financial Stability Report, 2009) capital ratios, in the immediately preceding period before the crisis event, did not show any significant difference! This suggests, but certainly does not prove, that the older (pre-1970s and pre-global finance) penchant for putting much more weight on liquidity ratios, and perhaps slightly less on capital ratios, might be sensible.

There is a counter argument, advanced by Willem Buiter (2008). This is that any asset is liquid if the Central Bank will lend against it. But the Central Bank can lend against anything. So long as the Central Bank takes an expansive approach to its own role as Lender of Last Resort, there should be no need for specific liquidity requirements. Interestingly Willem Buiter (2009) more recently came up with an entirely contrary argument, following Marvin Goodfriend (2009), that the Central Bank should restrict its operations to dealing in public-sector debt, because of the quasi-fiscal implications of dealing in private sector assets. I do not believe that either, but it does raise the point that operations (whether outright purchases, or lending against collateral), in private sector debt with narrower and more volatile markets, and hence less certain valuation, does raise the question of what price and terms should be offered by the Central Bank. Too generous terms and it provides a subsidy to the banks, and a potential cost and danger to both the Central Bank and the taxpayer. Too onerous terms, and it would not help the banks or encourage much additional liquidity injection. The advantage of having banks hold a larger buffer of public sector debt is that it both finesses the problem for the Central Bank of pricing its liquidity support and provides all concerned with more time to plan their recovery strategy.

A liquidity requirement is an oxymoron. If you have to continue to hold an asset to meet a requirement, it is not liquid. What is needed is a buffer, not a minimum requirement. There is a story of a traveler arriving at a station late at night, who is overjoyed to see one taxi remaining. She hails it, only for the taxi driver to respond that he cannot help her, since local by-laws require one taxi to be present at the station at all times! If the approach towards making banks safer is primarily through some form of insurance premia, a pricing mechanism (Perotti and Suarez, 2009), then the levy imposed on the TBTF intermediary can be an inverse function of its liquidity ratio, (possibly amongst other determinants). If the mechanism is to be external regulation, then the objective should be to ensure that it acts as a buffer, not a minimum. That should involve quite a high 'fully satisfactory' level with a carefully considered ladder of sanctions as the liquidity ratio becomes increasingly impaired. Devising a ladder of sanctions is essential and much more critical than the arbitrary choice of a satisfactory level at which to aim. It was the prior failure of the BCBS to appreciate this crucial point that vitiated much of their earlier work.

To recapitulate, there is a trade-off between the extent and degree of regulation on banks, to make them safer, and their capacity to intermediate between lenders and borrowers, in particular their ability to generate credit flows on acceptable terms to potential borrowers. One possible way to combine a smaller/safer banking system with a larger flow of credit is to restart securitization, the practice of originate to distribute. A problem with this latter is that it largely depended on trust that credit qualities were guaranteed by the ratings agencies, due diligence by the originators and liquidity enhancement by the support of the parent bank. Absent that trust, the duplication of information can be horrendously expensive. The attempt to restore trust, notably in due diligence, by requiring banks to hold a (vertical) share of all tranches in a securitized product can make the whole exercise less attractive to potential originators. So, the market for securitization remains becalmed.

Thus, the ability of our financial system to generate credit growth well in excess of deposit growth may be at an end, at a time when deposit growth itself may slow. Phasing the new regulation in gradually over some transitional period may do little more than prolong the adjustment. Quite how the financial system, and the broader economy, may adjust to this is far from clear. What is more worrying is that in the rush to reregulate and to 'bash the bankers' far too few participants are thinking about such structural problems.

Such structural problems are not, alas, the only ones facing regulators. We turn next to some of these.

The Border Problems

There are several generic problems connected with financial regulation. Amongst them, two perennial problems are connected with the existence of important, but porous, borders, or boundaries. The first such boundary is that between regulated and non-regulated (or less regulated) entities, where the latter can provide a (partial) substitute for the services of the former. The second, key, border is that between states, where the legal system and regulatory system differs from state to state.

I have dealt with the first boundary problem at some length, in the National Institute Economic Review (Goodhart, 2008) and in the Appendix to the Geneva Report (2009). Forgive me for reproducing a few paragraphs of this:-

> In particular if regulation is effective, it will constrain the regulated from achieving their preferred, unrestricted, position, often by lowering their profitability and their return on capital. So the returns achievable within the regulated sector are likely to fall relative to those available on substitutes outside. There will be a switch of business from the regulated to the non-regulated sector. In order to protect their own businesses, those in the regulated sector will seek to open up connected operations in the non-regulated sector, in order to catch the better opportunities there. The example of commercial banks setting up associated conduits, SIVs and hedge funds in the last credit bubble is a case in point.
>
> But this condition is quite general. One of the more common proposals, at least in the past, for dealing with the various problems of financial regulation has been to try to limit deposit insurance and the safety net to a set of 'narrow banks', which would be constrained to hold only liquid and 'safe' assets. The idea is that this would provide safe deposits for the orphans and widows. Moreover, these narrow banks

would run a clearing-house and keep the payments' system in operation, whatever happened elsewhere. For all other financial institutions outside the narrow banking system, it would be a case of 'caveat emptor'. They should be allowed to fail, without official support or taxpayer recapitalization.

In fact, in the UK something akin to a narrow banking system <u>was</u> put in place in the 19th century with the Post Office Savings Bank and the Trustee Savings Bank. But the idea that the official safety net should have been restricted to POSB and TSB was never seriously entertained. Nor could it have been. When a 'narrow bank' is constrained to holding liquid, safe assets, it is simultaneously prevented from earning higher returns, and thus from offering as high interest rates, or other valuable services, (such as overdrafts), to its depositors. Nor could the authorities in good conscience prevent the broader banks from setting up their own clearing house. Thus the banking system outside the narrow banks would grow much faster under normal circumstances; it would provide most of the credit to the private sector, and participate in the key clearing and settlement processes in the economy.

This might be prevented by law, taking legal steps to prohibit broader banks from providing means of payment or establishing clearing and settlement systems of their own. There are, at least, four problems with such a move. First, it runs afoul of political economy considerations. As soon as a significant body of voters has an interest in the preservation of a class of financial intermediaries, they will demand, and receive, protection. Witness money market funds and 'breaking the buck' (i.e. not being able to repay at par, or better; so involving a net loss to deposit funds) in the USA. Second, it is intrinsically illiberal. Third, it is often possible to get around such legal constraints, e.g., by having the broad bank pass all payment orders through an associated narrow bank. Fourth, the reasons for the authorities' concern with financial intermediaries, for better or worse, go well beyond insuring the maintenance of the basic payment system and the protection of small depositors. Neither Bear Stearns nor Fannie Mae had small depositors, or played an integral role in the basic payment system.

When a financial crisis does occur, it, usually, first attacks the unprotected sector, as occurred with SIVs and conduits in 2007. But the existence of the differential between the protected and unprotected sector then has the capacity to make the crisis worse. When panic and extreme risk aversion take hold, the depositors in, and creditors to, the unprotected, or weaker, sector seek to withdraw their funds, and place these in the protected, or stronger, sector, thereby redoubling the pressures on the weak and unprotected sectors, who are then forced into fire sales of assets, etc. The combination of a boundary between the protected and the unprotected, with greater constraints on the business of the regulated sector, almost guarantees a cycle of flows into the unregulated part of the system during cyclical expansions with sudden and dislocating reversals during crises.

In so far as regulation is effective in forcing the regulated to shift from a preferred to a less desired position, it is likely to set up a boundary problem. It is, therefore, a common occurrence, or response, to almost any regulatory imposition. A current (2010) example is the proposal to introduce additional regulatory controls on systemically important financial intermediaries (SIFIs). If SIFIs are to be penalized, there needs, on grounds of equity and fairness, to be some definition, some criteria, of what constitutes a SIFI, an exercise with considerable complication. But once such a definition is established and a clear boundary established, there will be an incentive for institutions to position themselves on one side or another of that boundary, whichever may seem more advantageous. Suppose that we started, say in a small country, with three banks, each with a third of deposits, and each regarded as TBTF, and the definition of a SIFI was a bank with over 20 percent of total deposits. If each bank then split itself into two identical clones of itself, to avoid the tougher regulation, with similar portfolios and interbank linkages, would there have been much progress? Similarity implies contagion. Indeed, regulation tends to encourage and to foster similarity in behavior. Does it follow then that regulation thereby enhances the dangers of systemic collapse that its purpose should be to prevent? Does the desire to encourage all the regulated to adopt, and to harmonize on, the behavior of the 'best' actually endanger the resilience of the system as a whole?

The second boundary of critical importance to the conduct of regulation is the border between states, each with their own legal and regulatory structures, the cross border problem. In a global financial system with (relatively) free movement of capital across borders, most financial transactions that are originated in one country can be executed in another. This means that any constraint, or tax, that is imposed on a financial transaction in a country can often be (easily) avoided by transferring that same transaction to take place under the legal, tax and accounting jurisdiction of another country, sometimes, indeed often, under the aegis of a subsidiary, or branch, of exactly the same bank/intermediary as was involved in the initial country.

This tends to generate a race for the bottom, though not always since the parties to a contract will prize legal certainty and contract reliability. Another aspect of this same syndrome is the call for 'a level playing field'. Any state which seeks to impose, unilaterally, tougher regulation than that in operation in some other country will face the accusation that the effect of the regulation will just be to benefit foreign competition with little, or no, restraining effect on the underlying transactions.

Moreover the cross-border concern may constrain the application of countercyclical regulation. Financial cycles, booms and busts, differ in their intensity from country to country. Housing prices rose much more in Australia, Ireland, Spain, UK and USA than in Canada, Germany and Japan in the years 2002–2007. Bank credit expansion also differed considerably between countries. But if regulation becomes countercyclically tightened in the boom countries, will that not, in a global financial system, just lead to a transfer of such transactions off-shore; and London has been at the centre of arranging such cross-border financial operations.

Are There Solutions?

Perhaps the greatest need is for a fundamental change in the way that we all, but especially regulators and supervisors, think about the purposes and operation of financial regulation, i.e., a paradigm shift. The old idea was that the purpose of regulation was to stop individual institutions assuming excessive risk, and that the way to do this was to encourage, or force, all institutions (banks) to harmonize on 'best practices' by requiring them to hold the appropriate ratios of capital, or liquidity, or whatever.

It is the thesis of this chapter that this approach has been fundamentally misguided along several dimensions. First, it should not be the role of the regulator/supervisor to seek to limit the risks taken by the individual institution, so long as those risks are properly internalized. The concern instead should be on externalities, i.e., limiting the extent to which adverse developments facing one actor in the financial system can lead to greater problems for other actors.

Various methodologies for measuring, and then counteracting, such externalities, such as CoVar, Expected Shortfall, CIMDO, are being developed, but much more needs to be done.[3]

Second, the attempt to limit such externalities should not be done by a process of setting minimum required ratios, whether for capital, liquidity or even, perhaps, for margins more generally. There are two main reasons why not. First, that process sterilizes, and makes unusable, the intra-marginal capital or liquidity. Second, no one can ever correctly determine what the 'correct' level of such a safeguard should be, and effort and time gets wasted in trying to do so. Instead, much more thought needs to be put into devising a, preferably continuous, ladder of penalties, whether pecuniary, e.g. in the form of a tax, or non-pecuniary in the form of prohibitions of increasing severity on the freedom of action of an intermediary as its capital, liquidity and margins decrease and its leverage increases.

One purpose of having a more continuous function of sanctions is that it might be possible to apply the regulation over a wider range of intermediaries, and thus avoid the boundary problem between the regulated and non-regulated.   Thus, all (leveraged) financial intermediaries would come under the regulations, small as well as large banks, and hedge funds and money markets mutual funds as well as banks, but so long as the leveraged institution was small, with few counterparties amongst other financial intermediaries (i.e., not inter-connected), with low leverage and satisfactory liquidity, it should not suffer any penalties. The more that a leveraged institution became a risky 'shadow bank', the greater the penalty (against the risk of externalities and thus imposing costs on society) that should be applied.   It will involve a considerable effort to try to recast regulation along such lines, but it could be one way of overcoming the boundary problem between the regulated and the non-regulated.

Incidentally, John Kay's 'narrow banks' (Kay, 2011) and Larry Kotlikoff's all equity-based financial intermediaries would, under this rubric, face no, or very few, penalties or sanctions, whereas there would

---

[3] This branch of analysis includes the Brunnermeier and Pedersen (2009), Adrian and Brunnermeier (2009), 'CoVaR'; Acharya, et al., 'Measuring Systemic Risk', (2010), 'Systemic Expected Shortfall'; Segoviano (2006, 2009, forthcoming); Segoviano and Goodhart (2009); Goodhart (2010), on 'CIMDO'. Also see the IMF Global Financial Stability Report, April 2009, Chapter 3.

be increasing penalties/sanctions as intermediaries took on increasingly risky strategies, where the ladder of penalties/sanctions should be calibrated to relate to the additional risk to society. While such calibration is surely hard to do, this would be preferable either to leaving all such 'risky' intermediation either completely unregulated, or banned entirely. Neither of these latter approaches would be sensible, or desirable.

In order to limit and control systemic risk, supervisors have to be able to identify it. That requires greater transparency. That is one reason, but not the only one, for requiring standardized derivative deals to be put through a centralized counter party, and for requiring that remaining over the counter (OTC) transactions be reported to, and recorded by, a centralized data repository. Similarly it would be desirable to simplify and increase the transparency of securitizations. Reliance on credit ratings was a means for enabling buyers in the past to disregard much (legal) detail. In this field the credit rating agencies have, for the time being, lost their reputation, even if in the exercise of sovereign debt rating their clout now seems stronger than ever!

However great the incentives provided for more prudent behavior, which implies penalties on imprudent behavior, failures and insolvencies will still occur. As noted earlier, the occasions of such bankruptcies are the main source of social risk and reliance on taxpayers. So the need is to try, first to limit and to prevent bankruptcy, and second to lessen its social ramifications should it occur, e.g. by internalizing losses.

In addition to the objective of controlling externalities, social risk and the need for reliance on taxpayers, there is also, as already noted in the second section, a rationale for some additional regulation based on asymmetric information and customer protection. It is largely, though not entirely, under this latter rubric that proposals such as Product Regulation and Deposit Insurance take their place. We will not discuss these further here, since both the difficulties of applying such regulation and the overall costs of regulatory failure are so much less than in the case of macro-prudential regulation.

Considerable weight had been placed by many economists on the concept of prompt corrective action (PCA) as a means of lessening the costs of failure. This had been incorporated into the FDIC Improvement Act of 1991, whereby any bank that was severely undercapitalized, under two percent (i.e., a leverage ratio greater than

50), either had to raise more equity rapidly or be closed, with the aim of doing so before there was a burden of losses to be somehow shared.

Yet this did not prevent the crisis in the USA, though the main initial failures, Fannie Mae, Lehman, AIG, occurred in intermediaries to which such PCA was not applicable. Even so, PCA was less effective than had been hoped. In crises the estimated residual value of equity can erode fast; and, prior to the final collapse, may be manipulated by accounting dodges (such as the Repo 105 used by Lehman Bros). In extremis, liquidity may be a better, or even more desirable supplementary, trigger than capital.

A widespread complaint has been that too little of the losses suffered have been internalized amongst bond holders and transferred to taxpayers instead, thereby increasing externalities and social cost. But we need to remind ourselves why this was done. This was because many such bond-holders were either themselves leveraged intermediaries, such as Reserve Primary Fund, whose 'breaking of the buck' unleashed the run on money-market mutual funds, or had sufficient power (the Chinese?) to threaten to withdraw funds massively from this market, and thereby unleash an even worse disaster. So, contagion was as much an issue amongst bond-holders as amongst depositors.

One conclusion is that if losses cannot, in the event of a financial crisis, be internalized amongst either bond-holders or depositors, then banks should be induced and encouraged (n.b., by a continuous ladder of penalties, not by a required minimum) to hold more tangible core equity. Another approach is to precommit, e.g. by contract, to make bond holders face equity-type losses in a crisis. This is one of the purposes of the proposed conditional contingent bonds (CoCos) which are to be forcibly transmuted into equity format under certain triggers of distress. As with ordinary bank bonds, this could lead to contagion if such CoCos were held by other levered financial intermediaries. Even absent such contagion, the relative cost, and market dynamics of such CoCos in a crisis, has yet to be clearly observed. And how far their use would be preferable to the simpler procedure of encouraging more equity holding, perhaps in countercyclical format, has yet to be fully worked out.

One important way of diminishing both the probability and the cost of failure is to get the levered institution and its supervisor(s) to plan for such adverse eventualities in advance. This is the purpose of the concept of the 'Living Will', or Special Resolution Regime (SRR) which has obtained (and rightly so) much traction recently as a desirable initiative in the field of financial regulation. Such a 'living will' has two parts, see Huertas 2010 (a, b and c). The first part consists of a recovery plan, which outlines how, in the face of a real crisis, a leveraged institution could bolster its liquidity and its capital, for example by disposing of non-core assets, so as to remain an on-going business. This could be agreed between an institution and its lead (home) supervisor, though there would be implications for host supervisors.

The second part of a 'Living Will' involves planning for the resolution of a failing financial institution, should the recovery plan be insufficient. In this case the supervisor(s) may require the financial institution to take certain preparatory actions, for example to maintain a data room (that would enable an outside liquidator/administrator to have sufficient knowledge of the current condition of a financial intermediary to wind it down) and, perhaps, to simplify its legal structure, for the same purpose. But the agreement on how to resolve the intermediary, and to share out residual losses, would need to be amongst its regulators/supervisors.

Even within a single country many, particularly large 'universal', intermediaries may have several supervisors, and each should know their role in advance. But almost all systemically important financial intermediaries (SIFIs) have significant cross-border activities, and, while they may be international in life, they become national in death. Indeed some of the worst complications and outcomes, following bankruptcy, arose from the difficulties of international resolution, notably in the cases of Lehman, the Icelandic banks, Fortis and Dexia.

Avgouleas, Goodhart and Schoenmaker (2010) have suggested building on the concept of 'living wills' in order to develop an internationally agreed legal bankruptcy procedure for SIFIs, but, given the entrenched preferences in each country for their historically determined legal traditions and customs, this may well be utopian. Instead Hüpkes (2009a and b) has proposed that, for each SIFI, an international resolution procedure be adopted on a case by case basis.

Such a procedure might, or might not, also include an ex ante burden sharing agreement (Goodhart and Schoenmaker, 2006). Apart from the difficulty of doing so, arguments against are that attempts would be made, ex post, to renegotiate; that the prior agreement might seem unfair or inappropriate in unforeseeable circumstances, and that it might involve moral hazard. While this last claim is often made, so long as the executives, who actually take the decision, are sacked whether, or not, the entity is kept as a going concern, it can be overstated. The arguments for such an ex ante exercise is that, without it, uncoordinated and costly failure and closures will be much more likely (Freixas, 2003).

More generally, financial globalization in general, and the cross-border activities of SIFIs in particular, mean that the level-playing-field argument is advanced to oppose almost any unilateral regulatory initiative. The main response to this, of course, is to try to reach international agreement, and a whole structure of institutions and procedures has been established to try to take this forward, with varying degrees of success. Inevitably, and perhaps properly, this is a slow process. Those who claimed that we were losing the potential momentum of the crisis for reforming financial regulation simply had no feel for the mechanics of the process. Moreover, any of the major financial countries, perhaps some three or four countries, can effectively veto any proposal that they do not like, so again the agreements will tend to represent the lowest common denominator, again perhaps desirably so.

Finally, there can be circumstances and instances when a regulator can take on the level-playing-field argument and still be effective. An example can be enforcing a margin for housing LTVs by making lending for the required down-payment unsecured in a court of law. Another example is when the purpose of the additional constraint is to prevent excessive leverage and risk taking by domestic banks, rather than trying to control credit expansion more widely (as financed by foreign banks).

Conclusion

The current crisis has forced a fundamental reconsideration of financial regulation; and rightly so since much of the focus, and of the effects, of the existing system were badly designed, with its concentration on individual, rather than systemic, risk and its procyclicality. In response now we have a ferment of new ideas, many touched on here. A great deal of further work needs to be done to discern which of these ideas are good and which less so.

References

Acharya, V., L.H Pedersen, T. Philippon and M. Richardson (2010a), 'Measuring Systemic Risk', AFA 2011 Denver Meetings Paper, Stern School of Business, New York University, available at SSRN: http://ssrn.com/abstract=1573171.

Acharya, V., L.H Pedersen, T. Philippon and M. Richardson (2010b), 'A Tax on Systemic Risk', Stern School of Business, New York University.

Acharya, V. and M. Richardson, (eds) (2009), *Restoring Financial Stability: How to Repair a Failed System*, New Jersey: John Wiley & Sons, Inc.

Adrian, T. and M.K. Brunnermeier (2009), 'CoVaR', *Federal Reserve Bank of New York Staff Reports*, No.348, August.

Adrian, T. and H.S. Shin (2008), 'Liquidity, Monetary Policy, and Financial Cycles', *Current Issues in Economics and Finance*, **14**, (1), January/February.

Avgouleas, E., C. Goodhart, and D. Schoenmaker (2010), 'Living Wills as a Catalyst for Action', Duisenberg School of Finance Policy Paper No. 4, Duisenberg School of Finance, Amsterdam, available at SSRN: http://ssrn.com/abstract=1533808.

Bebchuk, L.A. and J.M. Fried (2009), 'Paying for Long-Term Performance', *Harvard Law and Economics Discussion Paper* No. 658, December 1.

Bebchuk, L.A. and H. Spamann (2010), 'Regulating Bankers' Pay', *Georgetown Law Journal*, **98**(2), January, 247–287.

Beltratti, A. and R.M. Stulz, (2009), 'Why Did Some Banks Perform Better during the Credit Crisis? A Cross-Country Study of the Impact of Governance and Regulation', Fisher College of Business Working Paper No. 2009-03-012, July 13.

Brunnermeier, M.K. and L.H. Pedersen (2005), 'Predatory Trading', *Journal of Finance*, **LX**(4), August.

Brunnermeier, M.K. and L.H. Pedersen (2009), 'Market Liquidity and Funding Liquidity', *Review of Financial Stability*, **22**(6).

Brunnermeier, M.K., A. Crockett, C.A.E. Goodhart, A. Persaud, and H.S. Shin (2009), The Fundamental Principles of Financial Regulation, *Geneva Reports on the World Economy*, 11, Geneva: International Center for Monetary and Banking Studies, ICMB, and Centre for Economic Policy Research, CEPR.

Buiter W. (2008), 'Central Banks and Financial Crises', *Financial Markets Group Discussion Paper* 619, London School of Economics.

Buiter, W. (2009), 'Reversing Unconventional Monetary Policy: Technical and Political Considerations', Centre for Economic Policy Research Discussion Paper 7605, December.

Cardarelli, R., Elekdag, S., and S. Lall, (2009), 'Financial Stress, Downturns, and Recoveries', IMF Working Paper 09/100, May.

Chamley, C., and L. Kotlikoff, (2009), 'Toolbox: Limited Purpose Banking', in American Interest Online, 1 April.

Danielsson, J., (2002), 'The emperor has no clothes: Limits to risk modelling', *Journal of Banking and Finance*, **26**, pp 1252–1272.

Fahlenbrach, R., and R.M. Stulz, (2009), 'Bank CEO Incentives and the Credit Crisis', National Bureau of Economic Research Working Paper 15212.

Ferguson, N., and L. Kotlikoff, (2009), 'Reducing Banking's Moral Hazard', in *Financial Times*, 2 December.

Freixas, X., (2003), 'Crisis Management in Europe', in *Financial Supervision in Europe*, ed. J. Kremers, D. Schoenmaker, and P. Wierts, Cheltenham: Edward Elgar, pp 102–19.

Geneva Report, by Brunnermeier, M.K., Crockett, A., Goodhart, C.A.E., Persaud, A., and H.S. Shin, (2009), 'The Fundamental Principles of Financial Regulation', Geneva Reports on the World Economy, 11, (Geneva: International Center for Monetary and Banking Studies, ICMB, and Centre for Economic Policy Research, CEPR).

Goodfriend, M., (2009), 'Central Banking in the Credit Turmoil: An Assessment of Federal Reserve Practice', presented at the Conference on 'Monetary-Fiscal Policy Interactions, Expectations, and Dynamics in the Current Economic Crisis', May 22–3, Princeton University, Princeton, New Jersey.

Goodhart, C.A.E., (2008), 'The Boundary Problem in Financial Regulation', *National Institute Economic Review*, Vol. **206**, No. 1, pp 48–55.

Goodhart, C.A.E., (2010), 'The Role of Macro-Prudential Supervision', paper presented at the 2010 Financial Markets Conference of the Federal Reserve Bank of Atlanta, George, entitled 'Up from the Ashes: The Financial System after the Crisis', May 11–12.

Goodhart, C., and D. Schoenmaker, (2006), 'Burden Sharing in a Banking Crisis in Europe', Sveriges Riksbank Economic Review, No. 2, pp 34–57

Goodhart, C.A.E., Peiris, M.U., Tsomocos, D.P. and A.P. Vardoulakis, (2010), 'On Dividend Restrictions and the Collapse of the Interbank Market', *Annals of Finance*, **6**, 455–473.

Goodman, J.C., and L. Kotlikoff, (2009), 'The only way Obama can fix the economy is by changing the way banks do business', in The New Republic, 14 May.

Hart, O.D., and L. Zingales, (2009), 'A new capital regulation for large financial institutions', Centre for Economic Policy Research Discussion Paper no. DP7298.

Hellwig, M., (1996), 'Capital Adequacy Rules as Instruments for the Regulation of Bank', Swiss Journal of Economics and Statistics, Swiss Society of Economics and Statistics, vol. 132(IV), December, pp 609–612.

Hellwig, M., (2008), 'Systemic Risk in the Financial Sector: An Analysis of the Subprime-Mortgage Financial Crisis', Max Planck Institute for Research on Collective Goods, November; also found in De Economist, Springer, Vol. 157(2), pp 129–207, June 2009.

Huertas, T., (2010a), 'Improving Bank Capital Structures', speech by T.F. Huertas, Director, Banking Sector, FSA and Vice Chairman, CEBS, at London School of Economics, London, 18 January.

Huertas, T.F., (2010b), 'Living Wills: How Can the Concept be Implemented?', remarks before the Conference 'Cross-Border Issues in Resolving Systemically Important Financial Institutions', at Wharton School of Management, University of Pennsylvania, February 12.

Huertas, T.F., (2010c), 'Resolution and Contagion', Remarks before the Centre for Central Banking Studies/Financial Markets Group Conference, 'Sources of Contagion', 26 February.

Hüpkes, E., (2009a), 'Bank Insolvency: The Last Frontier', in Towards a New Framework for Financial Stability, edited by D. Mayes, R. Pringle and M. Taylor, London: Risk Books.

Hüpkes, E., (2009b), 'Complicity in complexity: what to do about the 'too-big-to-fail' problem', *Butterworths Journal of International Banking and Financial Law*, October.

International Monetary Fund, (2009a), 'Responding to the Financial Crisis and Measuring Systemic Risks, Global Financial Stability Report, April.

International Monetary Fund, (2009b), 'Detecting Systemic Risk', Chapter 3, in 'Responding to the Financial Crisis and Measuring Systemic Risks', Global Financial Stability Report, April.

Kay, J., (2010), 'Narrow Banking', World Economics, Vol. 11, No. 1, pp 1–10.

Kay, J., (2011), 'Should We Have 'Narrow Banking ?', Chapter 8 in *The Future of Finance: The LSE Report*, London: The London School of Economics and Political Science, see www.futureoffinance.org.uk.

Kotlikoff, L., and E. Leamer, (2009), 'A Banking System We Can Trust', in Forbes, 23 April.

Large, A., (2010), 'What Framework is Best for Systemic (Macroprudential) Policy?', Chapter 7 in *The Future of Finance: The LSE Report*, London: The London School of Economics and Political Science, see www.futureoffinance.org.uk.

Modigliani, F., and M.H. Miller, (1958), 'The Cost of Capital, Corporation Finance and the Theory of Investment', American Economic Review.

Perotti, E., and J. Suarez, (2009), 'Liquidity Insurance for Systemic Crises', Centre for Economic Policy Research Policy Insight No. 31.

Record, N., (2010), 'How to make the bankers share the losses', *Financial Times*, 6 January.

Schularick, M. and A.M. Taylor, (2009), 'Credit Booms Gone Bust: Monetary Policy, Leverage Cycles and Financial, Crises, 1870–2008', National Bureau of Economic Research Working Paper 15512, November.

Segoviano, M., (2006), 'Consistent Information Multivariate Density Optimizing Methodology', Financial Markets Group Discussion Paper No. 557, (London: London School of Economics).

Segoviano, M., (forthcoming), 'The CIMDO-Copula. Robust Estimation of Default Dependence under Data Restrictions', IMF Working Paper, (Washington: International Monetary Fund).

Segoviano, M. and C. Goodhart, (2009), 'Banking Stability Measures', IMF Working Paper 09/04, (Washington: International Monetary Fund).

Shleifer, A., (2010), 'Efficient Regulation', National Bureau of Economic Research Working Paper No. w15651, January.

Smithers, A., (2010), 'Can We Identify Bubbles and Stabilize the System?', Chapter 6 in *The Future of Finance: The LSE Report*, London: The London School of Economics and Political Science, see www.futureoffinance.org.uk.

Squam Lake Working Group on Financial Regulation, (2009), 'An Expedited Resolution Mechanism for Distressed Financial Firms: Regulatory Hybrid Securities', Council on Foreign Relations Press.

Squam Lake Working Group on Financial Regulation, (2010), 'Regulation of Executive Compensation in Financial Services', Council on Foreign Relations Press.

Treasury Select Committee, (2010), 'Too Important to Fail – Too Important to Ignore', Ninth Report of Session 2009–10, Volume 1, HC 261-1, 29 March.

13. Out-of-the-Box Thoughts about the International Financial Architecture

Barry Eichengreen[1]

Introduction

There is a good deal of conventional wisdom about what needs to be done to strengthen the international financial architecture in the wake of the global credit crisis. Countries must upgrade their supervision and regulation of financial markets and institutions. They must support demand while at the same time avoiding the reemergence of global imbalances. The IMF should strengthen its surveillance of policies and markets in order to better anticipate systemic risks. It should streamline its procedures for disbursing resources. It should reconfigure its seats and votes to better reflect the economic and political realities of the 21st century.

There is broad consensus on the desirability of these measures, though specifics are another matter. But there is also the question of whether these incremental changes are enough to make the world a significantly safer financial place. Aren't more radical reforms required? Shouldn't aspiring reformers set the bar higher?

The reality is that changes in the international financial architecture are almost always incremental. The membership of existing institutions is expanded rather than creating new institutions out of whole cloth. Regulations on the books are revised. Quota

[1] An earlier version of this work was published both in the 'Milken Review' and in the *Journal of International Commerce, Economics and Policy*, Vol. 1(1), pp. 1–20, April 2010. For comments I am grateful to Tam Bayoumi, Morris Goldstein and Peter Kenen, who certainly should not be implicated in anything that follows.

formulas are tweaked. Radical reform, like that at Bretton Woods in 1944, is the exception, not the rule.

The tendency to focus on marginal changes rather than throwing out the institutional inheritance and starting over reflects the fact that the public sector has already sunk significant costs in existing arrangements. The private sector has similarly sunk the costs of adapting to their existence. There would be high transactions costs of starting over. There is an obvious analogy with the history of technology, where it is argued that network technologies exhibit strong persistence. It makes little sense for any one agent to invest in radical improvements in technological practice when the payoff from such investments depends on whether or not others participating in the same network simultaneously make such investments. The existence of the network thus creates a coordination problem.[2] And what is the international monetary and financial system if not a network of monetary and financial institutions and arrangements which displays a similar tendency toward lock-in? And what is the obstacle to radical reform if not a coordination problem?

At the same time, the history of technology also points to key moments when existing networks are disrupted, opening the door to radical change.[3] If disruptions to the network are sufficiently serious, everyone will move away from the existing equilibrium. Hopefully they will then coordinate on a preferable one.

Imagine that the global credit crisis is such a moment for the international financial arrangements.[4] On what alternative equilibrium should participants in this system coordinate? To put it another way, what form would radical changes take?

---

[2] The Qwerty typewriter keyboard is only the most famous (and contested) illustration of the point. David (1985). See also Leibowitz and Margolis (1990).

[3] David speaks of 'critical phases' where it may be possible to alter an established technological trajectory. See David (1991).

[4] It will be objected that the Asian crisis of 1997/8 was an equally devastating shock for the countries involved, but this led to only incremental, not radical reforms of the international financial architecture. To the extent that the current crisis is global and not merely regional, there is reason to think that, like the Great Depression of the 1930s, it might occasion more radical reforms.

What follow are eight out-of-the-box ideas. Some of these are even further out of the box than others. They fall under three headings: measures to buttress financial stability, steps to smooth the operation of the international monetary system, and reforms of the IMF. Admittedly, none of these ideas will be adopted in the short term.[5] But they are the kind of things that policy makers should be pondering once they move beyond the current crisis.

Countercyclical IMF Capital Charges

It is widely recognized that the IMF's resources are inadequate for any new responsibilities that might be thrust on the institution. As of early 2009, the Fund had some $200 billion of quota resources, and could tap an additional $53 billion through borrowing arrangements under the General Arrangements to Borrow (GAB) and New Arrangements to Borrow (NAB).[6] At the G20 summit in early April it was agreed to increase those resources by a further $500 billion through, in the first instance, the New Arrangements to Borrow.[7] At the time of writing, roughly half this amount has been promised by G20 leaders (some of which will still require approval by their national parliaments or congresses, as in the United States, in order for those promises to become reality). Whether the balance will be delivered, time will tell.

A more radical departure, which should be adopted in addition to and not instead of the above, would be to index countries' contributions to Fund resources and have them contribute annually.[8]

---

[5] As I would be the first to acknowledge.

[6] By comparison, the new Short-Term Liquidity Facility (SLF), which allows applicants to draw up to 500 per cent of quota, exposes it to potential claims of more than $450 billion from 44 emerging market members alone.

[7] In addition, there was agreement in principle to authorize an additional $250 billion of Special Drawing Rights, to be issued in proportion to countries' quotas. These will not be resources for the IMF itself, strictly speaking, but for its members.

[8] Here regularization would require enabling legislation at the national level: the US Congress for example would have to adopt legislation under which the US would make annual contributions to the IMF based on growth rates in GDP. Note that routinizing quota increases by indexing them to the rate of growth of countries' GDP would not address the current need to appreciably

The goal might be to increase the IMF's real resources at an average annual rate of three percent, to reflect the three percent average real rate of growth of the global economy. [9]

A further innovation might be to make this additional capital charge countercyclical, in the same way that there is now increasing attention to the possibility of making bank capital ratios countercyclical. Thus, when global growth rises to four percent, countries might be asked to augment IMF real resources by five percent; when growth slips to two percent, they might be asked to augment IMF real resources by only one percent.[10] In this way more budgetary resources would be freed up to support demand in bad times, while fewer budgetary resources would be available to further goose demand in good times.

A further step in the direction of routinization would be to index these capital charges to national growth rates rather than global growth rates. In this way the countercyclical impulse would be felt most strongly by the countries most in need of it. Votes in the Fund might be adjusted annually along with these contributions; the problem of fast-growing countries with chronically inadequate quotas and voting rights would be automatically addressed. The legitimacy of the IMF would be enhanced.[11]

---

redistribute current quotas to better reflect 21st century global economic realities. It would not correct the current imbalance between quotas and economic size but only prevent it from recurring in the future. A separate initiative – a one-time adjustment of quotas – would be needed to address the immediate problem.

[9] Actual contributions would be in nominal terms of course. Contributions would thus be calculated as, say, three percent of the outstanding subscription plus an adjustment for global inflation.

[10] This two-for-one formula would imply cutting contributions to zero when global growth fell to 1 1/2 per cent or less. Symmetry would then suggest capping contributions at six percent when global growth rose to 4 1/2 percent or higher.

[11] It could conceivably be argued that this would be a disincentive to spurring growth. The same argument was offered in response to the issuance of GDP-indexed bonds, however, and proved exaggerated. It might be desirable to adjust votes to a moving average of past contributions rather than year by year so as not to penalize countries in recession or reward those experiencing an unsustainable boom.

A Price-Based Scarce Currency Clause

There have long been worries about asymmetric pressure to adjust felt by deficit and surplus countries – a problem that the Scarce Currency Clause (SSC) in the IMF's Articles of Agreement was designed to address. Recently discussions have focused on China and its chronic surpluses, though the point is more general. Authorizing other members to invoke the SCC against a country running chronic surpluses and to impose tariffs and other restrictions on its exports would be politically charged and difficult for the Executive Board. Reflecting the difficulties of doing so in a collegial institution, the SCC has never been invoked.

More efficacious in the long run would be to establish an automatic process that creates incentives for surplus countries to adjust. A country that had run a current account surplus in excess of three percent of GDP for three years, for example, might be required to transfer additional resources to the Fund at the end of every year in which that excess persisted. The transfer might equal one half of the current account surplus in excess of three percent of GDP.[12] Alternatively, one can imagine a tax on the increase in foreign exchange reserves when reserves had been increasing for three years and the increase in the current year exceeded three percent of GDP.[13] Nothing would prevent countries from running large and persistent external surpluses if they found it difficult and costly to raise investment or reduce savings, but doing so would entail an additional cost, in turn ratcheting up the pressure on the central bank and government to adopt policies of adjustment.[14]

Economists not liking tax schedules with discontinuities, one can imagine a tax on all increases in foreign reserves that started at

---

[12] Or the charge might initially be set at a lower level and raised to, say, 50 percent over time (as members who wished to minimize it had more time to adjust).

[13] Or if it increased the average rate of growth of the economy in the last three years by a certain percent.

[14] Of course, if the goal is to encourage adjustment by surplus countries, nothing requires that the tax revenues be paid in to the Fund. They equally well might go to the World Bank for development assistance or the United Nations for peacekeeping operations.

infinitesimal levels but rose fairly quickly as the increase in reserves rose as a share of GDP and as a function of its persistence.

This approach would have the advantage that it would not be necessary for IMF staff or anyone else to decide whether a surplus country was 'manipulating' its currency or whether that currency was 'fundamentally undervalued.' The country would not have to be cited as in violation of its obligations as an IMF member.

A tax on countries that undervalued their currencies to accumulate more reserves, requiring them to transfer dollars or the equivalent to the International Monetary Fund, could conceivably have the perverse effect of only encouraging them to undervalue their currencies by more so that they could replace the reserves that they had been forced by the provision to transfer to the Fund. In other words, the tax would have a relative price effect and an 'income effect' working in opposite directions. The desire to accumulate reserves is only one reason, of course, why some countries are inclined to maintain highly competitive real exchange rates and run chronic external surpluses. Rodrik argues for example that so-called undervalued exchange rates are associated with rapid economic growth because they encourage manufacturing employment.[15] To the extent that these other motives prevailed, the perverse 'income effect' would not dominate. But to the extent that reserve accumulation pure and simple was the motivation, marrying the tax to other reforms designed to guarantee emergency liquidity to countries in need (expansion, for example, of the IMF's Flexible Credit Line) would weaken the motive and address the problem.

This tax could be written into the Articles of Agreement so that collecting it would not require, inter alia, a decision by the Executive Board. It would presumably be easiest to implement in a period when it was not so obvious on which members it would predominantly fall.[16]

---

[15] Rodrik (2008).

[16] Tax compliance should probably not just be assumed. In the same way that the United States has been known to withhold its dues to the United Nations out of dissatisfaction with some of the organization's actions, one can imagine a country (a large country in particular) withholding its scarce-currency-clause tax payments to the IMF. A very strong international consensus (very strong peer pressure) would presumably be necessary to elicit compliance.

Convertible SDRs

In the 1950s and 1960s, Robert Triffin argued that an international monetary system in which a national currency serves as the dominant source of incremental foreign exchange reserves is intrinsically unstable.[17] Reserves at that time predominantly took the form of gold and the dollar, but the supply of new monetary gold was relatively inelastic; therefore the dollar played the largest part on the margin.

Triffin argued that this was undesirable on a number of grounds. For one thing it allowed the United States to run a chronic balance of payments deficit, fund it at low cost, and live beyond its means.[18] As a result, policy discipline in the United States was weakened. With other countries pegging their currencies to the dollar, the consequence was an inflationary bubble that infected the entire world economy.

In addition, as the world economy expanded, with other catch-up economies growing even faster than the United States, the official foreign dollar liabilities of the US grew both as a share of global foreign exchange reserves and relative to the size of the US economy. As those official foreign dollar liabilities grew large relative to US gold reserves, confidence in the ability of the United States to convert them into gold at a fixed price was liable to weaken. The result might be disorderly exchange rate changes and credit stringency in the United States if foreign central banks scrambled out of dollar claims.

These observations gave rise in 1969 to the creation of Special Drawing Rights and in the 1970s to proposals for a Substitution Account through which SDRs could be substituted for dollar reserves. As Henry Wallich once noted, there were always two arguments for a Substitution Account, one being to 'bail out the dollar from short-term difficulties' and the other to bring about a 'long-term structural improvement in the world monetary system.'[19]   In 2007 C. Fred Bergsten resuscitated the idea of a Substitution Account through which SDRs might be substituted for dollar reserves as a way of allowing central banks to diversify out of dollars without precipitating a dollar crash which might undermine confidence in US financial

---

[17] See inter alia Triffin (1960).
[18] This being the 'exorbitant privilege' of which Valery Giscard d'Estaing complained.
[19] Wallich (1980).

markets.[20] This was a reincarnation of Wallich's first argument for the Substitution Account – as a way of 'bailing out the dollar from short-term difficulties.' There was then a debate over whether such an initiative was necessary; in the event, there has been little evidence of central bank diversification out of dollars, at least as of the time of writing.[21]

The alternative is to rehabilitate Wallich's second argument of the need for an alternative to a national currency as international reserves as a way of smoothing the operation of the world monetary system. Assume, for simplicity, that strong network externalities/increasing returns result in a single instrument constituting the dominant share of reserves.[22] Imagine that this is the dollar. This allows the United States to run chronic external deficits, finance them at low cost, and live beyond its means. It weakens policy discipline on the United States. It is conducive to the growth of a financial bubble in the US capable of infecting the entire world. (This is one interpretation of the genesis of the global credit crisis.) The commitment to convert dollars into gold (or into anything else, for that matter) is no longer there, but there continue to be warnings about a loss of confidence in the dollar with the expansion of the Fed's balance sheet and the prospect of massive fiscal stimulus to offset the effects of accumulated financial problems. We know that speculative attacks (in the sense of large numbers of traders simultaneously taking positions against a currency) are possible when currencies float and not only when they are fixed. In the longer run the question is what would prevent all this from happening again – whether it were the dollar and the United States or some other currency and economy in the privileged but vulnerable position.[23]

---

[20] Bergsten (2007).

[21] There was also a debate over whether it was feasible (whether central banks would willingly hold SDR claims, given the instrument's limited liquidity) and whether it was equitable (given that someone, presumably the shareholders in the IMF, which assumed the dollar claims, would now bear the risk of capital losses in the event of dollar depreciation).

[22] An assumption about which I myself have doubts: see Eichengreen (2006). But leave those doubts aside for sake of argument. See however the next footnote.

[23] Imagining a world of more than one reserve currency (most plausibly, the dollar and the euro) alters this logic only slightly. On the one hand, the economy issuing the reserve unit(s) is now larger relative to the world as a whole (it is the US and Euro Area together, not just the US). But the same

One answer is that such problems can be avoided by creating a composite unit that central banks find as attractive to hold as dollars and which could be used not just in transfers with the IMF itself and between IMF members (that is to say, governments). This general idea was proposed by People's Bank of China Governor Zhou Xiaochuan in the run-up to the April 2nd 2009 G20 summit in London.

But making the SDR an attractive unit in which to hold central bank reserves presupposes deep and liquid markets in SDR claims. Central banks use their reserves to smooth their countries' international transactions and to intervene in foreign exchange markets. They need to buy and sell reserve assets without moving the markets or, for that matter, being noticed. This requires that the markets in which their reserve assets are traded be deep and liquid. Such liquidity does not spring up spontaneously. It requires a critical mass of SDR issuance, not only by the IMF itself but by other entities, such as governments, banks and nonfinancial firms, along with a critical mass of trading. In short, it requires commercializing the SDR.

There have been previous attempts to commercialize the SDR. A limited market in private SDRs emerged as early as 1975, when some banks began to accept time deposits in SDRs and some corporations began issuing long-term debt securities in SDRs. But these previous attempts were not especially successful.[24] The coordination problem – that many prospective issuers were reluctant to issue SDR denominated claims in the absence of evidence that others were prepared to do likewise – was substantial. The dollar's first-mover advantage proved impossible to overcome.

To be as attractive as dollar debt securities, SDRs would have to offer comparable liquidity and return. Historically, composite currencies traded commercially have not offered attractive

---

problem as before – that the US and Euro Area, the high-income countries with the most liquid markets, are likely to come to account for a shrinking share of the world economy over time, so that the demand for confidence-inspiring international reserves will grow faster than their capacity to supply them – continues to arise. In addition, there is the danger of sharp shifts in demand from one international currency to the other, since the two international units are likely to be close substitutes. Thus, while one source of fragility is less pressing in this alternative scenario, a second source of fragility is added.

[24] Sobol (1981).

combinations of liquidity and return.[25] For this to happen, someone would have to act as market maker and subsidize the operation of the market until it acquired scale and liquidity.

The obvious someone is the IMF. It could stand ready to buy and sell SDRs at bid-ask spreads comparable to those in US treasury and agency markets. It would be prepared to convert its SDR liabilities into any of the constituent currencies at those spreads. (Exchanging SDRs only into, say, dollars and asking market participants desiring another currency to pay the spread twice would not render the SDR particularly attractive or make it a true international currency.) Subsidies would have a cost, which members would have to agree to defray. They would presumably do so if they saw this as a worthwhile investment in reform of the international monetary system.

Transforming the SDR into a true international currency would require surmounting other hurdles. The IMF would have to be able to issue additional SDRs in periods of shortage, like the Fed provided dollar swaps to foreign central banks to ensure adequate dollar liquidity in the second half of 2008. At the moment, countries holding 85 percent of IMF voting power must agree before SDRs can be issued, which is no recipe for liquidity. IMF management would have to be empowered to decide on SDR issuance, just as the Federal Reserve can decide to offer currency swaps. For the SDR to become a true international currency, in other words, the IMF would have to become more like a global central bank and international lender of last resort.

Global Glass-Steagall

Any explanation for the global credit crisis must confront the questions: why the most serious banking crisis in 80 years, and why now? One answer runs as follows.[26] There is a conflict between banks' core functions of providing a safe repository for household savings and operating the payments system, on the one hand, and the advantages of diversifying into originating, distributing and investing in risky assets, utilizing wholesale funding and employing leverage,

---

[25] See Allen (1993).
[26] Eichengreen (2009).

on the other. The second strategy offers economies of scale, scope and diversification but may undermine banks' ability to carry out their safe-repository and payments-system functions.[27] Thus, the global credit crisis resulted from deregulation that permitted banks to branch into new lines of risky business and that ratcheted up competitive pressure, which induced gambling to survive. That deregulation and the intensification of competition occurred both at the national level, as with the elimination of Regulation Q and Glass-Steagall restrictions in the United States, and internationally, as capital controls were removed, restrictions on the activities of foreign banks were relaxed, and cross-border bank activity expanded. In the US, broker-dealers, no longer able to make a comfortable living off fixed commissions on stock trades, moved into concocting and issuing new kinds of derivative securities and into employing additional leverage in their own investment strategies. In Europe, universal banks, feeling the intensification of cross-border competition, resorted to even more leverage than North American commercial banks. The result was serious financial vulnerabilities of the sort from which we are currently suffering.

One conceivable response would be to reimpose Glass-Steagall-like restrictions dividing the banking and financial system into two components. In one component (what we used to call commercial banking) liabilities would be limited to retail deposits, while assets would be limited to low-risk instruments: cash, short-term treasuries,

---

[27] Although there is now an entirely predictable backlash according to which scale economies give way to scale diseconomies at a much lower level of activity than it was previously popular to argue. My own view is that economies of scale and scope exist, although there obviously comes a point where diseconomies set in. Consistent with this presumption is the observation that there had existed a noticeable tendency for financial firms in the United States to attempt to exploit the existence of such economies of scope even before the formal removal of Glass-Steagall in 1999. See Barth, Brumbaugh and Wilcox (2000). See also Hu (2002). Historical studies similarly suggest that the imposition of Glass-Steagall raised the cost of financial services: see Ramirez (1999). Whether the benefits in terms of greater efficiency that can be reaped over the relevant range dominate the costs in terms of greater scope for financial instability depends on how effectively one thinks the regulators can contain those instability effects. Recent experience clearly leads one to revise downward one's assessment of such effectiveness.

commercial paper, adequately-collateralized small business loans, and conforming mortgages.[28] This would guarantee confidence in the security of deposits, reduce the likelihood of bank runs, and ensure the stability of the payments system. The other component of the system would be allowed to invest in riskier assets. Investment banks would provide loans to sub-investment-grade borrowers and take companies public. Hedge funds and mutual funds would invest in these same entities (both riskier financial and nonfinancial companies) and in their securities. Other changes would presumably be required to make this second segment tolerably safe: capital requirements, limits on the use of leverage, disclosure requirements, requirements that firms in this segment purchase financial disaster (capital) insurance.[29] Another way of putting the point is that, in contrast to traditional proposals for narrow banking, it still may not be the case that large entities in this second segment can be safely allowed to fail even if the payments system is secure. And if they are going to be rescued, they should be regulated before the fact.

What earlier proposals along these lines have failed to acknowledge is that in a financially integrated world such reforms will be feasible only if coordinated internationally. Otherwise, Icelandic banks will be allowed to take deposits from British savers and invest them in risky assets. British banks will complain that they are unable to compete, given restrictions on their funding and investments, if foreign banks are free of such restrictions. To be both effective and politically acceptable, a new Glass-Steagall Act would have to be coordinated internationally. A relatively light-handed approach would be for such restrictions to be incorporated into the Basel Committee's Core Principles for Effective Banking Supervision. The IMF and World Bank could monitor compliance in their FSAP exercises. A more heavy-handed approach would make them an obligation of IMF members.

Some would go only part way toward the reimposition of Glass-Steagall-style restrictions; UK FSA head Adair Turner, for example, would limit the range of activities that could be undertaken by any one financial institution without necessarily dividing these activities into

---

[28] As argued in Chamley and Kotlikoff (2009). See also Bhide (2009); Johnson (2009); and Buiter (2009).

[29] On this see below.

two (or more) mutually-exclusive groups. But even these somewhat less restrictive schemes would pose the same issues for international coordination.[30]

A Global Systemic Risk Facility

A number of authors, following Kashyap, Rajan and Stein, have suggested protecting against systemic risk by requiring banks to purchase capital insurance.[31] Rather than holding additional capital at all points in time in order to protect against major shocks against which a bit of additional capital will be an inadequate buffer, they recommend that banks sell financial Cat bonds, paying insurance premia whose cost is equivalent to a bit of additional capital in good times in return for a large payout in the event that systemic risk materializes. This will give them large amounts of protection when they need it as opposed to small amounts both when they do and when they don't. And since the payout on the policy is indexed to a systemic rather than a bank-specific event, the moral hazard associated with the insurance will be limited.[32]

---

[30] Precisely the same argument applies to proposals to prevent financial institutions from growing beyond a certain size (or to apply heavier capital requirements as they get larger) to limit the too-big-to-fail problem. Such capital requirements in one country would put its financial institutions at a competitive disadvantage internationally, assuming the existence of some scale or scope economies over the relevant range. Again it would be necessary to coordinate such measures internationally to make them palatable in any one country.

[31] Kashyap, Rajan and Stein (2008); Nishimura (2008).

[32] A related scheme, due to Perotti and Suarez, envisages contingent liquidity rather than capital insurance. The problem, in this view, is not large losses leading to a hit to capital but temporary disruptions to market liquidity which hit banks relying on wholesale funding. Their scheme would require banks to pay a liquidity insurance premium to the central bank as a function of their reliance on wholesale funding (and also perhaps the tenor of that wholesale funding or the mismatch between the duration of their wholesale liabilities and assets). Banks would be discouraged from relying excessively on wholesale funding without being prohibited from resorting to it. The premium charges would compensate the central bank from having to provide emergency liquidity when market liquidity was disrupted. Unlike the capital

For this scheme to work there would have to be a counterparty prepared to put its own capital at risk. Put another way, for this scheme to be more attractive than self insurance, where each financial institution simply puts aside more capital on its own, the payoff in the event of the bad realization must be larger than what can be mobilized by liquidating the assets in which the banks' insurance premia have been invested. This is how Cat bonds issued to protect against earthquakes, floods and hurricanes work. The insured issues bonds that are purchased by investors (often hedge funds specializing in Cat bonds) using their own funds. Those investors receive an attractive return if the bad realization does not occur but lose part or all of their investment in the event it does.[33]

Cat bonds can be costly to issue because payoffs depend on rare events on which there may not exist reliable data, rendering the instrument difficult to value.[34] Underwriters require issuers to pay substantial up-front costs for research on the distribution of risks and returns (geological surveys, weather studies) that investors require before committing their funds. The result is that small countries tend to be rationed out of this market. This same problem is likely to arise in the case of financial Cat bonds insofar as the risks affecting bank capital have similarly proven to be difficult to forecast on the basis of, inter alia, banks' internal models and regulators' indicators of impending distress.

Moral hazard can also be a problem in the same way that the availability of catastrophe insurance encourages homeowners to build in a flood plain; this is another factor potentially elevating costs. Any scheme for the provision of capital insurance should therefore be

---

insurance scheme, this would appear something that can be organized on the national level; there does not appear to be a prima facie case for international coordination orchestrated by the IMF or any other institution. See Perotti and Suarez (2009).

[33] Some Cat bonds include principal protected tranches, which guarantee the return of principal. In their case the triggering event affects payment of interest and the timing of the repayment of principal, which might be extended from, say, three to ten years. One can imagine similarly applying this model to systemic-risk insurance.

[34] Another reason for the high premium demanded by investors is that there will be an incentive for the underwriter to retain its best risks while securitizing and selling off questionable ones.

married to strengthened supervision and regulation to prevent additional risk taking.

Finally, opportunistic behavior can be a problem if the triggering event is reported or controlled by the insured. In principal this can be addressed by indexing the payoff to an independently verifiable indicator not under the control of the insured: wind speed, rainfall or Richter Scale readings in the case of traditional Cat bonds, a global financial market indicator like the Ted spread or an index of bank shares in the case of financial Cat bonds. The problem here is basis risk (the Ted spread or an index of bank shares will be an imperfect indicator of capital needs), which renders insurance less effective (banks are paying for insurance that pays off at times other when the damage in question occurs). In addition the assumption that individual banks are too small to affect the Ted spread or a global index of bank shares may be unrealistic.[35]

But Cat bonds can also be attractive to investors and therefore relatively inexpensive to issue insofar as returns are uncorrelated with those on other financial assets. They are attractive because they offer diversification, in other words.[36] This is less likely to be true in the case of capital insurance, however. Returns to investors will decline in the event of systemic risk, which is precisely when the returns on their other investments will decline. It is not obvious therefore that financial Cat bonds will be attractive to hedge funds, pension funds, sovereign wealth funds, and sophisticated private investors.

A multilateral institution like the IMF could address these problems by creating a Global Systemic Risk Facility to underwrite systemic risk insurance for member countries. With similar countries facing similar risks, it could exploit the existence of economies of scale in the research needed at the underwriting stage.[37] This is analogous to what the World Bank has done with its Caribbean Catastrophe Risk Insurance Facility: each of a number of Caribbean islands facing similar catastrophic risk pays a premium to underwrite

---

[35] Can you say 'Lehman Brothers?'

[36] This is one explanation for why the market in Cat bonds has held up relatively well despite the severity of the credit crisis – in contrast to the markets in other complex financial instruments.

[37] Since the Fund is not profit oriented this would presumably also address the fear that the underwriter, enjoying private information, was retaining the best risks while selling off the others (see above).

the issuance of a common insurance instrument.[38] In the present context the IMF could organize research on systemic risk and underwrite issuance of the standardized bond, perhaps in cooperation with one or more private reinsurers like Swiss Re or Munich Re. An entity like the IMF would also be in a position to reassure investors about moral hazard. For example, countries could be disqualified from receiving payouts and paying in further premia in the event of an FSAP that identified significant problems with its financial system. Measurement of the parametric trigger should presumably be delegated to an independent agency following transparent rules.[39]

Insofar as systemic risk hits different countries at different times or with different degrees of severity, payouts would not have to be uniform across countries. What we might call the IMF Systemic Risk Facility could thus act as a risk aggregator. It would allow countries to pool their country-specific risks into a diversified portfolio, allowing for a substantial reduction in premium costs relative to a situation where a capital-insurance scheme was pursued at the country level. Even in the current global credit crisis, systemic risk and losses of bank capital have not affected all countries to the same extent.

Just why institutional and individual investors can't do the pooling themselves is not clear.[40] One possibility is that effective diversification is possible only when the bonds in question are issued by a range of different countries but the "After you, Alphonse" problem prevents anyone from going first. If this is the case, then a global scheme organized by an entity like the IMF is an appropriate solution. (In this instance it would be necessary for the IMF to provide the impetus but not the finance.) Similarly, if there were a tendency for countries to under-invest in systemic risk insurance because some of the costs of disruptions to the national financial system are incurred by other countries, then an IMF initiative to coordinate investments in

---

[38] See Guesquire et al. (2008).

[39] Given the IMF's politicized nature, this would be a function that the institution presumably would want to outsource. Just for fun, one is tempted to say 'to the rating agencies.' An alternative is to address the politicization of IMF decision making. On this see below.

[40] The success of entities like the World Bank's Caribbean facility suggests that there are, in fact, occasions where private investors do not themselves undertake these functions but become enthusiastic investors when someone else does the aggregation.

insurance would be the appropriate way of internalizing this externality.[41]

The details of this scheme would still have to be fleshed out.[42] Would the insurance premia be paid by banks directly to the IMF, which in the event of a systemic crisis would see that the payout went directly to those same banks? If so, which banks, and who would decide? Or would the premia be paid to the IMF by the bank regulator in the member country, which would make the decision on which banks participated, collect the premia from them, and distribute the payoff on receiving it from the Fund?

A Multilateral Insolvency Trust for International Banks

A gap in the international financial architecture pointed up by the crisis is the absence of a regime to deal with the insolvency of a major bank or bank-like institution doing business in multiple countries. International insolvencies, to the extent that they are managed, are managed by separate national insolvency regimes, each of which appoints a fiduciary (or trustee or administrator) to assume control of the firm and its assets, value and prioritize creditor claims, and reorganize or liquidate the firm so as to ensure that those claims are respected. But fiduciaries of different nationality see their priorities differently. Consistency will be difficult if different fiduciaries, following national practice, attach different weights to preserving economic value versus settling claims. A potentially viable enterprise may be driven out of business as a going concern if fiduciaries scramble for assets. Creditors may be treated unfairly if assets can be allocated by multiple fiduciaries. These difficulties are illustrated by the case of Lehman Bros. with its operations in both the US and UK.

There has been some progress in encouraging cooperation among trustees and national judicial systems. The International Association

---

[41] The other explanation for the absence of a private market – that individual country risks can become highly correlated in a systemic crisis and the counterparties who have bought the bonds default on their obligations under these extreme circumstances – points to a less reassuring interpretation.

[42] As with all the other schemes in this chapter.

of Restructuring, Insolvency and Bankruptcy Professionals (INSOL International), Committee J of the International Bar Association, and UNCITRAL (the United National Commission on International Trade Law) have all commissioned working papers, organized international meetings and established working groups to encourage informal cooperation, foster the recognition of foreign insolvency proceedings, and promote the adoption of model legislation. Financial firms have sought to promote the standardization of contract terms in different countries so that enforcement can be similarly standardized in insolvency proceedings. Examples of this are the International Foreign Exchange Master Agreement (IFEMA) and International Swaps and Derivatives Association Master Agreement (ISDA Agreement). In a limited number of cases, countries have negotiated bilateral treaties and conventions about how to cooperate in this process.

The argument that cooperation among national forums is neither reliable nor efficient leads to suggestions that international insolvency proceedings should occur in a single forum, which would reach all assets of the debtor, wherever located, and distribute those assets to all creditors, wherever located. The name for this approach to international insolvency is 'universalism.'[43] But in practice it is not obvious in what single national jurisdiction universal proceedings should take place. The one where the financial entity was first licensed, or the one where it has the most assets? It is not clear whether the authorities in that jurisdiction can be counted on to fairly distribute assets to creditors located in other countries.

These observations create an argument for a universal venue where cross-border insolvencies of internationally-active financial institutions can be administered. One can imagine an International Court of Insolvency comparable to the International Court of Justice, headed by experienced jurists who would in turn appoint respected, neutral administrators. Their actions would have to be guided by international law, build presumably on the UCITRAL's Model Law on Cross-Border Insolvency. That insolvency proceedings for internationally active banks would fall under their jurisdiction could be made an obligation of IMF members. This obligation would still, of course, have to be given the force of law in each individual country through the passage of the relevant law. And the international court

---

[43] See Buxbaum (2000).

will need staff support to gather necessary data on assets and liabilities and other information needed for restructuring and reorganization; this would presumably be provided by national regulators, whose efforts could be coordinated by the IMF.[44]

A World Financial Organization

The preceding has provided multiple examples of how problems arising in connection with supervision and regulation in one country can infect financial systems in other countries. Recent experience suggests that even small countries can be the source of significant spillovers.[45] Yet mechanisms for ensuring that national decisions regarding regulation are taken with external as well as domestic consequences in mind remain inadequate. Efforts to share information, apply peer pressure, and correct regulatory problems through the deliberations of the Financial Stability Forum, the Basel Committee on Banking Supervision and colleges of supervisors (as agreed to by the G7 in April 2008) have been shown by the recent crisis to not be up to the task.[46] International standards for supervision and regulation have not been sufficiently demanding. Compliance with such standards as exist has been spotty, since there exist no international sanctions on countries failing to comply.

The latest idea for strengthening existing arrangements would have the Financial Stability Forum define acceptable practice and the IMF assess whether national regulation meets that standard. But is the Financial Stability Forum sufficiently legitimate and accountable,

---

[44] Readers will be reminded of the debate over the viability of and need for an international insolvency regime or court for sovereign debtors; see Raffer (2005).

[45] Consider the cases of Iceland and Ireland, for example.

[46] For good theoretical reasons, argue a number of recent authors. Thus, Holthausen and Ronde (2005) show that cooperating supervisors will not in general reveal all relevant information if their interests to not perfectly coincide. Freixas (2003) shows that information asymmetries and information asymmetries will in general not lead to optimal supervision in the absence of a centralized process or an enforcement mechanism that produces its functional equivalent.

even given its recently expanded membership?[47] Does the Forum have adequate staff? Is the IMF, for its part, willing to take on its large shareholders when their national practices are not up to snuff?

An alternative would be to create a World Financial Organization analogous to the already-existing World Trade Organization (WTO).[48] In the same way that the WTO establishes principles for trade policy (nondiscrimination, reciprocity, transparency, binding and enforceable commitments) without specifying outcomes, the WFO would establish principles for prudential supervision (capital and liquidity requirements, limits on portfolio concentrations and connected lending, adequacy of risk measurement systems and internal controls) and without attempting to prescribe the structure of regulation in detail.[49] The WFO would define obligations for its members; the latter would be obliged to meet international standards for supervision and regulation of their financial markets and institutions. Membership would be obligatory for all countries seeking freedom of access to foreign markets for domestically-chartered financial institutions.[50] The WFO would appoint independent panels of experts to determine whether countries were in compliance with those obligations. Importantly, it would authorize the imposition of sanctions against countries that failed to comply. Other members would be within their rights to restrict the ability of banks and nonbank financial institutions

---

[47] At its plenary meeting in London on 11–12 March 2009, the FSF agreed to broaden its membership to add Argentina, Brazil, China, India, Indonesia, Korea, Mexico, Russia, Saudi Arabia, South Afica, and Turkey (the remaining members of the G20) along with Spain and the EU. This decision was confirmed by G20 leaders at their London Summit on April 2nd, when they announced that the FSF would be renamed the Financial Stability Board.

[48] Eichengreen (2008). In a similar proposal, Claessens (2008) has proposed creating an international charter for banks engaged in cross-border activity. Internationally active banks would be required to secure a charter from an international College of Supervisors and be subject to its supervision. When the members of the College determined that a bank was in violation of its charter, it could impose cease-and-desist orders, limit the operations of said institutions, and require remedial action.

[49] The Basel Core Principles for Effective Banking Supervision would be the obvious place to go when defining these principles.

[50] The move to a WFO would presumably occur after some years of satisfactory experience with a GATT-like predecessor (if the history of the WTO is any guide).

chartered in the offending country to do business in their markets. This would provide a real incentive to comply.

It will be objected that national governments would never let an international organization dictate their domestic regulatory policies. The rebuttal is that the WFO would not dictate. The specifics of implementation would be left to the individual country. Members would still be able to tailor supervision and regulation to the particularities of their financial markets. But those regulatory specifics would have to comply with the broad principles set down in the WFO charter and associated obligations.

We already do the equivalent for trade. Dispute settlement panels already determine whether, inter alia, US tariffs on timber imports from Canada are in compliance with US WTO obligations. If not, we have the choice of whether to change those laws or face sanctions and retaliation. If the US and other countries accept this in the case of trade, why should they not accept it for finance?[51]

Who would have the power to initiate cases under this WFO model? WTO cases are initiated by a country that feels it has been injured by foreign trade policies. One can imagine instances of this in the context of finance (other European countries objecting to Ireland's blanket deposit guarantees or Icelandic banks' offshore deposit-taking activities). But more generally, in the case of finance injury is likely to be more diffuse; the adverse financial repercussions are likely to be more widespread. And given the speed with which such markets work, it is even more important to correct problems before the fact.

The alternative would be for cases to be initiated at the volition of the WFO's panel of independent experts, who might choose to convene a panel in response to an ambiguous FSAP. The advantage of this approach over the FSF-IMF model is that it would not be necessary to imagine that the Fund could provide an up-or-down decision on the adequacy of national regulation; the "rating decision" would be outsourced to the independent panel of experts.

The alternative, of course, would be to make the IMF itself more independent, a possibility to which I now turn.

---

[51] One answer is that in certain countries, such as my own, finance is more powerful than industry as a source of political funding. Another is that financial intermediation is more complex and opaque than bananas, rendering governments less sure about the consequences of delegating authority over finance than trade.

IMF Governance

There is a broad consensus regarding what should be done to reform the governance of the IMF in order to enhance its legitimacy and accountability.[52] Quotas need further revision to give fast-growing countries louder voice and to otherwise reflect the realities of the 21st century. The 85 percent supermajority for substantial changes to the Articles of Agreement, new SDR issues and the like needs to be relaxed (perhaps to 80 per cent) so that no one country exercises a veto over key policy decisions and reforms. Voting procedures within the institution should be revised to better balance the interests of large and small countries. The Executive Board needs to be updated to better reflect the economic and political realities of the 21st century and downsized, perhaps to 20 members, to streamline decision making and allow for more emerging-market representation, something that can be most easily accomplished if the EU or even the euro area moves to a single chair. The leadership selection process needs to be opened up once and for all. The International Monetary and Financial Committee of 24 finance ministers from leading countries should be transformed into a Council, as envisaged by Article XII of the Articles of Agreement. The Council would then provide oversight of the Executive Board and its decisions through periodic meetings and could be canvassed regularly for its views on major issues through a written procedure.

A few moments of reflection are enough to convince one that many of the fashionable items on this menu have more symbolic than operational value. Virtually all important operational decisions are made on the basis of consensus, not votes. It can be argued that consensus is formed in the shadow of voting rules, but even then careful observers of the Fund have noted that the ability of a member's representative to present his arguments articulately and forcefully can shape board decisions above and beyond what one might expect on the basis of his voting share. Even if the supermajority requirement was brought down from 85 to 80 percent, it is hard to imagine that the United States, with its 17 percent of total votes, could not round up a few allies with three percent of total votes

---

[52] For a clear statement of this conventional wisdom see Center for International Governance and Innovation (2009).

between them to tip the balance. One can reasonably question whether decision making would be significantly streamlined by downsizing the Executive Board to 'only' 20 members. Finally, one can ask whether changing the name of the IMFC to the IMF Council and having the latter meet biannually would significantly alter decision making by a Board that works full time at absorbing staff reports and other documents and meets up to four days a week.[53]

More substantial reform would start with abolishing the Executive Board. Day-to-day decisions would be made by a majority vote of the managing director and deputy managing directors in the manner of a monetary policy committee of a central bank. These individuals would have the independence and autonomy to act quickly and take politically difficult decisions, such as, inter alia, publicly criticizing the exchange rate or fiscal policy of a large member or disbursing a large amount of money quickly.[54] They would not be slowed down by first having to obtain the approval of 24 mid-level bureaucrats, some of whom take instructions directly from the governments of those same large members. They would not be hindered in adopting radical departures from past policies, as required by radically new circumstances, by a large board representing a large collection of countries that, by its nature, is slow to accept modifications of past practice.

Everyone agrees what is needed to make the IMF more effective. The Fund needs to strengthen its surveillance of policies and markets and come clean when it perceives potential threats to national and global financial stability. It needs to be able to provide large amounts of emergency liquidity quickly when circumstances require. Modernizing the current 1940s-vintage structure to create an independent management team would allow the latter to move with the speed and flexibility of a modern central bank monetary policy committee confronted with serious regulatory problems and financial instability – something that is not true of present arrangements, which require it to first obtain the approval of the members of a large and

---

[53] Another argument for simply changing the name of the IMFC to IMF Council is that IMFC is also the name of a Dutch hedge fund administrator and trustee.

[54] To provide insulation from political pressures, members of the management team would have to be appointed/elected to long terms in office.

heterogeneous Executive Board that must in turn obtain the approval of their political masters.

But for such strong independence to be politically acceptable, the members of the management team would have to be equally strongly accountable for their actions. They would have to be more transparent about their decisions and their criteria for taking them. One could imagine delayed publication of minutes of their deliberations.[55] Alternatively, the Managing Director could hold regular press conferences summarizing the management team's decisions in the manner of the ECB. It might be necessary to relax the informal rule that IMF management does not appear before congressional/parliamentary committees.

Most importantly, management would have to be strongly accountable to the IMFC/Council in the same manner that the president and monetary policy committee of a central bank are accountable to their national parliament or congress. They would have to be required to justify their actions to the IMFC. They should be subject to a formal vote of no confidence. The management team would be not just more independent but also more accountable. The IMFC, for its part, would be accountable to the Board of Governors of the IMF.[56] It should be reconstituted as the IMF Council so that what are now recommendations become binding instruments to management, as provided for under the Articles of Agreement. There could be a commitment by its members to meet at least quarterly.

It would of course be necessary to do more than simply abolish the Executive Board. The convention that the managing director should be a European and his first deputy an American would have to be abolished and leadership selection structured so as to reward the most qualified candidates.[57] It would be necessary to devise a selection mechanism for the entire management team that both picked out high-

---

[55] In the manner of the Fed. This would be a small step technically, since minutes of Board meetings are already kept and a highly sanitized version is published as the conclusions of the chair.

[56] Readers will recognize the echoes of De Gregorio, Eichengreen, Ito and Wyplosz (1999), but also King (2006).

[57] As G20 finance ministers reportedly agreed at their mid-March 2009 meeting in Sussex, England.

quality candidates and ensured a reasonable degree of geographic and economic diversity.[58]

The most compelling objection to schemes of this sort is that the decisions of the IMF are more complex and therefore entail more discretion than those of a central bank and that they require the Fund to put taxpayer money more directly at risk. Since a central bank just sets interest rates rather than applying detailed prescriptions for changes in the fabric of social and economic policy, it is said, independence for its monetary policy committee is politically tolerable. Since it just sets interest rates, an action which is easily monitored and assessed, holding its independent management accountable for their actions is relatively straightforward. And since central banks accept only high-quality collateral in their lending operations, they do not put serious taxpayer money at risk (typically, in contrast, they are a profit center).

In the wake of the credit crisis of 2008–9, it is clear that none of these objections holds water. We have seen national central banks engage in very detailed interventions in financial and other markets. They have purchased all manner of collateral as required by policies of credit easing, exposing themselves to significant balance-sheet losses. The reality is that modern central banks, not unlike the IMF, are required to do much more than just set interest rates. This has created some discomfort among observers and demands that central bankers do a better job at justifying their actions; it has similarly

---

[58] This part of the problem is not straightforward. Competing five-person slates of one North American, one Latin American, one African, one Asian and one European candidate could be nominated (a slight expansion of the present four person managing director-deputy managing director team), and the entire slate could be voted on by the Board of Governors. This would not be optimal, since governors might be forced to vote for slate members for whom they had little desire in order to secure the election of other slate members. An alternative would be to have five regional candidates elected by the countries of the five respective regions; there would then be a second election in which the entire membership voted on who among the five winners they preferred as managing director. Or candidates could be nominated and voted for without reference to nationality/national origin, with the candidate receiving the most votes becoming MD and the next four becoming her deputies, the assumption being that the need for regional diversity would take care of itself. Solving this problem can only be done by a better political scientist than the present author.

created pressure that mechanisms for holding them accountable, be these oversight committees or appointed by the US Congress or the relevant committees of the European Parliament, be strengthened. But it has not given rise to the view that central bank independence is intolerable or, for that matter, undesirable.

Conclusion

None of these blue-sky ideas will come to fruition overnight. But in the meantime there is plenty of a more straightforward nature to do. The IMF can push ahead once shareholders recover their appetite for so doing with the reform of quotas and with reconstituting and streamlining the Executive Board. It can transform the IMFC into a Council that can issue binding instructions to management and the board. It can entice additional countries, Asian countries in particular, to sign up for its short-term liquidity facility, eliminating the stigma problem once and for all. It can make Financial Sector Assessment Programs mandatory rather than at the volition of the member. It can administer FSAPs at the regional rather than the national level, first in Europe and then other parts of the world, not least in order to be sure that FSAP exercises encompass banks' overseas subsidiaries and affiliates. These may all be 'in the box' initiatives but they are no less important and valuable for the fact.

At the same time, the existence of this 'in the box' agenda should not be an excuse for failing to engage in out-of-the-box thinking.

For out-of-the-box ideas to have legs, they must be accompanied by a roadmap for how to get from here to there in the space of, say, ten years. It is clear that reform of IMF governance is a prerequisite for many of the other ambitious ideas entailing a role for the Fund. Without meaningful governance reform, emerging market members would not agree to a significant expansion of the Fund's resources along the lines of the indexing scheme in the first section above. They would not agree to an automatic system of contributions, overseen by the Fund, from countries in chronic balance of payments surplus. They would not acquiesce to the IMF acting as secretariat to a World Financial Organization or even to the latter using FSAPs as the basis for its decisions. They would not agree that the IMF should be the source of staff support to the International Court of Insolvency. They would not agree to having the Fund pool and underwrite subscriptions to a Capital Insurance Facility or coordinate the move to a Global Glass-Steagall Act. They would not look favorably on efforts by the Fund to enhance the role of the SDR. Thus, progress on the other out-of-the-box ideas offered here hinges on prior governance reform.

This suggests a sequencing strategy. First, pursue business as usual – strengthening the FSAP process, streamlining the SLF. Next, proceed meaning governance reform, starting with the conventional agenda and then proceeding to the more ambitious reforms enumerated here. Finally, leverage the enhanced legitimacy and efficiency resulting from those governance reforms to implement the remaining items on the agenda. Were all or even many of the proposals enumerated here to be implemented in this manner, the result would be a safer financial world.

References

Allen, R. (1993) 'Composite Currencies: SDRs and ECUs,' *Open Economies Review,* **4**, 97–110.

Barth, J., D. Brumbaugh and J. Wilcox (2000), 'The Repeal of Glass-Steagall and the Advent of Broad Banking,' *Journal of Economic Perspectives,* **4**, 191–204.

Bergsten, C.F. (2007), 'How to Solve the Problem of the Dollar,' *Financial Times* (11 December 2007).

Bhide, A. (2009), 'In Praise of More Primitive Finance,' *The Economist's Voice,* **6**(3), February.

Buiter, W. (2009), 'Regulating the New Financial Sector,' *Vox EU* (9 March).

Buxbaum, H.L. (2000), 'Rethinking International Insolvency: The Neglected Role of Choice-of-Law Rules and Theory,' *Stanford Journal of International Law,* **36**, 23–71.

Center for International Governance and Innovation (2009), 'Advancing the Reform Agenda: A Proposal to the G-20 on International Financial Institution Reform', University of Waterloo, 23 February.

Chamley C. and L. Kotlikoff (2009), 'Limited Purpose Banking: Putting an End to Financial Crises,' Boston University, mimeo.

Claessens, S. (2008), 'The New International Financial Architecture Requires Better Governance' in B. Eichengreen and R. Baldwin (eds), *What G20 Leaders Must Do to Stabilize our Economy and Fix the Financial System, A VoxEU.org Publication*, 11 November, Centre for Economic Policy Research, CEPR, 29–32.

David P. (1985), 'Clio and the Economics of Qwerty,' *American Economic Review Papers and Proceedings*, 332–337.

David P. (1991) 'The Hero and the Herd in Technological History: Reflections on Thomas Edison and the Battle of the Systems' in P. Higonnet, D. Landes and H. Rosovsky (eds), *Favorites to Fortune* Cambridge, MA, USA: Harvard University Press, pp.72–119.

De Gregorio, J., B. Eichengreen, T. Ito and C. Wyplosz (1999), *An Independent and Accountable IMF*, Centre for Economic Policy Research.

Eichengreen, B. (2006), 'Sterling's Past, Dollar's Future,' in *Global Imbalances and the Lessons of Bretton Woods* Cambridge, MA, USA: The MIT Press, pp. 123–148.

Eichengreen B. (2008), 'Not a New Bretton Woods but a New Bretton Woods Process,' in B. Eichengreen and R. Baldwin (eds), *What G20 Leaders Must Do to Stabilize our Economy and Fix the Financial System,* VoxEU, 11 November.

Eichengreen, B. (2009), 'Origins and Responses to the Current Crisis,' *CESifo Forum,* (November), 6–11.

Freixas X. (2003), 'Crisis Management in Europe,' in J.J.M. Kremers, D. Schoenmaker and P.J. Wierts (eds), *Financial Supervision in Europe*, Cheltenham, UK and Northampton, MA, USA; Edward Elgar, pp.102–119.

Guesquire F. et al. (2008), *Caribbean Catastrophe Risk Insurance Facility: A Solution to the Short-Term Liquidity Needs of Small Island States in the Aftermath of Natural Disasters*, Washington, DC, USA: The World Bank.

Holthausen C. and T. Ronde (2005), 'Cooperation in International Banking Supervision,' CEPR Discussion Paper no. 4990.

Hu, L. (2002) 'On the Wealth and Risk Effect of the Glass-Steagall Overhaul: Evidence from the Stock Market,' University of Notre Dame Historical Studies, mimeo.

Johnson, S. (2009), 'High Noon: Geithner vs. the Oligarchs,' www.growthcommissionblog.org (9 February).

Kashyap, A., R. Rajan and J. Stein (2008), 'Rethinking Capital Regulation,' paper presented to the Jackson Hole Symposium of the Kansas City Fed (August).

King, M. (2006), 'Reform of the International Monetary Fund,' speech to the Indian Council for Research on International Economic Relations, Delhi (20 February).

Leibowitz S. and S. Margolis (1990), 'The Fable of the Keys,' *Journal of Law and Economics,* **33**, 1–26.

Nishimura, K. (2008), 'A Proposal for Public Capital Insurance,' Bank of Japan, mimeo. (22 November).

Perotti, E. and J. Suarez (2009), 'Liquidity Insurance for Systemic Crises,' www.ft.com (24 February).

Raffer, K. (2005), 'Considerations for Designing International Insolvency Procedures,' *Law, Social Justice and Global Development (LGD),* **1**.

Ramirez, C. (1999), 'Did Glass Steagall Increase the Cost of External Finance for Investment? Evidence from Bank and Insurance Company Affiliations,' *Journal of Economic History,* **59**, 372–396.

Rodrik, D. (2008), 'The Real Exchange Rate and Economic Growth,' *Brookings Papers on Economic Activity* (Fall), 365–412.

Sobol, D. (1981) 'The SDR in Private International Finance,' *Federal Reserve Bank of New York Quarterly Review,* (1981), 29–41.

Triffin, R. (1960) *Gold and the Dollar Crisis* Yale, USA: Yale University Press.

Wallich, H. (1980), 'The World Monetary System after the Postponement of the Substitution Account,' *Intereconomics* (July/August), 163–167.

14. Safe and Sound Banking: A Role for Countercyclical Regulatory Requirements?

Gerard Caprio[1]

Introduction

The financial crisis that began in the summer of 2007 and that has been termed the most serious crisis since the Great Depression has spawned not only a hunt for culprits and scapegoats, but also a search for regulatory solutions. A number of papers have already covered the diagnosis of the causes of the crisis and traced the propagation mechanisms (see Brunnermeier, 2009; Caprio, Demirgüç-Kunt, and Kane, 2008; Caprio, 2009; Greenlaw, Hatzius, Kashyap and Shin, 2008; and Gorton, 2009). Now the search is afoot in regulatory agencies in numerous countries, in fora such as the Basel Committee on Bank Supervision and the Financial Stability Board (formerly the Financial Stability Forum), and in academic circles, for ways to rebuild a regulatory framework in which the public will have confidence and which will promise to mitigate crises.

One idea that is gaining support among various groups is how to

[1] This chapter was prepared with support from the World Bank and was completed while I was on leave as a Fulbright Scholar at Trinity College, Dublin. Accordingly I would like to thank the Fulbright Program, the Institute for International Integration Studies at Trinity College, and the Williams College World Fellowship Program. I benefitted greatly from the first-rate research assistance of Pablo Cuba Bordo, in particular the material on Colombia and Spain. Comments from James Barth, Asli Demirgüç-Kunt, Giovanni Ferri, Jim Hanson, and Ross Levine are gratefully acknowledged, though responsibility for the views espoused here remains with the author.

make Basel II (or III) or any regulatory regime less procyclical (see Brunnermeier, Crockett, Goodhart, Persaud, and Shin, 2009 and Griffith-Jones and Ocampo, 2009). As witnessed in the run-up to the current crisis, prolonged periods of economic expansion can lead to increases in lending and leverage on the part of the banks (and others),with supervisors either swept along in the euphoria or swept aside by the political influence of bankers determined to expand rapidly in a supposedly safe and profitable environment. Basel II offered several ways in which procyclicality can become institutionalized. Those banks that would base their capital ratios on model estimates can do so, with the Basel Committee's blessing, with only five years of data, which at times might only include boom years and thus underestimate the probability of default. Alternatively, banks relying on ratings to set risk weights in the determination of minimum capital holdings may find that the ratings organizations are similarly influenced by the macro environment. Accordingly, the search for a more countercyclical regulatory framework seems worthwhile, and the fact that the aforementioned authors and important international groups are espousing this effort lends credence to the idea.

This Chapter reviews the pros and cons of countercyclical requirements and looks at the very limited experience with them. Section two addresses the rationale for attempting to cope with procyclicality and examines different ways to make credit less procyclical. Countercyclical provisioning is one way potentially to address this problem, and Section three therefore will then look at the efforts of the authorities in Spain and Colombia, two countries in which countercyclical provisioning has been tried, to see what the track record has been. As explained there, these experiments have been at best too recent and limited to put much weight on them, but they are much less favorable for supporting this practice than is commonly admitted.

Section four will address some concerns and implementation issues with countercyclical capital or provisioning requirements. First, although banks that add to their capital or provisions during boom times might be safer than banks with lesser holdings, other things equal, it is not clear from theory or empirical evidence that requirements for such changes will be effective in curbing risk taking. Second, countercyclical provisioning or capital requirements also must deal with the so-called boundary problem, namely that tightening requirements on some entities or in some geographical areas will induce a shift of the more costly or prohibited activity across institutional or geographic boundaries, leaving the world still exposed to risk. This type of regulatory arbitrage has characterized finance throughout its history. Regulatory avoidance can have positive effects, as when creditworthy borrowers gain access to finance, as well as negative consequences, as seen in the current crisis by the disguising or shifting of risk exposures through the creation of Structured Investment Vehicles (SIVs) by banks expressly to evade limits imposed by capital requirements. Third, it is quite possible that countercyclical provisioning or capital requirements will be applied in insufficient doses, as appears to have been the case thus far where implemented. The history of financial regulation suggests that such a development should not be unexpected, as for example seen with deposit insurance premia – where many countries underprice the risk, and where risk-based premia – an idea many economists would endorse – differed by so little in practice as to render them ineffective in restraining risk. After all, the US had risk-based premia (and prompt, corrective action, no less), and yet still suffered a record crisis. Section five concludes and offers advice to developing country authorities, who may be tempted to follow industrial countries down a path they seem determined to take. Countercyclical provisioning or capital requirements may well be oversold in their ability to rein in booms and alleviate busts, and authorities should look more to addressing underlying information and incentive problems in the sector.

Coping with Procyclicality: Why and How

> A sound banker, alas, is not one who foresees danger and avoids it, but one who, when he is ruined, is ruined in a conventional and orthodox way with his fellows, so that no one can really blame him. J.M. Keynes (1932), p. 176.

Rationale

Procyclicality in banking, meaning the tendency of banks to ease lending standards excessively in a boom and restrain them unreasonably in a contraction, is not new, as the quote from Keynes attests. Banking tends to be procyclical for a variety of reasons, not least of which is that in the presence of information asymmetries, bankers are willing to make more loans when borrower net worth and collateral values are high and unemployment rates among borrowers are low. To the extent that the value net worth and collateral at current prices, credit will become more readily available when asset prices are high.

However, there are a variety of reasons why societies, in their own long-term interest, might want banks to restrain procyclical tendencies in the expansionary phase of a credit boom. For example one can easily imagine that many who are having their houses foreclosed regret that they borrowed so much, or in other words that banks were so generous in making credit available to them, a sentiment shared by the many affected by the crisis. Both banks and borrowers might suffer from disaster myopia (Guttentag and Herring, 1986), which is basically a form of framing identified by Tversky and Kahneman (1981). When prices rise (whether the price in question is South Sea Company stock, oil, currencies, housing, etc.) or economies or businesses prosper for a sufficient time, many use simple extrapolation as their forecasting tool, forgetting the phenomenon of regression to the mean. Indeed, the title for Reinhart and Rogoff's 2009 book on crises employs the saying most frequently uttered in booms – 'This Time is Different' – an expression of the belief that an upward trend will continue, rather than revert back to the mean.[2] Bankers often note that when a long time has passed since mean reversion, those in risk-taking positions, such as loan officers, not having lived through lean periods, nor apparently having studied them, do not plan for this eventuality. Lack of experience is difficult to separate from a tendency to go with the herd. Keynes' quote at the

---

[2] The stories of why change is supposedly new and lasting – why land in Japan could suddenly become more scarce, why developing countries could take on tremendous amounts of debt, why housing prices cannot fall, etc. – vary but have in common the neglect of less recent history (e.g., when land was less valuable, debtors defaulted, or housing prices fell).

start of this section captured a key reason behind herding behavior in banking.

The most recent crisis revealed a less innocent cause, which in effect is herding at the level of remuneration, namely the payment of significant amounts of compensation based on generating large volumes of business – from mortgage origination, to the creation of securities, the production of optimistic ratings, etc. – without recourse in the event that outcomes are less favorable. So rather than an episode of collective amnesia or a failure to comprehend history, this explanation (Rajan, 2006) argues that many – from mortgage brokers to heads of banks and rating agencies – were handsomely compensated to look only on the upside because they would not be accountable for the losses on the downside, which was one of the key reasons behind Rajan's early warning of problems in the financial sector.

The prevalence of asset bubbles, especially in recent years, is another reason for the search for a more countercyclical regulatory framework. While not a new phenomenon, it has been noted that as early as the South Sea Bubble of 1719–20, some savvy insiders have 'ridden' the bubble, thereby exacerbating asset prices swings and the pain that they entail (Temin and Voth, 2004), suggesting to some the need for some regulatory counter-measures.

Banks and other financial intermediaries – especially the largest – have also become more interconnected than in generations past through a variety of markets in which they are counterparties or have the same exposure. Although interconnectedness has long been a feature of banking, formerly banks held substantial amounts of liquidity and more capital, whereas now they depend more heavily on markets – including other intermediaries – to provide that liquidity. This dependence heightens their fragility, commensurate with their greater leverage during booms, and makes countercyclical regulation more desirable. And the gains in the speed of communication and the transmission of information over the years, while a benefit in most respects, gives banks little time to adjust to liquidity demands.

Although shareholders, creditors, auditors, credit rating agencies, and supervisors all have a role in disciplining bank management, crises generally expose the weaknesses in corporate governance and the limits of each of these groups in overcoming the agency problem; in the boom preceding the current crisis, the outsized compensation paid for by originating business, with little thought of the future consequences, was a major governance failure. Shareholders' lack of attention to the downside is understandable, given that they at least benefit when risk taking pays off. Creditors' lack of discipline perhaps is the most puzzling, as they risk losses when banks fail yet do not benefit from upside gains when risky bets pay off. Although it is possible that they were merely anticipating a bailout by the government – uninsured creditors to US banks thus far largely have been protected from losses – the more plausible explanation is that they were swept up in the general euphoria. As creditors across the board drove down risk premia on most forms of debt, from spreads on emerging market debt to riskier corporate paper, bank creditors appeared to have been infected with the same optimism (perhaps fueled by high credit ratings) and failed to charge risky banks a sufficient default premium.

Procyclical lending – easing credit standards in boom times – also leads to greater losses and forced asset sales during the 'bust' phase. The term applied to the latter behavior, 'fire sale,' suggests the clear downside, in that asset prices will tend to overshoot their long-term value in the downturn, just as they did during the boom. Reducing procyclicality therefore has the potential to reduce asset price volatility, making it easier for individuals and firms to plan.

Procyclicality evidently was not reduced by discretionary supervision. Supervisory failures around the world in the current crisis – and not just in the countries in which intermediaries were originating dodgy assets but equally in those in which intermediaries were purchasing them – likely were due to the political influence of the regulatees, ideology, and/or incompetence. Disentangling these factors is no easy task. However, any of these answers suggests caution in basing too much of the responsibility for safe and sound banking on discretionary supervisory policies, as we have seen, and not just in this crisis, that they do not function well. Consequently, the interest in reducing reliance on supervisory discretion and installing some automaticity in regulatory standards is understandable.

Methods for countering procyclical behavior in banking

The above reasons provide ample justification for an attempt to slow excessive lending by banks during boom times. Until the current crisis, most regulatory attention has been on micro-prudential factors, that is those factors that are relevant for individual financial intermediaries. The earlier debate on restraining credit booms therefore not surprisingly centered on the role of monetary policy in deflating asset bubbles. Unfortunately, an ample literature did not produce a consensus (Posen, 2006; Roubini, 2005), nor was one evident in policy circles. The Federal Reserve Board led the debate in favor of not intervening until a bubble collapsed, and as late as the end of 2008 apparently had not changed its view, saying that it was more in the remit of regulatory policy as long as overall price stability targets were satisfied (Kohn, 2008). The European Central Bank made it known in several of its annual reports that it favored monetary policy intervention to reduce the amplitude of asset bubbles, though noting that this does not imply opposition to regulatory attempts to slow excessive credit expansion. The essence of the debate on using monetary policy to rein in bubbles turns on the benefits and costs of such intervention, with the Fed arguing that the difficulty of identifying bubbles in time to address them with monetary policy, as well as the likely ineffectiveness of relatively small increases in interest rates in restraining speculative bubbles (which are based on expectations of rates of return that are much larger than even the most vigorously countercyclical interest rate hikes by an activist central bank), implies that it is better to wait to use monetary policy if and when a bubble bursts. The opposing position puts less weight on the costs of bubble bursting and emphasizes the damage done by asset prices that are out of line with fundamentals. Demirgüç-Kunt and Serven (2010) review the pros and cons of using monetary policy to rein in asset bubbles. It would seem that some proactivity on the part of the central banks is especially important to the extent that countercyclical capital or provisioning requirements cannot be relied on to do that job.

Outside of the monetary policy area, perhaps the first way to limit the procyclicality of lending would be to reduce or eliminate features of the regulatory system that encourage it. Risk-based capital requirements are an example: because minimum capital holdings are based on a risk weighted average, factors that depress estimates of risk during booms and elevate them during recessions make capital requirements more procyclical than, for example, a simple and time-invariant leverage requirement. Using models with few years of data, or basing risk weights on ratings that might be higher in boom times than in recessions encourages procyclicality. And ratings do appear to be procyclical – as for example in the 1994 Mexican crisis, the 1997–99 East Asian crisis, and in the current one. In all cases, ratings stayed high until after difficulties were widely known. Consequently, the many requirements that different fund managers (e.g., those of pension funds) only hold rated instruments introduces some procyclicality. Ending the reliance of regulation on risk weights and ratings would thus help lessen procyclicality (see Caprio, Demirgüç-Kunt, and Kane, 2008); somehow compelling the risk weights and ratings to be based on 'through the cycle' estimates of vulnerability would help as well.

Aside from removing sources of procyclicality, there are several ways for officials to use regulatory policy to 'lean against the wind' of a vigorous credit expansion. Perhaps the easiest way for regulatory authorities to intervene is on an ad hoc basis, meaning that as they see credit expansion and/or asset prices increasing beyond some rate (admittedly difficult to determine), they would attempt to slow credit expansion, perhaps beginning with the banks that are growing the fastest, by using discretionary limits on the expansion of their balance sheet. In effect by operating one by one on the most rapidly expanding banks, such discretionary intervention, if actually implemented, could serve both micro-prudential and macro-prudential ends. However, as suggested earlier, discretionary supervision may not be dependable. Although US bank supervisors are quick to point to the role of non-bank financial intermediaries, such as investment banks and AIG (the American Insurance Group, which wrote credit default swaps (CDS) covering many securities that later experienced losses), in the current crisis, a number of large commercial banks clearly had excessive levels of leverage and needed access to government funds through a variety of channels. The malfunctioning of discretionary supervision in the US S&L crisis, which prompted the FDICIA legislation, provides some support for making regulatory interventions both automatic and easy to monitor, so that whether regulations are being enforced or not is readily apparent. As we will discuss in the last section, however, the fact that FDICIA malfunctioned in the current crisis might serve as a warning against putting too much stock on seemingly automatic policy levers.

It should be noted that supervisory breakdowns were not exclusive to the United States. High leverage – 20 or 30-to-1, or higher – also plagued banks in a number of high and middle-income countries (Barth, et al. 2006). Moreover, while much 'toxic waste,' the impaired securities that have been so widely vilified in this crisis, originated in the US, much was purchased by European and other non-US institutions. True, the securities largely were AAA-rated, but they were paying interest rates above other AAA securities. Which supervisory agency asked why this was the case and forced their institutions to hold additional capital against them? Apparently the answer is that none did so.

More concrete, formulaic means of interventions recently have been suggested to put regulation on automatic pilot. One way would be to have the models that either banks or supervisors use in setting minimum capital requirements be more conservative in the default probabilities that are employed. This could be accomplished for example by estimating default probabilities over entire business cycles, or even over (or giving extra weight to) the worst parts of business cycles; either method would generate higher default probabilities and therefore higher minimum capital holdings compared with the run up to the current crisis, when banks were able to use data from only the positive phase of the business cycle. To be sure, capital levels might still be insufficient; for example capital levels based on relatively short and mild recessions (such as 2001) would be insufficient for sharper slowdowns. More generally, there is a clear issue as to the optimum length of time over which models should be estimated and how safe society wants is banking system. If banks regard default probabilities as sufficiently high, they might choose not to lend to any but the very safest firms or in the limit just to the government, thereby limiting economic development and access to credit. This issue is revisited in the penultimate section below.

One method for dealing with an increase in systemic risk has been proposed by Adrian and Brunnermeier (2009), namely by measuring risk spillovers and tail risk correlations. As noted above, much of the focus of supervision and regulation prior to the current crisis has been on individual banks, and much attention has been on their assets, with much less to the asset-liability mismatches, let alone cross-institution risk. Adrian and Brunnermeier instead come up with essentially a series of measures that attempt to gauge an institution's contribution to systemic risk, or the value at risk of the financial sector given that an individual institution is at risk or in financial distress. They propose that institutions that contribute more to systemic risk should face greater regulation and/or restrictions. This very recent suggestion certainly looks to be worthy of more research.

Another proposal (Brunnermeier, Crockett, Goodhart, Persaud, and Shin, 2009, or henceforth BCGPS) is to make capital requirements a function not just of micro-prudential factors but of macro factors as well. BCGPS propose multiplying the basic minimum capital ratio, however derived (e.g., by Basel), by a factor that reflects leverage, maturity mismatches, and credit and asset prices. Although they state 'Highly levered and fast growing "systemic" *institutions* would be subject to higher capital requirements than the rest' (p. 31), they clearly intend that their multiplication factor would vary with macro indicators, and would be larger (greater than unity) during boom periods and smaller (less than unity) during slowdowns in credit growth and asset price increases. Thus their multiplier would presumably take account of economy-wide leverage and mismatches, in addition to overall asset prices and credit growth.

As explicated below, a different proposal, which has been adopted by the Spanish authorities, is to have banks build their provisions when credit is expanding rapidly. Provisions are the funds that banks set aside to take account of expected losses. As Borio, Furfine, and Lowe (2001) point out, from an economist's view, the economic value of a loan is the face amount less any provisions, which, as the difference between the face value of the loan and its current value, should equal the discounted value of losses minus the present value of any default premium that the bank collects.[3] The implication is that all future profits and losses matter, not just those in the current period. Accountants, whose primary concern is with the interpretation of accounts by shareholders, only look at the current period; hence their view is that provisions need to reflect what has actually happened, not what might occur. Accountants' focus is measuring accurately net income period by period, and contrasts sharply with the supervisory view (and certainly the view from a deposit insurance agency) that banks should be aggressively provisioning so as to avoid losses in the

---

[3] Borio et al. also note that if the risk premium is sufficient, there may be no need to set aside provisions.

future. As Wall and Koch (2000) mention, supervisors can demand additional information from banks, whereas most actual and potential shareholders cannot; in the absence of additional information, it will be difficult for shareholders to weigh the different future scenarios, hence the accountants' attitude (given their role in protecting the accuracy of accounts for current and potential shareholders) in focusing on what has materialized. Still, from the economist's view, if banks' provisions are less than their true expected losses, then their capital is overstated and potentially misleads investors and creditors.

Capital, on the other hand, is there to absorb unexpected losses. To be sure, there is a grey line separating expected and unexpected losses, due to the uncertainty of the distribution of various risks and the confidence interval applied. Still, countercyclical provisioning appeals to economists and supervisors – in effect it is a way of taking account of the finding that credit standards demonstrably deteriorate during booms and that credit then goes to riskier and less collateralized borrowers (Jimenez and Saurina, 2006).

Countercyclical Regulation in Practice

Although no country thus far has adopted a countercyclical capital requirement policy, as recommended by Brunnermeier et al. (2009), a few have been adopting countercyclical provisioning. The Spanish authorities were the first to do so, followed by Colombia and much more recently (November, 2008) Peru. In this section we will look at the first two cases in order to understand how countercyclical features were implemented. As will become clear with the individual descriptions, it is at best too soon, and the cases are too few, to put much weight on them as models for others. Section four will consider reasons why countercyclical measures might not be as effective as those who have designed them intend.

The Spanish example

The Spanish authorities first adopted the so-called statistical or dynamic provisioning in 2000, in part because of their loss of control of the money supply due to their membership in the Euro zone. Although authorities in other countries that are not in common currency areas at least have the option to 'lean against the wind' when asset prices begin rising sharply, Spanish authorities do not enjoy this ability; monetary policy is decided by the ECB and Euro zone conditions, not just those in Spain, will dominate policy decisions. Moreover, studies showed that Spain experienced sharply procyclical credit growth since the 1960s (Fernandez de Lis and Garcia Herrero, 2009). Jimenez and Saurina (2006) also found strong evidence that over the period 1984–2002 credit standards declined during booms, both in regard to the screening of borrowers – riskier projects/borrowers getting financing – and in the share of loans that were collateralized. Thus lending was both expanding and simultaneously deteriorating in quality, just as many bank supervisors had long asserted occurred in booms.

The attempt to reduce lending procyclicality began in July of 2000 with the creation of a new category of provisions, statistical provisions, which were merely added on to generic and specific provisions. Then in 2004, in order to deal with concerns from accountants, as noted in the discussion in the previous section, the system was modified so that statistical provisions were subsumed into generic provisions, which were set as Generic provisions = $\alpha \Delta$ Credit + β Credit-Specific provisions, where α is bounded by 0 and 2.5, and β by 0 and 1.64 (Fernandez de Lis and Garcia Herrero, 2009).

The first term, $\alpha \Delta$ Credit, captures what are normally termed general provisions, that is a small portion of all new loans is set aside to cover losses. The second term takes into account longer-term factors, and these calculations are done for each class of loan risk.

In setting β, bank assets were assigned different risk weights; alternatively, banks could use their own internal models to set these weights, subject to supervisory oversight. However, statistical provisions depended on the difference between a measure of 'latent exposure' (that is, losses that might emerge on the banks' balance sheets in the future, but which are not recognized by traditional accounting systems) and specific provisions (these due to specific problems already identified). Thus latent exposure depends in part on the credit cycle, and statistical provisions can be positive or negative. Statistical provisions accumulate in a fund and are limited to between zero and three times latent risk (Poveda, 2000, and Fernandez de Lis and Garcia Herrero,

2009). As can be seen in Figure 14.1, in the initial years, the impact on total provisions was modest, as statistical provisions were partly offset by a decrease in specific provisions.

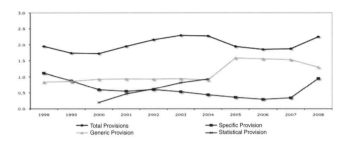

Source: Banking Supervision Report 2001–2008 and Statistical Bulletin, Bank of Spain

Figure 14.1 Provisions as Share of Total Credit (%)

Not surprisingly, there was resistance to statistical provisioning from the banks, as bankers felt that it made them less competitive, presumably because it entailed lower stated profits compared with those of banks in other regulatory jurisdictions. This claim is difficult to evaluate. At the level of the banking system, as seen above, the increase in provisions is tiny. Bankers could argue that it was reducing their profits and potentially making it more costly to issue stock (because their stated profits would look bad relative to other European banks not using statistical provisioning), but one would think that the dullest stockholder would see through to the underlying values, and realize that other banks would be underprovisioned compared with Spanish banks (again, to the extent that the effects were judged significant). And Spanish banks could help the market understand their positions better by disclosing more information about their statistical models and how they were being applied.

Some are quick to declare the Spanish system a success (Griffith-Jones and Ocampo, 2009, and *Wall Street Journal*, November 10, 2008), however it is still too soon to see how the Spanish financial system will fare in this crisis. An IMF report showed that as of 2005, Spain had a much higher ratio of provisions to NPLs, compared with other high-income countries, but the issue is how well the latter are estimated. Housing prices rose even more dramatically in Spain than they did in the U.S., growing by a factor of 2.5 over the period from 2000 to their peak in March of 2008 (Bank of Spain). As seen in Figure 14.2, total debt in Spanish financial institutions rose by a comparable amount. Moreover, the relationship between credit and GDP does not seem to have changed in the years following the adoption of countercyclical provisioning.

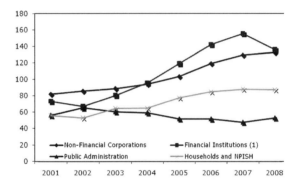

Source: Banking Supervision Report 2001–2008 and Statistical Bulletin, Bank of Spain

Figure 14.2 Total Debt in Spain (% of GDP)

As of June 2009, the latest estimate by the head of the Spanish Savings Bank Association was that loan losses were expected to more than double to over nine percent in 2010, from four percent in 2009; according to the same report, a rise of NPLs to ten percent of assets would put about 20 banks below the minimum eight percent capital ratio.[4] What is not yet clear is the extent to which the housing boom was financed through the banking system and how much larger a decline of housing prices – which fell by about seven percent in the year ending in March 2009 – will occur by the end of the crisis.

---

[4] See Thomson Reuters, UPDATE 2: CECA says Spanish banks may post losses in 2010, June 17, 2009.

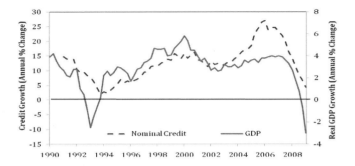

Source: Bank of Spain and National Institute of Statistics

Figure 14.3 Nominal Credit and GDP Growth (%)

Importantly, even if the Spanish banking system fares well during this cycle, it is by no means clear that their provisioning system is or would be the principal cause. First, as noted above, Spanish banks had been through their own serious crisis in the early 1980s and then experienced a series of losses related to their Latin American exposure in the 1990s and early 2000s. Banks traditionally become more risk averse following crises – as the world is discovering in the current one! – and tend to reduce the rate of growth of lending (and/or provision more conservatively), even when regulatory policy is being relaxed. Second, similar to Canada, Spanish authorities adopted a relatively conservative position related to securitization, so that off-balance sheet securitization accounts for less than seven percent of total securitization (Fernandez de Lis and Garcia Herrero, 2009) and involves far less complicated instruments than in the United States. This policy change could easily have been more important in reducing the scope of the crisis in Spain, compared with a realistic counterfactual. Third, there may be other regulatory and supervisory factors, should Spanish banks emerge from this crisis in better condition than those elsewhere, that account for their better performance. Thus Canadian banks, which seem to be faring well, do not have a system of countercyclical provisioning, yet seem to be among the better performing banking systems in the OECD region, notwithstanding the economic performance of their neighbor. Among the factors that could account for their relative stability are a higher franchise value (less competition), less financial innovation, avoidance of policies to encourage home ownership (though with the same home ownership rate as in the United States), and a policy of not allowing capital relief to banks who purchased CDS. In sum, *aficionados* of the Spanish approach must acknowledge a serious identification problem and be less quick to claim victory for countercyclical provisioning.

Colombia[5]

Authorities in Colombia adopted in 2002 a System for the Administration of Credit Risk (SARC), which is a collection of rules, procedures, methodologies, tools, knowledge, and human and physical capital aimed at the understanding, measurement and control of credit risk. According to the current legislation, expected losses related to credit risk have to be overcome using general or specific provisioning on the exposed portfolio, with expected losses estimated using the internal evaluation model(s) of each bank. The system explicitly acknowledges that provisioning should consider countercyclical adjustments, per the discussion of section two above. Interestingly, countercyclical provisioning can be performed either on an individual or a general basis. Prior to the adoption of SARC, provisioning in Colombia appeared to be firmly procyclical as seen in Figure 14.4; for example, provisions declined in the years after 1998 when growth was relatively strong and soared in the subsequent recession. Initially, legislation merely permitted countercyclical provisioning but did not require it or even define how it could be implemented.[6] As seen in

---

[5] This section draws on reports and circulars from the Banco de la Republica (2008, 2009), Fedesarrollo (2009), and Martinez, Pineda, and Salamanca (2005).

[6] Though intended to commence in 2003, the SARC had several revisions, extending the period that was allowed for institutions to present their internal models and to comply with the required data dissemination standards. There were difficulties in the construction of the internal models between 2003 and 2005 and on January 1st 2005 the Superintendencia Financiera de Colombia (SFC) presented a transition model or benchmark model for risk assessment while the internal models were evaluated and approved. The 2005 benchmark model included the use of countercyclical provisions but it did not have an explicit methodology for its use. In 2007 the SARC was modified and amended with a benchmark model for the constitution of countercyclical provisions for commercial credit only, and the following year a benchmark

Figure 14.5, provisioning behavior changes markedly in 2005, even though the system was still not mandatory. It is not clear if there was any attempt at 'moral suasion' on the part of the authorities to achieve this result.

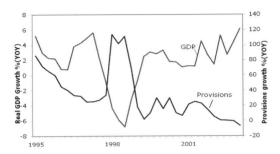

Figure 14.4 Provisions and GDP Growth (Before SARC implementation)

As with the Spanish system, the Colombian approach defines latent losses for each loan based on outstanding exposures and average provisions (over the previous cycle) for each credit category. In accordance with the 2005 measures, to the extent that latent losses are below provisions (calculated on each credit category), banks can put the difference into a fund, on which they can draw when losses rise above provisions. Specific provisions were split into two categories: individual provisions (IP) and individual countercyclical provisions (IPC). Thus the provisioning scheme can be summarized as follows:

$$TP_{i,t} = GP_t + IP_{i,t}(s_{i,t}) + IPC_{i,t}(s_{i,t}) \qquad (14.1)$$

where TP are the total provisions of category *i*, GP are the general provisions which remained at one percent of the portfolio, IP are the individual or specific provisions for credit category *i* calculated using the internal risk model and IPC are the countercyclical adjustment of the individual provisions within the credit category, for time t.

---

model was introduced for consumption credit lines. Thus between 2005 and 2007 the countercyclical scheme was voluntary.

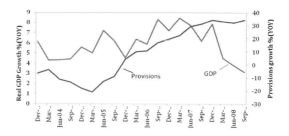

Figure 14.5 Provisions and GDP Growth (After SARC implementation)

Since the IP and IPC are state dependent, $s_{i,t}$ is an index capturing the current state of the economy, and each bank has to use a different set of parameters in their internal risk model to assess the amount of provisioning required. By construction, individual provisions are pro-cyclical, because in the expansionary phase of the cycle, credit risk – both the probability of default and the loss given default – will be overshadowed by the favorable environment and thus provisions will be moderate to low. To avoid an unnecessary tightening in provisions when the economy deteriorates, the IPC component is calculated during the expansionary phase using the parameters consistent with the bad state of nature and thus increasing total provisions before the downturn. When economic conditions worsen, IPC is set at zero and the bank can use the saved resources during the expansion to make up for the IP, thus reducing the burden of provisioning when the economy is contracting. By being able to determine the benchmark model and to define the state of the economy (and transition matrices), the authorities retain tight control of the system, so that provisioning behavior is not quite on automatic pilot.

Notwithstanding this control, as in the case of Spain, there was some substitution, as general provisions declined to offset some of the increase in countercyclical provisions (Figure 14.6). Overall credit growth in Colombia did decelerate markedly – from 34 percent in the year ending in March 2007 to 18 percent by December 2008. Again, however, a variety of factors played a role in the change, not least of which was a nearly 400 basis points tightening in the reference interest rate set by the central bank, as well as the global credit crunch and slowdown in trade that would have made banks more risk averse.

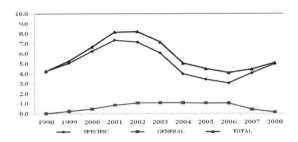

Figure 14.6 Columbia: Provisions as Share of Total Credit (%)

Overall, then, the experience of Spain and Colombia has to be judged as limited and a weak basis for other countries in deciding to adopt countercyclical policy. As we will see in the next section, there are good reasons for this ambiguity.

Limitations and Concerns Regarding Countercyclical Requirements

'If you entrench yourself behind strong fortifications, you compel the enemy to seek a solution elsewhere.' von Clausewitz

While some attempt to induce banks to build up capital or provisions in good times, and thus restrain the pace of their lending in a boom, is appealing, there are several reasons to be skeptical that such regulations will be effective, as well as some potential problems about their implementation. Regarding their efficacy, a serious concern is that the theoretical and empirical case for the effectiveness of countercyclical capital (and provisioning) requirements is weak. As numerous authors have noted, there is no theoretical consensus that higher capital ratios will reduce risk-taking behavior.[7] Many experts in the field have argued that higher capital requirements could induce risk-taking behavior to the extent

---

[7] See Barth, Caprio, and Levine (2006) for a short summary.

that shareholders and/or managers target some rate of return and that supervisors cannot monitor banks effectively or on a timely basis. The latter assumption would be difficult to dispute after the current crisis. So according to theory, raising capital requirements – which is what countercyclical capital requirements would do during boom times – could lead to an increase or a decrease in the risk that banks undertake. The issue is the adjustments that banks can make when the minimum required capital ratio is above that which they judge to be optimal, which is when they might have the incentive to engage in riskier activities.

Nor is there evidence that higher capital requirements lead to greater banking system stability. Barth, Caprio, and Levine (2006) assemble a large cross-country database on regulation and supervision and, among their other findings, see no evidence that the stringency of capital requirements have any impact on the stability of the banking system. A number of researchers have investigated these data and have not overturned this conclusion. Moreover, Laeven and Levine (2011) find that bank risk taking varies directly with the concentration of ownership among shareholders – in those countries with less (more) concentrated ownership, higher capital requirements result in greater (less) risk taking by banks, which provides confirmation of the ambiguous result obtained by Barth, Caprio, and Levine, and of the stalemate in the theoretical literature. Although there have not been tests on cross-country data about the stringency of provisioning requirements (in Barth, Caprio and Levine, provisioning is treated as part of their index of supervisory powers), conceptually provisions are similar to capital and therefore it is expected that the same empirical result would govern; compelling banks to set aside more provisions than they deem optimal should lead to the same behavior as forcing them to hold capital in excess of their optimal levels.

To be sure, the aforementioned empirical work holds for the range of capital regulation seen around the world in recent years; if in adopting countercyclical capital requirements, countries would effectively raise capital ratios in boom times to levels well outside the range in the data, then it is possible that there could be some effect. Perhaps for example if in a boom minimum capital requirements were raised from eight percent to 20 percent or 30 percent, it might be difficult for banks to take sufficiently large risks to offset this change. On the other hand, experience in the recent crisis belies this point –

after all, some banks were able to take leverage from a supposed limit of 12.5 to one to about 30 to one. Moreover, substantial changes in capital requirements of this magnitude likely will prove to be difficult politically – and Barth, Caprio and Levine (2006) also found that political factors are critical in determining the type of regulation that is implemented.

In effect, reliance on countercyclical provisioning or capital requirements is similar to depending on risk-based deposit insurance premia to rein in risk taking in banks. Here the idea was that if banks were made to pay for their increased risktaking through higher deposit insurance premia (similar to paying through higher provisions), they would take less risk. However, the difficulty is that it was hard to measure banks' risk, and bankers also may have had an influence on the legislation adopted in the countries that tried this experiment. The result was that the differences in premia appeared small relative to differences in risk profiles, and indeed in cases such as the United States, other features of deposit insurance legislation overrode attempts to used risk-based pricing – in this case, the feature of the US law that limited the size of the total premia collected meant that in fact for a number of years leading into the crisis, all banks were paying the identical premium – zero! Thus even if countercyclical provisioning or capital requirements survive other critiques, it would be unwise to rely on them to stabilize the banking system.

In addition to theory and related empirical work, there is much experience in finance with regulatory avoidance. Inasmuch as it is precisely in booms when, for all of the reasons noted in the second section (disaster myopia, etc.), banks want to lend and borrowers want access to credit, there will be great pressure to evade regulations that attempt to restrict lending in good times. This so-called boundary problem in finance has existed for as long as there has been a formal financial sector. For example, usury restrictions in Medieval times in Western Europe made it profitable to find ways around limitations on the payment of interest, leading to the creation of bills of exchange – selling a piece of paper (receiving funds) today with the agreement to buy it back (repay funds) in the future at a specified higher price (the difference being the interest rate). In the present context, countercyclical capital or provisioning requirements would be expected to induce banks to try to conceal or shift their lending, much as current capital requirements with differential risk weights led to the creation of off-balance sheet vehicles so as to allow banks to shed higher risk exposure and to leverage themselves well above levels consistent with existing requirements. In the above discussion on Spain, we do not know the extent to which such concealment or avoidance behavior was occurring, though the boom in real estate prices and in the growth of total debt make it likely that some avoidance was operating. [8]

Goodhart and Persaud, in their January 30, 2008 op-ed in the *Financial Times*, acknowledge that some shifting to NBFIs will occur and that some steps will be necessary to deal with this behavior, but they do not specify how this will be accomplished.

When countercyclical requirements are most binding is precisely when the *short-term* profits from lending would be the greatest. As long as banks have in place compensation systems that reward volume and short-term profits – generating new loans, bundling them in securities, etc. – one would expect that this pressure would be particularly intense. Thus if compensation systems do not change, it is unrealistic to expect that bank behavior would change. To be sure, specific regulatory changes from this crisis might well limit some forms of risk taking, but the history of finance (and the von Clausewitz quote at the start of this section) suggest that others will be invented. Thus it seems important to consider some regulatory response to the compensation issue (Caprio, 2009).

Another form of the boundary issue of course is that we would expect to see nonbanks take on some of the activity of banks to the extent that countercyclical requirements were binding. In this sense, as Goodhart (2009) notes, to the extent that the NBFIs are unregulated or less regulated, it could lead to more serious crises. Indeed, that type of interplay between more and less regulated parts of the financial sector has been key to understanding the present crisis – the practically nonexistent regulation of investment banks and of instruments such as CDS were important ingredients underlying its magnitude. The traditional response to these concerns is that institutions in the unregulated sector can be allowed to fail. However, another lesson of the current crisis is that when NBFIs grow sufficiently large, they will be rescued. Moreover, with less holdings

---

[8] See Brunnermeier, Crockett, Goodhart, Persaud, and Shin (2009) and Goodhart (2008) for an excellent discussion of the boundary problem.

of liquid assets, banks increasingly are linked through a variety of markets and instruments to NBFIs, so avoiding a rescue when the latter are in distress will be especially difficult. Thus to the extent that credit moves out of the banking system during booms, some type of regulation and supervision would seem necessary.

Goodhart (2009) has proposed '...to limit the periods in which regulation is effectively biting to those few in which it is essential, so that the overall costs of such regulation are reduced, and hence the incentive to avoid it is lessened' (p. 110). Although this is a clever idea, banks surely will see the danger it poses to their ability to leverage themselves when it most appears profitable to do so. Countercyclical provisioning and capital requirements have no or little cost[9] during recessions – banks would be allowed to reduce provisions and/or capital then – yet their cost could be quite high during a boom. Indeed, the greater and longer the boom period, the higher the costs. Thus dealing with the boundary problem has to be counted as a serious implementation issue.

Notwithstanding these concerns, authorities that proceed to implement countercyclical requirements still need to consider how to vary them through the cycle or how to set through-the-cycle provisioning requirements. As noted above, part of the rationale for countercyclical requirements is that merely leaving the decision on a discretionary basis to supervisory authorities regarding varying provisions (or capital) is questionable given the political opposition that banks could be expected to muster when the macro cycle picks up. Moreover, supervisory agencies or departments (even within central banks) do not have much macroeconomic expertise, and if the discretion is lodged elsewhere, that is where political pressure will be brought to bear. Even if the decision were left to the monetary authorities, this would have the effect of exposing them to greater political pressure, which could compromise their independence.

Thus if countercyclical provisioning rules or capital requirements are to be relied on to restrain booms, then a formula must be devised to do so. Should requirements vary based on credit growth? If so, at what rate(s) should provisioning escalate? Or should they be based on

---

[9] Banks can easily reduce their provisions in contractions and expand them later. Reducing capital in recessions only to expand it later imposes some transactions costs.

asset prices? If so, which prices and what rate of change should set off an increase in the requirement? And suppose a technological improvement takes place that increases the steady state rate of economic growth and the demand for credit. Will authorities be willing and able to sit by and watch their formula choke off economic growth? These are merely some of the questions that must be answered before governments proceed down the path of countercyclical requirements.

Finally, authorities implementing countercyclical requirements should understand that the effect could be asymmetric. It is possible that raising capital or provisioning requirements might have some effect during a boom, in particular if the increases were substantial – though really large increases were not seen in Spain and Colombia, and would undoubtedly engender significant political opposition. However, it is less likely that lowering these requirements would be effective in an economic slowdown. As is well known in the credit view of monetary policy, several transmission channels operate through credit markets that hamper attempts to encourage banks to lend (again, as seen in this crisis). As a slowdown takes hold and asset prices fall, borrowers' net worth declines, making them a less attractive target for bank loans. The value of collateral also declines, with the same effect, raising the cost of credit intermediation for the banks and cutting loan supply. Bank net worth would also decline as losses increase, reinforcing this effect. And banks' risk aversion would rise, for example if managers that had been encouraging expansion during a boom were removed and replaced by more conservative bankers.[10] In fact, by late 2009 it seems clear that banks are holding significant amounts of resources in short-term public debt that is paying a near-zero rate of return, rather than increasing their lending. Since loan provisioning is not the binding constraint, it is difficult to believe that easing provisioning further would stimulate lending. Instead, policy interventions that reduced risk premia (improvements in information, perhaps greater government spending) might be more successful in stimulating lending.

For all of these reasons, it would be risky to think that easing provisioning or capital requirements in a slowdown would be met with

---

[10] See Kuttner and Mosser (2002) for a good discussion of the various transmission channels.

an increase in lending. To the extent that countercyclical measures are only effective in the tightening phase – and there are good reasons to doubt even this effect – policy makers might save themselves the dilemmas as to how to set the formula for when and by how much requirements would increase and decrease, and instead just implement a simple leverage requirement. Stated alternatively, Goodhart's point on minimizing the pain from regulation might mislead authorities: although banks surely would oppose being forced to raise capital during a boom, when it might be difficult politically to do so, many banks would enjoy having higher capital ratios and/or provisions during a slowdown.

Conclusions and Advice for Developing Countries

The view that regulation should be more countercyclical certainly is appealing in light of the evidence that banking tends to be procyclical. And the appeal of using 'speed bumps,' meaning limits on credit expansion when asset prices appear to be rising well beyond what fundamentals suggest, would seem to be a useful approach for regulatory authorities. Since discretionary intervention by supervisors has not worked well in recent bubbles, some attempt to put regulation on automatic pilot, forcing banks to add to their capital or provisions in boom times and reduce the same in a bust, has much appeal. Two proposals are under consideration in various fora: to vary either minimum capital requirements or provisions on a countercyclical basis, the former being untried but recommended by an impressive group of experts and the latter being the methods used in Spain and Colombia.

The advantage of these proposals is that the current crisis has revealed the limitations of a static approach to regulation, which market participants will evade over time, much the same as the way in which the German army dealt with the Maginot line by going over and around it. Thus a more dynamic approach to regulation is laudable.

Unfortunately, as reviewed above, there is a dearth of theory, evidence, or practical experience that would support countercyclical regulatory requirements. While the Spanish and Colombian examples are cited favorably, it is important to recognize that neither case showed a clear ability to rein in or reduce an asset bubble. Before the regulatory community rushes off to adopt countercyclical regulation, it would be useful to understand the forces that led to the failure of the previous intellectual fad, namely the prompt corrective action features of FDICIA, and how these forces would be contained in preventing the failure of countercyclical regulation.[11] Although some would hold that ideology accounted for the failure of FDICIA and the crisis in the U.S., they would also have to explain the failure of discretionary supervision in Iceland, Ireland, the United Kingdom, Spain, and numerous Eastern European and some Central Asian countries, where asset bubbles and sharp increases in credit also occurred.

While waiting for more evidence on countercyclical regulation, what should developing country authorities do? First, as noted above, if countercyclical provisioning is not certain to reduce significantly the procyclicality of the banking system, then monetary authorities still must plan on using monetary policy to burst incipient asset bubbles before they get out of hand. Certainly improving the quality of information and a focus on incentives in the financial system should continue to be a high priority. Supervisors have a clear job in this process, both in compelling disclosure as well as verifying the accuracy of information. Also, authorities should look to removing or limiting procyclical features of the regulatory system, as noted above. Both ratings and internal models, underpinnings of pillar one of Basel II, accentuated procyclicality in the recent boom and bust cycle (Caprio, Demirgüç-Kunt, and Kane, 2008). To the extent that developing countries move in the direction of risk modeling, compelling banks to use more than a few years of data is critical, as are other attempts to take account of how assets will perform in the contractionary phase of the business cycle. Reliance on rated instruments in industrial countries amounted to an outsourcing of regulation – and was procyclical as well. Requirements for holding rated instruments need to be removed from legislation, so that fund managers can face civil lawsuits should they deviate from following the best fiduciary standards. Without officially-approved ratings organizations offering their highest rating on complex securities, it is

---

[11] The other notable fad is the drive to consolidate regulation in a single agency. Although the balkanization of regulation is blamed for the US crisis, the UK FSA is also viewed as having failed.

unlikely that banks would have been able to sell many of their loans in the run-up to the current crisis. For developing countries, this will mean much less reliance on securitization, compared to what was in place in many industrial economies up to the crisis. Moving to a simple leverage requirement, rather than a more complex risk weighting system for capital regulation, will help reduce the procyclicality of regulation.

Lastly, authorities should focus more attention on incentives in the financial sector. Banks will be more likely to hold more provisions and capital when it is in their self-interest to do so, which requires uninsured creditors – those who actually believe that they will lose money if banks take excessive risk – to help in the process of disciplining banks. Incentives also matter for regulators; despite much talk of holding regulators accountable, the consequences for them in the current crisis have been limited. Greater disclosure of the information available to regulators is a requirement if this is to happen. And if regulators are not accountable, why should we expect to be spared from serious crises in the future?

References

Adrian, T. and M. Brunnermeier (2009), 'CoVar,' mimeo.

Banco de la República (2008), 'Informe de Estabilidad Financiera,' and various circulars, Bogotá, Colombia.

Banco de la República (2009), 'Informe de Estabilidad Financiera' Bogotá, Colombia.

Barth, J.R., G. Caprio, Jr. and R. Levine (2006), *Rethinking Bank Regulation: Till Angels Govern*. New York: Cambridge University Press.

Borio, C., C. Furfine and P. Lowe (2001), 'Procyclicality of the Financial System and Financial Stability: issues and policy options,' in BIS *Marrying the macro- and micro-prudential dimensions of financial stability*, Policy Paper No. 1, March.

Brunnermeier, M.K. (2009), 'Deciphering the Liquidity and Credit Crunch 2007–2008,' *Journal of Economic Perspectives*, Winter, **23**(1).

Brunnermeier, M.K., A. Crockett, C. Goodhart, A. Persaud and H. Shin (2009), 'The Fundamental Principles of Financial Regulation,' *Geneva Reports on the World Economy*, 11.

Caprio, G. (1997), 'Safe and Sound Banking in Developing Countries: We're Not in Kansas Anymore,' in G. Kaufman (ed.), *FDICIA: Bank Reform Five Years Later and Five Years Ahead*, JAI Press, December.

Caprio, G. (2009), 'Financial Regulation in a Changing World: Lessons from the Recent Crisis,' Paper prepared for the VII Colloquium on 'Financial Collapse: How are the Biggest Nations and Organizations Managing the Crisis?' October 2, 2009 Ravenna.

Caprio, G., A. Demirgüç-Kunt and E. Kane (2008), 'The 2007 Meltdown in Structured Securitization: Searching for Lessons not Scapegoats,' World Bank Policy Research Working Paper 4756, November and forthcoming, *World Bank Research Observer*, 2010.

Demirgüç-Kunt, A. and L. Serven (2010), 'Are All the Sacred Cows Dead? Implications of the Financial Crisis for Macro and Financial Policies,' forthcoming, *World Bank Policy Research Observer*.

Fedesarrollo (2009) 'Regulación financiera y provisiones anti-cíclicas' en Tendencia Económica, No 89 – Febrero, 2009.

Fernandez de Lis, S. and A. Garcia Herrero (2009), 'The Spanish Regulatory Approach to Procyclicality: Dynamic Provisioning and Other Tools,' BBVA Economic Research Department, No. 0904, February.

Financial Services Authority (2009), 'The Turner Review: A regulatory response to the global banking crisis,' March.

Goodhart, C. (2008), 'The Regulatory Response to the Financial Crisis,' mimeo, LSE Financial Markets Group Paper Series, February.

Goodhart, C. and A. Persaud (2008), 'A party pooper's guide to financial stability,' Letter to the Editor, *The Financial Times*, June 4.

Gorton, G. (2009), 'Slapped in the Face by the Invisible Hand: Banking and the Panic of 2007,' Paper prepared for the Federal Reserve Bank of Atlanta's 2009 Financial Markets Conference: Financial Innovation and Crisis, May 11–13, 2009, mimeo.

Greenlaw, D., J. Hatzius, A.K. Kashyap, H. Song Shin (2008), 'Leveraged Losses: Lessons from the Mortgage Market Meltdown,' paper prepared for US Monetary Policy Forum Conference,' February.

Griffith-Jones, S. and J.A. Ocampo (2009), 'Building on the Counter-cyclical Consensus: A Policy Agenda,' Initiative for Policy Dialogue, October.

Guttentag, J.M. and R.J. Herring (1986), 'Disaster Myopia in International Banking.' *Princeton Essays in International Finance*, No. 164, September.

Jimenez, G. and J. Saurina (2006), 'Credit Cycles, Credit Risk, and Prudential Regulation,' *International Journal of Central Banking*, 2(2), June, 65–98.

Keynes, J.M. (1932), 'The Consequences to the Banks of the Collapse of Money Values,' in *Essays in Persuasion*, New York, New Jersey, USA: Harcourt, Brace, and Co.

Kindleberger, C.P. (1978), *Manias, Panics, and Crashes: A History of Financial Crises*, New York: John Wiley and Sons.

Kohn, D. (2008), 'Monetary Policy and Asset Prices Revisited,' mimeo.

Kuttner, K. and P. Mosser (2002), 'The Monetary Transmission Mechanism: Some Answers and Further Questions,' Federal Reserve Bank, Economic Policy Review, 8(1).

Laeven, L. and R. Levine (2011), 'Bank governance, regulation and risk taking,' *Journal of Financial Economics*, forthcoming.

Martinez O., F. Pineda and D. Salamanca (2005), 'Esquema de provisiones anti-cíclicas para Colombia' in Informe de Estabilidad Financiera, 2005. Banco de la República. Bogotá, Colombia.

Minsky, H.P. (1986), *Stabilizing an Unstable Economy*, New Haven: Yale University Press.

Posen, A.S. (2006), 'Why Central Banks Should Not Burst Bubbles,' Peterson Institute for International Economics Working Paper No. 06-01.

Poveda, R. (2000), 'Reform of the System of Insolvency Provisions,' Speech given at the APD, Madrid, 18 January.

Rajan, R. (2006), 'Has Financial Development Made the World Riskier?' *European Financial Management,* 12(499).

Reinhart, C. and K. Rogoff (2008), 'This Time is Different: A Panoramic View of Eight Centuries of Financial Crises,' mimeo.

Roubini, N. (2005), 'Why Central Banks Should Burst Bubbles,' mimeo.

Temin, P. and H.J. Voth (2004), 'Riding the South Sea Bubble,' *American Economic Review*, **94**(5).

Tversky, A. and D. Kahneman (1981), 'The Framing of Decisions and the Psychology of Choice,' *Science*, New Series, **211**(4481), 453–458.

Wall, L. and T. Koch (2000), 'Bank Loan-Loss Accounting: A Review of Theoretical and Empirical Evidence,' Federal Reserve Bank of Atlanta Economic Review, Second Quarter.

15. Quality of Financial Sector Regulation and Supervision Around the World

Martin Čihák and Alexander Tieman [1]

Introduction

How good is financial sector regulation and supervision around the world? That is a rather grand question, given that there are many different regulatory frameworks around the world, operating in different institutional environments. But it is a valid and important question, because the financial globalization made individual country financial systems much more closely linked, and differences in regulatory and supervisory quality can become exposed in a stressful situation, as illustrated in the recent global financial crisis.

This chapter addresses the question about the quality of regulation and supervision around the globe by using data from International Monetary Fund (IMF)–World Bank assessments of countries' compliance with international standards.[2] Unlike some of the existing databases and studies that collect only information on regulation and

[1] The views expressed in this paper are those of the authors and do not necessarily represent those of the IMF or IMF policy. The chapter is an updated and shortened version of Čihák and Tieman (2008). We would like to thank, without implicating, Jörg Decressin, Jennifer Elliott, Alessandro Giustiniani, Bernard Laurens, Jan-Willem van der Vossen, and Graham Colin-Jones for useful comments, Mark Swinburne for guidance, and Kalin Tintchev for research assistance. All remaining errors are our own.

[2] As used in this chapter, the term 'country' does not in all cases refer to a territorial entity that is a state as understood by international law and practice. As used here, the term also covers some territorial entities that are not states but for which statistical data are maintained on a separate and independent basis.

supervision 'on the books,' this study, by making use of the underlying data, can also assess the practical implementation of regulation and supervision.[3]

Our main findings are that (i) on average, countries' regulatory frameworks score one notch below full compliance with the standards (on a four-notch scale); (ii) per capita income is significantly linked to cross-country differences in regulatory quality; (iii) higher regulatory quality in banking is correlated with better banking sector performance; and (iv) there are substantial differences in regulatory quality across regions, some but not all of which can be explained by differences in economic development.

The finding that high-income countries are characterized by better supervisory structures needs to be put in a context. These countries tend to have more developed and more complex financial systems, and this is taken into account in the assessment process that leads to the gradings used in this chapter. Nonetheless, despite the higher grades, the supervisory frameworks in high-income countries clearly still leave much to be desired. Indeed, the recent global financial crisis illustrates that the higher quality of supervisory systems in many high-income countries has still been insufficient considering the complexity of their financial systems.

Measuring supervisory quality is a Herculean task. Regulation should aim at supporting the efficient allocation of resources across the economy in normal times. Arguably, the ultimate test of a well-functioning regulatory framework is whether it contributes to the financial system's intermediation capacity, while decreasing the likelihood and costs of systemic financial crises. However, achievement of these goals is next to impossible to measure, because they are either very broad ('efficient allocation') or involve analyzing causality in 'tail events.' This chapter uses an alternative approach to measuring regulatory quality: it analyzes the data from assessments of compliance with international standards aimed at identifying good supervisory practices. Specifically, we examine a unique dataset derived from assessments of regulatory and supervisory frameworks around the globe carried out under the IMF–World Bank Financial

---

[3] To economize on words, the subsequent text sometimes refers only to 'supervision' or 'supervisors' as a shorthand expression for 'regulation and supervision' and 'regulators and supervisors.'

Sector Assessment Program (FSAP). The FSAP has so far covered about two-thirds of the IMF's 185 member countries, and is therefore an important source of broadly comparable information on the quality of supervisory frameworks. This chapter analyzes the findings from the FSAP assessments in a comprehensive way, relying on a combination of quantitative and qualitative approaches.

Are international standards good measures of supervisory quality? A full theoretical discussion of what constitutes an optimal supervisory framework would go well beyond the scope of this chapter. In fact, rigorous theoretical work on what constitutes good prudential regulation and supervision is limited, especially for non-bank financial institutions, and remains a topic for future research.[4] For the purpose of this chapter, let us just say that we acknowledge at the outset that compliance scores do not necessarily give the full picture of supervisory quality, but nevertheless: (i) the standards assessments are results of detailed consultations among top international experts; (ii) the gradings have proven useful in previous research that tried to explain cross-country differences in financial sector performance (e.g., Podpiera, 2004).

The chapter contributes to the literature in two important ways: (i) it provides an analysis of prudential frameworks around the world that covers the practical implementation of regulation; and (ii) it covers all the key segments, i.e., banking, insurance, and securities regulation. Substantial work has been done on analyzing banking sector laws and regulations (in particular, through the work of Barth, Caprio, and Levine, 2006). However, that work has focused only on regulations 'on the books' and on those pertaining to banks. Regulatory quality is assessed in the World Bank governance database (Kaufman, Kraay, and Mastruzzi, 2007), but this is a survey-based broad measure of regulation in general, and does not specifically focus on financial sector regulation. A global analysis of the quality of regulation in the securities area was carried out by Carvajal and Elliot (2007); our chapter uses a similar dataset, but in addition to securities regulation also covers banking and insurance supervision.

---

[4] For banks, Dewatripont and Tirole (1994) provide an interesting analysis of an optimal 'outside intervention policy,' focusing on solvency ratios. A somewhat more general discussion of what constitutes optimal regulation is contained in Herring and Santomero (2000).

The structure of the chapter is as follows. Section two explains the data and methodology being used. Section three provides a basic overview of the data on compliance with the various core principles. Section four presents the results of the regression analysis that tries to explain the factors behind cross-country differences in regulatory quality. Section five analyzes some additional relevant findings from the FSAP program, which were not captured in the assessments of standards. Section six concludes.

Data and Methodology

To analyze the quality of regulation and supervision, this chapter uses data on countries' observance of internationally accepted standards in banking, insurance, and securities regulation ('standards'). The data are unique, because they reflect not only the laws and regulations 'on the books' (data on that are widely available, for example, through the work of Barth, Caprio, and Levine, 2006); their key feature is that they reflect also detailed expert assessments of the practical implementation 'in the field.'

The standards covered in this analysis are the Basel Core Principles for Effective Banking Supervision (BCP); the Insurance Core Principles (ICP), issued by the International Association of Insurance Supervisors (IAIS); and the International Organization of Securities Commissions' (IOSCO's) Objectives and Principles of Securities Regulation.[5] The BCP contains 25 Core Principles and the ICP and IOSCO standards also comprise a number of principles (Tables 15.1, 15.2, and 15.3). Although the terminology differs, the extent to which each principle in the three standards is observed is rated on a four-point scale, ranging from fully observed to nonobserved.[6] Most of the assessments used in the analysis were

---

[5] See http://www.imf.org/external/standards/index.htm for a full listing of the standards and other relevant materials.

[6] In addition to the principles for effective supervision, the standard-setters have also identified a number of 'preconditions,' which include the general policy, environmental conditions, and institutional infrastructure. In the BCP, these are discussed separately from the individual core principles, while in the ICP and IOSCO, they are incorporated into the code. We have not explicitly

Table 15.1 Banking Supervision Dictionary

Standard 1/	Basel Core Principles for Effective Banking Supervision (BCP)	
Principle No.	Topic	Component 2/
1	Objectives, Autonomy, Powers, And Resources	REG
2	Permissible Activities	PRF
3	Licensing Criteria	PRF
4	Ownership	PRF
5	Investment Criteria	REP
6	Capital Adequacy	REP
7	Credit Policies	REP
8	Loan Evaluation and Loan-Loss Provisioning	REP
9	Large Exposure Limits	REP
10	Connected Lending	REP
11	Country Risk	REP
12	Market Risks	REP
13	Other Risks	REP
14	Internal Control and Audit	REP
15	Money Laundering	FIN
16	On-Site and Off-Site Supervision	PRF
17	Bank Management Contact	PRF
18	Off-Site Supervision	PRF
19	Validation of Supervisory Information	REG
20	Consolidated Supervision	PRF
21	Accounting Standards	FIN
22	Remedial Measures	PRF
23	Globally Consolidated Supervision	PRF
24	Host Country Supervision	PRF
25	Supervision Over Foreign Banks' Establishment	PRF

1/ See http://www.imf.org/external/standards/index.htm for details on assessment methodology.

2/ See IMF (2004) for more details. REG is regulatory governance, PRF is prudential framework, REP are regulatory practices, and FIN is financial integrity and safety nets.

prepared as part of an FSAP, under which the gradings are normally confidential, and therefore the analysis in this chapter is presented so as to respect this confidentiality.[7] The sample comprises all countries for which formal assessments are available.

---

incorporated the banking system preconditions into the core principle gradings, but our subsequent analysis of governance variables suggests that incorporating cross-country differences in the preconditions into the analysis would reinforce our results.

[7] For the published assessments, see http://www.imf.org/external/standards/index.htm.

Table 15.2 Insurance Supervision Dictionary

Standard 1/	International Association of Insurance Supervisors Insurance Core Principles (ICP)	
Principle No.	Topic	Component 2/
	2000 IAIS standard	
1	Organisation of the supervisor	REG
2	Licensing	PRF
3	Changes in control	PRF
4	Corporate governance	PRF
5	Internal controls	PRF
6	Assets	REP
7	Liabilities	REP
8	Capital adequacy and solvency	PRF
9	Derivatives and off-balance sheet items	REP
10	Reinsurance	REP
11	Market conduct	FIN
12	Financial reporting	PRF
13	On-site inspection	PRF
14	Sanctions	REP
15	Cross-border business operations	PRF
16	Coordination and cooperation	REP
17	Confidentiality	PRF
	2003 IAIS standard	
1	Conditions for effective insurance supervision	REG
2	Supervisory objectives	REG
3	Supervisory authority	REG
4	Supervisory process	REG
5	Supervisory cooperation and information sharing	REP
6	Licensing	REP
7	Suitability of persons	REP
8	Changes in control and portfolio transfers	REP
9	Corporate governance	PRF
10	Internal control	PRF
11	Market analysis	REP
12	Reporting to supervisors and off-site monitoring	REP
13	On-site inspection	REP
14	Preventive and Corrective Measures	REP
15	Enforcement or sanctions	REP
16	Winding-up and exit from the market	REP
17	Group-wide supervision	REP
18	Risk assessment and management	PRF
19	Insurance activity	PRF
20	Liabilities	REP
21	Investments	REP
22	Derivatives and similar commitments	REP
23	Capital adequacy and solvency	PRF
24	Intermediaries	FIN
25	Consumer protection	FIN
26	Information, disclosure & transparency towards the market	FIN
27	Fraud	FIN
28	Anti-money laundering, combating the financing of terrorism (AML/CFT)	FIN

1/ See http://www.imf.org/external/standards/index.htm for details on assessment methodology.
2/ See IMF (2004) for more details. REG is regulatory governance, PRF is prudential framework, REP are regulatory practices, and FIN is financial integrity and safety nets.

Table 15.3 Securities Supervision Dictionary

Standard 1/	International Organization of Securities Commissions (IOSCO) Objectives and Principles of Securities Regulation	
Principle No.	Topic	Component
1	Responsibilities of the regulator	REG
2	Operational independence and accountability	REG
3	Powers, resources, and capacity to perform the functions and exercise the powers.	REG
4	Clear and consistent regulatory processes.	REG
5	Professional standards including standards of confidentiality	REG
6	Appropriate use of Self-Regulatory Organizations (SROs)	REG
7	Standards for SROs	REG
8	Comprehensive inspection, investigation and surveillance powers	PRF
9	Comprehensive enforcement powers	PRF
10	Effective and credible use of inspection, investigation, surveillance and enforcement powers and implementation of an efective compliance program.	PRF
11	Authority to share both public and non-public information with domestic and foreign counterparts	PRF
12	Setting up information sharing mechanisms	PRF
13	Assistance to foreign regulators who need to make inquiries in the discharge of their functions and exercise of their powers.	PRF
14	Full, accurate and timely disclosure of financial results and other information that is material to investors'	FIN
15	Fair and equitable treatment of holders of securities in a company	FIN
16	High and internationally acceptable quality of accounting and auditing standards	FIN
17	Standards for the eligibility and the regulation of those who wish to market or operate a collective investment scheme	REP
18	Rules governing the legal form and structure of collective investment schemes and the segregation and protection of client assets	REP
19	Disclosure necessary to evaluate the suitability of a collective investment scheme for a particular investor and the value of the investor's interest in the scheme	FIN
20	Proper and disclosed basis for asset valuation and the pricing and the redemption of units in a collective investment scheme	REP
21	Minimum entry standards for market intermediaries	REP
22	There should be initial and ongoing capital and other prudential requirements for market intermediaries	REP
23	Standards for internal organization and operational conduct	REP
24	Procedure for dealing with the failure of a market intermediary	FIN
25	Regulatory authorization and oversight of the establishment of trading systems	REP
26	Ongoing regulatory supervision of exchanges and trading systems	FIN
27	Transparency of trading.	REP
28	Detecting and deterring manipulation and other unfair trading practices.	FIN
29	Proper management of large exposures, default risk and market disruption.	PRF
30	Systems for clearing and settlement of securities transactions	FIN

1/ See http://www.imf.org/external/standards/index.htm for further details on the assessment methodology.
2/ See IMF (2004) for details. REG=regulatory governance, PRF=prudential framework, REP=reg. practices, and FIN=financial integrity, safety

Following the previous literature on this subject (e.g., IMF, 2004; Čihák and Podpiera, 2006, 2008; and Čihák and Tieman, 2007), we have used these calculations to process the input data:

- *Principle-by-principle gradings.* For each standard and each principle, there is a grading on a four-point scale. This grading was transformed into a numeric value from 0 percent (nonobserved) to 100 percent (fully observed). The value of 67 percent corresponds to the 'largely compliant' rating and the value of 33 percent to the "materially noncompliant" rating in the BCP assessment.
- *Summary grading.* An unweighted average of the principle-by-principle gradings was calculated to arrive at a summary grading for each standard. This summary grading is also a number between 0 percent (nonobserved) and 100 percent (fully observed).

- *Component gradings.* Given that the individual principles cover different subjects and that the composition of the principles differs for the three standards, it is easier to carry out cross-sectoral comparisons if the principles are aggregated into comparable groups that cover similar topics. As in IMF (2004), the principles are grouped into the following four components of a good supervisory framework: (i) regulatory governance, which includes the aims, independence, and accountability of regulators; (ii) prudential framework, which consists of regulations covering risk management, capital adequacy, internal controls, and corporate governance; (iii) regulatory practices, which include monitoring and supervision, enforcement, conglomerates, and licensing; and (iv) financial integrity and safety nets, including consumer protection and addressing financial crimes. Table 15.4 maps the individual principles into the four components. For each of the four components, an observance index was calculated as an unweighted average of the individual principles included in that component.

It is important to emphasize that we did not originate the underlying gradings. The information used in this chapter is a result of coordinated work by the IMF, the World Bank, and other cooperating institutions and their experts over a number of years. The only thing that we are doing as far as the input data are concerned is to convert them from the gradings on a 4-notch scale into gradings on a 0–100 scale and aggregating. All the underlying methodology for the assessments and some of the principle-by-principle gradings are available at the IMF's website at http://www.imf.org/external/np/fsap/fsap.asp. The full principle-by-principle grading information is available for countries that agreed to publication of the detailed assessments;[8] for other countries that have undergone the assessments,

---

[8] Australia is an example of a country that agreed to the publication of the full gradings. The relevant input data can be found on the above website or directly by going to http://www.imf.org/external/pubs/ft/scr/2006/cr06415.pdf. Tables 2, 5, and 8 in that document contain the principle-by-principle gradings for BCP, IAIS, and IOSCO, respectively, which we have used as input data for our calculations.

Table 15.4 Financial Sector Standards and Their Four Main Components

Four Main Components (Abbreviation)	Sub-components	Sector (Principles)		
		Banking (BCP)	Insurance (ICP) 1/	Securities (IOSCO)
Regulatory Governance (REG)	Objectives of regulation Independence and adequate resources Enforcement powers and capabilities Clarity and transparency of regulatory process External participation	1, 19	2000 IAIS: 1	1,2,3,4,5,6, 7
			2003 IAIS: 1,2,3,4	
Prudential Framework (PRF)	Risk management Risk concentration Capital requirements Corporate governance Internal controls	2,3,4,6,16, 17,18,20,22,23,24, 25	2000 IAIS: 2,3,4,5,12, 13,15,16, 17	8,9,10,11,12 ,13, 29.
			2003 IAIS: 9,10,18,19, 23	
Regulatory Practices (REP)	Group-wide supervision Monitoring and on-site inspection Reporting to supervisors Enforcement Cooperation and information sharing Confidentiality Licensing, ownership transfer, corporate control Qualifications	5,6,7,8,9,10,11,12,13, 14	2000 IAIS: 6,7,9, 10, 14, 16	17,18,20,21, 22, 23,25, 27
			2003 IAIS: 5,6,7,8,11, 12,13,14, 15,16,17,18,20,21,22	
Financial Integrity and Safety Nets (FIN)	Markets (integrity, financial crime) Customer protection Information, disclosure, transparency	15, 21	2000 IAIS: 11	14,15,16,19, 24, 26, 28, 30
			2003 IAIS: 24,25,26,27,28	

Note: 1/ For each component, the upper row corresponds to the original (2000) IAIS standard, and the lower row corresponds to the revised (2003) IAIS standard.

Source: Adapted from IMF (2004).

the data are not publicly available on an individual country basis, but are included in our calculations and presented on an aggregate basis.

How precise are these assessment gradings? Grading is not an exact science, and there are some obvious limitations. In particular, individual assessments may be influenced by factors such as the assessors' experience and the regulatory culture they are most familiar with. For each standard, there are methodology documents and assessors' templates, which add a degree of direction to the assessments, but the assessments still have an element of subjectivity and require exercise of judgment on the part of the individual assessor. Also, standards assessments are not designed to address political economy issues, or issues associated with financial regulation such as crisis management, the bankruptcy code, or deposit insurance. Finally, the assessments are a one-time measurement of the regulatory system and are therefore limited by time.

While we need to be mindful of these limitations, there are also reasons to be confident that these assessments capture relevant information. Each assessment is based on a standardized methodology issued by an internationally recognized standard-setting body (e.g., the Basel Committee on Banking Supervision in the case of the BCP). The assessment is carried out by a team of senior international assessors, assembled by the IMF and the World Bank. The assessors are drawn from a diversified pool of experts with different backgrounds, which limits the effect of individual assessors' experience and background. When carrying out their assessment, they are usually part of a broader team ('FSAP team') that also includes IMF and World Bank staff and that carries out a broader assessment of the financial system in a country. The team spends several weeks in the assessed country, and several more months preparing detailed reports, which include the gradings as one component. The country authorities (i.e., the relevant supervisory agencies) have an opportunity to read the assessment and point out any factual errors or mistakes. To help ensure internal consistency and cross-country comparability, all assessments are subject to a thorough review at the IMF and World Bank headquarters. And, as mentioned above, the gradings have been successfully used in previous literature (e.g., Podpiera, 2004; Carvajal and Elliott, 2007).

The gradings are relatively robust with respect to time. When interpreting the results, one must bear in mind that the gradings are a series of country-by-country snapshots. The individual assessments were undertaken at different points since 2000, and some of the earlier gradings may have become outdated subsequent to the FSAP. The existence of lags between regulatory developments and a reassessment of the gradings means that older assessments are likely to underestimate the true quality of current regulation and supervision in a country. Interestingly, statistical tests do not suggest a strong link between the 'vintage' of an assessment and the overall grading (specifically, we did not find a significant relationship between the year of the assessment and the overall grading, controlling for the country's income per capita). Nonetheless, to address this concern, updated gradings were taken into account for those countries for which reassessments took place in the context of FSAP Updates; for others, the FSAP gradings represent the most recent assessment information available.

Supervisory frameworks include elements that are not easy to quantify, and information may be lost if the focus is solely on quantitative analysis. Each assessment therefore contains a rich set of underlying, qualitative information from the FSAPs. Moreover, not all principles are equally relevant in all countries, and there are issues that may not be captured by the standards assessments. To address this, the FSAP reports use the standards assessments in combination with other analytical tools to form an integrated analysis of the financial sector. The key messages from these overall analyses are surveyed in the next section of this chapter.

An Introductory Analysis of the Quality of Supervision

Overall Findings

Based on the overall results for all economies in the sample (Figure 15.1 and Table 15.5), the regulatory quality seems to be remarkably similar in the three sectors. Both in banking and in insurance supervision, the average overall level of compliance is 67 percent, in both cases with a standard deviation of 19 percent. The average for securities is marginally (insignificantly) higher, with the same standard deviation. Given that a value of 67 percent corresponds to the third point on the four-point scale used in the three standards, it is possible to say that on average, the regulatory systems are 'largely compliant.'[9]

---

[9] To be precise, 'largely compliant' is the rating that corresponds to 67 percent in the BCP terminology; the corresponding ICP and IOSCO terms are 'largely observed' and 'broadly implemented,' respectively.

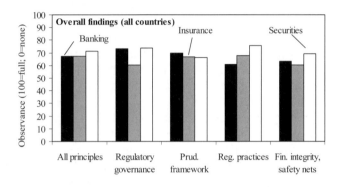

Source: Authors' calculations, based on IMF's standards database.

Figure 15.1 Overall Compliance with International Standards

This overall assessment overlooks important differences among banking, insurance, and securities regulation in terms of the main regulatory components. Specifically, insurance regulation lags behind both banking and securities regulation in terms of regulatory governance. This reflects the fact that many insurance supervisory agencies lack clear autonomy from the government. In terms of prudential framework, banking scores somewhat higher than insurance and securities regulation, but the difference is small compared to the cross-country variation. Finally, in terms of both regulatory practices as well as financial integrity and safety nets, securities regulation is more aligned with international standards than banking and insurance.

Table 15.5 Supervisory Quality by Level of Development

	Banking		Insurance		Securities	
	Average	St.dev.	Average	St.dev.	Average	St.dev.
All economies	67	19	67	19	71	19
Regulatory governance	73	20	60	27	74	19
Prud. framework	70	19	67	21	67	24
Reg. practices	61	24	68	22	76	22
Fin. integrity, safety nets	63	27	61	32	69	23
High income	86	10	79	14	85	16
Regulatory governance	90	12	76	20	84	18
Prud. framework	88	10	75	21	83	18
Reg. practices	84	15	81	14	86	18
Fin. integrity, safety nets	85	14	76	24	85	17
Middle income	60	17	57	17	62	17
Regulatory governance	66	20	49	25	67	17
Prud. framework	62	18	57	18	55	20
Reg. practices	52	20	57	20	68	22
Fin. integrity, safety nets	56	27	47	31	59	18
Low income	56	13	54	15	52	9
Regulatory governance	69	17	58	17	60	25
Prud. framework	59	12	56	18	42	16
Reg. practices	49	15	48	19	64	8
Fin. integrity, safety nets	40	23	58	32	44	18

Note: Standard deviation of the relevant index across the country sample.
Source: Authors' calculations based on IMF's standards and codes database.

These general comparisons, however, should not overlook important cross-country differences, which are indicated by the high standard deviation. In the next sub-section, we therefore focus on groups of countries by income level and region.

Differences by Income Level and Geographic Region

Differences by income level

There are important differences in the level of compliance based on a country's income level (Figure 15.2).[10] In all the three sectors, wealthy economies have clearly higher levels of compliance than poorer ones; the difference is bigger between high-income and medium-income economies than between medium-income and low-income

---

[10] The standards were designed to be universal. In principle, therefore, economic development does not need to be taken into account. However, in practice, the level of compliance is positively correlated with economic development. It is thus useful to analyze the gradings not only for all countries, but also by peer groups of countries.

economies.[11] The text chart illustrates the relationship between compliance and income level for the overall gradings. Table 15.5 shows the numbers and confirms that this general conclusion also applies when one looks at the four main regulatory components (regulatory governance, prudential framework, regulatory practices, and financial integrity and safety nets).

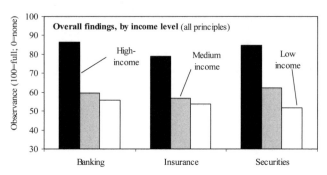

Source: Authors' calculations, based on IMF's standards database.

Figure 15.2 Overall Compliance by Income Level

Differences by geographic region

There are also notable regional differences in supervisory quality (Figure 15.3 and Table 15.6). In particular, European economies show, on average, higher levels of observance than economies in all the other four regions.[12] A large part of this difference can be attributed to differences in income levels: the average (unweighted) GDP per capita in the European sample is $19,566, compared to $5,800 in the non-European sample.

---

[11] We use here the World Bank's classification of economies into high-income (those with GDP per capita above USD 11,115), low-income (those with GDP per capita below USD 906), and medium-income (those in between).
[12] The definitions of the five regions follow the country classification in the IMF's *World Economic Outlook*.

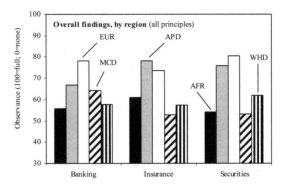

Source: Authors, based on IMF's standards database.

Figure 15.3 Overall Compliance by Geographic Region

The difference in regulatory quality is even more notable if one compares European Union (EU) countries with non-EU countries, both European and non-European. The degree of observance of the three standards and their subcomponents was on average about 8 percentage points higher in the EU countries than in the non-EU countries (for details, see Čihák and Tieman, 2007).

EU member countries also show a more even level of observance than non-EU countries. Usual measures of cross-country variability (such as the standard deviation or the difference between minimum and maximum) suggest that EU member countries have a lower variability in quality of regulation and supervision. Cross-country variability in the EU tended to be higher in regulatory governance than in other aspects of the supervisory framework. Both in banking and in insurance, regulatory governance showed higher cross-country variability than the prudential framework, regulatory practices, or financial integrity and safety nets. In securities regulation, the prudential framework was the component with the highest cross-country variability.

Despite the relatively favorable performance vis-à-vis non-EU countries, compliance in the EU countries was far from perfect. The overall level of compliance ranged from 79 percent in insurance to 85

Table 15.6 Supervisory Quality by Geographic Region

	Banking		Insurance		Securities	
	Average	St.dev.	Average	St.dev.	Average	St.dev.
All economies	67	19	67	19	71	19
Regulatory governance	73	20	60	27	74	19
Prud. framework	70	19	67	21	67	24
Reg. practices	61	24	68	22	76	22
Fin. integrity, safety nets	63	27	61	32	69	23
Africa	56	10	61	22	54	17
Regulatory governance	67	20	61	25	64	33
Prud. framework	59	12	64	23	45	18
Reg. practices	48	12	56	26	68	19
Fin. integrity, safety nets	42	24	61	33	45	24
Asia and Pacific	67	23	78	14	76	15
Regulatory governance	73	23	65	21	80	12
Prud. framework	69	24	77	13	70	24
Reg. practices	60	29	76	24	78	19
Fin. integrity, safety nets	58	23	84	17	76	21
Europe	78	16	74	16	81	17
Regulatory governance	82	18	67	25	81	17
Prud. framework	81	15	71	20	80	21
Reg. practices	73	21	76	17	83	21
Fin. integrity, safety nets	78	22	64	31	78	20
Middle East and Central Asia	64	14	53	17	53	15
Regulatory governance	77	13	53	34	57	20
Prud. framework	67	16	52	13	46	11
Reg. practices	57	18	53	18	59	22
Fin. integrity, safety nets	54	28	40	36	51	16
Western Hemisphere	58	19	57	20	62	14
Regulatory governance	61	20	41	20	67	10
Prud. framework	60	19	60	24	48	14
Reg. practices	49	24	56	22	67	20
Fin. integrity, safety nets	59	27	55	31	64	19

Source: Authors' calculations based on IMF's standards and codes database.

percent in securities regulation.[13] For example, in banking, two EU countries observed all core principles, but no principle was observed fully across the EU. On average, there were about nine less-than-fully-compliant EU countries for each principle. For some principles, more than half of EU countries were less than fully compliant.

Looking at the other regions, Europe is followed (in terms of supervisory quality) by Asia and the Pacific, the Middle East and Central Asia, the Western Hemisphere, and Africa. Again, one should note that these aggregate differences are driven to a large extent by

---

[13] As mentioned, the value of 67 percent corresponds to the 'largely compliant' grading, and so it could be said that on average, the EU regulatory systems were more than 'largely compliant.' However, they were significantly less than 'fully compliant' (100 percent), and some were not even 'largely compliant.'

differences in income per capita, and also that there is substantial variability within each of the regions.

The lowest values are generally reached in the area of financial integrity and safety nets. This is particularly true in African banking supervision (42 percent), in Middle East and Central Asian insurance supervision (40 percent), and in African securities regulation (45 percent). The highest levels of observance are generally reached in Europe, in particular in regulatory governance in banking (82 percent) and in regulatory practices in securities regulation (83 percent).

Main Strengths and Areas for Improvement

This section highlights the main strengths and the main areas for improvement that are relatively consistently highlighted in the BCP, ICP, and IOSCO assessments. The discussion is based on a detailed principle-by-principle analysis of the results, a summary of which is provided in Figure 15.4 (banking), Figure 15.5 (insurance), and Figure 15.6 (securities). A more detailed discussion is provided in the Appendix.

Each of the figures consists of the following two closely related charts: the first one shows the average degree of compliance for each principle across all the countries in the sample; the second one shows the percentage of countries that were less-than-fully compliant with the particular principle.[14] So, for example, for the first Basel core principle (objectives, autonomy, powers, and resources of banking supervisors), the first chart in Figure 15.4 illustrates that the average degree of compliance over the whole sample was 73 percent, while the second chart illustrates that 61 percent of countries were less than fully compliant with this principle (the exact numbers are available upon request).[15] As one could expect, there is a negative correlation between the average degree of compliance and the percentage of less-than-fully compliant countries, but the correlation is lower (in absolute value) than 1, so each of the charts has a separate informational value.

---

[14] An exception is Figure 15.5, which contains two charts for the 2000 IAIS standard, and two for the 2003 standard.

[15] We have also carried out this analysis by peer groups of countries in terms of income level and regions. However, these breakdowns do not yield much additional useful information to that reported in Section three.

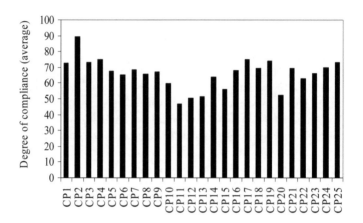

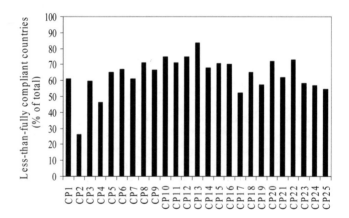

Source: authors' calculations, based on IMF's standards database.

Figure 15.4 Compliance in Detail: Basel Core Principles

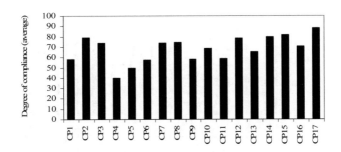

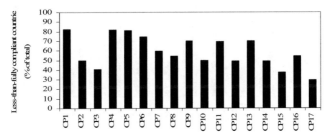

(i) 2000 IAIS Standard

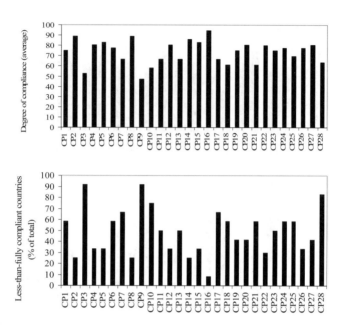

(ii) 2003 IAIS Standard

Source: authors' calculations, based on IMF's standards database.

Figure 15.5 Compliance in Detail: IAIS Principles

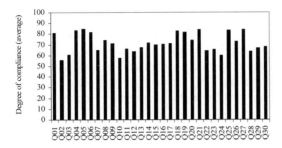

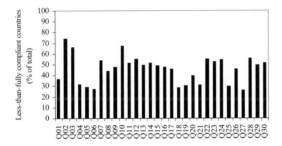

Source: authors' calculations, based on IMF's standards database.

Figure 15.6 Compliance in Detail: IOSCO's Objectives and Principles

The specific strengths and areas for attention include the following:

- In *banking regulation*, the strongest observance has been recorded in the area of licensing, specifically in the principle that deals with definition of permissible activities for the licensed institutions. In contrast, the areas most in need of improvement included supervision of other risks; connected lending; issues related to money laundering; supervisory objectives, autonomy, powers, and resources; remedial measures; and consolidated supervision.
- In *insurance regulation*, the highest degree compliance has been recorded in the areas of confidentiality and winding-up. In contrast, areas with low observance include market conduct issues to internal controls, derivatives and off-balance-sheet items, organization of the

supervisor, corporate governance, assets, onsite inspection, and licensing.
- In *securities regulation*, the areas of strength include clarity and consistency of the regulatory process, professional standards, the appropriate use of self-regulatory organizations, and the rules on transparency of trading. The areas for improvement relate to enforcement powers and compliance program; capital and other prudential requirements; powers, resources, and capacity; and operational independence and accountability.

Regression Analysis

Quality of regulation and supervision is positively correlated with the level of economic development. This finding, indicated in previous literature (e.g., Čihák and Podpiera, 2006, 2008), has been confirmed by our study (Figure 15.7).

We have calculated correlations between the 'supervisory quality' data studied here, and the regulatory database by Barth, Caprio, and Levine (2006, henceforth BCL). The main difference between the two is that the latter focuses on regulations 'on the books,' while the former includes both regulations on the books and their actual implementation in practice. We have found correlations between the two datasets low, all below 50 percent, and many in the 20–30 percent range (Table 15.7). This is consistent with the notion that the two datasets describe different phenomena, given that the standards database incorporates also practical implementation of regulations.

We have calculated correlations between all BCP, IAIS, and IOSCO categories, and the World Bank governance database by Kaufman, Kraay, and Mastruzzi (2007, henceforth KKM) as of 2002 and 2006. This database reflects the views on governance by experts from the public sector, private sector, and non-government organizations, as well as thousands of citizen and firm survey respondents worldwide. With many correlations between 50 and 60 percent, a few readings higher than 60 percent, and about half below 50 percent, the correlation between these survey data and our regulatory quality indicators is higher than the correlation between the regulatory database of BCL and our supervisory quality data (Tables

15.8 and 15.9).[16] Apparently, as both our dataset and the KKM governance data aim to measure implementation and actual practice,

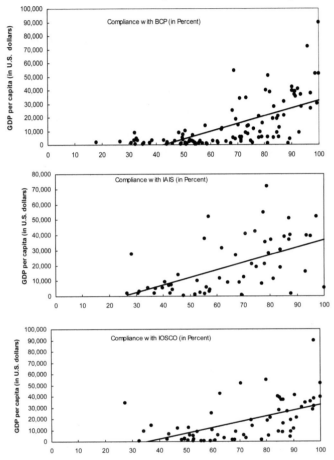

Source: authors' calculations, based on IMF's standards database.

Figure 15.7 Regressions of Compliance on Income Per Capita

---

[16] We have also calculated correlations between the KKM governance data of 2002 and 2006. Somewhat surprisingly, about half of these correlations are below 90 percent, with many of between 70 and 80 percent. Slightly below half of the changes in these variables between 2002 and 2006 were improvements.

the relationship between these data is closer than the relationship between implementation and regulation on the books, as measured by BCL.

We tested which macroeconomic variable best explained standards. As expected, we found this to be gross domestic product per capita. It performed better than alternative variables, such as domestic credit and claims to the private sector, or proxies for the size of the financial sector,[17] which all exhibited lower explanatory power.

Subsequently, we gauged whether information embedded in the international standards added information to that contained in a country's level of development (as measured by its GDP per capita), and its governance regime (as measured by the individual KKM indicators). To do so, we regressed all standards on the individual KKM governance variables and per capita GDP, i.e., we estimated:[18]

$$SC_{ij} = \alpha + \beta \cdot KKM_i + \gamma \cdot GDP_j + \varepsilon, \qquad (15.1)$$

With:

SC_{ij} = standards variable i for country j, i = regulatory governance, prudential framework, regulatory practice, financial integrity, for all three standards (BCP, IAIS, and IOSCO),

KKM_i = KKM variable i for country j, i = Voice and Accountability, Political Stability, Government Effectiveness, Regulatory Quality, Rule of Law, Control of Corruption,

GDP_j = GDP per capita in country j.

We ran these regressions for all standards being considered, and for the KKM data from both 2002 and 2006. For GDP per capita we use the value from the same years as the KKM data (i.e. either 2002 or

---

[17] As we do not have data about the size of the financial sector for all countries in the sample, we employed the ratios of domestic credit and claims to the private sector over GDP as simple proxies.

[18] Even though the KKM variables do correlate with GDP per capita, the correlation is far from perfect, and multicollinearity problems do not seem to arise in the regressions.

2006).[19] This results in matrices of coefficients and t-values (Tables 15.10 and 15.11), discussed below:[20]

- *For the BCP*, the coefficient estimates for GDP per capita always exhibit the expected positive sign, and are often significant at the 5 percent uncertainty level (in 80 percent of the cases, both for the 2002 and the 2006 data). At the same time, the KKM governance variables are also significant most of the time. We interpret this as indication that the BCP captures information contained in the level of development, which is not contained in the World Bank governance data. We paid specific attention to KKM's 'regulatory quality' variable, which comes closest to our BCP data. For the BCP regressions including this explanatory variable, significance at the 5 percent uncertainty level for this variable is found in about 50 percent of the cases for 2006 data, and about 75 percent of the cases for 2002 data, while the GDP per capita variable is almost always significant. Taken together, these results suggest rather clearly that the BCP contains information beyond the regulatory governance data.
- *For IAIS and IOSCO*, the results are less strong. Still, around a half of the regressions featured GDP per capita with a coefficient with the expected sign and significantly different from zero at the 5 percent uncertainty level. In particular, this is the case for IAIS Regulatory Practice, and IOSCO Prudential Framework and Financial Integrity. The KKM governance variables were not significant most of the time. We interpret this as the BCP 'core' banking regulations being better reflected in the general regulatory quality variable of KKM, whereas the 'more obscure' insurance and securities regulations feature less prominently in the survey responses of the KKM study.

---

[19] It is not always the exact year in which the standards assessment was performed, but it is reasonably close.

[20] One explanatory variable not included in the above regression is the degree of sectoral integration of supervision in a country, which was found to be significant in previous research (Čihák and Podpiera, 2006, 2008).

Table 15.7 Correlation of Standards Assessments with the BCL Database 1/

			Barth, Caprio, Levine Database						
		Q3.4	Q 3.8.1	Q 3.8.2	Q 6.1	Q 6.2	Q 9.4	Q 12.4	Q 12.5
	Regulatory governance	-0.18	-0.20	-0.08	0.32	0.24	-0.06	-0.10	-0.10
	Prudential Framework	-0.13	-0.33	0.08	0.27	0.07	-0.31	-0.07	0.14
	Regulatory Practice	-0.19	-0.25	-0.01	0.29	0.13	-0.26	0.04	0.06
BIS	Financial Integrity	-0.15	-0.34	0.09	0.19	0.13	-0.39	-0.07	-0.10
	Regulatory governance	-0.35	-0.17	-0.23	0.18	0.17	-0.35	0.05	0.31
	Prudential Framework	-0.15	-0.28	0.05	0.06	-0.22	-0.37	-0.09	0.19
	Regulatory Practice	-0.30	-0.30	-0.07	0.15	0.00	-0.47	-0.17	0.30
IAIS	Financial Integrity	0.05	-0.12	0.05	0.07	-0.33	-0.13	-0.09	0.06
	Regulatory governance	-0.10	-0.18	0.02	0.21	0.09	-0.33	-0.04	0.12
	Prudential Framework	-0.21	-0.25	0.08	0.32	0.11	-0.34	-0.07	0.15
	Regulatory Practice	-0.27	-0.04	0.01	0.07	0.19	-0.23	-0.02	-0.01
IOSCO	Financial Integrity	-0.15	-0.10	-0.01	0.20	0.05	-0.43	-0.10	0.12

(Standards & Codes)

Note: 1/ Explanatory Note. The questions used from the BCL database are:

Q 3.4 'What is the actual risk-adjusted capital ratio in banks as of yearend 2005, using the 1988 Basel Accord definitions?'

Q 3.8.1 'What fraction of the banking system's assets is in banks that are 50 percent or more government owned as of yearend 2005?'

Q 3.8.2 'What fraction of the banking system's assets is in banks that are 50 percent or more foreign owned as of yearend 2005?'

Q 6.1 'Can the supervisory authority force a bank to change its internal organizational structure? 1=Yes, 0 = No'

Q 6.2 'Has this power been utilized in the last 5 years? 1=Yes, 0 = No'

Q 9.4 'What is the ratio of nonperforming loans to total assets as of year-end 2005?'

Q 12.4 'How many professional bank supervisors are there in total?'

Q 12.5 'How many onsite examinations per bank were performed in the last five years?'

Sources: IMF standards codes database and World Bank BCL Database

Table 15.8 Correlation of Standards Assessments with KKM 2006 Database 1/

| | | Kaufman, Kraay, and Mastruzzi Database 2006 | | | | | |
		Voice and Acc.	Pol. Stability	Gov. Effectiveness	Reg. Quality	Rule of Law	Control of Corruption
		Regulatory governance	0.34	0.29	0.49	0.51	0.42	0.46
		Prudential Framework	0.52	0.43	0.63	0.64	0.55	0.60
		Regulatory Practice	0.49	0.36	0.62	0.64	0.54	0.57
	BIS	Financial Integrity	0.56	0.48	0.65	0.66	0.59	0.63
		Regulatory governance	0.31	0.11	0.37	0.41	0.40	0.40
		Prudential Framework	0.39	0.39	0.52	0.51	0.49	0.50
		Regulatory Practice	0.52	0.36	0.60	0.61	0.58	0.59
	IAIS	Financial Integrity	0.27	0.12	0.31	0.31	0.38	0.33
		Regulatory governance	0.47	0.27	0.45	0.45	0.41	0.41
		Prudential Framework	0.63	0.48	0.57	0.59	0.56	0.55
		Regulatory Practice	0.38	0.19	0.33	0.35	0.33	0.32
Standards & Codes	IOSCO	Financial Integrity	0.55	0.39	0.59	0.59	0.57	0.57

Note: 1/ The KKM data relate to Voice and Accountability, Political Stability, Government Effectiveness, Regulatory Quality, the Rule of Law, and the Control of Corruption.

Sources: IMF's standards database; and World Bank's KKM database

We have also performed the above regressions for regions (following the IMF's *World Economic Outlook* classification, i.e., Europe, Middle East and Central Asia, Asia and Pacific, Africa, and Western Hemisphere)[21] and by income level (following the World Bank country classification through the Atlas method,[22] and adding the OECD as a separate group). The results generally show less significance, reflecting the much smaller samples. For the BCP regression, however, the GDP per capita variable is significant at the 5 percent uncertainty level in a number of cases, specifically for both

---

[21] See, for example, http://www.imf.org/external/pubs/ft/weo/2008/01/pdf/stat-app.pdf.

[22] See http://go.worldbank.org/K2CKM78CC0.

the low income and the high income (and OECD) countries. It therefore seems that the results for the BCP are driven in particular by low- and high-income countries.

Table 15.9 Regressions of Standards on KKM 2002 Variables and GDP Per Capita

		Voice and Acc.	Pol. Stability	Gov. Effectiveness	Reg. Quality	Rule of Law	Control of Corruption
		Kaufman, Kraay, and Mastruzzi Database 2002					
		Coefficient Estimates for Constant					
BIS	RegGov	67.30	67.66	58.99	53.97	61.58	60.14
	Prud	54.11	56.61	45.91	42.76	49.76	50.80
	RegPract	43.57	47.24	33.67	29.21	37.73	38.44
	FinInt	35.54	38.84	24.85	21.87	29.12	31.87
IAIS	RegGov	52.53	49.86	38.26	34.12	36.44	36.91
	Prud	53.77	50.18	41.49	41.25	43.26	43.30
	RegPract	50.92	52.02	38.45	37.36	41.55	43.28
	FinInt	45.66	53.23	27.50	30.67	29.50	26.09
IOSCO	RegGov	52.63	60.11	42.75	49.40	53.08	56.09
	Prud	34.30	42.49	30.96	35.30	39.27	41.60
	RegPract	59.56	65.99	53.23	55.65	59.12	62.17
	FinInt	44.02	52.41	33.03	35.44	41.54	42.46
		t-values for Coefficient Estimates for Constant					
BIS	RegGov	16.17	18.44	12.59	11.07	13.92	14.66
	Prud	15.12	17.78	11.91	10.69	13.38	14.61
	RegPract	11.11	13.48	8.07	6.85	9.36	10.26
	FinInt	6.85	8.41	4.48	3.75	5.47	6.36
IAIS	RegGov	5.30	5.84	3.03	3.21	3.54	3.90
	Prud	6.95	7.51	4.24	4.95	5.47	5.79
	RegPract	7.38	8.69	4.46	5.16	5.95	6.49
	FinInt	3.78	4.94	1.75	2.20	2.25	2.25
IOSCO	RegGov	8.55	11.07	5.34	6.38	7.78	8.54
	Prud	5.44	7.56	3.59	4.31	5.43	6.00
	RegPract	8.97	11.51	6.07	6.74	8.13	8.92
	FinInt	7.07	9.56	4.12	4.69	6.14	6.60
		Coefficient Estimates for KKM coefficient					
BIS	RegGov	-0.04	-0.06	0.15	0.25	0.10	0.14
	Prud	0.12	0.07	0.31	0.36	0.24	0.22
	RegPract	0.15	0.07	0.45	0.61	0.31	0.30
	FinInt	0.33	0.29	0.57	0.61	0.52	0.46
IAIS	RegGov	-0.04	0.02	0.25	0.35	0.34	0.33
	Prud	0.01	0.09	0.24	0.27	0.25	0.25
	RegPract	0.05	0.03	0.28	0.33	0.26	0.23
	FinInt	0.08	-0.10	0.42	0.38	0.45	0.55
IOSCO	RegGov	0.29	0.15	0.44	0.32	0.28	0.22
	Prud	0.37	0.23	0.39	0.31	0.27	0.22
	RegPract	0.17	0.03	0.26	0.22	0.18	0.11
	FinInt	0.25	0.08	0.43	0.39	0.31	0.29
		t-values for Coefficient Estimates for KKM coefficient					
BIS	RegGov	-0.53	-0.76	1.55	2.61	1.00	1.52
	Prud	1.66	1.00	3.88	4.56	2.91	2.84
	RegPract	1.88	0.92	4.37	5.38	3.45	3.58
	FinInt	3.17	2.88	5.01	5.27	4.41	4.15
IAIS	RegGov	-0.20	0.14	1.07	1.75	1.57	1.69
	Prud	0.05	0.71	1.39	1.72	1.55	1.65
	RegPract	0.38	0.24	1.85	2.43	1.89	1.71
	FinInt	0.34	-0.44	1.50	1.47	1.68	2.29
IOSCO	RegGov	2.51	1.32	3.13	2.33	2.12	1.71
	Prud	3.18	2.00	2.57	2.16	1.91	1.63
	RegPract	1.33	0.25	1.72	1.53	1.25	0.82
	FinInt	2.17	0.73	3.05	2.93	2.36	2.35
		Coefficient Estimates for Per Capita GDP					
BIS	RegGov	6.3E-04	6.6E-04	4.1E-04	3.1E-04	4.6E-04	4.0E-04
	Prud	5.9E-04	6.3E-04	3.6E-04	3.3E-04	4.2E-04	4.3E-04
	RegPract	6.8E-04	7.5E-04	4.1E-04	3.5E-04	4.6E-04	4.5E-04
	FinInt	5.7E-04	5.6E-04	2.6E-04	2.6E-04	2.7E-04	3.2E-04
IAIS	RegGov	6.1E-04	5.4E-04	3.2E-04	1.8E-04	1.6E-04	1.5E-04
	Prud	5.5E-04	4.5E-04	3.1E-04	2.7E-04	2.7E-04	2.5E-04
	RegPract	6.7E-04	6.9E-04	4.3E-04	3.7E-04	4.1E-04	4.3E-04
	FinInt	5.1E-04	7.1E-04	1.8E-04	2.0E-04	6.4E-05	-6.6E-05
IOSCO	RegGov	1.5E-04	2.6E-04	1.8E-05	1.3E-04	1.2E-04	1.8E-04
	Prud	4.1E-04	5.1E-04	4.1E-04	4.8E-04	4.8E-04	5.3E-04
	RegPract	3.1E-04	4.4E-04	2.2E-04	2.6E-04	2.7E-04	3.4E-04
	FinInt	4.5E-04	6.1E-04	3.0E-04	3.3E-04	3.5E-04	3.6E-04
		t-values for Coefficient Estimates for Per Capita GDP coefficient					
BIS	RegGov	4.8	4.7	2.8	2.2	2.9	2.6
	Prud	5.2	5.3	3.0	2.8	3.2	3.3
	RegPract	5.5	5.7	3.1	2.8	3.2	3.2
	FinInt	3.5	3.2	1.5	1.5	1.4	1.7
IAIS	RegGov	2.2	2.0	1.1	0.7	0.5	0.5
	Prud	2.6	2.2	1.4	1.3	1.1	1.1
	RegPract	3.6	3.7	2.2	2.0	2.0	2.1
	FinInt	1.5	2.1	0.5	0.6	0.2	-0.2
IOSCO	RegGov	0.9	1.4	0.1	0.7	0.6	0.9
	Prud	2.3	2.7	2.1	2.5	2.3	2.5
	RegPract	1.7	2.2	1.1	1.3	1.3	1.6
	FinInt	2.6	3.3	1.6	1.8	1.8	1.9

Source: Authors' estimates.

Table 15. 10 Regressions of Standards on KKM 2006 Variables and GDP Per Capita

		Kaufman, Kraay, and Mastruzzi Database 2006					
		Voice and Acc.	Pol. Stability	Gov. Effectiveness	Reg. Quality	Rule of Law	Control of Corruption
		Coefficient Estimates for Constant					
BIS	RegGov	63.9	66.4	55.5	52.4	59.4	58.0
	Prud	51.8	56.9	45.3	43.6	50.6	49.3
	RegPract	41.9	48.9	33.0	30.6	38.4	38.9
	FinInt	34.4	40.8	22.0	20.2	30.4	27.2
IAIS	RegGov	49.6	60.9	38.4	30.5	36.6	36.9
	Prud	53.3	50.4	36.7	37.9	43.5	43.2
	RegPract	48.2	54.3	34.9	34.3	41.7	41.1
	FinInt	43.0	54.5	33.3	35.5	27.4	33.6
IOSCO	RegGov	50.8	63.6	45.0	45.5	54.1	54.6
	Prud	32.7	46.0	29.9	28.9	38.3	39.1
	RegPract	58.7	70.0	58.4	57.4	61.9	63.4
	FinInt	44.1	56.8	33.3	33.5	41.5	41.9
		t-values for Coefficient Estimates for Constant					
BIS	RegGov	15.3	18.1	11.7	10.7	13.4	13.1
	Prud	14.6	17.9	11.4	10.6	13.4	13.1
	RegPract	10.7	13.9	7.7	6.9	9.4	9.4
	FinInt	6.6	8.7	3.9	3.5	5.6	5.1
IAIS	RegGov	4.9	7.1	2.9	2.4	3.3	3.5
	Prud	6.7	7.3	3.7	3.8	5.1	5.2
	RegPract	6.8	8.8	3.9	4.0	5.6	5.6
	FinInt	3.5	5.1	2.1	2.1	2.0	2.6
IOSCO	RegGov	8.1	11.4	5.0	5.1	7.4	7.6
	Prud	5.1	7.9	3.1	3.1	5.0	5.2
	RegPract	8.6	12.1	6.0	5.9	7.9	8.3
	FinInt	6.9	10.2	3.7	3.8	5.7	5.9
		Coefficient Estimates for KKM coefficient					
BIS	RegGov	0.0	0.0	0.2	0.3	0.2	0.2
	Prud	0.2	0.1	0.3	0.3	0.2	0.2
	RegPract	0.2	0.0	0.4	0.4	0.3	0.3
	FinInt	0.4	0.2	0.6	0.6	0.5	0.5
IAIS	RegGov	0.0	-0.2	0.2	0.4	0.3	0.3
	Prud	0.0	0.1	0.3	0.3	0.2	0.2
	RegPract	0.1	0.0	0.4	0.4	0.3	0.3
	FinInt	0.1	-0.1	0.3	0.3	0.5	0.4
IOSCO	RegGov	0.3	0.1	0.4	0.4	0.2	0.2
	Prud	0.4	0.1	0.4	0.4	0.3	0.3
	RegPract	0.2	-0.1	0.2	0.2	0.1	0.1
	FinInt	0.2	0.0	0.4	0.4	0.3	0.3
		t-values for Coefficient Estimates for KKM coefficient					
BIS	RegGov	0.4	-0.3	2.3	3.0	1.6	1.9
	Prud	2.5	0.9	3.9	4.2	2.6	3.0
	RegPract	2.4	0.3	4.4	4.9	3.2	3.0
	FinInt	3.4	2.3	5.5	5.6	4.0	4.8
IAIS	RegGov	0.1	-1.4	1.0	1.7	1.4	1.5
	Prud	0.1	0.6	1.9	1.8	1.4	1.5
	RegPract	0.8	-0.2	2.2	2.4	1.7	1.8
	FinInt	0.6	-0.6	1.1	0.9	1.8	1.3
IOSCO	RegGov	2.8	0.5	2.5	2.4	1.8	1.8
	Prud	3.4	1.2	2.4	2.6	1.9	1.8
	RegPract	1.4	-0.6	0.9	1.1	0.7	0.5
	FinInt	2.1	-0.3	2.7	2.7	2.2	2.2
		Coefficient Estimates for Per Capita GDP					
BIS	RegGov	5.5E-04	6.1E-04	3.3E-04	2.7E-04	4.0E-04	3.6E-04
	Prud	5.3E-04	6.5E-04	3.7E-04	3.4E-04	4.6E-04	4.3E-04
	RegPract	6.4E-04	8.1E-04	4.2E-04	3.8E-04	5.0E-04	5.2E-04
	FinInt	5.3E-04	6.7E-04	2.3E-04	2.2E-04	3.5E-04	2.6E-04
IAIS	RegGov	5.4E-04	7.9E-04	3.2E-04	1.7E-04	2.0E-04	2.0E-04
	Prud	5.4E-04	4.8E-04	2.2E-04	2.5E-04	2.8E-04	2.8E-04
	RegPract	6.0E-04	7.4E-04	3.7E-04	3.6E-04	4.4E-04	4.1E-04
	FinInt	4.4E-04	7.1E-04	2.9E-04	3.4E-04	4.9E-05	2.0E-04
IOSCO	RegGov	1.1E-04	3.7E-04	9.8E-05	9.7E-05	1.7E-04	1.8E-04
	Prud	3.7E-04	6.3E-04	4.3E-04	4.1E-04	4.8E-04	5.0E-04
	RegPract	2.9E-04	5.5E-04	3.3E-04	3.1E-04	3.5E-04	3.9E-04
	FinInt	4.5E-04	7.4E-04	3.4E-04	3.4E-04	3.9E-04	3.9E-04
		t-values for Coefficient Estimates for Per Capita GDP coefficient					
BIS	RegGov	4.1	4.7	2.3	1.9	2.7	2.4
	Prud	4.7	5.8	3.1	2.9	3.6	3.4
	RegPract	5.1	6.5	3.2	2.9	3.6	3.7
	FinInt	3.2	4.0	1.3	1.3	1.9	1.4
IAIS	RegGov	1.8	3.3	1.1	0.6	0.6	0.7
	Prud	2.4	2.5	1.0	1.1	1.3	1.2
	RegPract	3.1	4.4	1.8	1.8	2.1	2.0
	FinInt	1.2	2.4	0.8	0.9	0.1	0.5
IOSCO	RegGov	0.6	2.4	0.5	0.5	0.9	0.9
	Prud	2.1	3.3	2.2	2.1	2.3	2.4
	RegPract	1.5	2.9	1.6	1.5	1.7	1.9
	FinInt	2.6	4.0	1.8	1.8	2.0	2.0

Source: Authors' estimates.

A similar approach for the BCL regulation and supervision database shows several interesting results (Table 15.11). First, while higher government ownership of banks is associated with a lower BCP ranking (significant in two out of four regressions), higher foreign ownership is weakly associated with a better BCP ranking (not significant). This indicates that market discipline, in the form of bank ownership by parties not directly under the influence of government has a positive relationship with banking supervision quality, as measured by BCP. Second, the supervisor's authority to ask a bank to change its structure is associated with higher BCP scores (significant).

Table 15.11 Regressions of Standards on BCL Variables and GDP Per Capita

		Barth, Caprio, Levine Database 1/							
		Q3.4	Q 3.8.1	Q 3.8.2	Q 6.1	Q 6.2	Q 9.4	Q 12.4	Q 12.5
		Coefficient Estimates for Constant							
BIS	RegGov	64.3	68.0	65.5	55.4	61.8	63.0	66.9	64.5
	Prud	56.3	63.2	56.6	54.1	60.4	62.4	60.8	60.4
	RegPract	53.4	54.3	49.1	41.0	49.5	53.4	50.7	52.7
	FinInt	54.8	59.9	49.4	48.0	52.3	60.8	55.8	53.0
IAIS	RegGov	70.7	57.1	53.5	43.4	48.4	60.5	49.2	38.1
	Prud	64.3	57.9	52.1	55.3	58.1	60.6	52.8	52.0
	RegPract	69.4	59.3	54.4	52.3	55.2	63.4	55.7	52.8
	FinInt	44.1	51.0	47.7	47.1	50.9	51.3	47.9	43.8
IOSCO	RegGov	68.1	64.9	64.2	58.6	62.2	70.5	64.2	64.0
	Prud	66.4	54.4	51.4	41.1	51.5	57.2	50.2	51.3
	RegPract	84.2	66.2	67.0	67.0	66.2	72.4	67.0	66.6
	FinInt	70.8	57.2	57.6	51.0	56.8	65.7	57.6	56.2
		t-values for Coefficient Estimates for Constant							
BIS	RegGov	8.0	19.1	15.6	13.8	19.0	18.2	18.9	18.0
	Prud	8.0	22.4	16.7	15.5	21.3	22.0	20.5	20.4
	RegPract	6.5	16.4	12.5	10.6	15.5	16.5	15.5	16.4
	FinInt	5.6	15.1	10.3	9.1	12.8	15.6	13.4	12.6
IAIS	RegGov	4.8	7.6	5.5	5.3	6.9	8.0	6.4	4.6
	Prud	5.1	11.1	7.6	8.5	10.2	9.8	7.8	8.1
	RegPract	6.8	13.0	8.8	9.7	11.6	12.7	10.1	9.1
	FinInt	2.4	5.6	4.1	4.5	6.5	5.4	4.6	3.9
IOSCO	RegGov	6.6	14.5	13.3	8.3	12.4	14.8	12.7	11.5
	Prud	6.2	10.3	9.1	5.9	9.7	10.3	9.3	8.5
	RegPract	7.9	13.4	12.4	9.4	12.7	13.7	12.7	11.1
	FinInt	8.0	13.7	12.6	7.8	12.8	14.8	12.9	12.0
		Coefficient Estimates for BCL coefficient							
BIS	RegGov	0.8	-12.2	1.9	14.9	8.7	29.7	0.0	0.0
	Prud	23.1	-19.1	9.4	9.9	1.8	-52.7	0.0	0.0
	RegPract	-13.0	-15.0	7.8	15.1	3.9	-38.9	0.0	0.0
	FinInt	9.0	-29.2	13.7	7.9	5.4	-120.7	0.0	0.0
IAIS	RegGov	-113.9	-34.5	-2.4	10.4	5.1	-122.7	0.0	0.0
	Prud	-63.4	-25.6	8.3	-2.0	-6.0	-92.1	0.0	0.0
	RegPract	-77.5	-28.0	6.0	2.8	2.4	-112.8	0.0	0.0
	FinInt	30.0	-6.9	3.6	-0.9	-14.9	5.2	0.0	0.0
IOSCO	RegGov	-12.7	-4.2	1.4	8.6	1.4	-78.6	0.0	0.0
	Prud	-84.2	-11.8	2.8	14.9	4.1	-68.5	0.0	0.0
	RegPract	-97.2	9.2	3.7	1.4	5.7	-64.4	0.0	0.0
	FinInt	-70.3	2.6	1.9	6.1	0.1	-104.3	0.0	0.0
		t-values for Coefficient Estimates for BCL coefficient							
BIS	RegGov	0.0	-1.0	0.3	3.3	2.1	0.8	-0.7	-1.4
	Prud	0.6	-2.0	1.7	2.6	0.5	-1.7	-0.1	0.5
	RegPract	-0.3	-1.4	1.2	3.5	1.0	-1.1	1.0	-0.2
	FinInt	0.2	-2.2	1.7	1.4	1.0	-2.7	-0.3	-1.4
IAIS	RegGov	-1.4	-1.0	-0.2	1.2	0.7	-1.6	0.6	0.2
	Prud	-0.9	-1.1	0.8	-0.3	-1.0	-1.4	0.2	0.0
	RegPract	-1.4	-1.4	0.7	0.5	0.5	-2.2	-0.3	0.2
	FinInt	0.3	-0.2	0.2	-0.1	-1.8	0.1	0.1	-0.3
IOSCO	RegGov	-0.2	-0.3	0.2	1.2	0.2	-1.5	0.2	0.4
	Prud	-1.3	-0.6	0.3	2.0	0.7	-1.1	0.3	0.5
	RegPract	-1.5	0.5	0.4	0.2	1.0	-1.1	0.1	-0.2
	FinInt	-1.3	0.2	0.3	0.9	0.0	-2.1	0.0	0.3
		Coefficient Estimates for Per Capita GDP							
BIS	RegGov	6.3E-04	5.3E-04	5.4E-04	5.1E-04	5.5E-04	6.1E-04	5.3E-04	6.5E-04
	Prud	6.9E-04	6.1E-04	6.6E-04	6.3E-04	6.4E-04	6.3E-04	6.4E-04	6.5E-04
	RegPract	7.5E-04	7.0E-04	7.4E-04	7.4E-04	7.7E-04	7.2E-04	7.7E-04	7.7E-04
	FinInt	7.3E-04	6.7E-04	7.6E-04	7.6E-04	7.5E-04	6.6E-04	7.3E-04	8.2E-04
IAIS	RegGov	3.8E-04	4.5E-04	5.5E-04	5.7E-04	5.7E-04	3.3E-04	7.7E-04	1.1E-03
	Prud	4.4E-04	4.8E-04	5.5E-04	5.5E-04	5.0E-04	3.6E-04	4.4E-04	5.9E-04
	RegPract	5.1E-04	6.0E-04	6.6E-04	6.7E-04	6.1E-04	4.5E-04	5.7E-04	8.7E-04
	FinInt	5.7E-04	4.7E-04	5.3E-04	6.5E-04	4.3E-04	4.3E-04	6.7E-04	6.7E-04
IOSCO	RegGov	3.8E-04	4.7E-04	4.9E-04	4.2E-04	4.7E-04	3.6E-04	3.8E-04	2.9E-04
	Prud	6.5E-04	6.9E-04	7.5E-04	7.1E-04	6.9E-04	6.7E-04	7.3E-04	6.8E-04
	RegPract	3.5E-04	4.5E-04	4.4E-04	4.4E-04	3.9E-04	3.5E-04	3.6E-04	2.8E-04
	FinInt	3.9E-04	6.2E-04	6.1E-04	6.7E-04	6.2E-04	4.6E-04	5.6E-04	5.1E-04
		t-values for Coefficient Estimates for Per Capita GDP coefficient							
BIS	RegGov	5.0	4.2	4.6	4.9	4.9	3.9	3.9	
	Prud	6.3	6.1	7.0	6.9	6.6	6.2	5.7	4.5
	RegPract	6.0	6.0	6.8	7.4	7.1	6.2	6.2	5.1
	FinInt	4.7	4.8	5.6	5.6	5.4	4.7	4.6	4.1
IAIS	RegGov	1.6	2.0	2.4	3.0	2.8	1.4	3.1	2.8
	Prud	2.2	3.0	3.3	3.5	3.0	1.9	2.0	1.9
	RegPract	3.0	4.3	4.3	5.0	4.4	3.0	3.1	3.1
	FinInt	1.9	1.7	1.9	2.8	3.0	1.5	1.5	1.3
IOSCO	RegGov	2.4	3.2	3.6	2.8	3.1	2.4	2.3	1.3
	Prud	3.9	4.0	4.7	4.8	4.3	3.7	4.2	2.9
	RegPract	2.1	2.8	2.9	2.9	2.4	2.0	2.1	1.2
	FinInt	3.9	4.5	4.8	4.8	4.6	3.3	3.8	2.8

1/ Explanatory Note: The questions used from the BCL database are:
Q 3.4 'What is the actual risk-adjusted capital ratio in banks as of yearend 2005, using the 1988 Basel Accord definitions?'
Q 3.8.1 'What fraction of the banking system's assets is in banks that are 50 percent or more government owned as of year-end 2005?'
Q 3.8.2 'What fraction of the banking system's assets is in banks that are 50 percent or more foreign owned as of year 2005?'
Q 6.1 'Can the supervisory authority force a bank to change its internal organizational structure?1=Yes, 0 = No'
Q 6.2 'Has the power been utilized in the last 5 years? 1=Yes, 0 = No'
Q 9.4 'What is the ratio of nonperforming loans to total assets as of year-end 2005?'
Q 12.4 'How many professional bank supervisors are there in total?'
Q 12.5 'How many onsite examinations per bank were performed in the last five years?'

Source: Authors' estimates.

A possible explanation is that this is probably the case in only the better regulated systems. Third, a higher ratio of nonperforming loans to total assets is associated with lower BCP scores (significant in only one out of four regressions). This could be because systems with high nonperforming loan ratios are generally the ones that are less well-run.

Analysis of Other FSAP Recommendations

In addition to the quantitative findings derived from gradings, several recurrent themes emerge from a qualitative survey of the main overall messages in the FSAP assessments on EU countries. To complement the quantitative analysis above, this section reviews the available Financial System Stability Assessment (FSSA) reports, and presents the results of a survey of IMF leaders of FSAP missions.

A majority of the available FSSAs described the country's financial system to be well supervised. However, issues and gaps were identified in virtually all cases. In a minority of countries, 'substantial weaknesses' or 'important shortcomings' were identified. This is consistent with the findings of the quantitative analysis, which finds a majority of countries in the high-compliance range, but a relatively small minority with very low levels of compliance. For instance, in securities regulation, more than a half of the countries had an overall grading in the 80–100 percent range, but some five percent of the countries had overall gradings lower than 40 percent.

Most FSSAs highlighted the need to adjust the supervisory frameworks to meet new challenges, in particular those relating to cross-sector and cross-border financial integration. A majority of FSSAs stressed that the consolidation of the financial markets has increased the importance of effective cooperation within and across national jurisdictions. In several countries, this issue was raised in the context of strengthening consolidated supervision.[23] Additionally, a number of the FSSAs urged continued work, both domestically and internationally, in the areas of crisis management, deposit insurance, cross-border payment and settlement systems, and day-to-day cross-border supervisory cooperation. As a recent example, the 2006 FSAP for Belgium recommended that the supervisory agency position itself to meet new challenges stemming from the following cross-sector and cross-border issues: (i) the dominant role of conglomerates in the domestic market and their increasingly international character; (ii) the demands of Basel II and Solvency II; (iii) the implementation of the Financial Services Action Plan and the ongoing integration within the

---

[23] This is consistent with the finding of Section three that the principles on consolidated supervision have been among those with the lowest level of observance.

European market; and (iv) the changes in, and special requirements of, new cross-border financial market infrastructures, such as Euronext and Euroclear. As another example, the 2004 FSAP for the Netherlands included key recommendations on cross-border securities settlement and cross-border crisis management, both of which require close cooperation with foreign counterparts, and a recommendation on the deposit guarantee system, suggesting that it take into account the broader European context of depositor/investor protection arrangements.

Although the FSAPs often note the importance of cross-border issues, the process offers only limited scope to analyze them. In particular, FSAP missions have limited or no interaction with relevant foreign parties (both public and private), which means that the perspective of such parties is often not analyzed in depth.[24] A survey of IMF FSAP mission leaders suggests that this is primarily due to resource constraints and to a lesser extent to constraints on access to data and people abroad. FSAPs have also been able to give only limited coverage to important cross-border issues relating to crisis management, lender-of-last-resort support, safety nets, and risk management in international conglomerates, because their country focus does not lend itself to studying such supranational issues.[25] A study that specifically focused on these cross-border issues was done for the Nordic-Baltic region in 2006–07 (Wajid and others, 2007).

With respect to domestic prudential issues, several themes emerged:

- *Improving the monitoring of systemwide risks.* Virtually all FSSAs highlighted the need to improve the monitoring of new systemwide

---

[24] However, the U.K. FSAP team met with the German supervisory agency BaFin and US supervisors, and the Belgian FSAP team held discussions with Euroclear entities and customers abroad.

[25] In a sense, the FSAPs for euro area countries are only partial, because they could not fully assess important elements of the financial stability framework that are wholly or partially determined at the European level. The FSAP's country-based format also limits its ability to assess vulnerabilities related to cross-border conglomerates if an important part of the risk management of these conglomerates takes place abroad. Bottom-up stress tests of such conglomerates might not reflect the full nature of the risks presented by a particular scenario when the foreign risk management team has not been involved in the exercise.

risks. This was typically worded in terms of a need to improve macro-prudential surveillance processes and outputs, related to monitoring and analyzing new risks, implementing stress tests, and collecting and disseminating additional or more timely indicators.

- *Strengthening of regulations in specific segments.* Substantial improvements in insurance regulation were recommended most frequently (in about half of the surveyed FSSAs), which is consistent with the relatively lower level of compliance in this area. In some FSSAs, regulators were urged to focus on certain types of activities, for example, risks related to large and growing portfolios of residential mortgage loans.
- *Strengthening of regulatory governance.* The need to strengthen regulatory governance was raised in a majority of FSSAs. This is consistent with the quantitative findings of the previous section. The exact recommendations ranged from the need to reduce the potential for political interference in day-to-day supervision, to issues such as the need to strengthen the legal protection of supervisors or the lack of budgetary independence.
- *Improving corporate governance and disclosures.* This was also a recurrent theme, with about one-third of the FSSAs highlighting the need for improvements in corporate governance of financial institutions and their public disclosures.

Other issues not explicitly covered by the standards have been prominent in some country FSAPs. This includes the role of public ownership in the financial sector (for example, in Germany) and the relationship between concentration, competition, and stability (for example, in France and Italy). Prudential regulation can play a role, but only a secondary one, in addressing these issues.

Conclusions

We find that on average, countries' regulatory frameworks score one notch below full compliance with the international supervisory standards (on a four-notch scale). At the same time, there is substantial cross-country differentiation.

Perhaps the main finding of this chapter is a confirmation that there are significant differences in the quality of regulatory and supervisory frameworks across countries, and that the level of economic development is an important explanatory factor. This is evident from an analysis of the data by country peer groups (which is consistent with previous findings for smaller or narrower samples in IMF, 2002; IMF, 2004), and confirmed by regression analysis.

The regression analysis finds that banking supervision quality can be explained by governance variables and by income level (GDP per capita). For insurance supervision and securities regulation, the conclusion is similar, even though less strong. Also, we find that datasets focusing only on regulations 'on the books' have low correlation with the standard assessments used in this chapter. When we break down our analysis by geographic regions, we find substantial differences in regulatory quality across regions, some (but not all) of which can be explained by differences in economic development.

The analysis suggests that financial supervisory systems in high-income economies are generally of higher quality than those in medium- or low-income economies. However, supervision in high-income countries also faces bigger challenges, as they are characterized by more complex financial systems. On balance, therefore, our research cautions that despite the higher grades obtained by high-income countries, the supervisory knowledge about the financial strength of their institutions may not be higher than that for low- or middle-income countries. Indeed, the recent global financial crisis suggests that the higher quality of supervisory systems in many high-income countries was in fact insufficient given the complexity of their financial systems.

Many of the gaps identified in the assessments have been recognized by country authorities and are being addressed as part of their reform plans. Progress in regulatory frameworks was confirmed by recent FSAP updates and other IMF surveillance work (FSAP updates have so far been completed for some 1/10 of the countries assessed under the original FSAP); however, the updated assessments also indicated that the financial environment has changed substantially in recent years, presenting new challenges.

The analysis of the assessments points out a need to close gaps in existing frameworks and also to adjust them to meet emerging challenges. Some of the gaps are relatively small and may have already been closed since the respective assessments were carried out, but new challenges have emerged as financial systems have become more integrated. These include those posed by the growing role of conglomerates and their increasingly international character, ongoing financial integration, and in some cases the emergence of cross-border financial market infrastructures. To a substantial extent, international standards are evolving to take these new challenges into account. The Basel Core Principles, for example, have recently been revised in part to better address cross-border banking and the increased importance of supervisory cooperation, as well as to ensure consistency with Basel II. Such evolution of best practices and standards ensures that compliance with the standards will to some extent always remain a moving goal. Therefore, attention for compliance with international standards should remain an important aspect of financial sector assessments.

Appendix: Main Areas for Improvements in Regulation and Supervision

Banking Regulation and Supervision

Based on the analysis summarized in Figure 15.4, the areas most in need of improvement in banking included supervision of other risks; connected lending; issues related to money laundering; supervisory objectives, autonomy, powers, and resources; remedial measures; and consolidated supervision.

- *Supervision of other risks:* The relevant Core Principle (CP13) requires that banking supervisors be satisfied that banks have in place a comprehensive risk management process to identify, measure, monitor, and control all other material risks and, where appropriate, to hold capital against these risks. The reasons for less-than-full compliance varied from country to country; in some cases the reason was lack of specific guidelines on interest rate risk and operational risk, and in other cases, the reason was weak guidelines on liquidity risk.

- *Connected lending:* The relevant principle (CP10) requires that – to prevent abuses arising from connected lending – banking supervisors have in place requirements that banks lend to related companies and individuals on an arm's-length basis, that such extensions of credit are effectively monitored, and that other appropriate steps are taken to control or mitigate the risks. The most frequent issues include absence of legal prohibition to lend to connected parties on more favorable terms than to nonrelated counterparts, absence of a limit above which exposures to connected parties are subject to board approval, absence of supervisory power to deem that a connection exists in cases other than those specified in the law, and absence of power to deduct connected lending from capital or require it to be collateralized.

- *Money laundering:* The relevant principle (CP15) requires that banking supervisors determine that banks have adequate policies, practices, and procedures in place (including strict know-your-customer rules) that promote high ethical and professional standards in the financial sector and prevent the bank being used, intentionally or unintentionally, by criminal elements. One of the common issues was low frequency of the relevant onsite inspections.

- *Supervisory objectives, autonomy, powers, and resources:* The relevant principle (CP1) requires clear responsibilities and objectives for each agency involved in the supervision of banks. The most frequent weaknesses related to the potential for political interference in day-to-day supervision, the lack of budgetary independence, and the need to strengthen the legal protection of supervisors.

- *Remedial measures:* The relevant principle (CP22) requires that banking supervisors have at their disposal adequate supervisory measures to bring about timely corrective action when banks fail to meet prudential requirements, when there are regulatory violations, or when depositors are threatened in any other way. The most frequent problems included limited powers to remove individuals, lack of statutory "prompt corrective action" procedures, and lack of powers to restrict dividend payments.

- *Consolidated supervision:* The relevant principle (CP20) notes that an essential element of banking supervision is the ability to supervise a banking group on a consolidated basis. The assessments often noted that supervisors need to rise to the challenge posed by the conglomerization of systems, which can provide systems with more stability, but can also pose additional challenges resulting from possible draining of capital from one type of institution to another. It can also create opportunities for arbitrage when prudential requirements are not well aligned across the different business lines. The most common issues include insufficient resources in insurance supervision or the absence of a fully articulated structure for sharing of information and assessments.

Insurance Regulation and Supervision

In insurance regulation, areas with low observance (Figure 15.5) ranged from market conduct issues to internal controls, derivatives and off-balance-sheet items, organization of the supervisor, corporate governance, assets, onsite inspection, licensing, and cross-border business operations. Specifically:

- *Market conduct issues:* The relevant principle (CP11)[26] requires insurance supervisors to ensure that insurers and intermediaries exercise the necessary knowledge, skills, and integrity in dealings with their customers. The most frequent weaknesses relate to ensuring that market conduct issues are better handled at the point of sale when the agent is actually selling the product. Some assessments noted that this is especially relevant for unit-linked products, which may not be suitable for all customers (from a risk tolerance perspective) and may be purchased on the basis of unrealistic expectations.
- *Internal controls:* The relevant principle (CP5) requires the insurance supervisor to be able to: review the internal controls that the board of directors and management approve and apply; request strengthening of the controls where necessary; and require the board of directors to provide suitable prudential oversight, such as setting standards for underwriting risks and setting qualitative and

---

[26] For simplicity, the references to individual ICP principles are based on the 2000 IAIS standard. ICP assessments based on the 2003 IAIS standards were also included in the analysis and are reflected in this summary.

quantitative standards for investment and liquidity management. The reasons for less-than-full compliance usually included lack of legislative support for internal controls in the operations of insurance companies.

- *Derivatives and off-balance-sheet items:* The relevant principle (CP9) requires the insurance supervisor to be able to set requirements with respect to the use of derivatives and off-balance-sheet items. In many cases, the assessments concluded that the onsite inspection programs generally need to be amended to state more precisely the work that has to be done by supervisors with regard to derivatives.

- *Organization of the supervisor:* The relevant principle (CP1) requires that the insurance supervisor be organized so as to be able to accomplish its primary task, which is to maintain efficient, fair, safe, and stable insurance markets for the benefit and protection of policyholders. The most common reasons behind less-than-full compliance were potential political interference in supervision and lack of adequate resources.

- *Corporate governance:* The relevant principle (CP4) requires establishing standards to deal with corporate governance. The most frequent reasons for less-than-full compliance were insufficient powers of the supervisory agency.

- *Assets:* The relevant principle (CP6) requires that standards be established with respect to the assets of companies licensed to operate in the jurisdiction. The most common reason for less-than-full compliance was the lack of specificity in the standards for establishing internal controls for managing assets in accordance with the overall investment policy.

- *On-site inspection:* The relevant principle (CP13) requires that the insurance supervisor be able to conduct onsite inspections to review the business activities and affairs of the company, including the books, records, accounts, and other documents. In most countries, the main reason for less-than-full compliance was the extended period between inspections for most companies and less than full implementation of a risk-based approach.

- *Licensing:* The relevant principle (CP2) requires that companies wishing to underwrite insurance in the domestic insurance market be licensed.

- *Cross-border business operations:* The relevant principle (CP15) notes that the insurance supervisor should ensure that all foreign insurance establishments and all insurance establishments of international insurance groups and international insurers are subject to effective supervision; that all newly created cross-border insurance establishments are subject to consultation between host and home supervisors; and that all foreign insurers providing insurance coverage on a cross-border services basis are subject to effective supervision. The reasons for less-than-full compliance varied from country to country, but one main concern was a lack of resources for supervisors to actively supervise branches of financial institutions abroad.

Securities Regulation and Supervision

In securities regulation, the number of low-compliance areas was relatively smaller than in banking and insurance. The main areas for improvement (Figure 15.6) relate to enforcement powers and the compliance program; capital and other prudential requirements; powers, resources, and capacity; and operational independence and accountability.

- *Enforcement powers and compliance program:* The relevant principle (Q10) requires an effective and credible use of inspection, investigation, surveillance, and enforcement powers as well as implementation of an effective compliance program. The most frequent reason for less-than-full compliance was the limited ability of the supervisor to carry out full inspections, investigations, surveillance, and enforcement.
- *Capital and other prudential requirements:* The relevant principle (Q22) requires that there be initial and ongoing capital and other prudential requirements for market intermediaries that reflect the risks these intermediaries undertake. A common issue under this principle was that capital requirements have insufficient risk component, because regulators had a weak understanding of market intermediary operations.
- *Powers, resources, and capacity:* The relevant principle (Q03) requires that the regulator has adequate powers, proper resources,

and the capacity to perform its functions and exercise its powers. Most of the countries less-than-fully compliant with this criterion were found needing more supervisory resources and some clarification of supervisory powers and institutional arrangements.

- *Operational independence and accountability:* The relevant principle (Q02) requires that the regulator be operationally independent and accountable in the exercise of its functions and powers. The most frequent reasons for less-than-full compliance were a lack of budgetary independence and the potential for political interference.

References

Barth, J. R., G. Caprio and R. Levine (2006), *Rethinking Bank Regulation: Till Angels Govern*, Cambridge, MA, USA: Cambridge University Press.

Carmichael, J., A. Fleming, and D. T. Llewellyn (2004), *Aligning Financial Supervisory Structures with Country Needs,* Washington, DC, USA: World Bank.

Carvajal, A. and J. Elliott (2007), 'Strengths and Weaknesses in Securities Market Regulation: A Global Analysis,' IMF Working Paper No. 07/259, Washington: International Monetary Fund.

Čihák, M. and R. Podpiera (2006), 'Is One Watchdog Better Than Three? International Experience with Integrated Financial Sector Supervision,' IMF Working Paper No. 06/57, Washington, DC, USA: International Monetary Fund.

Čihák, M. and R. Podpiera (2008), 'Integrated Financial Supervision: Which Model?,' *North American Journal of Economics and Finance*, doi:10.1016/j.najef.2008.03.003.

Čihák, M. and A. Tieman (2007), 'Assessing Current Prudential Arrangements,' in J. Decressin, H. Faruqee and W. Fonteyne (eds.), *Integrating Europe's Financial Market,* Washington, DC, USA: International Monetary Fund.

Čihák, M. and A. Tieman (2008), 'Quality of Financial Sector Regulation and Supervision Around the World,' IMF Working Paper No. 08/190, Washington, DC, USA: International Monetary Fund.

Das, U. S., M. Quintyn and K. Chenard (2004), 'Does Regulatory Governance Matter for Financial System Stability? An Empirical Analysis.' IMF Working Paper 04/89, Washington, DC, USA: International Monetary Fund.

Dewatripont, M. and J. Tirole (1994), *The Prudential Regulation of Banks,* Cambridge, MA, USA: The MIT Press.

Herring, R. and A. Santomero (2000), 'What is Optimal Regulation?,' Financial Institution Center, University of Pennsylvania.

International Monetary Fund (2002), 'Implementation of the Basel Core Principles for Effective Banking Supervision, Experiences, Influences, and Perspectives', Washington, DC, USA: International Monetary Fund.

International Monetary Fund (2004), Financial Sector Regulation: Issues and Gaps', Washington, DC, USA: International Monetary Fund.

Kaufmann, D., A. Kraay and M. Mastruzzi (2003), 'Governance Matters III: Governance Indicators for 1996–2002', Washington, DC, USA: The World Bank.

Kaufmann, D., A. Kraay and M. Mastruzzi (2007), 'Governance Matters IV: Governance Indicators for 1996–2006', Washington, DC, USA: The World Bank.

Podpiera, R. (2004), 'Does Compliance with Basel Core Principles Bring Any Measurable Benefits?' IMF Working Paper No. 04/204, Washington, DC, USA: International Monetary Fund.

Wajid, S. K., A. Tieman, M. Khamis, F. Haas, D. Schoenmaker, P. Iossifov and K. Tintchev (2007), *Financial Integration in the Nordic-Baltic Region*', Washington, DC, USA: International Monetary Fund.

16. Regulating the Regulators: The Changing Face of Financial Supervision Architectures Before and After the Financial Crisis

Donato Masciandaro and Marc Quintyn

Introduction

In June 1998 the responsibility for banking supervision in the United Kingdom (UK) was transferred from the Bank of England to the newly established Financial Services Authority (FSA), which was charged with supervising all segments of the financial system. For the first time a large industrialized country – as well as one of the main international financial centers – had decided to assign the task of supervising the entire financial system to a single authority, other than the central bank. After that symbolic date, the number of unified supervisory agencies has grown rapidly.

In Europe, this trend has seemed rather strong. True, the UK was not the first one to unify its supervisory structure. The Scandinavian countries (Norway (1986), Iceland and Denmark (1988) and Sweden (1991)) had preceded the UK. But it is no exaggeration to state that the establishment of the FSA really opened the gate to widespread reforms worldwide. In addition to the UK, three 'old' European Union member states – Austria (2002), Belgium (2004), and Germany (2002) – have since assigned the task of supervising the entire financial system to a single authority other than the central bank. In Ireland (2003) and the Czech and Slovak Republics (2006) the supervisory responsibilities were concentrated in the hands of the central bank.

Five countries involved in the EU enlargement process – Estonia (1999), Latvia (1998), Malta (2002), Hungary (2000) and Poland (2006) – have also reformed their structures, concentrating all powers in a single authority. Outside Europe unified agencies have been established in Kazakhstan, Korea, Japan and Nicaragua.

In general, the financial supervision architecture remains in a state of flux (Goodhart, 2007): many countries have profoundly modified the shape of their financial supervision architectures, while other countries refrained from drastic overhauls but nonetheless made some changes to the supervisory landscape (e.g., by merging two or three sectoral supervisors). The upshot of this wave of reforms is a much more diversified supervisory landscape than ever before in history.

The experience of the past few years provides evidence that the move towards even more integrated and complex financial markets has exposed the system to a growing risk of costly financial turmoil. The consequent concern for the health of the banking and financial industry has caused renewed attention to the supervisory settings. Policymakers and supervisors in all the countries, shaken by the financial crisis of 2007–2008, are wondering if they need to reshape their supervisory regimes (yet again).

In response to the supervisory reform trend, a new line of research on the determinants of the reform process and on the impact of the new architectures of financial supervision, has emerged. This chapter surveys and updates the existing literature on the topic.

The chapter is organized as follows. In section two we describe the current landscape of the financial supervision architecture and the correspondent role of the central bank in a cross-country perspective, drawing upon a database that includes 102 countries for the period 1998–2008. In our chapter we distinguish between regulation and supervision, focusing on the second one only.[1] Focusing on supervision is today more easy than in the past, given that an important development of the last fifteen years has been the shift towards separation of regulatory and supervisory authority (Monkiewicz, 2007). The focus of this chapter is on micro-prudential

---

[1] While regulation refers to the rules that govern the conduct of the intermediaries, supervision is the monitoring practice that one or more public authorities implement in order to ensure compliance with the regulatory framework (Barth et al., 2006).

supervision and consumer protection, while macro prudential supervision is usually carried out by the central bank and competition policy is in the hands of a specialized authority (Borio, 2003; Kremers, Schoenmaker and Wierts, 2003; Čihák and Podpiera, 2007; Herrings and Carmassi, 2008). The review of the recent body of research performed in sections three and four allows us to shed light, firstly on the factors affecting the choice of a given supervisory architecture and then on the impact of the supervisory setting in influencing the banking and financial performances. Section five concludes.

Cross-Country Comparison of Financial Supervision Architectures after a Decade of Reforms

In the last decade many countries have reformed the structure of their financial supervision. Let us consider a dataset consisting of an heterogeneous sample of 102 countries, belonging to all continents. Table 16.1 describes all the relevant features of the 102 supervisory regimes in the sample. In the ten years since 1998, 64 percent of the countries included in our sample – 66 on 102 – chose to reform their financial supervisory structure (Figure 16.1), by establishing a new supervisory authority and/or changing the powers of one – at least – of the already existing agencies.

Table 16.1 Supervisory Authorities in 102 Countries: FSU Index and CBFA Index (year: 2008)

Countries	Banking Sector (b)	Securities Sector (s)	Insurance Sector (i)	Rating	Weight	FSU INDEX[a]	CBFA INDEX[b]
Albania	CB	SI	SI	3	1	4	2
Algeria	CB,B1,B2	S	-	1	-1	0	2
Argentina	CB	S	I	1	0	1	2
Australia	BI,S	BI,S	BI,S	7	-1	6	1
Austria	U, CB	U	U	7	-1	6	1
Bahamas	CB	S	I	1	0	1	2

Table 16.1 Continued

Countries	Banking Sector (b)	Securities Sector (s)	Insurance Sector (i)	Rating	Weight	FSU INDEX	CBFA INDEX
Bahrain	CB	CB	CB	7	0	7	4
Belarus	CB	S	I	1	0	1	2
Belgium	U	U	U	7	0	7	1
Bolivia	B	SI	SI	3	0	3	1
Bosnia	CB,B1,B2	S	I	1	-1	0	2
Botswana	CB	S	I	1	0	1	2
Brazil	CB	S	CB,I	1	1	2	3
Bulgaria	CB	S	I	1	0	1	2
Cameroon	B	S	I	1	0	1	1
Canada	BI	Ss(**)	BI	3	0	3	1
Chile	CB,B	CB,S	I	1	-1	0	3
China	B	S	I	1	0	1	1
Colombia	BI	BI,S1,S2	BI	3	-1+1	3	1
Costa Rica	B	S	I	1	0	1	1
Croatia	CB	SI	SI	3	1	4	2
Cyprus	CB	S	I	1	0	1	2
Czech Republic	CB	CB	CB	7	0	7	4
Denmark	U	U	U	7	0	7	1
Ecuador	BI	S	BI	3	0	3	1
Egypt	CB	S	I	1	0	1	2
El Salvador	BI	S	BI	3	0	3	1
Estonia	U	U	U	7	0	7	1
Finland	BS	BS	I	5	0	5	1
France	CB,B1,B2	CB,S	I	1	-1+1	1	3
Georgia	U	U	U	7	0	7	1
Germany	U,CB	U	U	7	-1	6	1
Ghana	CB	S	I	1	0	1	2
Greece	CB	S	I	1	0	1	2
Guatemala	BI	S	BI	3	0	3	1
Haiti	CB	-	Is (**)	1	0	1	2
Hungary	U	U	U	7	0	7	1
Iceland	U	U	U	7	0	7	1
India	CB,B	S	I	1	-1	0	2
Iran	CB	CB	I	5	0	5	3
Ireland	CB	CB	CB	7	0	7	4
Israel	CB	S,I	I	1	1	2	2

Table 16.1 Continued

Countries	Banking Sector (b)	Securities Sector (s)	Insurance Sector (i)	Rating	Weight	FSU INDEX	CBFA INDEX
Italy	CB,S	CB,S	I	1	1	2	3
Jamaica	CB	S1,S2	S1,S2	3	-1	2	2
Japan	U,CB	U	U	7	-1	6	1
Jordan	CB	S	I	1	0	1	2
Kazakhstan	U,CB	U	U	7	-1	6	1
Kenya	CB	S1, S2	I	1	-1	0	2
Korea	U	U	U	7	0	7	1
Kyrgyzstan	CB	S	I	1	0	1	2
Latvia	U	U	U	7	0	7	1
Lebanon	B, CB	CB	I	1	1	2	3
Libya	CB	SI	SI	3	0	3	2
Lithuania	CB	S	I	1	0	1	2
Luxembourg	BS	BS	I	5	0	5	1
Macedonia	CB	S	I	1	0	1	2
Madagascar	BS	BS	I	5	0	5	1
Malaysia	CB	S	CB	3	0	3	3
Malta	U	U	U	7	0	7	1
Mauritius	CB	SI	SI	3	0	3	2
Mexico	CB,B	CB,S	I	1	1	2	3
Moldova	CB	S	I	1	0	1	2
Montenegro	CB	S	I	1	0	1	2
Morocco	CB,B	S,B	I,B	1	-1+1	1	2
Namibia	CB	SI	SI	3	0	3	2
Netherlands	CB,S	CB,S	CB,S	7	-1	6	4
New Zealand	CB	S	I	1	0	1	2
Nicaragua	U	U	U	7	0	7	1
Norway	U	U	U	7	0	7	1
Pakistan	CB	SI,Ss**	SI	3	-1	2	2
Panama	B	S	I	1	0	1	1
Peru	BI	S	BI	3	0	3	1
Philippines	CB	CB,S,Ss**	I	1	1	2	3
Poland	U	U	U	7	0	7	1
Portugal	CB	S	I	1	0	1	2
Romania	CB	S	I	1	0	1	2
Russia	CB	S	I	1	0	1	2
Rwanda	CB	CB	I	5	0	5	3

Table 16.1 Continued

Countries	Banking Sector (b)	Securities Sector (s)	Insurance Sector (i)	Rating	Weight	FSU INDEX	CBFA INDEX
Saudi Arabia	CB	S	CB	3	0	3	3
Singapore	CB	CB	CB	0	0	7	4
Slovak Republic	CB	CB	CB	7	0	7	4
Slovenia	CB	S	I	1	0	1	2
South Africa	CB,B	SI	SI	3	-1	2	2
Spain	CB.Bs(**)	CB,S	I	1	1-1	1	3
Sri Lanka	CB	S	I	1	0	1	2
Sweden	U	U	U	7	0	7	1
Switzerland	U	U	U	7	0	7	1
Tajikistan	CB	CB	I	5	0	5	3
Tanzania	CB	S	I	1	0	1	2
Thailand	CB	S	I	1	0	1	2
Trinidad Tobago	CB	S,CB	I,CB	1	2	2	4
Tunisia	CB	S	I	1	0	1	2
Turkey	B	S	I	1	0	1	1
Ukraine	CB	SI	SI	3	0	3	2
UAE	CB	S	I	1	0	1	2
Uganda	CB	S	I	1	0	1	2
UK	U	U	U	7	0	7	1
USA	CB,B	S,Ss**	I,Is(**)	1	-1	0	2
Uruguay	BC,BS	BC,BS	I, BC	5	1	6	4
Venezuela	B	S	I	1	0	1	1
Vietnam	CB	S	I	1	0	1	2
Zimbabwe	CB	S	I	1	0	1	2

Notes: The initials have the following meaning: B = authority specialized in the banking sector; BI = authority specialized in the banking sector and insurance sector; CB = central bank; G= government; I = authority specialized in the insurance sector; S = authority specialized in the securities markets; U = single authority for all sectors; BS = authority specialized in the banking sector and securities markets; SI = authority specialized in the insurance sector and securities markets.

(*) (b) = banking or central banking law; (s) = securities markets law; (i) = insurance law; (**) = state or regional agencies

[a] **FSU INDEX:** The index was built on the following scale: 7 = Single authority for all three sectors (total number of supervisors=1); 5 = Single authority for the banking sector and securities markets (total number of supervisors=2); 3 = Single authority for the insurance sector and the securities markets, or for the insurance sector and the banking sector (total number of supervisors=2); 1 = Specialized authority for each sector (total number of supervisors=3). We assigned a value of 5 to the single supervisor for the banking sector and securities markets because of the predominant importance of banking intermediation and securities markets over insurance in every national financial industry. It also interesting to note that, in the group of integrated supervisory agency countries, there seems to be a higher degree of integration between banking and securities supervision than between banking and insurance supervision; therefore, the degree of concentration of powers, *ceteris paribus*, is greater. These observations do not, however, weigh another qualitative characteristic: there are countries in which one sector is supervised by more than one authority. It is likely that the degree of concentration rises when there are two authorities in a given sector, one of which has other powers in a second sector. On the other hand, the degree of concentration falls when there are two authorities in a given sector, neither of which has other powers in a second sector. It would therefore seem advisable to include these aspects in evaluating the various national supervisory structures by modifying the index as follows: adding 1 if there is at least one sector in the country with two authorities, and one of these authorities is also responsible for at least one other sector; subtracting 1 if there is at least one sector in the country with two authorities assigned to supervision, but neither of these authorities has responsibility for another sector; 0 elsewhere.

[b] **CBFA INDEX:** For each country, and given the three traditional financial sectors (banking, securities and insurance), the CBFA index is equal to: 1 if the central bank is not assigned the main responsibility for banking supervision; 2 if the central bank has the main (or sole) responsibility for banking supervision; 3 if the central bank has responsibility in any two sectors; 4 if the central bank has responsibility in all three sectors. In evaluating the role of the central bank in banking supervision, we considered the fact that, whatever the supervision regime, the monetary authority has responsibility in pursuing macro financial stability. Therefore, we chose the relative role of the central bank as a rule of thumb: we assigned a greater value (2 instead of 1) if the central bank is the sole or the main authority responsible for banking supervision.

Source: Masciandaro (2004 and 2006) and our calculation

The trend of reforms is even more evident when we add a regional and country-income perspective. Figure 16.2 provides a breakdown

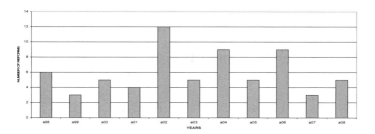

Figure 16.1 Reforms of the Supervisory Architectures per Year (1998–2008)

by country groups and shows that the European, the EU and OECD countries account for respectively 82 percent, 77 percent and 73 percent of the countries that have undertaken reforms. Therefore, the shape of the supervisory regime seems to be a relevant issue in particular in the more advanced countries, and particularly in Europe.

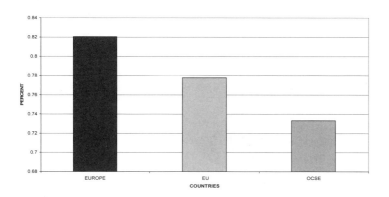

Figure 16.2 Reforms of the Supervisory Architectures (1998–2008, %)

There are signs that in the advanced countries the reform wave will continue – whether or not stimulated by the 2007–08 crisis. Switzerland adopted a unified structure at the beginning of 2009, and Italy and Spain are considering changes. However, most eyes are fixated on the US where, in March 2008, US Secretary Henry N. Paulson announced that his Department would undertake a comprehensive examination of the regulatory overlaps in the US financial supervision architecture (Department of the Treasury 2008). Its shortcomings were evident well before the 2007–08 financial crisis (Brown, 2005), but the crisis demonstrated the failure and the obsolescence of the argument for regulatory competition, which was most often used as the rationale to justify the US supervisory structure (Coffee, 1995; Scott, 1997).

Figure 16.3 summarizes the state of affairs. We group the current supervisory regimes taking into account the three main models of supervision that theory so far proposed: the vertical (silos) model, which follows the boundaries of the financial system in different sectors of business, and where every sector is supervised by a different agency; the horizontal (peaks) model, which follows the difference among the public goals of regulation, and where every goal is supervised by a different authority (Taylor, 1995); and the unified (integrated) model, where a single authority supervises all the financial system in pursuing all the public goals. We do not consider the model by function, which follows the functions performed by banking and financial firms, given its very limited historical use.

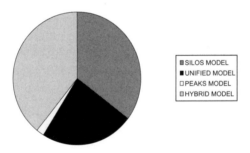

Figure 16.3 Models of Financial Supervision Architectures (102 countries)

In several situations – 36 countries, 35 percent of our sample – the supervisory regime still follows the vertical model, with separate agencies for banking, securities, and insurance supervision. The classic silos model worked well in a structure of the financial industry where a clear demarcation existed between banking, security markets and insurance companies. In the regimes consistent with this model, supervision is performed per sector of the financial market and is assigned to a distinct authority. In each sector a monopolist agency operates.

In another 24 percent of our sample (24 countries), a new regime of supervision has been established with the introduction of a single authority, where the supervision covering banking, securities and insurance markets is completely integrated. The single supervisory regime is based on just one control authority, which acts as a monopolistic agency on the overall financial system. In the small 'peaks' group we classify the two countries – Australia and the Netherlands, two percent of our sample – that adopted the so-called vertical model, which groups supervision aimed at preserving systemic stability in one peak, and the conduct of business supervision in another. Both the unified model and the peaks model represent examples of the consolidation process that seems to dominate the reforms of the supervisory architectures.

Finally, other countries adopted hybrid supervisory regimes, with some supervisors monitoring more than one segment of the market and others only one. We bring them all together in a residual class (40 countries, 39 percent of our sample); The group comprises countries such as France, Italy and the US, where the structure of the supervision can be explained using history – or political economy, as we will see below – rather than economic models.

The evolution in the supervisory regimes becomes more clear if we focus our attention on the 66 countries that implemented reforms in the period 1988–2008 (Figure 16.4): the weights of the three main regimes (unified, silos and hybrid) become substantially equal – respectively 30 percent, 33 percent and 33 percent – while the peaks regime is the least common one (four per cent). In other words, 40 percent of the sample (20 countries) adopted an innovative regime of supervision – unified or peaks regime – while the remaining 60 percent (31 countries) chose a 'conservative' approach, i.e., maintaining the more traditional regime (silos or hybrid regime).

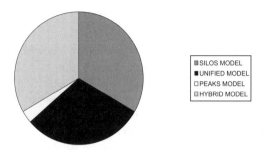

Figure 16.4 Model of Financial Supervision Regimes after the Reforms (66 countries)

One more interesting fact can be highlighted (Figure 16.5): the 'conservative' countries show a common feature, i.e. the central bank is the sole (or the main) banking supervisor in 80 percent of the sample (61 on 76).

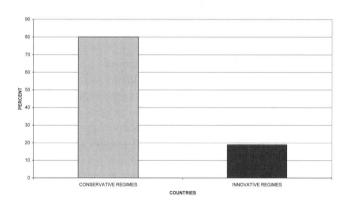

Figure 16.5 Central Bank as Main Supervisor: Conservative vs. Innovative Regimes (%)

At the same time, the adoption of an innovative model of supervision is centered on the role of the central bank in only very few cases (5 on 26 cases, 20 percent). In other words the conservative approach seems to be more likely to occur when the central bank is deeply involved in supervision, while the innovative approach seems to be more likely to occur if the main supervisor is different from the central bank.

Therefore, it is not surprising that the recent literature on the economics of the financial supervision architectures zooms in on this crucial fact. An increasing number of countries show a trend towards a certain degree of consolidation of powers, which in several cases has resulted in the establishment of unified regulators, that are different from the national central banks. Different studies (Barth, Nolle, Phumiwasana and Yago, 2002; Arnone and Gambini, 2007; Čihák and Podpiera, 2007) claim that the key issues for supervision are (i) whether there should be one or multiple supervisory authorities and (ii) whether and how the central bank should be involved in supervision. More importantly, these two crucial features of a supervisory regime seem to be related. The literature tried to go in depth in the analysis of the supervisory reforms measuring the key institutional variables (Masciandaro, 2004, 2006, 2007 and 2008), i.e., the degree of consolidation in the actual supervisory regimes, as well as the central bank involvement.

How can the degree of unification of financial supervision be measured? This is where the financial supervision unification index (FSU Index) comes in (description in Table 16.1). This index was created through an analysis of which, and how many, authorities in each of the examined countries are empowered to supervise the three traditional sectors of financial activity: banking, securities markets and insurance. The country sample depends on the availability of institutional data.

To transform the qualitative information into quantitative indicators, a numerical value has been assigned to each regime, in order to highlight the number of the agencies involved. The rationale by which the values have been assigned simply considers the concept of unification (consolidation) of supervisory powers: the greater the degree of unification, the higher the index value.

Figure 16.6 shows the distribution of the FSU Index. On the one hand there are countries (44) with a low consolidation of supervision (the index is equal to 0 or 1). On the other, there are countries (27) that established a unified supervisor or that adopted the peaks model, with a high level of supervisory consolidation (the index takes the value 6 or 7).

Now we can consider what role the central bank plays in the various national supervisory regimes. We use the index of the central bank's involvement in financial supervision (Masciandaro, 2004, 2006, 2007 and 2008): the Central Bank as Financial Authority Index (CBFA) (description in Table 16.1).

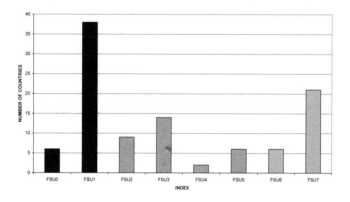

Figure 16.6 The Financial Supervision Unification Index

Figure 16.7 shows the distribution of the CBFA Index. In the majority of countries in our sample (46) the central bank is the main bank supervisor (the Index is equal to 2), while in very few countries (8) the central bank is involved in the overall financial supervision (the Index is equal to 4).

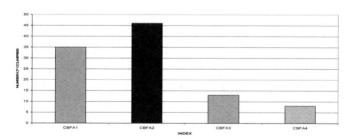

Figure 16.7 Central Bank as Financial Supervisor Index

Figure 16.8 brings both indexes together and shows that the two most frequent regimes are polarized: on the one hand, the Unified Supervisor regime (16 cases); on the other, Central Bank Dominated Multiple Supervisors regime (31 cases). The figure seems to depict a trade-off between supervision unification and central bank involvement, with two outliers.

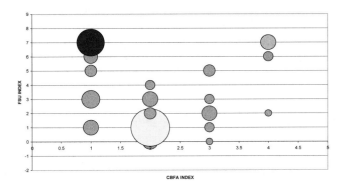

Figure 16.8 Financial Supervision Regimes

Therefore the descriptive analysis (Masciandaro, 2004, World Bank and IMF, 2005) signaled an intriguing result: the national choices on how many agencies should be involved in supervision seems to be strictly dependent on the existing institutional position of the central bank. The degree of consolidation seems to be inversely related to the central bank involvement in supervision; this effect was labeled 'central bank fragmentation effect'.

Determining the Shape of the Financial Supervision Architecture: Economics, Political Economy and Econometrics

How can the supervision consolidation trend outside the central banks be explained? The first natural answer should be to pursue a classic cost-benefit analysis, doing comparisons among the alternative models from a social welfare standpoint, calculating for each of them, on the one side the expected benefits and, on the other side the expected risks.

Economics

In general, different arguments for consolidation of supervision can be identified and related to effectiveness and efficiency. The key reasons for having a unified supervision can be classified into three categories, regarding respectively the governance, the relationships with the political system, and the relationships with the market participants:

1. Governance

a. Economies of Scale and Scope: a unified supervisor is more likely to achieve economies of scale in the use of the physical infrastructure as well as in employing human capital. At the same time, it is easier for a single agency to monitor banking and financial firms that are increasingly involved in more than one sector and/or line of business (Abrams and Taylor, 2002; De Luna Martinez and Rose, 2003; Čihák and Podpiera, 2007; Llewellyn, 2005; Herrings and Carmassi, 2008);
b. National Trade Off Resolution: the unified supervisor is more effective in dealing with conflicts that may arise between different goals of the national supervision, internalizing those conflicts (Wall and Eisenbeis, 2000);
c. International Trade Off Resolution: the more domestic banks become international financial conglomerates, the greater is the need for international cooperation and coordination, which is more easy to achieve if the supervisor is one (Abrams and Taylor, 2002);
d. Regulatory Flexibility: the single supervisor is likely to be more flexible in dealing with supervisory problems (Abrams and Taylor, 2002; Čihák and Podpiera, 2007);

2. Relationships with the Political System:

a. Accountability and Transparency: the unified agencies are by definition solely responsible for supervision and therefore it is easier for politicians, consumers and supervised firms to understand their policies; besides, the single supervisor cannot 'pass the buck' if problems arise, while this happens more easily with multiple supervisors (Briault, 1999; Abrams and Taylor, 2002; Čihák and Podpiera, 2007);

3. Relationships with the Markets:

a. Regulatory Arbitrage: as banking institutions grow bigger and more complex, they may include financial firms that are involved in different business areas; under a multiple supervisor regime financial conglomerates may engage in so-called regulatory arbitrage, while a single agency could avoid gaps that can arise with a model based on several authorities (Čihák and Podpiera, 2007; Llewellyn, 2005; Herrings and Carmassi, 2008);

b. Regulatory Costs: a unified supervisor is likely to reduce the cost of compliance, given that the supervised firms face one agent rather than many regulators (Briault, 1999; Abrams and Taylor, 2002; Čihák and Podpiera, 2007; Llewellyn, 2005; Herrings and Carmassi, 2008).

However, there are also several arguments against unification. They can be grouped under the same three headings as above:

1. Governance

a. Diseconomies of Scale and Scope: a bigger supervisor instead of multiple specialized agencies can produce inefficiencies in resource allocation as well as in the monitoring activity (Kahn and Santos 2005) and can lose the possibility to have diversification in approaching supervision, mainly in the financial systems where the businesses are not fully integrated (Abrams and Taylor, 2002; Čihák and Podpiera, 2007; Llewellyn, 2005; Herrings and Carmassi, 2008);

b. Regulatory Rigidity: the single supervisor is likely to be less flexible in dealing with supervisory problems, if there is uncertainty regarding the optimal regulation and how it may change over time (Herrings and Carmassi, 2008);

2. Relationship with the Political System:

a. Bureaucratic Overpower: a single supervisor can become a bureaucracy with excessive powers (Kane, 1996);

3. Relationship with the Markets

a. Regulatory Rent Costs: the single agency represents a monopoly in implementing supervision and consequently risks of rents can arise, for example considering the risks of excessive forbearance (Kahn and Santos, 2005; Čihák and Podpiera, 2007), while the multiple authorities-setting produces competition in supervision with benefits in terms of policy quality (Kane, 1996; Herrings and Carmassi, 2008).

Also on the second important issue in the architecture design, concerning the involvement of the central bank in the financial supervision, the literature offers arguments for and against.

A deeper involvement of the central bank in the supervision can be costly for different reasons. First of all, any extension of the central bank powers in the field of supervision can increase the classic moral hazard risks (Goodhart and Schoenmaker, 1995; Llewellyn, 2005; Herrings and Carmassi, 2008) (moral hazard effect).

Secondly, the more the central bank is involved in supervision the greater the risks of conflict among different goals (Goodhart and Schoenmaker, 1995; Padoa Schioppa, 2003); for example, costs can arise in delegating the conduct of business controls to the central bank, which has not traditionally sought to become involved in such matters of transparency (Goodhart, 2000; Bini Smaghi, 2007) (conflict of interests effect). Thirdly, the risk of reputational loss may be likely to increase if the central bank is deeply involved in supervision, while the reputational benefits are less likely to emerge, given the nature of the supervision policies, where failures are more visible than successes (Goodhart, 2000) (reputation effect). Finally, the society has to take into account the risks of increasing the bureaucratic powers of the central bank (bureaucracy effect) (Padoa Schioppa, 2003; Masciandaro, 2006).

The main argument in favor of the involvement of the central bank in supervision is linked to the positive effect stemming from information gains. Having supervisory powers may assist the central bank in making monetary policy more effective and/or making crisis management more effective (Goodhart and Schoenmaker, 1995; Bernanke, 2007; Herrings and Carmassi, 2008). An additional argument is related to the central bank capacity in attracting more skilled staff (Abrams and Taylor, 2002; Quintyn and Taylor, 2007).

In conclusion, different review essays (Abrams and Taylor, 2002; Lumpking, 2002; Arnone and Gambini, 2007; Čihák and Podpiera, 2007; Wymeersch, 2006; Holopainen, 2007; Monkiewicz, 2007) have demonstrated that there are no strong theoretical arguments in favour of any particular architecture of financial supervision and of any specific involvement of the central bank, given that it is possible to list advantages and disadvantages of each theoretical model. Arguments in favor of, or against, the unified model can be taken into account also to consider specific country studies (Gugler, 2005).

Political Economy

Thus, if the main driver of the supervisory reform is not the classic social welfare perspective, it is necessary to explore alternative views. Starting from the above findings, and the associated critique, a strand of the literature has addressed the question from a different perspective, focusing on the role of the political actors in the (re)design of supervisory architectures (Masciandaro, 2004, 2006 and 2008; Dalla Pellegrina and Masciandaro, 2008; Masciandaro and Quintyn, 2008).

This literature assesses that all the policymakers are politicians. Hence, they are held accountable at the elections for how they have pleased the voters. However, there are two types of politicians, with different objective functions, that can produce dissimilar outcomes in defining the financial supervision landscape. The main difference between the two concerns which voters they wish to please in the first place. On the one hand, the politician can be of the helping hand-type (HH), motivated by improving the general welfare. On the other hand, the politician can be of the grabbing hand-type (GH), motivated by the aim of pleasing vested interests.

The political economy approach for studying the determinants of the supervisory architectures is based on three crucial hypotheses. First, gains and losses of a supervisory model are variables calculated by the policymaker in charge, who decides to maintain or reform the supervisory regime. Second, the decisions of policymakers, whatever their own specific goals are, will likely be influenced by structural variables, that may vary from country to country. Among them, central bank involvement in supervision can play a crucial role. Finally, economic agents have no information on the true preferences of the policymaker: the latter's optimal degree of financial supervision concentration is a *hidden variable*.

The crucial element of this approach in considering the policymaker's objective as a factor in the design of the supervisory architecture is the identification of his preferences. The first approach to identifying the policymaker's function is the *narrative approach*, in which official documents and statements are interpreted to gauge the choices of policymakers (Westrup, 2007). One drawback of this approach is that there is often substantial room for difference between a policymaker's pronouncements and the actual, revealed preferences.

The second approach, the *factual approach*, is to consider the actual choices of policymakers in determining the level of financial supervision concentration. At each point, we can observe the policymaker's decision to maintain or reform the financial supervision architecture. In other words, we consider that policymakers are faced with discrete choices. Using the factual approach, we can investigate if the features of the financial markets play any role in determining the actual shape of the supervisory architecture. By taking a political-economic view, we can test the hypothesis that politicians may wish to use reform (or status quo) to gain or keep influence through the supervisory process. The relevant players in this theoretical framework are the policymakers, the community and the financial constituency.

In the economic literature, there is just one formal model that considers the policymaker's objective function in determining the degree of unification of the financial supervision regime (Masciandaro, 2008), which proposed a specific application of the general model developed by Alesina and Tabellini (2003) to investigate the criteria with which to allocate policy tasks to elected politicians.

Let us summarize the main findings of the model. The design of the financial supervision unification is modeled as a delegation problem, where the policymaker follows a sequential process: given the institutional position of the central bank, he chooses the supervisory design. If we take into account the existence of two constituencies with different preferences – the citizens and the financial industry – we can analyse the behavior of two alternative policymakers: the HH type versus the GH type.

If the policymaker acts as an HH type, central bank involvement in supervision can be viewed as an obstacle in the supervision consolidation if at least one of the three theoretical effects – moral hazard effect, conflict of interest effect and bureaucracy effect – holds. The so-called central bank fragmentation effect is likely to occur.

If the policymaker chooses to please the financial community acting as a GH type, the central bank fragmentation effect is less likely to occur, provided that the financial community likes a more consolidated supervision, and central bank involvement is a proxy of the financial constituency power.

If and only if these assumptions hold it is possible to disentangle the effect of different types of policymakers on the relationship between the financial supervision unification and the central bank involvement. Otherwise a signal extraction problem occurs. For example, other things being equal, if the central bank is not a captured one and the policymaker acts as a GH type, the central bank fragmentation effect is likely to occur again.

Therefore, theory predicts the possibility of different degrees of unification in the design of the supervisory structure, depending on the type of the policymaker involved, and on the features of the parameters of the model (i.e., the structural environment in which the policymaker takes his decisions). In the real world, the type of the policymaker – as well as all the structural and institutional channels which influence his behavior – is a hidden variable. At each point in time, we can only observe the politicians' decision to maintain or reform the supervisory governance structure, in particular its degree of unification.

Econometrics

The next step in the research (Masciandaro, 2007 and 2008; Masciandaro and Quintyn, 2008) was to empirically investigate the robustness of the relationship between the degree of financial supervision unification and central bank involvement, using the institutional variables – FSU Index and CBFA Index – described above and applying ordered models. Alternatively, it is possible to focus on the choice in terms of overall supervisory architecture, rather than just on the concentration of the supervisory powers (Dalla Pellegrina and Masciandaro, 2008).

The main result that emerges from the empirical work is the confirmation of a significant inverse relationship between supervision unification and central bank involvement. The central bank fragmentation effect – instead of the central bank unification effect – dominates. Given that the type of the policymaker is unknown, the story goes as follows. Each policymaker, in determining the degree of supervisory unification, could be influenced by the involvement of the central bank, but under different conditions. If the policymaker is of an HH type, he should care about the effectiveness of the supervision, in order to please the citizens. If the policymaker sees the supervision consolidation as a welfare improvement, then central bank involvement could be viewed as an obstacle, but only if at least one of the three effects – moral hazard, conflict of interest and bureaucracy – holds. If the policymaker is of a GH type, he wishes to please the financial constituency. In this case the central bank fragmentation effect holds if, and only if, the financial constituency dislikes unified supervision and the central bank is a captured agency. Furthermore, different proxies of the central bank power were used, other than the involvement in supervision: central bank age (Dalla Pellegrina and Masciandaro, 2008; Masciandaro, 2008), assuming that an old central bank is more influential; and central bank independence (Freytag and Masciandaro, 2007; Dalla Pellegrina and Masciandaro, 2008). The effects of the alternative indicators of the central bank role were mixed and in general weak.

Other variables were tested as well. The quality of public sector governance and the size of the country seem to matter in the decision making process on the degree of supervisory unification. With respect to the role of political governance in the decision making process, it can indeed be assumed that in countries characterized by good public sector governance, an HH type of policymaker is more likely to occur, which in turn would promote supervision unification if this is welfare-improving. Including population as an exogenous scale factor yielded a significant estimated parameter, highlighting the so-called small country effect (Taylor and Fleming, 1999): whatever the policymaker type, with relatively few people the expertise in financial supervision is likely to be in short supply, and concentration is more likely to occur.

Other potential drivers of the consolidation process turned out to be weak or not relevant at all. First of all, almost all the studies devoted to the analysis of the recent evolution in supervision design stressed the importance of the characteristics of the financial markets – with particular attention to the role of financial conglomerates – as determinants in the choice for a total or partial unification of the supervisory regimes. Some evidence (Masciandaro and Quintyn, 2008) seems more consistent with the GH view, when considering the degree of banking concentration as a proxy of the capture risk, and presuming the market demonstrates a preference for consolidation of supervisory powers. The results of a survey among financial CEOs in Italy (Masciandaro and Quintyn, 2008) confirms a market preference for a more consolidated supervisory regime but reveals only weak consistency between the views of the policymakers and those of market operators.

The possible presence of some sort of 'mimic effect' among neighboring countries has also been tested. Geographical dummies were used to capture the existence of international agreements between countries – such as the European Union, or the OECD membership – which may influence their behavior at home. The geographical testing did not produce any results.

The same fate befell the use of temporal variables. The use of this variable started from the finding that the number of countries that are reviewing their supervisory structures has been increasing year after year (until 2006). So a legitimate question about whether there was a kind of *fashion effect* (or bandwagon effect) at work arose, i.e., if recent reformers were inspired by the type of changes in supervisory arrangements introduced by earlier reformers, producing a trend towards unification (Monkiewicz, 2007). The results were not significant.

The possible effect of the legal origin has also been investigated. The law and finance literature claims that legal origin is associated with a variety of aspects of policymakers' performance. Countries of English (market friendly) legal origin perform better than countries with legal systems rooted in French, German, Scandinavian or other (socialist, Muslim) traditions. According to these sources, market friendly law traditions offer better protection against bad public policy (as in expropriation by the State) and greater incentive in providing public goods (as in good regulation). In countries with market friendly law origins, an HH policymaker is more likely to occur. Our results were puzzling: the level of supervision unification is linked with the Civil Law root, in particular with German and Scandinavian law jurisdictions. The testing of the legal origins effect produced mixed results in the empirical works.

Finally, the occurrence of a financial crisis as a reason for reform of the supervisory institutional set-up has also been considered (as has been suggested by Carmichael, Fleming and Llewellyn, 2005; and Monkiewicz, 2007). We can imagine that the decision making process of both types of policymakers can be affected by such a crisis, although the impact of a crisis experience on the degree of supervision consolidation is far from clear. The results were not significant.

Does the Financial Supervision Architecture Matter?

The emerging literature on the financial supervision architecture has also tried to shed some light on the impact of the supervisory structure on the performance of the banking and financial industry. Two main questions have been addressed: is a single supervisor to be preferred over multiple authorities? Should the central bank be involved in supervision? Unfortunately, despite the debate on the features of the supervisory regimes and their drivers, the empirical evidence is still very limited, probably given the fact that the wave of reforms is recent.

The first empirical analysis (Barth, Nolle, Phumiwasana and Yago, 2002) provided a cross country comparison of the banking supervision architectures, using a difference of means test to ascertain whether differences in the supervisory architecture correlate in a significant way with key differences in banking industry structure. The study gathered information on national banking supervisors in 133 countries, for the years 1996–1999.

The study found no correlation between the number of supervisory authorities and any of the key features of a banking system. On the other hand, central bank involvement in supervision seems to matter. In fact countries where the central bank is the banking supervisor have banking systems with a smaller average size, and have greater government ownership of banks and banking assets. Regarding the entry conditions, a greater number of applications to start a new bank were denied and a lower percent of foreign owned banks is present. These countries tend to allow a narrower range of banking powers. Furthermore, regimes with the central bank as supervisor are less likely to allow the use of subordinated debt as a component of capital and are less likely to have explicit deposit insurance systems; the index of moral hazard – calculated by the authors – is lower. The authors concluded that the issue of single versus multiple supervisory authorities was less urgent than the issue of the central bank powers in supervision. At the time however, the wave of consolidation was more an anecdotal phenomenon than a trend.

These results need to be interpreted with care. The authors did not test for causality. It is not clear that central bank involvement in banking supervision *per se* leads to the dominance of the above features of the banking system. Their findings may simply reflect a strong correlation in developing countries between the features mentioned. Many developing countries' financial systems still exhibited during the period under review the features that the authors list (presence of state-owned banks, barriers to entry and low presence of foreign banks), while supervision was housed in the central bank because of capacity constraints in the country.

A subsequent analysis (Čihák and Podpiera, 2007) suggested that the unified regime is associated with higher quality and consistency of supervision across supervised institutions, where the quality of supervision is measured using the degree of compliance with internationally accepted standards in banking, insurance and security regulation. At the same time the unified regime is not associated with a significant reduction in the supervisory staff. Finally, whether the integrated supervision is located inside or outside the central bank does not have a significant impact on the quality of supervision.

Finally, in a third piece of research (Arnone and Gambini, 2007), the degree of compliance with the Basel Core Principles for Effective Banking Supervision (BCP) is used to investigate the possible relationship between the compliance capacity of each country and the way these countries have organized their supervisory architecture, with particular reference to the two fundamental questions: the supervisory model and the role of the central bank. The article provides a description of the current institutional organization of banking supervision for a sample of 116 countries between 1999–2004.

The descriptive analysis provides several hints in favor of integration of supervisory powers. When considering the two most diffused models of supervisory architecture, the authors find a stronger (and significant) positive correlation between integrated supervisory regimes outside the CB and compliance with the BCPs, compared to CB-dominated multiple-agencies supervisory regimes. Furthermore two econometric tests, based on an OLS specification with heteroskedasticity-robust standard errors, show that a higher degree of compliance is achieved by those countries applying a unified model, with some evidence in favor of doing so inside the central bank.

Conclusion

The worldwide wave of reforms in supervisory architectures that we have witnessed since the end of the 1990s leaves the interested bystander with a great number of questions regarding the key features of the emerging structure, their true determinants, and their effects on the banking and financial industries. This chapter has tried to provide an overview of the answers to these questions by reviewing the recent literature that has been devoted to this topic.

The evolution of the supervisory regimes was described by drawing upon a database on 88 countries for the period 1998–2008. Inspection of this database highlights a supervision consolidation trend outside the central banks, where the outliers are central banks without the monopoly in monetary policy responsibilities.

In other words the tendency of the supervision structures to change seems to be characterized by two distinctive features: consolidation and specialization. The reforms were driven by a general tendency to reduce the number of agencies, to reach the unified model – unknown before 1986 – or the vertical model. In both models the supervisors are specialized, having a well defined mission. The trend towards specialization becomes particularly evident if we observe the route that national central banks are following. Those banks with full responsibility for monetary policy – the FED, the ECB, the Bank of England, the Bank of Japan – do not have full responsibility of supervisory policy. This does not mean that these banks are not concerned with financial stability – on the contrary, as we have observed over the last few months – but they tend to deal with it from a macroeconomic perspective, in function of their primary mission i.e. monetary policy. Amidst the central banks which do not have full responsibility for monetary policy, such as those of the countries belonging to the European Monetary Union, the most prudent banks chose or are about to choose the route of specialization in vigilance: we can look at the most emblematic cases of Czech Republic, Ireland, Netherlands and the Slovak Republic. In general, it has been noted (Herrings and Carmassi, 2008) that the central banks of members of the EMU have become financial stability agencies.

To explain this trend a political–economic approach has been used, where the decision-making process regarding the shape of the supervisory regime seems to be related to the influence of the institutional setting of the central bank and to the role of political governance: the consolidation is more likely to occur in countries characterized by a good public sector governance *and* where the central bank is only weakly involved in supervision. The consolidation trend seems to be correlated with a striving for better quality of the supervisor, while the effects of the central bank involvement are so far mixed. However the limited number of tests and data do not allow us to make any further comments.

Now, in the face of 2007–08 financial turmoil, which are the lessons from the past that can be useful for the future? The events that shook the world will force the actors to reconsider the architectures of financial supervision. The starting point is to recognize that in these years financial markets have grown bigger and more complex almost everywhere. How can we best supervise the ever-changing markets, which are becoming increasingly complex and intertwined with each other? The general formula for an effective supervision is always the same: it is necessary to have exhaustive and up-to-date information. But it is the application of the classical formula that is tricky today. In markets that were fundamentally static and segmented – banks, the stock exchange, insurance – a simple 'photograph' of the situation every now and then was sufficient; the vertical model was the natural and effective answer. Nowadays, to have an exhaustive and up-to-date informative patrimony it is necessary to explore in depth the innovative models of supervision: the unified model and the horizontal model.

However, the economic rationale for modifying the supervisory settings is not always sufficient. Politics matter as well. To stress the role of politics and of politicians it is fundamental to understand where, why and how reforms about supervision can see the light of day. Why do politicians not take action? And when are they going to do so? In order to find the answers to these questions more research is still warranted; if government's helping or grabbing hand can leave fingerprints all over the topic, the mission of the researcher is to find them.

References

Abrams, R.K. and M.W. Taylor (2002), 'Assessing the Case for Unified Sector Supervision' *Financial Markets Group Special Papers* No.134, FMG, LSE, London.

Alesina, A. and G. Tabellini (2003), 'Bureaucrats or Politicians? Part II: Multiple Policy Task.' Discussion Paper No.2009, Harvard Institute of Economic Research, Harvard University, MA, USA.

Arnone, M. and A. Gambini (2007), 'Architecture of Supervisory Authorities and Banking Supervision' in Masciandaro D. and M. Quintyn (eds), *Designing Financial Supervision Institutions: Independence, Accountability and Governance*, Cheltenham, UK and Northampton, MA, USA: Edward Elgar, pp. 262–308.

Barth, J.R., D.E. Nolle, T. Phumiwasana, and G. Yago (2002), 'A Cross Country Analysis of the Bank Supervisory Framework and Bank Performance', *Financial Markets, Institutions & Instruments*, **12**(2), 67–120.

Barth, J.R., G. Caprio and R. Levine (2006), *Rethinking Bank Regulation. Till Angels Govern.* Cambridge, MA, USA: Cambridge University Press.

Bernanke B. (2007), 'Central Banking and Banking Supervision in the United States', Allied Social Sciences Association, Annual Meeting, Chicago, mimeo.

Bini Smaghi L. (2007), 'Independence and Accountability in Supervision' in D. Masciandaro and M. Quintyn (eds), *Designing Financial Supervision Institutions: Independence, Accountability and Governance*, Cheltenham, UK and Northampton, MA, USA: Edward Elgar, pp. 41–62.

Borio C. (2003), 'Towards a Macroprudential Framework for Financial Regulation and Supervision?', BIS Working Papers, N.128, Bank of International Settlements, Geneva.

Briault C. (1999), 'The Rationale for a Single National Financial Services Regulator', Financial Services Authority Occasional Paper, Series 2.

Brown, E.F. (2005), 'E Pluribus Unum – Out of Many, One: Why the United States Need a Single Financial Services Agency', American Law and Economics Association Annual Meeting.

Carmichael J., A. Fleming and D.T. Llewellyn (eds.) (2005), *Aligning Financial Supervision Structures with Country Needs*, Washington DC, USA: World Bank Publications.

Čihàk, M. and R. Podpiera (2007), 'Experience with Integrated Supervisors: Governance and Quality of Supervision,' in Masciandaro D. and M. Quintyn (eds), *Designing Financial Supervision Institutions: Independence, Accountability and Governance*, Cheltenham, UK and Northampton, MA, USA: Edward Elgar, pp.309–341.

Coffee, J. (1995), 'Competition versus Consolidation: the Significance of Organizational Structure in Financial and Securities Regulation', *Business Lawyer*, **50.**

Dalla Pellegrina, L. and D. Masciandaro (2008), 'Politicians, Central Banks and the Shape of Financial Supervision Architectures', *Journal of Financial Regulation and Compliance*, **16**, 290–317.

De Luna Martinez, J. and T.A. Rose (2003), 'International survey of integrated financial sector supervision', Policy Research Working Paper Series, No.3096, World Bank, Washington DC.

Department of the Treasury (2008), Blueprint for a Modernized Financial Regulatory Structure, Washington DC.

Freytag, A. and D. Masciandaro (2007), 'Financial Supervision Fragmentation and Central Bank Independence' in D. Masciandaro and M. Quintyn (eds.) *Designing Financial Supervision Institutions: Independence, Accountability and Governance*, Cheltenham, UK and Northampton, MA, USA: Edward Elgar.

Goodhart, C.A.E. (2000), 'The Organizational Structure of Banking Supervision', Financial Services Authority Occasional Paper, Series 1.

Goodhart, C.A.E. (2007), Introduction in D. Masciandaro and M. Quintyn (eds.) *Designing Financial Supervision Institutions: Independence, Accountability and Governance*, Cheltenham, UK and Northampton, MA, USA: Edward Elgar, pp.12–26.

Goodhart, C.A.E and D. Schoenmaker (1995), 'Should the Functions of Monetary Policy and Banking Supervision be Separated?' Oxford Economic Papers, 47(4), 539–560.

Gugler P. (2005), 'The Integrated Supervision of Financial Markets: The Case of Switzerland', *The Geneva Papers*, **30**, 128–143.

Herrings R.J. and J. Carmassi (2008), 'The Structure of Cross-Sector Financial Supervision', *Financial Markets, Institutions and Instruments*, **17**(1), 51–76.

Holopainen H. (2007), 'Integration of Financial Supervision, Discussion Papers', Bank of Finland, No.12.

Kahn, C. and J. Santos (2005), 'Allocating Bank Regulatory Powers: Lender of Last Resort, Deposit Insurance and Supervision', *European Economic Review*, 49, 2107–2136.

Kane E.J. (1996), 'De Jure Interstate Banking: Why Only Now?', *Journal of Money, Credit and Banking*, **28**.

Kremers J., D. Schoenmaker and P. Wierts (2003), 'Cross-Sector Supervision: Which Model?', in R. Herrings and R. Litan (eds), *Brookings Wharton Papers on Financial Services*: 225–243.

Llewellyn, D.T. (2005), 'Institutional Structure of Financial Regulation and Supervision the Basic Issues' in A. Fleming, D.T. Llewellyn and J. Carmichael (Eds.), *Aligning Financial Supervision Structures with Country Needs*, World Bank Publications, Washington DC, pp. 19–85.

Lumpking, S. (2002), *Supervision of Financial Services in OECD Area*, Paris, OECD.

Masciandaro, D. (2004), 'Unification in Financial Sector Supervision: The Trade-off Between Central Bank and Single Authority,' *Journal of Financial Regulation and Compliance*, **12**(2), 151–169.

Masciandaro, D. (2006), 'E Pluribus Unum? Authorities Design in Financial Supervision: Trends and Determinants', *Open Economies Review*, **17**(1), 73–102.

Masciandaro, D. (2007), 'Divide et Impera: Financial Supervision Unification and the Central Bank Fragmentation Effect', *European Journal of Political Economy*, **23**(2), 285–315.

Masciandaro, D. (2008), 'Politicians and Financial Supervision Outside the Central Bank: Why Do They Do it?' *Journal of Financial Stability,* **5**(2), 124–146.

Masciandaro, D. and M. Quintyn, (2008), 'Helping Hand or Grabbing Hand? Politicians, Supervision Regime, Financial Structure and Market View,' *North American Journal of Economics and Finance* **19**(2), 153–173, August.

Monkiewicz J. (2007), 'Consolidated or Specialized Financial Market Supervisors: Is there an Optimal Solution?', *The Geneva Papers,* **32**, 151–161.

Padoa Schioppa, T. (2003), 'Financial Supervision: Inside or Outside the Central Banks?' in J. Kremers, D. Schoenmaker, P. Wierts (eds), *Financial Supervision in Europe*, Cheltenham, UK and Northampton, MA, USA: Edward Elgar, pp. 160–175.

Quintyn, M. and M. Taylor (2007), 'Building Supervisory Structures in sub-Saharan Africa – An analytical framework'. IMF Working Papers WP 07/18.

Quintyn, M., S. Ramirez, and M. Taylor (2007), 'The Fear of Freedom. Politicians and the Independence and Accountability of Financial Supervisors,' in Masciandaro D. and M. Quintyn (eds), *Designing Financial Supervision Institutions: Independence, Accountability and Governance*, Cheltenham, UK and Northampton, MA, USA: Edward Elgar.

Scott, K. (1977), 'The Dual Banking System: a Model of Competition in Regulation', *Stanford Law Review*, **30**.

Taylor, M. (1995) *'Twin Peaks: A Regulatory Structure for the New Century'*, London: Centre for the Study of Financial Innovation.

Taylor, M. and A. Fleming (1999), 'Integrated Financial Supervision. Lessons from Northern European Experience,' *Policy Research Working Paper,* No. 2223, The World Bank.

Wall, L.D. and R.A. Eisenbeis (2000), 'Financial Regulatory Structure and the Resolution of Conflicting Goals', *Journal of Financial Services Research*, **17**, 223–245.

Westrup, J. (2007), 'Independence and Accountability: Why Politics Matter', in Masciandaro D. and M. Quintyn (eds), *Designing Financial Supervision Institutions: Independence, Accountability and Governance*, Cheltenham, UK and Northampton, MA, USA: Edward Elgar.

World Bank and IMF (2005), *Financial Sector Assessment: A Handbook*, Washington DC, World Bank and IMF.

Wymeersch, E. (2006), 'The Structure of Financial Supervision in Europe: About Single, Twin Peaks and Multiple Financial Supervisors', Financial Law Institute, Ghent University, mimeo.

17. Will They Sing the Same Tune? Measuring Convergence in the New European System of Financial Supervisors

Donato Masciandaro, Maria J. Nieto and Marc Quintyn[1]

Introduction

The development of a single financial market has been a long-term objective of the European Union (EU) and the achievement of this objective received a significant impetus with the introduction of the Euro, which has acted in many ways as a catalyst for financial integration. Soon after the establishment of the European Central Bank (ECB), a debate emerged about the desirable structure of financial supervision in this single financial market. In many circles it was indeed felt that, in order to support EU financial integration and preserve financial sector soundness, a substantive degree of coordination of regulatory and supervisory actions was needed.

For a long time, the debate remained dominated by divergences in academic and policy circles between, on the one hand, proponents of light forms of coordination among national supervisors and on the

---

[1] The views expressed in this paper do not necessarily represent those of the Bank of Spain and of the IMF. The authors would like to thank, without implication, Rosaria Vega Pansini for skillful research assistance and Martin Čihàk, Sylvester Eijffinger, Wim Fonteyne, Tomislav Galac, Daniel Hardy, Fabio Recine, Jan Willem van der Vossen and participants at the Finlawmetrics 2009 Conference (Milan, 18–19 June 2009) for helpful comments and suggestions.

other, those in favor of more centralized approaches.[2] Meanwhile, some initiatives in support of more regulatory and supervisory coordination among member states saw the light of day. The most important ones were: (i) on the *regulatory* side, the establishment of the Lamfalussy framework, an elaborate structure aiming at speeding up the legislative process governing the European financial system, delivering more uniform and better technical regulation, and facilitating supervisory convergence in support of financial integration and stability; and (ii) on the *supervisory* side, the establishment of supervisory colleges in charge of monitoring large cross-border groups.[3]

However, as is often the case, it takes a crisis to reform. The impact of the current financial crisis on EU members introduced a sense of urgency to the coordination/centralization debate. Indeed, two issues for regulatory and supervisory reform that have been gaining worldwide acceptance in the wake of the crisis are: (i) the expansion of the cross-institutional and cross-border scope for regulation while safeguarding constructive diversity; and (ii) the need for putting in place mechanisms for effective and coordinated supervisory actions (Sacasa, 2008). With 46 banking groups with significant holdings of cross-border assets and liabilities active on the EU's territory at end 2007, the relevance of these recommendations is great indeed. These cross-border banks operate in a multi-jurisdictional environment and do need to interact with multiple national supervisors. Against this background, the consensus has been growing that the efficiency and effectiveness of existing frameworks for banking regulation and supervision needs to be (re)assessed.

In October 2008, the European Commission mandated a group of experts, under the chairmanship of Jacques de Larosière to formulate recommendations on the future of European financial regulation and supervision. The group presented its report to the Commission in early

---

[2] See CEPS (2008) and Fonteyne and van der Vossen (2007) for overviews. Kremers et al. (2003) provides a good overview of the debate in the earlier years. Individual contributions include Nieto and Peñalosa, (2004) and Lastra (2006) on the need to harmonize regulatory frameworks; Prati and Schinasi (1999) and Goodhart (2000) on the establishment of integrated financial oversight; and Holthausen and Ronde (2005) and Mayes, Nieto and Wall (2008) on incentives for cooperation among national supervisors.

[3] For overviews, see CEPS (2008) and Fonteyne and van der Vossen (2007).

Spring of 2009.[4] Since then, developments at the policy level gained momentum. On 27 May 2009, the European Commission published its proposal for the structure of European financial supervision (based on the de Larosiere recommendations), which was adopted by ECOFIN on June 9 and by the European Council on 18–19 June 2009. [5][6]

The adopted structure consists of a macro-prudential supervisory framework centered around the European Systemic Risk Board (ESRB) and a micro-prudential supervisory framework, the European System of Financial Supervisors (ESFS), consisting of a steering committee, three sectoral European Supervisory Authorities (ESA) and the network of national supervisors.

This chapter focuses on the micro-prudential framework and is motivated by the finding that this relatively complex three-layered framework for micro-prudential supervision is composed, at the bottom layer, of a large group of a very heterogeneous set of national supervisory architectures (approximately 47 agencies for 27 countries), with a wide variety of governance arrangements, supervisory cultures and regulatory frameworks. Thus far, these features, and their implications for the working of the ESFS, have not really been the topic of any discussion (or concern) in the reform debate. [7][8]

---

[4] The de Larosière Report (2009).

[5] Commission of the European Communities (2009), and Council of the European Union (2009).

[6] In the months leading up to the recent decision, other proposals were floated as well. See for instance Wirtschaftswoche (2009) where ECB vice-president Papademos suggested that the ECB be in charge of the supervision of the large banks with cross-border operations. Hardy (2009) suggested the adoption of a 'European mandate' for national supervisors as a first step towards more coordination. Note that this proposal is not necessarily incompatible with the adopted framework. Defining such a mandate could actually be a stepping stone to make the new structure more incentive-compatible (see later).

[7] The de Larosière Report (2009, p. 53) recommends that '....organization, competences and independence of national supervisory authorities...' be evaluated, which should lead to concrete recommendations for improvement. On some occasions, the European authorities (Commission and ECB) have issued opinions on planned reforms in regulatory frameworks in member countries. Europe-specific studies that compared regulatory governance arrangements among members based on findings of IMF-World Bank

So, this chapter intends to fill this void in our understanding of the potential implications of heterogeneous supervisory architectures and governance arrangements for the quality of future EU financial regulation and supervision. Starting from an analysis of the current landscape of supervisory architectures and governance practices of the main supervisor (mainly banking supervisor) in each country, we identify those areas where lack of cross-country convergence could lead to failures in providing national supervisors the right incentives to cooperate across borders, and hence, could undermine the efficiency and effectiveness of EU supervision. We finish by formulating some recommendations to address these issues.

Following a brief overview in the next section of the main features of the European supervisory structure endorsed by the European Council, we devote a section to an analysis of the current European landscape of supervisory architectures. In line with the suggestions of the new research in the field, we analyze both the overall architecture and the role of the central bank therein. This review will (i) help us in detecting preferences among the 27 EU countries regarding their supervisory architectures, and (ii) allow us to make an assessment of some of the issues that could stand in the way of efficient and effective cooperation at the European level. The next section will analyze the degree of similarity in the governance of national financial supervisory authorities. We focus on two main dimensions of supervisory governance, independence and accountability. It will be pointed out that some differences in governance arrangements at the national level could potentially have a negative impact on European

---

Financial Sector Assessments Programs (FSAP) include Čihàk and Tieman (2007 and 2008), and Čihàk and Fonteyne (2009).

[8] As a short aside, a preliminary comparison with the process of establishing the ECB and the ESCB in the 1990s illustrates some of the more complex issues that policymakers will face when making the ESFS operational. First, some governance reforms in the national central banks were put forward as a prerequisite for joining the Euro-system. This convergence process was facilitated by the fact that central banks have always been more similar than supervisory agencies in terms of governance and mandates. In addition, the main task of the national central banks – formulation and implementation of monetary policy – was centralized in the ECB, whereas in the case of the ESFS the national authorities retain (at least in the foreseeable future) all their powers and responsibilities.

supervisory coordination – and thus European financial stability. This leads us to argue that (i) harmonization of governance principles towards the highest levels is essential in order to maximize effectiveness and efficiency of the new supervisory structure, and (ii) that such best practices should serve as a reference for the design of the governance arrangements of the supranational structures that will be put in place.

A European Supervisory Structure is Born

Following years of debate and slow action on this front, European supervisory reform got the center stage since the middle of 2008 (the UK was severely hit in 2007), when the financial crisis hit the EU financial system in all its layers and laid bare the weaknesses in the regulatory and supervisory coordination framework. In response to these events, the EU Commission mandated in late 2008 a group of experts under the chairmanship of Jacques de Larosière to present an analysis of the causes of the financial crisis as well as recommendations for supervisory reform in Europe.

The group presented its report in early Spring of 2009. The report proposed a strengthening of the Level Three committees of the Lamfalussy framework in a first stage (Recommendation 20). In a second stage an integrated European System of Financial Supervisors (ESFS) should be established (Recommendation 21). At a later stage, only two authorities would emerge: one for banking and insurance supervision and any other issue relevant for financial stability, and the other for conduct of business and market issues across sectors (Recommendation 22).

The proposal by the Commission (Commission of the European Communities, 2009) in fact collapses stages one and two for micro-prudential supervision, and establishes a second pillar for macro-prudential supervision. The central body of the latter is the ESRB. For micro-prudential supervision, the ESFS is a three-layered structure, with a Joint Committee, three European Supervisory Authorities (ESA) and the national supervisory agencies at the bottom layer. The three ESA emanate from the existing Level-Three authorities in the Lamfalussy framework. In line with the practice in this framework, they have sectoral responsibilities: the European Banking Authority

(EBA), the European Insurance and Occupational Pension Authority (EIOPA), and the European Securities Authority (ESA). A complex set of arrows indicates all the lines of communication between the two pillars as well as with the national authorities and the European authorities. The proposal of the Commission received the full support of ECOFIN on 9 June and the European Council adopted it as the European Supervisory Framework for the future during the 18–19 June 2009 Summit.

In the remainder of the chapter we focus on the ESFS, the micro-prudential framework. The framework, consisting of three sectoral authorities at the supranational level, belongs to the category of the traditional, or silo, approach to supervision (see next section). The Commission recognizes that many member countries have different architectures, but states that at the European level, this silo-approach was the most evident one.

The document remains vague with respect to the governance arrangements for the three new authorities. These need to be further elaborated in specific enabling legislation. The document states that the three authorities (ESA) should:

1. be independent from the political world; they should, among others, have budgetary independence;
2. have accountability arrangements toward the European institutions (Commission, Parliament and Court);
3. adhere to high transparency standards;
4. also liaise with all stakeholders, notably consumers.

The document also foresees wide-ranging powers vis-à-vis the national supervisory authorities to enforce harmonization of the regulatory framework and to correct non compliance by national supervisors. They should also play a role in harmonizing supervisory cultures among the latter.

While many of these arrangements and powers need to be further defined and specified, and more importantly, adopted by the European political authorities, it is clear that the national supervisors are entering a multiple principals – multiple agents framework, implying that all players involved need to have an incentive-compatible governance framework in order to make this supervisory network operational, efficient and effective. This network becomes even more complex if the lines of communication with the macro-prudential pillar are taken into account.[9] This short overview sets the stage for our analysis of national supervisory architectures and governance arrangements in the next sections.

Review of Supervisory Architectures[10]

In recent years, we have witnessed a profound change in the design of the institutions responsible for supervising financial markets and banks. The landscape of financial supervision has been going through a deep (r)evolution on all fronts, and many countries have undertaken important changes in their overall architecture, redefining who is responsible for what. Only 15 years ago, the issue of financial supervisory architecture was considered irrelevant. The fact that only banking systems were subject to robust supervision kept several of the current organizational questions in the sphere of irrelevance. In such a context, the supervisory design was considered either deterministic (i.e., an exogenous variable), or accidental (i.e., a completely random variable).[11] Since then, financial market development, resulting in the growing importance of insurance, securities and pension fund sectors, has made supervision of a growing number of non-bank financial intermediaries, as well as the investor protection dimension of supervision, highly relevant.

---

[9] See e.g., Bini Smaghi (2009).

[10] This section draws on Masciandaro, Nieto and Quintyn (2009).

[11] For an historical perspective, see the discussions in Goodhart (2007) and Capie (2007).

As a result of these changes, financial supervisory architectures are now less uniform than in the past. In some countries the architecture still reflects the classic sectoral model, with separate supervisors for banking, securities and insurance (e.g., France, Spain and Italy).[12] This model dominated until the end of the 1990s (Figure 17.1A).

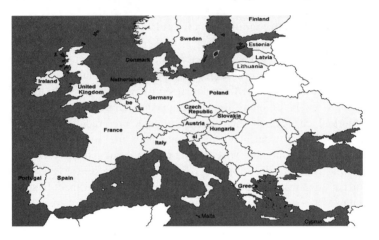

Figure 17.1A

However, an increasing number of countries have shown a trend towards consolidation of the supervisory responsibilities (Figure 17.1B), which has resulted in the establishment of unified supervisors in a number of countries (e.g., UK and Germany) (dark shading in the Figure 17.1B), which are different from the national central banks, while in a few cases (e.g., Czech Republic, Ireland and Slovakia) (light shading in the same Figure) the central bank emerged as the unified supervisor. Furthermore, Figure 17.1B also shows that one

---

[12] Political authorities in Italy and Spain have recently expressed their intention to reorganize their supervisory architectures. In Italy, the Parliament discussed in 2005 the 'hybrid' supervisory institutional setting, introduced a marginal reform of the antitrust responsibilities, reduced central bank involvement in supervision and shortened the Governor's term of office. In Spain, the government has announced its intention to reform the architecture of financial supervision separating financial stability and business conduct supervision in order to build an objectives-based model (see below in the text).

country – the Netherlands – adopted the so-called objectives-based (peaks) model (patterned in the Figure).

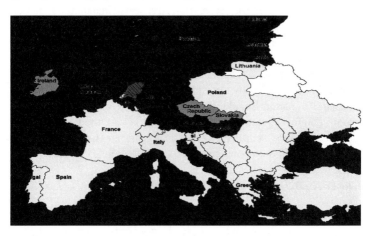

Figure 17.1B

The dynamic character of these reforms is highlighted by the fact that the present financial crisis is leading to a reassessment of the recent reforms (e.g., Austria in 2008, the debate in the United Kingdom following the Northern Rock debacle as well as a reconsideration of the latest reforms in Germany and Belgium), or has opened the debate in those countries that stayed out of the previous round of reforms (most prominently the United States).

The model of supervisory architecture and its degree of consolidation are two distinctive dimensions of the reform, although they can be highly correlated. In fact the same model of financial supervision can be designed with different degrees of supervisory consolidation. The single supervisory model, where the supervision of banking, securities and insurance markets is completely integrated, is based on just one control authority; but some powers (i.e., information gathering) can be shared with other authorities (typically the central bank).[13] In the (classic) specialized (sectoral) model, with separate supervisors for banks, securities and insurance, at least three separate

---

[13] García and Nieto, 2005, Table 1 presents the central bank access to banks' prudential information.

supervisors exist and more than one agency can supervise the same sector (as is the case in the US). The objectives-based model has one authority responsible for each objective of financial regulation (prudential supervision and business conduct). So, at least two authorities can be identified. However, some countries have identified more than two goals of supervision. As such, Australia has developed a 'four peaks model.' The Australian Securities and Investments Commission (ASIC) promotes fairness in the conduct of business, the Australian Prudential Regulation Authority (APRA) is responsible for micro prudential regulation (individual institutions), the Reserve Bank cares about macro stability, while the Australian Competition and Consumer Commission is in charge of antitrust policies.

A Closer Analysis of the EU Supervisory Landscape

For the purposes of this study, we concentrate on the degree of consolidation of financial supervision in the individual EU countries. This degree is measured by the financial supervision unification index (FSU Index) developed in Masciandaro (2004, 2005 and 2006) (description in Box 17.1). The index is created through an analysis of which, and how many, authorities are empowered to supervise the three traditional sectors of financial activity: banking, securities markets and insurance.[14] The qualitative information has been transformed into quantitative indicators by assigning a numerical value to each type of regime, in order to highlight the number of the agencies involved. The rationale by which the values are assigned simply considers the concept of unification of supervisory powers: the greater the degree of unification, the higher the index value.[15] This

---

[14] Sources: for all countries, official documents and websites of the central banks and the other financial authorities. The information is updated through 2006. See Box 17.1.

[15] There are five qualitative characteristics of supervisory regimes that we decided not to consider in constructing this index. Firstly, we did not consider the legal nature – public or private – of the supervisory agencies nor their relationship to the political system (degree of independence, level of accountability). Secondly, we excluded from this analysis the authority in charge of competition and market regulation. Since such an agency exists in all EU 27 countries, it was left out for the purposes of this analysis. We also did not include the agency in charge of the management of the deposit insurance schemes. In general, we consider only the three traditional sectors

gives us for each European country the level of financial supervision unification.

Box 17.1 The Institutional Indicators

FSU INDEX

The index was built on the following scale: 7 = Single authority for all three sectors (total number of supervisors=1); 5 = Single authority for the banking sector and securities markets (total number of supervisors=2); 3 = Single authority for the insurance sector and the securities markets, or for the insurance sector and the banking sector (total number of supervisors=2); 1 = Specialized authority for each sector (total number of supervisors=3).

We assigned a value of five to the single supervisor for the banking sector and securities markets because of the predominant importance of banking intermediation and securities markets over insurance in every national financial industry. It is also interesting to note that, in the group of integrated supervisory agency countries, there seems to be a higher degree of integration between banking and securities supervision than between banking and insurance supervision; therefore, the degree of concentration of powers, *ceteris paribus*, is greater. These observations do not, however, weigh another qualitative characteristic: There are countries in which one sector is supervised by more than one authority. It is likely that the degree of concentration rises when there are two authorities in a given sector, one of which has other powers in a second sector. On the other hand, the degree of concentration falls when there are two authorities in a given sector, neither of which has other powers in a second sector. It would therefore seem advisable to include these aspects in evaluating the various national supervisory structures by modifying the index as follows: adding one if there is at least one sector in the country with two authorities, and one of these authorities is also responsible for at least one other sector; subtracting 1 if there is at least one sector in the country with two authorities assigned to supervision, but neither of these authorities has responsibility for another sector; zero elsewhere.

CBFA INDEX

For each country, and given the three traditional financial sectors (banking, securities and insurance), the CBFA index is equal to: 1 if the central bank is not assigned the main responsibility for banking supervision; 2 if the central bank has the main (or sole) responsibility for banking supervision; 3 if the central bank has responsibility in any two sectors; 4 if the central bank has responsibility in all three sectors. In evaluating the role of the central bank in banking supervision, we considered the fact that, whatever the supervision regime, the central bank has responsibility in pursuing macro financial stability. Note that the countries of the Euro area are not monetary authorities. Therefore, we chose the relative role of the central bank as a rule of thumb: we assigned a greater value (two instead of one) if the central bank is the sole or the main authority responsible for banking supervision.

Source: Masciandaro (2007)

(banking, securities and insurance markets) that have been the subject of supervision. Finally, the financial authorities may perform different functions in the regulatory as well as in the supervisory area. However, at this first stage of the institutional analysis, we prefer to consider only the number of the agencies involved in the supervisory activities.

Figure 17.2 shows a polarized distribution of the countries according to the FSU Index with some EU countries (nine)[16] showing the lowest level of consolidation of supervision (Index equal to one), and others who have a unified supervisor (11),[17] the highest level of consolidation (Index equal to seven) (eight outside and three inside the central bank). Note that the new EU structure shows a relatively low level of consolidation.

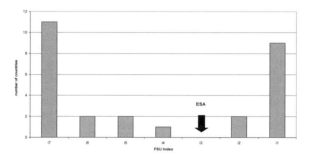

Figure 17.2 FSU Index Distribution

These different architectures are compatible with different levels of central bank involvement. Masciandaro (2006) uses the index of the central bank's involvement in financial supervision (Central Bank as Financial Authority Index – CBFA – described in Box 17.1). Figure 17.3 shows the frequency distribution of the CBFA Index. Again a polarization holds. In the majority of EU countries (13) the central bank is not the main bank supervisor (Index equal to one), while in just three countries (Czech Republic, Ireland and Slovakia) the central bank is monopolistic in the overall financial supervision (Index equal to four).

---

[16] Bulgaria, Cyprus, France, Greece, Lithuania, Poland, Romania, Slovenia, Spain .
[17] Belgium, Czech Republic, Denmark, Estonia, Hungary, Ireland, Latvia, Malta, Slovak Republic, Sweden, UK.

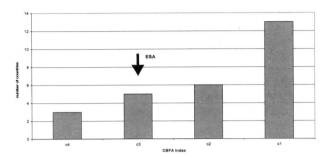

Figure 17.3 CBFA Index Distribution

Considering the FSU and the CBFA indices jointly for the EU countries, Figure 17.4 seems to depict a trade-off between supervision unification and central bank involvement, with three outliers (Czech Republic, Ireland and Slovakia – dotted bubble). The two most frequently adopted regimes are polarized: on the one hand, Unified Supervisor regime (eight countries[18]– black bubble); on the other, Central Bank Dominated Multiple Supervisors regime (seven countries[19] – white bubble). The position of the new EU structure (black star in Figure 17.4) reflects the three sectoral supervisors, without ECB involvement in micro-prudential supervision.

The EU situation confirms a general finding of the recent literature: the national choices on how many agencies should be involved in supervision seem to be closely correlated with the existing institutional position of the central bank. In general, the degree of supervisory unification seems to be inversely related with the central bank's involvement in supervision. The trade-off – and the related, so called central bank fragmentation effect [20] – was confirmed first using a cross-country analysis of the reforms in the supervisory regimes (Masciandaro 2004, 2005 and 2006) and analyzing the economics of the central bank fragmentation effect (Masciandaro 2007 and 2008,

---

[18] Belgium, Denmark, Estonia, Hungary, Latvia, Malta, Sweden, UK.

[19] Bulgaria, Cyprus, Czech Republic, Greece, Lithuania, Romania, Slovenia.

[20] Meaning, the presence of the central bank in the supervisory field typically leads to fragmentation of supervisory responsibilities, as opposed to unification.

Masciandaro and Quintyn 2008, Dalla Pellegrina and Masciandaro 2008). From a political economy point of view, the central bank fragmentation effect can be explained as a peculiar case of path dependence effect: the incumbent policymaker, in choosing the level of financial supervision consolidation, is influenced by the characteristics that already exist in terms of the central bank position. The policymaker's choices are viewed as a sequential process in which the institutional position of the central bank matters.

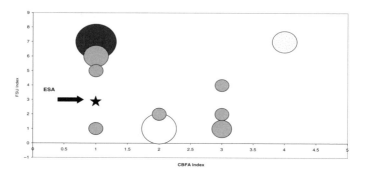

Note: The axes represent the two indices, while the diameter represents the number of countries for each regime.

Figure 17.4 Financial Supervision Regimes

It is evident that the degree of convergence among the EU countries is low. Furthermore, it has been claimed that no 'superior' model of supervision exists (see Schoenmaker 2003, and Quintyn et al., 2007, among others). Different contributions (Abrams and Taylor, 2002; Arnone and Gambini, 2007; Fleming, Lewellyn and Carmichael, 2004; Čihàk and Podpiera, 2007a, and 2007b) claim that there are no strong theoretical arguments in favor of any particular architecture of financial supervision. Advantages and disadvantages can be associated with each model.

Potential Policy Implications of Polarization

Even though there is no best practice with respect to the supervisory architecture, the existence of a polarized field of supervisory architectures, as it has emerged from domestic political and economic preferences, could potentially have a number of implications for the efficiency and effectiveness of European supervisory processes. The lack of uniform national architectures is likely to render supervisory coordination among countries and with the three European authorities difficult. Several studies (e.g. Čihàk and Tieman, 2007 and 2008, based on FSAP results, and Seelig and Novoa, 2009 based on a worldwide survey) show that supervisory cultures and governance practices differ significantly among sectoral supervisors (with banking supervisors typically having the strictest supervisory culture and the most stringent governance arrangements).[21] So, the wide variety of supervisory architectures, and the number of agencies on the EU territory could in the first place create hiccups in the coordination of supervisory actions and initiatives because of the multiple lines of communication.

In the second place, the wide variety of architectures goes hand in hand – almost in a one-to-one relationship – with a wide variety of supervisory cultures and governance arrangements which could make coordination even more difficult. While the obstacles created by such heterogeneity are not insurmountable, they could certainly throw sand in the wheels of smooth and efficient supervisory coordination at the EU level. This is a reality that European policymakers did not face when setting up the ECB and the ESCB. Central banks' cultures are less diverse than supervisory cultures. Moreover, central banks transferred their monetary policy prerogatives to the ECB, while supervisors retain under the adopted framework their powers over the domestic financial system. So the coordination and communication issues are of a different order now. Some of the implications of the co-existence of a wide variety of architectures will come out more clearly when the architectures are considered in conjunction with their governance structures in the next section.

---

[21] Several representatives of national authorities have also in private conversations with the authors of this paper alluded to the problems that these differences created at the time they were establishing a unified supervisor.

Finally, one also needs to bear in mind that a number of studies (e.g., Masciandaro, 2006, Westrup, 2007, and Masciandaro and Quintyn, 2008) show that revealed preferences with respect to national supervisory architectures often stemmed from political considerations (such as politicians fearing that independent central banks in charge of supervision would prevent politicians from keeping or having any influence on financial sector developments). In other cases, central banks were able to throw their weight in the discussion and managed to secure (or expand) their supervisory powers. Against the background of this reform record, it now remains to be seen whether individual countries will be inclined to revisit their supervisory architectures in light of the emerging European framework. Given that the European framework can also be subject for revision, one could also imagine some emerging competition among various architectures going forward.

Convergence in Supervisory Governance

In sharp contrast with the debate on independence of the central bank's monetary policy function, the terrain with respect to financial regulatory and supervisory governance remained relatively uncharted until recently. Somehow, it was assumed in the literature that, for those central banks that also performed supervisory functions, the independence in monetary policy spilled over into the supervisory functions. Almost no attention went to the governance of those supervisory agencies that were not housed in the central bank.

As argued in Das and Quintyn (2002) and Quintyn (2007), attention for governance arrangements for supervisors is needed because the job content of supervisors has been changing profoundly in response to the worldwide liberalization of financial sectors. Prudential supervisors are nowadays 'governance supervisors' who monitor, on behalf of depositors and tax payers, the quality of the supervised institutions' governance arrangements (Dewatripont and Tirole, 1994). Quintyn (2007) shows that solid governance arrangements for financial supervisors – built around arrangements for independence, accountability, transparency and integrity – are a precondition for effective supervision. More specifically, Quintyn and Taylor (2003 and 2007) and Hüpkes et al. (2005) made the case for independence and accountability of supervisory agencies and spelled out the operational implications.

These papers also argue that accountability arrangements of financial supervisors in a democratic environment must necessarily be more complex than for monetary policy authorities owing to: (i) their multiple, and harder to measure objectives; (ii) the existence of a multiple principals environment; and (iii) the extensive legal powers typically conferred on them in combination with their legal immunity. It has been further argued that from a social welfare standpoint independence and accountability should not be regarded as mutually exclusive but are complementary to the extent that well-designed accountability arrangements can help to buttress agency independence.

Assuming that the theoretical case for independence and accountability is accepted, this section draws on the earlier work of Quintyn, Ramirez and Taylor (2007) (hereafter called QRT), which established a framework for analyzing and rating independence and accountability arrangements for bank supervisors based on their legal frameworks (*de iure* measurements).[22] QRT define 19 criteria to measure supervisory independence and 22 for the quality of accountability arrangements (Table 17.1). We refer to QRT (2007) for a detailed discussion of the methodology and the sources of information (mainly national regulations). A rating of 'two' is given if the law satisfies the criteria, a 'one' is given for partial compliance, and a 'zero' for non compliance. In some cases a '-1' is given for what are considered practices that undermine independence or accountability.[23] The individual ratings are summed and normalized

---

[22] We focus on bank supervision, given its central and crucial role in preserving the overall financial stability in the EU, and by extension in most countries around the globe. We are aware that, where the institutional setting is the sectoral model, a complete analysis would require the examination of the other agencies as well.

[23] For example in some European countries the Minister of Finance has retained (some) oversight power on supervision – Austria, Cyprus, Denmark, Estonia, Germany, Greece, Hungary – or a government representative is on the agency's policy board – Estonia, Finland, France, Germany, Latvia, Poland, Spain and Sweden.

between zero and one.[24] Our sample contains 14 countries where bank supervision is part of the central bank's responsibilities[25] and 13 countries where an agency, separate from the central bank is in charge of banking supervision.[26]

Table 17.1 Independence Criteria (19)

1. Institutional Independence
The agency has a legal basis (law, act, …)
The law states that the institution is independent
The chairman and senior executives appointed by two branches of government
The decision-making body a board (not a single person)
All agency staff have legal immunity for actions done in good faith
No parliamentarians are sitting on policy board of agency
There is no government official on the agency policy board
The law/act does not give the minister of finance the right to intervene in policy decisions made by the agency
The law defines clear criteria for dismissal of the president of the agency
2. Regulatory and Supervisory Independence
The agency can autonomously issue legally binding prudential regulations for the sector
The agency has the sole right to issue licenses
The agency has the sole right to withdraw licenses
The agency has the sole right to impose sanctions on supervised institutions
The agency has the right to enforce supervisory sanctions
3. Budgetary Independence
The agency is funded through fees from the supervised entities
The agency need not submit the budget to the government for a priori approval
The agency has autonomy in defining salaries and salary structure of staff
The agency can autonomously hire staff
The agency can autonomously define the internal organizational structure

Source: QRT (2007).

Measuring Independence

The criteria for independence are regrouped hereafter into three different dimensions: institutional; regulatory and supervisory, and budgetary independence. Regulatory and supervisory independence form the core, while institutional and budgetary independence are

---

[24] Given an indicator, for each country the normalized value of the ranking is the ratio between the absolute value of the indicator and the maximum value reached in the sample of the 27 EU countries.

[25] Bulgaria, Cyprus, Czech Rep., France, Greece, Ireland, Italy, Lithuania, Netherlands, Portugal, Romania, Slovak Rep., Slovenia and Spain.

[26] Austria, Belgium, Denmark, Estonia, Finland, Germany, Hungary, Latvia, Luxembourg, Malta, Poland, Sweden and UK.

essential to support the execution of the core functions. The Basel Committee on Banking Supervision recognized the importance of supervisory independence by making it part of its first 'Core Principle for Effective Bank Supervision' (Basel Committee, 1997 and 2006):

> *Basel Core Principle 1:* 'An effective system of banking supervision will have clear responsibilities and objectives for each agency involved in the supervision of banks. Each such agency should possess operational independence and adequate resources...'

Institutional Independence

Institutional independence refers to the status of the agency as an institution separate from the executive and legislative branches of government. The following are two critical elements of institutional independence. First, independence is best served if there are clear rules on the terms of appointment and dismissal of the agency's senior personnel. Under such rules regulators would enjoy security of tenure, enabling them to speak and take action without fear of dismissal by the government of the day. Ideally, both the executive and legislative branches of government should be involved in the appointment process. Second, regarding the agency's governance structure, collegial decision-making structures are considered better than systems where the chairperson solely takes the decisions.

QRT consider nine criteria to assess institutional independence. Figure 17.5 shows that ten countries have a high degree of compliance (throughout, we use as rule of thumb a level of the index equal or greater than 75 percent to indicate high compliance), while two countries have granted less institutional independence to their unified supervisory agency.

From the point of view of coordination/centralization in the EU, three criteria for institutional independence seem super-critical and therefore warrant a more detailed analysis: legal immunity of supervisors; presence of government officials on policy boards, and dismissal procedures for presidents and senior management.

Legal immunity. Despite the high degree of compliance on independence, we notice that, on this dimension, supervisors in a large number of EU 27 countries do not possess legal immunity when exercising their job in good faith. Legal immunity is unanimously considered a *conditio sine qua non* for effective supervision. Lack of immunity may prevent supervisors from taking decisive actions, thereby creating forbearance. In a system that relies heavily on home-country supervision, forbearance in one country could easily and quickly spread across the EU, thereby reducing the incentives to cooperate. Legal immunity (or the lack thereof) must also be seen in conjunction with judicial accountability (see below).

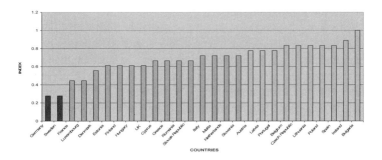

Figure 17.5 Institutional Independence: Cross-country Convergence

Government officials on policy boards. The EU countries are relatively heterogeneous with respect to the presence of government officials on supervisory policy boards, often as chairpersons. More specifically, several recent members from Central and Eastern Europe have kept or adopted this practice. Having government officials in decision-making positions undermines supervisory independence from the political process. Our findings also show that in those countries where government officials are on policy boards, accountability towards legislative and executive branches is relatively underdeveloped, which in itself opens the door to other forms of unequal treatment of supervisors. Having politicians in decision-making positions could potentially lead to issues such as slowing down the adoption of EU Directives, favoring national interests through regulatory processes, promoting national financial institutions or champions, shifting the regulatory burden to other countries, or domestically applying forbearance for short-term political gain. All these outcomes would have an impact on coordination among national supervisors and, ultimately on the effectiveness of the European supervisory framework. While such practices may also emerge under independent supervisors, they are more likely to surface when politicians have a direct say in the supervisory process.

Dismissal procedures. Several EU countries do not stipulate specific dismissal procedures for agency presidents and senior management. Again, this could potentially undermine political independence of the regulatory and supervisory process and foster self capture.

In an analysis of the quality of regulatory and supervisory arrangements in Europe, based on the IMF-WB FSAPs, Čihàk and Tieman (2007) come to similar conclusions, based on scores with respect to the Basel Core Principles which are less detailed on regulatory governance than our criteria. They find that 'The most frequent weaknesses relate to the potential for *political interference in day-to-day supervision,* the lack of budgetary independence and *the need to strengthen the legal protection of supervisors*' (italics are ours).

Regulatory and Supervisory Independence

Regulatory independence refers to the ability of the agency to have an appropriate degree of autonomy in setting those fundamental prudential rules and regulations for the sectors under its supervision, within the confines of the country's broader legal framework.[27] A high degree of autonomy in setting prudential regulations is expected to help in ensuring that the financial sector complies with international best standards and practices. Lack of autonomy introduces risks that revisions are unnecessarily spun out over time, or that regulatory capture by government or industry may result in regulatory forbearance.

Supervisory independence concerns the independence with which the agency is able to exercise its judgment and powers in such matters

---

[27] Prudential regulations cover general rules on the stability of the business and its activities (e.g., fit and proper requirements for senior management), as well as specific rules that follow from the special nature of financial intermediation (risk-based capital ratios, limits on off-balance sheet activities, definition of limits on exposure to a single borrower, limits on connected lending, loan classification rules, and loan provisioning rules).

as licensing, on-site inspections and off-site monitoring, sanctioning, and enforcement of sanctions (including revoking licenses), which are the supervisors' main tools to ensure the stability of the system. The need for adequate authority is also recognized by the Basel Committee on Banking Supervision:

> *Basel Core Principle 23:* Banking supervisors must have at their disposal adequate supervisory measures to bring about timely corrective action when banks fail to meet prudential requirements (such as minimum capital adequacy ratios), when there are regulatory violations, or where depositors are threatened in any other way. In extreme circumstances, this would include the ability to revoke the banking license or recommend its revocation.

Supervisory independence is arguably the most difficult aspect of independence to guarantee. To preserve its effectiveness, the supervisory function typically involves private ordering between the supervisor and the supervised institution. But the privacy of the supervisory process makes it vulnerable to interference, from both politicians and supervised entities. Such interference can take many forms and can indeed be very subtle, making it difficult to shield the supervisors from all forms of interference. Some argue therefore that critical supervisory actions (such as 'intervening' in a financial institution) should be rules-driven to avoid that too much discretion leads to forbearance.[28]

QRT identify five criteria to assess regulatory and supervisory independence. Figure 17.6 shows that EU countries are highly compliant in this regard. Two criteria deserve particular attention: regulatory independence and licensing powers.

Regulatory independence. Supervisors in a minority of EU countries do not have the autonomy to define the prudential regulatory framework. In a number of countries constitutional rules do not allow the rulemaking prerogative to be given to agencies. These limitations could hinder cross-border coordination of regulation and an homogeneous transposition of the EU Directives.

---

[28] See Nieto and Penalosa (2004) for arguments why EU countries should adopt rules-based intervention policies.

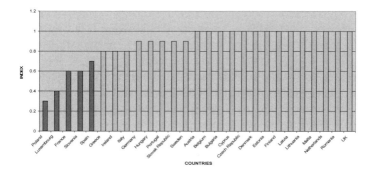

Figure 17.6 Regulatory and Supervisory Independence: Cross-country Convergence

Licensing and withdrawing licenses. This remains a sensitive area in a number of EU members. Several countries in the EU prefer to keep a role for the government in the area of licensing – and even more withdrawing licenses (e.g., Italy and Spain). Unlike for some other criteria, there is no dividing line here between the 'old' and 'newer' members. While some governments have retained this role only as a formality, several others wish to keep an active role in the process of closing a financial institution. An active government role in withdrawing licenses delays, at the minimum, supervisory action and increases supervisors' incentives to forbear, which could be particularly conspicuous in cross-border supervision. In the worst case, it opens the door to political considerations with respect to the composition and operation of a country's financial system.

Budgetary Independence

Budgetary independence refers to the ability of the agency to determine the size of its own budget and the specific allocations of resources and priorities that are set within the budget. Regulatory agencies that enjoy a high degree of budgetary independence are better equipped to withstand political interference (which might be exerted through budgetary pressures), to respond more quickly to newly emerging needs in the area of supervision and to ensure that salaries are sufficiently attractive to hire competent staff.

Funding via a levy on the regulated reduces the risks typically associated with funding from the government budget. To avoid industry capture and ensure that the fees are reasonable, in some countries, their level is determined jointly by the regulatory agency and the government. Fee-based funding is also vulnerable to the risk that the regulator's resources will be most limited when the industry is under strain. If, for whatever reason, there is a consensus that funding needs to come from the government budget, the budget of supervision should be proposed and justified by the agency, based on objective criteria related to developments in the markets. Masciandaro, Nieto and Prast (2007) analyze the financing of banking supervision in 90 countries (including the EU countries). They show that supervisors housed in the central bank are in most cases funded through the latter's budget, while supervision funded via a levy on the regulated banks is more likely in the case of a separate financial authority, with some countries applying mixed funding. In general, there seems to be a trend toward more private funding. At the EU level, some degree of cross-country convergence in matters of budgetary independence is desirable. Large discrepancies in fee structures may disturb level playing field conditions among supervisors in the EU with respect to their input of supervisory efforts.

QRT use five criteria to assess the degree of budgetary independence. Figure 17.7 shows that 16 EU countries are highly compliant with the criteria, with only one country – Malta – significantly diverging. Čihàk and Tieman (2007) listed the lack of budgetary independence among the main weaknesses in the European supervisory frameworks.

Measuring Accountability

The criteria for accountability, defined in QRT, are regrouped into three dimensions: political accountability, judiciary accountability and transparency – mainly accountability arrangements versus other stakeholders (Table 17.2).

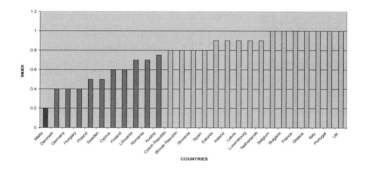

Figure 17.7 Budgetary Independence: Cross-country Convergence

Political Accountability (Toward Legislative and Executive Branches)

In most systems of government the legislative branch plays a vital role overseeing the activities of the executive branch in virtue of its representative character. The objective of its oversight is to ensure that public policy is administered in accordance with legislative intent. The key is that the supervisors should be accountable *'ex post'* to the political authorities for the appropriateness of their actions.

Since the principles of regulatory regimes are normally promulgated by parliament, the latter should be a primary actor charged with holding the financial regulator accountable for meeting the stated objectives in its mandate.[29] This can be achieved through regular institutionalized contacts between the regulatory agency and

---

[29] In Westminster-type systems, accountability to parliament typically goes through the minister who bears the final responsibility for the activities of the financial regulator. This helps explain the low rate of compliance for the UK.

parliament (or a parliamentary committee). Parliament's influence on the regulatory activities ought to be exerted primarily through its law-making powers, i.e., by making changes to the legal framework when needed.

An independent agency also needs to have a direct line of accountability to the executive branch because the latter bears the ultimate responsibility for the general direction and development of financial policies, and the minister of finance needs to be aware of developments in the financial system, given the government's active role in financial crisis management. Formal channels of communication should include the annual report, as well as regular reporting (monthly, quarterly). Masciandaro, Nieto and Prast (2007) find anecdotal evidence that public financing of supervisory agencies is more associated with accountability towards Parliament, while private financing seems to go hand in hand with an emphasis on accountability towards government.

Table 17.2 Accountability Criteria (22)

1. Political Accountability
The agency's mandate is defined in the enabling legislation
With multiple mandate, the objectives are prioritized
There is an obligation in the law to present annual report to legislative branch
The law provides for possibility of regular hearings before committees (e.g. quarterly)
Accountability to the legislature is not delegated to finance minister (i.e., not the chair of the agency presents the report to parliament but the minister of finance).
There is an obligation in the law to present the annual report to executive branch
The law provides for a possibility of regular briefing meetings with minister of finance (e.g., quarterly, …)
The law provides for the possibility for ad hoc hearings
2. Accountability to the judiciary branch
Supervised entities have the right to appeal supervisory decision to courts
Distinct judicial processes are in place to handle these appeals
Appeals are handled by specialized judges
The law provides for penalties for faulty supervision
3. Transparency
There is a process whereby the agency presents and discusses its budget ex post
There is a practice of disclosure of supervisory policies and of decisions (website)
The agency has issued a mission statement
The annual report is available to the general public
There is a possibility for inquiries by the general public (email, ombudsman)
The law provides for a consumer consultation board in the framework of regulation and supervision
The law requires a formal ex ante consultation process with the industry about new regulations
The law requires a formal consultation process with the public at large about new regulations
The agency has an internal audit process in place
The agency has an external audit process in place

The executive branch also has an important role to play in the appointment of the senior officials of the regulatory agency. In many countries, they are appointed by the government or by the head of state upon recommendation by the government or finance minister. Best practice would imply the involvement of two branches of government to ensure checks and balances: the legislative branch appointing senior officials, upon recommendation of the government. While the right to appoint the chief executive and/or members of the agency's board for a fixed term enhances independence, the right for removal on clearly specified grounds, is an indispensable accountability mechanism.[30]

QRT identify eight criteria to assess the degree of the political accountability. Figure 17.8 shows that four countries have the highest ratios, while two countries – Denmark and UK – are at the bottom.

Judicial Accountability (Toward Judiciary Branch)

Given the extensive legal powers typically conferred on regulatory agencies in combination with their legal immunity, judicial review is a cornerstone of their accountability relations in respect of supervisory measures. Any independent agency should be accountable 'ex post' to the judicial system for the legality of its actions. The former should have some right of legal redress in court. Judicial review provides a procedure whereby the courts oversee the exercise of public power. Traditionally, the purpose of judicial review of administrative action is to ensure that the decision-maker acts within its powers.

---

[30] Dismissal procedures are of relative value if dismissal is limited to cases of malfeasance. In no instance is serious misconduct interpreted as including the failure to discharge functions properly in accordance with the statutory objectives of the financial regulator and thus in terms of bad performance.

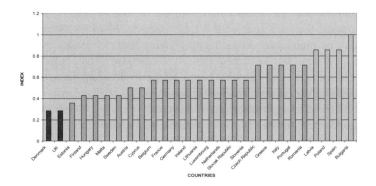

Figure 17.8 Political Accountability: Cross-country Convergence

Individuals or institutions subject to the agency's decisions should also have the right to apply to a judicial authority for review of those decisions. The agency must indeed observe a number of due process requirements when it takes decisions such as issuing or withdrawing licenses and imposing sanctions. Once a formal decision has been taken, the party to whom the decision is addressed must be informed of his or her legal remedies. The purpose of these requirements is to ensure the procedure is as transparent as possible and that it results in a fair and just decision.

There should also be a form of substantive accountability (judicial review of the substance of supervisory measures). The difficulty here is that the discretion conferred on a supervisor is typically broad and courts in practice prefer to exercise restraint and defer to the expert knowledge of the supervisor given that they do not normally possess the expertise in financial matters and are therefore reluctant to substitute their judgment on supervisors. Substantive accountability is therefore often limited to review of legality with a view to ensuring that discretion is not exercised in bad faith or for improper purposes.[31] Substantial review needs to be limited and time-bound in order to avoid that the process will stand in the way of regulatory and supervisory efficiency and effectiveness and ultimately undermine agency independence.

---

[31] Hüpkes (2000).

In the event that a regulatory agency is found to have breached its legal duties, the plaintiff must have some remedy available. However, the need to ensure agency independence means that there should be a variety of limitations on liability for faulty supervisory action. Any official of an agency who took action in good faith should not be held personally liable for damages caused in the exercise of his functions. Because rules on immunity and limited liability of the supervisor are correlates of independence, their existence needs to be compensated by appropriate accountability arrangements including judicial review and a procedure that offers administrative compensation in cases where loss was suffered due to unlawful action by the agency.

QRT identify the criteria to assess the accountability to the judiciary branch. Figure 17.9 shows that compliance with this aspect of accountability is somewhat problematic in the EU: only seven countries – Finland, Ireland, Netherlands, Malta, Portugal, Sweden, and UK – reach high ratios, while as many as twelve do not. Only few EU countries have elaborate mechanisms of judicial accountability. Several countries do not provide for rights of appeal by institutions affected by supervisory decisions. Likewise, only few countries' legislation provides for penalties for supervisory mistakes. Lack of proper mechanisms for judicial accountability could have several repercussions. On the one hand, the need for judicial accountability mechanisms must be seen as a counterweight against the right to legal immunity (see above) and the broad sanction and enforcement powers typically conferred to supervisors. This is a clear example of a case where independence can become ineffective, if not put in a context of accountability arrangements. Extreme differences in judicial accountability could potentially lead to regulatory arbitrage – financial institutions looking for countries where arrangements are most favorable – or forms of regulatory capture – weaker judicial practices that lead financial institutions to influence the regulatory process in specific countries.

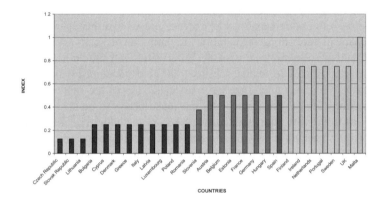

Figure 17.9 Judiciary Accountability: Cross-country Convergence

Transparency

The critical elements of transparency relate to the decision making of supervisory action to all stakeholders. Inherent in financial supervision is the fact that many decisions involve commercially sensitive material that it would be delicate to disclose. But the presumption should be in favor of openness in the decision-making process, making it possible for both the public and the industry to scrutinize regulatory decisions minimizing the risk of political interference. Moreover, in the prevailing institutional framework in the EU based on the principle of 'home control,' and the existence of 'supervisory colleges'[32] the possibility of asymmetric information tends to reduce or undermine mutual trust and incentives to cooperate among supervisory agencies. In order to address these potential problems, supervisors need to be assured that their counterparts in other jurisdictions comply with all accountability and transparency arrangements and that there is maximum openness towards peers.

An important instrument of agency accountability is the presentation of financial accounts, demonstrating the regularity of

---

[32] For an earlier account of the problems with home country control, see Mayes and Vesala (1998).

expenditures. Masciandaro, Nieto and Prast (2007) find that, in the case of prudential supervisors housed in central banks and financed exclusively through seigniorage, the budgeting process and financial statements are in general those of the central bank (e.g., The Netherlands, Spain and Portugal). They also share financial statements in the case of prudential supervisors financed by supervised institutions that operate within central banks and, as a consequence, do not have separate assets and liabilities (e.g., Ireland).

In order that this aspect of accountability should not undermine agency independence by the back door, financial accountability should be limited to ex post accountability, focusing on a review of the annual accounts and balance sheets by independent auditors to determine whether there has been proper financial management, whether the authority is managing its resources in an efficient way, and whether financial reports represent a true and fair view.

The EU countries show a high degree of compliance with the transparency criteria. Some areas of accountability and transparency vis-à-vis stakeholders, such as consultation processes with supervised entities, and consultation with the public at large, are not very developed in most EU countries (although the process is well established at the EU level in the context of the Lamfalussy architecture). Insufficient consultation and transparency may result in an uneven transposition of EU directives at the national level as well as in limited convergence of supervisory practices. Figure 17.10 shows that ten countries are highly compliant with the ten criteria defined in QRT. No country seems to be way out of line.

Is the Governance Convergence within the EU?

Governance, in the words of Williamson (2000) ' ... is an effort to craft *order*, thereby to mitigate *conflict* and realize neutral *gains*. So conceived a governance structure obviously reshapes incentives' (italics are ours). By extension, and in the context of the ESFS, governance arrangements serve to (i) craft order, *internally* in the agency, and *between* the agency and its stakeholders which include in the new European setting, the other national agencies and the European-level agencies; (ii) mitigate conflict between the agencies and their stakeholders; and (iii) assist in realizing neutral gains for all stakeholders, i.e. to assure that the division of labor and the delegation of powers to the different layers in the ESFS is a socially optimal solution. Hence, the ESFS, and the individual countries have an interest in harmonizing their governance arrangements to align their incentive structures in order to achieve the EU-wide supervisory objectives.

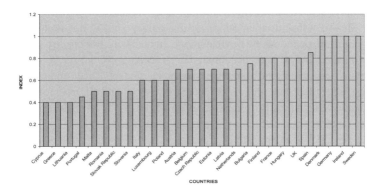

Figure 17.10 Transparency: Cross-country Convergence

So, do we see convergence in governance arrangements among EU countries? The general answer is a cautious 'yes' but with some important provisos nevertheless. Indeed, close inspection of the results reveals some issues that deserve attention in the run-up to the implementation of the ESFS. Before we enter into details, it is worthwhile emphasizing the positive aspects of our analysis. First of all, the analysis in Čihàk and Tieman (2007) and (2008), QRT (2007), and Masciandaro, Quintyn and Taylor (2008) show that regarding regulatory governance, European supervisors have, on average, the highest degrees of compliance in a worldwide sample. QRT (2007) also show that governance arrangements have on average improved more than in the rest of the world. Finally, these studies, and Čihàk and Fonteyne (2009) also show that governance arrangements in the 'old' Europe have on average higher degrees of compliance than those in 'new' Europe, a finding that we also pointed out in this paper for a number of issues.[33]

Despite these positive trends, weaknesses and lack of convergence certainly remain. More specifically, four broad themes emerge from our analysis. First, regarding total independence and accountability, from Figure 17.11 we observe a fair degree of convergence on independence, with 16 countries above the 75 percent mark.

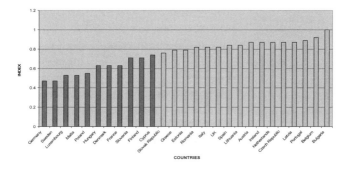

Figure 17.11 Total Independence: Cross-country Convergence

There is clearly a lesser degree of compliance *and* convergence on accountability (Figure 17.12). Only one country is above the 75 percent of compliance and the scores are for all countries much lower. These findings are in line with earlier findings in QRT (2007) and Masciandaro, Quintyn and Taylor (2008) for broader samples of countries.

---

[33] As indicated before, Čihàk and Tieman (2007) and (2008) and Čihàk and Fonteyne (2009) rely on Basel Core Principles assessments to evaluate regulatory governance. The criteria used in these assessments are less detailed than the ones used in this chapter.

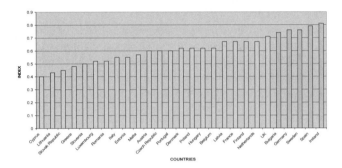

Figure 17.12 Overall Accountability: Cross-country Convergence

From this finding follows a second one. Levels of independence and accountability seem to be only weakly correlated. To illustrate this, Figure 17.13 plots the two dimensions against each other, as well as the median values for each dimension.

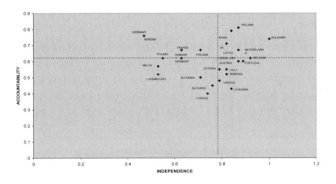

Figure 17.13 Independence and Accountability: Scatter Plot

Our separation of the countries into four quadrants illustrates the heterogeneity of the sample. Countries in the above right quadrant show the highest levels of independence and accountability; the countries in the above left quadrant have only high levels of accountability; finally, the countries in the lower right quadrant show only high levels of independence. This finding is also in line with Masciandaro, Quintyn and Taylor (2008) who empirically find that degrees of supervisory independence and accountability are determined by different sets of variables in the countries: levels of independence are more related to some sort of demonstration effect (others have it, so we should have it too) and the level of democracy, while levels of accountability are more driven by the quality of public sector governance and the levels of supervisory unification. More integrated supervisors, who are also the 'newer' institution tend to pay more attention to well-structured accountability arrangements. More generally, this means that countries have not really grasped the idea that accountability and independence are mutually reinforcing institutional arrangements.

Thirdly, elaborating on this last observation, differences in independence and accountability scores are observed according to the location of financial supervision (Figure 17.14).

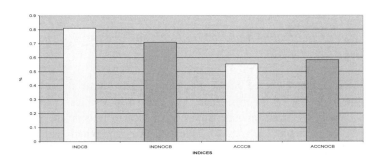

Note: Indices: INDCB = Independence of the supervisors located inside the central banks; INDNOCB = Independence of the supervisors located outside the central banks; ACCCB = Accountability of the supervisors located inside the central banks; ACCNOCB = Accountability of the supervisors located outside the central banks.

Figure 17.14 Independence and Accountability Inside and Outside the Central Bank

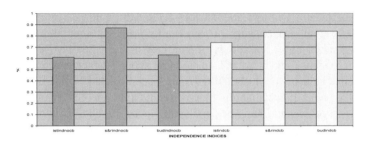

Note: Indices: ISTINDCB = Institutional Independence of the supervisors located inside the central banks; S&RINDCB = Regulatory and Supervisory Independence of the supervisors located inside the central banks; BUDINDCB = Budgetary Independence of the supervisors located inside the central banks; ISTINDNOCB = Institutional Independence of the supervisors located outside the central banks; S&RINDNOCB = Regulatory and Supervisory Independence of the supervisors located outside the central banks; BUDINDNOCB = Budgetary Independence of the supervisors located outside the central banks

Figure 17.14A Independence Indices Inside and Outside the Central Bank

Supervisors located inside the central bank have typically the highest degree of independence, but have also the least elaborate accountability arrangements. Supervisors located outside the central bank enjoy lower degrees of independence, combined with more developed accountability arrangements. Figures 17.14A and 17.14B show respectively the level of three dimensions of independence and accountability, disentangling supervisors located inside and outside the central bank. Supervisors located inside central banks enjoy higher degrees of institutional and budgetary independence – they 'piggy back' on the arrangements ensuring monetary policy independence. On the other hand, supervisors outside central bank score higher on regulatory and supervisory independence, most likely because this is their sole mandate, whereas for central banks, supervision is not their prime task. Regarding accountability, supervisors in central banks score higher on political accountability but fall behind on judicial accountability and transparency. These two are 'newer' forms of accountability and the fact that supervision is not their main mission,

combined with inertia in institutional reform, could explain why these
newer forms have not (yet) penetrated central banks to the same extent
as new supervisory agencies.

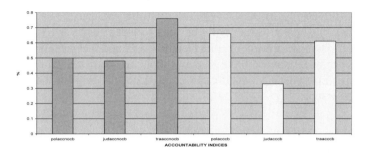

Note: Indices:ACCCB = Accountability of the supervisors located inside the
central banks; ACCNOCB = Accountability of the supervisors located outside
the central banks

*Figure 17.14B Accountability Indices Inside and Outside the Central
Bank*

Finally, our analysis shows that the devil is in the details. It is
indeed necessary to go beyond the general levels of independence and
accountability. For both we singled out a number of individual criteria
that are more crucial than some others for smooth European
supervisory coordination, and where we identified significant
differences among countries. The most critical ones are the lack of
legal protection for supervisors, the presence of politicians on
decision-making boards, the shared responsibilities regarding the right
to license and withdraw licenses on the independence side, and weak
judicial accountability mechanisms. We pointed out how weaknesses
(and great differences) in these areas could potentially undermine
cooperation and coordination in supervisory matters because they
could undermine national (and European) supervisors' trust in each
other's information gathering capacities, intervention powers and
supervisory intentions and actions – the cornerstones of the European
supervisory edifice. Upward harmonization of governance
arrangements is necessary to reshape and align incentive structures of
the national supervisors in the European context.

It should be noted that this analysis only (or mainly) covers the main supervisor in each country. A broader analysis that includes governance arrangements for other supervisors (securities markets, insurance) is outside the scope of this paper. However, without going into the details, as indicated before, one can see that the issues we have highlighted here will be compounded once all sectoral supervisors are brought into the picture. Čihàk and Tieman (2008) and Seelig and Novoa (2009) show that, in particular, insurance supervisors typically have weaker governance arrangements than bank supervisors.

Conclusions and Policy Considerations

The EU authorities have taken decisive steps to strengthen the European financial supervisory framework in response to the financial crisis which damaged the EU financial system and (the reputation of) its supervisory framework fairly badly. The new framework will consist of a macro- and a micro-prudential pillars. The micro-prudential pillar – the focus of this chapter – will consist of three levels: a Joint Committee, three supranational supervisory authorities (ESA), and at the lower level, the network of national supervisory authorities.

The ESAs will have far-reaching powers vis-à-vis the national supervisory authorities. However, the latter will also retain their full powers with respect to the oversight of the domestic financial system. Intertwined in this network of European and national supervisors are also the existing home-host supervisor relations, as well as the supervisory colleges, in charge of oversight of cross-border institutions. So, the emerging structure is a complex multiple principals–multiple agents web, which, in order to produce efficient and effective supervision needs to be governed by incentive-compatible arrangements.

The network of national supervisors is characterized by two crucial features – their architecture and their governance arrangements – that have a great impact on the incentives.[34] These are two separate

---

[34] The quality of the regulatory framework is a third crucial feature, but is outside the scope of this paper.

features, but they also interact with each other in a number of important ways. A systematic comparison of the two features across the EU members and an analysis of their impact on future cooperation has thus far not been undertaken.

This chapter intends to fill some of the voids in our understanding of the potential implications of differing supervisory architectures and governance arrangements for the effectiveness of future EU financial regulation and supervision. We start from an analysis of the current landscape in supervisory architectures and governance practices of the main supervisor (mainly banking supervisor) in each country. Subsequently, we identify those areas where lack of cross-country convergence could lead to failures in providing national supervisors the right incentives to cooperate across borders, and hence, could undermine the effectiveness of EU supervision.

On supervisory architecture, the paper finds that the EU landscape is polarized with, at the one extreme, a number of unified supervisors, and, at the other, a large number of fragmented systems (sector-specific supervisors), with a few countries not belonging to these groups. Typically in the fragmented systems, the central banks are in charge of banking supervision (hence, the central bank-fragmentation effect). Building on the Lamfalussy-framework, the politically-endorsed plan for the EU also establishes a sector-specific system at the supranational level. While there is no such thing as best practice in terms of supervisory architecture, it is clear that inter-agency coordination issues could arise from this heterogeneous supervisory landscape, particularly when we take into account the diverse supervisory cultures and governance arrangements that are associated with these diverse architectures. It also remains to be seen what the reactions to this heterogeneity will be, at both the supranational and the national levels, once frictions and coordination failures surface. Will there be another (spontaneous) round of reforms at the national level (a process that should be interesting to observe, given that several national architectures have emerged from country-specific political-economic considerations)? Or will there eventually be some pressure for harmonization coming from the European level?

On governance arrangements, the chapter finds that the degree of independence is relatively high among EU members, while the degree of compliance with accountability is much lower, and compliance is also less homogeneous. From this, we deduce that independence and accountability are not perceived as two sides of the same coin, which certainly hampers the solidity of the agencies' governance. Our findings also showed that supervisory architecture matters: supervisors housed in central banks are more independent than others, while their accountability arrangements are less developed (or to a lesser extent geared towards the supervisory tasks).

Unlike for the architectures, a set of best governance practices is emerging in the literature and our analysis shows that, given the complexities involved in establishing coordination and cooperation in the emerging European supervisory framework, intra-European harmonization towards best practices in independence and accountability is highly desirable, including for the new ESAs. Such upward harmonization would align the incentive structures of all partners by (i) increasing incentives to reduce forbearance of national supervisors and to cooperate among them; (ii) limiting self capture and industry capture by strengthening the principle-agent relation between the tax payer and the supervisor; (iii) promoting independence from the political branch of power; and (iv) fostering a level playing field among supervisors and supervised institutions.

While not all aspects of independence and accountability need to be fully harmonized, we pointed out some crucial issues that need to be addressed, such as (i) the need for legal protection for supervisors handling in good faith and (ii) budgetary independence; (iii) the issue of the presence of politicians on decision-making bodies; (iv) the need for supervisory autonomy in matters of licensing and withdrawing licenses; and lastly, (v) the need for mechanisms for judicial accountability. Upward harmonization of governance arrangements will be crucial in order to have incentive-compatible structures conducive to interagency information sharing, building mutual trust and cooperation to achieve the pan-European goal of financial stability.

In order to expedite, or facilitate, this process, and secure the right outcomes, this chapter finishes with two possible policy recommendations:

- First, one may wonder if guidance from the European level with respect to the harmonization of governance arrangements could be useful. The creation of the ECB and the ESCB was preceded by a number of mandatory changes in the governance structure of the prospective members' central banks under the Maastricht Treaty. Some similar process – through recommendations or mandatorily – could be envisaged now for the ESFS.

- Second, one could also think about the introduction of a *European mandate* for national supervisors (Hardy, 2009) in order to better align incentives among the network-participants. While attractive from the point of view of aligning incentives, the promulgation of a European mandate would raise another set of governance issues. Adopting a European Mandate would imply that lines of accountability from national supervisors to (some) European institutions (this could be the ESA) be established. Keeping the lines of accountability to the national branches of government only would not guarantee proper compliance with the European mandate because national legislative and executive branches may be tempted to still look at their national interests in the first place, or fail to grasp the European dimension of financial stability related to the issues posed before them.

References

Abrams, R.K. and M.W. Taylor (2002), 'Assessing the Case for Unified Sector Supervision' *Financial Markets Group Special Papers* No.134, FMG, LSE, London.

Arnone, M. and A. Gambini (2007), 'Architecture of Supervisory Authorities and Banking Supervision' in Masciandaro D. and M. Quintyn (eds), *Designing Financial Supervision Institutions: Independence, Accountability and Governance*, Cheltenham, UK and Northampton, MA, USA: Edward Elgar, pp. 262–308.

Basel Committee on Banking Supervision (1997), 'Core Principles for Effective Banking Supervision' Basel, April.

Basel Committee on Banking Supervision (2006), 'Core Principles for Effective Banking Supervision' Basel, October.

Bini Smaghi, L. (2009), 'Going Forward: Regulation and Supervision after the Financial Turmoil,' paper presented at Finlawmetrics Conference 2009 'After the Big Bang: Reshaping

Central Banking, Regulation and Supervision', Bocconi University, Milan, 18–19 June.

Capie, F. (2007), 'Some Historical Perspective on Financial Regulation,' in D.G. Mayes and G.E. Wood (eds) *The Structure of Financial Regulation,* London and New York: Routledge, pp. 43–65.

CEPS (2008), 'Concrete Steps towards More Integrated Financial Oversight,' CEPS Task Force Report, December.

Čihàk, M. and W. Fonteyne (2009), 'Five Years After: European Union Membership and Macro-Financial Stability in the New Member States,' *IMF Working Paper WP/09/68.*

Čihàk, M. and R. Podpiera (2007a), 'Experience with Integrated Supervisors: Governance and Quality of Supervision,' in Masciandaro D. and M. Quintyn (eds), *Designing Financial Supervision Institutions: Independence, Accountability and Governance*, Cheltenham, UK and Northampton, MA, USA: Edward Elgar.

Čihàk, M. and R. Podpiera (2007b), 'Does More Integrated Supervision mean Better Supervision? paper presented at Finlawmetrics Conference 2007, Bocconi University, Milan.

Čihàk, M. and A. Tieman (2007), 'Assessing Current Prudential Arrangements' in Decressin, J., H. Faruqee and W. Fonteyne (eds) *Integrating Europe's Financial Markets,* Washington, DC: International Monetary Fund pp 171–198.

Čihàk, M. and A. Tieman (2008), 'Quality of Financial Sector Regulation and Supervision around the World,' *IMF Working Paper WP/08/190.*

Commission of the European Communities (2009), 'Communication from the Commission. European financial supervision,' COM 252 final.

Council of the European Union (2009), 'Council conclusions on strengthening EU financial supervision,' 2948th Economic and Financial Affairs, Luxembourg, 9 June 2009.

Dalla Pellegrina, L. and D. Masciandaro (2008), 'Politicians, Central Banks and the Shape of Financial Supervision Architectures', *Journal of Financial Regulation and Compliance*, **16**, 290–317.

Das, U. and M. Quintyn (2002), 'Financial Crisis Prevention and Crisis Management – The Role of Regulatory Governance,' in R. Litan, M. Pomerleano and V. Sundararajan (eds) *Financial Sector*

Governance: The Roles of the Public and Private Sectors, Washington, DC: Brookings Institution Press.

de Larosière Report (2009), 'Report of the High Level Group on Supervision.'

Dewatripont, M. and J. Tirole (1994), 'A Theory of Debit and Equity: Diversity of Securities and Manager-Shareholder Congruence,' *The Quarterly Journal of Economics*, MIT Press, **109**(4), 1027–54, November.

European Shadow Financial Regulatory Committee (2005), 'Reforming Banking Supervision in Europe,' Statement No. 23.

Fleming A., D.T. Llewellyn and J. Carmichael (2004), *Aligning Financial Supervision Structures with Country Needs*, Washington DC: World Bank Publications.

Fonteyne, W. and J.W. van der Vossen (2007), 'Financial Integration and Stability,' in J. Decressin, H. Faruqee and W. Fonteyne (eds) *Integrating Europe's Financial Markets,* Washington, DC: International Monetary Fund.

García, G.H. and María J. Nieto (2005), 'Banking Crisis Management in the European Union: Multiple Regulators and Resolution Authorities,' *Journal of Banking Regulation*, **6**(3), 206–226.

Goodhart, C.A.E. (ed.) (2000), *Which Lender of Last Resort For Europe?*, London: Central Banking Publications.

Goodhart, C.A.E. (2007), 'Financial Supervision from an Historical Perspective: Was the Development of Such Supervision Designed, or Largely Accidental?' in D.G. Mayes and G.E. Wood (eds) *The Structure of Financial Regulation,* London and Chapman and Hall, New York: Routledge.

Hardy, D. (2009), 'A European Mandate for Financial Sector Supervisors in the EU,' *IMF Working Paper WP/09/5*, Washington DC: International Monetary Fund.

Holthausen, C. and T. Ronde (2005), 'Cooperation in International Banking Supervision,' Discussion Paper Series No. 4990, Center for Economic Policy Research.

Hüpkes, E.H.G. (2000), 'The Legal Aspects of Bank Insolvency.' The Hague, The Netherlands: Kluwer Law International.

Hüpkes, E.H.G., M. Quintyn and M. Taylor (2005), 'The Accountability of Financial Sector Supervisors: Theory and Practice,' *European Business Law Review,* **16**, 1575–1620.

Kremers, J., D. Schoenmaker and P. Wierts (eds) (2003), *Financial Supervision in Europe,* Cheltenham, UK and Northampton, MA, USA: Edward Elgar.

Lastra, R.M. (2006), *Legal Foundations of International Monetary Stability*, London: Oxford University Press.

Masciandaro, D. (2004), 'Unification in Financial Sector Supervision: The Trade-off Between Central Bank and Single Authority,' *Journal of Financial Regulation and Compliance*, **12**(2), 151–169.

Masciandaro, D. (ed.) (2005), *Handbook of Central Banking and Financial Supervision in Europe*, Cheltenham, UK and Northampton, MA, USA: Edward Elgar.

Masciandaro, D. (2006), 'E Pluribus Unum? Authorities Design in Financial Supervision: Trends and Determinants', *Open Economies Review*, **17**(1), 73–102.

Masciandaro, D. (2007), 'Divide et Impera: Financial Supervision Unification and the Central Bank Fragmentation Effect', *European Journal of Political Economy,* **23**(2), 285–315.

Masciandaro, D. (2008), 'Politicians and Financial Supervision Outside the Central Bank: Why Do They Do it?' *Journal of Financial Stability,* **5**(2), 124–146.

Masciandaro, D., M. Nieto, and H. Prast (2007), 'Who Pays for Banking Supervision? Principles and Trends,' *Journal of Financial Regulation and Compliance,* **3**(3), 303–326, July.

Masciandaro, D., M. Nieto, and M. Quintyn (2009), 'Financial Supervision in the EU: Is there convergence in the National Architectures? ' *Journal of Financial Regulation and Compliance,* **17**(2), 86–95, May.

Masciandaro, D. and M. Quintyn, (2008), 'Helping Hand or Grabbing Hand? Politicians, Supervision Regime, Financial Structure and Market View,' *North American Journal of Economics and Finance* **19**(2), 153–173, August.

Masciandaro, D., M. Quintyn and M. Taylor (2008), 'Inside and Outside the Central Bank: Independence and Accountability in Financial Supervision. Trends and determinants,' *European Journal of Political Economy,* **24**(4), 833–848, December.

Mayes, D. and J. Vesala (1998), 'On the problems of Home Country Control', *Bank of Finland Discussion Paper 20/1998*.

Mayes, D., M. J. Nieto and L. Wall (2008), 'Multiple Safety Net Regulators and Agency Problems in the EU: Is Prompt Corrective

Action partly the Solution?' *Journal of Financial Stability*, **4**(3), 223–257.

Nieto, M. J. and J. M. Penalosa (2004), 'The European architecture of regulation, supervision and financial stability: A central bank perspective', *Journal of International Banking Regulation,* **5**(3), 228–242.

Nieto, M. and L. Wall (2007), 'Prompt Corrective Action: Is There a Case for an International Banking Standard?' in D. Evanoff, G. Kaufman and J. La Brosse (eds) *International Financial Instability: Global Banking and National Regulation*, World Scientific Studies in International Economics, Vol. 2.

Prati, A. and G. Schinasi (1999), 'Financial stability in European economic and monetary union,' *Princeton Studies in International Finance,* vol.86.

Quintyn, M. and M. Taylor (2003), 'Regulatory and Supervisory Independence and Financial Stability,' *CESifo, Economic Studies* No. 49, 259–94.

Quintyn, M. (2007), 'Governance of Financial Supervisors and its Effects–A Stocktaking Exercise,' *SUERF Studies 2007/4.*

Quintyn, M. and M. Taylor (2007), 'Robust Regulators and Their Political Masters,' in Masciandaro D. and M. Quintyn (eds), *Designing Financial Supervision Institutions: Independence, Accountability and Governance*, Cheltenham, UK and Northampton, MA, USA: Edward Elgar.

Quintyn, M., S. Ramirez, and M. Taylor (2007), 'The Fear of Freedom. Politicians and the Independence and Accountability of Financial Supervisors,' in Masciandaro D. and M. Quintyn (eds), *Designing Financial Supervision Institutions: Independence, Accountability and Governance*, Cheltenham, UK and Northampton, MA, USA: Edward Elgar.

Sacasa, N. (2008), 'Preventing Future Crises,' *Finance and Development,* **45**(4) (December), 11–14.

Schoenmaker, D. (2003),'Financial Supervision: From National to European?', *Financial and Monetary Studies* **22**(1), NIBE-SVV, Amsterdam.

Seelig, S. and A. Novoa (2009), 'Governance Practices at Financial Regulatory and Supervisory Agencies', *IMF Working Paper,* forthcoming.

Westrup, J. (2007), 'Independence and Accountability: Why Politics Matter', in Masciandaro D. and M. Quintyn (eds), *Designing Financial Supervision Institutions: Independence, Accountability and Governance*, Cheltenham, UK and Northampton, MA, USA: Edward Elgar.

Williamson, O. (2000), 'The New Institutional Economics: taking stock, looking ahead.' *Journal of Economic Literature*, **38**(3), 595–613.

Wirtschaftswoche (2009), 'EZB fordert Verantwortung für Europäische Bankenaufsicht,' January 3.

18. How Do Joint Supervisors Examine Financial Institutions? The Case of State Banks

Marcelo Rezende[1]

Introduction

Banks in the United States are supervised by multiple regulators. Three federal regulators together with state banking departments supervise commercial banks and their powers and responsibilities often overlap. This fragmented regulatory structure has often been blamed for duplicating compliance costs, causing ineffective communication of information and motivating regulators to supervise and regulate institutions leniently.

Supervisors, however, alleviate these inefficiencies by coordinating bank examinations. Federal supervisors are required to coordinate examinations with each other and with state banking departments to minimize the disruptive effects of multiple examinations on the operations of depository institutions.[2] Banks themselves demand that supervisors cooperate too. In a recent survey, financial institutions in the United States recommended that, to reduce compliance costs, regulators increase collaboration and consistency among themselves and reduce the number of examinations where

---

[1] I thank Rosalind Bennett, Marc Escrihuela, David Jones, Edward Kane and seminar participants at the Central Bank of Brazil, EESP/FGV, Ibmec-Rio, IPEA-Rio, PUC-Rio, the University of São Paulo, the 2010 International Industrial Organization Conference and Finlawmetrics 2010 for comments. The views expressed herein are my own and do not necessarily reflect those of the Board of Governors or the staff of the Federal Reserve System.
[2] See the Riegle Community Development and Regulatory Improvement Act of 1994.

different regulators examine the same issue (Deloitte Center for Banking Solutions, 2007).

Although most banks are jointly supervised, little is known about what determines how their supervisors examine them. In this chapter, I study the characteristics of states and their respective banking departments that determine how state banking departments and federal regulators examine state-chartered banks in the United States. I use variation in characteristics across states and over time to study how they affect the examinations of banks jointly supervised with the Federal Reserve (Fed) and the Federal Deposit Insurance Corporation (FDIC). Such a setting is convenient for two reasons. First, by focusing on variation within the United States, I eliminate any potential impact of unobserved country characteristics – even time varying – that can affect examinations. Second, since the federal regulators are the same throughout the country, I can also control for unobservable characteristics that determine how they examine banks, and therefore I isolate the effects of states' and banking departments' characteristics on examinations.

I investigate how these characteristics determine the number and the types of examinations conducted. State banking departments examine banks independently, concurrently and jointly. An independent examination is conducted by a regulator alone. In a concurrent examination a state banking department and a federal regulator examine an institution together but issue separate reports, while in a joint investigation they collaborate on the same report.

The results indicate that state and federal supervisors determine how they examine banks in order to support states with lower budgets and capabilities and more banks to supervise: States with larger budgets examine more banks independently. For instance, in 1992 all the states that conducted less than 40 percent of their examinations independently allocated less than US$ one million to commercial bank supervision, while every state with more than US$ five million allocated to it performed at least 60 percent of examinations independently. Regarding the number of banks, joint or concurrent examinations are found to increase by around 0.88 percent for each one-percent increase in the number of state banks, while independent examinations increase by at most 0.58 percent for the same increase in the number of banks. Also, the fraction of joint examinations in the total examinations with federal regulators decreases by at least 14 percent when states are accredited by the Conference of State Bank Supervisors.

Examinations are also determined by regulation and banks' characteristics in an intuitive way: joint or concurrent examinations increase with bank size, while independent examinations decrease with branching deregulation, which is consistent with the fact that deregulation consolidated banks within fewer independent firms and that state and federal supervisors tend to examine large and complex institutions together instead of independently. These results indicate that regulation affects examinations both by determining banks' characteristics and by determining regulators' responsibilities over them, and therefore they have strong implications for regulatory policy.

Bank examinations have been intensely studied in the literature, but the questions that researchers have addressed so far differ from those I raise here. This literature has mostly evaluated the information contained in bank examinations (Flannery, 1983; Hirschhorn, 1987; Berger and Davies, 1998; Cole and Gunther, 1998; Hirtle and Lopez, 1999; Berger, Davies and Flannery, 2000; Allen, Jagtiani and Moser, 2001; DeYoung, Flannery, Lang and Sorescu, 2001) and, more recently, the impact of disclosing such information on supervisors' effectiveness (Feldman, Jagtiani and Schmidt, 2003) and the impact of exams on institutions (Gunther and Moore, 2003). I differ from these authors by analyzing how banks are examined as opposed to evaluating the effects of examinations or of the information obtained through them.

This chapter therefore contributes to the empirical literature on what determines how financial institutions are supervised.[3] This literature has analyzed how the official power granted to bank

---

[3] As opposed to what determines the characteristics of bank supervision, the empirical literature has mostly studied its effects. For instance, evidence has been presented that requiring banks to disclose information to the public and favoring private-sector control of banks succeed relative to traditional supervisory policies, such as direct intervention, in fostering the bank industry and in helping firms to raise external finance (Barth, Caprio and Levine, 2004, 2006; Beck, Demirgüç-Kunt and Levine, 2006). The literature has also found evidence that changing supervisors' obligations, powers and incentives impacts bank recovery and how insolvency is resolved (Kane, Bennett and Oshinsky, 2008).

supervisors is determined by countries' political systems (Barth, Caprio and Levine, 2006), how politics influences supervisors' decisions to intervene in problem banks (Brown and Dinç, 2005; Imai, 2009), and how the skills and size of supervisory staffs vary with countries' and other regulators' characteristics (Goodhart, Schoenmaker and Dasgupta, 2002). This chapter contributes to this literature by studying examinations, which is the main tool of supervision and perhaps the most understudied.

This chapter is also the first empirical analysis of what determines how supervisors coordinate their work. Recent theoretical papers have studied how supervisors' incentives to monitor, share information and close banks vary with the allocation of powers. They monitor banks more and share more information depending on how the responsibilities of lender of last resort, deposit insurance and supervision are distributed among them (Kahn and Santos, 2005). National supervisors also exchange information or close jointly supervised multinational banks depending on the allocation of the power to close institutions (Holthausen and Rønde, 2005). This chapter, on the other hand, analyzes coordination among supervisors empirically and focuses on how they examine banks.[4]

This chapter is organized as follows. The next sections offer a background on bank examinations, describe the data, present the empirical strategy and show the results on what determines the number and distribution of examinations. A final section concludes.

Background on Bank Examination

In this chapter I study how supervisors examine two categories of state-chartered banks: commercial and savings banks. Commercial banks make up the large majority and account for most of the assets of these banks. For instance, in 2000 there were 6,153 state-chartered commercial banks and only 336 savings banks, holding US$ 2,371

---

[4] Related to coordination in bank supervision, the literature has analyzed coordination and harmonization of bank regulation across countries. For example, see White (1994), Acharya (2003), Kane (2005), Dell'Ariccia and Marquez (2006), Eisenbeis and Kaufman (2008) and Morrison and White (2009). See also Hardy and Nieto (2010) for a study on optimal bank supervision and deposit insurance with cross-border banking.

billion and US$ 244 billion in assets, respectively. Also, while every state banking department charters commercial banks, in 2000 only 28 of them issued savings bank charters.

Every state-chartered bank is supervised by its respective state banking department and primary federal regulator. The primary federal regulator is determined by whether the bank is a member of the Federal Reserve or not. Member and nonmember banks have the Fed and the FDIC as their primary federal regulators, respectively.[5] State-chartered savings banks, in their turn, are necessarily supervised by their respective states and the FDIC. Because state-chartered commercial banks are larger in number and assets, and every state, the Fed and the FDIC supervise this category of banks, most of the data on the bank industry used in this chapter refer to them.

The main tool of bank supervision is the bank examination. In an examination, supervisors assess the financial condition of the bank, the quality of its management and procedures, whether it complies with applicable laws and regulations, and identify areas that may require corrective actions. They then communicate their conclusions to management. The examination consists of three major parts: off-site monitoring, on-site examination, and preparation of a final report of the findings.

Off-site monitoring presents a number of benefits, but also some serious limitations that prevent supervisors from relying solely on it. It is typically based on Call Report data submitted quarterly by banks and therefore it can be conducted frequently and require minimal contact with banks, lowering the burden of examinations. Besides having the direct effect of identifying banks in financial distress through the data analysis, off-site surveillance also allows an initial screening of banks before on-site reviews. Hence, it helps to allocate resources for these reviews more efficiently. Off-site monitoring also has important limitations, mostly due to the characteristics of Call

---

[5] Banks in these categories are necessarily insured by the FDIC. A third category, corresponding to state nonmember banks not insured by the FDIC, existed in the past but was eliminated as all states eventually started requiring FDIC insurance from their chartered depository institutions and the Federal Deposit Insurance Corporation Improvement Act (FDICIA) of 1991 established extremely costly requirements for noninsured banks. However, even before these regulatory changes, FDIC insurance was considered very advantageous competitively, with only a few commercial banks opting out.

Report data.[6] In some cases, however, such information can be obtained directly from banks during on-site reviews. For various reasons, it is often argued that 'the best way for supervisors to track the condition of banks is to conduct frequent, periodic on-site examinations of banks' (FDIC, 1997).

On-site examinations are conducted by teams of examiners. Examiners plan their on-site review beforehand and analyze documents that may assist in their work, such as past examination reports, information about the bank's holding company (if any), and descriptions of models, processes or the organization of the bank prepared by the institution itself. Teams vary in size, experience and skills depending on the scope of the exam, the size and complexity of the bank and supervisors' expectations about its financial condition.

Supervisors are required to perform on-site examinations frequently. State banking departments vary from 12 to 36 months in the maximum interval between examinations in the period analyzed in the chapter. The FDIC required that nonmember banks be examined at least every 12 to 36 months depending on their supervisory ratings, while for the Fed the maximum interval between examinations of its member banks ranged between 12 and 18 months from the early eighties until the early nineties (FDIC, 1997). Since the Federal Deposit Insurance Corporation Improvement Act of 1991 (FDICIA) became effective in December 1992 Federal supervisors must examine banks every 12 to 18 months, depending on their size and risk profile. These frequencies may be altered, however, for both federal and state supervisors if they participate in alternate examination agreements or if they can accept each other's examination reports as substitutes for their own.

When assessing the safety and soundness of an institution on-site, examiners evaluate six main areas and prepare an individual assessment of each one in their final report. The areas are Capital Adequacy, Asset Quality, Management, Earnings, Liquidity, and Sensitivity to Market Risk. Based on the evaluation of these six areas, a composite CAMELS rating is assigned. The rating ranges from one

---

[6] Call Report data do not contain soft information that may be relevant to risk assessments, such as the quality of management and their practices. Moreover, the level of data aggregation in the Call Reports often prevents accurate risk assessments. For instance, Call Report data have no information about loan distribution across industries or geographic areas.

to five, where one is assigned to banks that raise no supervisory concern and five is assigned to institutions that warrant immediate attention from supervisors.[7]

Once the examination is finished, the findings are discussed with the bank's senior management. Supervisors provide comments and recommendations for improvements and, if necessary, obtain a commitment from the bank to solve the deficiencies identified. Depending on the bank's condition, supervisors also discuss with senior management the need for corrective actions. Examiners disclose to senior management the CAMELS rating assigned after the review.[8] A final report of the findings is sent to the bank's senior management. It describes the bank's overall condition, justifies the CAMELS rating assigned, summarizes the on-site communications with senior managers, including the commitments they made, and recommends improvements.

Data

The data used in this chapter are a panel where the unit of observation is a state-year pair. The data were obtained from the biannual publication 'A Profile of State-Chartered Banking' by the Conference of State Bank Supervisors (CSBS) from 1982 until 2004 and from Call Reports submitted by banks during the same period. Because the Profile is intended to be published biannually but was late a few times, observations in these twenty-two years are separated by intervals that range from two to three years. These data offer a unique opportunity to study what determines how supervisors examine banks. Because they range from 1982 to 2004, they start before CSBS accredited any state banking department and they cover a period when most states

---

[7] The sixth component of the CAMELS rating, Sensitivity to Market Risk, was added in 1997.

[8] Knowledge of the CAMELS ratings was restricted to regulators until 1982. Between 1982 and 1988 supervisors started disclosing the composite ratings to bank senior management and directors and between 1996 and 1997 their components also started being communicated. See Feldman, Jagtiani and Schmidt (2003) for details.

were accredited and lifted bank branching restrictions allowing me to better identify the impact of these policies on bank exams.[9]

Bank Examinations

The data separate the number of examinations performed by state banking departments into five different types: independent, concurrent with the FDIC, concurrent with the Fed, joint with the FDIC, and joint with the Fed. These data were obtained from the volumes of the *Profile of State-Chartered Banking* and the definitions of bank examinations and of types of banks in the publication change over time. Thus, I had to make some judgments in order to maximize the consistency of the time series, as discussed in the appendix. The data used in the chapter are summarized in Table 18.1.

Figure 18.1 presents the distribution of independent, joint and concurrent bank examinations performed by state banking departments over time.[10] The graph shows that independent examinations predominated throughout the period: they increased from 79 percent in 1980 to 89 percent in 1990 and since then declined, reaching 70 percent in 2004. Joint and concurrent examinations account for the remainder of the distribution and evolved differently over the study period. Concurrent examinations corresponded to 13 percent of the total in 1980 and decreased to less than one percent in 2004, while joint examinations jumped from eight to 30 percent in the same period.

Data on joint and concurrent examinations are available for member banks (jointly supervised with the Fed) and nonmember ones (jointly supervised with the FDIC) independently. Their percentages are shown for the two federal regulators in Figure 18.2. Joint

---

[9] Other examination datasets, such as the National Examination Database (NED), contain more recent observations and thus register fewer state-year pairs before these policies were introduced. NED officially starts in 1989, although it contains exam observations from as early as 1980. However, a large number of exams are missing until 1989. For instance, the first exam led by a state that this dataset registers is from 1985 only.

[10] To guarantee consistency over the years, the sample used in this figure is restricted to the twenty states with valid observations in every edition of the *Profile*. The data used in the regression analysis, however, do include states that did not have valid observations in every edition.

examinations with the FDIC range between 41 and 65 percent from 1980 until 1993, but they increase sharply after 1995, reaching 98 percent by 2004. Joint examinations with the Fed rise from 8 percent in 1980 to 100 percent in 2004.

Table 18.1 Summary Statistics

Variable	Mean	Std. Dev.	Min	Max	Num. Obs.
Independent Examinations	98.37	132.69	0	1156	450
Joint Examinations with the FDIC	8.29	18.77	0	203	482
Joint Examinations with the Fed	3.41	10.46	0	182	481
Concurrent Examinations with the FDIC	5.80	16.49	0	211	483
Concurrent Examinations with the Fed	2.04	7.49	0	97	477
Number of State Member Banks	21.63	22.04	1	103	495
Number of Nonmember Banks	146.32	154.92	3	788	495
Median Assets of State Member Banks (million)	785	3,674	10	40,445	495
Median Assets of Nonmember Banks (million)	116	366	16	6,779	495
90th Percentile Assets of State Member Banks (million)	3,445	11,118	14	102,858	495
90th Percentile Assets of Nonmember Banks (million)	596	1,186	50	13,419	495
Budget of State Banking Department (million)	5.39	6.95	0.43	71.42	390
Allocated to Commercial Bank Supervision (million)	3.15	2.98	0.01	18.35	350
Simulated Revenues from Assessment Fees (million)	5.08	6.65	0.13	54.49	495
CSBS Accreditation	0.48	0.50	0	1	495
Intrastate Branching Permitted	0.78	0.41	0	1	495
Interstate Branching Permitted	0.71	0.45	0	1	495
Personal Income (billion)	132.50	156.24	7.67	1,133.10	485
Examiner Salary	35,433	7,433	21,169	67,096	303
State Member Bank Failures and Assistance	0.09	0.48	0	6	495
State Nonmember Bank Failures and Assistance	0.64	2.43	0	31	495
Cooperative Program with the FDIC	0.80	0.40	0	1	178
Cooperative Program with the Fed	0.75	0.43	0	1	178
Required Frequency of Examinations (years/exam)	1.63	0.51	1	3	181
FDIC or Fed Examination Acceptable in Lieu of State	0.90	0.29	0	1	220

Note: Variables in US$ were deflated using the GDP deflator and normalized by the year 2000 values.

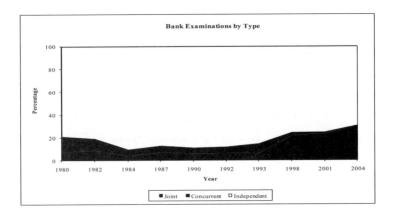

Note: The data used in the figure are restricted to states with valid observations in all the editions of the Profile of State-Chartered Banking from 1981 to 2004/2005. The states included are AL, CA, DE, FL, GA, IA, ID, IL, MI, MT, NC, ND, NJ, NM, OH, OK, OR, PA, TN and WA. The 2000 edition of the profile does not include data on examinations of state-chartered banks.

Figure 18.1 Independent, Joint and Concurrent Examinations

The sharp increase in the percentage of joint examinations at the expense of independent and concurrent ones between 1993 and 1998 shown in Figures 18.1 and 18.2 can be explained by initiatives undertaken by supervisors to foster coordination among them. As mentioned above, the FDICIA mandated that federal supervisors examine banks at least every 12 to 18 months, depending on their risk profile, which motivated supervisors to substitute concurrent examinations by joint ones because both count as one examination for the minimum frequency requirement but the latter demand less work. Also, the Riegle Community Development and Regulatory Improvement Act of 1994 mandated that federal supervisors coordinate examinations with their state counterparts and in 1996, the Fed, the FDIC and the CSBS (on behalf of state banking departments) signed an agreement with the objective of minimizing regulatory burden and of improving efficiency by conducting more joint examinations or alternating independent ones (Federal Reserve, 1996). All these initiatives favored joint examinations as opposed to concurrent or independent ones.

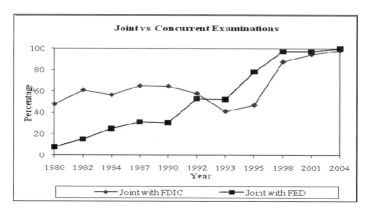

Note: The data used in the figure are restricted to states with valid observations in all the editions of the Profile of State-Chartered Banking from 1981 to 2004/2005. The states included are AL, CA, DE, FL, GA, IA, ID, IL, MI, MT, NC, ND, NJ, NM, OH, OK, OR, PA, TN and WA. The 2000 edition of the profile does not include data on examinations of state-chartered banks.

Figure 18.2 Joint and Concurrent Examinations with Federal Regulators

The data have three important limitations: First, they do not describe the choice of exam type at the bank level, only the aggregate number of each type by state. Second, data on independent examinations conducted by the FDIC or the Fed are not available. Third, the number of independent examinations performed by state banking departments is not separated by member and nonmember banks.

These three facts have different consequences for my analysis. Aggregate data by states imply, of course, that the dependent variables – which are based on bank examinations – must be defined at the state level. This limitation however does not prevent an adequate empirical analysis because examination choices within states are not independent and therefore the state-year pair may be the preferable unit of analysis. The lack of data on independent examinations performed by federal regulators implies that all the empirical analysis must be based on examinations performed by state banking departments. Moreover, it must be assumed that the number of independent examinations performed by federal regulators is not correlated with the observables that enter in the empirical specification, because this number is not observed. Finally, the data do not report independent and non independent examinations separately by member and nonmember banks. Thus, little can be said, for instance, about differences in the fraction of independent examinations between member and nonmember banks. However, some inference on differences in examination practices applied to member and nonmember banks can still be made because the numbers of joint and concurrent examinations are discriminated by member and nonmember banks. I thus can study how departments choose between these two types of examinations together with a federal regulator separately for the cases when this regulator is the Fed or the FDIC.

Due to these restrictions, the dependent variables measure (i) the number of different types of examinations performed by state banking departments and (ii) the fraction of joint examinations relative to the total number of joint and concurrent examinations, discriminated by member and nonmember banks.

States' and Banking Departments' Characteristics

The data on state banking departments' characteristics were obtained either from the Profile or directly from the CSBS. The CSBS accredits state banking departments based on their ability to supervise banks. The CSBS accreditation is considered by federal regulators in deciding how to share the supervision with state regulators and measures the quality of the latter (FDIC, 2002). The CSBS reports which departments are accredited and the date of their accreditation.[11] Based on this, I created a dummy variable that is equal to one if the department is accredited and zero otherwise. Data from the Profile record commercial bank examiners' salaries, departments' required bank examination frequencies, whether they can accept federal supervisors' reports as substitutes for their own, whether they participate in cooperative examination programs with federal regulators, and two measures of financial resources available to bank

---

[11] These data are available at www.csbs.org.

supervision: departments' annual budgets and the amount they allocate to commercial bank supervision.[12]

Whether state banking departments can accept federal supervisors' examination reports as substitutes for their own and whether they participate in cooperative examination programs with federal regulators determine the frequency of safety and soundness examinations and also which banks should be examined alternately and which ones should be examined independently, concurrently or jointly.[13] These agreements generally establish the pre-examination procedures, the responsibilities of each regulator for preparing reports, the responsibilities for conducting specialty examinations, the procedures for coordinating informal and formal enforcement actions, for reviewing and deciding on bank applications, and for sharing supervisory information and developing uniform requirements, the communication with bank management and directors, and invitations for each other's staff to participate in training programs (FDIC, 2004; Federal Reserve, 2008).[14] Data on departments' required bank examination frequencies, whether they can accept federal supervisors' reports as substitutes for their own, and whether they participate in

---

[12] A few observations reported salaries as a single number as opposed to the minimum and the maximum commercial bank examiner salary. I eliminated these observations in empirical specifications that included salary as an independent variable.

[13] Banks may be separated across these types of examinations either by broad categories such as rating, size and location, or by listing institutions directly. See also Flannery (1983) for evidence that the FDIC and the state bank departments reach similar conclusions in their examinations, therefore supporting the use of states' reports as adequate substitutes for the FDIC's.

[14] It must be emphasized, though, that a formal agreement between a federal and a state supervisor is neither a sufficient nor a necessary condition for them to coordinate bank examinations. Supervisors may alternate with each other or perform joint examinations even without a formal agreement. Moreover, these agreements are limited in their scope. They typically exclude problem banks, which are then examined by both supervisors. They allow supervisors to conduct independent examinations or to change their own schedules subject only to notification to the other supervisor. Also, under alternate examination agreements, each supervisor's staff reviews the other's reports to ensure that the conclusions are adequate. Supervisors, however, may disagree with the assigned rating or reject the examination reports. In these cases they must discuss the causes of disagreement with each other. In practice, however, reports are almost never rejected (FDIC, 2004).

cooperative examination programs with federal regulators however are missing for a significant number of state-year pairs (see Table 18.1 and the note of Figure 18.3). For this reason, I do not include them among the independent variables in the regressions.

Figure 18.3 shows the percentage of state banking departments participating in the Divided Examination Program with the FDIC and in the Alternate Examination Program with the Fed over time. Agreements with both federal supervisors have a similar and positive trend. Starting at 45 and 32 percent of states with agreements with the FDIC and the Fed, respectively, in 1981, the percentage of such agreements reached 100 and 87 percent in 2002.[15]

The two measures of financial resources contained in the Profile – departments' annual budgets and the amount allocated to commercial bank supervision – are important for two reasons, although they are possibly endogenous. First, one must be able to separate its impact on the financial resources available to banking departments (a supply side effect) from any other channel to understand how the number of banks affects the choice of examinations. Second, federal supervisors consider whether state banking departments are adequately budgeted when deciding if they can rely on their examinations (e.g., FDIC, 2002). However, both state banking departments' annual budgets and in particular the amount allocated to commercial bank supervision are possibly endogenous to examination types. These two variables can be endogenous, for example, if the technical sophistication of banking departments is not observable, because it determines both the types of examinations performed and resources available to them. In this case, both variables would be correlated with the disturbance. Taking that into account, I constructed a third variable intended to measure the resources available to banking departments that is exogenous to their examinations.

---

[15] Even though federal supervisors and state banking departments have established alternate examination agreements since the late seventies, in 1994 the Riegle Community Development and Regulatory Improvement Act required the Federal Financial Institutions Examination Council (FFIEC) to issue guidelines for when federal supervisors could rely on their state counterparts' examinations, which happened in the year after (FFIEC, 1995; Federal Reserve, 1995).

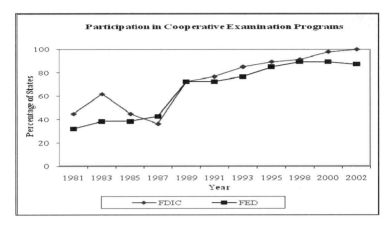

Note: The data used in the figure are restricted to states with valid observations in all the editions of the Profile of State-Chartered Banking from 1981 to 2004/2005. The states included are AK, AL, AR, AZ, CA, CO, CT, DE FL, GA, HI, IA, ID, IL, IN, KS, KY, LA, MD, ME, MI, MN, MO, MS, MT, NC, ND, NE, NH, NJ, NM, NV, NY, OH, OK, PA, RI, SD, TN, TX, UT, VA, VT, WA, WI, WV AND WY. The 2004 edition of the Profile does not include data on participation in cooperative examination programs.

Figure 18.3 Cooperative Examinations Programs with Federal Regulators

This variable is an estimate of the supervisory fees that state banking departments would earn from their respective state banks if their fee schedules were the same as those of the Office of the Comptroller of the Currency (OCC), the national banks' regulator, in 2004. Most state banking departments and the OCC have their budgets covered by fees charged from the banks they supervise, i.e., state and national banks respectively. Thus, a natural candidate for a proxy for the resources available to state banking departments would be their revenues from assessment fees, which are a function of the characteristics of the banks they supervise and of their assessment fee schedules. However, while the population of banks they supervise is arguably exogenous to the examinations they perform, their assessment fee schedules may not be, for the very reasons discussed above. Thus, I use the OCC's General Assessment Fee schedule effective January 2004 (OCC, 2003) – which is exogenous to examinations performed by states – and apply it to the state banks corresponding to each state-year pair. This schedule is a concave function of a bank's total assets and the simulated revenues of a given state-year pair are the sum of the values this function takes for each bank in that pair.[16] These simulated revenues replicate what states' revenues from assessment fees would be if their schedules were the same as the OCC's in 2004. Since this schedule is held constant over time and across states, all the variation in simulated revenues across these two dimensions is due to differences in the population of state banks. Moreover, because the simulated revenues are a function of the whole distribution of state bank's assets, they contain information beyond that encompassed by the other state banks' characteristics I control for in the regressions.

These data are complemented by other independent variables obtained from Call Reports and from the FDIC. The Call Reports data measure the number and the assets of state member and nonmember banks in each state. I use the median and the 90th percentile of bank's assets as measures of their size distribution.[17] The FDIC data are used to control for the number of banks that failed or were assisted by this regulator in each state-year pair.

The data also include information on intrastate and interstate branch deregulation. I use two dummy variables that are equal to one if intrastate or interstate deregulation occurred and zero otherwise, respectively. Intrastate deregulation is defined as the year in which a state allowed banks based in it to open new branches through mergers and acquisitions, which typically precedes branch deregulation. Interstate deregulation is defined as the year in which a state allowed banks from other states to acquire its incumbent banks either unconditionally or conditional on reciprocity from those states. These data are obtained from Amel (1995) and have been widely used in the literature on branch deregulation.[18] They may be correlated with the

---

[16] To apply this schedule to bank data from different years, I deflated assets using the GDP Implicit Price Deflator. A Matlab code constructed to perform this simulation is available upon request.

[17] The empirical results in the paper are mostly robust to changes in the percentile of banks' assets.

[18] Jayaratne and Strahan (1996), Kroszner and Strahan (1999) and Demyanyk, Ostergaard and Sørensen (2007) use the same data and the same definition of

types of examinations conducted for two reasons. First, deregulation should affect the distribution of examinations because it is both cause and consequence of changes in banks' characteristics. Deregulation allowed more entries, mergers and acquisitions and thus changed the characteristics of banks. Changes in banks' characteristics – such as the diffusion of automated teller machines – in turn have also contributed to deregulation. Second, states also removed branching restrictions when they needed potential buyers for their troubled banks during periods of high bank risk. Thus, controlling for deregulation is important to identify precisely the effect of bank risk on the distribution of examinations.

Empirical Strategy

The purpose of this chapter is to investigate what determines how institutions are examined by joint supervisors. For this purpose, I use a regression with the form:

$$Y_{ijst} = \alpha + \beta X_{st} + \gamma_s + \delta_t + \varepsilon_{ijst} \qquad (18.1)$$

Where Y_{ijst} is the natural logarithm of the number or the fraction of examinations of type i in banks of category j in state s and year t, α and β are coefficients to be estimated, X_{st} is a vector containing observed time-varying characteristics of states, γ_s and δ_t are state and time-fixed effects, respectively, and ε_{ijst} represents an unobservable error specific to each combination of its four arguments.

For Y_{ijst} I use either the natural logarithm of the number or the fraction of examinations of different types. When using the number of examinations, I separate them between independent and joint or concurrent ones.[19] Joint and concurrent examinations are added

---

intrastate deregulation but different definitions of interstate deregulation dummies from mine.

[19] The ratio between independent examinations and the total number of examinations or the ratio between independent examinations and the total number of banks could be used as dependent variables to study what determines how supervisors choose between independent and joint or concurrent examinations instead of the natural logarithms of the number of independent examinations and of the number of joint or concurrent ones.

because of the large number of state-year pairs with no concurrent examinations, which causes many observations to be dropped when their logarithms are taken. When using fractions of examinations, I consider the ratios of joint over the total of joint and concurrent examinations discriminated by member and nonmember banks. These ratios measure the number of examinations in which federal and state supervisors prepared a joint report with a single message relative to the number of examinations they performed together but for which they prepared separate reports. For this reason, supervisors consider joint examinations more cooperative than concurrent ones.

The number of independent examinations relative to the number of joint and concurrent ones, however, cannot be given such interpretation because it is ambiguously related with cooperation. On the one hand, joint and concurrent examinations should be more frequent the more supervisors cooperate for two reasons. First, the better they coordinate their schedules and resources, the easier it becomes for them to examine banks together. Second, the more they rely on each other's reports and the more they alternate with each other in examining banks, the fewer independent examinations they need to perform. On the other hand, when supervisors cooperate in alternate examination programs, they actually reduce the number of joint or concurrent examinations, therefore lowering their number relative to independent ones.

Banks' characteristics enter in X_{st} separately by member and nonmember banks. This is motivated both by the fact that these two types of banks differ substantially and because the characteristics of each respective category of banks should in principle explain more of its respective number and distribution of examinations, i.e., the number of nonmember banks should explain more their own number of examinations than the number of member banks and vice versa. Moreover, I control for the characteristics of both member and nonmember banks even in regressions where exams of only one of

---

However, the ratio of independent on the total number of examinations cannot discern whether supervisors increase the number of independent examinations or decrease the number of joint or concurrent ones in response to changes in the independent variables, which is a relevant question in the chapter. Similarly, the ratio between independent examinations and the number of banks would not allow me to analyze how supervisors change the examinations they perform in response to changes in the number of banks.

these two categories of banks only are included in Y_{ijst} to compare the results when different dependent variables are used.

Results

In this section I present the regression results based on equation (18.1). I start with the results when state fixed effects, i.e. the term γ_s, are not included in the regression. Although in this case I cannot account for unobserved heterogeneity across states, the results without fixed effects should be analyzed first for two reasons. First, banks' assets and numbers and departments' budgets vary substantially across states at any point in time compared to how much they do for each state over time and these characteristics should have a relevant impact on examinations that cannot be measured when fixed effects are included. Second, supervisors may differ in how they respond to differences in characteristics across states compared to changes over time. Indeed, the results presented in this section indicate that this is actually the case.

Table 18.2 shows the regression results without state fixed effects. In this table I give special attention to the coefficients on the number of banks and on state banking departments' budgets. The first column shows the results when the dependent variable is the total number of examinations. Both the coefficients of the number of member and nonmember banks are positive and significant but the latter is naturally much larger given that there are more nonmember than member banks. The coefficient on departments' budgets is also positive and significant, implying that the elasticity of examinations with respect to the budget is equal to 0.121.

To better understand how the numbers of banks and departments' budgets determine the number of examinations, I now divide examinations between independent and joint or concurrent ones. Column two shows the results for the same specification in column one, but now with independent examinations as the dependent variable. The coefficients of the number of banks in column two are larger than their counterparts in column one, where the dependent variable is the total number of examinations. The coefficient of member banks, however, is no longer significant. These results are consistent with the fact that nonmember banks are more likely to be examined independently than member ones. The coefficient of the budget allocated to commercial bank supervision in column two is more than twice as large as the same coefficient in column one, indicating that independent examinations are more elastic to the resources available than are examinations together with a federal regulator.

Table 18.2 Determinants of the Number of Examinations without State Fixed Effects

Variable	All Examinations	Independent Examinations				Joint or Concurrent Examinations		
	(1)	(2)	(3)	(4)		(5)	(6)	(7)
Number of Nonmember Banks	0.627	0.730	0.795	0.524		0.193	0.174	0.485
	(0.053)***	(0.111)***	(0.116)***	(0.156)***		(0.209)	(0.198)	(0.257)*
Number of State Member Banks	0.082	0.103	0.100	0.024		0.170	0.169	0.310
	(0.034)**	(0.066)	(0.073)	(0.066)		(0.111)	(0.111)	(0.095)***
Median Assets of Nonmember Banks	0.016	-0.102	-0.015	-0.016		0.294	0.340	0.385
	(0.070)	(0.151)	(0.202)	(0.193)		(0.228)	(0.231)	(0.227)*
90th Assets of Nonmember Banks	0.000	0.005	-0.005	-0.134		0.064	0.096	0.261
	(0.064)	(0.137)	(0.153)	(0.131)		(0.189)	(0.179)	(0.157)
Median Assets of State Member Banks	0.128	0.301	0.169	0.136		0.012	0.029	0.019
	(0.071)*	(0.116)	(0.099)*	(0.096)		(0.131)	(0.109)	(0.098)
90th Assets of State Member Banks	-0.098	-0.187	-0.145	-0.152		0.059	0.090	0.138
	(0.031)***	(0.052)***	(0.049)***	(0.048)***		(0.101)	(0.091)	(0.103)
Commercial Bank Supervision Budget	0.121	0.294				-0.231		
	(0.057)**	(0.118)**				(0.121)*		
Budget of State Banking Department			0.300				-0.032	
			(0.138)**				(0.223)	
Simulated Revenues from Assessment Fees				0.413				-0.574
				(0.162)**				(0.244)**
CSBS Accreditation	0.031	0.080	0.057	0.158		-0.134	-0.172	-0.075
	(0.077)	(0.119)	(0.118)	(0.111)		(0.278)	(0.251)	(0.191)
Intrastate Branching Permitted	-0.088	0.095	0.038	0.031		-0.172	-0.137	-0.185
	(0.092)	(0.125)	(0.163)	(0.154)		(0.271)	(0.272)	(0.266)
Interstate Branching Permitted	-0.019	-0.170	-0.321	-0.283		0.261	0.223	0.186
	(0.074)	(0.128)	(0.136)**	(0.132)		(0.267)	(0.258)	(0.258)
Personal Income	0.097	0.017	0.011	0.128		0.267	0.100	0.192
	(0.040)**	(0.084)	(0.100)	(0.089)		(0.144)*	(0.185)	(0.124)
Number of Observations	323	334	371	425		274	310	400
R-squared	0.836	0.741	0.734	0.728		0.186	0.213	0.233

Note: All regressors are the natural logarithms of the respective variable with the exception of dummy variables and of terminated and failed banks, for which the natural logarithm of the respective variable plus one is used because of the large number of observations with a value of zero. All specifications include year fixed effects. Standard errors are clustered by states. Robust standard errors are in parentheses. *, ** and *** denote significant at the 10, 5 and 1 percent level, respectively.

The specifications in columns three and four differ from those on column two only by the variable used to measure the resources available to the state banking department: the total department budget and the simulated revenues from assessment fees, respectively. The three different measures are used to check if the results are robust. Moreover, since the budget allocated to commercial bank supervision and the total budget are likely to be endogenous to the number of examinations performed, it is important to estimate equation (18.1) not only with actual figures, but also with the simulated revenues, which are not endogenous to examinations. The estimates from column two are very similar to those in column three, where the total department budget is used, but they differ from those in column four, where the simulated revenues are used. The main coefficient in these regressions – on the number of nonmember banks – drops from 0.730 and 0.795 in columns two and three, respectively, to 0.524 in column four, which can be attributed to the endogeneity of the budget measures used in columns two and three.[20] However, even in this case the coefficient estimate implies a substantial impact of the number of nonmember banks on the number of independent examinations.

Columns five to seven repeat the specifications in columns two to four but now use the number of examinations with a federal supervisor as the dependent variable. The coefficients of the number of nonmember banks are much lower compared to their counterparts when independent examinations were used as the dependent variable and are never significant at a five percent level. On the other hand, the coefficients of the number of member banks in columns five to seven are larger than those in columns two to four, although they become significant only when the simulated revenues from assessment fees are used. These results can be justified by the fact that member banks are typically larger than nonmember ones and thus are more likely to be examined jointly or concurrently with a federal supervisor. Still, I found little evidence that states with more banks are more likely to

---

[20] The lower coefficient in column four might also be attributed to the larger sample used compared to columns two and three. In order to test this possibility I also estimated the specification in column four restricting the sample to the observations used in column two only. The coefficient on the number of nonmember banks decreases even further to 0.393 but remains statistically significant at the five percent level, which supports the hypothesis that endogeneity is the main cause of the difference in estimates when simulated revenues are used. These results are not included in the paper for the sake of brevity but are available from the author upon request.

examine banks either independently or together with a federal supervisor.[21]

Departments' budgets on the other hand impact the number of examinations with a federal supervisor very distinctly compared to independent examinations. As shown in columns five to seven, the coefficients of the three measures employed are always negative and are significant at the five percent level only when the simulated revenues are used. Given the previous results from columns two to four, where these coefficients were always positive, large and statistically significant, I conclude that state banking departments with larger budgets conduct more independent examinations relative to joint or concurrent ones. This result is actually very clearly illustrated by Figure 18.4, which shows how the proportion of independent examinations relates to the budget allocated to commercial bank supervision in 1992. I chose 1992 simply because it is the median of my panel. The graph shows that states with small budgets such as Hawaii and Nevada rely mostly on examinations with a federal regulator, while states with large budgets such as Illinois and Texas perform most of their examinations independently. This result can be interpreted straightforwardly: Independent examinations are costlier and therefore departments with smaller budgets should demand more support from federal supervisors in examinations.

Table 18.3 presents the regression results with state fixed effects. The first column reports the results for the total number of examinations by state-year pairs. The coefficient of the number of nonmember banks implies that a one percent increase in their number increases the number of examinations by 0.74 percent and this effect is statistically significant. The coefficient of the number of member banks is not significant, which is consistent with the fact that the numbers of member and nonmember banks are highly correlated and that the former are typically fewer and therefore should have a weaker impact on the total number of examinations.

---

[21] I also did not find any evidence that the number of banks had any impact on the distribution of examinations based on regressions with the percentage of independent examinations used as the dependent variable and without state fixed effects. These regressions are not reported in the chapter for the sake of brevity.

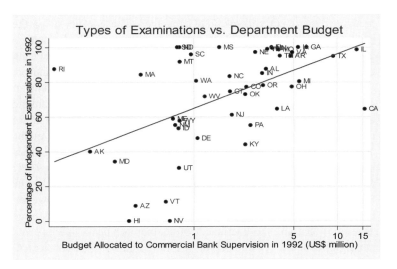

Note: Accreditation data were obtained from www.csbs.org. The data do not contain information on the budget allocated to commercial bank supervision for NH and NY in 1992.

Figure 18.4 Percentage of Examinations in 1992 and Budget Allocated to Supervision

The coefficient of the number of nonmember banks decreases to 0.577 when independent examinations only are used as the dependent variable and it increases to 0.880 when joint or concurrent examinations only are used, in columns two and three respectively. These results together imply that the proportion of joint or concurrent examinations over the total number increases with the number of these banks. These results also contrast with those in the previous table, where state fixed effects were not included in the regressions and there was no evidence that the number of banks affected the distribution of examinations. Taken together they indicate that while differences in the number of banks across states do not determine how they examine institutions, states accommodate shocks in their number over time mostly by examining more or fewer banks together with federal supervisors.

In column four, joint or concurrent examinations of nonmember banks alone are considered, i.e., examinations performed by a state banking department and the FDIC together. The coefficient of the number of nonmember banks remains roughly unchanged, equal to 0.854, consistent once again with the fact that nonmember bank examinations dominate the total number of joint and concurrent examinations. In column five, joint or concurrent examinations of member banks only are considered, i.e., performed by a state banking department and the Fed together. Now the coefficient of the number of nonmember banks decreases and is not significant while the coefficient of the number of member banks increases to 0.670 and is statistically significant. This result is obviously expected because the number of examinations with the Fed should be determined by the number of member banks as opposed to nonmember banks. However, the fact that the coefficient of the number of member banks is large and significant and the coefficient of nonmember banks is small and not significant when examinations with the Fed only are considered, and that the opposite holds when examinations with the FDIC only are considered, indicates that these estimates measure a true causal effect of the number of banks on the number of examinations instead of resulting from unobservable state characteristics correlated with either the number of member or nonmember banks. If the estimates were driven by unobservable state characteristics, they would most likely be similar if the dependent variable was either the number of examinations with the Fed or the FDIC.

The table also shows that banks' characteristics determine the examinations performed. The coefficient on bank size – measured by the 90th percentile of nonmember bank assets – is small and not significant when the dependent variable is the total number of examinations or the number of independent examinations. On the other hand, when the dependent variable is the number of joint or concurrent examinations of both member and nonmember banks or of nonmember banks alone, it is significant and larger, equal to 0.583 and 0.588 respectively. This result corroborates the fact that state and federal supervisors are more likely to alternate with each other in conducting independent examinations of small institutions and examine together the largest and most complex institutions. The estimates suggest that for every one percent increase in the size of the 90th percentile institution, the number of joint or concurrent examinations increases by around 0.58 percent, while the total number or the number of independent examinations remains constant.

When joint or concurrent examinations with the Fed are used as the dependent variable, this coefficient is smaller and significant only at the 10 percent level, consistent once again with the fact that member bank examinations should not be affected by the characteristics of nonmember banks.

Table 18.3 Determinants of the Number of Examinations

Variable	All Examinations	Independent Examinations	Joint or Concurrent Examinations	Joint or Concurrent with the FDIC	Joint or Concurrent with the Fed
Number of Nonmember Banks	0.740	0.577	0.880	0.854	0.071
	(0.151)***	(0.204)***	(0.290)***	(0.313)***	(0.338)
Number of State Member Banks	-0.057	0.023	0.119	-0.048	0.670
	(0.067)	(0.089)	(0.127)	(0.133)	(0.143)***
Median Assets of Nonmember Banks	0.044	0.113	-0.305	-0.308	-0.239
	(0.101)	(0.213)	(0.224)	(0.216)	(0.304)
90th Assets of Nonmember Banks	0.093	-0.028	0.583	0.588	0.278
	(0.084)	(0.116)	(0.157)***	(0.174)***	(0.153)*
Median Assets of State Member Banks	-0.053	-0.005	-0.059	-0.099	-0.023
	(0.072)	(0.093)	(0.101)	(0.114)	(0.107)
90th Assets of State Member Banks	-0.058	-0.067	-0.060	-0.055	0.007
	(0.036)	(0.043)	(0.061)	(0.069)	(0.059)
Commercial Bank Supervision Budget	0.034	0.022	-0.057	-0.107	0.181
	(0.068)	(0.066)	(0.120)	(0.115)	(0.166)
CSBS Accreditation	0.127	0.016	0.083	0.020	-0.188
	(0.070)*	(0.098)	(0.174)	(0.178)	(0.219)
Intrastate Branching Permitted	-0.147	-0.085	0.150	-0.135	0.206
	(0.072)**	(0.091)	(0.187)	(0.204)*	(0.195)
Interstate Branching Permitted	-0.191	-0.240	-0.023	0.025	-0.103
	(0.086)**	(0.121)**	(0.193)	(0.245)	(0.187)
Personal Income	-0.003	-1.359	1.517	1.543	1.140
	(0.310)	(0.600)**	(0.825)*	(0.928)*	(0.803)
Number of Observations	323	334	274	261	223
R-squared	0.884	0.861	0.727	0.717	0.724

Note: All regressors are the natural logarithms of the respective variable with the exception of dummy variables and of terminated and failed banks, for which the natural logarithm of the respective variable plus one is used because of the large number of observations with a value of zero. All specifications include state and year fixed effects. Robust standard errors are in parentheses. *, ** and *** denote significant at the 10, 5 and 1 percent level, respectively.

Branching deregulation also impacts the number of examinations performed by states. According to the first column in the table, both intrastate and interstate branching deregulation have a negative impact on the total number of examinations, decreasing them by 0.147 and 0.191, respectively. The latter therefore has a stronger effect on the total number of examinations and also decreases the number of independent examinations strongly, by almost a quarter, according to the second column. On the other hand, branching deregulation does not have any meaningful impact on examinations with either the FDIC or the Fed. These results are consistent with the fact that after deregulation, institutions were more likely to be acquired and consolidated within holding companies, therefore requiring fewer examinations. Such effect should be observed even after controlling for the number of banks, because consolidation within holding companies may leave the number of banks unchanged while reducing the number of independent institutions. Consistent with the evidence presented here, the impact of deregulation should be stronger on independent examinations than on joint or concurrent ones because, as mentioned above, smaller institutions are more likely to be examined independently and as institutions consolidate the size distribution of banks shifts rightwards.

Table 18.4 investigates whether the results for independent examinations are robust to changes in the empirical specification. Columns one and two repeat the specification presented in the second column of Table 18.3, but now substitute the budget allocated to commercial bank supervision with the department's budget and the simulated revenues from assessment fees, respectively. I find that the coefficient of the number of nonmember banks decreases substantially, to 0.358 and 0.320, respectively, and loses its statistical significance. The coefficient is also lower in column three when I control for examiners' salary – 0.366 – even though the sample is drastically reduced from the original 334 observations to only 193 in this case. In column 4 the number of failed and assisted state banks is added to the basic specification. The estimate of the coefficient of the number of nonmember banks remains roughly unchanged compared to the baseline specification.[22] In column five, I restrict the sample to states that accepted FDIC or Fed examination reports as substitutes for their own in 1991 in order to control for the impact of this form of

---

[22] This result also did not change when I replaced the number of failed and assisted banks with the ratio between their assets and total banks' assets.

cooperation between federal and state supervisors on the number of independent examinations.

Table 18.4 Determinants of the Number of Independent Examinations

Variable	(1)	(2)	(3)	(4)	(5)
Number of Nonmember Banks	0.358	0.320	0.366	0.570	0.651
	(0.230)	(0.229)	(0.198)*	(0.207)***	(0.222)***
Number of State Member Banks	0.004	0.049	0.067	0.020	0.103
	(0.079)	(0.091)	(0.078)	(0.089)	(0.121)
Median Assets of Nonmember Banks	-0.012	-0.067	-0.056	0.110	0.000
	(0.212)	(0.184)	(0.239)	(0.214)	(0.222)
90th Assets of Nonmember Banks	0.005	0.018	-0.141	-0.028	-0.035
	(0.118)	(0.106)	(0.135)	(0.116)	(0.121)
Median Assets of State Member Banks	-0.033	-0.039	-0.032	-0.006	0.024
	(0.066)	(0.060)	(0.071)	(0.093)	(0.096)
90th Assets of State Member Banks	-0.060	-0.031	-0.031	-0.066	-0.083
	(0.040)	(0.037)	(0.037)	(0.043)	(0.045)*
Commercial Bank Supervision Budget			0.046	0.025	0.059
			(0.054)	(0.068)	(0.067)
Budget of State Banking Department	0.113				
	(0.104)				
Simulated Revenues from Assessment Fees		-0.074			
		(0.154)			
CSBS Accreditation	-0.020	0.037	0.135	0.018	0.028
	(0.091)	(0.088)	(0.087)	(0.097)	(0.120)
Intrastate Branching Permitted	-0.167	-0.111	-0.060	-0.074	-0.063
	(0.108)	(0.116)	(0.100)	(0.096)	(0.121)
Interstate Branching Permitted	-0.261	-0.287	-0.052	-0.234	-0.258
	(0.123)**	(0.122)**	(0.083)	(0.125)*	(0.157)
Personal Income	-1.268	-1.091	-0.446	-1.346	-1.700
	(0.564)**	(0.551)**	(0.855)	(0.593)**	(0.679)**
Examiner Salary			0.124		
			(0.202)		
State Bank Failures and Assistance				0.029	
				(0.070)	
Number of Observations	371	425	193	334	265
R-squared	0.859	0.840	0.962	0.861	0.860

Note: All regressors are the natural logarithms of the respective variable with the exception of dummy variables and of terminated and failed banks, for which the natural logarithm of the respective variable plus one is used because of the large number of observations with a value of zero. All specifications include state and year fixed effects. Robust standard errors are in parentheses. *, ** and *** denote significant at the 10, 5 and 1 percent level, respectively.

The coefficient of the number of nonmember banks is now equal to 0.651, thus higher but close to the basic specification's. In summary, the coefficient of the number of nonmember banks when the number of independent examinations is the dependent variable ranges between 0.320 and 0.651 and therefore is always below the estimate when the number of joint or concurrent examinations is employed.

I now investigate in more detail whether the results for examinations conducted with federal regulators are robust. Table 18.5 employs as the dependent variable the number of joint and concurrent examinations performed by state banking departments together with the FDIC. The coefficients of the number of nonmember banks and of the 90th percentile of nonmember banks' assets remain large and statistically significant throughout a variety of specifications. Columns one to five vary the basic specification by replacing the budget allocated to commercial bank supervision with the department's budget and with the simulated revenues from assessment fees, by including examiners' salary and failed and assisted state banks as independent variables, and by restricting the sample to states which had a valid cooperation agreement with the FDIC in 1991. Across these specifications, the coefficient of the 90th percentile of assets of nonmember banks ranges from 0.452 to 0.888, which implies a moderate effect of bank size on examinations. The 0.588 estimate from column four in Table 18.3 implies that increasing the assets of the nonmember bank in the 90th percentile of asset distribution by one standard deviation increases the number of examinations with the FDIC by 3.8 percent. The coefficient of the number of nonmember banks varies from 0.843 when bank failures and terminations are controlled for to 1.311 when examiners' salary is included in the regression, but in the latter case the sample is reduced to only 147 observations. All these estimates are higher than the baseline specifications in column four of Table 18.3 and thus always higher than those in regressions using independent examinations as the dependent variable. Depending on the specification in Table 18.5, the coefficient of the number of nonmember banks is more than three times the corresponding estimate in Table 18.4. Taken together these results reinforce the idea that joint or concurrent examinations increase with the number of banks more than independent examinations do.

In Table 18.6 the dependent variable is the number of joint and concurrent examinations performed by state banking department together with the Fed. Columns one to four, respectively, show that the results obtained in column five of Table 18.3 are also robust to replacing the budget allocated to commercial bank supervision with the whole budget of the state banking department or with the simulated revenues from assessment fees and to including examiners' salary and failed and assisted banks as independent variables. In column five, the sample is restricted to states which had a valid cooperation agreement with the Fed in 1991. The coefficient of the number of member banks is always statistically significant, ranging between 0.527 and 0.699, and therefore always close to the baseline estimates of 0.670 presented in Table 18.3. The coefficient of the number of nonmember banks is never significant – as in the baseline specification – which once again corroborates the idea that they measure a true relation between the number of banks and the number of examinations instead of the effects of unobservable variables on examinations.

Table 18.5 Determinants of the Number of Examinations with the FDIC

Variable	(1)	(2)	(3)	(4)	(5)
Number of Nonmember Banks	0.919	1.255	1.311	0.843	1.040
	(0.320)***	(0.311)***	(0.639)**	(0.316)***	(0.356)***
Number of State Member Banks	-0.052	0.048	-0.051	-0.053	-0.098
	(0.132)	(0.117)	(0.174)	(0.133)	(0.153)
Median Assets of Nonmember Banks	-0.151	0.003	0.261	-0.297	-0.549
	(0.217)	(0.212)	(0.339)	(0.219)	(0.305)*
90th Assets of Nonmember Banks	0.486	0.452	0.888	0.589	0.626
	(0.157)***	(0.152)***	(0.339)***	(0.177)***	(0.202)***
Median Assets of State Member Banks	0.004	0.010	-0.037	-0.099	-0.187
	(0.087)	(0.078)	(0.201)	(0.114)	(0.136)
90th Assets of State Member Banks	0.010	0.047	0.064	-0.050	-0.004
	(0.063)	(0.062)	(0.074)	(0.068)	(0.075)
Commercial Bank Supervision Budget			-0.378	-0.103	-0.070
			(0.102)***	(0.115)	(0.164)
Budget of State Banking Department	-0.136				
	(0.205)				

Table 18.5 Continued

Variable	(1)	(2)	(3)	(4)	(5)
Simulated Revenues from Assessment Fees		-0.387			
		(0.229)*			
CSBS Accreditation	0.099	0.050	-0.345	0.039	0.063
	(0.171)	(0.149)	(0.259)	(0.180)	(0.210)
Intrastate Branching Permitted	-0.034	-0.134	-0.271	-0.094	-0.042
	(0.199)	(0.192)	(0.339)	(0.210)	(0.238)
Interstate Branching Permitted	0.010	0.084	0.000	0.029	0.180
	(0.214)	(0.209)	(0.297)	(0.245)	(0.247)
Personal Income	1.300	1.234	1.620	1.613	2.211
	(0.847)	(0.713)*	(1.704)	(0.922)*	(1.071)**
Examiner Salary			0.514		
			(0.757)		
State Bank Failures and Assistance				0.083	
				(0.102)	
Number of Observations	297	381	147	261	197
R-squared	0.680	0.633	0.820	0.718	0.711

Note: All regressors are the natural logarithms of the respective variable with the exception of dummy variables and of terminated and failed banks, for which the natural logarithm of the respective variable plus one is used because of the large number of observations with a value of zero. All specifications include state and year fixed effects. Robust standard errors are in parentheses. *, ** and *** denote significant at the 10, 5 and 1 percent level, respectively.

Table 18.6 Determinants of the Number of Examinations with the Fed

Variable	(1)	(2)	(3)	(4)	(5)
Number of Nonmember Banks	0.082	0.267	-0.276	0.098	0.835
	(0.324)	(0.305)	(0.631)	(0.341)	(0.392)**
Number of State Member Banks	0.642	0.579	0.527	0.673	0.699
	(0.119)***	(0.098)***	(0.187)***	(0.144)***	(0.171)***
Median Assets of Nonmember Banks	-0.134	0.039	-0.203	-0.235	0.632
	(0.234)	(0.224)	(0.473)	(0.300)	(0.446)
90th Assets of Nonmember Banks	0.205	0.152	0.160	0.275	0.603
	(0.132)	(0.114)	(0.396)	(0.153)*	(0.218)***
Median Assets of State Member Banks	0.012	0.040	0.119	-0.023	0.151
	(0.065)	(0.058)	(0.164)	(0.106)	(0.136)
90th Assets of State Member Banks	-0.020	-0.036	0.009	0.002	0.001
	(0.048)	(0.049)	(0.085)	(0.059)	(0.078)
Commercial Bank Supervision Budget			0.386	0.174	0.316
			(0.246)	(0.168)	(0.223)

Table 18.6 Continued

Variable	(1)	(2)	(3)	(4)	(5)
Budget of State Banking Department	0.416				
	(0.195)**				
Simulated Revenues from Assessment Fees		0.083			
		(0.259)			
CSBS Accreditation	-0.236	-0.179	-0.435	-0.200	-0.173
	(0.191)	(0.158)	(0.337)	(0.219)	(0.279)
Intrastate Branching Permitted	0.121	-0.071	0.063	0.180	0.492
	(0.175)	(0.154)	(0.355)	(0.198)	(0.234)**
Interstate Branching Permitted	-0.252	-0.264	-0.070	-0.092	-0.145
	(0.201)	(0.196)	(0.239)	(0.187)	(0.224)
Personal Income	0.999	0.460	0.181	1.104	1.289
	(0.746)	(0.622)	(1.911)	(0.798)	(0.998)
Examiner Salary			-0.384		
			(0.681)		
Terminated and Failed Nonmember Banks				-0.075	
				(0.113)	
Number of Observations	252	331	125	223	162
R-squared	0.723	0.696	0.768	0.725	0.753

Note: All regressors are the natural logarithms of the respective variable with the exception of dummy variables and of terminated and failed banks, for which the natural logarithm of the respective variable plus one is used because of the large number of observations with a value of zero. All specifications include state and year fixed effects. Robust standard errors are in parentheses. *, ** and *** denote significant at the 10, 5 and 1 percent level, respectively.

Table 18.7 Determinants of the Fraction of Joint among All Examinations with a Federal Regulator

Variable	with the FDIC			with the Fed		
	(1)	(2)	(3)	(4)	(5)	(6)
Number of Nonmember Banks	0.068	0.060	-0.005	0.105	-0.014	-0.170
	(0.154)	(0.130)	(0.128)	(0.178)	(0.159)	(0.148)
Number of State Member Banks	0.086	0.100	0.326	0.077	0.113	0.054
	(0.051)*	(0.044)**	(0.043)	(0.070)	(0.056)**	(0.047)
Median Assets of Nonmember Banks	0.093	0.093	-0.070	-0.103	-0.084	-0.210
	(0.096)	(0.087)	(0.087)	(0.151)	(0.123)	(0.103)**
90th Assets of Nonmember Banks	-0.068	-0.066	-0.029	0.018	-0.053	-0.048
	(0.075)	(0.062)	(0.058)	(0.086)	(0.082)	(0.060)

Table 18.7 Continued

Variable	with the FDIC			with the Fed		
	(1)	(2)	(3)	(4)	(5)	(6)
Median Assets of State Member Banks	-0.006	0.018	0.021	-0.059	-0.030	-0.049
	(0.043)	(0.032)	(0.032)	(0.054)	(0.036)	(0.030)
90th Assets of State Member Banks	-0.027	-0.033	-0.034	-0.013	-0.014	-0.005
	(0.025)	(0.023)	(0.023)	(0.034)	(0.029)	(0.027)
Commercial Bank Supervision Budget	-0.029			-0.069		
	(0.063)			(0.078)		
Budget of State Banking Department		0.048			0.011	
		(0.084)			(0.096)	
Simulated Revenues from Assessment Fees			0.153			0.119
			(0.097)			(0.106)
CSBS Accreditation	-0.138	-0.152	-0.186	-0.154	-0.190	-0.231
	(0.075)*	(0.069)**	(0.059)***	(0.089)*	(0.080)**	(0.068)***
Intrastate Branching Permitted	0.141	0.152	0.153	0.025	0.069	0.019
	(0.086)	(0.077)*	(0.074)**	(0.086)	(0.076)	(0.074)
Interstate Branching Permitted	0.045	0.041	0.050	-0.041	-0.015	0.003
	(0.100)	(0.090)	(0.094)	(0.116)	(0.110)	(0.106)
Personal Income	-0.380	-0.310	-0.186	-0.375	-0.239	-0.171
	(0.386)	(0.335)	(0.294)	(0.388)	(0.379)	(0.312)
Number of Observations	261	297	381	223	252	331
R-squared	0.697	0.685	0.628	0.712	0.701	0.664

Note: All regressors are the natural logarithms of the respective variable with the exception of dummy variables and of terminated and failed banks, for which the natural logarithm of the respective variable plus one is used because of the large number of observations with a value of zero. All specifications include state and year fixed effects. Robust standard errors are in parentheses. *, ** and *** denote significant at the 10, 5 and 1 percent level, respectively.

These results confirm the previous evidence that the percentage of independent examinations performed by state banking departments decreases the larger the number of banks. Indeed, federal regulators support states with limited staff or capabilities that are responsible for supervising a large number of banks. Thus, when the number of banks a state supervises increases, federal and state supervisors increase the number of examinations they perform together in order to alleviate the burden on the latter.

I now investigate further whether federal and state supervisors coordinate examinations to help the most burdened and least capable state banking departments. Table 18.7 shows the estimates when the dependent variable is the fraction of joint examinations among all examinations together with the FDIC or the Fed. The first three columns of the table present the results for examinations with the FDIC and the last three columns for examinations with the Fed. The results on the effect of the number of banks on the distribution of examinations are weak: The coefficient of the number of nonmember banks varies in sign depending on the specification employed for both member and nonmember bank examinations and it is never statistically significant. The coefficient of member banks is significant at the five percent level only when the state banking department's budget is used for both nonmember and member banks, as shown in columns two and five respectively. Moreover, the coefficients imply a very modest impact of the number of these banks on the fraction of joint examinations. For example, the 0.100 coefficient on the number of state member banks in column two implies that doubling the number of these banks would cause the fraction of joint examinations to increase by ten percent only. CSBS accreditation, on the other hand, appears to impact the fraction of joint examinations for both nonmember and member banks. The estimate of the coefficient in column 1 implies that accreditation decreases the fraction of joint examinations with the FDIC by 13.8 percent. This impact is larger in absolute terms when the budget of the department or the simulated revenues is employed, in columns two and three, respectively. The result is very similar for examinations together with the Fed. The baseline estimate in column four implies that CSBS accreditation decreases the fraction of joint examinations by 15.4 percent, and this effect is larger when different measures of resources are used in columns five and six. The coefficient on CSBS accreditation is not significant at the five percent level only when the budget allocated to commercial bank supervision is used as a measure of resources, but that can be justified by the fact that the sample size is reduced in this case. When the department's budget or the simulated revenues are used, this coefficient is significant at the five percent level.

Even though accreditation is correlated with other independent variables, the empirical evidence suggests that it affects the distribution of joint versus concurrent examinations. Indeed, state banking departments with larger and more numerous banks tend to be accredited by the CSBS earlier. Figures 18.5 and 18.6 show the relation between accreditation date and the number and total assets of state banks, respectively, in 1984, the year Illinois became the first state with an accredited department. States with many state banks such as Illinois were accredited in the eighties, while states with few state banks such as Alaska had to wait two decades. Similarly, states with a large volume of state bank assets such as New York were accredited two decades before states with little volume such as South Dakota. Other states with small state bank industries, such as Nevada or Rhode Island, have not been accredited yet. However, in Table 18.7 the coefficients on CSBS accreditation are statistically significant in most specifications, while those on banks' size and characteristics are not. Moreover, when CSBS accreditation was removed from the regressions in this table, the coefficients of these variables remained roughly unchanged.[23]

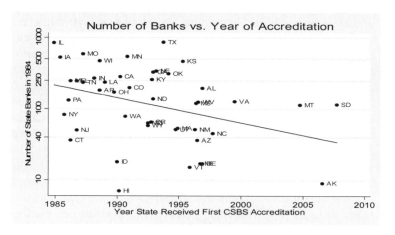

Note: Accreditation data were obtained from www.csbs.org. DC, NV, NH, RI and SC had not been accredited yet as of November 2009.

Figure 18.5 Number of State Banks in 1984 and Year of First Accreditation

---

[23] The results of regressions that do not include CSBS accreditation were not included for the sake of brevity but are available upon request.

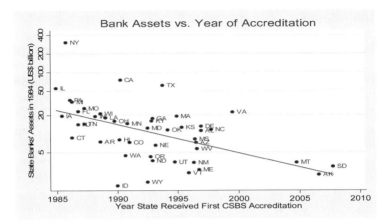

Note: Accreditation data were obtained from www.csbs.org. DC, NV, NH, RI and SC had not been accredited yet as of November 2009.

Figure 18.6 State Banks' Assets in 1984 and Year of First Accreditation

Given these results, why does CSBS accreditation increase the share or concurrent versus joint examinations? The CSBS evaluates departments' ability to supervise institutions by reviewing examination staff, policies and practices, among other aspects. To the extent that accreditation measures departments' ability to examine institutions adequately, accredited departments should rely less on federal regulators to prepare examination reports and therefore should have a larger share of concurrent versus joint examinations compared to departments that are not accredited. The results from this table thus corroborate the hypothesis that federal and state supervisors coordinate examinations in order to compensate for the lower ability of some states, which are not accredited by the CSBS. Other variables that were found to determine the number of independent and the total of joint and concurrent examinations, such as the number and characteristics of banks and branch deregulation, do not appear to affect it.

Conclusion

This chapter studies what factors determine whether state banking departments examine banks independently, concurrently or jointly with a federal regulator. Departments with large budgets examine more banks independently. Joint or concurrent examinations increase more with the number of state banks than independent examinations. Joint or concurrent examinations also increase with bank size, while independent examinations decrease with branching deregulation. This is consistent with the fact that deregulation consolidated banks within fewer independent firms and state and federal supervisors tend to examine large and complex institutions together instead of independently. The number of joint versus concurrent examinations decreases when states are accredited by the CSBS, suggesting that federal and state supervisors coordinate their work in order to support the least capable state banking departments.

These results have important implications for bank supervision and regulation. They show that the number and size distribution of banks determine the examinations performed. However, banks open, close, merge or grow depending on how they are regulated. Thus, policymakers should integrate bank regulation and supervision by anticipating how regulation affects examinations. To be fair, policymakers typically consider how supervision can be affected by regulation but only to the extent that it defines the jurisdictions of supervisors over existing banks. The results in this paper instead call attention to the fact that regulation must also take into account how it impacts supervision, by determining the number and size distribution of banks even when it does not affect these jurisdictions.

Whether these results can be used for policy, however, depends on how supervisors modify their examination strategies over time. For example, federal and state supervisors have strived to coordinate their work and this contributed to increase the fraction of joint versus concurrent examinations of state banks in the two decades studied. In a more recent example, the Federal Reserve has recently emphasized the importance of consolidated supervision of large and complex financial institutions, recognizing that they are managed to a great extent as a whole instead of separated by their legal, corporate or national boundaries (Bernanke, 2009). Thus, the relation between banks' characteristics and the exams estimated here may change over time. Future research should investigate whether this relation will persist over time and how it will interact with recent and future changes in supervisors' strategies.

Future research may also reveal more about banks' characteristics that determine examinations, about other forms of cooperation and about examinations by national supervisors. Banks' individual characteristics determine the type of examinations they are subject to and bank level data would help to identify these characteristics. Other forms of cooperation should also be analyzed, including communication and information sharing among supervisors. Additional research is welcome on international coordination among supervisors as well. For instance, as banks have increased their activities across national borders, regulators are sharing more information and conducting joint examinations more often (*Economist*, 2008). The results in this paper are based on examinations by federal and state supervisors within the United States and they may not apply directly to international banks. A similar study on examinations across national borders would impose new challenges because the researcher would have to take into account the heterogeneity in bank supervision and regulation across countries. However, such research would be extremely valuable considering that the current concerns about the safety and soundness of international banks have motivated most of the interest in how joint supervisors examine financial institutions.

Appendix

This appendix describes the bank examination data obtained from the Profile. It details the types of examinations reported in each edition and reports which ones were used and how they were used to construct the panel of bank examinations employed in the paper.

The 1981, 1984, 1986, 1988, 1990, 1992, 1994 editions of the Profile report the number of independent, concurrent with the FDIC, concurrent with the Fed, joint with the FDIC and joint with the Fed commercial and mutual savings bank examinations performed in 1980, 1982, 1984, 1987, 1990, 1992 and 1993, respectively. All these variables were used in the panel.

The 1996 edition reports the total number of safety and soundness examinations, the total number of compliance examinations and the number of examinations concurrent with the FDIC, concurrent with the Fed, joint with the FDIC and joint with the Fed conducted in 1995. The first two variables were not used in the paper. Because the number of independent examinations was not explicitly reported in this edition, data on examinations in 1995 were not used in the estimations when the dependent variable was the share of independent examinations. The last four variables were used when the dependent variable was the share of joint versus concurrent examinations.

The 1998 edition reports the total number of safety and soundness examinations, the total number of compliance examinations and the number of examinations concurrent with the FDIC, concurrent with the Fed, joint with the FDIC, joint with the Fed conducted, alternate year (independent) with the FDIC and alternate year with the Fed conducted until November 1998. The first two variables were not used and the other six were. The last two variables were added to calculate the total number of independent examinations. It should be noted that the 1998 edition is the only one that separates independent examinations of member and nonmember banks. I assumed that the shares of examinations until November 1998 correctly approximate the respective shares for the whole year.

The 2000 edition does not include data on examinations of state-chartered banks.

The 2002/2003 edition reports the total number of safety and soundness examinations and the number of safety and soundness examinations concurrent with the FDIC, concurrent with the Fed, joint with the FDIC, joint with the Fed and state only alternate year/independent safety and soundness examinations conducted in 2001. The first variable was not used but the other five were. Since these data are restricted to safety and soundness examinations, I implicitly assumed that the shares of examination types are the same for compliance and safety and soundness examinations or that they differ by a constant value across states in 2001. Such constant would be captured by the year fixed effects introduced in the specifications used in the paper. This assumption was necessary in order to use these data together with the data from previous editions, which may also include compliance examinations. This edition also reports the number of IS examinations, which were not used.

The 2004/2005 edition reports the total number of safety and soundness examinations and the number of safety and soundness examinations concurrent with the FDIC, concurrent with the Fed, joint with the FDIC with state lead, joint with the FDIC with federal lead, joint with the Fed with state lead, joint with the Fed with federal lead and state only independent safety and soundness examinations conducted in 2004. The first variable was the only one not used. The values of each examination type with federal and state lead were added to calculate the number of examinations concurrent with the FDIC, concurrent with the Fed, joint with the FDIC and joint with the Fed. Similarly to the previous edition, these data are restricted to safety and soundness examinations, and here I implicitly imposed the same assumption as with the 2001 examination data. This edition also reports the number of IS examinations, which were not used either.

References

Acharya, V. V. (2003), 'Is the International Convergence of Capital Adequacy Regulation Desirable?,' *Journal of Finance*, **58**(6), December, 2745–2781.

Allen, L., J. Jagtiani and J. T. Moser (2001), 'Further Evidence on the Information Content of Bank Examination Ratings: A Study of BHC-to-FHC Conversion Applications,' *Journal of Financial Services Research*, **20**(2–3), October, 213–232.

Amel, D. (1995), 'State Laws Affecting the Geographic Expansion of Commercial Banks,' unpublished manuscript, Board of Governors of the Federal Reserve System.

Barth, J. R., G. Caprio Jr. and R. Levine (2004), 'Bank Regulation and Supervision: What Works Best?,' *Journal of Financial Intermediation*, **13**(2), April, 205–248.

Barth, J. R., G. Caprio Jr. and R. Levine (2006), *Rethinking Bank Regulation: Till Angels Govern*, Cambridge, MA, USA: Cambridge University Press.

Beck, T., A. Demirgüç-Kunt, and R. Levine (2006), 'Bank Supervision and Corruption in Lending,' *Journal of Monetary Economics*, **53**, 2131–2163.

Berger, A. N. and S. M. Davies (1998), 'The Information Content of Bank Exams,' *Journal of Financial Services Research*, **14**(2), October, 117–144.

Berger, A. N. and S. M. Davies and M. J. Flannery (2000) 'Comparing Market and Supervisory Assessment of Bank Performance: Who Knows What When?' *Journal of Money, Credit and Banking*, **32**(3), Part 2, August, 641–667.

Bernanke, B. S. (2009), 'Financial Regulation and Supervision after the Crisis: The Role of the Federal Reserve,' Speech at the Federal Reserve Bank of Boston 54th Economic Conference, Chatham, MA, October 23, http://www.federalreserve.gov/newsevents/speech/bernanke2009 1023a.htm.

Brown, C. O. and I. S. Dinç (2005), 'The Politics of Bank Failures: Evidence from Emerging Markets,' *Quarterly Journal of Economics*, **120**(4), November, 1413–1444.

Cole, R. A. and J. W. Gunther (1998), 'Predicting Bank Failures: A Comparison of On- and Off-Site Monitoring Systems,' *Journal of Financial Services Research*, **13**(2), April, 103–117.

Conference of State Bank Supervisors (1981, 1984, 1986, 1988, 1990, 1992, 1994, 1996, 1998, 2000, 2002, 2004), 'A Profile of State Chartered Banking,' Conference of State Bank Supervisors, Washington, DC.

Dell'Ariccia, G. and R. Marquez (2006), 'Competition among Regulators and Credit Market Integration,' *Journal of Financial Economics*, **79**(2), February, 401–430.

Deloitte Center for Banking Solutions (2007), 'Navigating the Compliance Labyrinth: The Challenge for Banks,' http://www.deloitte.com/dtt/cda/doc/content/us_fsi_NavigatingCompLabyrinth1–08.pdf.

Demyanyk, Yuliya, Charlotte Ostergaard and Bent Sørensen (2007), 'US Banking Deregulation, Small Businesses, and Interstate Insurance of Personal Income,' *Journal of Finance*, Vol. **62**, No. 6, pp. 2763–2801.

DeYoung, R., M. J. Flannery, W. W. Lang and S. M. Sorescu (2001), 'The Information Content of Bank Exam Ratings and Subordinated Debt Prices,' *Journal of Money, Credit and Banking*, **33**(4), November, 900–925.

Economist (2008), 'The Next Crisis: Cross-border Supervision Needs More Attention,' May 17, A Special Report on International Banking.

Eisenbeis, R. and G. Kaufman (2008), 'Cross-border Banking and Financial Stability in the EU,' *Journal of Financial Stability*, **4**(3), September, 168–204.

Federal Deposit Insurance Corporation (1997), 'History of the Eighties – Lessons for the Future,' Vol. 1, Federal Deposit Insurance Corporation, Washington, DC.

Federal Deposit Insurance Corporation (2002), 'Manual of Examination Policies,' February, Federal Deposit Insurance Corporation, Washington, DC.

Federal Deposit Insurance Corporation (2004), 'FDIC's Reliance on State Safety and Soundness Examinations,' March 26, Audit Report No. 04-013, Federal Deposit Insurance Corporation, Washington, DC.

Federal Financial Institutions Examination Council (1995), 'Guidelines for Relying on State Examinations,' Federal Financial Institutions Examination Council, Washington. DC.

Federal Reserve (1995), 'SR Letter 95–40,' Board of Governors of the Federal Reserve System, Washington, DC.

Federal Reserve (1996), 'SR Letter 96–33,' Board of Governors of the Federal Reserve System, Washington, DC.

Federal Reserve (2008), 'Commercial Bank Examination Manual,' Board of Governors of the Federal Reserve System, Washington, DC.

Feldman, R., J. Jagtiani and J. Schmidt (2003), 'The Impact of Supervisory Disclosure on the Supervisory Process: Will Bank Supervisors be Less Likely to Downgrade Banks?,' in G.G. Kaufman (ed.) *Market Discipline in Banking: Theory and Evidence*, pp. 33–56, London: Elsevier Ltd.

Flannery, M. J. (1983), 'Can State Bank Examinations Data Replace FDIC Examination Visits?,' *Journal of Bank Research*, **13**(4), Winter, 312–316.

Goodhart, C., D. Schoenmaker, and P. Dasgupta (2002), 'The Skill Profile of Central Bankers and Supervisors,' *European Finance Review*, **6**(3), 397–427.

Gunther, J. W. and R. R. Moore (2003), 'Loss Underreporting and the Auditing Role of Bank Exams,' *Journal of Financial Intermediation*,**12**(2), April, 153–177.

Hardy, D. and M. Nieto (2010), 'Cross-border Coordination of Prudential Supervision and Deposit Guarantees,', *Journal of Financial Stability*, forthcoming.

Hirschhorn, E. (1987), 'The Informational Content of Bank Examination Ratings,' Federal Deposit Insurance Corporation, *Banking and Economic Review*, July/August, 6–11.

Hirtle, B. J. and J. A. Lopez (1999), 'Supervisory Information and the Frequency of Bank Examinations,' Federal Reserve Bank of New York, *Economic Policy Review*, 5, April, 1–20.

Holthausen, C. and T. Rønde (2005), 'Cooperation in International Banking Supervision,' CEPR working paper No. 4990, April.

Imai, M. (2009), 'Political Influence and Declarations of Bank Insolvency in Japan,' *Journal of Money, Credit and Banking*, **41**(1), February, 131–158.

Jayaratne, J. and P. E. Strahan (1996), 'The Finance-Growth Nexus: Evidence from Bank Branch Deregulation,' *Quarterly Journal of Economics*, **111**(3), August, 639–670.

Kahn, C. M. and J. Santos (2005), 'Allocating Bank Regulatory Powers: Lender of Last Resort, Deposit Insurance and Supervision,' *European Economic Review*, **49**, 2107–2136.

Kane, E. J. (2005), 'Confronting Divergent Interests in Cross-Country Regulatory Arrangements,' NBER Working Paper No. 11865, December.

Kane, E. J., R. Bennett and R. Oshinsky (2008), 'Evidence of Improved Monitoring and Insolvency Resolution after FDICIA,' NBER Working Paper No. 14576, December.

Kroszner, R. S. and P. E. Strahan (1999), 'What Drives Deregulation? Economics and Politics of the Relaxation of Bank Branching Restrictions,' *Quarterly Journal of Economics*, **114**(4), November, 1437–1467.

Morrison, A. and L. White (2009), 'Level Playing Fields in International Financial Regulation,' *Journal of Finance*, **64**(3), June, 1099–1142.

Office of the Comptroller of the Currency (2003), 'OCC Bulletin 2003-45,' Office of the Comptroller of the Currency, Washington, DC, http://www.occ.treas.gov/ftp/bulletin/2003-45.txt.

White, L. J. (1994), 'On the International Harmonization of Bank Regulation,' *Oxford Review of Economic Policy*, **10**(4), Winter, pp. 94–105.

19. Credit Rating Agencies

Jakob De Haan[1] and Fabian Amtenbrink

Introduction

Since John Moody started in 1909 with a small rating book, the rating business has developed into a multi-billion dollar industry. Credit rating agencies (CRAs) play an important role in financial markets through the production of credit risk information and its distribution to market participants. Issuers, investors and regulators use the information provided by rating agencies in their decision-making. For instance, sovereigns seek ratings so that they can attract foreign investors. Likewise, ratings of structured products have been a key factor in the development of the originate-to-distribute model.[2] Credit ratings also play an important role in financial market regulation. For instance, under Basel II financial institutions can use credit ratings from approved agencies when calculating their capital requirements.

CRAs essentially provide two services. First, they offer an independent assessment of the ability of issuers to meet their debt obligations, thereby providing 'information services' that reduce information costs, increase the pool of potential borrowers, and promote liquid markets. Second, they offer 'monitoring services' through which they influence issuers to take corrective actions to avert downgrades via 'watch' procedures.[3]

CRAs have come under attack due to their role in the recent financial crisis. According to many observers, CRAs underestimated the credit risk associated with structured credit products. For instance, according to the International Monetary Fund (IMF), more than three

---

[1] The views expressed do not necessarily reflect the views of De Nederlandsche Bank
[2] IMF (2010).
[3] Ibid.

quarters of all private residential mortgage backed securities issued in the United States from 2005 to 2007 that were rated AAA by Standard & Poor's are now rated below BBB-, i.e., below investment grade. This led the IMF to conclude that 'While downgrades are expected to some extent, a large number of them – in particular when they involve several notches at the same time or when the downgrading takes place within a short period after issuance or after another downgrade – are evidence of rating failure.'[4]

Pagano and Volpin (2010, p.404) argue that the ratings of securitized instruments played a crucial role in the drying up of the markets for these instruments, once the crisis had set in:

> 'in the process of securitization and rating much detailed information about the risk characteristics of the underlying assets was lost: ratings provide very coarse and limited information about these characteristics. This information loss is particularly serious in view of the heterogeneity of the collateral and the great complexity of structured debt securities. Once a scenario of widespread default materialized, this detailed information would have been essential to identify the 'toxic assets' in the maze of existing structured debt securities, and to price them correctly. Absent such information, structured debt securities found no buyers, and their market froze.'

CRAs have also been criticized for responding with a considerable time lag, i.e., ratings were not immediately downgraded once the problems in the sub-prime market became clear. Also on many other occasions, CRAs were slow in adjusting their ratings. For instance, the day before Lehman went bankrupt the major CRAs gave the bank still investment grade ratings. To be sure, at that time this issue had been long recognized. Already following the 2000–2001 collapse of Enron, a 2002 Staff Report of the US Senate Committee on Governmental Affairs had noted that 'Not one of the watchdogs was there to prevent or warn of the impending disaster: [...] not the credit rating agencies, who rated Enron's debt as investment grade up until four days before the company filed for bankruptcy; and not the SEC, which did not begin to seriously investigate Enron's practices until after the

---

[4] Ibid, at p. 4.

company's demise became all but inevitable.'[5] Moreover, criticism has been raised concerning the CRAs' communication with users of credit ratings, affecting market participants' confidence in the performance of CRAs and the reliability of their ratings.

CRAs have also come under fire for their sovereign rating activities. CRAs were condemned for failing to predict the Asian crisis, and for exacerbating the crisis when they downgraded the countries in the midst of the financial turmoil.[6] More recently, in the context of the euro area crisis, CRAs have been criticized for downgrading European sovereigns thereby exacerbating the fiscal problems of countries like Greece, Ireland, Portugal and Spain. Some of these adjustments surprised markets, in particular with regard to their scale. Specifically, the four-notch downgrade of Greece by Moody's in June 2010 caught markets by surprise, with spreads widening significantly following the event.[7] According to the President of the European Commission, 'ratings appear to be too cyclical, too reliant on the general market mood rather than on fundamentals – regardless of whether market mood is too optimistic or too pessimistic.'[8]

This chapter critically reviews the debate on CRAs and, in the light thereof, analyses the European regulatory approach to CRAs, thereby combining insights from economics and law. The next section provides some basic background on the function of CRAs. Thereafter, the next two sections focus on the two main tasks for which CRAs have come under criticism, namely the issuing of sovereign ratings and the rating of structured instruments. Section five zooms in on the question of whether and how CRAs should be regulated given their function, focusing on recent European legislation that aims to standardize the conduct of CRAs. Finally, section six offers our conclusions.

---

[5] Senate Committee on Governmental Affairs (2002), p. 2. The Staff Report meticulously plots the chronology of Enron's ratings by CRAs.
[6] However, Mora (2006) questions the view that credit rating agencies aggravated this crisis by excessively downgrading countries, reporting that ratings were, if anything, sticky rather than procyclical.
[7] IMF (2010).
[8] Barroso (2010).

The Function of Credit Rating Agencies[9]

CRAs assess credit risk of borrowers (governments, financial, and non-financial firms). A credit rating can be defined as 'an opinion regarding the creditworthiness of an entity, a debt or financial obligation, debt security, preferred share or other financial instrument, or of an issuer of such a debt or financial obligation, debt security, preferred share or other financial instrument, issued using an established and defined ranking system of rating categories'.[10] A rating only refers to the credit risk; other risks, like market risk (the risk due to unfavorable movements in market prices) or liquidity risk (the risk that a given security or asset cannot be traded quickly enough in the market to prevent a loss) are not covered.

There are around 150 CRAs, but the three largest competitors share roughly 95 percent of the market. Standard & Poor's Ratings Services and Moody's Investors Service have 40 percent of the market while Fitch Ratings holds 15 percent.[11] Box 19.1 illustrates how the three largest CRAs regard their ratings. While most CRAs are regional or product-type specialists, the three biggest players are truly global and broad in their product coverage. What is more, the sovereign rating coverage of the big three dwarfs that of other CRAs. As of 30 July 2010, Standard & Poor's rated 125 sovereigns, Moody's 110, and Fitch 107.[12]

Credit ratings are expressed on a scale of letters and figures (see Table 19.1). The Standard & Poor's rating scale is, for example, as follows: AAA (highest rating), AA, A, BBB, BB, B, CCC, CC, C, D (lowest rating). Modifiers are attached to further distinguish ratings within classification. Whereas Fitch and Standard & Poor's use pluses and minuses, Moody's uses numbers. CRAs typically signal in advance their intention to consider rating changes, using 'outlooks' and rating reviews (so-called 'watchlists').

---

[9] This section builds on previous work by the authors, namely Amtenbrink and De Haan (2009).

[10] Article 3(1) (a) Regulation (EC) 1060/2009 of the European Parliament and of the Council of credit rating agencies (O.J. 2009, L 302/1).

[11] White (2010).

[12] IMF (2010).

Box 19.1 Credit Ratings by the Big Three

Fitch	"Credit ratings express risk in relative rank order, which is to say they are ordinal measures of credit risk and are not predictive of a specific frequency of default or loss. Fitch Ratings' credit ratings do not directly address any risk other than credit risk, ratings do not deal with the risk of a market value loss on a rated security due to changes in interest rates, liquidity and other market considerations."
Moody's	"There is an expectation that ratings will, on average, relate to subsequent default frequency, although they typically are not defined as precise default rate estimates. Moody's ratings are therefore intended to convey opinions of the relative creditworthiness of issuers and obligations...Moody's ratings process also involves forming views about the likelihood of plausible scenarios, or outcomes—not forecasting them, but instead placing some weight on their likely occurrence and on the potential credit consequences. Normal fluctuations in economic activity are generally included in these scenarios, and by incorporating our views about the likelihood of such scenarios, we give our ratings relative stability over economic cycles and a sense of horizon."
Standard & Poor's	"Standard & Poor's credit ratings are designed primarily to provide relative rankings among issuers and obligations of overall creditworthiness; the ratings are not measures of absolute default probability. Creditworthiness encompasses likelihood of default and also includes payment priority, recovery, and credit stability."

Source: IMF (2010)

Whereas outlooks represent agencies' opinions on the development of a credit rating over the medium term, watchlists focus on a much shorter time horizon – three months, on average. The watch and outlook procedures are considered to be generally strong predictors of rating changes relative to other public data.[13]

Two explanations have been provided for the introduction of outlooks and watchlists.[14] First, their introduction may reflect a heightened demand for accurate and timely credit risk information from financial markets.[15] Second, they may be interpreted as an agency's means of engaging in an implicit contract with the borrowing firm. In a theoretical model, Boot et al. show that the watchlist procedure is the institutionalized form of monitoring.[16] By threatening the listed companies with imminent rating deteriorations, the agencies may induce them to abstain from further risk-enhancing actions in order to uphold the initial rating level. Bannier and Hirsch find that, particularly for low-quality borrowers, the watchlist instrument seems to have developed into an active monitoring device that allows CRAs to exert real pressure on the reviewed companies.[17]

---

[13] Hill et al. (2010).
[14] Bannier and Hirsch (2010).
[15] Also referred to as the 'delivery of information' argument.
[16] Boot et al. (2006).
[17] Bannier and Hirsch (2010).

Table 19.1 Credit Ratings

Interpretation	Fitch and S&P	Moody's
Highest quality	AAA	Aaa
High quality	AA+	Aa1
	AA	Aa2
	AA–	Aa3
Strong payment capacity	A+	A1
	A	A2
	A–	A3
Adequate payment capacity	BBB+	Baa1
	BBB	Baa2
	BBB–	Baa3
Likely to fulfill obligations, ongoing uncertainty	BB+	Ba1
	BB	Ba2
	BB–	Ba3
High-risk obligations	B+	B1
	B	B2
	B–	B3
Vulnerable to default	CCC+	Caa1
	CCC	Caa2
	CCC–	Caa3
Near or in bankruptcy or default	CC	Ca
	C	C
	D	D

Source: IMF (2010)

CRAs frequently provide different ratings for the same entity. Alsakka and ap Gwilym show that rating disagreements across agencies are more frequent for sovereign ratings than for corporate ratings.[18] The authors report that in their sample of sovereign ratings, Moody's and Standard and Poor's disagree on 50.6 percent of daily rating observations.[19] Moody's and Fitch have different sovereign ratings in 46.9 percent of the observations. Standard and Poor's and Fitch have by far the lowest frequency of disagreement (35.9 percent). In seeking an explanation for the high frequency of disagreements across agencies three reasons have been identified. Firstly, rating agencies use different factors and place different weights on these

---

[18] Alsakka and ap Gwilym (2009).
[19] Alsakka and ap Gwilym (2010).

factors.[20] Secondly, rating agencies may disagree to a greater extent about more speculative-grade rated issuers, and, finally, some agencies may tend to rate issuers in their 'home region' more favorably. As to the last argument however, Güttler and Wahrenburg come to the conclusion that credit ratings by Moody's and Standard and Poor's are not subject to any home preference.[21] Their analysis is based on near-to-default issuers with multiple ratings by both CRAs for the period 1997 to 2004. In fact, the authors find that both CRAs assigned more conservative ratings to US issuers than to non-US issuers. This might be due to their better forecasting ability in the home market, or to the high quality of accounting information in the US, or to different national bankruptcy legislation.

Ratings play a crucial role in financial markets as investors use them to evaluate the credit risk of financial instruments (see the next section for more details). The assessment of these instruments requires specific knowledge and is highly time-consuming, making it attractive for individual investors to rely on the rating of the CRAs. The ratings have an important influence on the interest rate that borrowers have to pay. A downgrading may lead to a higher interest rate on loans. Portfolio manager performance is often benchmarked against standard indices that are usually constructed on the basis of credit ratings. This implies that a downgrade to below the investment-grade threshold often triggers immediate liquidation, leading to herd behavior. This kind of behaviour may increase market volatility and may even cause a self sustaining downward spiral of asset prices with potential negative effects for financial stability.[22]

CRAs also play a role in the supervision of financial institutions and as such arguably serve a public function in both the EU and the US. In the EU, in order to cover various risks, financial institutions are required to hold a minimum level of own financial resources, i.e., capital. These capital requirements serve as a buffer against unexpected losses, thereby protecting depositors and contributing to the overall stability of the financial system. The EU Capital Requirements Directive, which effectively implements the Basel II framework, provides for the use of external credit assessments to

---

[20] See IMF (2010) for further discussion.
[21] Güttler and Wahrenburg (2007).
[22] European Commission (2010b).

determine capital requirements applied to a bank or investment firm's exposure. An external credit assessment may only be used for this purpose, if the institution providing the risk assessment has been recognized by the competent authorities.[23] In a nutshell, this requires that the agency's assessment methodology complies with the requirements of objectivity, independence, on-going review and transparency, and that the resulting credit assessments meet the requirements of credibility and transparency. Moreover, based on the Capital Requirements Directive, the Committee of European Banking Supervisors (CEBS) in the past has issued non-legally binding guidelines on the recognition of external credit assessment institutions with the aim of a consistent decision-making across jurisdictions, the enhancement of the single market level playing field, and the reduction of administrative burdens for all participants, including potentially eligible credit rating agencies, institutions, and supervisory authorities. In the US, CRAs play a similar role. Only the ratings of a nationally recognized statistical rating organization (NRSRO) can be used for regulatory purposes.[24] In fact, White concludes that: 'Essentially, the creditworthiness judgments of these third-party raters had attained the force of law.'[25]

The key-role of CRAs is moreover underlined by the fact that central banks often require that assets have a minimum rating to be acceptable as collateral for financial institutions if they want to borrow from the central bank. For instance, until recently the European Central Bank (ECB) required marketable assets to have at least one BBB- credit rating from one of the four accepted external credit assessment institutions (with the exception of asset-backed securities, for which the credit rating at issuance should be AAA).

Given the crucial role of CRAs for the functioning of today's financial markets it is vital that ratings are indeed as objective and reliable as possible.[26] Yet, arguably the current practice reveals serious

---

[23] Critically on the effects of ratings-depend banking capital requirements on the financial system: Weber and Darbellay (2008).

[24] For a brief overview see Senate Committee on Governmental Affairs (2002), p. 97 et seq.; Richards (2009).

[25] White (2010), at p. 213.

[26] Cantor and Mann (2007) argue that there is a trade-off between accuracy and stability. This is due to the preference for stable ratings: 'Users of rating systems value stability because they sometimes take actions based in part on

shortcomings. In the early half of the twentieth century, ratings were subscription-based, and purchased by the investors, but later on CRAs switched to an issuer-based compensation scheme, meaning that the agencies are paid by the issuers of these instruments to publish a rating. Currently, the 'issuer pays' model is by far the dominant remuneration model used by credit rating agencies, generating more than two-thirds of total CRA revenues.[27] While CRAs also provide unsolicited ratings, i.e., CRA-initiated ratings, they are generally thought to be less reliable and less accurate than solicited ratings due to the fact that they are based on publicly available data.[28] The 'issuer pays' model is not unproblematic, as it creates partly irreconcilable incentives. On the one hand, with CRAs being paid by the issuers of financial products, agencies face an incentive to overstate the creditworthiness of a particular product in order to build a good relationship with the issuer. On the other hand it may be argued that CRAs must safeguard their credibility with investors, as their ratings would otherwise be of no value in the market. In this perspective, CRAs must balance any short-term gain from satisfying the issuer with their long-run reputation in the market.[29] Yet, it is doubtful whether the potential loss of reputation sufficiently restrains CRAs and can indeed function as an effective form of sanction. Caprio et al. argue that CRAs in the past faced a moral hazard problem as the fees too strongly influenced their evaluations.[30] As a consequence, in the context of the subprime mortgage crisis the undervaluation of the riskiness of pools of mortgages led buyers to purchase very risky assets they assumed had low risk. Likewise, Mathis et al. argue that when rating complex financial products becomes a major source of income for a CRA, the latter is always too lax with a positive probability that it inflates its ratings.[31] What is more, CRAs may be

---

rating changes. These actions imply costs that may be unrecoverable if they need to be reversed in response to future rating changes. Stability is important because ratings affect behavior, and the actions taken in response to rating changes have consequences.' (p. 60).

[27] European Commission (2010b) at p. 26.
[28] Kormos (2008).
[29] European Economic Advisory Group (2009), at p. 67.
[30] Caprio et al. (2008).
[31] Mathis et al. (2009).

manipulated by issuers by outsmarting the rating standards and by rating shopping.[32]

At least partly explaining this lack of restraint may be the domination of the market for credit ratings by only a handful of big CRAs, as 'the dominant agencies do not have to fear any significant qualitative cut-throat competition, with the consequence that the temptation exists to keep their resource input down.'[33] This lack of competition has been recognized by regulators on both sides of the Atlantic.[34] Indeed, as Utzig observes: 'Self-regulation does not work effectively when the pressure of reputation as a controlling power exists only to a limited degree due to a lack of competition.'[35] The Issing Committee has come to the conclusion that 'the self-disciplining role of reputation cannot always be relied upon, even under normal market conditions' and, moreover, that 'It would need very long periods to verify statistically that rating standards have been compromised, and it therefore remains unclear how agencies that cheated would be punished by the market.'[36]

Credit Ratings of Sovereigns

Sovereign credit ratings are an assessment by rating agencies of a government's ability and willingness to repay its public debt (both principal and interest) on time. These ratings are thus forward-looking qualitative measures of the probability of default.[37] A sovereign defaults when it fails to make timely payment of principal or interest on its debt, or if it offers a distressed exchange for the original debt.[38]

---

[32] Issing Committee (2008).

[33] Blaubock (2007), p. 6.

[34] See e.g. the preamble to the US Credit Rating Agency Reform Act of 2006 (S. 3850 [109th]): 'An Act [...] To improve ratings quality for the protection of investors and in the public interest by fostering accountability, transparency, and competition in the credit rating agency industry.' See also European Commission (2010a), Proposal p. 5.

[35] Utzig (2010), p. 6.

[36] Issing Committee (2008), at p. 9–10.

[37] Afonso et al. (2007).

[38] IMF (2010).

Figure 19.1 highlights that the three major CRAs publish credit ratings for a high and increasing number of sovereigns.[39]

Hill et al. (2010) have examined differences in sovereign rating levels across CRAs employing sovereign ratings data for 129 countries spanning the period 1990–2006. The study concludes that more often than not credit rating agencies disagree about the rating of a sovereign obligor. However, disagreement tends to be within one or two notches on the finer scale. This may be explained by the fact that the available information is comparable across the CRAs.[40] Each of the big three CRAs identifies a different set of key drivers that determine its sovereign credit ratings, but there is significant overlap in the underlying information that is considered. An important factor that makes the rating of sovereigns different compared to the rating of firms is the concept of 'willingness to pay.' This reflects the potential risk that the sovereign may not be willing to pay if it considers the social or political costs to be too great. To capture this element, CRAs assess a range of qualitative factors such as institutional strength, political stability, fiscal and monetary flexibility, and economic vitality. In addition, a country's track record of honoring its debt is an important indicator of willingness to pay.[41] These qualitative factors are complemented with quantitative factors such as the level of debt and official international reserves, the composition of debt, and interest costs. Various empirical studies have made an effort to infer the relative weighting of these different factors in determining the ultimate rating.[42] A good example is the study by Afonso et al., who examine the determinants of sovereign debt credit ratings of the big three rating agencies.[43] Using a panel of 130 countries from 1970 to 2005, these authors find that GDP per capita, real GDP growth, government debt, government effectiveness, external debt and external reserves, sovereign default indicator, and a dummy for EU membership, are the most important determinants of the sovereign debt ratings. Two more recent studies come to slightly different

---

[39] As the sovereign rating generally sets a ceiling for the ratings assigned to domestic banks and companies, it therefore also affects private financing costs (Jaramillo, 2010).

[40] IMF (2010).

[41] Ibid.

[42] See Jaramillo (2010) for an overview.

[43] Afonso et al. (2007).

conclusions.[44] Using a random effects binomial logit model estimated with data for a sample of 48 emerging market economies during the period 1993–2008, Jaramillo finds that investment grade rating status can be explained by external public debt, domestic public debt, political risk, exports, and broad money.[45] In contrast to previous papers, the author employs a binary variable for investment grade status as dependent variable. Hill et al. find that six variables are common determinants of all three agencies' assessments of credit quality, namely GDP per capita, GDP growth and its square, debt history, the Institutional Investor rating and the risk premium.[46] The authors also find non-uniform results in relation to the external balance and external debt (significant only for Moody's and Standard and Poor's), inflation (significant only for Standard and Poor's) and the fiscal balance (significant only for Moody's).

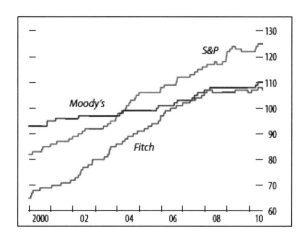

Source: IMF (2010).

Figure 19.1 Total Number of Sovereigns Rated by the Three Major Credit Rating Agencies

---

[44] Jaramillo (2010) and Hill et al. (2010).
[45] Jaramillo (2010).
[46] Hill et al. (2010).

Sovereign credit ratings have a notable effect on financial market developments, as they affect sovereign bond prices.[47] For instance, Sy finds for emerging markets sovereigns that a one-notch upgrade decreases their bond spread on average by 14 percent. Sovereign ratings also affect a country's stock market.[48] Brooks et al. report that sovereign rating downgrades have a strong negative impact on stock returns (1-day abnormal return of 197 basis points), but there is limited evidence of abnormal returns linked to upgrades.[49] Furthermore, downgrades of one country may affect financial markets in other countries. For instance, Gande and Parsley, who use sovereign credit ratings from 1991 to 2000, find that a ratings change in one country has a significant effect on sovereign credit spreads of other countries.[50] This effect is asymmetric: positive ratings events abroad have no discernable impact on sovereign spreads, whereas negative ratings events are associated with an increase in spreads. On average, a one-notch downgrade of a sovereign bond is associated with a 12 basis point increase in spreads of sovereign bonds of other countries. However, Ismailescu and Kazemi, who employ daily data for dollar denominated Credit Default Swaps (CDS) written on high-yield sovereigns for the period 2 January 2001 to 22 April 2009 for 22 emerging markets, report that premiums display a strong reaction to positive announcements, but respond weakly to negative events.[51]

---

[47] Various studies have examined the impact of credit ratings on private sector bond prices and/or CDS spreads. See, for instance, Daniels and Jensen (2005) who examine the relationship between CDSs and bonds, using cross-sectional data covering 72 corporations spanning a wide range of industries over the period 2000–2002. They find that credit rating is a significant determinant of both CDS spreads and credit spreads for investment-grade issues and especially for non-investment-grade issues. Jorion and Zhang (2007) analyze the impact of credit rate changes on stock prices. They find that the rating prior to the announcement is extremely important for predicting the size of the stock price reaction: stock price effects are much stronger for low-rated firms relative to high-rated firms. Their sample consists of 1,195 downgrades and 361 upgrades by Standard and Poor's and Moody's during the period of January 1996 to May 2002.

[48] Sy (2002).

[49] Brooks et al. (2004).

[50] Gande and Parsley (2005).

[51] Ismailescu and Kazemi (2010). A CDS is an insurance contract that provides protection against the risk of default by a corporation or a sovereign. The regular payment made by the CDS buyer to the CDS seller is expressed as a percentage (usually basis points) of the contract's notional value, and is

Arezki et al. have examined the spillover effects of selected European sovereign rating downgrades during the 2007–2010 period using daily sovereign CDS spreads and stock market indices.[52] The main result of this study is that sovereign rating downgrades impact not only the financial markets in the country that was downgraded but also other euro area countries. For instance, Austrian CDS spreads and stock market indices moved sharply following the downgrades of Baltic countries, while the Austrian credit rating remained unchanged. One possible explanation for this effect is the exposure of Austrian banks to the Baltic countries.

It has also been noted that financial markets may react differently to rating changes made by different CRAs. For instance, Brooks et al. report an unequal reaction to sovereign rating changes across agencies. Whereas Standard & Poor's and Fitch induce a significant market reaction only when they downgrade a sovereign rating, upgrade announcements by Moody's only are associated with a positive abnormal return.[53] Moreover, there is evidence for a certain degree of interaction between CRAs. Alsakka and ap Gwilym investigate the presence of lead–lag relationships among sovereign ratings assigned by five CRAs, namely Moody's, Standard & Poor's, Fitch, Japan Credit Rating Agency, and Japan Rating & Investment Information.[54] They find that Moody's seems to be the first mover in upgrading sovereign issuers, but Standard & Poor's tends to lead Moody's rating downgrades. The Japanese agencies are influenced by the rating dynamics of Standard & Poor's and Fitch, but not vice versa.

Investors prefer stable ratings due to the certification role played by ratings, and the transaction costs induced by trading when ratings change frequently. Therefore, CRAs use several mechanisms to promote stability.[55] Figure 19.2 summarizes Moody's upgrades and downgrades during the recent financial crisis. Sovereigns on the 45-degree line maintained their ratings while those below (above) were

---

known as the CDS premium (or the CDS spread). When entering into a CDS contract, the counterparties choose the settlement method (e.g., cash settlement or physical settlement) and also specify which credit event (e.g., default, repudiation, or moratorium) will trigger the settlement.

[52] Arezki, Candelon, and Sy (2010).

[53] Brooks et al. (2004).

[54] Alsakka and ap Gwilym (2010).

[55] IMF (2010). See also Cantor and Mann (2007).

downgraded (upgraded). The figure shows that 63 percent of ratings remained unchanged (so far). The IMF concludes that the 'analysis suggests that the way that CRAs try to smooth their rating changes may make them prone to procyclical cliff effects. Furthermore, the market impact of these rating changes is exacerbated by the overreliance on ratings in legislation, regulations, and private sector contracts.'[56]

Finally, conflict of interest issues may not only arise in the context of the rating of (complex) financial products, but also for sovereign debt ratings. In a recent working document the European Commission observes that 'credit rating agencies' remuneration policies for sovereign debt ratings are not uniform. While most of the countries participate in the rating process, not all of them are charged for having their debt rated. The fact that many countries pay for the rating service they receive may raise concerns with regard to conflicts of interest inherent in the issuer-pays model.'[57]

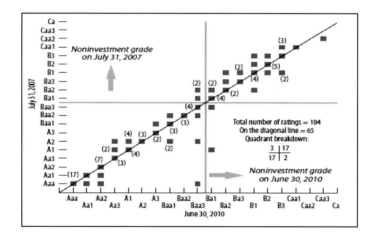

Source: IMF (2010).

Figure 19.2 Sovereigns Rated by Moody's between July 31, 2007 and June 30, 2010

---

[56] Ibid, p. 27.
[57] European Commission (2010b), p. 14.

Rating Structured Instruments

The important role of CRAs in the financial system is highlighted by the fact that for many observers CRAs played a significant part in the making and unfolding of the recent global financial crisis. The origin of this crisis is commonly placed in a particular segment of the US mortgage market, namely the subprime mortgage market. Subprime is lending to individuals with a high level of default risk, because they have a low income or a less than perfect credit history relative to the standards of 'prime' borrowers. The share of subprime in origination of all mortgages rose steadily between 2001 and 2006, from 7.2 to 20.1 percent. The outstanding stock amounted to 1.4 trillion dollars.[58] When housing prices started declining while interest increased, losses on these loans rapidly increased. According to recent estimates, these losses amounted to 1.4 trillion dollars in the course of 2008. Although these losses were huge, their magnitude was by no means unprecedented – the losses from the dot-com crash wiped out 5 trillion dollars in the market value of technology companies between March 2000 and October 2002.[59] What led to the subsequent financial turmoil was the securitization of these mortgages and it is in this securitization process that CRAs played a crucial role.

What needs to be realized in this context is that securitization developed against the background of a strong and growing demand for highly rated assets by individual and institutional investors, the latter often restricted in their portfolio choice by rules setting quality standards for the securities in their portfolios. Hence, the goal of securitization was to satisfy this demand at the least cost, i.e., by creating the largest possible pool of standardized, highly rated securities from the underlying pool of mortgages. The way in which risky cash flows from heterogeneous mortgage contracts could be turned into standardized so-called Asset Backed Securities (ABS) was by slicing the cash flow from a well-diversified pool of mortgages into tranches of increasing risk/return profiles, thereby making it possible to create a tranche with relatively low risk. The cash accruing from the pool of assets is used first to pay interest and the principal to the tranche with the highest and most senior status; the remaining cash is then used to

---

[58] The EEAG Report on the European Economy (2009), p. 63.
[59] Ibid, p. 63.

pay the holders of a second tranche, with lower status; what is left is paid to a third tranche, and so on.[60]

According to the Financial Stability Forum (FSF), poor credit assessments of complex structured credit products by CRAs contributed to both the build-up and the unfolding of the financial crisis.[61] CRAs assigned high ratings to complex structured sub-prime debt based on inadequate historical data and in some cases flawed models. Structured credit products are designed to take advantage of different risk preferences of investors. They are therefore structured for each tranche to achieve a particular credit rating. CRAs generally give these first tranches the highest ratings possible. If during this structuring process CRAs discuss with issuers the rating implications of particular structures, there is a clear potential for conflicts of interest. These conflicts are exacerbated when CRAs also sell consulting services to entities that purchased ratings. What is more, there is increasing evidence that the methods used by agencies yielded ratings that were too high.[62] In the 2009 European Economic Advisory Group Report on the European Economy it is shown that about 80 percent of subprime mortgages' origination was converted into triple-A pools, while less than five percent of these mortgages were converted into triple-B or lower rate assets. As it is stated in this report:

'These percentages obviously contained the seed of the crisis, as securitization flooded the market with triple-A products whose risk and prices were obviously quite sensitive to housing market conditions. The evidence [...] raises the key issue concerning the extent to which a risky cash flow from mortgages could back triple-A securities. Even after accounting for credit enhancement, a percentage as high as 80 percent may hardly survive proper stress testing of the market conditions underlying securitization. In this dimension (with the benefit of hindsight) the models adopted by financial intermediaries to assess risk appeared to be far from adequate.'[63]

---

[60] Ibid, pp. 63–64.

[61] FSF (2008).

[62] Benmelech and Dlugosz (2009) examined 4,000 structured bonds that were backed by loan portfolios. The average rating of the loans was B+, yet 70 percent of the bonds were rated AAA.

[63] The EEAG Report on the European Economy (2009), p. 68.

Investors have arguably over-relied on these ratings. A 2008 IMF report comes to the conclusion that

> 'Credit ratings have been a key input for many investors in the valuation of structured credit products because they have been perceived to provide a common credit risk metric for all fixed-income instruments. In particular, when reliable price quotations were unavailable, the price of structured credit products often was inferred from prices and credit spreads of similarly rated comparable products for which quotations were available. For example, the price of AAA ABX subindices could be used to estimate the values of AAA-rated tranches of mortgage-backed securities (MBS), the price of BBB subindices could be used to value BBB-rated MBS tranches, and so on [...]. In this way, credit ratings came to play a key mapping role in the valuation of customized or illiquid structured credit products, a mapping that many investors now find unreliable.'[64]

There also seems to have been a 'false sense of security' concerning ratings of structured financial products despite the fact that 'credit rating agencies insist that ratings measure only default risk, and not the likelihood or intensity of downgrades or mark-to-market losses'.[65] At the same time, new structured securities found eager investors who were attracted by the high rates of return during a period with low interest rates.

Not only investors, but also regulators, who tied bank capital requirements to ratings, effectively outsourced their due diligence to rating agencies without sufficient consideration of whether credit ratings meant the same thing for structured finance as for other securities. None of the key parties seemed to recognize that small errors in rating individual instruments are significantly magnified in case of structured instruments. Recently, the Financial Stability Board published a document containing principles for reducing reliance on CRA ratings, reflecting that policymakers also have come to the conclusion that serious risks are involved in relying mechanistically on ratings. According to the document, 'The principles aim to catalyze a significant change in existing practices, to end mechanistic reliance by market participants and establish stronger internal credit risk assessment

---

[64] Brackets added. IMF (2008), p. 55.
[65] The IMF (2008), p. 55 links this to 'the benign performance of credit markets since the early part of this decade'.

practices instead. They set out broad objectives, for standard setters and regulators to follow up by defining the more specific actions that will be needed to implement the changes over time.'[66]

Credit rating agencies in all probability did not fully appreciate the fragility of their estimates or the possible effects of modest errors in assumptions in their models. This lack of understanding of 'complex and difficult-to-value structured finance products',[67] which was also highlighted by the fact that they 'were forced to make precipitous downgrades on a large number of structured finance products backed by US subprime mortgages, on which default rates had risen abruptly relative to earlier assumptions.'[68] They did so with a considerable time lag, i.e., ratings were not immediately downgraded, once the problems in the subprime market became clear.[69]

Regulating CRAs[70]

Until recently, CRAs were mainly governed by the International Organization of Securities Commissions (IOSCO), which sets international standards for security markets. These standards come in the shape of the 'Code for Conduct Fundamentals for Credit Rating Agencies' (IOSCO code), which has been updated in the wake of the global financial turmoil. However, this code is based on voluntary compliance and lacks enforcement mechanisms (self-regulation). In the wake of the financial crisis, many countries have taken steps to enhance the regulatory framework for credit rating agencies, focusing on registration, enhanced oversight, and transparency.[71] This included very prominently also the European Union (EU) with its internal (financial) market. The question that arises in this context and that is explored hereafter for the EU regulatory initiatives is, whether these measures actually correct the shortcomings of the previously applicable regime.

---

[66] Financial Stability Board (2010).

[67] Ibid., p. 54.

[68] Ibid., p. 55.

[69] Ibid., p. 57–58.

[70] This part draws on Amtenbrink and De Haan (2009) and (2010).

[71] See IMF (2010) for an overview.

In response to the crisis, several international expert bodies made concrete proposals for reforms. The FSF recommended that CRAs should improve the quality of the rating process and manage conflicts of interest related to the issuer-pays model; should differentiate ratings on complex structured credit products from those on 'regular' bonds as these ratings have different risk properties; and should enhance their review of the quality of the data received from issuers and of the due diligence performed on underlying assets by all parties involved.[72] The FSF stressed that investors should address their over-reliance on ratings. However, the FSF did not go as far as proposing a more stringent supervisory regime for CRAs. Instead, it advised that competent authorities should monitor, individually or collectively, the implementation of the revised IOSCO code by CRAs, in order to ensure that CRAs quickly translate it into action.[73] In Europe this rejection of a comprehensive regulatory approach was supported by the European Securities Markets Expert Group (ESME) and the Committee of European Securities Regulators (CESR). In a 2008 report ESME expressed the opinion that the incremental benefits of regulation would not exceed the costs and accordingly it is not recommended.[74] CESR for its part shared the view of market participants that there is no evidence that regulation of the credit rating industry would have had an effect on the issues which emerged with ratings of US subprime backed securities.[75] Preference was thus given to market driven improvements, albeit under a closer supervision.[76]

In the face of this expert advice the European Commission opted for regulation, claiming that the legislative option had clear advantages over the other policy options especially with regard to its effectiveness and certainty, because the other options (self-regulatory approaches or a recommendation) cannot produce legally binding

---

[72] FSF (2008), p. 32–39.

[73] Ibid., p. 58.

[74] ESME (2008). The report emphasizes that this opinion is based on the assumption that an enhanced self regulatory model is made to work and is seen in the market to be effective.

[75] CESR (2008), p. 3. However, as a quasi stick-behind-the-back the report also states that if such a body did not succeed, a regulatory response would be called for.

[76] See CESR (2008) and ESME (2008).

rules and an enforcement mechanism.'[77] While the European Commission considers the revised IOSCO code to be 'the global benchmark', it maintained that its substance had to be made more specific, to make it easier to apply in practice, and more efficient. In its own perception, the Commission has thus opted for more robust, stringent and enforceable rules. The Commission concluded that 'EU legislation appears to be the only option that could sufficiently protect investors and European financial markets against the risk of malpractice by credit rating agencies.'[78] Interestingly, neither the Commission Proposal nor the subsequent European Regulation expressly refer to sovereign credit ratings. Nevertheless it can be assumed that Regulation 1060/2009 and namely its rules referring to rating process in principle also apply to this category of ratings.

The European Regulation on Credit Agencies was finally approved by the European Parliament (EP) and the Council of the European Union in September 2009.[79] As part of a wider strategy to strengthen financial market supervision in the EU, already in June 2010 the European Commission put forward a proposal to amend this Regulation, aiming at simplifying the present regulatory framework by centralized CRA supervision and creating better access to the market for credit ratings through enhanced transparency.[80] From the outset the fact that the European Commission has proposed the amendment of a Regulation only months after it has been enacted is hardly a sign of the sustainability of EU financial market legislation. This also suggests that the initial Regulation was drafted rather hastily in the face of the on-going financial crisis. Indeed, almost in parallel to the process of seeking legislative approval for Regulation 1060/2009 the Commission could be seen making plans for a much broader approach to financial market supervision in the EU, thereby reforming the Lamfalussy framework and its committee structure.[81] Against the background of the findings of the De Larosière Group, in September 2009 the European Commission adopted a whole package of

---

[77] European Commission (2008), Explanatory Memorandum, p. 5.

[78] Ibid, 6.

[79] Regulation (EC) 1060/2009 of the European Parliament and of the Council of credit rating agencies (O.J. 2009, L 302/1).

[80] European Commission (2010a). At the time of writing, this proposal was discussed by the European Parliament and the Council.

[81] Lastra (2003).

legislative proposals basically aimed at strengthening macro-prudential supervision through the establishment of a European Systemic Risk Board (ESRB) and micro-prudential supervision through the setting up of a European System of Financial Supervisors (ESFS). The supervision of financial institutions is supposed to take the shape of the cooperation between the existing competent national authorities of the Member States and three new European regulatory agencies, namely the European Banking Authority (EBA), the European Insurance and Occupational Pensions Authority (EIOPA), and the European Securities and Markets Authority (ESMA). According to the corresponding Commission proposal for a Regulation of the European Parliament and of the Council, ESMA would effectively be put in charge of the registration of CRAs and – to a large extent – also of their supervision.[82]

Three main elements of the European regulatory approach to CRAs can be identified, namely the registration requirement, rules of conduct for registered CRAs, and the supervision of registered CRAs.[83]

The European registration regime

In principle the Regulation applies to credit ratings issued by CRAs registered in the EU and which are disclosed publicly or distributed by subscription.[84] Registration forms a condition for being recognized as an External Credit Assessment Institution (ECAI) in accordance with the Capital Requirements Directive,[85] and thus a precondition for an application of the separate certification procedure by the competent national authority for CRAs whose

---

[82] European Commission (2009). See also Commission proposal to amend Regulation (EC) No 1060/2009 of the European Parliament and of the Council on credit rating agencies (COM (2010) 289 final).

[83] For details, see Amtenbrink and De Haan (2009).

[84] Article 2(1) Regulation 1060/2009. At the time of writing of this contribution the first registration based on the new European regulatory regime was done by the German Bundesanstalt für Finanzdienstleistungsaufsicht (BaFin) on 16 November 2010, concerning Euler Hermes Rating GmbH.

[85] Namely Directive 2006/48/EC of the European Parliament and of the Council of 14 June 2006 relating to the taking up and pursuit of the business of credit institutions (O.J. 2006 L 177/1).

ratings are used as external credit assessments to determine risk weights and the resulting capital requirements applied to a bank or investment firm's exposure.[86] It can thus not be concluded that Regulation 1060/2009 replaces the procedure foreseen in the Capital Requirements Directive. In order for a CRA with a registered office outside the EU to be able to qualify for registration, it has to set up a subsidiary in the EU. Alternatively it can make use of the endorsement system or the equivalence procedure also foreseen in the Regulation. This approach seeks to ensure one of the aims of the Regulation that is the efficient supervision of the activities of CRAs located outside the EU. While the Regulation does not close the European market for third-country CRAs, credit rating activities by third-country CRAs are effectively subjected to the European supervisory standards. This becomes most notably clear from the need for an equivalence decision by the European Commission in order for third-country ratings that are not endorsed by a EU-based CRA to be used in the EU.[87]

The Regulation states the conditions and the procedure for granting or withdrawal of registration.[88] While the preamble to the Regulation refers to 'a single point of entry for the submission of application for registration', it foresees a rather complex decision-making process involving not only CESR and the Member State in which the CRA has its registered office (home Member State), but also the competent authorities of other Member States. The procedure commences with the forwarding of the application for registration by CESR, to which it has to be initially addressed, to the competent national authority of the home Member State. The Regulation foresees the establishment of a so-called college of competent authorities on a case-by-case basis. This college consists of the competent authority of the Member State where the CRA has its registered office and the competent authorities of other Member States. The latter have the right to join the college, if either a branch which is a part of the CRA in question or of one of the undertakings

---

[86] In accordance with the said Directive CRAs have to comply with requirements such as objectivity, independence, continuous review, credibility, and transparency.

[87] The endorsement system and equivalence procedure are not further discussed in this contribution.

[88] Articles 14–20.

in the group of credit rating agencies is established within its jurisdiction, or if the use for regulatory purposes of credit ratings issued by the CRA, or if the group of CRAs is 'widespread or has or is likely to have a significant impact within its jurisdiction'. The members of this college have to elect a so-called 'facilitator', whose main task is to chair the meetings of the college and coordinate its action. In principle the home country competent authority and the college have to reach an agreement on granting registration based on the compliance of the CRA concerned with the conditions set out in the Regulation. In the case of the absence of an agreement in the college, which continues after mediation by CESR, the home country has no other alternative but to adopt a fully reasoned refusal decision, whereby the dissenting competent authorities must be identified and their opinions be stated.

Arguably the current legal regime does not feature an effective mechanism to deal with disagreements between national authorities. This is particularly crucial since the criteria, which competent national authorities have to apply in assessing the compliance of the applicant with the provisions of the Regulation and its Annex I leave ample room for value judgments. CESR is not given any effective tools to challenge a decision rejecting registration. As pointed out by the European Commission, the division of responsibilities between the competent authority of the home Member State and the other competent authorities is not a long-term solution for the oversight of CRAs as credit ratings are used throughout the EU.[89] Indeed, even before the Regulation had entered into force, the European Commission was preparing a package of legislative proposals aimed at strengthening financial supervision in Europe. In the future, ESMA will become the single European supervisor for CRAs, assuming competence in matters relating to the registration of registered credit rating agencies. Different to the present system, a single Member State cannot effectively block the decision to register a CRA.[90] Moreover, also the decision to withdraw a registration rests with ESMA. While the competent authorities of a Member State in which the ratings of a

---

[89] European Commission (2010a).

[90] Within ESMA the registration decisions will be taken by the Board of Supervisors and therein by the heads of the competent authority in each Member State who principle decide by simple majority.

CRA are used can request ESMA to examine whether the conditions for withdrawal of registration are met, the latter is under no obligation to withdraw the registration. Any negative decision of ESMA following a request by a national competent authority does, however, require a full reasoning.

European rules of conduct for CRAs

The rules of conduct for registered CRAs according to the current European regime under Regulation 1060/2009 reflect in large parts the substance of the IOSCO code. Indeed, the European Commission itself has recognized that 'many of its substantive provisions are inspired by the IOSCO code.'[91] The European regulatory regime builds on a combination of specific rules of conduct and, more generally, enhanced transparency.

Ratings for structured finance instruments must ensure that those credit rating categories attributed to structured finance instruments are clearly differentiated using a symbol, which distinguishes them from rating categories used for any other entities, financial instruments, or financial obligations. This coincides with the approach taken in the IOSCO code, which states that a CRA should differentiate ratings of structured finance products from traditional corporate bond ratings, preferably through a different rating symbology. This should make it clear to investors that the ratings of structured finance instruments are different from the ratings of other financial instruments. Indeed, in the past investors did not always realize that a triple A rating of, say a government bond, is something different than a triple A rating of a structured instrument.[92]

For the first time in the EU, registered CRAs are also obliged to disclose to the public the methodologies, models, and key rating assumptions such as mathematical or correlation assumptions used in their credit rating activities as well as any material changes. In the case of the adjustment of the methodologies, models, or key rating assumptions the CRA must immediately disclose the likely scope of credit ratings affected by this change and review and possibly re-rate them promptly. CRAs must also continually review ratings in order to

---

[91] European Commission (2008), Explanatory Memorandum, p. 6.
[92] Goodhart (2009), p. 17.

prevent them from concentrating on the initial rating and neglecting subsequent monitoring against the background of macroeconomic or financial market developments, which can be detrimental to the on-going quality of the ratings. Under the current regime of Regulation 1060/2009 it is not entirely clear to what extent CRAs can be expected to reveal their methodologies. While full disclosure of methodologies can contribute to a better understanding of the value of credit ratings, full disclosure could create strong disincentives to use the best available methodologies and to invest in better rating methodologies, i.e., to innovate, since the outcome could be immediately copied by competing CRAs.

Overall, the Regulation clearly aims at improving the transparency of CRAs, including their past performance. With regard to the latter, CRAs must also disclose ratings on a non-selective basis and in a timely manner. This also applies to ratings that are only distributed by subscription. CRAs must also make available a list of the largest 20 clients by revenue and must periodically disclose data on the historical default rates of rating categories and make available in a central repository – to be established by CESR – information on its historical performance data including the rating transition frequency and information about credit ratings issued in the past and on their changes. Finally, CRAs must publish an annual transparency report and keep extensive records of their activities.

CRAs are obliged to disclose conflicts of interest in a complete, timely, clear, concise, specific, and prominent manner and record all significant threats to the rating agency's independence or that of its employees involved in the credit rating process, together with the safeguards applied to mitigate those threats.[93] For instance, the administrative or supervisory board of a CRA must include at least one third, but no less than two, non-executive members who are independent with a non-renewable term in office not exceeding five years.[94] At the same time, CRAs may no longer provide consultancy or advisory services to the rated entity or a related third party.[95] Yet this does not also exclude so-called 'ancillary services', which

---

[93] Article 6 Regulation 1060/2009 and Annex I, section A on organizational requirements and section B on operational requirements.
[94] Ibid, Annex I, section A. 2.
[95] Regulation 1060/2009, Annex I, section B. 4.

Regulation 1060/2009 defines as 'market forecasts, estimates of economic trends, pricing analysis and other general data analysis as well as related distribution service'.[96] The CRA must ensure that such activities do not result in conflicts of interest with its credit rating activity and the final ratings report must reveal any ancillary services provided for the rated entity or any related services.[97] By including at least some global indication of what these ancillary activities amount to, one of the major concerns stated in the 2008 CESR Report, i.e., that the updated IOSCO code still did not satisfactorily address the issue of ancillary and advisory services and that there is 'a need for more clarity', has been addressed to some extent.[98] At the same time, it can hardly be argued that the Regulation introduces a comprehensive definition of ancillary business and core rating services as recommended by CESR.[99] It is to be welcomed in this context that the Regulation at least obliges CRAs to disclose a list of their ancillary services.[100]

The Regulation furthermore seeks to address potential conflicts of interests in the rating process by obliging CRAs to introduce adequate internal policies and procedures to insulate rating analysts, employees and other persons involved in the rating activities from conflicts of interest and ensure appropriate rotation arrangements for analysts and persons approving credit ratings for a particular entity.[101] This includes *inter alia* that the compensation arrangements of employees involved in the rating process may not be contingent on the amount of revenue that the CRA derives from the rated entities or related third parties to which the analyst or persons approving the credit ratings provide services.[102] Moreover the Regulation bans the employment by rated entities or related third parties of CRA employees in a 'key management position' for a period of 6 months after the credit rating.[103] What remains unclear and thus a potential loophole for

---

[96] Ibid, Annex 1, section B. 4.
[97] Ibid.
[98] CESR (2008), at p. 3.
[99] Ibid, at p. 35.
[100] Regulation 1060/2009, Annex I, Section E. I.2.
[101] Ibid, Article 7(4) and Annex I, Section C.
[102] Ibid, Article 7(5).
[103] Ibid, Annex I, Section C. 7.

creative workarounds is what exactly 'key' management positions amount to.

In the context of the general reform of the European financial supervisory regime, the European Commission has argued in favor of additional measures to "avoid possible conflicts of interest arising for the CRA under the issuer-pays model which are particularly virulent regarding the rating of structured finance instruments" and, moreover, 'to enhance transparency and to increase competition among CRAs.'[104] Next to the centralization of the registration and supervision process, the proposed amendment of Regulation 1060/2009 is most notable for its enhanced transparency regime. It is foreseen that CRAs registered or certified in accordance with the European regulatory regime must be granted access upon request to the information that issuers of a structured finance instrument or a related third party have provided to the CRA, which has been selected to rate an instrument. For this purpose, an issuer must provide to the appointed CRA, on a password-protected website that it manages, all information necessary for the CRA to initially determine or monitor a credit rating of a structured finance instrument.[105] Other CRAs must be granted access to this information upon request without delay under two conditions:

1. the CRA must have the systems and organizational structure in place to ensure the confidentiality of the information to which it gains access, and
2. the CRA provides ratings on a yearly basis for at least 10 percent of the structured finance instruments for which it requests access to information.[106]

CRAs other than the one that has actually rated the structured financial instrument thus will gain access to the information, which the issuer of such an instrument has given to the CRA he/she has hired for the purpose of the rating of such an instrument. Moreover, a credit rating issuing CRA has to maintain a password-protected website which includes a list of the structured finance instruments for which it

---

[104] European Commission (2010a), Explanatory Memorandum, p. 5.
[105] European Commission (2009), Article 8a(1) of the proposed Regulation establishing a ESMA.
[106] Ibid, Article 8a(2).

is in the process of providing a credit rating, identifying the type of the structured finance instrument, the name of the issuer and the date when the rating process was initiated. Other CRAs must, under the same conditions stated above, be granted access to that information as well.[107]

Amtenbrink and De Haan have criticized Regulation 1060/2009 for not addressing the high concentration of the CRA market or the financing of the CRAs.[108] Arguably, these features increased over-dependence on the ratings of CRAs in the past. One of the main objectives of the proposed amendment of Regulation 2060/2009 is to 'increase competition in the rating market and increase the number of ratings per instrument so that users of ratings will be able to rely on more than one rating for the same instrument.'[109] Yet, it is not self-evident whether this access to information will indeed increase competition in the light of the relatively high market access barriers that will be set up both with regard to the registration system and the conditions under which CRAs can gain access to rating information. With regard to the former, the example of the US CRA registration system introduced by the Credit Rating Agency Reform Act of 2006 leaves little room for optimism. White argues in this context that the designation as Nationally Recognized Statistical Rating Organization (NRSRO) was a significant barrier for entry into the rating business. New rating firms would risk being ignored by most financial institutions (the 'buy' side of the market), and since financial institutions would ignore the would-be rater, so would issuers of financial instruments (the 'sell' side of the market). Although the Credit Rating Agency Reform Act 2006 led to an increase of NRSROs, new entrants could not quickly overcome the inherent advantage of the 'Big Three'.[110] It cannot be seen why the situation should be any different in the EU.[111]

---

[107] Ibid, Article 8b.

[108] Amtenbrink and De Haan (2009).

[109] European Commission (2009), Explanatory Memorandum, section 4.3.2.

[110] White (2010).

[111] The European Parliament raised the issue of the creation of a new independent, preferably European, credit rating agency. Recital 73 of the Regulation states that the European Commission should submit a report to the European Parliament and the Council by December 2012 assessing, inter alia, the appropriateness of the issuer-pays model, including the assessment of the

Moreover, the requirement in the proposed amendment to Regulation 1060/2009 that a CRA can ask only for all the information so that it can issue unsolicited ratings if it has a market share of 10 percent could in practice be an important entry barrier. Indeed, the wording of the proposed new provisions is anything but clear on the exact meaning of this condition.[112] If this provision actually has to be interpreted in such a way that a CRA must already have a market share in the rating of the structured finance instruments of least ten percent, this raises the question how CRAs that are entirely new to the market can actually make use of this possibility. Moreover, it is also entirely unclear in what ways an access to information under these conditions can actually 'mitigate conflicts of interest due to the issuer-pay model', as claimed by the European Commission.[113] Arguably, access to the information that the issuer of an instrument has submitted to the rating CRA will neither prevent nor uncover cases of conflicts of interest. It should be noted in this context that the proposed amendment does not address the current system of financing of CRAs, as the 'issuer pays model' is left untouched.

While the proposed reform of Regulation 1060/2009 is supposed to increase transparency, the European Commission proposal offers little in terms of monitoring the performance of CRAs. ESMA will host a central repository in which CRAs will become obliged to make available information on their historical performance data including the ratings transition frequency and information about credit ratings issued in the past and on their changes. ESMA must make that information publicly available and must publish summary information on the main developments observed on an annual basis.[114] However, it is not envisaged that ESMA will actually undertake and publish an analysis of

---

creation of a public EU credit rating agency. In a recent consultation document, the European Commission outlines some options, including a new independent European Credit Rating Agency, set up as a public/private structure. Another option mentioned is that European small and medium-sized credit rating agencies establish a European network of agencies (European Commission, 2010b).

[112] In fact, according to Article 8a(3) of the proposed amendment (European Commission, 2010a), the European Commission has to establish detailed rules specifying the conditions of access.

[113] European Commission (2009), Explanatory Memorandum, section 4.3.2.

[114] Ibid, Article 11(2).

that performance or indeed compare the performance of different CRAs. These arrangements do thus not greatly facilitate benchmarking of CRA performance. It is clear, that the advice of the Issing Committee has not been followed. This committee recommended that 'rating performance (i.e. the long-term statistics relating initial ratings to subsequent defaults) should be monitored by the regulators, applying high statistical standards. Rating performance relative to outcomes should be published regularly (e.g., once a year).'[115]

In this context, Goodhart has argued in favor of an independent institution, a CRA Assessment Centre (CRAC), whose only task would be to assess the accuracy of CRA estimates and to publish comparative studies of such accuracy.[116] All CRAs in all countries should be required to place with CRAC a record of each product rated and a measure of the uncertainty of this rating. This might help competition. Goodhart argues that

'A new entrant could establish a track record for greater accuracy (again independently assessed) in a particular niche by exploiting a comparative advantage, say in rating one particular product line, with a small staff and build from that. What investors want is forecast accuracy. At present they have no simple or straightforward way of checking that [...] So most investors fall back on reliance on brand names, which reinforces oligopoly.'[117]

However, the IMF has pointed out that 'event studies suggest that the arrival of an additional CRA to a market has led to lower rating quality/higher ratings, in part reflecting enhanced opportunities for rating shopping, while not enhancing the information content.'[118] For example, Becker and Milbourn examine how the quality of ratings issued by Standard & Poor's and Moody's, responds to the new competition presented by Fitch.[119] These authors find that the ratings issued by Standard and Poor's and Moody's rose as competition increased, while the ratings are less informative about the value of bonds when raters face more competition. Finally, the ability of firm

---

[115] Issing Committee (2008), p. 10.
[116] Goodhart (2008).
[117] Ibid., p. 31–32. Brackets added.
[118] IMF (2010).
[119] Becker and Milbourn (2010).

level ratings to predict default is lower when Fitch has a higher market share.

With regard to sovereign debt ratings, a recent European Commission Public Consultations document suggests that additional measures are required to increase, first of all, the level of transparency of these rating by obliging CRAs *inter alia* to[120]

1. 'inform the country for which they are in the process of issuing a rating at least three working days before the publication of the rating on the principle grounds on which the rating is based, in order to give the country the opportunity to draw the attention of the credit rating agency to any factual errors and to any new developments which may influence the rating.'
2. 'disclose free of charge their full research reports on sovereign debt ratings.'
3. substantially reduce the maximum time period after which sovereign debt ratings have to be reviewed.

With regard to the methodology and the process of rating sovereign debt, the same European Commission document suggests that in addition to today's requirements under Regulation 1060/2009 one or more of the following new obligations should be introduced for CRAs:[121]

1. a detailed explanation of the assumptions, parameters, limits and uncertainties surrounding the models and methodologies used when establishing sovereign credit ratings;
2. regular (e.g. semi-annual) meetings where the CRA presents and discusses its methodologies on sovereign debt ratings, open to all interested parties (rated countries, financial institutions, and other users of ratings);
3. the publication of sovereign debt ratings only after the close of business of European trading venues;
4. to provide sovereign debt ratings free of charge for Member States.

---

[120] European Commission (2010b), p. 15–16.
[121] Ibid., p. 17.

Supervision of CRAs

As the authors of this contribution have argued elsewhere, it is with regard to enforcement that the binding legal regime introduced by Regulation 1060/2009 is most distinct from the previous voluntary IOSCO code.[122] While the latter had to rely on a comply-or-explain approach, Regulation 1060/2009 introduces instruments to actually enforce the new rules.

Under the European regulatory regime of Regulation 1060/2009, Member States have to identify competent national authorities, which have to ensure that CRAs comply with the Regulation.[123] EU national legislators must provide competent authorities with an arsenal of more or less severe supervisory measures at their disposal, including the temporary prohibition of issuing or suspension of the use, for regulatory purposes, of credit ratings with effect throughout the EU, the issuing of public notices when a CRA breaches the obligations set out in the Regulation, the possibility to refer matters for criminal prosecution to the competent jurisdiction, and ultimately the withdrawal of the registration.[124] For this purpose, the competent authorities have to have 'all the supervisory and investigatory powers that are necessary for the exercise of their functions'.[125] Moreover, the Member States must lay down rules on penalties in their national legislation which 'at least, cover cases of gross professional misconduct and lack of due diligence', whereby these penalties must be 'effective, proportionate and dissuasive'.[126] Similar to the registration procedure, before taking any measures the competent authority of the home Member State must inform the facilitator of the relevant college and aim at reaching an agreement on the necessity to take any measures. In case that such an agreement cannot be reached advice can be sought from CESR. If the disagreement continues the competent authority can nevertheless take the envisaged measures, whereby any deviation from the opinions of members of the college and/or an advice issued by CESR must be fully reasoned. The Regulation enables the home country competent authority to take a

---

[122] Amtenbrink and De Haan (2009).
[123] Article 22 and 23 Regulation 1060/2009.
[124] Ibid, Article 24(1).
[125] Ibid, Article 23.
[126] Ibid, Article 36 and preamble, para. 66.

final decision within 15 working days after it has notified the facilitator of the relevant college.[127]

The competent authorities of a Member State on whose territory credit ratings are used of a CRA that has its registered office in another Member State can initiate supervisory measures in case the CRA is considered to breach the obligations arising from the Regulation.[128] The competent authorities of that Member State can issue public notices and refer matters for criminal prosecution to its relevant national authorities and, more generally, adopt appropriate measures to ensure that a CRA complies with legal requirements.[129] This also includes a suspension of the use of credit ratings of a particular CRA.[130] Similar to the case of sanctions initiated by the home state competent authority, the college has to be consulted with the aim to reach agreement on the measures to be taken, whereby in the end the competent authority of the other Member State can take measures even against the will of the home Member State and/or the advice by CESR.[131]

Ultimately it is for the home Member State to effectively address misconduct by a CRA.[132] The Member State that issued the registration also has to decide on its withdrawal.[133] Apart from a breach of the operating conditions for CRAs as laid down in the Regulation, the discovery of false statements during the registration process, as well as instances in which a CRA no longer meets the conditions under which it was registered can justify a withdrawal of the registration.[134] While the competent authority in principle must withdraw the registration, if one of the situations described in the Regulation[135] arises, as has been observed above for the registration process, the conditions for operations leave room for interpretation.

---

[127] Ibid, Article 24(3).
[128] See namely Article 30 Directive 2006/48/EC.
[129] Article 25(1) regulation 1060/2009. When taking measures pursuant to Article 25(1) (b), the competent authority of the other Member State has to take into account any measures already taken or envisaged by the home Member State.
[130] Ibid, Article 25(1) (c) in conjunction with Article 4(1).
[131] Ibid, Article 25(3).
[132] Ibid, Article 25(4).
[133] Ibid, Article 20.
[134] Ibid, Article 20(1) (a)–(d).
[135] Namely Article 20(1) thereof.

Similar to the registration process, the relevant college has to be consulted with the aim to reach agreement on the necessity to withdraw the registration to the CRA based on a joint assessment. In case of disagreement CESR can be consulted. The competent authority of the home Member State can take an individual withdrawal decision with immediate effect throughout the EU in principle regardless of whether an agreement is reached in the college.[136] However, this decision needs to be fully reasoned in case it deviates from the opinions expressed in the college and/or the advice by CESR. While the competent authority of another Member State can thus request the withdrawal of registration, the home Member State cannot be forced to act in this regard.[137]

In line with the approach taken with regard to the registration of CRAs, in its present form Regulation 1060/2009 does not put a European body in charge of the oversight of CRA operations. Moreover, competent authorities of other Member States in which a CRA may operate are also not issued any effective instruments by the Regulation to enforce a withdrawal of registration. As to situations where cooperation between national authorities breaks down, apart from non-binding mediation, the only option left to compel a national competent authority to withdraw a registration, it seems, would be the initiation of a judicial procedure before the Court of Justice of the European Union. A CRA whose registration is refused or withdrawn would have to seek legal remedies in the national legal order of the Member State concerned.[138]

It is only after the implementation of the general supervisory reform and the establishment of the ESMA, as envisaged at the time of the writing of this contribution, that CRA supervision will be much more centralized. ESMA will gain competence in matters relating to the on-going supervision of registered CRAs, thereby cooperating with the new European Banking Authority. The instruments at the

---

[136] Ibid, Article 20(2) and (4). A transitional period applies for the use of credit ratings.

[137] For more details see Amtenbrink and De Haan (2009).

[138] See, e.g., case 77–69, *Commission v. Belgium,* [1970] ECR 237. In the context of Article 258 TFEU it needs to be noted that the Commission is under no legal obligation to act, whereas natural or legal persons cannot force the Commission to act. See, e.g., case 200/88, *Commission versus Greece*, [1990] ECR I-4299.

disposal of ESMA largely correspond to those that national competent authorities have in enforcing Regulation 1060/2009 in its current form, including inter alia general investigative rights and the possibility of on-site inspections. However, even under the proposed new regime some tasks will remain with national competent authorities of the Member States of the EU. This applies *inter alia* to the enforcement of the prohibition, namely for credit institutions, investment firms and insurance undertakings, to use credit ratings other than those issued in accordance with Regulation 1060/2009 for determining capital requirements in accordance with the before mentioned Capital Requirements Directive.[139] Moreover, ESMA will have the competence to delegate specific supervisory tasks to national authorities, including in particular information requests, investigations and on-site inspections.[140]

Conclusion

Throughout this contribution it has been argued that CRAs play a crucial role in the global financial system as it is currently organized. This role is not limited to the elimination of an information asymmetry in favor of investors that readily take over the advice provided by CRAs in the form of credit ratings, but actually extents to the fulfillment of a quasi-regulatory and thus public function in determining capital requirements for financial institutions, a crucial aspect of the prudential supervision and thus ultimately of financial stability as such. What is more, CRAs do not only cast a judgment on the creditworthiness of companies, such as financial institutions and their financial products, but also on states. The current euro area crisis highlights the vast implications, which a sovereign downgrading can have not only in the financial markets but also for the respective state itself.

The recent global financial crisis highlights that assigning such a key role to CRAs bears considerable risks when not accompanied by an adequate regulatory framework. Certainly in the past, the business model of CRAs left room for conflicts of interest, while their rating

---

[139] European Commission Proposal (2010a), Article 25a.
[140] Ibid., Article 30.

methodologies remained opaque and arguably ill-suited for the application to the complex structured financial products that currently make such a large portion of the rating business of CRAs. Moreover, a large concentration in the rating business has left little or no room for new CRAs with other business models and rating methods to enter the market.

The answer to the question how these shortcomings should be addressed involves more than one dimension. Firstly, there is a clear overreliance of investors on credit ratings. In the past due diligence has not been effectively promoted by the (non-binding) regulatory regime and the insistence by CRAs that their ratings only measure credit risk seems to have been ignored by many investors. More is needed in this regard. Moreover, the acceptance of external credit assessment for the determining of capital requirements has effectively resulted in the 'outsourcing of regulatory judgment', whereby not the CRA bears the final risk, but rather the taxpayer that may have to come to the rescue of a failing systemic relevant institution.

Turning to the recent efforts in the EU to address these issues, the authors of this contribution have previously expressed their doubts as to whether the regime under Regulation 1060/2009 will make a decisive difference compared to the previously existing mix of regulation and self-regulation under the Capital Requirements Directive and the IOSCO code. Indeed, it is still unclear on the basis of what evidence it is assumed that the regulation of the credit rating industry will have an effect on the issues that have emerged with ratings of US subprime backed securities, which lay at the root of the global financial crisis. The main concern raised by several advisory bodies, including CESR, FSF and EMSE, persists that comprehensive regulation may actually result in more reliance on the ratings of structured financial instruments by investors that are given the false impression that the ratings of EU registered CRAs are more reliable. Put differently, the (amended) Regulation implies that CRAs have to adhere to various requirements, creating the impression that their ratings can be trusted.[141] Also the fact that ESMA and not an

---

[141] The European Commission seems to be aware of this. In a recent consultation document, it reads: 'references to ratings in the regulatory framework should be reconsidered in light of their potential to implicitly be regarded as a public endorsement of ratings and their potential to influence behavior in an undesirable way, for instance due to sudden hikes in capital

independent institution monitors rating performance may add to this impression.

However, oversight by either competent national authorities or, in the future, the ESMA does not imply an improvement of the ratings. Utzig rightly argues that

> 'there is broad consensus that rating methodologies should not be monitored. This is not only for competitive reasons, but above all because regulation of this kind could result in the state being considered partly responsible for published ratings. This would be incompatible with the concept of private-sector credit rating agencies. Given that states themselves are also issuers of debt, moreover, a new conflict of interests would arise if the state were in a position to influence the methodologies used for assigning sovereign ratings.'[142]

In line with this view, the Issing Committee recommended that 'Authorities should continue to review their use of structured finance ratings in the regulatory and supervisory framework and reduce the use to the extent possible in order to limit the pressure on agencies, e.g. in consumer protection regulation.' White even argues that authorities should not rely on credit ratings in capital requirements. The withdrawal of these delegations would not imply that 'anything goes', but safety judgments should remain the responsibility of the regulated institutions with oversight by the regulators.[143] The IMF goes one step further, even questioning the benefits of structured financial products as such: The conclusion of this chapter is that, although structured finance can be beneficial by allowing risks to be diversified, some complex and multi-layered products added little economic value to the financial system. Further, they likely exacerbated the depth and duration of the crisis by adding uncertainty relating to their valuation as the underlying fundamentals deteriorated.[144] The way in which the issue of the desirability of

---

requirements resulting from rating downgrades.' (European Commission (2010b) p. 5). The Financial Stability Board (FSB) recently endorsed principles to reduce authorities' and financial institutions' reliance on credit ratings (FSB (2010)).

[142] Utzig (2010), p. 5.

[143] White (2010). In a recent consultation document, the European Commission identifies several ways to reduce reliance on CRA ratings (European Commission 2010b).

[144] IMF (2008), p. 54.

certain types of financial products takes a backseat in the current debates on regulatory reforms is conspicuous, to say the least.

Be that as it may, due diligence of investors will also not be enhanced as a result of the proposed amendment of Regulation 1060/2009. The only notable novelty in this area relates to the prohibition of CRAs in the future to use the name of ESMA or any competent authority in such a way that would indicate or suggest endorsement or approval by that authority of its credit ratings or any credit rating activities. In our view, this is a missed opportunity. It is also not in line with Directive 2009/111/EC, which enables due diligence requiring that

> 'Sponsor and originator credit institutions shall ensure that prospective investors have readily available access to all materially relevant data on the credit quality and performance of the individual underlying exposures, cash flows and collateral supporting a securitization exposure as well as such information that is necessary to conduct comprehensive and well informed stress tests on the cash flows and collateral values supporting the underlying exposures. For that purpose, materially relevant data shall be determined as at the date of the securitization and where appropriate due to the nature of the securitization thereafter.'

References

Afonso, A., P. Gomes, and P. Rother (2007), 'What "Hides" Behind Sovereign Debt Ratings?' *ECB Working Paper* No. 711.

Alsakka, R., and O. ap Gwilym (2009), 'Heterogeneity of sovereign rating migrations in emerging countries', *Emerging Markets Review*, **10**, 151–165.

Alsakka, R., and O. ap Gwilym (2010), 'Leads and lags in sovereign credit ratings', *Journal of Banking and Finance*, **34**, 2614–2626.

Amtenbrink, F., and J. de Haan (2009), 'Regulating Credit Ratings in the European Union: A Critical First Assessment of Regulation 1060/2009 on Credit Rating Agencies', *Common Market Law Review*, **46**, 1915–1949.

Amtenbrink, F., and J. de Haan (2011), 'Regulating Credit Rating Agencies in the European Union', in F. Delimatsis and N. Herger (eds), *Financial Regulation at the Crossroads: Implications for*

Supervision, Institutional Design and Trade, Alphen aan den Rijin, the Netherlands: Kluwer Law International, pp. 97–112.

Arezki, R., B. Candelon, and A. Sy, (2010), 'Sovereign Ratings News and Financial Markets Spillovers', *IMF Working Paper*.

Bannier, C.E. and C.W. Hirsch (2010), 'The economic function of credit rating agencies. What does the watchlist tell us?', *Journal of Banking and Finance*, **32**(12), 3037–3049.

Barroso, J.M. Durão (2010), 'Statement to the European Parliament prior to the meeting of the Heads of State and Government of the Euro Area', European Parliament Plenary, Brussels, 5 May 2010.

Becker, B. and T. Milbourn (2010), 'How Did Increased Competition Affect Credit Ratings?' Available at: http://www.hbs.edu/research/pdf/09-051.pdf

Benmelech, E. and J. Dlugosz (2009), 'The Alchemy of CDO Credit Ratings', *Journal of Monetary Economics*, **56**, 617–634.

Blaubock, U. (2007), 'Control and Responsibility of Credit Rating Agencies', *Electronic Journal of Comparative Law*, **11.3** (December 2007), http://www.ejcl.org.

Boot, A.W.A., T.T. Milbourn, and A. Schmeits (2006), 'Credit Ratings as Coordination Mechanisms', *Review of Financial Studies,* **19** (1), 81–118.

Brooks, R., R. Faff, D. Hillier, and J. Hillier (2004), 'The national market impact of sovereign rating changes', *Journal of Banking and Finance*, **28**, 233–250.

Cantor, R. and C. Mann (2007), 'Analyzing the Tradeoff Between Ratings Accuracy and Stability', *Journal of Fixed Income*, **16**, 4, 60–68.

Caprio, G., A. Demirgüç-Kunt and E. Kane (2008), 'The 2007 Meltdown in Structured Securitization: Searching for Lessons, not Scapegoats', *World Bank Policy and Research Working Paper* No. 4756.

Committee of European Securities Regulators (CESR) (2008), *CESR's Second Report to the European Commission on the compliance of credit rating agencies with the IOSCO code and the role of credit rating agencies in structured finance*, CESR/08-277.

Coval, J.D., J. Jurek and E. Stafford (2009), 'The Economics of Structured Finance', Harvard Business School, Working Paper 09-060.

Daniels, K.N. and M.S. Jensen (2005), 'The Effect of Credit Ratings on Credit Default Swap Spreads and Credit Spreads', *Journal of Fixed Income*, **14**, 16–33.

European Commission (2008), 'Proposal of a Regulation of the European Parliament and of the Council on Credit Rating Agencies' (COM (2008), 704 final).

European Commission (2009), 'Proposal for a Regulation of the European Parliament and of the Council Establishing a European Securities and Markets Authority' (COM(2009) 503 final).

European Commission (2010a), 'Proposal for a Regulation of the European Parliament and of the Council on amending Regulation (EC) No 1060/2009 on credit rating agencies', SEC(2010) 678.

European Commission (2010b), 'Public Consultation on Credit Rating Agencies', 5 November 2010. Available at http://ec.europa.eu/ internal_market/consultations/docs/2010/cra/cpaper_en.pdf (accessed 27 November 2010).

European Economic Advisory Group (EEAG) (2009), 'The EEAG Report on the European Economy 2009', CESifo Group Munich, Germany. Available at http://www.cesifo-group.de/portal/page/ portal/ifoHome/ B-politik/70eeagre port/20PUBLEEAG2009 (accessed 10 October 2010).

European Securities Markets Expert Group (ESME) (2008), 'The Role of Credit Rating Agencies', June 2008, available at http://ec.europa.eu/ internal_market/securities/esme/index_en.htm (accessed 6 July 2010).

Financial Stability Board (FSB) (2010), 'Principles for Reducing Reliance on CRA Ratings', available at: http://www.financialstability board. org/publications/r_101027.pdf (accessed 30 November 2010).

Financial Stability Forum (FSF) (2008), *Report of the Financial Stability Forum on Enhancing Market and Institutional Resilience*, 7 April 2008, available at: http://www.fsforum.org/publications /r_0804.pdf (accessed 9 March 2008).

Gande, A., and D.C. Parsley (2005), 'News spillovers in the sovereign debt market', *Journal of Financial Economics*, **75**, 691–734.

Goodhart, C.A.E. (2008), 'How, if at all, should Credit Ratings Agencies (CRAs) be Regulated?', Special papers 181, LSE Financial Markets Group Paper Series.

Goodhart, C.A.E. (2009), *The Regulatory Response to the Financial Crisis,* Cheltenham, UK and Northampton, MA, USA: Edward Elgar.

Güttler, A. and M. Wahrenburg (2007), 'The adjustment of credit ratings in advance of defaults', *Journal of Banking and Finance*, **31**, 751–767.

Hill, P., R. Brooks, and R. Faff (2010), 'Variations in sovereign credit quality assessments across rating agencies', *Journal of Banking and Finance*, **34**, 1327–1343.

IMF (2008), *Global Financial Stability Report*. The International Monetary Fund.

IMF (2010), 'The uses and abuses of sovereign credit ratings', in IMF *Global Financial Stability Report.*

Ismailescu, I. and H. Kazemi (2010), 'The Reaction of Emerging Market Credit Default Swap Spreads to Sovereign Credit Rating Changes', *Journal of Banking and Finance*, **34**, 2861–2873.

Issing Committee (2008), *New Financial Order: Recommendations by the Issing Committee*, Frankfurt: Center for Financial Studies. Available at http://www.ifk-cfs.de/fileadmin/downloads/ publications /white_paper/White_Paper_No_1_Final.pdf (accessed 10 October 2010).

Jaramillo, L. (2010), 'Determinants of Investment Grade status in Emerging Markets', *IMF Working Paper*, 10/117.

Jorion, P. and G. Zhang (2007), 'Information Effects of Bond Rating Changes: The Role of the Rating Prior to the Announcement', *Journal of Fixed Income*, **16**, 4, 45–59.

Kormos, B.J. (2008), 'Quis Custodiet Ipsos Custodes? Revisiting Rating Agency Regulation', *International Business Law Journal*, **4**, 569–590.

Lastra, R. (2003), 'The Governance Structure for Financial Supervision and Regulation in Europe', *Columbia Journal of European Law*, **10** (1), 49–68.

Mathis, J., J. McAndrews, and J-C. Rochet (2009), 'Rating the raters: Are reputation concerns powerful enough to discipline rating agencies?' *Journal of Monetary Economics*, **56**, 657–674.

Mora, N. (2006), 'Sovereign credit ratings: Guilty beyond reasonable doubt?', *Journal of Banking and Finance*, **30**, 2041–2062.

Pagano, M. and P. Volpin (2010), 'Credit ratings failures and policy options', *Economic Policy*, April 2010, 403–431.

Richards, M.L. (2009), 'Credit-Rating-Agency Reforms', *Mortgage Banking*, **69**, 7, 40–44.

Senate Committee on Governmental Affairs (2002), 'Financial Oversight of Enron: The SEC and Private-Sector Watchdogs', Staff Report, October 8, 2002.

Sy, A. (2002), 'Emerging market bond spreads and sovereign credit ratings: Reconciling market views with economic fundamentals', *Emerging Markets Review*, **3**, 380–408.

Utzig, S. (2010), 'The Financial Crisis and the Regulation of Credit Rating Agencies: A European Banking Perspective', ADBI Working Paper Series No. 188.

Weber, R.H. and A. Darbellay (2008), 'The regulatory use of credit ratings in bank capital requirement regulations', *Journal of Banking Regulation*, **10**, 1, 1–16.

White, L.J. (2010), 'The Credit Rating Agencies', *Journal of Economic Perspectives*, **24**, 211–226.

Index